SAP PRESS Books: Always on hand

Print or e-book, Kindle or iPad, workplace or airplane: Choose where and how to read your SAP PRESS books! You can now get all our titles as e-books, too:

- By download and online access
- For all popular devices
- And, of course, DRM-free

Convinced? Then go to www.sap-press.com and get your e-book today.

Plant Maintenance with SAP® — Practical Guide

# SAP PRESS

SAP PRESS is a joint initiative of SAP and Galileo Press. The know-how offered by SAP specialists combined with the expertise of the Galileo Press publishing house offers the reader expert books in the field. SAP PRESS features first-hand information and expert advice, and provides useful skills for professional decision-making.

SAP PRESS offers a variety of books on technical and business-related topics for the SAP user. For further information, please visit our website: www.sap-press.com.

Lorri Craig, John Hoke
Maximize Your Plant Maintenance with SAP
2008, 372 pp., hardcover
ISBN 978-1-59229-215-8

Jawad Akhtar
Production Planning and Control with SAP ERP
2013, 1040 pp., hardcover
ISBN 978-1-59229-868-6

Jochen Balla, Frank Layer
Production Planning with SAP APO (2nd Edition)
2010, 408 pp., hardcover
ISBN 978-1-59229-354-4

Marc Hoppe et al.
Materials Planning with SAP
2009, 564 pp., hardcover
ISBN 978-1-59229-259-2

Karl Liebstückel

Plant Maintenance with SAP® — Practical Guide

Bonn • Boston

Galileo Press is named after the Italian physicist, mathematician, and philosopher Galileo Galilei (1564–1642). He is known as one of the founders of modern science and an advocate of our contemporary, heliocentric worldview. His words *Eppur si muove* (And yet it moves) have become legendary. The Galileo Press logo depicts Jupiter orbited by the four Galilean moons, which were discovered by Galileo in 1610.

Editor Eva Tripp
English Edition Editor Katy Spencer
Translation Lemoine International, Inc., Salt Lake City, UT
Copyeditor Miranda Martin
Cover Design Mai Loan Nguyen Duy, Graham Geary
Photo Credit Shutterstock.com/99077531/© donatas1205_BEA; iStockphoto/19740303/© TommL; iStockphoto.com/20991969/© Alexander Bauer
Layout Design Vera Brauner
Production Kelly O'Callaghan
Typesetting SatzPro, Krefeld (Germany)
Printed and bound in the United States of America, on paper from sustainable sources

ISBN 978-1-59229-929-4

© 2014 by Galileo Press Inc., Boston (MA)
3rd edition 2014
3rd German edition published 2013 by Galileo Press, Bonn, Germany

Library of Congress Cataloging-in-Publication Data
Liebstückel, Karl.
[Instandhaltung mit SAP. English]
Plant maintenance with SAP : practical guide / Karl Liebstückel. -- Third edition.
pages cm
Includes bibliographical references and index.
ISBN 978-1-59229-929-4 (print : alk. paper) -- ISBN 1-59229-929-6 (print : alk. paper) --
ISBN 978-1-59229-930-0 (e-book : alk. paper) --
ISBN 978-1-59229-931-7 (print and e-book : alk. paper) 1. Plant maintenance--Data processing. I. Title.
TS192.L55 2014
658.2'020285--dc23
2013037975

All rights reserved. Neither this publication nor any part of it may be copied or reproduced in any form or by any means or translated into another language, without the prior consent of Galileo Press, Rheinwerkallee 4, 53227 Bonn, Germany.

Galileo Press makes no warranties or representations with respect to the content hereof and specifically disclaims any implied warranties of merchantability or fitness for any particular purpose. Galileo Press assumes no responsibility for any errors that may appear in this publication.

"Galileo Press" and the Galileo Press logo are registered trademarks of Galileo Press GmbH, Bonn, Germany, SAP PRESS is an imprint of Galileo Press.

All of the screenshots and graphics reproduced in this book are subject to copyright © SAP AG, Dietmar-Hopp-Allee 16, 69190 Walldorf, Germany.

SAP, the SAP logo, ABAP, BAPI, Duet, mySAP.com, mySAP, SAP ArchiveLink, SAP EarlyWatch, SAP NetWeaver, SAP Business ByDesign, SAP BusinessObjects, SAP BusinessObjects Rapid Mart, SAP BusinessObjects Desktop Intelligence, SAP BusinessObjects Explorer, SAP Rapid Marts, SAP BusinessObjects Watchlist Security, SAP BusinessObjects Web Intelligence, SAP Crystal Reports, SAP GoingLive, SAP HANA, SAP MaxAttention, SAP MaxDB, SAP PartnerEdge, SAP R/2, SAP R/3, SAP R/3 Enterprise, SAP Strategic Enterprise Management (SAP SEM), SAP StreamWork, SAP Sybase Adaptive Server Enterprise (SAP Sybase ASE), SAP Sybase IQ, SAP xApps, SAPPHIRE NOW, and Xcelsius are registered or unregistered trademarks of SAP AG, Walldorf, Germany.

All other products mentioned in this book are registered or unregistered trademarks of their respective companies.

Contents at a Glance

1	About This Book	17
2	Plant Maintenance and SAP: A Contradiction?	25
3	Organizational Structures	41
4	Structuring of Technical Systems	55
5	Business Processes	149
6	Integrating Applications from Other Departments	375
7	Plant Maintenance Controlling	441
8	New Information Technologies in Plant Maintenance	501
9	Usability	577
A	List of Sources	631
B	Overviews	637
C	The Author	651
D	Acknowledgments	653

Dear Reader,

We all know that there is so much more to plant maintenance than tightening a loose bolt. Whether you are on the plant floor or managing the entire logistic process, you are responsible for the nuts, the bolts, and the day-to-day functioning of your plant. This practical, must-have guide to SAP Enterprise Asset Management (EAM) will become a trusted resource in your arsenal of tools. With this updated and expanded edition, explore how to structure your functional locations, capture shift notes and shift reports, and manage both time based and performance based preventative maintenance, and much more.

Like the editors before me, it was a pleasure to work with Karl Liebstückel and witness such dedication and expertise in SAP. I'm confident that you will find this new edition up to the same standard of its predecessors. It is often said that the third time is the charm; I think this third edition is just the title you need to reduce the complexity of your daily plant maintenance tasks.

As always, we appreciate your business and welcome your feedback. What did you think about *Plant Maintenance with SAP—Practical Guide?* Your comments and suggestions are the most useful tools to help us improve our books for you, the reader. We encourage you to visit our website at *www.sap-press.com* and share your feedback.

Katy Spencer
Editor, SAP PRESS

Galileo Press
Boston, MA

katy.spencer@galileo-press.com
www.sap-press.com

Contents

Preface to the Third Edition 13
Preface to the First Edition 15

1 About This Book 17

    1.1   Target Audience 19
    1.2   What This Book Can and Cannot Do 20
    1.3   Structure of This Book 21

2 Plant Maintenance and SAP: A Contradiction? 25

    2.1   Plant Maintenance Today: New Ideas Need
           New Space 26
    2.2   New Maintenance Terminology 28
    2.3   Maintenance Strategies over the Course of Time 32
    2.4   SAP Plant Maintenance over the Course of Time 34
    2.5   SAP ERP 6.0 35

3 Organizational Structures 41

    3.1   SAP Organizational Units 41
           3.1.1   The Plant from a Maintenance Perspective 41
           3.1.2   Maintenance-Specific Organizational Units 42
           3.1.3   Other General Organizational Units 44
           3.1.4   Plant-Specific and Cross-Plant Maintenance 45
    3.2   Work Centers 47

4 Structuring of Technical Systems 55

    4.1   Actions before Mapping Your Technical Systems in
           the SAP System 56
    4.2   SAP Elements for Structuring Technical Systems and
           How to Use Them 71
           4.2.1   Functional Locations and Reference Functional
                    Locations 71
           4.2.2   Equipment and Serial Numbers 83
           4.2.3   Links and Object Networks 93

		4.2.4	Linear Asset Management	94
		4.2.5	Material and PM Assemblies	103
		4.2.6	BOMs	110
		4.2.7	Classification	114
		4.2.8	Product Structure Browser	120
		4.2.9	Special Functions	122

5 Business Processes ... 149

5.1	What You Should Do before You Map Your Business Processes in the SAP System		150
5.2	Planned Repairs Business Process		158
	5.2.1	Notification	160
	5.2.2	Planning	176
	5.2.3	Controlling	207
	5.2.4	Processing	221
	5.2.5	Completion	223
5.3	Immediate Repairs Business Process		232
5.4	Shift Notes and Shift Reports		238
5.5	External Processing		245
	5.5.1	Basic Principles of External Processing Assignment	245
	5.5.2	External Services as an Individual Purchase Order	248
	5.5.3	External Services with External Work Centers	253
	5.5.4	External Services with Service Specifications	257
5.6	Refurbishment Business Process		262
5.7	Subcontracting Business Process		273
5.8	Preventive Maintenance Business Process		280
	5.8.1	Basic Principles of Preventive Maintenance	281
	5.8.2	Objects of Preventive Maintenance	283
	5.8.3	Maintenance Task Lists	287
	5.8.4	Preventive Maintenance, Time-Based	296
	5.8.5	Preventive Maintenance, Performance-Based	316
	5.8.6	Preventive Maintenance, Time-Based and Performance-Based	326
	5.8.7	Inspection Rounds	333
5.9	Condition-Based Maintenance Business Process		341
5.10	Calibration of Test Equipment Business Process		344

5.11	Pool Asset Management Business Process		356
5.12	Project-Based Maintenance Business Process		363
	5.12.1	SAP Project System	364
	5.12.2	Maintenance Event Builder	370

6 Integrating Applications from Other Departments 375

6.1	How Other Departments Are Involved		375
6.2	Integration within SAP ERP		376
	6.2.1	Materials Management	377
	6.2.2	Production Planning and Control	386
	6.2.3	Digression: In-house Production of Spare Parts for Stock	391
	6.2.4	Quality Management	396
	6.2.5	Environment, Health, and Safety	397
	6.2.6	Financial Accounting	400
	6.2.7	Asset Accounting	402
	6.2.8	Controlling	405
	6.2.9	Real Estate Management	415
	6.2.10	Human Capital Management	418
	6.2.11	Service and Sales	423
6.3	Integration with Other SAP Systems		426
	6.3.1	Integration with SAP NetWeaver MDM	426
	6.3.2	Integration with SAP SRM	428
6.4	Integration with Non-SAP Systems		431
	6.4.1	Operations Monitoring Systems	432
	6.4.2	Operations Information Systems	435
	6.4.3	Service Specifications and Entry of Services Performed	438

7 Plant Maintenance Controlling 441

7.1	What Plant Maintenance Controlling Involves		441
7.2	SAP Tools for Obtaining Information and How to Use Them		446
	7.2.1	SAP List Viewer	446
	7.2.2	SAP Quick Viewer	454
	7.2.3	SAP ERP Logistics Information System	459
	7.2.4	SAP NetWeaver BW	469

		7.2.5	Comparison of LIS and SAP NetWeaver BW	479
	7.3		SAP Tools for Budgeting and How to Use Them	481
		7.3.1	Order Budgeting	481
		7.3.2	Cost Center Budgeting	483
		7.3.3	Budgeting with IM Programs	485
		7.3.4	Budgeting Using WBS Elements	488
		7.3.5	Maintenance Cost Budgeting	492

8 New Information Technologies in Plant Maintenance ... 501

	8.1		SAP NetWeaver Portal	502
		8.1.1	Role Concept	503
		8.1.2	Service Maps, Overviews, and Reports	504
		8.1.3	After-Event Recording	507
		8.1.4	Technical Structure View	509
	8.2		Electronic Parts Catalogs	511
	8.3		Easy Web Transaction	514
	8.4		Collaboration Folders	516
	8.5		Vision or Reality?	518
		8.5.1	Electronic Data Exchange	518
		8.5.2	Vendor Portal	520
		8.5.3	Virtual Spare Parts Storage	521
		8.5.4	Virtual Personnel Capacities	522
		8.5.5	Sell Rather Than Scrap	523
	8.6		SAP NetWeaver Business Client	524
		8.6.1	General Functions	525
		8.6.2	Roles, Task Lists, Overviews, and Reports	527
		8.6.3	Confirming Unplanned Jobs	528
		8.6.4	Asset Viewer	529
		8.6.5	Side Panels	531
		8.6.6	SAP Visual Enterprise Viewer	532
	8.7		Mobile Maintenance	535
		8.7.1	Fundamentals of Mobile Maintenance	535
		8.7.2	Paging	541
		8.7.3	Mobile Asset Management	543
		8.7.4	SAP Work Manager	550
		8.7.5	SAP Rounds Manager	560

		8.7.6	Other Aspects of Mobile Platforms	561
		8.7.7	RFID	562
	8.8		Service-Oriented Architecture	566
	8.9		SAP HANA	571

9 Usability 577

	9.1		What is Meant by Usability?	578
	9.2		Assessing Usability	583
	9.3		Why Usability Does Not Mean User Acceptance	584
	9.4		The Importance of User Acceptance in Plant Maintenance	587
	9.5		SAP System Options to Improve Usability	590
		9.5.1	General User Parameters	592
		9.5.2	Maintenance-Specific User Parameters	593
		9.5.3	Roles and Favorites	594
		9.5.4	List Variants	596
		9.5.5	Personalizing Input Help	596
		9.5.6	Buttons and Key Combinations	597
		9.5.7	Table Controls	598
		9.5.8	Transaction Variants	601
		9.5.9	Customizing	603
		9.5.10	Action Box	604
		9.5.11	GuiXT	606
		9.5.12	Upstream Transactions	607
		9.5.13	Web User Interface	610
		9.5.14	Customer Exits	611
		9.5.15	Other Programming Techniques	613
	9.6		Usability Study for SAP ERP 6.0	616
		9.6.1	Preparation and Execution	616
		9.6.2	Results	621
		9.6.3	Conclusions	626

Appendices 629

A		List of Sources	631
B		Overviews	637
	B.1	Functional Comparison of Structuring Resources	637
	B.2	Functions of Notifications and Orders	638

	B.3	Integration Aspects	642
	B.4	Standard Reports of PM-IS	648
C	The Author		651
D	Acknowledgments		653

Index 655

Preface to the Third Edition

Dear Readers,
This is the third edition of the maintenance manual, and, as you may have noticed, its title was slightly modified this time to *SAP Plant Maintenance—Practical Guide*. Are you wondering why it was modified?

Due to the positive experience with other applications, SAP PRESS has decided to publish a second book for area of Plant Maintenance, *Configuring SAP Plant Maintenance* which will be released in the summer of 2014. There, you will find all the appropriate answers to your questions related to the implementation and customization of EAM. While these aspects were dealt with only briefly in the previous two editions of this book, they are discussed in the appropriate breadth and depth in *Configuring SAP Plant Maintenance*.

Consequently, the previous Chapter 9 of *SAP Projects in Plant Maintenance* and all the more detailed information on Customizing settings will be moved from the previous edition to the new EAM Configuration book.

They are now replaced by the following new sections:

- Linear Asset Management
- Production of spare parts
- Integration with SAP Environment, Health, and Safety Management (EHS Management)
- SAP NetWeaver Business Client as the new user interface
- SAP Work Manager and SAP Rounds Manager as new mobile solutions
- SAP HANA as the new database
- Additional information on usability (user acceptance, table controls, action box)

In addition, all enhancements from Enhancement Packages 5 and 6 (a few even from Enhancement Package 7) were included—and there were quite a few.

Finally, you will find a supplementary fold-out map (a "reference card"), which includes the most important maintenance transactions. If you were an SAP R/2 user, you know it from RM-INST and have sorely missed it in SAP R/3 and SAP ERP. You now have one again! You will also find a document with all transactions for download at *http://www.sap-press.com/H3316*.

I now hope you enjoy reading this manual, and good luck in your SAP maintenance projects.

Yours,

Preface to the First Edition

The ongoing technicalization of production, combined with the continually increasing automation of production processes, means that the availability of production facilities and the quality of production are exerting an ever-increasing influence on the success of enterprises. The maintenance of technical systems has a direct effect on the competitiveness of modern enterprises and makes an important contribution to financial results. Plant maintenance does not just involve ensuring that technical systems are in working order and available; it also has to do with other aspects of operating technical systems, such as plant safety, product quality, and environmental protection.

Modern maintenance operations, therefore, are much more than simply maintenance and repair teams, as they represent a comprehensive asset management concept that is incorporated into the processes along the entire lifecycle of technical systems, from procurement to operations, plant rebuilds and modernization, to reinvestments.

Furthermore, the demands made of plant maintenance teams have evolved over time, such that modern asset management technology is now essential. The increasing proportion of complex technical systems and the growing popularity of electronic components and assemblies are creating increased demand for specialists in areas such as electronics and information technology, alongside the traditional setups. In many cases, there is a need for external experts who collaborate as service providers and service partners with enterprises' own in-house plant technicians and take care of the entirety of technical systems in companies.

These developments mean that maintenance management systems must be able to deal with the changing circumstances in asset management, provide flexibility when it comes to the structuring of technical systems, and work with the different work processes of both internal and external maintenance teams.

Preface to the First Edition

The topic of *plant maintenance* was an important focus of SAP as far back as the early years of application development. Right from the start, SAP was aware of the need for a comprehensive definition of asset management and therefore extended its focus beyond the basic topics of inspection, maintenance, and repair. Processes such as building a new plant or modernizing an existing one, calibrating test equipment, and refurbishing repairable spares were taken into account in the development of a comprehensive asset management solution.

Maintenance processes in their various forms are now part of a variety of industries. In addition to the repair, inspection, and maintenance processes that are common to several industries, there are also company-specific elements and special requirements unique to individual industries. These can include special approval procedures (such as the work clearance procedure for power generators), complex maintenance planning techniques (such as those in aircraft maintenance), and project-based plant maintenance (large-scale revision).

With *Enterprise Asset Management*, SAP has developed a flexible asset management and maintenance system that has proved its value in numerous installations in a wide variety of industries worldwide. Asset management is also a permanent part of the *Solution Maps* of the various asset-intensive industries. Following on from this, the concept of an asset as a resource in the form of Enterprise Asset Management (EAM) is also part of the overall *Enterprise Resource Planning* (ERP) system.

This book introduces readers to the wide range of potential uses of asset management within the SAP system. Thanks to his role right from the start as a consultant on a wide range of customer projects in various industries, the author has extensive SAP experience and has influenced and was actively involved in the development of the SAP *Plant Maintenance* solution. Thus, he is able to offer a plethora of useful, first-hand information in this manual.

I hope this book will give you the ideas and information you need and that you can implement them successfully in your own projects.

Rolf Peter Westhues
Former Vice President, SAP AG

Genius is one percent inspiration and ninety-nine percent perspiration.
—Thomas A. Edison

1   About This Book

Slowly but surely, a new concept of plant maintenance in enterprises is establishing itself in the minds of decision makers. It is a concept that is moving away from the notion of plant maintenance as purely a cost driver and toward the realization that goal-oriented, modern plant maintenance can be a success factor and a competitive advantage in one's own company. In other words, the trend is moving away from terms like *cost factor* and toward descriptions such as a component that ensures machine availability, increases production, and ensures plant safety. At the same time, it must be acknowledged that, in many industries, more than 40% of enterprise costs are either directly or indirectly attributable to plant maintenance.[1] Even the sale of internal plant maintenance services to interested companies no longer seems ruled out by any company. Thus, the plant maintenance area can contribute to the increase in revenue.

Is plant maintenance purely a cost factor?

While the transition from cost factor to success factor is taken for granted in most other enterprise areas, when it comes to plant maintenance, many enterprises are only now slowly coming to the realization that it can be accomplished only with the support of modern communication and information technology. The chosen IT solution should, ideally, have the following features:

Plant maintenance and IT

▸ It should be embedded in the heterogeneous network of enterprise processes.

---

[1] According to a press release of Forum Vision Instandhaltung (FVI) – Vision Maintenance Forum – of 08.24.2007

- It should flexibly support all plant maintenance–specific business processes—from the elimination of malfunctions via preventative plant maintenance to new plant maintenance strategies, such as condition-based maintenance (CBM) or reliability-based maintenance (RCM).
- It should be oriented toward future challenges in the enterprise and the market.
- It should be able to integrate modern technologies, such as cloud computing, the Internet, and mobile services.
- It should be easy to use because, unlike with other enterprise areas such as purchasing or accounting, you encounter users in plant maintenance for whom IT is not one of the daily tools of the trade.

Plant maintenance and SAP

SAP's response to these requirements is *Enterprise Asset Management* (EAM), which is part of Release SAP ERP 6.0. This book is based on this current release level. This third, updated and expanded edition not only provides an overview of the current range of functions, but also illustrates completely different uses of EAM. As a result, each company must find its own solution in plant maintenance; thus, a pure description of the functions is insufficient here. On the basis of my 25-plus years of experience in plant maintenance with SAP and my work on more than 70 customer projects, I will show you in this book how you can use EAM functionality in your enterprise, and also how you should not use it.

It's all about practice.

The book uses customer examples to illustrate what other companies have done, and I also provide numerous practical tips that will be equally useful whether you are a beginner or an advanced user of a previous release of the system.

SAP and usability—is that possible?

Unfortunately, it is a widespread prejudice that usability is not necessarily a major feature of SAP applications. It has always been a special concern of mine not to let this prejudice become the final verdict. This topic is particularly significant in plant maintenance. Therefore, I devote an entire chapter to a range of measures that will help you to increase usability and, thus, user acceptance of the SAP system in your enterprise. Furthermore, I will present the results of a study we conducted at the university that clearly prove that such measures yield an effective advantage in the processing of business processes to improve usability, as well as the extent to which they do so.

Other highlights of the book include the following: You will receive numerous tips and tricks for daily operations and learn what you should and should not do in the course of your daily work.

Other highlights

1.1 Target Audience

This book always addresses you directly. So, who are *you*? What can you expect from this book?

Who are you?

- You are a *project lead* and are responsible for an SAP plant maintenance project. In reality, you are also a technical expert, maintenance planner, workshop manager, IT expert, and a member of the organizational team, among other things. This book gives you lots of advice on project management, IT strategy, and the other strands of your job.
- You are a *member of the project team* and are interested in creating a particular kind of SAP plant maintenance system. Therefore, your actual daily activities mean that you are also a maintenance planner, a workshop manager, an IT expert, a company engineer, a technical expert, a group leader, and a member of the organizational team, among other things. You, too, will find a lot of helpful advice in this book on business processes and procedures.
- You are a *manager* and have to decide whether or not to implement SAP plant maintenance. In your daily work, you are a technical leader, a maintenance manager, a facility manager, an IT manager, and an organizational manager, among other roles. This book gives you specific information about what the SAP system can and cannot do.
- You are a *key user*, which means that you help your colleagues in their daily work of processing business processes, and you therefore need more background information on the system than the standard user. This book gives you a lot of information about why something may or may not happen in the system, what you can do about it, and what you should not do.

- You are a *consultant*. This book will be useful to you whether you work in management consulting and need strategic advice or are a specialist consultant looking for application information. You will obtain this information here.
- You are interested in SAP plant maintenance on a *general level*. This book offers you an overview and basic understanding of the subject matter, and a certain level of detail.

Who are you not?
Whom does this book not address? What will you not find here?

- If you are a *developer* who is looking for help with programming (for example, for interfaces or add-ons), this is not the book for you.
- If you are an *end user* and need a user guide for your enterprise's SAP system, this book will only partly fulfill your needs. This is because individual installed systems are too multi-faceted for all possible variations to be included in a single book.
- You are an *(internal or external) consultant*, *key user*, or *member of the project team* and are hoping for in-depth explanations and tips on Customizing. You will not find such information here. A separate book on this topic, *Configuring SAP Plant Maintenance*, is expected to be published by SAP PRESS in the Summer of 2014.

1.2 What This Book Can and Cannot Do

There is neither Customizing information nor programming information in this book, and it is not end-user documentation (as it is not the SAP documentation either). The book does, however, provide the following for you:

- It gives you a basic understanding of the philosophy of SAP in the area of plant maintenance.
- It describes the functionality of the SAP system in order to illustrate the options it provides, and also to make you aware of the limits of this functionality.
- It uses reference processes and typical examples (such as the structuring of technical systems) to demonstrate how you can map your plant maintenance processes in the SAP system.

- It gives you information on whether and where you can adapt the system to your own needs by cross-referencing to Customizing. The actual Customizing settings can be found in the aforementioned book, *Configuring SAP Plant Maintenance*.
- It gives you arguments that will enable you to decide whether to implement SAP Plant Maintenance.
- It provides you with advice on making usability a central feature of your SAP system.
- It gives you many useful tips and tricks for your SAP plant maintenance system.

There is one thing that I have learned from my experience of projects in the past: every enterprise has its own idea of how the SAP system should be used. This means, for example, that every enterprise will map its technical systems differently, every enterprise will set up its business processes differently, every enterprise needs to connect to different IT systems, and so on. Therefore, you should regard the information presented in this book as a starting point for your own ideas on how to adapt the system to your enterprise's individual needs and thus to create "your" SAP Plant Maintenance system.

1.3 Structure of This Book

This book is divided into nine chapters:

Chapter 2, Plant Maintenance and SAP: A Contradiction?, lays the business foundations and gives you a basic understanding of SAP's commitment to the area of plant maintenance. In this chapter, you will also learn how maintenance strategies have developed over the years, what stages of development SAP has gone through in the plant maintenance area, and what SAP's position is today.

SAP and plant maintenance

Organizational structures are the basis of everything in an SAP system. In **Chapter 3**, Organizational Structures, I explain the generic SAP organizational units and demonstrate to you the maintenance-specific organizational units required for other procedures.

Organizational structures

Structuring of technical systems

A requirements-oriented approach to the structuring of technical systems is a prerequisite for processing business processes in SAP plant maintenance. SAP provides various elements for mapping your own asset structure, and like every other enterprise, you have to decide which elements you want to use for which purpose. In **Chapter 4**, Structuring of Technical Systems, I describe the options and limitations that apply when it comes to the structuring of technical systems, give advice, and make recommendations. I also provide tips on what you need to consider before you actually start to work in the system.

Business processes

Chapter 5, Business Processes, forms the core of the book. The focus here, as before, is on the uniqueness of the business processes within each enterprise. SAP provides tools that you, and every enterprise, can tailor to suit individual requirements. This chapter includes typical reference processes to show you the options and limitations of the SAP system. It also contains recommendations on how you can best use the system and what preparations you need to make before starting to work in the system.

Integration with other departments

Your plant maintenance concept is constantly interacting with and, thus, exchanging data with other departments in your enterprise. This is reflected in the system in the wide and in-depth level of integration between plant maintenance with the applications used in other departments. These applications can be in SAP ERP, in other SAP systems, or in non-SAP systems. **Chapter 6**, Integrating Applications from Other Departments, illustrates the integration options in the system, analyzes the interfaces, and, again, provides you with recommendations and tips.

Plant maintenance controlling

There are two types of controlling in plant maintenance: *operational controlling* controls ongoing business processes, and *analytical controlling* is used to prepare for decisions. Therefore, in **Chapter 7**, Plant Maintenance Controlling, I show you the options for budgeting maintenance activities, on one hand, and the options and limitations of the tools provided by SAP for the analytical area on the other.

Modern technologies

Modern information and communication technologies, such as cloud computing, the Internet, mobile services, and service-oriented architectures have become established in plant maintenance, as in almost every other area. In **Chapter 8**, New Information Technologies in Plant Maintenance, I describe state-of-the-art technologies, focusing particularly on their prerequisites, options, and limitations in plant maintenance. I also make some predictions about what we can expect from these technologies in the future.

In **Chapter 9**, Usability, I first present the options that the SAP system provides for improving usability. I then conclude the book with the results of an empirical laboratory test. In the SAP Laboratory at the Würzburg-Schweinfurt University of Applied Sciences, we set up real-world conditions and tested how long it takes to process business processes when every effort is made to increase usability, as well as when usability measures are not implemented. Even I was surprised by the results. | Usability

The **Appendix** contains a wealth of useful, additional information, such as overviews in tabular form, suggestions for further reading, and much more. | Appendix

To make it easier for you to use this book, particular information is highlighted using the following special icons: | Special icons used in this book

- **Caution** [!]
  Boxes with this icon contain important information about the topic under discussion. I also use this icon to warn you about potential error sources or stumbling blocks.

- **Practical tip** [+]
  This book contains lots of tips and recommendations that I have learned from my own professional experience. This kind of information is contained in boxes marked with this symbol.

| Online material for this book | [⊕] |

At *http://www.sap-press.com/H3316*, you will find the following document for download:

An overview of the plant maintenance *transaction codes*, as well as a PDF version of the reference card.

Now, it only remains for me to hope that you obtain many ideas and a great deal of inspiration for your own enterprise from reading this book.

And, true to the spirit of the quote from Thomas A. Edison (which, as far as I am concerned, is the best quote of all), I wish you the energy, patience, and stamina required to implement them in your enterprise.

Sincerely,
Karl Liebstückel

This chapter first takes a look at the increasing significance of plant maintenance and the associated change in perspective, which has also given rise to new terminology. It then outlines the environment of SAP's Plant Maintenance component.

2 Plant Maintenance and SAP: A Contradiction?

In the past few years and decades, plant maintenance has become more and more important for the following business, economic, and technological reasons:

- **Business factors**
  - Rising acquisition values for technical systems
  - A disproportionate increase in costs resulting from losses
  - A higher, modified requirements profile for maintenance activities
  - On-time collaboration with customers and vendors
  - Reduced vertical integration
- **Economic factors**
  - An increasing proportion of maintenance costs attributable to the gross national product (GNP)
  - Continuous growth in the number of people gainfully employed in the maintenance sector
  - More stringent environmental regulations and occupational health and safety regulations
  - Globalization of product markets
  - Expansion of the services sector

- **Technological factors**
  - Increased innovation speed[1]
  - Increased automation
  - Increasingly interlinked, complex technical systems

This chapter closely examines these influencing factors, all of which interact with each other, and the associated changes to plant maintenance. Furthermore, this chapter introduces the many changes that the maintenance components in the SAP system have undergone, without referring to releases.

2.1 Plant Maintenance Today: New Ideas Need New Space

Plant maintenance: a cost driver?

More and more companies are abandoning the outdated view that plant maintenance is a necessary evil or simply a cost factor. The ever-increasing pressure to be competitive in terms of quality and productivity is driving companies toward plant maintenance, which today occupies a much higher position in a company's priority list of objectives than ever before. This extends to the realization that the company can sell its plant maintenance services in the market and, thus, contribute to an increase in revenue in addition to a reduction in costs.

Collaboration with customers and vendors

Market globalization is increasingly leading to close collaboration with customers and vendors. Vertical integration is decreasing more and more. Thus, in the automotive industry, for example, the last 10 years have witnessed a considerable drop in vertical integration, to just 26.7%, and to 15% in individual cases. That is, the automotive industry produces just 15–25% of the end product itself, and everything else comes from upstream production stages, the suppliers.[2] This has led to a

---

1 See Matyas, K.: Instandhaltungslogistik – Qualität und Produktivität steigern, 4. Auflage, München: Hanser Verlag 2010 (*Plant Maintenance Verlag, 2010 Logistics: Increasing Quality and Productivity* 4th edition, Munich: Hanser Verlag, 2010).
2 Institut für Wirtschaftsforschung (IFO) (Institute for Economic Research): press release from 11.21.2005. Something similar is also expressed in the IKB report "Automotive Industry: New Opportunities, Increasing Investment and Financing Needs" (2003).

proportionate increase in dependency on the availability of technical systems at upstream production levels.

In the past, it was possible to take internal counter-measures against malfunctions within the production flow of deeply structured production processes, but this is entirely inconceivable for globalized production flows. Thus, today's goals of *preventing failures* and *increasing or ensuring system availability* are increasingly the focus of plant maintenance goals.

System availability

Preventive maintenance is another goal of today's plant maintenance. This can be achieved by changing the design of the technical system or machine. Another important aspect of preventive maintenance is sharing with production employees the responsibility (keyword: TPM[3]) of ensuring that no unscheduled outages occur, if possible. First Line Maintenance tasks (on-call services for breakdown clearance) can also support the process.

Preventive maintenance

In recent years, machines and technical systems have undergone enormous development in terms of their structure and the technology deployed. However, this also means that it is becoming more and more difficult to record the condition of individual components or assemblies because modern technical systems have considerably more weak points than the original machines. In addition, design engineers no longer tend to build oversized developments, but rather space-saving, lightweight technical systems. As a result, however, numerous components are more sensitive to signs of wear and defects.

New designs

Plants and machinery are constructed in a much more modular manner today than previously. Thus, maintenance is applied very differently to individual components of a system (component maintenance) and no longer refers to the complete system.

Component maintenance

---

3 TPM: Total Productive Management or Total Productive Manufacturing. The eight TPM pillars include autonomous maintenance (inspections and minor repairs by the plant operator) and the scheduled plant maintenance.

2 Plant Maintenance and SAP: A Contradiction?

Other goals Other goals may include the following:

- Increased, optimal use of the life cycle of technical systems and devices
- Improved quality of finished products
- Improved operating safety
- Optimized operating procedures
- Future-oriented cost planning
- Lower restart costs
- Compliance with legal requirements, particularly environmental regulations
- Compliance with manufacturer guidelines, so you can make a claim under warranty, if required

However, other objectives may also be of interest to you, depending on your industry, the objects to be maintained, the size of the company, the company's organization, and other influencing factors. If, for example, you are a maintenance service provider, customer satisfaction will be of primary importance to you. If you work in real estate, maintenance tasks may contribute to strengthening your negotiating position when selling real estate. Therefore, each company should develop clear maintenance objectives and communicate these to everyone involved (for example, employees, customers, and so on).

Two unavoidable consequences resulted from this change within plant maintenance: new maintenance terminology had to be coined for organizations with responsibilities both nationally and internationally, and companies had to react to these challenges by changing their maintenance strategies.

2.2 New Maintenance Terminology

In June 2003, a new version of the German standard DIN 31051—Fundamentals of Maintenance—was published to replace the older version from 1985. It was necessary to revise the older version as a result of EN 13306, published in 2001 (current version: EN 13306:2010), which compiled new terminology for plant maintenance. Maintenance is divided accordingly in the current version of DIN 31051:2012-09 into four basic measures[4] (see Figure 2.1). While this is a German standard, the concepts and the four basic measures are still globally applicable.

Maintenance includes "combinations of all technical and administrative measures as well as of management measures throughout the life cycle of a unit, which are aimed at preserving or restoring its functional state so that it can perform the required function." It essentially comprises the following four tasks: *inspection*, *maintenance*, *repair*, and *improvement*, each of which is described in more detail below.

Maintenance: definition

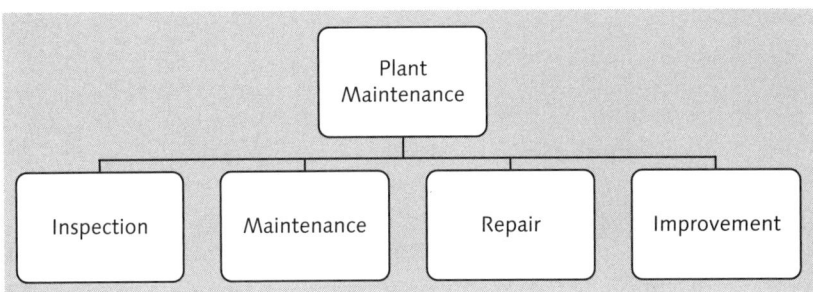

Figure 2.1 New Maintenance Terminology

To ensure both the high availability and operating safety of the machines, technical systems, and equipment, regular inspections are required to determine their technical condition and to define the necessary maintenance tasks. DIN 31051 defines inspection as all tasks for determining and assessing the actual condition of a unit, including identifying the cause of wear and tear and deducing the consequences necessary to ensure its future use. In contrast, the old DIN 31051 defined inspection as all tasks for determining and assessing the actual condition. The inspection includes the following measures in particular:

Inspection

- Check
- Measure
- Observe

---

4 In this case, see *DIN 31051:2012-09: Fundamentals of Maintenance*, issued by Deutschen Institut für Normung (DIN) (German Institute for Standardization), Berlin/Vienna/Zurich: 2012.

- Assess
- Derive consequences

Maintenance Whereas the old DIN 31051 defined maintenance as all tasks for preserving the target condition, the new DIN 31051 defines maintenance as all tasks for delaying the reduction of the wear reserve. Maintenance tasks include the following tasks in particular:

- Visual inspection
- Adjust
- Replace
- Supplement
- Lubricate
- Preserve
- Clean
- Functional testing

To obtain the required functional efficiency and availability of machines, technical systems, and equipment, it is necessary to regularly implement maintenance tasks based on the manufacturer guidelines, maintenance plans, and customer needs, while taking into account the changing, operation-specific processes and conditions.

Repairs The old DIN 31051 defined repairs as all tasks for restoring the target condition. In contrast, the new DIN 31051 defines as repairs all physical tasks that are carried out to restore the functioning of a faulty unit. Via maintenance and repairs, non-functioning components, assemblies, and so on in machinery, plant, and equipment, both unscheduled (breakdown clearance) and scheduled (planned shutdowns) are replaced and full functionality is, thus, restored. Repairs, thus, consist in particular of the following activities:

- Replacement
- Restoration of functions
- Elimination of breakdowns

New to DIN 31051 is the improvement. This is defined as the combination of all technical and administrative tasks, as well as management tasks, to improve the reliability and/or maintainability and/or safety of a unit without changing its original function. The constant improvement of the plant serves to increase the operational and functional safety of machines, plants, and equipment. At the same time, a corresponding potential for improvement is identified, solutions are designed, and specified measures are implemented. The inspection comprises the following tasks in particular:

Improvement

- Elimination of weak points
- Improvement in machinery and plant design
- Optimization of business processes
- Acceleration of the exchange of information

A summary comparison is shown in Table 2.1.

	DIN 31051:1985-01	DIN 31051:2012-09
Inspection	Tasks for determining and assessing the actual condition	Tasks for determining and assessing the functional condition with determination of the causes of wear and tear and derivation of the necessary tasks
Maintenance	Tasks for maintaining the target condition	Tasks for delaying the the reduction of the wear reserve
Repairs	Tasks for restoring the target condition	Tasks carried out to restore the functioning of a faulty unit
Improvement	—	Tasks to improve the reliability and/or maintainability and/or safety of a unit without changing its original function

Table 2.1 The Old and New DIN 31051

2.3 Maintenance Strategies over the Course of Time

Not only have the responsible organizations responded to the changed business conditions, but also the companies themselves have adopted the new challenges posed by their changed maintenance strategies (see Figure 2.2).

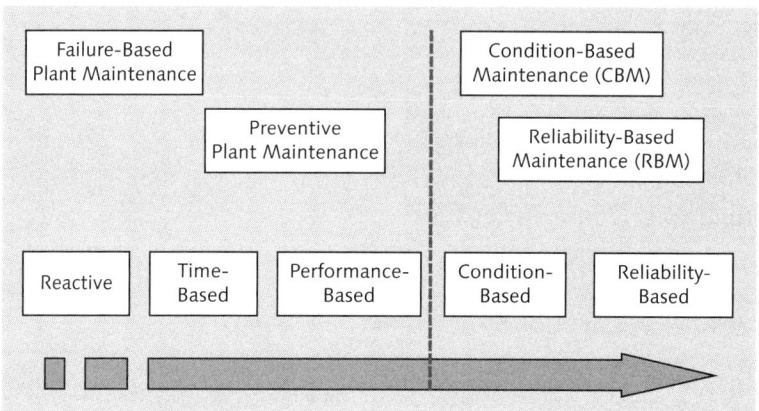

Figure 2.2 Strategies over the Course of Time

From reactive to preventive maintenance

The new challenges of the market and technology are reflected in the development of maintenance strategies and concepts. The classic reactive maintenance, which provides for the repair of the plant after its downtime, was replaced successively by preventive maintenance focused on proactive maintenance and inspection tasks. The "firefighting strategy" had to be replaced at the latest update with the increasing linking of assets, since the failure of a machine would stop the entire production line and result in very high downtime costs.

Preventive maintenance can be performed in a time-based (that is, calendar-based) or performance-based (that is, counter-based) manner.

Time-based or performance-based?

Why is this distinction so important, especially against the backdrop of the possible use of IT? This is because performance-based maintenance requires significantly more administrative effort than time-based maintenance.

With time-based maintenance, you define only the maintenance plans with fixed or sequential cycles. The maintenance planning and control system can, thus, calculate all maintenance dates and automatically generates an order for the calculated date.

However, performance-based maintenance requires a counter (kilometers, operating hours, quantities, and so on) and works correctly only if meter readings are recorded at regular intervals. Organization, planning, and recording meter readings leads to an administrative burden that should not be underestimated. The maintenance planning and control system can correctly calculate the updated maintenance schedules only if the current meter readings are available regularly.

The ratio of executed and planned maintenance orders was at 90:10 for a long time in many companies that followed the "firefighting strategy." For many companies, this ratio may still apply, but numerous companies are already on the way to more and better planning and may have reached a ratio of 70:30 or even of 50:50. If you have reached a better ratio in your company, you can be proud of your level of organization.

What is the reality?

With condition-based maintenance (CBM), maintenance activities are executed if a measuring point on a technical object has reached a certain condition. This requires the regular inspection of a assets, including the recording of inspection results, or the presence of upstream systems that constantly monitor the condition of a plant and trigger a message to the maintenance planning and control system in the event of an emergency (for example, exceeding or falling below predetermined value limits). Possible upstream systems may be, for example, the following:

Condition-based maintenance

- Mobile data acquisition systems
- Process control systems (PCS)
- Central building control systems
- Supervisory Control and Data Acquisition (SCADA) systems

Reliability-based maintenance (RBM) determines the maintenance tasks, operating rules, and structural adjustments necessary for the desired reliability of a technical system. RBM is a method of analysis that contains rules for the decisions and is based on the analysis of the functions of a machine. Possible malfunctions and their causes are derived from here. A failure impact assessment is carried out for each cause. This collection of information is called an *information worksheet* and is largely a

Reliability-based maintenance

failure mode and effects analysis (FMEA). A decision diagram is then used for any cause of a failure in the information sheet to check whether a condition-related, preventive, or reactive task is recommended. If none of these measures are useful, design changes or amended operating rules are considered.

2.4 SAP Plant Maintenance over the Course of Time

From RM-INST ... The history of SAP plant maintenance dates back to 1986. In this year, the first version of SAP plant maintenance was put on the market with RM-INST within the SAP R/2 system. More releases of RM-INST appeared in 1988 (4.3) and 1991 (5.0).

... Via R/3 PM ... In 1994, the first version of the Plant Maintenance (PM) module of SAP R/3 was put on the market. The SAP R/3 releases experienced a varied naming convention: from SAP R/3 to SAP R/3 Enjoy and mySAP.com to SAP R/3 Enterprise. The term for plant maintenance—PM—remained constant until the mySAP.com release. In Release SAP R/3 Enterprise, SAP referred to Asset Lifecycle Management (ALM). Figure 2.3 shows an overview of the history of SAP plant maintenance.

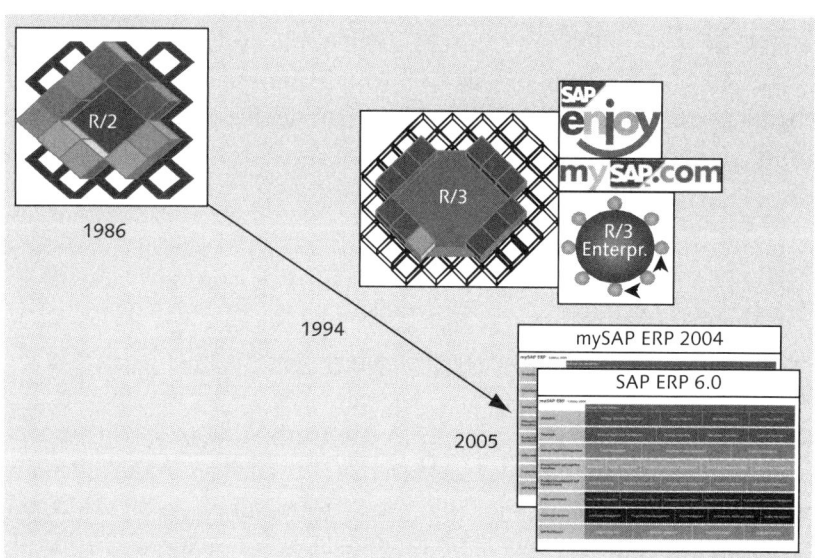

Figure 2.3 The History of SAP Plant Maintenance

When SAP 2005 launched the first ERP release on the market, we had to adapt yet again to a new term for plant maintenance: Enterprise Asset Management (EAM). The release names changed often since then: it was first mySAP ERP 2005, then the *my* disappeared, and the release was renamed SAP ERP 2005. A short time later, SAP replaced the year with the continuous release number; it has been SAP ERP 6.0 since then.

... to SAP ERP EAM

2.5 SAP ERP 6.0

SAP ERP 6.0 is composed of SAP ERP ECC (where *ECC* means Enterprise Core Component), all SAP industry solutions, additional components, and SAP NetWeaver 7.3 as a technological basis.

SAP ERP ECC is not a *revolutionary*, but rather an *evolutionary* development of SAP R/3, and includes solutions for the following areas (see Figure 2.4):

SAP ERP ECC

- Finance (formerly FI and CO, now SAP ERP Financials)
- Human resources (formerly HR, now SAP ERP Human Capital Management [HCM])
- Purchasing and warehouse management (formerly MM and WM, now SAP ERP Procurement and Logistics)
- Product development and production planning (formerly PP and PDM, now SAP ERP Product Development and Manufacturing)
- Sales and service (formerly SD and CS, now SAP ERP Sales and Service)
- Generic business functions, such as facility management/real estate management, project system, environment, health and safety, quality management, and travel management (formerly RE, PS, EHS Management, QM, and TM, now grouped together as SAP ERP Corporate Services)

Consequently, EAM is also included among SAP ERP Corporate Services. The essential aspects of the integration of EAM into SAP ERP ECC applications are presented in Section 6.2.

2 Plant Maintenance and SAP: A Contradiction?

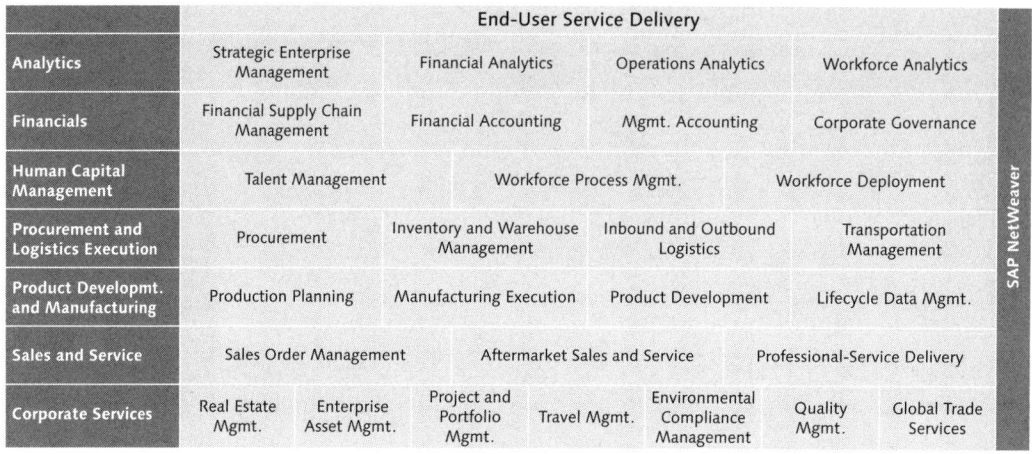

Figure 2.4 Solution Map of SAP ERP 6.0

Industry solutions
SAP offers a total of 28 industry solutions (for example, SAP for Automotive, SAP for Utilities, and SAP for Chemicals). These are delivered together with SAP ERP 6.0. You activate one or more industry solutions via the Switch Framework. I will not elaborate on this topic here, however, but would like to refer you to the extensive documentation and literature.

SAP Business Suite
In addition to SAP ERP, SAP offers the following applications within the SAP Business Suite:

- SAP Customer Relationship Management (SAP CRM) provides functions for sales, marketing, and service as a solution for customer relationship management.
- SAP Product Lifecycle Management (SAP PLM) provides functions for the product development process, such as ideas management, Computer-Aided Design (CAD) interfaces, document management, and so on, as a solution for the product life cycle.
- SAP Supplier Relationship Management (SAP SRM) provides functions for electronic purchasing, such as catalog management, self-service for suppliers and employees, and so on, as a solution for supplier relationship management.

► SAP Supply Chain Management (SAP SCM) includes functions for sales, production, and distribution planning as a solution for supply chain management.

Since SAP ERP 6.0, SAP has delivered Enhancement Packages once per year, on average. In the past, developments were delivered only in the context of new releases, which customers could manage only via migration projects and which, thus, led to a great deal of work. In contrast to new releases, Enhancement Packages provide a continuous, but cautious, functional development of the SAP system, without involving the major work of a migration project.

Development via Enhancement Packages

These developments were initially delivered as so-called Enterprise Extensions (see Figure 2.5). The extension that is important from the perspective of plant maintenance is EA-PLM, which you can activate via Transaction SFW5.

Enterprise Extensions and Business Functions

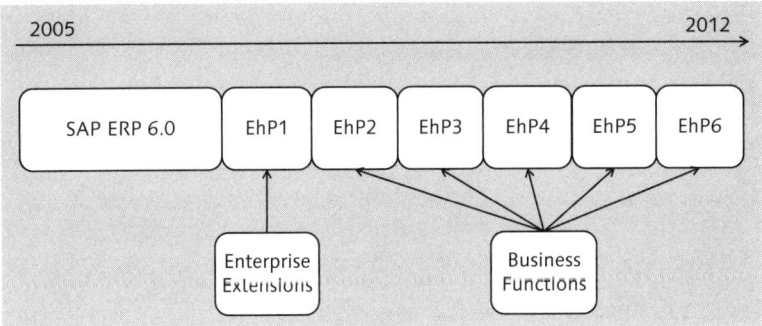

Figure 2.5 Enterprise Extensions and Business Functions

Activating EA-PLM [+]

In SAP ERP ECC, you can use certain functions of EAM (for example, mass change of messages and orders) only if you have activated *Enterprise Extension EA-PLM*. Activate Enterprise Extension EA-PLM via Transaction SFW5 if you want to use this maintenance function. However, note that you cannot undo this activation.

As of Enhancement Package 2, the enhancements have been delivered as Enterprise Business Functions, which you can also activate via the Switch Framework using Transaction SWF5 (see Figure 2.6). From the perspective of plant maintenance, the most important Business Functions are the following:

- **Enhancement Package 2**
  - LOG_EAM_CI_1 (for example, digital signature of operations)
  - LOG_EAM_POM (for example, Maintenance Event Builder)
  - LOG_EAM_SIMP (for example, simple order view)
- **Enhancement Package 3**
  - LOG_EAM_CI_2 (for example, new BAPIs and BAdIs for plant maintenance)
  - LOG_EAM_PAM (Pool Asset Management)
  - LOG_EAM_TOHO (Takeover/Handover of Technical Objects)
- **Enhancement Package 4**
  - LOG_EAM_CI_3 (for example, tour planning)
  - LOG_EAM_POM_2 (for example, enhancements in the Maintenance Event Builder)
  - LOG_EAM_ROTSUB (Refurbishment & Subcontracting)
  - LOG_MM_SERNO (serial numbers in the purchasing documents)

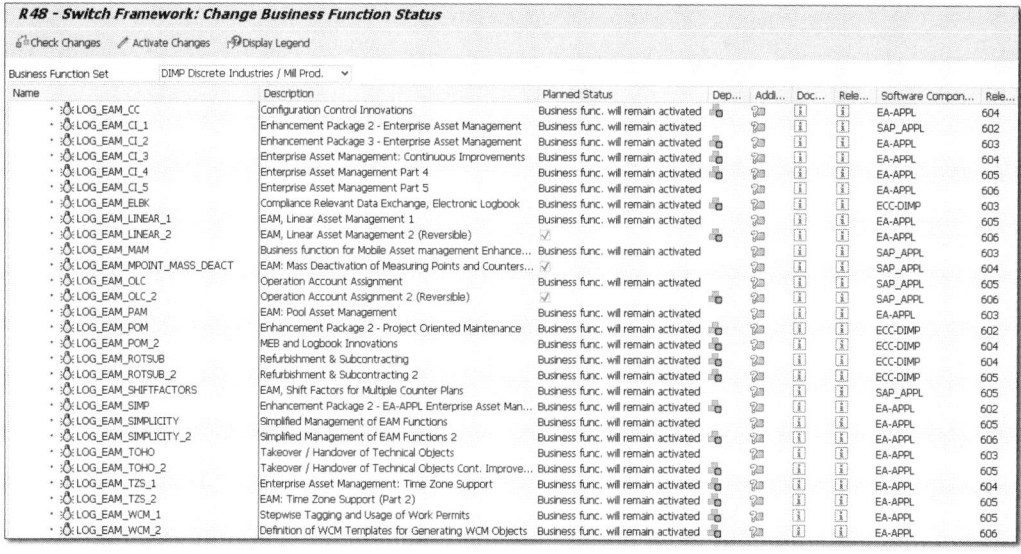

Figure 2.6 Transaction SWF5: Switch Framework

- **Enhancement Package 5**
  - LOG_EAM_CI_4 (for example, enhancements for tour planning)
  - LOG_EAM_SHIFTFACTORS (shift factors for multiple counter plans)
  - LOG_EAM_LINEAR_1 (Linear Asset Management)
  - LOG_EAM_OLC (Operation Account Assignment)
- **Enhancement Package 6**
  - LOG_EAM_CI_5 (for example, mass change of operations)
  - LOG_EAM_CI_6 (for example, opening period, in days)
  - LOG_EAM_OLC_2 (Enhancements for Operation Account Assignment)
  - LOG_EAM_LINEAR_2 (Enhancements for Linear Asset Management)

> **Activating Business Functions** [+]
>
> In SAP ERP ECC, you can use certain functions of EAM (for example, mass change of equipment and functional locations) only if you have activated *Enterprise Business Functions*. Activate the desired Business Functions via Transaction SFW5 if you want to use these maintenance functions.

The following SAP components are delivered together with SAP ERP 6.0:

- SAP SRM (only classic self-service procurement scenario)
- SAP E-Recruiting
- SAP Learning Solution
- SAP Financial Supply Chain Management
- Employee Self-Services/Manager Self-Services
- SAP cProjects Suite
- SAP Internet Sales Web Application Component

SAP NetWeaver is the technological platform for all SAP applications (see Figure 2.7) and is delivered together with SAP ERP 6.0. SAP NetWeaver combines the functions of many different SAP technology

SAP NetWeaver

products and distinguishes three major integration layers at the same time: the process level (process integration), the information level (information integration) and the user level (people integration). The application platform constitutes the common runtime environment.

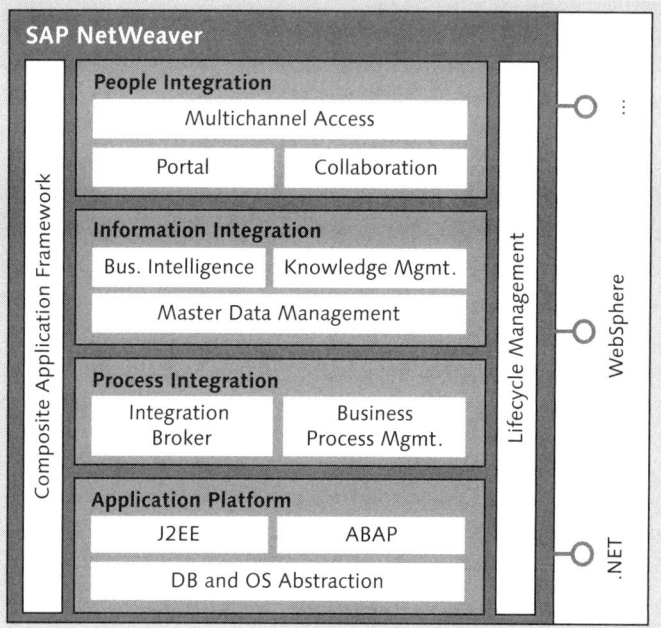

Figure 2.7 The Integration Levels and Components of SAP NetWeaver 7.3

The following components of SAP NetWeaver are of particular interest in terms of EAM, and I will discuss their possible uses in relation to EAM again in the following sections of this book:

- SAP NetWeaver Multi-Channel Access (see Section 8.7)
- SAP NetWeaver Portal (see Section 8.1)
- SAP NetWeaver Collaboration (see Section 8.4)
- SAP NetWeaver Business Warehouse (see Section 7.2.4)
- SAP NetWeaver Business Process Management (see Section 8.8)
- SAP NetWeaver Master Data Management (see Section 6.3.1)

This chapter provides information about the essential elements for maintenance processing in the SAP system: the general organizational units, maintenance-specific organizational units, and work center.

3   Organizational Structures

The definition of organizational structures covers the following areas: the general SAP organizational units (for example, controlling area, company code, plant, and storage location), definition of maintenance-specific organizational units (for example, location or plant section), and finally, definition of maintenance work centers (for example, mechanical workshop, electrical workshop, measurement, and control).

3.1   SAP Organizational Units

The organizational units form the basis of all master data and business processes in SAP ERP. In the following sections, you will learn about the most important organizational units from a maintenance perspective.

> **Organizational Units in the SAP Project** [+]
>
> Note: If you implement EAM, the general organizational units in the SAP system (for example, the company code, controlling area, and plant) are usually already defined. This is because they were defined when other applications (such as CO, MM, and so on) were implemented. Therefore, you can influence the design only if EAM is implemented from the outset or if you define separate organizational units from a pure maintenance perspective.

3.1.1   The Plant from a Maintenance Perspective

The plant is undoubtedly the most important organizational unit for plant maintenance. It fulfills several maintenance functions:

Functions of the plant

- A plant is responsible for planning maintenance activities. In this context, this plant is known as a *planning plant*. To convert a plant to a planning plant, you use the Customizing function MAINTAIN PLANNING PLANT.
- All technical objects to be maintained are physically located in a plant (functional location, equipment, serial number). Here, this plant is known as a *maintenance plant*. A plant becomes a maintenance plant if you create a technical object there. To assign the planning plant responsible for the maintenance plant, you use the Customizing function ASSIGN MAINTENANCE PLANNING PLANT.
- You require a plant with a storage location in which you can store spare parts.
- Furthermore, some technical objects (serial numbers) can be stored in a plant with a storage location.

3.1.2 Maintenance-Specific Organizational Units

Maintenance plant–specific or planning plant–specific?

Additional maintenance-specific organizational units (either maintenance plant–specific or planning plant–specific) play an important role within a plant (see Figure 3.1).

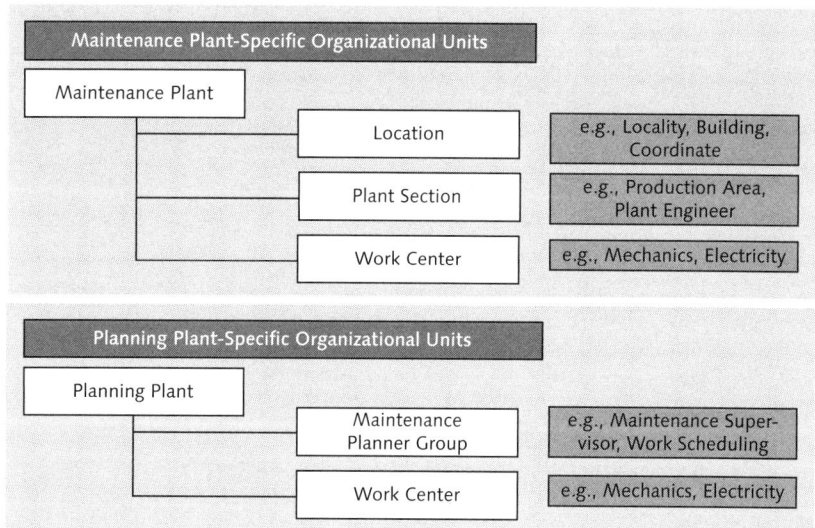

Figure 3.1 Maintenance Plant and Planning Plant

Technical objects (functional location, equipment) also contain all of the maintenance plant–specific and planning plant–specific data, which is then copied to notifications and purchase orders. This data is explained in more detail next.

Work centers perform maintenance tasks or are responsible for such tasks. Work centers relate to either the planning or maintenance plant (see Section 3.2).

Work center

A planner group is responsible for planning maintenance tasks and also relates to a planning plant. You maintain planner groups using the Customizing function DEFINE PLANNER GROUPS.

Planner group

Using Planner Groups	[+]
You set up maintenance planner groups, for example, if you want to map work scheduling or individual maintenance planners known by name.	

You use a label to indicate the physical location of a technical object. A location is always defined with reference to a maintenance plant; you maintain locations using the Customizing function MAINTAIN LOCATION.

Location

Naming Locations	[+]
In practice, either building numbers (for example, F141 or WDF21) or, if they exist, plant coordinates (for example, A01 or K15) have become commonly used locations.	

You define the responsibilities for the operation of the (production) plant as the plant section; you maintain plant sections using the Customizing function DEFINE PLANT SECTIONS.

Plant section

Responsibilities for the Plant Section	[+]
In practice, either the plant engineer responsible for the technical system or the production area belonging to the technical system is commonly used as a plant section.	

3.1.3 Other General Organizational Units

In addition to the maintenance-specific organizational units, there are other general organizational units that are also relevant for EAM.

Company code
You assign a plant to the company code (see Figure 3.2). The company code is the smallest organizational unit for which a complete, self-contained set of accounts can be drawn up for the purposes of external reporting ("the company"). This involves recording all relevant transactions and generating balance sheets and profit and loss statements.

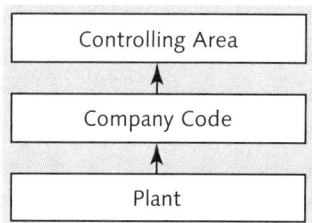

Figure 3.2 General Organizational Units

When you assign a technical object to a maintenance plant, you also automatically assign its company code in the background.

Controlling area
The controlling area is an organizational unit within a company for which a self-contained cost accounting can be performed. A controlling area may include one or more company codes.

When you assign a technical object to a maintenance plant, you not only create its company code, but also determine its controlling area. Similarly, when you assign a work center to a plant, you also assign its controlling area.

[+] **Controlling Areas Involved**

From a plant maintenance perspective, it is always favorable if the controlling area of the technical object and the controlling area of the work center are identical.

You may now be wondering why this is favorable. This will be explained in the next section.

3.1.4 Plant-Specific and Cross-Plant Maintenance

For business processes in plant maintenance, you need to differentiate between order planning and execution in the same plant and order planning and execution in different plants.

Plant-Specific Maintenance

In practice, you most frequently encounter a situation in which the maintenance requirement is planned in the same plant in which it originates, the purchase orders are fulfilled by workshops in the same plant, and the spare parts are stored within the same plant. In Figure 3.3, this plant is known as Plant 1000. The following applies here: maintenance plant = planning plant = plant with spare parts storage.

Requirements, planning, and execution in the same plant

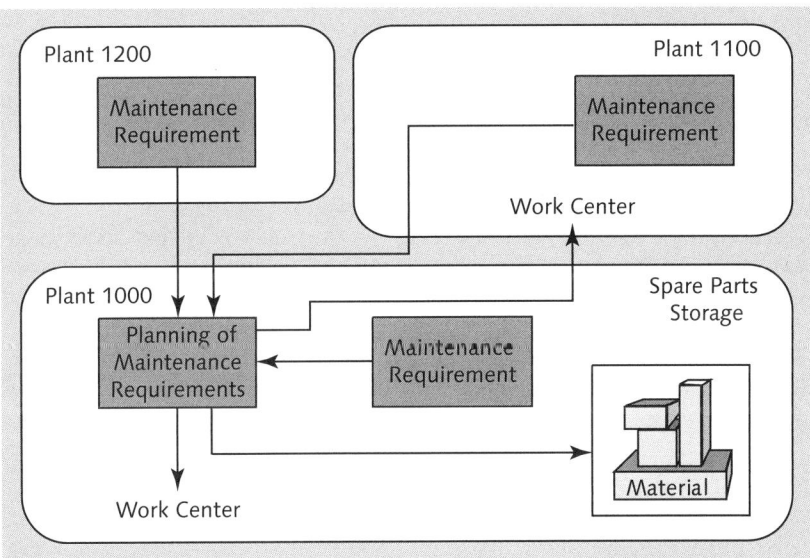

Figure 3.3 Plant and Plant Maintenance

Cross-Plant Maintenance

In addition to plant-specific maintenance, other situations are also to be found:

Requirements and execution in different plants

- In a plant (here, for example, 1200), there is a requirement because a technical system is to be maintained there (that is, in the maintenance plant), but all other functions (planning, order execution, spare parts storage) are the responsibility of another plant (here, for example, 1000).
- There is a requirement in a plant (here, for example, 1100), and additional sub-functions (order execution) are also the responsibility of this plant, but other sub-functions (order planning, spare parts storage) are the responsibility of other plants (here, for example, 1000).

Cross-plant maintenance is not problematic if the maintenance plant of the technical object and the plant of the executing work center have the same company code.

The same applies if the plants have different company codes but the same controlling area. This is also a typical scenario.

Different controlling areas It becomes problematic when the plants belong to different controlling areas. This is not a typical scenario, but results in a customer/supplier relationship. In this case, the maintenance plant (customer) should trigger purchase orders. At the work center plant (supplier), a customer order is triggered for which a billing document is then created. The billing document is entered, in turn, as an incoming invoice in the maintenance plant. This is a very tedious process overall. How can you simplify it?

[+] **Plants in Different Controlling Areas**

If you use cross-plant maintenance and the plants are in different controlling areas, the following procedure is recommended:

- Create a cost center for the actual maintenance plant in the work center plant.
- Assign all technical objects to the work center plant as a maintenance plant and its cost center.
- Process all maintenance orders in the work center plant.
- Manually perform periodic billing documents (for example, monthly) from the work center plant at the expense of the customer maintenance plant and for the benefit of the cost center.

This approach avoids creating purchase orders and sales orders, creating individual billings, and posting individual incoming invoices.

3.2 Work Centers

From a maintenance perspective, a work center represents either an individual person (for example, the engineer M. Huber) or a workshop, thus a group of persons. The following workshops are often found in practice:

Definition and basic principles

- Mechanics
- Electrics
- Measurement and control technology
- Machine center
- Welding shop
- Paint shop
- Cleaning team
- Building services engineering

> **No Individual Persons as a Work Center** [+]
>
> Avoid using individual persons as a work center. You could jeopardize your chances of capacity planning. Furthermore, work center data requires a great deal of maintenance. For person-specific responsibilities, it is better to use partner functions (see Section 4.2.9).
>
> If you, nevertheless, record work centers for each person, please note the legal regulations for each country. In Germany, for example, you can do this only if you have given your employee representatives a written company agreement in which, among other things, you state that the information will not be used to compare employee performance.

In plant maintenance, work centers are used as the following:

- Main work center in the equipment master record and functional location master record
- Main work center in a maintenance item
- Main work center in the header of a maintenance task list
- Executing work center in the operations of a maintenance task list
- Main work center in the notification

3 | Organizational Structures

- Main work center in the order header
- Executing work center in the operations of an order

[+] **Need for Work Centers**

Work centers are the individual master records that you must create in order to use EAM. You can implement business processes, for example, without technical objects (functional locations, equipment, and so on), but not without work centers.

Creating a Work Center

You use Transaction IR01 to maintain work centers. Here, you first assign a work center number and then assign the work center to a plant.

[+] **Choice of Work Center Numbers**

Frequently, you have to specify the work center in EAM processing. Therefore, you should keep work center numbers as short as possible (for example, M for mechanical workshop, E for electrical workshop, and so on).

Basic data The work center contains essential information for EAM processing (see Figure 3.4). Work centers contain basic data. You maintain this data on the BASIC DATA tab.

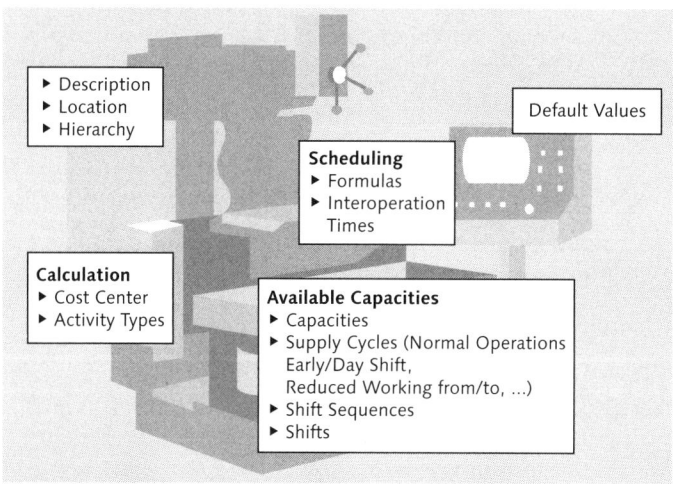

Figure 3.4 Contents of a Work Center

Characteristics of the Task List Usage [+]

When maintaining basic data for a work center, make sure you set the task list usage to 004 (maintenance tasks lists) or 009 (all task list types) so that the work center can be used in EAM processing.

Furthermore, the standard value key must be set to SAP0, so that standard values such as setup times or machine times are not required later.

Work centers contain default values that are copied into the operations or referenced when creating maintenance task lists and maintenance orders. Referencing means that the data cannot be changed in the maintenance task list. You maintain default values on the DEFAULT VALUES tab. The most important default value is the control key, via which you can subsequently control the following, in order:

Default values

1. Whether the operation should be part of costing
2. Whether the operation should be scheduled
3. Whether the operation should generate capacity requirements
4. Whether a confirmation is expected for the operation
5. Whether the operation should be processed externally
6. Whether service specifications should be set up in the operation

You maintain the control key in Customizing using the function MAINTAIN CONTROL KEY.

Using the Control Key [+]

Using the control key, you can control, in detail, the business functions that an operation should have (cost, print, confirm, assign externally, schedule, and so on).

You require at least two control keys: one key for internal processing and one key for external processing; the use of another control key depends on the respective needs.

You should always define the control key in the work center as a default value so that you do not always have to manually enter it in the maintenance task list and maintenance order.

3 | Organizational Structures

Scheduling data Work centers contain scheduling data required for lead time scheduling. You maintain scheduling data on the SCHEDULING tab (see Figure 3.5).

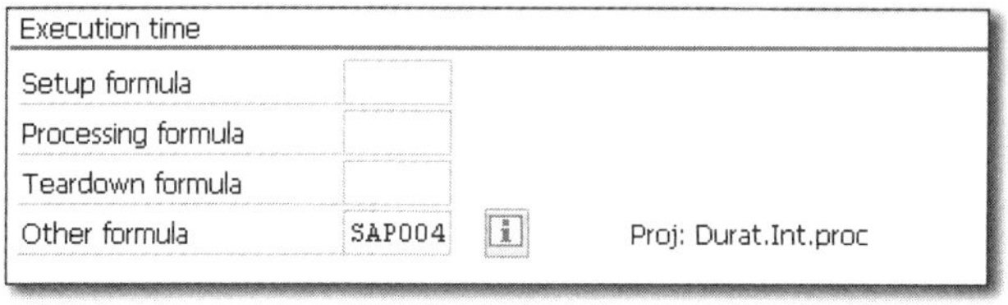

Execution time			
Setup formula			
Processing formula			
Teardown formula			
Other formula	SAP004	[i]	Proj: Durat.Int.proc

Figure 3.5 Scheduling

[+] **Formula for the Duration of Internal Processing**

If you want to schedule the purchase orders later, your work center requires a formula in the field DURATION OF INTERNAL PROCESSING. This must point to the DAUNO field—that is, to the duration from the operation. The formula SAP004 is defined in the standard SAP version.

You can check or define the formula for the duration of internal processing using the Customizing function DEFINE FORMULA PARAMETERS FOR WORK CENTERS.

Available capacity Work centers contain available capacity data required for capacity planning. Available capacity specifies which service provides capacity for each work day. A capacity is always assigned to a work center and, in plant maintenance, generally expressed in hours per week. The capacity data is maintained on the CAPACITIES tab (see Figure 3.6).

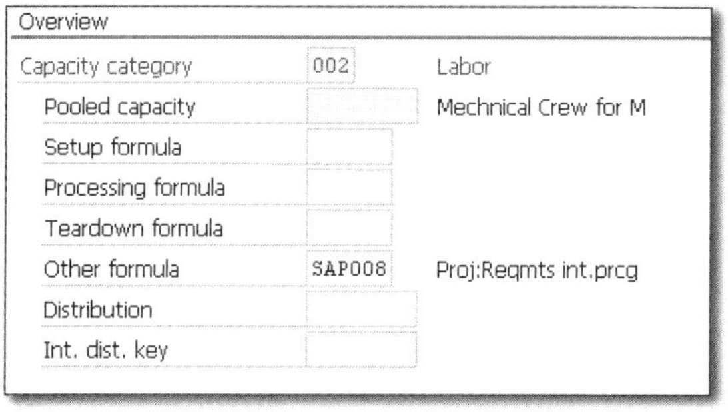

Overview		
Capacity category	002	Labor
Pooled capacity		Mechnical Crew for M
Setup formula		
Processing formula		
Teardown formula		
Other formula	SAP008	Proj:Reqmts int.prcg
Distribution		
Int. dist. key		

Figure 3.6 Capacities

Formula for the Requirements of Internal Processing   [+]

If you subsequently want to execute capacity planning for your work center, your work center requires a formula in the field REQUIREMENTS OF INTERNAL PROCESSING. This must point to the ARBEI field—that is, the work from the operation. By default, this is the SAP008 formula.

You can check or define this using the Customizing function DEFINE FORMULA PARAMETERS FOR WORK CENTERS.

In the work center, the available capacity is maintained on the CAPACITIES tab by choosing the Capacity button. Figure 3.7 shows which information you can specify for the available capacity.

Standard available capacity				
Start	08:00:00			
Finish	17:00:00	Capacity utilization	75	
Length of breaks	01:00:00	No. of indiv. cap.	8	
Operating time	6.00	Capacity	48.00	HR

Figure 3.7 Available Capacity

Most details you must enter, for example, in the fields WORK START, WORK FINISH, LENGTH OF BREAKS, and NUMBER OF INDIVIDUAL CAPACITIES (number of craftsmen) are not critical and are easily determined.

If you work in different time periods with different staff assignments, you can maintain intervals. You can also define multilayer models.

The rate of capacity utilization is critical: this specifies (as a percentage) the portion of gross capacity available to the craftsmen (net) for planned purchase orders. The following must be subtracted from 100%:

- Additional, necessary personal time (toilet breaks, unplanned breaks, work meetings, and so on)
- Illness
- Leave
- Unplanned purchase orders

The proportion of unplanned purchase orders can be only very roughly estimated and, thus, is a very critical factor in maintenance.

[+] **Rates of Capacity Utilization in Practice**

Without considering unplanned purchase orders, a rate of capacity utilization of between 65% and 75% is most common in practice.

When considering unplanned purchase orders, there are two possibilities:

- You consider them in the rate of capacity utilization; then, the rate of capacity utilization is reduced according to your proportion of unplanned purchase orders to a value between 30% and 50%.
- You reserve some personnel beyond the number of individual capacities specified in the available capacity (that is, the number of craftsmen) and deploy them only for unplanned purchase orders, so that the data specified in the available capacity is available only for planned purchase orders.

Costing   Work centers contain costing data that enables you to cost operations; it is maintained on the COSTING tab (see Figure 3.8).

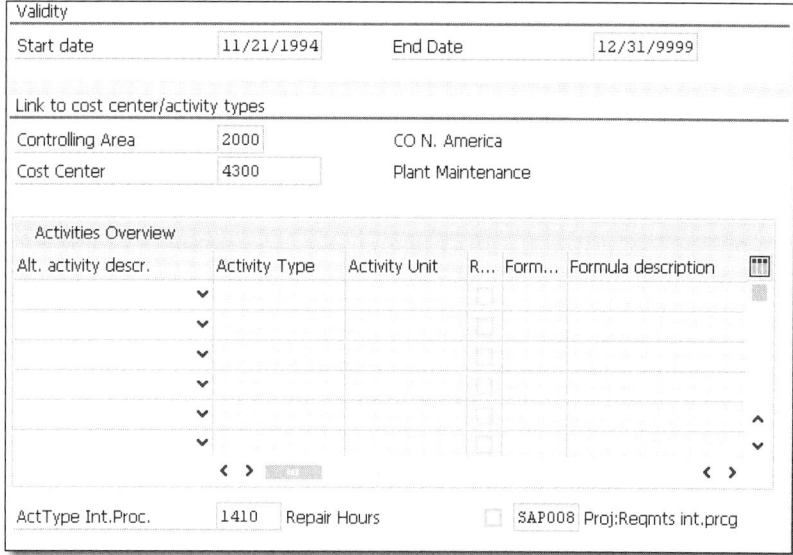

Figure 3.8 Costing

> **Prerequisites for Costing** [+]
>
> If you subsequently want to perform costing for your work center, your work center requires the following:
>
> - A cost center
> - An activity type
> - A formula in the field REQUIREMENTS FOR INTERNAL PROCESSING. This must point to the ARBEI field—that is, the work from the operation. By default, this is the SAP008 formula.

You can check or define this using the Customizing function DEFINE FORMULA PARAMETERS FOR WORK CENTERS.

Section 6.2.8 provides information on how to define the associated Cost rate in Controlling.

This chapter introduces you to the structuring elements of EAM. I will show you the purposes for which you can and cannot use each resource, and provide you with numerous tips on aspects you should observe in the structuring of technical systems.

4   Structuring of Technical Systems

A suitable structuring of technical systems is the basis for being able to use EAM to map business processes in plant maintenance and subsequently process them. If my experience with previous projects has shown one thing, it is that every company has its own idea of how it wants to map its technical systems in EAM, and each company thus does it differently—no two companies that I have encountered used the same approach in structuring their technical systems. This means that each company develops its own requirements within the implementation project, especially in relation to the following questions:

- Which structuring elements should be used?
- How deep should the structure be?
- As of which structure level should a particular resource be used?
- Which information should you store?
- Which functions should you use?
- At which levels should the technical systems be mapped?

If you are considering implementing EAM and want to map your technical systems there, then before doing so, you should ask yourself some questions and answer them to the best of your current knowledge.

4 Structuring of Technical Systems

4.1 Actions before Mapping Your Technical Systems in the SAP System

This section first outlines the questions you should ask yourself and also answer before you start the structuring of technical systems, and then provides tips on how to answer the questions.

Principle When you are trying to find the answers, the following principle should apply: as much as is necessary, but as little as possible.

For you, this means the following: find out what your business and technical requirements are and look for the easiest way to map these requirements in EAM. Throughout the rest of the book, the chapters will use lots of examples to show you how to apply this principle.

Question 1: Which Structuring Elements Should Be Used?

EAM provides you with a broad range of potential structuring elements: functional locations, reference functional locations, equipment, object links, serial numbers, maintenance assemblies, materials, and different types of bills of material.

Functional location Functional locations represent a complex, generally multilevel structure for technical systems, whereby you create each element of the technical system structure as a functional location. Therefore, functional locations are used to establish a vertical technical system structure. Functional locations usually represent immovable, functional units. Examples include process plants in the chemical and pharmaceutical industries, power plants, production lines, buildings, conduits, infrastructure, and computer networks.

Reference functional location Reference functional locations are only templates for generating "real" functional location structures or subsequently passing on data to "real" functional locations. Reference functional locations cannot be business processes (for example, malfunction reports), but serve as only a reference template.

Equipment Equipment represents movable, individual aggregates (inventories). Examples include machines, pumps, engines, production resources and tools (PRTs), vehicles (cars, trucks, fork lift trucks, and industrial trucks), and IT inventories (PCs, printers, monitors, notebooks, and projectors). Equipment categories that are seldom moved (for example, pumps) are designed in a way that enables them to be installed at functional locations; other equipment categories (for example, vehicles) are not installed at functional locations due to their permanent mobility.

You establish object links between different technical objects (pieces of equipment or functional locations). Such links exist, for example, between individual production units, between production plants and supply systems, and between supply systems and disposal systems. You use object links to form an object network. In this way, your technical systems can have a horizontal structure. Object links cannot be business processes (for example, malfunction reports), but serve only as information and visualization.
Object link

Linear assets (Linear Asset Management) are technical systems with a linear infrastructure whose properties and conditions can change from section to section (dynamic segmentation). Examples of linear assets include pipelines, road networks, rail networks, power lines, pipes, and so on. You can create linear assets as technical objects (for example, functional locations and equipment) and store linear data there.
Linear assets

Unlike a piece of equipment, a material does not represent an individual item, but rather a type of object, for example, the type pump normal 400–100 or the type three-phase normal engine SM/I, 220/380V, 50Hz, 0.18kW. A material includes a specific amount of the corresponding type; you require materials for spare parts and for pieces of equipment and maintenance assemblies (PM assemblies) that are suitable for storage.
Material

A PM assembly serves to provide a functional location or piece of equipment with a deeper structure. Thus, for example, a fork lift truck could comprise the following PM assemblies: *lift type, chassis, brake system,* and *drive assembly*. To specify the location of any damage, you assign a PM assembly to a notification, order, or maintenance plan.
PM assembly

You create serial numbers for a material number, whereby a material number can have several serial numbers. A serial number is an individual item and corresponds to a piece of equipment. The serial number
Serial number

4 | Structuring of Technical Systems

function enables you to place the equipment in storage. With regard to its use, a material serial number corresponds to a piece of equipment.

Equipment BOM
An equipment bill of material generally comprises a list of spare parts and is assigned directly to a piece of equipment. This means that only this piece of equipment can use this bill of material.

Functional location BOM
A bill of material for a functional location generally comprises a list of spare parts and is assigned directly to a functional location. This means that only this functional location can use this bill of material.

Material BOM
A material BOM also comprises a list of spare parts. However, you can make it available for any number of pieces of equipment or functional locations by using an indirect assignment.

You could now use all the above production resource tools. However, avoid doing so if possible. Instead, consider the following principle.

> [+] **As Few elements as Possible for Structuring**
>
> Use as few different structuring elements as possible. The more structuring elements you use, the more difficult it becomes to decide, in individual cases, how to classify a particular object, and the more errors may occur. Is this a piece of equipment, or is it perhaps an assembly or maybe even a material?

If you follow this principle, defining and recording your technical systems will not only be easier, but it will also have a positive effect on how you map and implement your business processes. Section 4.2 introduces you to the structuring elements and describes the available options, as well as the functions associated with each of these structuring elements. In Section 4.2, I provide you with information not only on the structuring elements you can use for specific purposes, but also the point especially at which you should not use any structuring elements. This valuable information will then enable you to decide which of the structuring elementson offer makes the most sense to you.

Question 2: How Deep Should the Structure Be?

How many levels?
In concrete terms, the question concerning the depth of the structure is as follows: how many structure levels do you form in EAM for your

technical systems? Do you prefer a detailed structure for technical systems in which you structure to the last spare part? Or do you prefer a rough structure in which you form only the first three to four levels for your technical systems? Each company must find its own answer to this question.

Unfortunately, this book cannot provide you with one general recipe for success. It can only highlight the advantages and disadvantages associated with both options (see Table 4.1).

Detailed Technical System Structure	Rough Technical System Structure
Better able to detect weak points	Less time and effort required to record and maintain technical system data
Better able to detect cost drivers	Fewer maintenance plans
More accurate definition of default values	Easier assignment for notifications and orders
	Fewer notifications and orders

Table 4.1 Detailed Versus Rough Technical System Structure

If your structure is as detailed as possible, you are then able to subsequently perform analyses that are as accurate and as specific as possible in order to detect weak points or cost drivers, for example. Detailed structures enable you to accurately define default values, such as cost centers, addresses, maintenance planner groups, or main work centers. Accurate default values increase user acceptance and accelerate business processes.

Detailed structure

However, all the above comes with some disadvantages: a great deal of time and effort required to record and maintain the master data, more maintenance plans, a higher volume of orders, and problems when assigning notifications and orders.

The disadvantages of the detailed technical system structure result in the following advantages of the rough technical system structure: less time

Rough structure

4 Structuring of Technical Systems

and effort required to record and maintain technical system data, fewer maintenance plans to be recorded, simple assigning of notifications and orders, and fewer notifications and orders.

Numerical example Let's take a look at a numerical example to clarify the problem associated with the quantity structure: normally, there is a multiplier of 4–6 from level to level, so if you structure a functional location in a lower level, there are, on average, four to six functional locations below it.

What does this mean for you? Let's assume that you have 50 technical systems and, on average, five items in the next structure level; this would then result in the number of technical objects shown in Table 4.2. You can see how many technical objects you would have for each structure level you choose to have, regardless of whether the objects are pieces of equipment, functional locations, or something else.

If you had … structure level(s), …	… you would have … technical objects
1	50
2	300
3	1,500
4	7,500
5	37,500
6	187,500
7	937,500
8	4,687,500

Table 4.2 Number of Technical Objects

Therefore, the number of technical objects does not experience linear growth, but rather exponential growth, depending on the number of structure levels. This simple example clarifies the meaning of exponential growth in numerical terms.

Structuring Broadly or Deeply? [+]

From my experience in various projects, the following strategy is recommended for the structuring of technical systems, and it has already been tried and tested by many users.

First, use a rough structure to map your technical systems across the entire area. Later on, break down only the parts of this structure that require further detail—not all of it.

For example, you can refine the structure wherever you feel the information value of the weak point analysis is insufficient or wherever you have identified cost-intensive technical systems.

The approach whereby you map deep structures across the entire area from the outset poses the problem of possibly requiring removal of some structure levels. This approach, in turn, if at all possible, requires a great deal of time and effort and has many disadvantages.

Question 3: Which Criteria Should Be Applied to the Structuring of Technical Systems?

Once again, there is no clear-cut answer to this question. It depends on your requirements, especially in relation to manageability, reporting, and so on. In principle, you can structure your technical systems according to the following criteria:

- Spatial criteria (for example, technical systems in Building A, Building B, and so on)
- Functional criteria (for example, all pumps receive one superior structure)
- Production-oriented, procedure-oriented, or process-oriented criteria (for example, production line C, chemical installation D, power supply E, air conditioning unit F, and so on)

Question 4: As of Which Structure Level Should a Particular Structuring Element Be Used?

In practice, the most frequently used structuring sequence is Functional Location → Equipment → Bill of Material (see Figure 4.1).

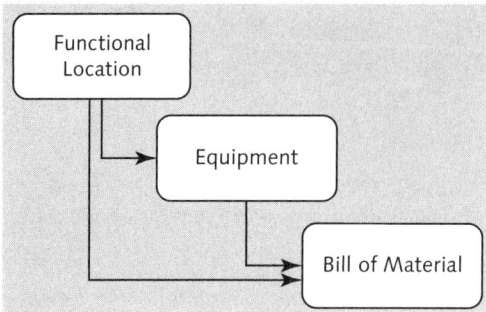

Figure 4.1 Structuring Sequence

The question "As of which structure level should a particular resource be used?" can be broken down into three sub-questions, as follows.

Question 4.1: Where Is the Boundary between a Functional Location and a Piece of Equipment?

The answer to this question will help you determine which functions you want to map in the system and whether you can fulfill them better with functional locations or pieces of equipment. In the beginning, functional locations and pieces of equipment differed greatly from each other. However, with each release, the functions have become more and more similar. Therefore, today, both of these technical objects have almost the same functions. However, the following key differences remain between functional locations and pieces of equipment:

- The fundamental difference between functional locations and pieces of equipment is illustrated by the fact that functional locations are designed to map complex multilevel structures for technical systems, while pieces of equipment are supposed to map individual units. Conversely, this means that multilevel structures for technical systems can basically be mapped even with pieces of equipment, but this approach quickly reaches its limits. The mapping of individual devices using functional locations is also only possible to a limited extent.

- Functional locations cannot be stored, whereas equipment can be stored using serial numbers.

- Pieces of equipment represent movable inventories; that is, they are installed in different technical systems over time and, thus, can document a usage history.
- Special vehicle data can be maintained for equipment only.
- The equipment has an internal and external number assignment, while the functional location number is assigned only externally.
- You can subsequently change the number of a functional location, while the number of a piece of equipment is always permanently assigned.
- The *refurbishment* business process (see Section 5.6) works only with equipment (more precisely, material serial numbers), but not for functional locations.
- The *subcontracting* business process (see Section 5.7) works only with equipment (more precisely, material serial numbers), but not for functional locations.
- The *Calibration Inspection Test Equipment* business process (see Section 5.10) works only with equipment, but not for functional locations.
- The *Pool Asset Management* business process (see Section 5.11) works only if the pool is created as a functional location and the devices to be lent are created as pieces of equipment.

Table 1.3 illustrates a clear comparison between the different properties of equipment and functional locations.

	Equipment	Functional Location
Mapping complex structures	In certain cases	Yes
Mapping individual devices	Yes	In certain cases
Internal number assignment	Yes	No
External number assignment	Yes	Yes
Changing numbers	No	Yes
Suitable for storage	Yes	No

Table 4.3 Overview of the Differences between Pieces of Equipment and Functional Locations

	Equipment	Functional Location
Usage history	Yes	Yes
Refurbishment	Yes	No
Subcontracting	Yes	No
Calibration	Yes	No
Pool Asset Management	Yes	Yes

Table 4.3 Overview of the Differences between Pieces of Equipment and Functional Locations (Cont.)

> [+] **Complex Structures and Individual Devices**
>
> Map multilevel structures for technical systems via a hierarchy of functional locations and individual devices, such as machines or vehicles, as pieces of equipment.

Question 4.2: Where Is the Boundary between a Functional Location and a Bill of Material?

This question is also best answered by looking at the relevant functions:

- Functional locations represent individual aggregates and, thus, permit an individual history. However, the items in a bill of material are represented by material numbers and, thus, represent an aggregate type and, as a result, do not permit an individual history or cost monitoring, and so on.
- Functional locations can act as reference objects in notifications, orders, and maintenance plans, whereas bills of material cannot act as reference objects.
- Functional locations are not suitable for storage, whereas BOM items are.

Table 4.4 compares the characteristics of BOMs and functional locations.

	BOM Item	Functional Location
Individual aggregates	No	Yes
Reference object of notifications, orders, and maintenance plans	In certain cases	Yes
Storage capable	Yes	No

Table 4.4 Overview of the Differences between BOM Items and Functional Locations

Functional Location or BOM Item? [+]

If you require an individual history for functional units, you should map these as functional locations. If you do not require any individual history for parts in storage, you should map these parts as material numbers in the bill of material.

Question 4.3: Where Is the Boundary between a Piece of Equipment and a Bill of Material?

Since you now know that equipment can be stored using serial numbers, only the two following functional difference remain between equipment and bills of material:

- Pieces of equipment represent individual inventories and, thus, permit an individual history and cost monitoring. However, the items in a bill of material are represented by material numbers and, thus, represent an aggregate type and do not permit an individual history.
- Pieces of equipment can be reference objects in notifications, orders, and maintenance plans, whereas bills of material cannot be reference objects.

Table 4.5 compares the characteristics of pieces of equipment and BOMs.

	BOM Item	Equipment
Individual history	No	Yes
Reference object of notifications, orders, and maintenance plans	In certain cases	Yes
Storage capable	Yes	Yes

Table 4.5 Overview of the Differences between Pieces of Equipment and BOMs

[+] **Equipment or BOM Item?**

If you require an individual history for inventories, you should map them as pieces of equipment; if you do not require an individual history for inventories, you should map them as material numbers or in the bill of material.

Question 5: How Are Numbers Assigned?

Essentially, there are two types of number assignment for IT systems:

- **Internal number assignment**
  You determine a number range interval and, when required, the SAP system assigns the next available number.

- **External number assignment**
  When required, you manually assign the number of a technical object.

Question 5.1: How Are Numbers Assigned to Functional Locations?

Structure indicator   You always assign an external number to a functional location in accordance with the structure indicator. You manually assign the functional location number according to the specifications made using the structure indicator.

You define the structure indicator in Customizing and determine the following (see Figure 4.2):

- How many levels the technical system structure should have.
- How many decimal places the numbers at each level should have and according to which rule the number of functional locations should be created:
  - A: alphabetic characters
  - N: numeric characters
  - X: alphanumeric characters

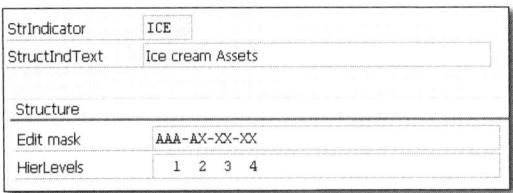

Figure 4.2 Structure Indicator

A common misconception is that SAP systems permit only generic numbers, for example:

1. Level: ICE
2. Level: ICE-M1
3. Level: ICE-M1-01

This is incorrect because the SAP system permits you to break away from the naming convention, for example:

1. Level: ICE
2. Level: ICE-M1
3. Level: P1001

Generic number assignment?

Number of Functional Location [+]

If you are already using other systems (for example, CAD or DMS) that use the functional location number, you can also use the existing number in EAM and not assign generic numbers.

Take time to carefully consider the numbering you wish to use and discuss with other users and experts the best way to manage it.

> Even though you can subsequently change the number of the functional location under certain conditions (for example, if you activate alternative labeling), it may be very time-consuming.
>
> Avoid using organizational abbreviations in functional location numbers (for example, company code, plant, and cost center). If reorganization were necessary, then you would have to rename the functional locations.

Question 5.2: How Are Numbers Assigned to Pieces of Equipment?

You can choose whether you want to assign the equipment numbers internally or externally. Table 4.6 gives you an overview of the advantages and disadvantages of the two possible procedures. You must decide for yourself which procedure is most suitable for your company.

Advantages	Disadvantages
▸ Easy to retain ▸ Good information value when manually editing documents ▸ Easy to synchronize with different systems ▸ Conclusions made using the number	▸ Lengthy preparation time ▸ Considerable effort required to agree on a common assignment with other plants ▸ The defined key "bursts"—that is, it eventually contains an insufficient number of characters. ▸ Assignment frequently difficult or impossible if there are boundaries ▸ Unable to change numbers

Table 4.6 External Equipment Numbers—Advantages and Disadvantages

Question 6: Which Information Should You Store?

The master records of the technical objects have predefined, allocated data. You can differentiate between the following data types here:

- Data that you want or have to store because of your requirements
- Data that should be stored because of the mapping in the SAP system (for example, the cost center)

However, the following principle must also apply here: as much as is necessary, but as little as possible. It does not make sense to have a data graveyard that is established for its own sake, of interest to no one, and viewed by no one and that requires considerable time and effort to record and maintain its data.

> **Data and Information** [+]
>
> Only enter data that is also information for you.

Furthermore, SAP offers flexible options for configuring master data:

- You can define the layout of the master record yourself (number, sequence, tab name, and tab contents).
- The definition of the layout can be divided into object types (vehicles, technical systems, pumps, PC, and so on).
- The field selection option enables you to differentiate important information from unimportant information or hide fields that you do not require.

> **Defining Your Own Layouts** [+]
>
> Use the option to determine the layout of the master data yourself and design your own layouts for your master data. For example, place the most important information on the first tab and hide unimportant fields (see Section 4.2).

Question 7: How Is the Master Data Transferred into the SAP System?

There are always two options for incorporating master data into the SAP system: manually or automatically.

If you switch from another maintenance planning and control system to EAM, or if the technical system data exists in another electronic form, you should try to automatically transfer this data into the SAP system. For this purpose, SAP provides the standard tools Transaction IBIP and the Data Transfer Workbench (Transaction LSMW).

If the data is not in electronic form, you require a plan for data entry. These aspects are discussed in the book *Configuring SAP Plant Maintenance*, which will be published by SAP PRESS in Summer 2014.

Question 8: Is It Easy to Delete Data Records?

SAP archiving is the only way to remove functional locations or pieces of equipment that have been set up once in the system. Scarcely feasible requirements had to be fulfilled in order to delete. This is because the following dependencies, among other things, are checked when deleting:

- Whether notifications still exist
- Whether orders still exist
- If so, whether there are still purchase requisitions, purchase orders, invoices, or material withdrawal documents for the orders
- Whether measurement documents were recorded
- Whether confirmation documents still exist

[+] **Deleting Master Records Is Not Possible**
You cannot delete a piece of equipment or functional location that has already been in use for some time.

What other alternatives do you have now? Obsolete functional locations and pieces of equipment should be reassigned to a "scrap yard" (see Section 4.2.1).

Question 9: Which of the Available Functions Should Be Used?

The SAP system provides you with a range of functions within each structuring resource that you will not find in this scope and scale in any other maintenance planning and control system. The functions are accurately described in Section 4.2 and are compared in a table in Appendix B.1.

This functional diversity presents you with many options, but also carries the risk of overloading the system and placing excessive demands on the users.

> **Deleting Functions** [+]
>
> Take the list of all functions of the master data, and delete those that you do not want to use, both physically from the piece of paper and also from the back of your mind.

Question 10: Which Strategy Should You Pursue When Recording Master Data?

The tenth and final question applies to the strategy for recording master data—that is, the steps or scope in which the master data should be transferred to the system: all master data from all plants at once, or completely for one plant, or for one area only?

There is no general answer to this question. Each company must find its own way here, on the basis of its general conditions (size, structure, competencies, organization, technical system types, and so on). More detailed information and tips on implementation strategies can be found in the aforementioned book, *Configuring SAP Plant Maintenance*.

Following this preparatory work and pre-considerations, absolutely nothing should prevent you from being able to structure your technical systems in EAM.

4.2 SAP Elements for Structuring Technical Systems and How to Use Them

The following sections explain each of the technical objects. I will differentiate among the individual object types, describe the range of functions available, and outline possible areas of use.

4.2.1 Functional Locations and Reference Functional Locations

The previous section provided a general definition of functional locations: functional locations represent a complex, generally multilevel,

Definition

immovable structure for technical systems. Therefore, functional locations are used to establish a vertical technical system structure.

Examples Practical examples include the following:

- Process plants in the chemical, pharmaceutical, and food industries
- Power plants, such as coal-fired power plants, hydroelectric power plants, or nuclear power plants
- Production lines in discrete manufacturing
- Complex machines, such as automated systems or flexible production cells
- Real estate
- Power systems, gas systems, water systems, and heating systems
- Conduits
- Infrastructure, such as streets, locations, tracks, tunnels, and bridges
- Computer networks
- Complex vehicles, such as locomotives, high-speed trains, and tractors
- Aircraft

Figure 4.3 shows an example of a process-oriented technical system structure.

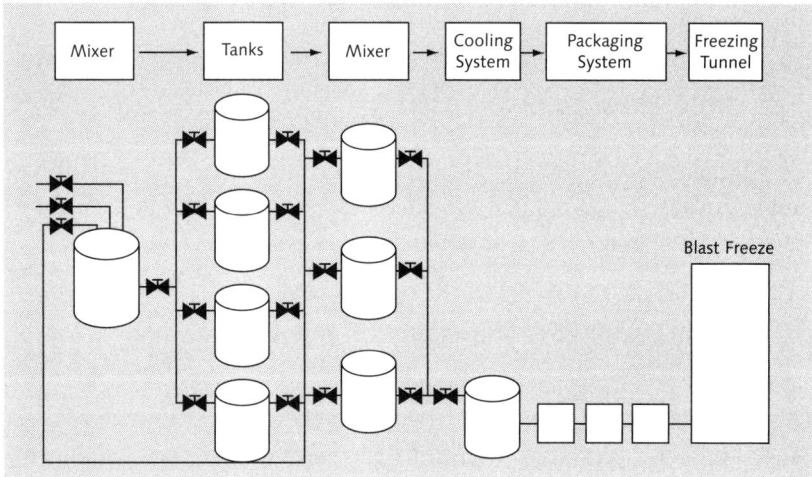

Figure 4.3 Technical System Structure of an Ice Cream Plant

For which items in the technical system do you now create a functional location in the SAP system? You create a functional location in EAM in the following cases:

Criteria

- You want to manage individual data from a maintenance perspective (technical data such as performance data, or organizational data such as the work center).
- You want to create notifications, orders, or maintenance plans.
- You want to manage an asset pool.
- You have documentation obligations and must provide evidence of maintenance tasks performed.
- You want to collate and analyze technical data, such as causes of damage, measurement readings, or counter readings.
- You want to verify costs.
- You require different perspectives for the technical systems (for example, one perspective for electrical engineering and one perspective for measurement and control).

You can define the technical system from Figure 4.3, as illustrated in Figure 4.4, in EAM (called via Transaction IH01).

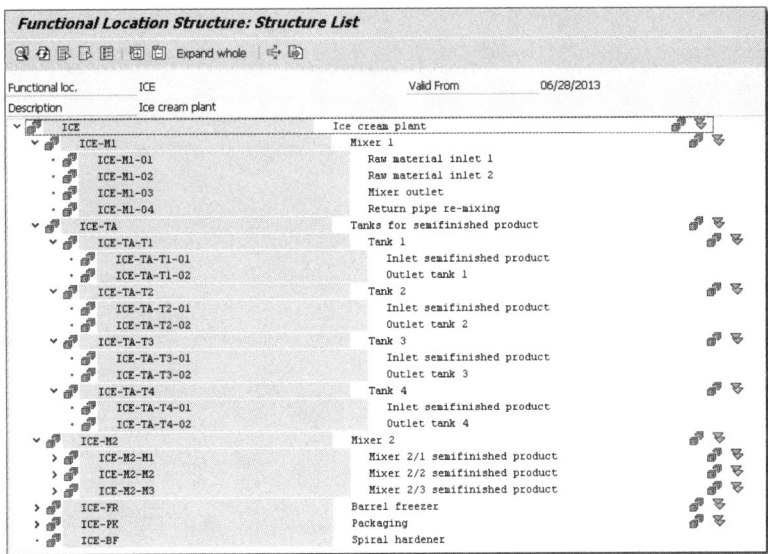

Figure 4.4 Structural Display of the Ice Cream Plant

Creating Functional Locations — Single Entry

If you want to create only one new functional location, call Transaction IL01. You then choose a suitable structure indicator and assign a new number.

Functional location numbers can have a maximum of 30 characters and, if alternative labeling is activated (see the section entitled "Alternative Labels"), they can have a maximum of 40 characters.

[+] **Highest Functional Location: Plant**

If you use the SAP system in several plants, I generally recommend that you create the plant itself as a functional location and as the first level. However, avoid using the SAP plant number, for the following reason.

You assign the functional location number at the client level; the system, thus, cannot simultaneously manage functional location ICE in plant 01 and plant 02. Therefore, I recommend that you create functional locations 01 and 02 respectively for plants 01 and 02, and the numbers 01-ICE and 02-ICE for the actual technical system.

For all other levels, the following applies: as a result of the number assigned, the system tries to arrange the new functional location within an existing technical system structure.

[+] **Setting Superior Functional Location**

If the system cannot automatically assign the new functional location to a superior functional location, you must manually enter any superior functional location in the initial screen in Transaction IL01 to avoid problems when subsequently maintaining data.

Figure 4.5 shows you the initial screen for the single entry of functional locations.

[+] **Setting Up a Scrap Yard**

Since it is very difficult, if not impossible, to delete master data from the SAP system, you should create a "scrap yard" in addition to the "real" functional locations and reassign all obsolete functional locations and pieces of equipment there.

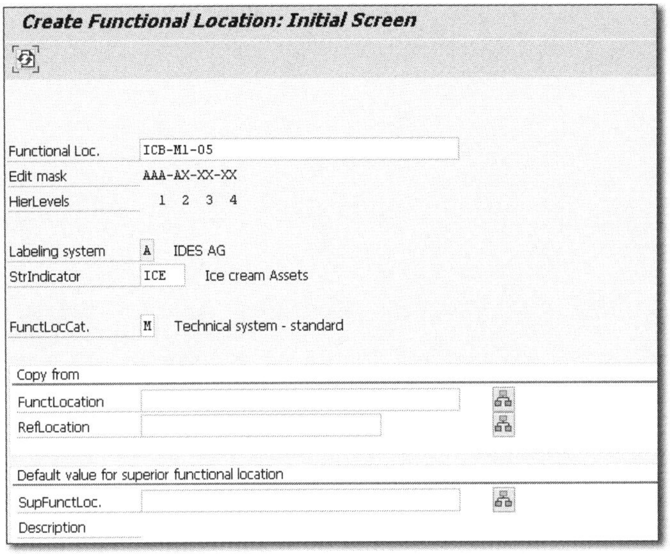

4.2 SAP Elements for Structuring Technical Systems and How to Use Them

Figure 4.5 Creating Functional Locations

Figure 4.6 shows a sample layout of a functional location.

Layout

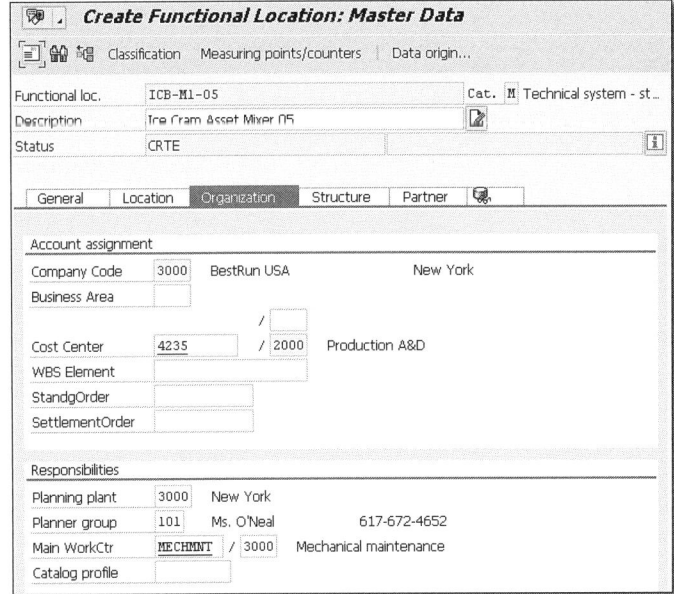

Figure 4.6 Layout of Functional Locations

The layout of the master records (functional location, equipment, and serial number) can be configured relatively flexibly. You can use the Customizing function SET VIEW PROFILES FOR TECHNICAL OBJECTS to define multiple tabs, and you can assign up to four screen groups to each tab.

The following screen groups are available:

- General data (for example, size, weight, and inventory number)
- Reference data (for example, vendor, acquisition value, and acquisition date)
- Manufacturing data (for example, manufacturer, year of construction, and month of construction)
- Location data (for example, maintenance plant, location, and room)
- Address (for example, zip code, town, telephone number, and fax number)
- Account assignment (for example, cost center, technical system, and company code)
- Responsibilities (i.e., planner group, main work center)
- Structuring (for example, superior functional location, position)
- Equipment (installed equipment)
- Customer/vendor data
- Standard class (full screen or sub-screen)
- Partner (for example, partner function, name, and address)
- Long text
- Warranty (customer warranty, vendor warranty)
- Documents (full screen or sub-screen)
- User data with their own fields
- Log book data
- Linear data for functional locations and characteristics

| Hide Fields | [+] |

You can use the screen control to adjust the individual fields; that is, you can hide unnecessary fields or declare important fields as mandatory. In this case, use the Customizing function DEFINE FIELD SELECTION FOR FUNCTIONAL LOCATIONS.

Position

In many application scenarios, it is desirable to display the functional locations and pieces of equipment in the sequence in which they appear in the production steps. If you use only numeric functional location numbers, you can achieve this by using the number assignment. However, if you use alphabetical or alphanumeric characters, EAM sorts the functional locations and pieces of equipment alphabetically and not in the sequence in which they appear in the process steps.

Thus, for example, the sequence M1 → TA → M2 → FR → PK → BF can be found in the second level of the ice cream plant in Figure 4.4; you achieve this by assigning position numbers in ascending order to the functional locations and pieces of equipment, in this case 10 → 20 → 30 → 40 → 50 → 60. The POSITION field itself has four alphanumeric characters.

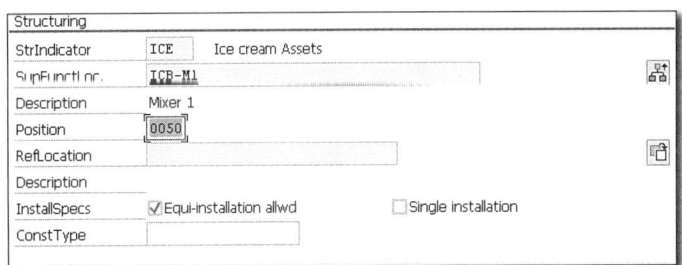

Figure 4.7 Position Number

| Use the Position | [+] |

Use the POSITION field in the STRUCTURING screen group to arrange your functional locations and pieces of equipment. Pay attention to standard conventions because, for example, the value 20 is sorted before 3. The best option is to use four-digit position numbers (for example, 0001 instead of 1, or 0030 instead of 30).

4 | Structuring of Technical Systems

Work Center and Main Work Center

The fields WORK CENTER in the LOCATION DATA screen group and MAIN WORK CENTER in the RESPONSIBILITIES screen group are often confused (see Figure 4.8).

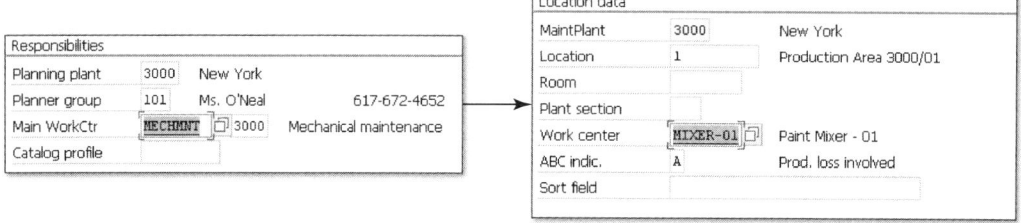

Figure 4.8 Work Center and Main Work Center

Assign a work center to the functional location if you want the planned maintenance orders to subsequently appear in the planning table of the production planners (Transaction CM21) to show machine unavailability, for example.

Assign a main work center to a functional location if, in maintenance processing, you want this work center to be proposed in notifications and/or orders as the executing maintenance workshop.

> [!] **Work Center versus Main Work Center**
>
> The work center represents the functional location as a production resource (production work center in SAP module Production Planning and Control [PP]). The main work center corresponds to a maintenance workshop.

Construction Type

In the CONSTRUCTION TYPE field in the STRUCTURING screen group, you enter a material number with which all similar objects are grouped together (see Figure 4.9). You are then able to access the same bills of material and general maintenance task lists, for example. For more information, refer to Section 4.2.5, Section 4.2.6, and Section 5.2.5.

> [!] **Construction Type as a Link**
>
> You use the CONSTRUCTION TYPE field if you want to create a link to a material number, the bill of material for this material, or general maintenance task lists.

4.2 SAP Elements for Structuring Technical Systems and How to Use Them

```
Structuring
StrIndicator      ICE       Ice cream Assets
SupFunctLoc.      ICB-M1
Description       Mixer 1
Position          0050
RefLocation
Description
InstallSpecs      ☑ Equi-installation allwd      ☐ Single installation
ConstType         P-1000                         ⬚ Pump GG Etanorm 200-1000
```

Figure 4.9 Construction Type

Creating Functional Locations—Collective Entry

If you want to record several functional locations at once or copy a functional location structure that you created previously, use Transaction IL04. Figure 4.10 shows you how you can copy an existing structure ICE as a template to a structure known as ICB. For this purpose, you choose 🖫 Capacity and determine which objects are to be copied from the template.

The system now generates a completely new functional location structure, ICB, containing all the functional locations, and, before you save it, the system displays the complete list so that you can make any necessary corrections.

Figure 4.10 Copying a Functional Location

Reference Functional Locations

Reference functional locations do not represent technical systems that actually exist, but are solely for the purpose of acting as a template for real functional locations. This means that you can copy functional location structures from reference structures. Unlike a copy with a functional location structure as a reference, changes to the reference structure are transferred to the resulting functional location structures.

However, the reference functional location contains much less information than a functional location. A reference functional location contains the following information:

- Responsibilities (i.e., planner group, main work center)
- Structuring (for example, superior reference functional location, position)
- Standard class
- Texts
- Documents

Alternative Labeling

Alternative labeling systems can be used for different purposes:

Numbers for different perspectives — You can assign several numbers to a functional location structure or each individual location within the structure for different perspectives (as shown in Figure 4.11, for example, your own naming conventions versus customer naming conventions).

Primary and secondary structures — You can create primary and secondary functional location structures (as shown in Figure 4.12, for example, a primary structure for the power supply and a secondary structure for building services).

You assign several numbers at the lowest level, where the same physical location is involved, and the functional location appears in several lists (Transaction IL05). The primary functional location structure is always displayed in the structural display (Transaction IH01).

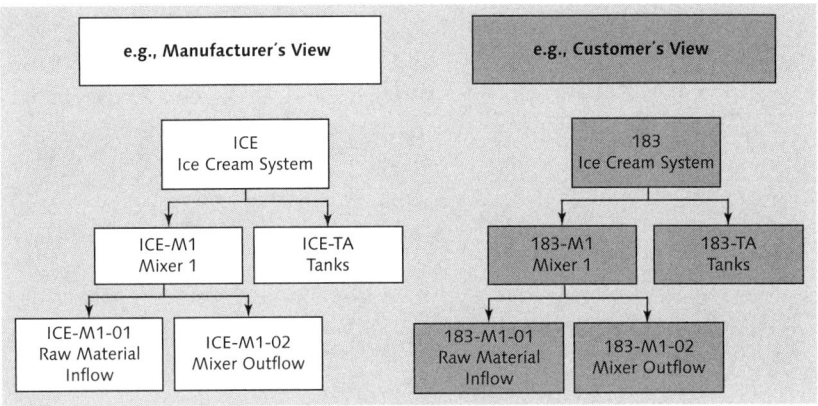

Figure 4.11 Alternative Labeling for a Complete Technical System Structure

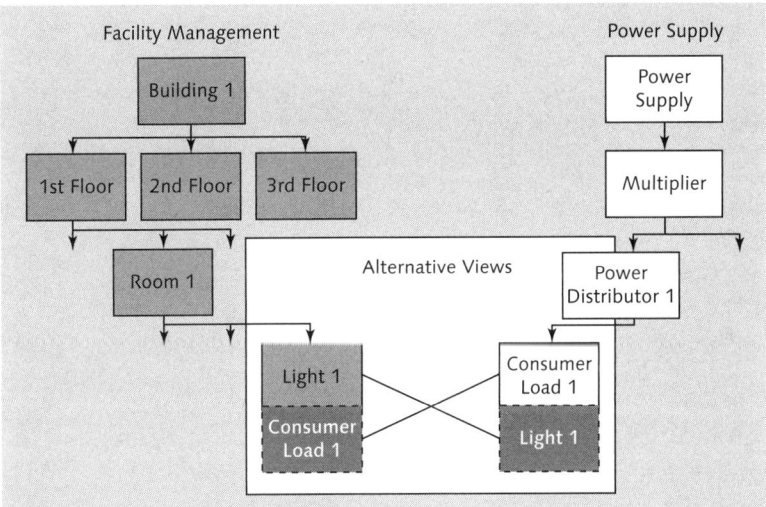

Figure 4.12 Alternative Labeling for Individual Functional Locations

You can change a functional location number. This is necessary, for example, in the following cases:

Renaming functional locations

- If you have assigned an incorrect number
- If you scrap a technical system, but use some of its parts in another technical system
- If part of a technical system is used in another technical system (see Figure 4.13).

4 | Structuring of Technical Systems

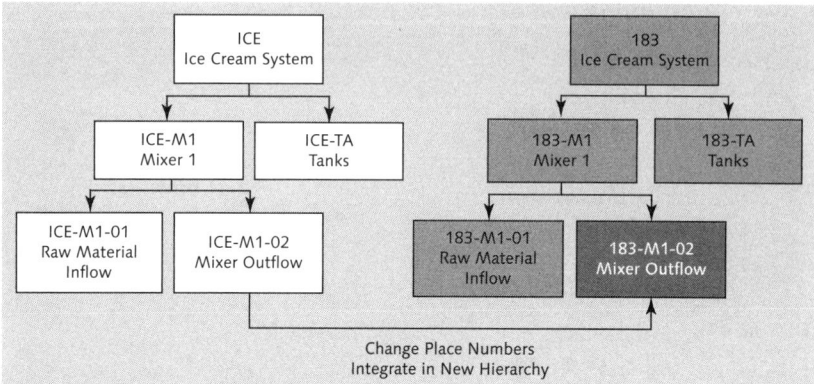

Figure 4.13 Alternative Labeling to Change Functional Location Number

> [+] **Activate the Alternative Labeling**
>
> You activate alternative labeling via the Customizing function ACTIVATE ALTERNATIVE LABELING, and you can then change the number of the functional location. Once you activate alternative labeling, however, you cannot deactivate it.

You use the Customizing function DEFINE LABELING SYSTEMS FOR FUNCTIONAL LOCATIONS to define the different perspectives that you want to manage for functional locations.

Within a functional location, you can now view or change the functional location number using EXTRAS • ALTERNATIVE LABELING • OVERVIEW (see Figure 4.14).

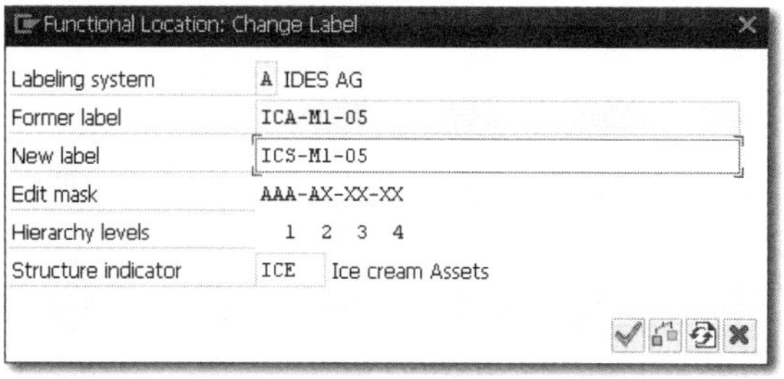

Figure 4.14 Changing Number of Functional Location

4.2.2 Equipment and Serial Numbers

Equipment represents movable, individual aggregates (inventories). For example, such equipment could include the following:

Definition and examples

- Machines
- Production equipment (pumps, engines)
- Production resources/tools (PRTs)
- Test equipment (scales, gauges)
- Vehicles (cars, trucks, fork lift trucks, and industrial trucks)
- IT inventories (PCs, printers, monitors, notebooks, and projectors)
- Robots

For which devices do you now create an equipment master record in the SAP system? You create a piece of equipment in the following cases:

- You install devices on functional locations and want to prove a usage history.
- You want to store the devices.
- You want to manage individual data from a maintenance perspective (technical data such as performance data, or organizational data such as the work center).
- You want to create notifications, orders, or maintenance plans.
- You have documentation obligations and must provide evidence of maintenance tasks performed.
- You collate technical data such as causes of damage, measurement readings, or counter readings and want to analyze them.
- You want to verify costs.
- You want to perform refurbishments on a device.
- You want an external vendor to perform subcontracting.
- You manage devices in a pool and want to support the lending process.
- You want to or need to perform calibrations and tests.

4 Structuring of Technical Systems

A piece of equipment can be configured in exactly the same way as a functional location. As a result, an equipment master record could look as shown in Figure 4.15.

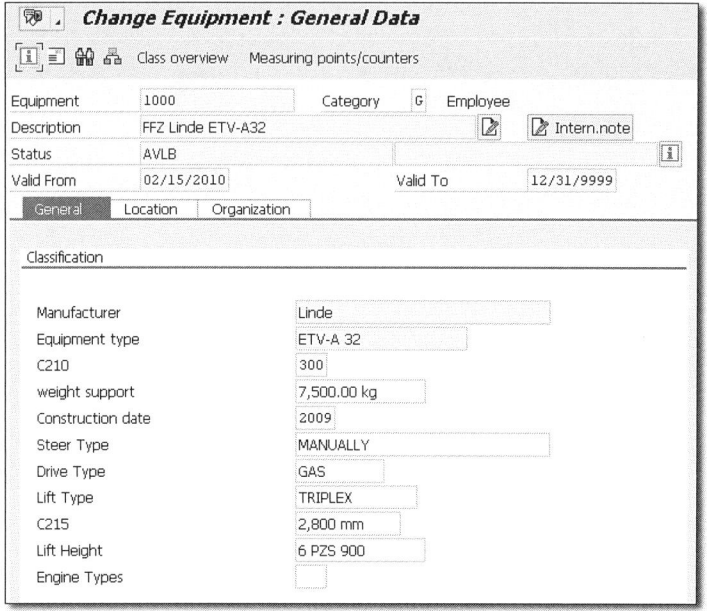

Figure 4.15 Equipment Master Record

Installing Equipment on Functional Locations/Dismantling Equipment from Functional Locations

On the one hand, some equipment categories have, from their design perspective, a layout that enables them to be installed at functional locations; this applies, for example, to pumps, engines, or robots. This is not the case for other equipment categories (for example, vehicles, tools, and so on).

On the other hand, however, there are also functional locations where you want to prevent the installation of equipment, for example, if you have created the plant as a functional location. There are also functional locations that constitute installation positions and are thus intended for the installation of equipment.

4.2 SAP Elements for Structuring Technical Systems and How to Use Them

Consequently, certain prerequisites must be fulfilled so that you can install a piece of equipment at a functional location.

Requirements

In the master record of the functional location, you must set the EQUIPMENT INSTALLATION ALLOWED switch in the STRUCTURING screen group (see Figure 4.16).

Figure 4.16 Installation Specifications for Functional Location

Furthermore, if you want only one piece of equipment to be installed at a certain time, also activate the SINGLE INSTALLATION switch.

From an equipment perspective, you must use the Customizing function DEFINE INSTALLATION AT FUNCTIONAL LOCATION to define which equipment categories can and cannot be installed (see Figure 4.17).

Category	Equipment category description	RefCat.	Inst. at FunctLoc.
A	Machines	S	☐
B	Machines with Serial Number	M	☑
C	RFID Equipment with Serial Num	M	☑
D	DSD vehicle	M	☐
E	Rolling stock serialized comps	M	☐
F	Vehicles	M	☑
G	Employee	M	☑
H	Medical Devices	M	☑
I	IT-Equipment	M	☑
J	Containers	M	☐
K	Vehicles	M	☑
L	MX Equipment	M	☐
M	Machines	M	☑
N	Mining Equipment	M	☑
O	Transmitter Equipments	M	☐
P	Production resources/tools	P	☐

Figure 4.17 Installation Specifications for the Equipment Category

If these prerequisites are fulfilled, you can install the equipment from an equipment perspective (Transaction IE02) or from a functional location perspective (Transaction IL02).

Equipment installation

If you restructure from an equipment perspective, use the function CHANGE INSTALLATION LOCATION. There, you dismantle the equipment in the old location in the first step and install it in the new installation location in the second step (see Figure 4.18).

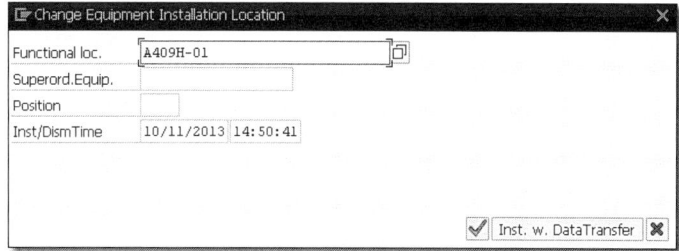

Figure 4.18 Restructuring a Piece of Equipment

Usage history   Furthermore, if you have used the Customizing function Usage History Update to activate the usage history for each equipment category, the history is automatically updated. The history lists the functional locations and the time periods in which a piece of equipment was installed. You can use the Usage List (Transaction IE02/03) to view this history from an equipment perspective or use the multilevel functional location list (Transaction IL07) to view this history from a functional location perspective. Figure 4.19 shows the usage list from an equipment perspective.

Figure 4.19 Usage List for a Piece of Equipment

Placing Equipment in Storage/Removing Equipment from Storage

Requirements   If you want to use the function for placing equipment in storage or removing it from storage, certain prerequisites must be fulfilled.

You must add the material/serial number segment to the equipment master. You do this by activating the Serial Number segment in the equipment master under EDIT • VIEW SELECTION and assigning the equipment a material number (see Figure 4.20).

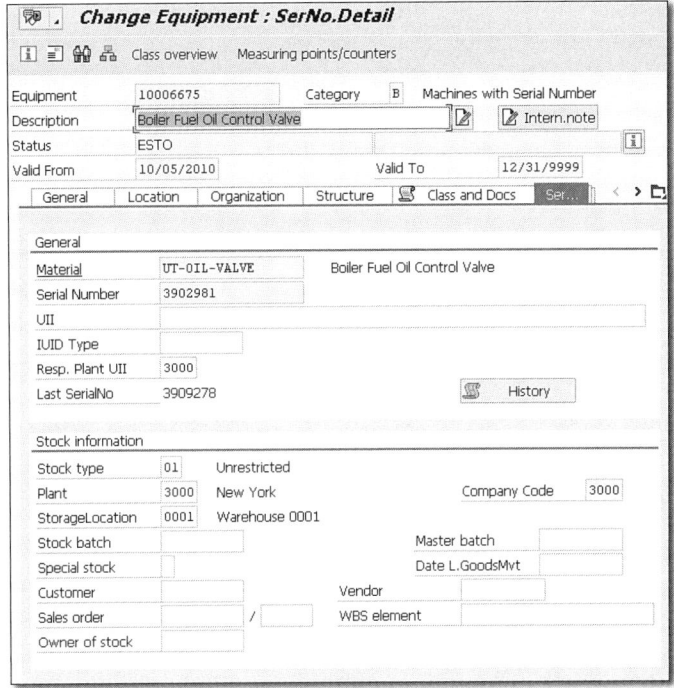

Figure 4.20 Equipment with Serial Data

You assign the material master in the GENERAL PLANT PARAMETERS screen group a SERIAL NUMBER PROFILE (see Figure 4.21).

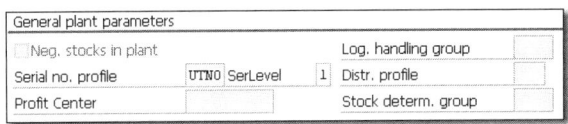

Figure 4.21 Serial Number Profile in the Material Master

You use the SERIAL LEVEL switch to determine whether the serial number and equipment number are to be synchronized.

To maintain serial number profiles, you use the Customizing function DEFINE SERIAL NUMBER PROFILES. Here, you determine whether it is mandatory to specify a serial number for goods movements and whether only existing serial numbers must be moved or new serial numbers can also be created for equipment that you place in storage/remove from storage.

Place in storage/ remove from storage

If these prerequisites are fulfilled, you can place the piece of equipment or material/serial number in storage. This can be done using the general transactions for inventory management (for example, MIGO) or Transaction IE4N, a special maintenance transaction (see Figure 4.22). This enables one of the following two processes to be used:

- Placing equipment in storage while simultaneously removing it from the functional location
- Removing equipment from storage while simultaneously installing it at a functional location

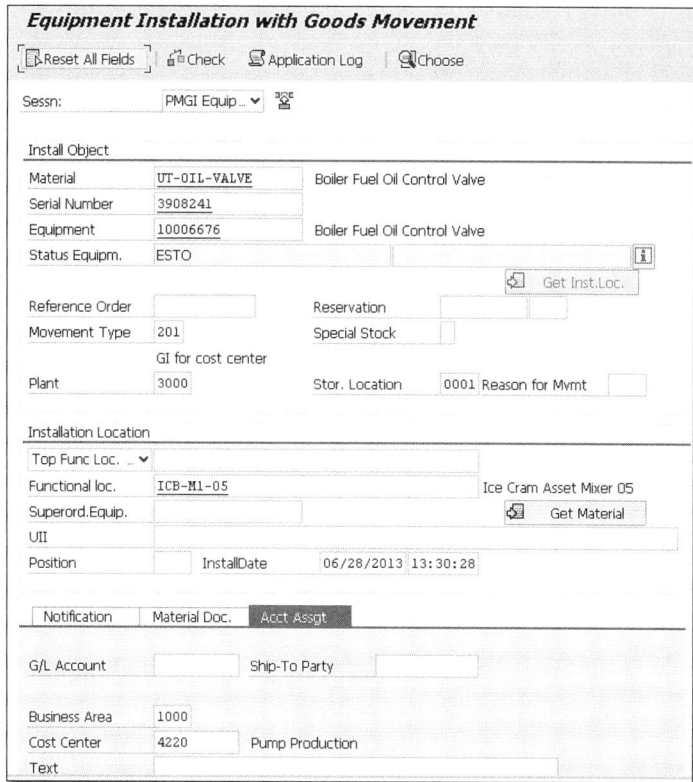

Figure 4.22 Removing Equipment from Storage and Installing It at a Functional Location

4.2 SAP Elements for Structuring Technical Systems and How to Use Them

The installed equipment is displayed in inventory management, for example, Transaction MMBE (see Figure Figure 4.23).

Stock overview

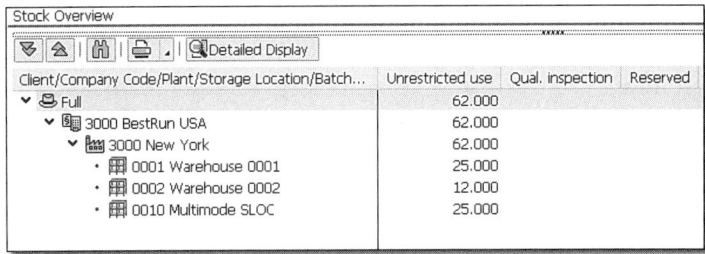

Figure 4.23 Stock Overview

Call ENVIRONMENT • EQUIPMENT/SERIAL NO. to display a list of all equipment installed (see Figure 4.24).

Material	Serial No.	Plant	SLoc	Equipment	Descriptn	SysStatus	Batch	PP	S
1268	10006249	3000	0001	10006249	PDA	ESTO		01	
1268	10006248	3000	0001	10006248	PDA	ESTO		01	
1268	10006247	3000	0001	10006247	PDA	ESTO		01	
1268	10006246	3000	0001	10006246	PDA	ESTO		01	
1268	10006245	3000	0001	10006245	PDA	ESTO		01	
1268	10006244	3000	0001	10006244	PDA	ESTO		01	
1268	10006243	3000	0001	10006243	PDA	ESTO		01	
1268	10006242	3000	0001	10006242	PDA	ESTO		01	
1268	10006241	3000	0001	10006241	PDA	ESTO		01	
1268	10006240	3000	0001	10006240	PDA	ESTO		01	
1268	10006239	3000	0001	10006239	PDA	ESTO		01	
1268	10006238	3000	0001	10006238	PDA	ESTO		01	
1268	10006237	3000	0001	10006237	PDA	ESTO		01	
1268	10006236	3000	0001	10006236	PDA	ESTO		01	

Figure 4.24 Stock Overview of Equipment

Equipment Hierarchies

Definition

In addition to the cases in which a single piece of equipment is installed on a functional location or removed from a functional location, in practice, there are also cases in which not just one piece of equipment, but rather an entire equipment group comprising several pieces of equipment, is replaced. Typical examples include the following:

- Roller conveyors comprising several pieces of equipment—for example, a rack, rolls, and drive motors
- (Motor) bogies for rail vehicles comprising several pieces of equipment—for example, suspension, wheels, motor, and gear wheels
- Painting stations, which include several pieces of equipment, such as the painting station itself, a circulating pump, and an agitator
- Robots that consist of several pieces of sub-equipment, such as design, robotic arm, and tool

If, for example, there is a problem with one of the bogie's wheels, the wheel is not usually replaced, but rather the entire bogie is. There are equipment hierarchies for such combinations whereby the entire piece of equipment (bogie) comprises sub-equipment (motor, wheel, and so on) (see Figure 4.25).

Figure 4.25 Bogie

You could map this bogie as an equipment hierarchy, similar to the hierarchy shown in Figure 4.26.

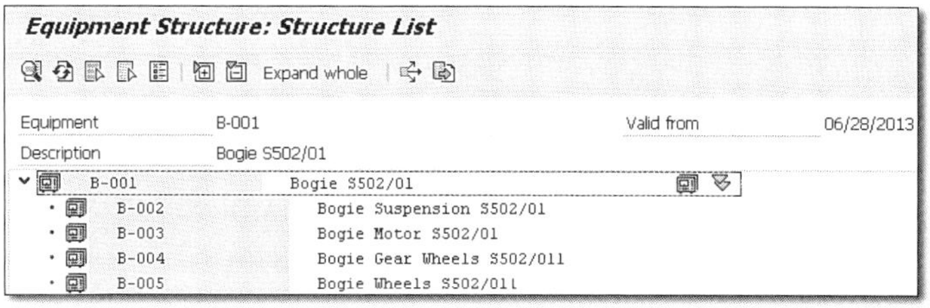

Figure 4.26 Equipment Hierarchy

> **Equipment Group as Equipment Hierarchy** [+]
>
> If you always consider an entire equipment group, you should work with equipment hierarchies.
>
> An order and notification history is always updated on the equipment that is specified in the order or notification. It is not directly updated for the superior equipment. Therefore, you should check whether equipment hierarchies fulfill your reporting and analysis requirements.

Functional Comparison between Pieces of Equipment and Functional Locations

This section recapitulates the differences between a piece of equipment and a functional location.

A piece of equipment provides the following options:

Which tasks can a piece of equipment fulfill?

- You can serialize a piece of equipment by assigning it a material and a serial number. As a result, inventory management is possible for the piece of equipment.
- You can install equipment at functional locations or on other pieces of equipment.
- In fleet management, a vehicle can be a piece of equipment; it then has special vehicle data.
- A piece of equipment installed at a functional location can save its usage history. The system writes an equipment usage period for each installation location, which enables you to trace the entire usage history.
- In addition to the standard tabs for the equipment master record, you can, if required, call additional tabs (such as SALES DATA, PRT DATA, or CONFIGURATION DATA) from the menu without having to make the relevant settings in Customizing.

When using equipment, the following features should be noted:

What are the considerations associated with equipment?

- When structures are created, pieces of equipment do not automatically find their location in the structure, but must be assigned manually for each master record.

- You can no longer change the equipment number after it is created.
- You cannot analyze equipment hierarchies on the basis of the superior piece of equipment.

Which tasks can a functional location fulfill?

The functional location provides the following options:

- You can change a functional location label after it is created if you have activated the alternative labeling function.
- Additional labeling is also possible for functional locations.
- As a result of the structure indicator, functional locations automatically find their location in the structure when you create them (in accordance with the top-down principle).
- The strictly hierarchical structure enables data (for example, costs) to be summarized at any hierarchy level.
- A functional location can be a piece of real estate in the Real Estate Management application (Real Estate Management, RE-FX; for more information, see Section 6.2.9).
- You can define a functional location in Investment Management (SAP module IM). Therefore, orders can automatically be assigned to an investment program (for more information, see Section 7.3.3).

What are the considerations associated with functional locations?

Functional locations also have some features you should note:

- You must create at least one structure indicator, but you usually create several structure indicators in Customizing.
- Functional locations are usually installed in superior functional locations. However, they can also exist as individual objects.
- A functional location installed at another functional location cannot save the history of its installation locations. Instead, it can only show its current installation location.
- Automatic assignment no longer works when you restructure functional location structures that have different structure indicators. As with pieces of equipment, you must manually assign the superior functional location.

4.2.3 Links and Object Networks

For the sake of completeness, it should also be mentioned that EAM functions are available to map links between different technical objects or systems (pieces of equipment or functional locations). Such links exist, as follows:

- Between production units
- Between production plants and supply systems
- Between supply systems and disposal systems

You use Services for Object to form an object network, and your technical systems can, thus, have a horizontal structure.

You can define links only between two pieces of equipment (Transaction IN07) or between two functional locations (Transaction IN04; see Figure 4.27).

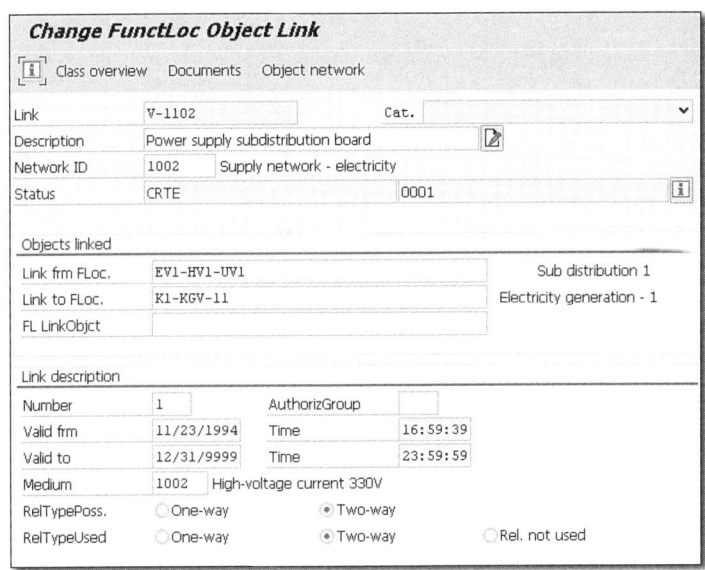

Figure 4.27 Object Link

The link itself can also be a piece of equipment or a functional location, but this is not necessary. You cannot establish a link between one piece of equipment and one functional location.

4 | Structuring of Technical Systems

You form an object network by creating several individual, logically consecutive object links. You can display an object network by viewing the graphic for a list of functional location links (Transactions N15/16) or the graphic for a list of equipment links (Transactions IN18/19) (see Figure 4.28).

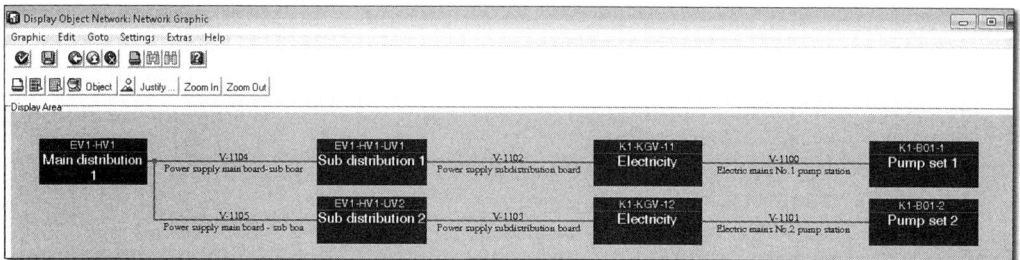

Figure 4.28 Object Network

[!] **Should You Use the Object Links?**

In practice, link and network mapping play a minor role in the SAP system for the following reasons:

- Object links cannot be integrated in business processes, that is, you cannot write any notifications, orders, maintenance plans, and so on, to an object link.
- Suitable, industry-specific systems (such as geographic information systems [GIS], network monitoring systems, and measuring and control technology systems) are generally used and coupled with the SAP system (see Section 6.4).

4.2.4 Linear Asset Management

Definition   Linear assets (Linear Asset Management) are technical systems with a linear infrastructure whose properties and conditions can change from section to section (dynamic segmentation). Examples of linear assets include the following:

- Pipelines
- Road networks
- Rail networks

- Power lines
- Pipes

From the aforementioned examples, you can see that this functionality, among other things, is of particular interest to the oil and gas industry, utility companies (electricity, gas, and water), road maintenance companies, public authorities, and rail operators.

Before we go into more detail, I'll first explain some aspects of linear asset management and the underlying problems using the practical example of a highway (see Figure 4.29):

Concept

The example is based on the following information:

- First of all, the total length of the highway (for example, the A81, which is 293 km in length) is of interest.
- The highway should be divided into several sections—for example, from interchange to interchange or from junction to junction (such as junctions 002 and 003, which are separated by a distance of 13 km).
- The highway has specific properties that can change over its course, such as road surface (for example, a change from tar to asphalt for 11.5 km), speed restrictions in some locations (for example, 120 km/h), and a varying number of lanes (between two and four).
- Stationary equipment, such as emergency phones, toll plazas, bridges, parking lots, or rest areas (emergency telephones at 3 km and 7 km), are located along the route.
- On 30.11., a maintenance order must be performed in the section *2 to 4.5 km*.
- Operation 10 concerns the quarterly grass cuttings in section *2.1 to 2.7 km*.
- Operation 20 concerns the twice yearly cleaning of the lateral boundary indicators in section *2.7 to 4.5 kms*.
- Various necessary repair measures are described in a notification sent on 15.11., which concern the section *2.5 to 5 kms*.
- Notification item 10 describes various holes in the road surface for the section *2.0 to 2.6 kms*.

4 | Structuring of Technical Systems

- Notification item 20 describes corroded surfaces in the central guardrail for the section *2.3 to 4.8 kms*.
- The noise level is measured in the section *2.0 to 10.0 kms*.
- On 23.11., a noise level of 75.6 decibels was measured in the section *3.5 to 5.0 kms*.

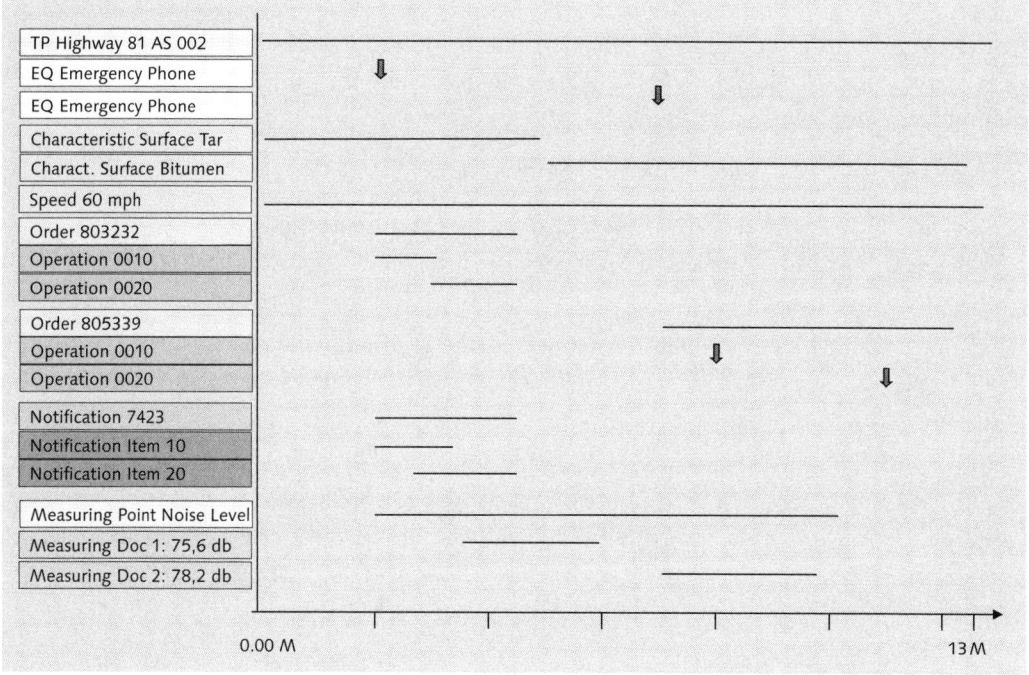

Figure 4.29 Highway Example

Linear data   You can store the following linear data for your technical objects:

- General linear data, such as starting point, end point, length, and unit of measurement
- Offset data, such as horizontal or vertical offset with respect to a starting point and unit of measurement
- Marker data, such as marker type, distance between two markers, and unit of measurement

You can assign linear data to the following objects: Objects

- Equipment
- Functional locations
- Measuring points
- Measurement documents
- Notification
- Notification item
- Order
- Confirmation
- Maintenance item

> **Fully Integrated in Processing** [+]
>
> In contrast to links, linear asset management is integrated consistently in the maintenance business processes. You can thus record linear data not only in the master data, but also in planning (maintenance plans, notifications, and orders) and in the confirmation.

To be able to use linear asset management to its full extent, you must have satisfied the following prerequisites in advance: Requirements

- In the classification system Customizing, you have used the function MAINTAIN OBJECT TYPES AND CLASS TYPES to create an organizational area—for example, the organizational area L for linear objects.
- In Customizing for linear asset management, you have used the function DEFINE OFFSET TYPES to define offset types—for example, the horizontal offset and the vertical offset.
- In Customizing for linear asset management, you have used the function ORGANIZATIONAL AREA FOR CHARACTERISTICS WITH LINEAR DATA to assign the equipment and functional locations an organizational area—for example, the organizational area L for linear data.
- To be able to record linear data for measuring points and measurement documents, you have defined a measuring point type using the function DEFINE MEASURING POINT TYPES and have set the indicator LINEAR SYSTEM there.

- Using the function SET VIEW PROFILES FOR TECHNICAL OBJECTS, you have defined a view profile for functional locations and one for equipment and have assigned the field groups for linear data there.
- To be able to store linear data for functional locations, you have used the function DEFINE TYPE OF FUNCTIONAL LOCATION to define a functional location type, assigned the view profile in particular there, and set the indicator LINEAR SYSTEM.
- To be able to store linear data for equipment, you have used the function MAINTAIN EQUIPMENT CATEGORY to define an equipment category, assigned the view profile in particular there, and set the indicator LINEAR SYSTEM.

Creating linear objects

If you now want to create a linear functional location, first call Transaction IL01. You then choose a suitable structure indicator and assign a new number.

If you want to create a linear piece of equipment, call Transaction IE01. Assign an equipment number or let the system assign a number.

In either case, make sure that you select the equipment category or functional location type that is defined as a linear object.

Linear data

After the view profiles have been correctly set and assigned, you start maintaining the linear data (see Figure 4.30), as follows:

- **Starting point**
  In the START POINT field, which determines the beginning of a section, you enter the value 7,000 in our example.
- **End point**
  In the END POINT field, you also enter the value 7,000 and thus define that the end of the section is to be identical to the starting point because our example involves a stationary system.
- **Length and unit of length**
- **Offset data**
  In the dropdown menu of the field OFFSET TYPE 1 in the area OFFSET 1, select the option HORIZONTAL OFFSET, and in the field VALUE OF OFFSET 1, enter the value 10.5. For OFFSET TYPE 2 in the area OFFSET 2,

select VERTICAL OFFSET, and in the field VALUE OF OFFSET 2, enter the value 5.25. The device is thus offset 10.5 m from the side of the road (horizontal offset) at a height of 5.25 m (vertical offset).

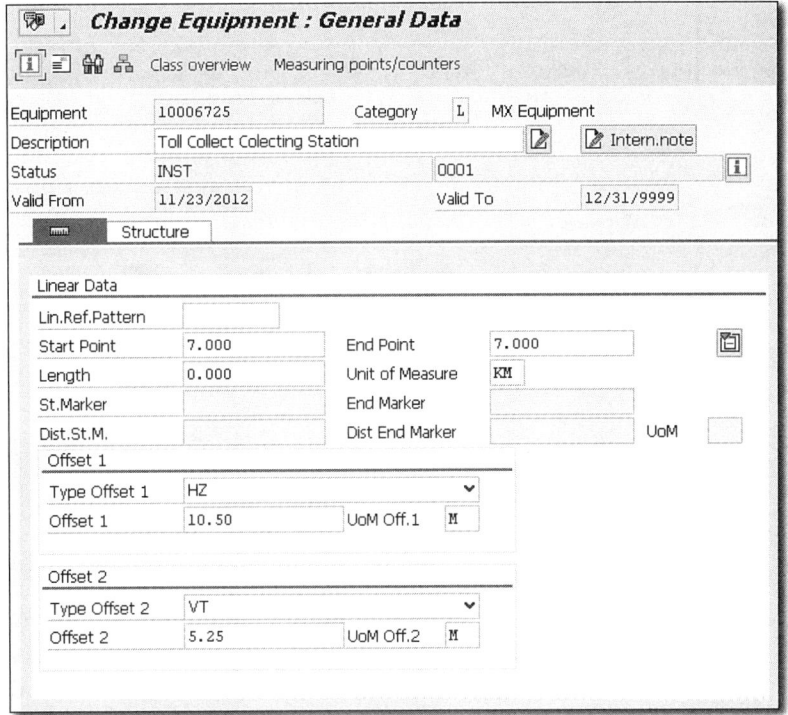

Figure 4.30 Linear Data

If you have also assigned a suitable class, you can now also maintain the stored characteristic values (see Figure 4.31).

Description	Char. Value	Start Point	End Point	Length	UoM
Traffic Lanes	2	3,000	17,000	14,000	KM
Traffic Lanes	3	17,000	21,000	4,000	KM
Surface	Bitumen	3,000	12,000	9,000	KM
Surface	Bitumen	17,000	21,000	4,000	KM
Surface	Tar	12,000	17,000	5,000	KM
Speed Limit	120 km/h	5,000	10,000	5,000	KM

Figure 4.31 Linear Characteristics

4 | Structuring of Technical Systems

[+] Dynamic Segmentation

What is special about the maintenance of linear characteristics is that you can assign the same characteristic with the same or different values with length specification. Thus, the surface changes in the example shown (bitumen on the section *3 to 12 kms*, tar on the section *12 to 17 kms*, and bitumen on the section *17 to 21 kms*), while a speed restriction of 120 km/h applies only on the section *5 to 10 kms*. This functionality is called *dynamic segmentation*.

Figure 4.32 shows a completed linear technical system structure, which has been called via Transaction IH01 (structural display).

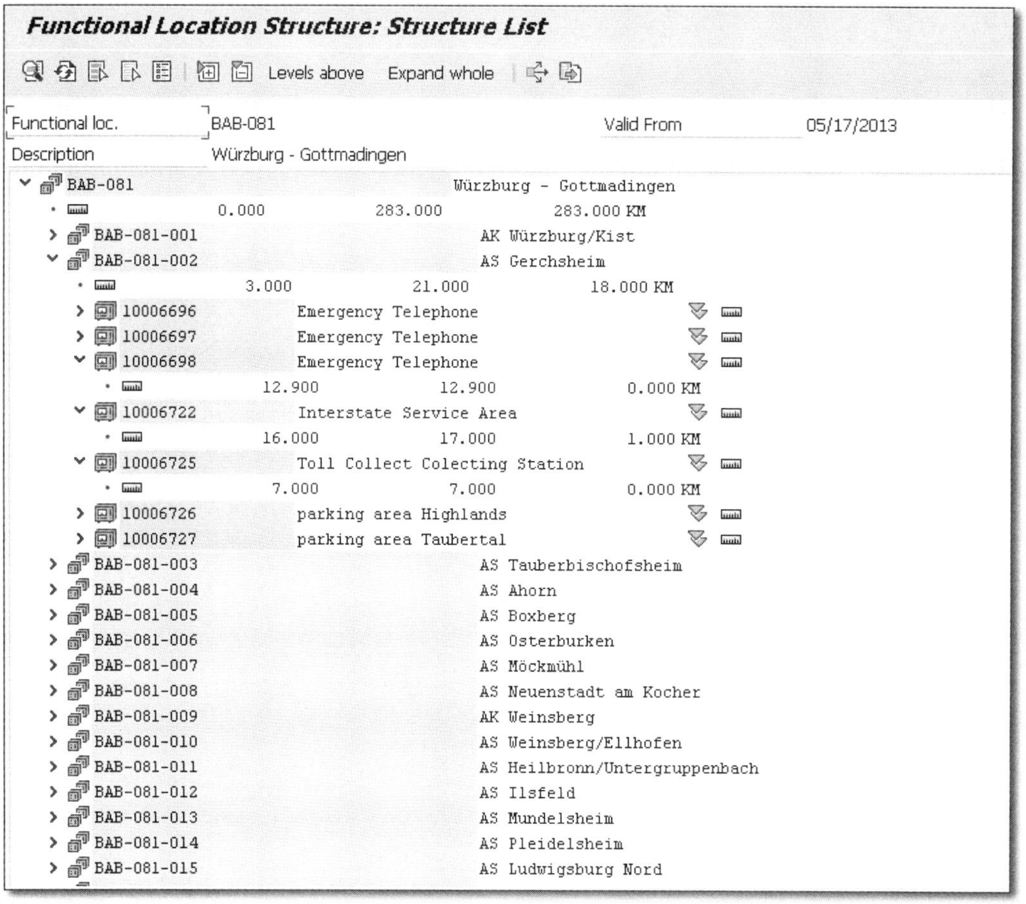

Functional Location Structure: Structure List

Functional loc.	BAB-081	Valid From	05/17/2013
Description	Würzburg - Gottmadingen		

```
> BAB-081                            Würzburg - Gottmadingen
  •          0.000      283.000      283.000 KM
  > BAB-081-001                      AK Würzburg/Kist
  > BAB-081-002                      AS Gerchsheim
    •        3.000      21.000       18.000 KM
    > 10006696          Emergency Telephone
    > 10006697          Emergency Telephone
    > 10006698          Emergency Telephone
      •      12.900     12.900       0.000 KM
    > 10006722          Interstate Service Area
      •      16.000     17.000       1.000 KM
    > 10006725          Toll Collect Colecting Station
      •      7.000      7.000        0.000 KM
    > 10006726          parking area Highlands
    > 10006727          parking area Taubertal
  > BAB-081-003                      AS Tauberbischofsheim
  > BAB-081-004                      AS Ahorn
  > BAB-081-005                      AS Boxberg
  > BAB-081-006                      AS Osterburken
  > BAB-081-007                      AS Möckmühl
  > BAB-081-008                      AS Neuenstadt am Kocher
  > BAB-081-009                      AK Weinsberg
  > BAB-081-010                      AS Weinsberg/Ellhofen
  > BAB-081-011                      AS Heilbronn/Untergruppenbach
  > BAB-081-012                      AS Ilsfeld
  > BAB-081-013                      AS Mundelsheim
  > BAB-081-014                      AS Pleidelsheim
  > BAB-081-015                      AS Ludwigsburg Nord
```

Figure 4.32 Linear Technical System Structure

You can also graphically display such a linear technical system structure over the course of the route. To do so, call Transaction IL07 (multilevel functional location list). Select the correct filter on the initial screen (see Figure 4.33).

Filter		
✓ FunctLoc	☐ Partners	☐ Permit
☐ EquipUsagePeriod	✓ Equipment	☐ Notification
☐ Order	☐ Class	✓ Characteristic
☐ Document	☐ Object link	✓ Measuring point
☐ MeasDocument	☐ Maintenance Item	☐ Maintenance Date
☐ Maintenance Packages	☐ Operations	
✓ Linear Data	✓ Linear Data Charact.	

Figure 4.33 Filter for Multilevel Functional Location List

Now, call the graphic linear technical system structure within the list using the 🗐 Linear Data button (see Figure 4.34).

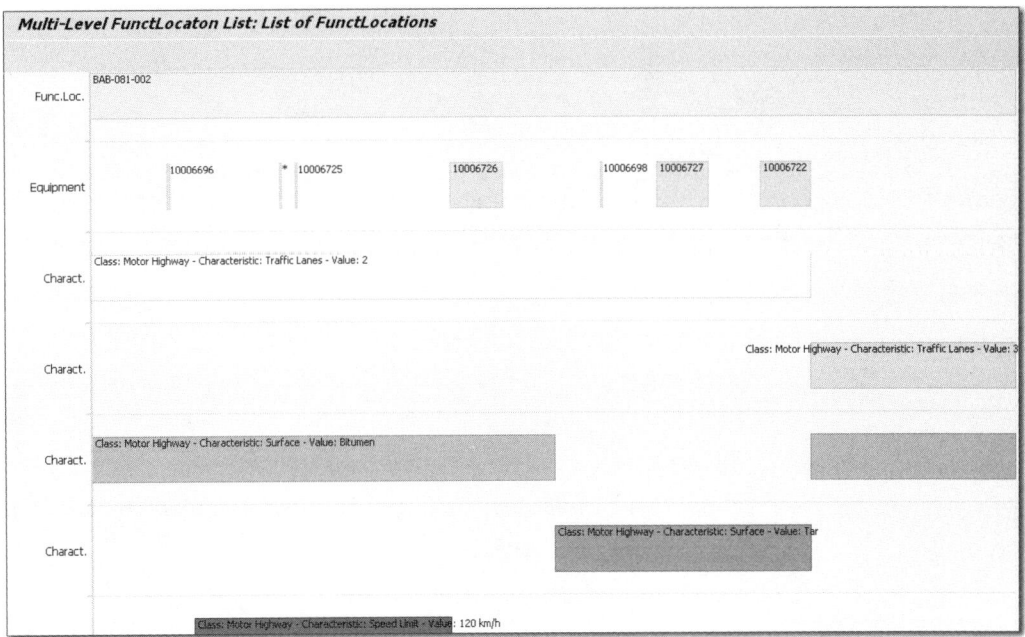

Figure 4.34 Graphic Linear Technical System Structure

4 | Structuring of Technical Systems

Mass maintenance of linear data

Instead of individual transactions, you can also use the list transactions to directly maintain the linear data for multiple objects. Proceed as follows in this case:

1. Call Transaction IL05 for the maintenance of functional locations or Transaction IE05 for the maintenance of equipment.
2. Narrow the selection, and then start the list.
3. Call the linear data using the [Linear Data] button.
4. You can maintain all linear data in the displayed list (see Figure 4.35).

Functional Location	Description of functional location	Start Point	End Point	Length	UoM	LRP	Type Off.1	Offs 1	UoM	Type Off.2	Offs 2	UoM
BAB-081	Würzburg - Gottmadingen	0,000	283,000	283,000	KM		HZ		M	VT		M
BAB-081-001	AK Würzburg/Kist	0,000	3,000	3,000	KM		HZ		M	VT		M
BAB-081-002	AS Gerchsheim	3,000	21,000	18,000	KM	BAB-081	HZ		M	VT		M
BAB-081-003	AS Tauberbischofsheim	21,000	32,000	11,000	KM		HZ		M	VT		M
BAB-081-004	AS Ahorn	32,000	40,000	8,000	KM		HZ		M	VT		M
BAB-081-005	AS Boxberg	40,000	50,000	10,000	KM		HZ		M	VT		M
BAB-081-006	AS Osterburken	50,000	68,000	18,000	KM		HZ		M	VT		M
BAB-081-006-R01	Raststätte Jagsttal											
BAB-081-007	AS Möckmühl	68,000	73,000	5,000	KM		HZ		M	VT		M
BAB-081-008	AS Neuenstadt am Kocher	73,000	83,000	10,000	KM		HZ		M	VT		M
BAB-081-009	AK Weinsberg	83,000	86,000	3,000	KM		HZ		M	VT		M
BAB-081-010	AS Weinsberg/Ellhofen	86,000	92,000	6,000	KM		HZ		M	VT		M
BAB-081-011	AS Heilbronn/Untergruppenbach	92,000	95,000	3,000	KM		HZ		M	VT		M
BAB-081-012	AS Ilsfeld	95,000	102,000	7,000	KM		HZ		M	VT		M
BAB-081-012-R01	Raststätte Wunnenstein											
BAB-081-013	AS Mundelsheim	102,000	107,000	5,000	KM		HZ		M	VT		M
BAB-081-014	AS Pleidelsheim	107,000	114,000	7,000	KM		HZ		M	VT		M
BAB-081-015	AS Ludwigsburg Nord	114,000	118,000	4,000	KM		HZ		M	VT		M

Figure 4.35 Mass Maintenance of Linear Data

Linear reference patterns

Linear reference patterns are created to be able to assign a descriptive reference point to the real technical objects or documents (order, notification, and so on). Thus, you can then send a notification, such as "the damage occurred 10 km after the Jagsttal rest area."

You maintain linear reference patterns using Transactions IK81 (create), IK82 (change), and IK83 (display).

The following are relevant as pattern types (see Figure 4.36):

- General markers (for example, 10, 20, 30, … km)
- Distinctive functional locations (for example, Weinsberg interchange)
- Distinctive pieces of equipment (for example, Jagsttal service area)

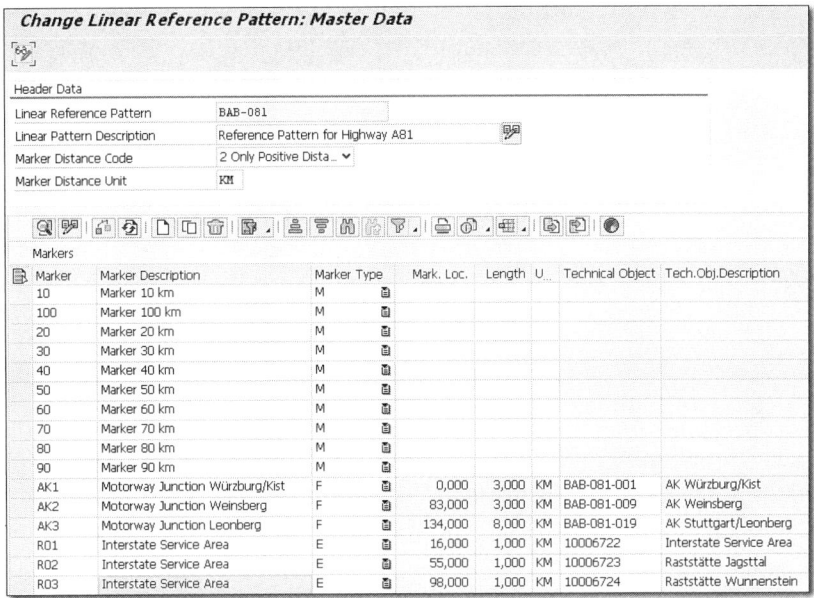

Figure 4.36 Linear Reference Patterns

4.2.5 Material and PM Assemblies

The material master contains information about materials that a company designs, procures, produces, stores, and sells and integrates data from the various areas of a company—for example, purchasing or accounting. Unlike a piece of equipment or functional location, a material master record does not describe just one thing, but rather similar items. This means that a material master record generally represents several similar spare parts, assemblies, raw materials, and so on.

Definition

From a maintenance perspective, material master records are used for the following purposes:

Material master records in plant maintenance

- Some material master records are purchased as spare parts and then stored.
- Some material master records are purchased as equipment and then placed in storage as material/serial numbers.
- Some material records are construction types that encompass only similar pieces of equipment or functional locations in order to execute

shared functions—for example, management of shared bills of material or general maintenance task lists.

- Some material master records serve as PM assemblies for sub-structuring pieces of equipment or functional locations.
- Some material master records fulfill the same function as spare parts, with the difference that they are not placed in storage, but, rather, procured each time as non-stock items, for example, because they are too expensive, too large, or rarely used.
- Some material master records are used as production resource tools for maintenance tasks, but not as spare parts (for example, tools or protective clothing).

Structure of the material master

The material master record has a hierarchical structure (see Figure 4.37) that resembles the organizational structure of your company. Some material data is valid at all organizational levels, and some is valid only at certain levels.

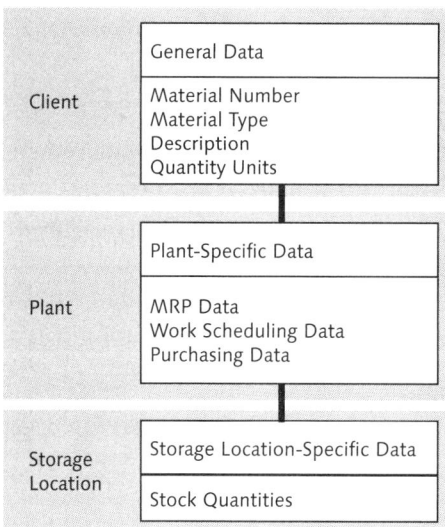

Figure 4.37 Structure of the Material Master

- At the client level, the following applies: general material data that is valid for the entire company is saved at this level. This includes, among other things, the material group, the base unit of measure, the material short texts, and the conversion factors for alternative units of measure.

- All the data that is valid in a specific plant and in the associated storage locations is saved at the plant level. This includes, for example, accounting data, purchasing data, material requirements planning (MRP) data, and forecast data.
- All data that refers to one particular storage location is saved at the storage location level. This primarily concerns storage location stock.

You must create a material master record, identified by a unique material number, for each material used by your company. As with equipment, you can assign an external or internal number.

Material number

You group together materials that have the same basic characteristics by assigning them to one common material type. This enables you to manage different materials in a uniform manner according to your company's requirements.

Material type

You use the material type to determine the following:

- Which user departments (purchasing, production, sales and distribution, accounting, and so on) can maintain the material master record
- Whether the material number is assigned internally or externally
- The number range interval from which the material number originated
- Which screens appear and in which sequence
- Which user department–specific data is available for entry
- Whether quantity and value changes are updated
- The procurement type of a material—that is, whether the material is produced in house or procured externally
- Which accounts are posted to if a material is placed in storage or removed from storage

Figure 4.38 provides an overview of potential material types.

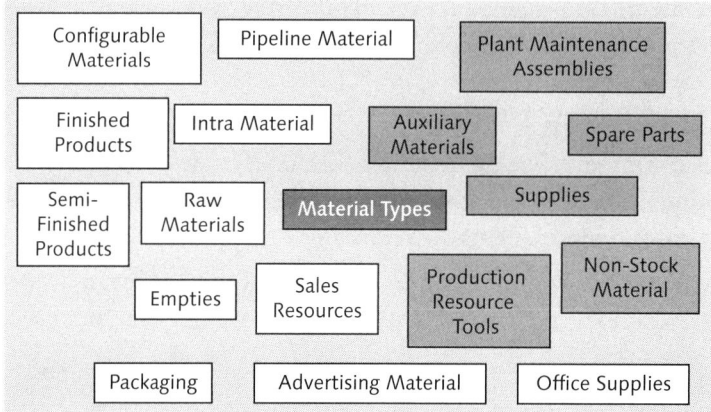

Figure 4.38 Overview of Material Types

From a maintenance perspective, the following material types are relevant in practice (indicated in the dark boxes in the figure):

- **Auxiliary materials**
  Auxiliary materials are those materials that form part of a finished product, but are insignificant and barely seen in the finished product (for example, screws, adhesive, welded joints).

- **Operating supplies**
  Operating supplies are not part of the finished product, but are required for the production process (for example, lubricant, power, grease, oil, and so on).

- **Spare parts**
  Spare parts are used to replace defective parts. They can be purchased and placed in storage.

- **PM assemblies**
  PM assemblies are not standalone objects, but, rather, logical elements that divide the technical objects in plant maintenance into clearly defined units. A forklift, for example, can be a technical object; the lifting plant, gear shift, chassis, and so on, can be the associated maintenance assemblies.

- **Production resource tools**
  Production resource tools are required for maintenance tasks (for example, tools and devices, test equipment, protective clothing, and

safety devices). Unlike operating supplies, they do not perish, but, rather, wear out with use over time.

▶ **Non-stock materials**
Non-stock materials are not held in storage, but are procured as required and used immediately. This may be the case, for example, because the parts are too expensive, very rarely required, or difficult to store (too large, too heavy, or too bulky). The master data of non-stock materials comprises purchasing data only.

> **[!] Define Your Own Material Types**
> You can determine which material types you require with which controls for your company using the function DEFINE PROPERTIES OF MATERIAL TYPES.

Because, in our example, several departments in a company work with the same material and each department uses different information about the material, the data in a material master record is arranged by user department (see Figure 4.39).

User departments, views, and data

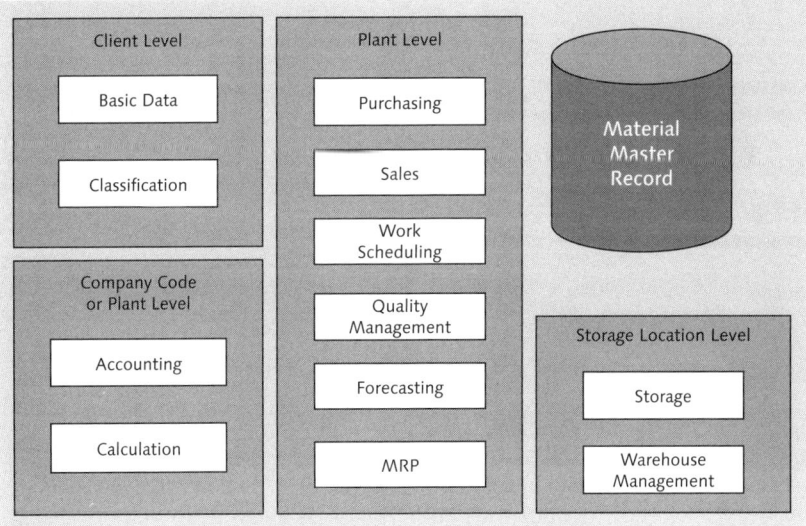

Figure 4.39 Material Views

Here, the BASIC DATA and CLASSIFICATION views are at the client level; that is, the views are valid for all plants and storage locations.

In the case of the ACCOUNTING view, you can choose whether to manage all the data together at the company code level for all plants assigned to a company code or separately at the plant level for each plant.

The views PURCHASING, MATERIAL REQUIREMENTS PLANNING, SALES AND DISTRIBUTION, WORK SCHEDULING, QUALITY MANAGEMENT, and FORECAST are at the plant level. That is, the views are valid for all storage locations assigned to the plant.

The STORAGE and WAREHOUSE MANAGEMENT views are at the storage location level.

The maximum value of the material master consists of more than 30 screens. Because these screens usually have to be maintained in only a rudimentary manner from a maintenance perspective, you should adapt the layout of the material master record. This restricts the selection of views (see Figure 4.40).

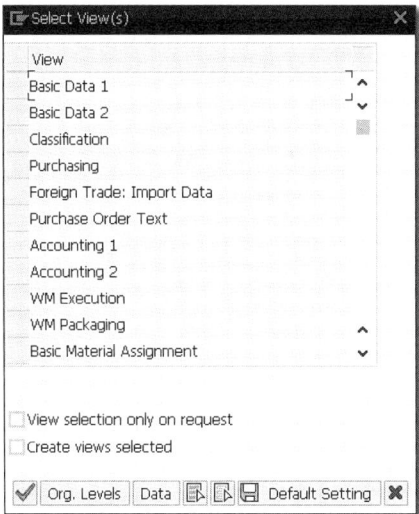

Figure 4.40 View Selection of an Adjusted Material Master

Furthermore, the screen templates contain only fields that you can actually use and that provide information (see Figure 4.41).

4.2 SAP Elements for Structuring Technical Systems and How to Use Them

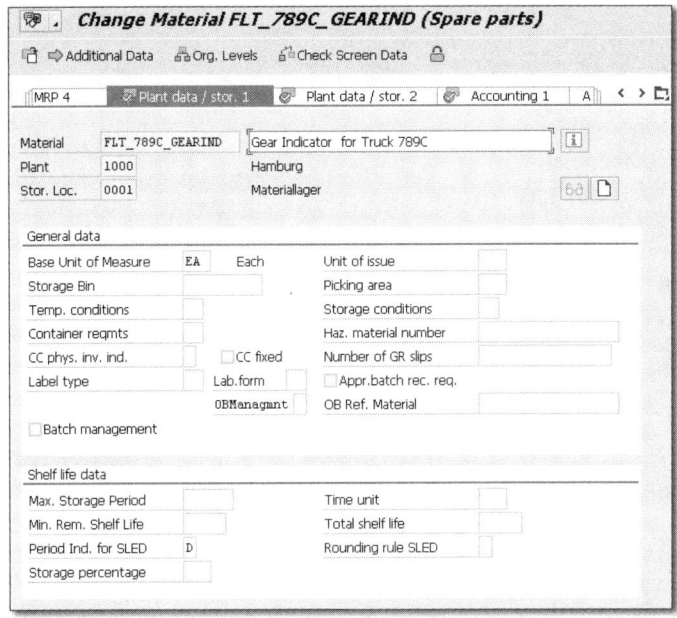

Figure 4.41 Layout of an Adjusted Material Master Record

> **Adjusting the Layout of the Material Master Record** [!]
>
> You should not use the layout of the material master record provided by SAP in the standard system because it contains too many views, too many screen groups, and too much data.
>
> You should define your own layout with selected views, screen groups, and data. You define this layout using the Customizing functions under CONFIGURING THE MATERIAL MASTER.

The book will not describe this material master in any further detail. Instead, let me refer you to some additional reading material.[1]

---

1 See Liebstückel, K.: Anwendungssysteme in Produktentstehung und Logistik, Modul: Beschaffung und Lagerhaltung, Stuttgart: AKAD-Verlag 2005 (*Application Systems in Product Development and Logistics, Module: Procurement and Warehousing*, Stuttgart: AKAD Publishing Company, 2005) or Liebstückel, K.: Anwendungssysteme in Produktentstehung und Logistik, Modul: Produktion und Fertigung, Stuttgart: AKAD-Verlag 2005 (*Application Systems in Product Development and Logistics, Module: Production and Manufacturing*, Stuttgart: AKAD Publishing Company, 2005).

4.2.6 BOMs

Definition A bill of material is essentially a complete, formally structured list of all components that belong to a product or assembly. It contains the material numbers of the individual components, as well as their quantity and unit of measure (see Figure 4.42). The components can be parts or assemblies that can or cannot be kept in storage. There may be BOMs, in turn, for the assemblies, which describe them in more detail. This results in a multilevel bill of material structure.

Item Number	Description	Material Number	Quantity	Quantity Unit
1	Spiral Casing	T-B00	1	ST
2	Blade Wheel	100-200	1	ST
3	Shaft	100-300	1	ST
4	Outrigger	100-600	2	ST
5	Pressure Lid	100-400	1	ST

Figure 4.42 Design Drawings and a Derived BOM

In the SAP system, bills of material are used not only in plant maintenance, but also in other areas, as follows:

- In production as production BOMs
- In controlling as costing BOMs
- In sales as sales order BOMs

Usage in plant maintenance In plant maintenance, you can primarily use bills of material for the following two purposes:

- **Structure description**
  You can use the BOM to describe the structure of a technical object or material. You can use the bill of material to pinpoint the location of the damage or the location where maintenance tasks are performed for a technical object.

- **Spare parts assignment**
  You can use the BOM to describe the assignment of spare parts for a technical object or material.

> **Spare Parts BOMs** [!]
>
> In practice, maintenance BOMs are primarily used as spare parts BOMs.

From a plant perspective, you must distinguish between three different BOM categories (see Figure 4.43):

- **Equipment BOM**
  You create an equipment bill of material for exactly one piece of equipment (Transaction IB01). Therefore, you can use the bill of material only in connection with this piece of equipment.

- **Functional location BOM**
  The same also applies for a functional location BOM (Transaction IB1).

- **Material BOM**
  You can indirectly make a material BOM (Transaction CS01) available for several pieces of equipment and/or functional locations. Here, you use the CONSTRUCTION TYPE field in the master record for the piece of equipment or functional location in the STRUCTURING screen group. This means that all pieces of equipment and functional locations for which a material number is entered in the CONSTRUCTION TYPE field can access the material BOM (see Figure 4.44).

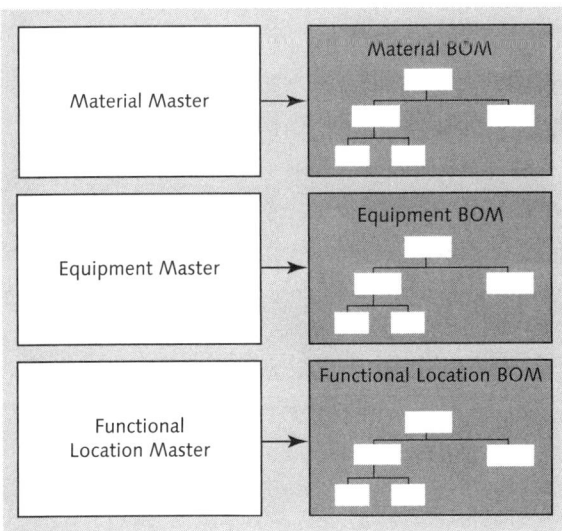

Figure 4.43 BOM Categories

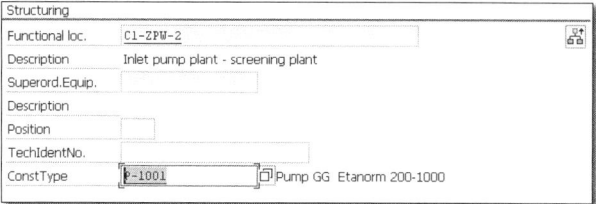

Figure 4.44 Construction Type

Consequently, these two assignment procedures are described as direct and indirect assignments (see Figure 4.45).

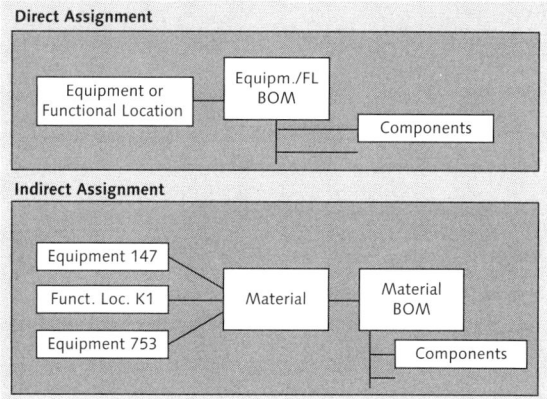

Figure 4.45 BOM Assignment

[!] **Using BOMs**

If you use bills of material in plant maintenance, note the following:

- Pieces of equipment and functional locations can have both directly and indirectly assigned bills of material.
- Bills of material for pieces of equipment and functional locations are triggered simultaneously in maintenance processing.
- If you use bills of material, you should create material BOMs as much as possible and assign them as construction types to the pieces of equipment and functional locations.
- Record the parts that are the same for the relevant equipment or functional location category as a material BOM. Record the parts in which a piece of equipment or functional location has a different category as an equipment BOM or a functional location BOM.

In the upper part of Figure 4.46, you see a structure list for a piece of equipment (Transaction IH04) in the form of a multilevel spare parts bill of material, which was assigned indirectly by construction type P-1000 to piece of equipment 10001031. The last three items are spare parts from the directly assigned equipment bill of material.

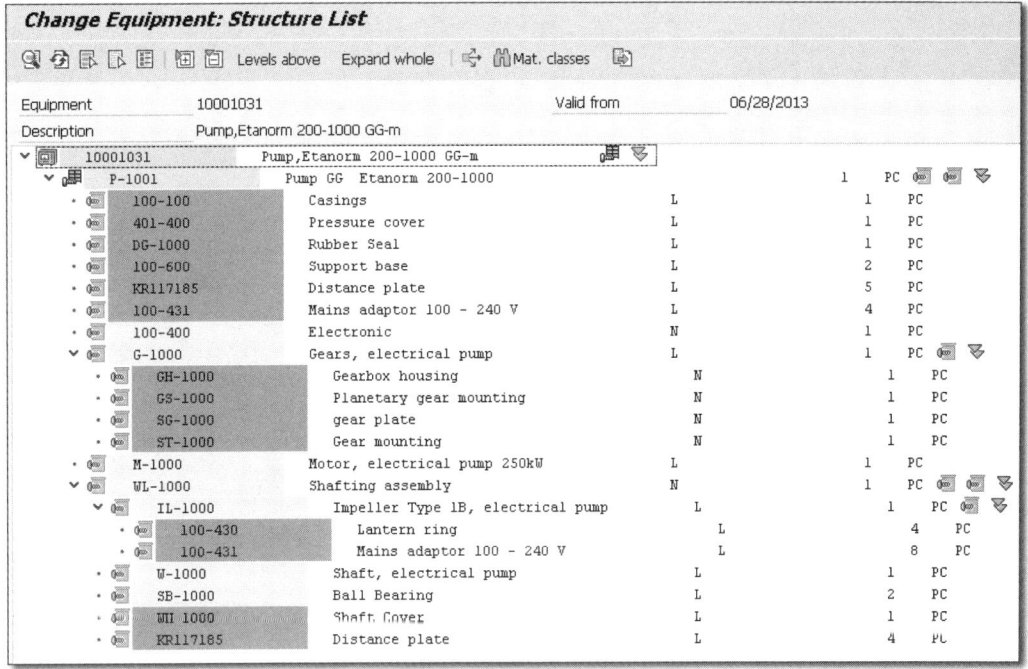

Figure 4.46 BOM Structure

> **[!] No Usage of Other BOM Categories**
>
> The BOM categories usually found in other applications, such as variant BOMs or multiple BOMs that are used, for example, in production, are practically insignificant in plant maintenance.

The where-used list (Transaction CS15) is the mirror image of a bill of material—thus, unlike a BOM from the top to the bottom, but from the bottom to the top. The where-used list shows you the bills of material that contain a specific spare part or assembly.

In Figure 4.47, you see that material 100-100 (control electronics casing) is in equipment BOMs (BOM category E), material BOMs (BOM category M), and functional location BOMs (BOM category T).

L	Usage	Plant	Obje..	Alt.	Item	RQex	RqQt	Un	ResQt	BOMcat	Functional loc.	Equipment	Material
1	4	1000			0010		1.000	PC	1.000	E		E-7045-77	
1	4	1000			0010		1.000	PC	1.000	E		E-7049	
1	4	1000			0010		1.000	PC	1.000	E		E-7049-01	
1	4	1000			0010		1.000	PC	1.000	E		E-7054	
1	4	1000			0010		1.000	PC	1.000	E		E-7054U	
1	4	1000			0010		1.000	PC	1.000	E		E-7089	
1	4	1000			0010		1.000	PC	1.000	E		E-NNNN	
1	4	1000			0010		1.000	PC	1.000	E		P-1000-N001	
1	4	1000			0010		1.000	PC	1.000	M			P-1000
1	4	1000			0010		1.000	PC	1.000	M			P-1001
1	4	1000			0010		1.000	PC	1.000	M			P-2000
1	4	1000			0010		1.000	PC	1.000	M			P-7000
1	4	1000			0010		1.000	PC	1.000	M			T-FP400
1	4	1000			0010		1.000	PC	1.000	T	00		
1	4	1000			0010		1.000	PC	1.000	T	01-B02-1		
1	4	1000			0010		1.000	PC	1.000	T	02-B01-2		
1	4	1000			0010		1.000	PC	1.000	T	03-B02-1		
1	4	1000			0010		1.000	PC	1.000	T	04-B02-1		
1	4	1000			0010		1.000	PC	1.000	T	05-B02-1		
1	4	1000			0010		1.000	PC	1.000	T	06-B02-1		

Figure 4.47 Material Where-Used List

4.2.7 Classification

Tasks of classes

In the SAP system, a *class* represents a group of similar objects that are described by means of the characteristics that they have in common. From a maintenance perspective, a class system offers you the following options:

- By means of classes, you can technically describe any objects (for example, equipment, functional locations, and material) using the characteristics beyond the master records fields.

- You can group similar objects, from a technical viewpoint, into classes.

- Whenever necessary, the SAP system provides you with search functions that make it easier for you to find objects by using classes and characteristics.
- You can use classes to describe the dynamic segmentation in the objects of linear asset management (see Section 4.2.4).

The class system structure comprises three steps:

In the first step, you describe the properties of an object, which are represented by characteristics, in Transaction CT04). The individual characteristics are created centrally in the SAP system.

Step 1: Definition of characteristics

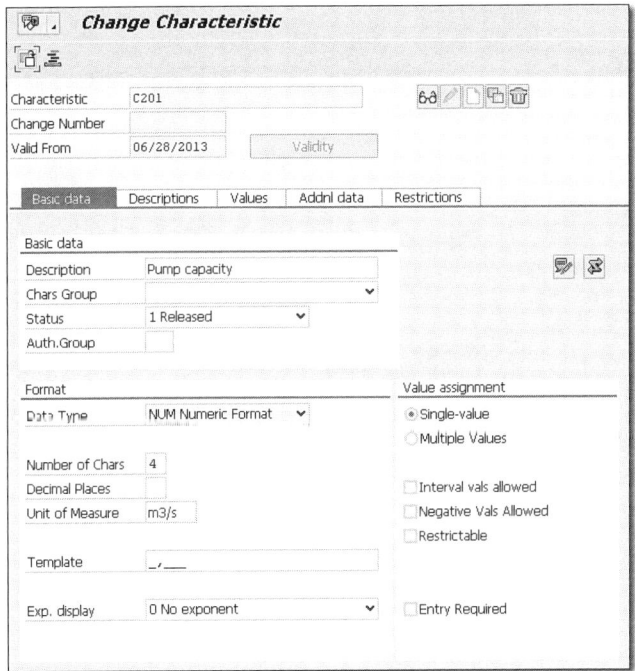

Figure 4.48 Defining Characteristic

In a characteristic, you define, for example, the following properties (see Figure 4.48):

- The name and the keywords (multilingual)
- The status (released, locked, and so on)
- The value assignment (one value or multiple values)

4 | Structuring of Technical Systems

- Whether intervals are allowed
- The data type (character, date, numeric)
- The number of characters
- Whether negative values are allowed
- A table of allowed values
- The link to a database field
- Whether the characteristic is to be restricted to certain class types

Step 2: Definition of classes

In the second step, you define the classes in Transaction CL02 and store the objects to be classified there. You then assign characteristics to the classes you created (see Figure 4.49).

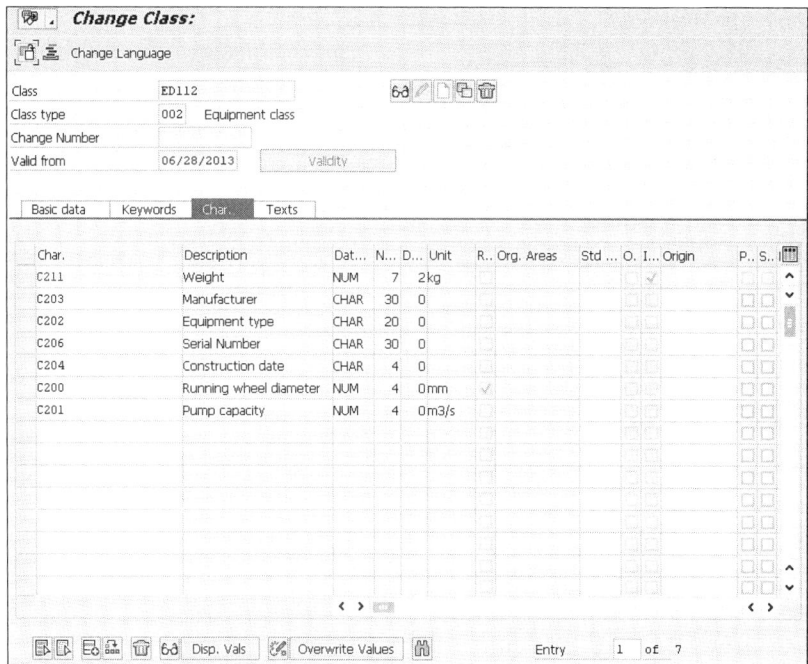

Figure 4.49 Defining Classes

The class types are pre-assigned by SAP, and they define the object type for which a class is to apply (for example, 001 Material, 002 Equipment, 003 Functional Location, and so on).

You can assign any alphanumeric name to the classes.

> **Take Care when Using the "Same Classification" Parameter** [!]
>
> The SAME CLASSIFICATION parameter checks whether the class has objects with the same characteristic values (see Figure 4.50). Set this parameter to DO NOT CHECK because, otherwise, unintentionally long runtimes or performance problems occur during the classification.

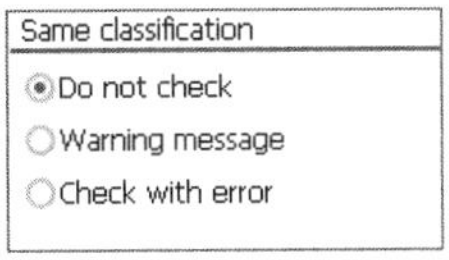

```
Same classification
⦿ Do not check
○ Warning message
○ Check with error
```

Figure 4.50 Check Classification

The most important elements within a class are the characteristics that define the technical properties of the class. In the aforementioned example, class ED112 (water pumps) contains technical properties, such as a running wheel diameter or pump capacity.

On the KEYWORDS tab, you can specify objects of this class. In the above example, you can use this class for pressurized water pumps, sewage water pumps, or industrial water pumps.

The classification provides you with a wide range of options that go beyond the scope of this book. Examples include using object dependencies to derive characteristics, using the variant configuration to define complete characteristic value tables, transferring characteristic values from the relevant functional location or piece of equipment, or defining value tables.

> **Using a Class System** [+]
>
> If you have carefully considered your class system and have a manageable number of characteristics (less than one page of characteristics works best), there will be a high level of acceptance among your users. Your EAM will become an production resource tools database; additional records or parallel systems are superfluous.

It is very time consuming to set up a class and characteristics system; it requires both an organizational effort to create a concept and a technical effort to record the data in the system. You can considerably reduce this time and effort by using a predefined class system, such as eCl@ss.

> **[+] Template for a Class System**
>
> At *http://www.eclass.de*, you will find a template for a complete class system, including all the characteristics and keywords. eCl@ss is a hierarchical system for grouping materials, products, and services according to product-specific idiosyncrasies described using characteristics. At present, eCl@ss comprises approximately 38,000 classes in four hierarchical levels, approximately 16,000 characteristics, and approximately 52,000 keywords. This is probably much more than you will ever require, but it would be easier for you to choose the elements you require from a template than to start from scratch.

Furthermore, you can also use the relevant data transfer programs of SAP for classification and transfer of characteristics in order to transfer the classification of eCl@ss. These are available in Transaction SXDA with the bus objects BUS3060, BUS1003, and BUS1088, or in Transaction LSMW under the data transfer objects 0130, 0140, and 0150.

Not only are well-known companies and associations from all industries (for example, Audi, BASF, Cognis, DB, and E.ON) involved in the development of eCl@ss, but SAP is also represented as a full member of the steering committee.

Step 3: Classification The third step is to assign objects—that is, to actually classify them. Once you create the classes you require for the classification, you can assign individual objects to them. The objects are described using the characteristics contained in the class.

You assign the objects using a central transaction (CL20N) or classify the objects directly in the master record itself, which is normally the case. For example, you classify the equipment using Transaction IE02 (see Figure 4.51), the material using Transaction MM02, or the functional locations using Transaction IL02.

> **[+] Set a Standard Class**
>
> When assigning a class to a functional location or piece of equipment, always set the checkbox for the standard class. This is the only way to ensure that the class-related object statistics of the Plant Maintenance Information System (PM-IS) are updated.

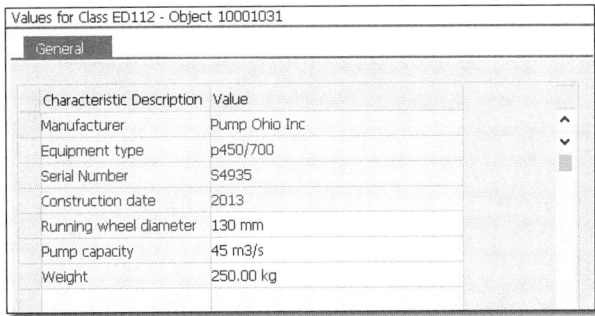

Figure 4.51 Classifying a Piece of Equipment

For more information about PM-IS, see Section 7.2.3.

Whenever necessary, the SAP system provides you with search functions that allow you to find objects with certain technical characteristics again. The following usage areas are typical for search functions:

- You require a list of all pumps that cross certain performance boundaries.
- An engine has failed, and you require an equivalent replacement.
- A spare part on the technical system is defective, but the original spare part is no longer in storage, so you look for an alternative.
- Since the delivery procedure from the warehouse is to be changed, you require a list containing the maximum payload of all of your industrial trucks.

You can use the following transactions for the search functions:

- Transaction CL30N, which enables you to find objects within a class according to characteristic restrictions
- Transaction CL20, which enables you to find objects across classes by restricting one or more characteristics
- Transaction CL6B, which enables you to create a complete object list for a class
- Transactions IE05 and IH08, which enable you to create a list of equipment with organizational (for example, cost center, plant) and technical restrictions (a class with characteristic value assignments) (see Figure 4.52)

4 | Structuring of Technical Systems

Change Equipment: Equipment List

S	Equipment	Equipment descriptn	Functional Location	Manufacturer	Equipment type	Serial Number	Construction date
	10005686	Electric pump 001	80LAC30AP001	Vereinte Mechanische Werke AG	P-I		
	EQ-01	Equipment	FL-01				
	MQ-09122-15	Electric pump 001	14-B02	Vereinte Mechanische Werke AG	P-I		
	P-1000-DF01	Electric pump 001	K1-B01-1	Vereinte Mechanische Werke AG	P-I		
	P-1000-DF02	Electric pump 001	K1-B01-1	Vereinte Mechanische Werke AG	P-I		
	P-1000-DF03	Electric pump 001	K1-B01-1	Vereinte Mechanische Werke AG	P-I		
	P-1000-N001	Electric pump 001	00-B02	Vereinte Mechanische Werke AG	P-I	001	1993
	P-1000-N002	Electric pump 002	K1-B01-2	Vereinte Mechanische Werke AG	P-I	002	1993
	P-1000-N003	Electric pump 003	K1-B02	Gerätefabrik Holst GmbH	P-II	003	1993
	P-1000-N004	Electric pump 004	K1-BR2-11	Gerätefabrik Holst GmbH	P-II	004	1993
	P-1000-N005	Electric pump 005	K1-BR2-12	Gerätefabrik Holst GmbH	P-I	005	1994
	P-1000-N006	Electric pump 006	K1-BR2-21	Solms&Söhne KG	P-III	006	1992
	P-1000-N007	Electric pump 007	K1-BR2-22	Vereinte Mechanische Werke AG	P-I	007	1993
	P-1000-N008	Electric pump 008		Gerätefabrik Holst GmbH	P-II	008	1993
	P-1000-N009	Electric pump 009		Solms&Söhne KG	P-III	009	1992
	P-1000-N010	Electric pump 010		Solms&Söhne KG	P-III	010	1991
	P-1000-N011	Electric pump 011		Solms&Söhne KG	P-III	011	1992
	P-1000-N012	Electric pump 012		Vereinte Mechanische Werke AG	P-I	012	1992
	P-1000-N013	Electric pump 001		Vereinte Mechanische Werke AG	P-I		
	P-2000-N002	Electric pump 001	00-B02	Vereinte Mechanische Werke AG	P-I		
	P-2000-N004	Electric pump 004	K1-BR2-11	Gerätefabrik Holst GmbH	P-II		
	P-2000-N005	Electric pump 004	K1-BR2-12	Gerätefabrik Holst GmbH	P-II		
	P-6000-N001	Pump GG Etanorm 200-10...		Vereinte Mechanische Werke AG	P-I		
	TEP-00	Elektrische Pumpe	00-BR2-12	Vereinte Mechanische Werke AG	P-I		
	TEQ-00	Electric pump 001	00-B02	Vereinte Mechanische Werke AG	P-I		1993
	TEQ-01	Electric pump 001	01-B02	Vereinte Mechanische Werke AG	P-I		1993

Figure 4.52 Equipment Lost with Characteristic Value Assignments

- Transactions IL05 and IH06, which enable you to create the same list for functional locations
- Transaction IQ08, which enables you to create the same list for serial numbers
- Transaction IE20, which enables you to find a replacement piece of equipment with the same performance data as the original piece of equipment

4.2.8 Product Structure Browser

Definition I now wish to introduce you to a function that is often unknown, even among very experienced users: the product structure browser (Transaction CC04). The product structure browser is a general tool from the product data management area in Logistics that enables you to set up, manage, and display complex product structures. Since the product structure browser enables you to manage not only functional locations and pieces of equipment, but also practically all logistics objects (documents, bills of material, maintenance task lists, classifications, and so on), you can use it not only in plant maintenance, but also in engineering/design, production, and so on.

From a maintenance perspective, the product structure browser (see Figure 4.53) is very similar to the display format for the structural display (Transactions IH01 and IH03).

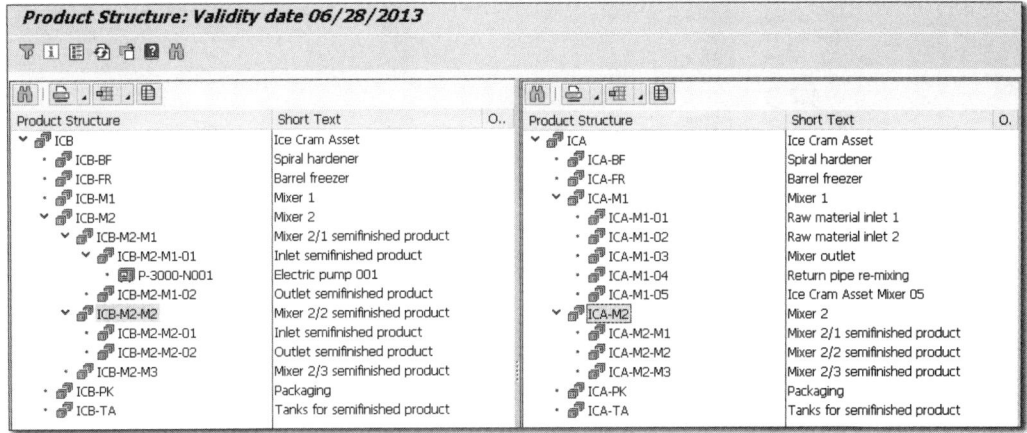

Figure 4.53 The Product Structure Browser

However, there are some considerable differences between the two display formats. The advantages of the product structure browser compared to the structural display are as follows:

Product structure browser vs. structural display

- You can use drag and drop to move technical objects (for example, install a piece of equipment on another functional location).
- You can create new technical objects or implement existing technical objects in the structure.
- You can change existing objects in the structure (for example, renumber a functional location).
- You can display not only functional locations, pieces of equipment, and bills of material, but also documents, classes, and characteristics.

- You can change the status of technical objects (deletion flag, inactive/active).
- You can generate a workflow task for a technical object and send technical objects.

> **[+] Use the Product Structure Browser**
>
> The product structure browser is a suitable resource for displaying and changing object structures. However, note that the changes are immediately posted to the database.

4.2.9 Special Functions

Some additional functions will be introduced below that are available to you when working with technical objects. Let's start with the data transfer.

Data Transfer

Definition — Data is automatically transferred within structures or across objects. If you use reference functional locations, functional locations, and pieces of equipment to structure your technical systems, the hierarchical structures you create frequently have the same master record data. For easier, more straightforward maintenance when creating structures, and during engineering change management, you have the option of using the data transfer function, with which you can execute the following actions:

- **Hierarchical data transfer**
  Transfer data in superior objects to lower-level objects in a hierarchy

- **Horizontal data transfer**
  Transfer data across objects (from a reference functional location to a functional location and from a functional location to a piece of equipment)

Hierarchical data transfer — If you change data within an object structure (reference functional location structure, functional location structure, or equipment hierarchy), this change is automatically transferred to the lower-level objects (see Figure 4.54).

4.2 SAP Elements for Structuring Technical Systems and How to Use Them

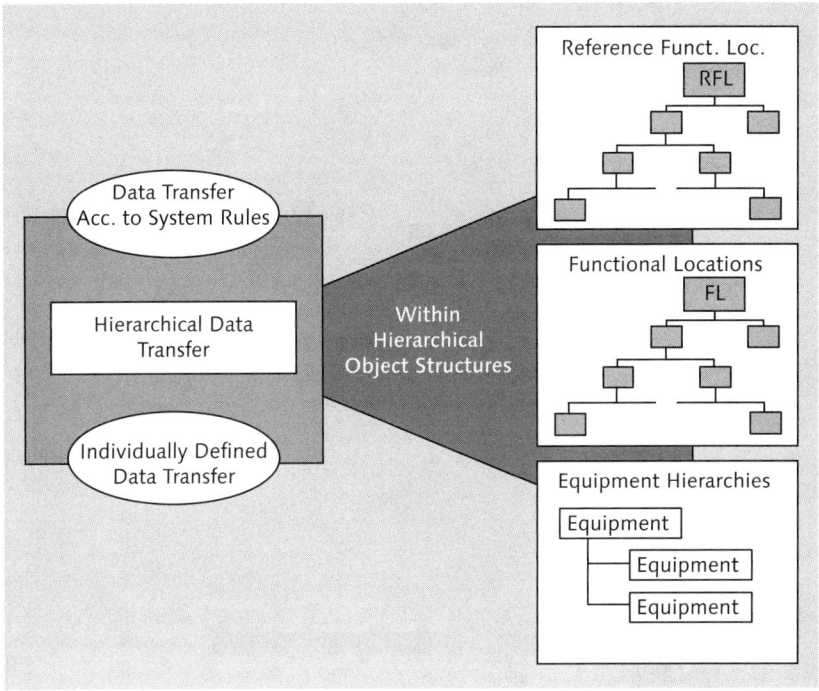

Figure 4.54 Hierarchical Data Transfer

In the case of the horizontal data transfer (see Figure 4.55), the data is automatically transferred between two different object types. In this case, you have the following two options, in turn:

Horizontal data transfer

- You change the data in the reference functional locations. These changes are then automatically transferred to all functional locations derived from these reference functional locations.
- You change data in functional locations on which pieces of equipment have been installed. The data changes are then automatically transferred to the pieces of equipment.

Pay Attention to the Indicators for the Data Origin	[+]
By structuring the functional locations and pieces of equipment in an intelligent manner, you can avoid extensive data maintenance, for example, if cost centers or responsibilities change.	

123

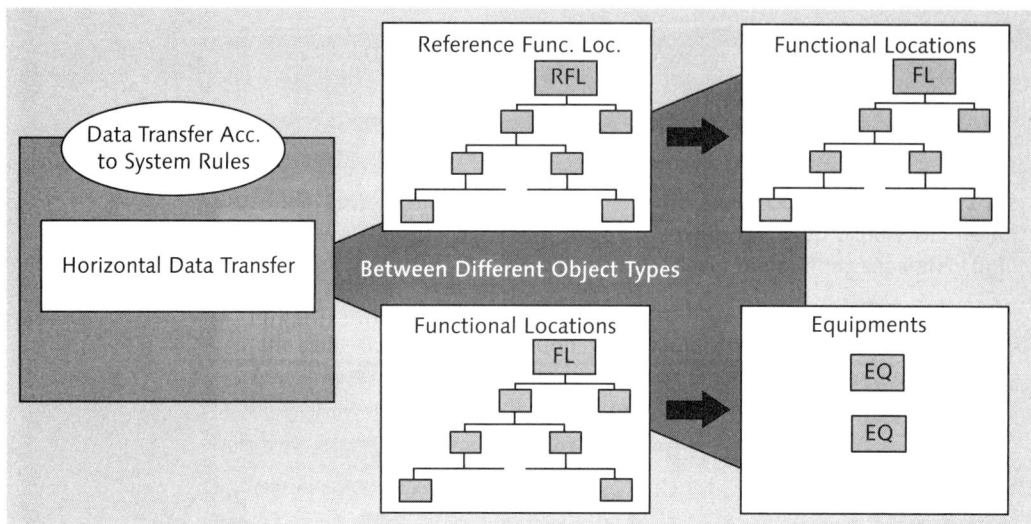

Figure 4.55 Horizontal Data Transfer

How does data transfer work?
Each field of a technical object has an indicator (see Figure 4.56) to show whether this field references its content from a superior object or from a reference functional location or is individually maintained.

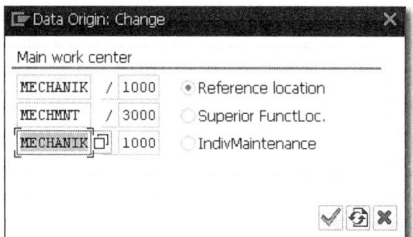

Figure 4.56 Data Origin

[+] **Changing Data Origin**

In the case of a hierarchical data transfer, you can manually change the indicator for each field at any time. In the case of a horizontal data transfer, you can determine this indicator only when the data is transferred—that is, only when the equipment is installed at the functional location.

4.2 SAP Elements for Structuring Technical Systems and How to Use Them

[+] Data Origin and Individual Maintenance

If you manually maintain a field once at a lower level, this field is assigned the INDIVIDUAL MAINTENANCE indicator. Consequently, if data is changed at a higher level, the object itself and its lower-level objects remain unchanged.

Mass Change of Pieces of Equipment and Functional Locations

In addition to data transfer, you can change specific field contents in a targeted manner in several pieces of equipment or functional locations. To do this, use the relevant list change transaction (Transaction IE05: Equipment list change or Transaction IL05: Functional location list change) and select the master records you want to change. To access the mass change function itself, choose GOTO • PERFORM MASS CHANGE. A dialog box opens, where you can enter the fields to be changed and the new field contents (see Figure 4.57).

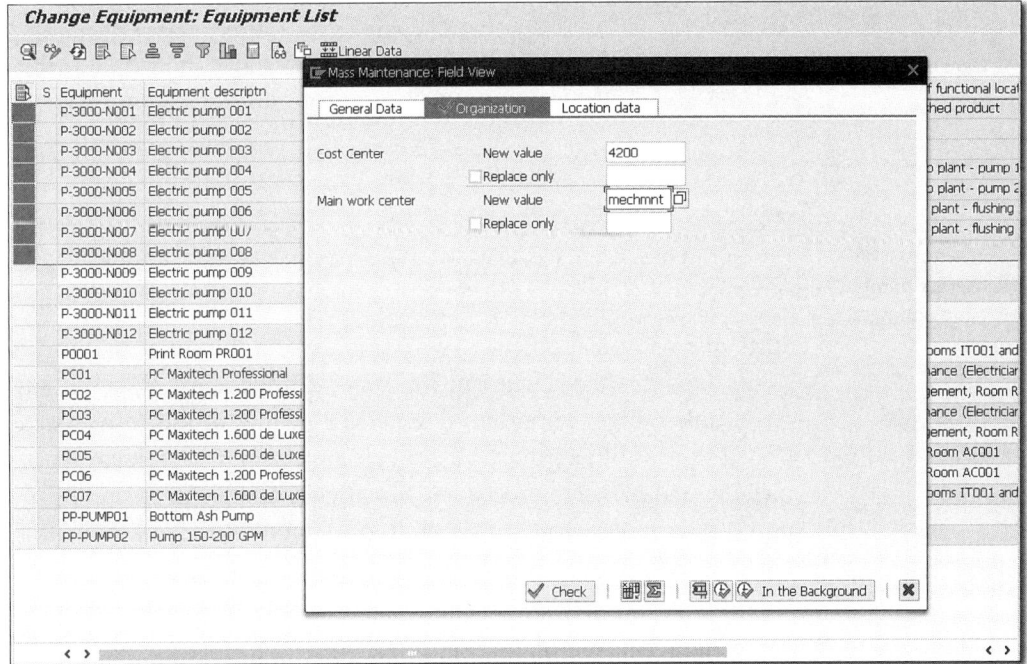

Figure 4.57 Mass Change of Technical Objects

If you use the option EXECUTE or EXECUTE IN THE BACKGROUND, the field contents are changed in all the objects you selected. In order for this function to work, the inheritance indicator must be set to INDIVIDUALLY MAINTAINED. Conversely, this means that an inheritance indicator set to SUPERIOR FUNCTIONAL LOCATION or SUPERIOR EQUIPMENT correctly has precedence over the mass change function.

Unfortunately, not all fields can be changed using the mass change function. You can change fields such as AUTHORIZATION GROUP, COST CENTER, or PLANT SECTION, whereas you cannot change the fields TECHNICAL IDENTIFICATION NUMBER, SORT, or CONSTRUCTION TYPE.

Business function The LOG_EAM_SIMP business function must be activated in order for you to use the mass change function to change functional locations and equipment.

[+] **Mass Processing of Equipment and Functional Locations**

The mass processing function enables quick and easy changes to the field contents of several technical objects at the same time. Note, however, that hierarchically inherited field contents are not changed and that this function cannot be used for all fields.

Measuring Points and Counters

Use cases for measuring points and counters

In the following three scenarios, it makes sense to record measurement documents and counter readings:

- **State of a technical object**
  Here, the aim is to document the state of a technical object at any given time. This is important if detailed evidence of the correct state of a technical object must be provided by law. This evidence may include critical values recorded for environmental protection purposes, hazardous working areas that are monitored for industrial hygiene and safety reasons, the condition of equipment in clinics, and measurements of emissions and pollution for objects of all types.

- **Performance-based maintenance**
  You want to perform performance-based maintenance. In the case of counter-based maintenance, maintenance activities are always performed

if the counter of the technical object has reached a particular counter reading (for more information, see Section 5.8).

- **Condition-based maintenance**
  You want to perform condition-based maintenance. In the case of condition-based maintenance, maintenance activities are always performed if one of the measuring points of a technical object exceeds or falls below a threshold value (for more information, see Section 5.9).

Measuring points mark those locations at which the current condition of a technical system is described, for example:

Measuring points

- Temperature
- Number of revolutions
- Pressure
- Level of contamination
- Viscosity

You can specify target values and upper/lower limits on individual measuring points. Figure 4.58 shows you a measuring point for a location where the operating temperature is measured.

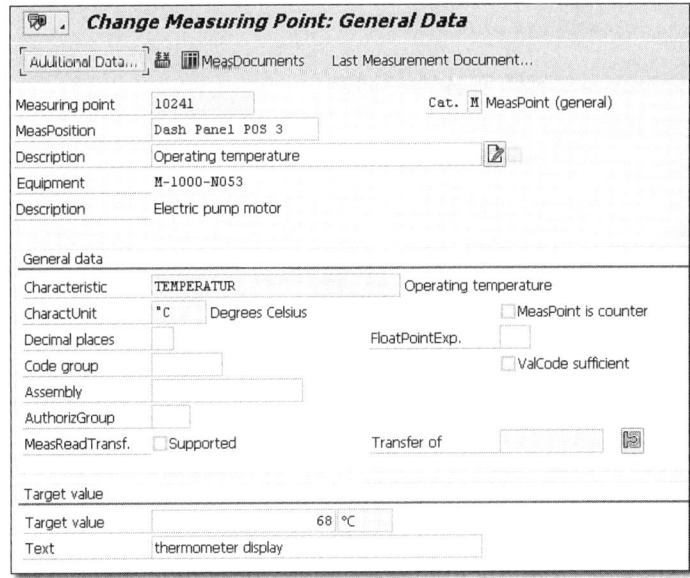

Figure 4.58 Measuring Point

If a measuring point to which a linear object is assigned is involved, the linear data also appears (see Figure 4.59).

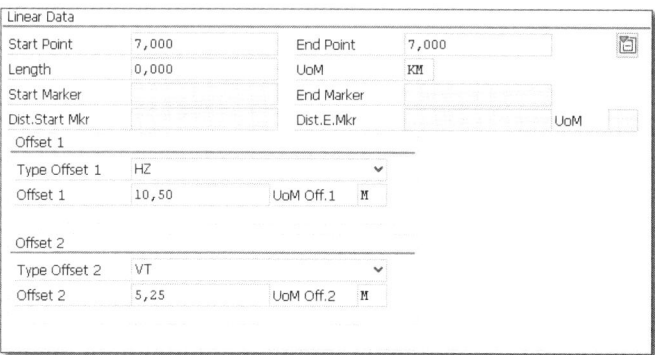

Figure 4.59 Measuring Point with Linear Data

Measurement readings

At measuring points, measurement documents are recorded that contain discontinuous values—for example, an internal engine temperature of 95° C is recorded in a measurement document at 10:25, a temperature of 98° C is recorded at 11:05, a temperature of 89° C is recorded at 12:10, and so on. Measuring points are always in technical objects—that is, in pieces of equipment or functional locations. Figure 4.60 shows the fluctuating measurement readings.

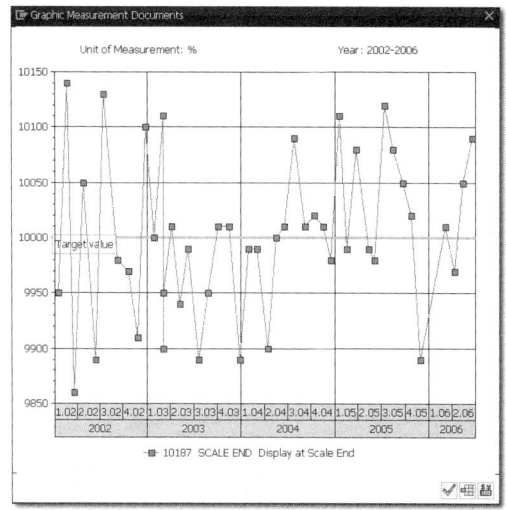

Figure 4.60 Measurement Readings over Time

Counters mark the locations in the SAP system where you can represent object wear, consumption, or reduction of a working supply—for example, a kilometer counter, operating hours counter, number of pieces, quantity produced in tons, and so on. Figure 4.61 shows you a counter for measuring operating hours.

Counters

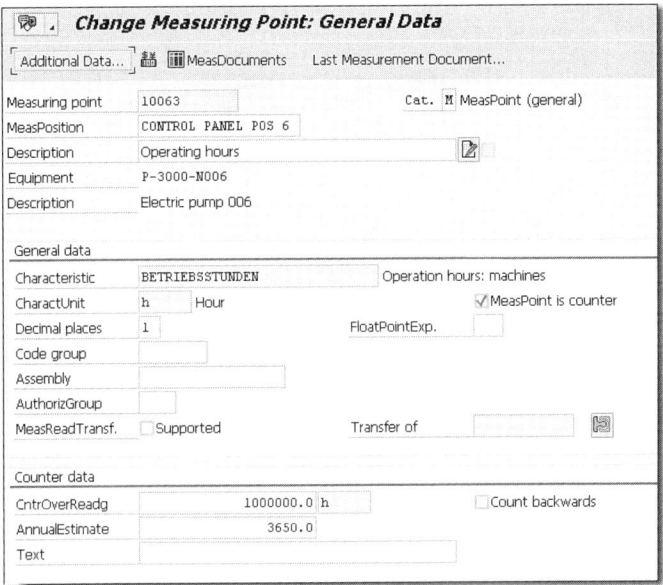

Figure 4.61 Operating Hours Counter

The following two values are particularly important when counters are used for performance-based maintenance:

- **Counter overflow reading**
  The counter overflow reading in the field COUNTEROVERREADING is the first value that a counter cannot display. For example, in the case of a four-digit counter, this value would be 10,000.
- **Annual estimate**
  The system uses the annual estimate in the field ANNUAL ESTIMATE to forecast the next maintenance date based on the current counter reading.

Detailed explanations are provided in Section 5.8.

Counter readings Counter readings are recorded for counters. These readings contain values that continuously rise or continuously fall. For example, in the case of a forklift, 1,250 operating hours were recorded on January 20, 1,274 operating hours were recorded on January 25, and 1,295 operating hours were recorded on February 1. Counters are always in technical objects—that is, in pieces of equipment or functional locations. An example of counter reading development is shown in Figure 4.62.

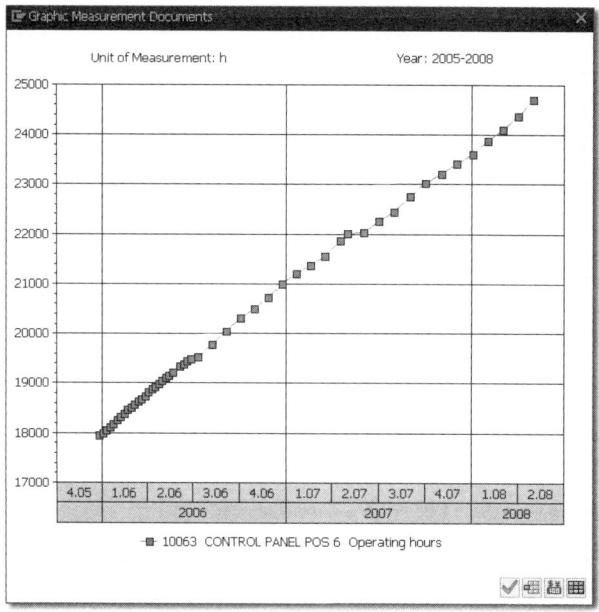

Figure 4.62 Counter Reading Development over a Period of Two Years

Measurement document transfer You can also transfer measurement documents from one measuring point to another measuring point. Both measuring points can be in the same technical system hierarchy (functional location structure, installed equipment), but they do not have to be. You can also establish a separate measuring point hierarchy. Figure 4.63 shows you a measurement document transfer oriented toward a functional location structure.

If the measurement document concerns measurement readings, the absolute readings are transferred. If the measurement document concerns counter readings, however, the differences between the counter readings are transferred.

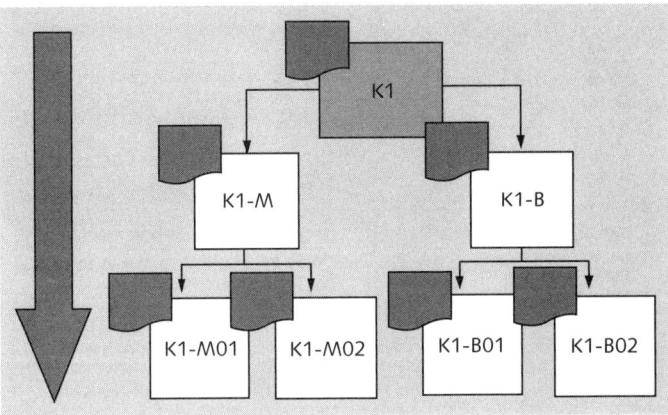

Figure 4.63 Measurement Document Transfer

> **Using Counters and Measuring Points** [!]
>
> Both the counter definition and regular recording of counter readings form the basis of performance-based, preventive maintenance.
>
> Both the measuring point definition and regular recording of measurement readings form the basis of condition-based maintenance.

Documents

In many companies, it is preferable to link the technical objects to documents, such as the following, for example:

Examples of documents

- Design drawings
- Work instructions
- Checklists
- Images
- Inspection instructions
- Exploded drawings
- Measuring and control technology profiles
- 3-D models

In Figure 4.64, for example, you can view a 3-D model.

4 | Structuring of Technical Systems

Figure 4.64 3-D Model

When linking objects to documents, you have two options: the path via document master records or via object links.

Document master records

You can manage your drawings in the SAP system as document master records (Transactions CV01N to CV04N). You then establish a link to the original in the document master record. To be able to assign the document to a technical object, you must embed the LINKED DOCUMENTS screen group (see Figure 4.65) or establish the link in the document master record using the view profile (Customizing function SET VIEW PROFILES FOR TECHNICAL OBJECTS), which you assigned to your functional location category or equipment category.

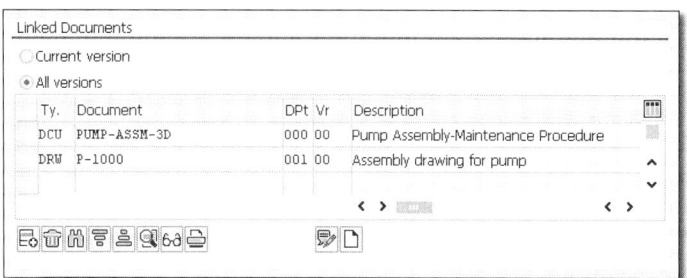

Figure 4.65 Links to Document Master Records

If you work with document master records, you can assign the same document to several technical objects, or a technical object can have several document links.

SAP Easy Document Management (SAP Easy DMS) provides a simple means of checking documents into the SAP system and assigning them to technical objects.

SAP Easy Document Management

The following prerequisites must be fulfilled:

▶ You have installed SAP Easy Document Management on a local or virtual machine. The installation creates a START icon on the desktop and generates two folders (PRIVATE DOCUMENTS and PUBLIC DOCUMENTS), which you can display with your explorer.

▶ You have successfully completed the Customizing settings for SAP Easy DMS.[2]

To assign a document to a technical object, follow the steps below:

1. Start SAP Easy Document Management with the DESKTOP button and log on to the system in which you want to manage the documents (see Figure 4.66).

Figure 4.66 SAP System Logon

---

[2] For more information, see the appropriate references, for example, Heck, R.: Geschäftsprozessorientiertes Dokumentenmanagement mit SAP, Bonn: SAP PRESS 2009.

2. The folders and documents that have already been created are displayed (see Figure 4.67).

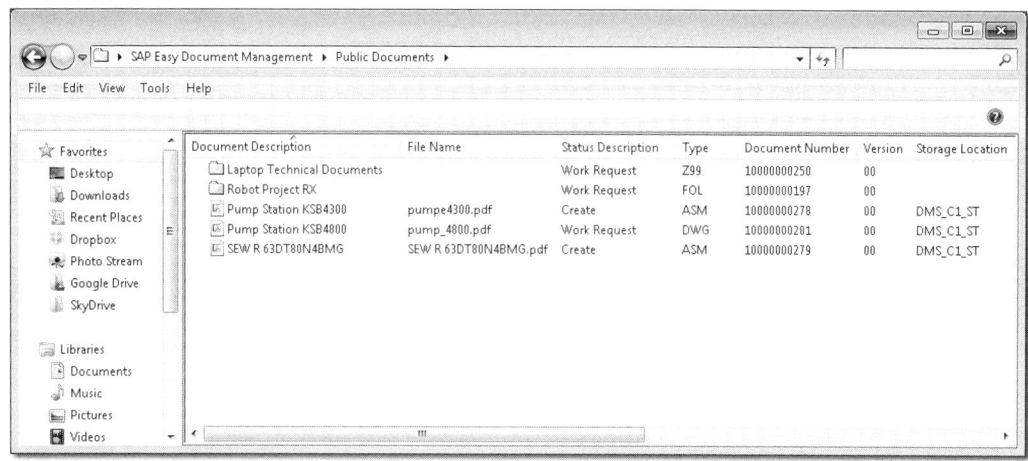

Figure 4.67 List of Documents in the Explorer

3. Use drag and drop to move a document from another folder into an SAP Easy DMS folder.

4. When you do this, a pop-up window opens, where you are asked to specify, among other things, the object (equipment, functional location) to which the relevant document is to be assigned. However, you also have the option of assigning the document to several objects simultaneously (se Figure 4.68).

5. A document master record is then created in the background and immediately assigned to the selected objects. The new document is displayed in the master record of the technical object (see Figure 4.69).

[+] **SAP Easy DMS**

SAP Easy Document Management offers a simple option for creating and managing document master records in the SAP system. You can then assign these document master records to several technical objects directly.

4.2 SAP Elements for Structuring Technical Systems and How to Use Them

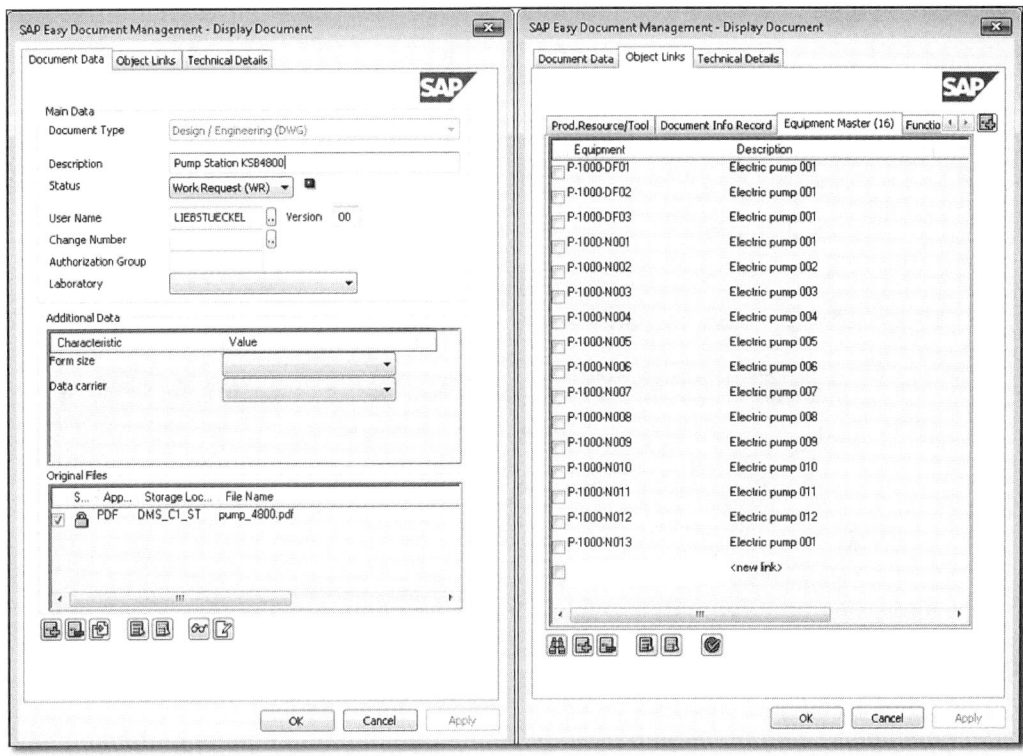

Figure 4.68 Document Data and Object Links

Figure 4.69 Linked Documents

In addition to the document master records, you can use object services to assign documents to your technical objects. You can access object services under SYSTEM • OBJECT SERVICES or by choosing the 🗐 button

Object service

135

(Object Services). Then, choose ☐ (CREATE • ATTACHMENT) in the displayed toolbar. You can now define the following information as attachments:

- PC files, such as PDF documents, images, or Office files
- Internal notes
- External URL addresses

This generates an attachment list (see Figure 4.70) from which you can call the original documents again at any time.

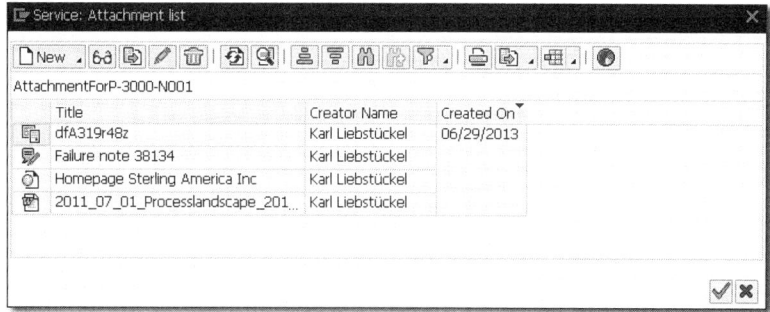

Figure 4.70 List of Attachments

Decision-making criteria

In practice, it is often difficult to choose between document master records and object service. Table 4.7 compares and contrasts the most important similarities and differences.

Document Master Records	Object Links
Document master records required	No document master records required
Complex handling	Simple handling
Original document linked	Original document copied to SAP database
N:M link possible (that is, an object with several documents and a document to several objects)	1:M link possible (that is, an object with several documents, but not a document to several objects)

Table 4.7 Differences Between Document Master Records and Object Services

Document Master Record or Object Service?	[+]
The more N:M links you require, the more worthwhile it is to spend time maintaining document master records. If you predominantly have 1:M links, it is advisable to use the simple procedure of object links.	

Address Management

The SAP system deploys uniform address management, which also integrates the following objects in plant maintenance (see Figure 4.71):

- Functional locations
- Equipment
- Notifications
- Orders
- Purchase requisitions for non-stock materials

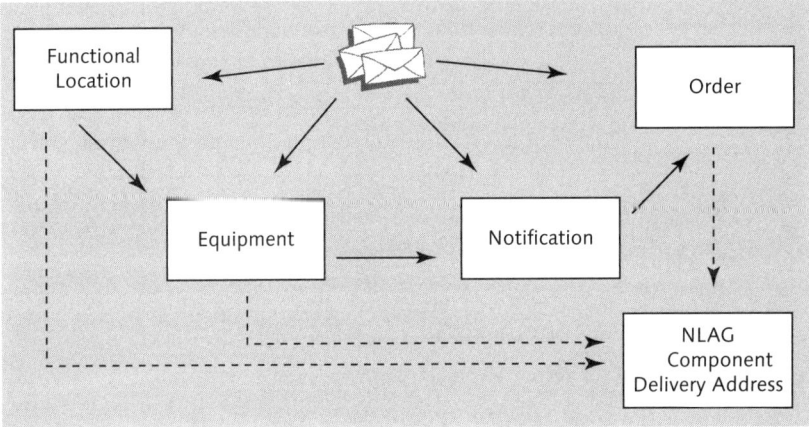

Figure 4.71 Central Address Management

If you define an address in a technical object, this address is then transferred to the notification. The address is also transferred to the order, where you can then choose to define a separate order address if it differs from the object address. You can use the Customizing function DEFINE ACCESS SEQUENCE FOR DETERMINING ADDRESS DATA to define which of these addresses is to be used as the ship-to address for non-stock materials

(NLAG in the figure); you can also define a separate ship-to address for each item.

Figure 4.72 shows a window in which an address has been maintained for a functional location.

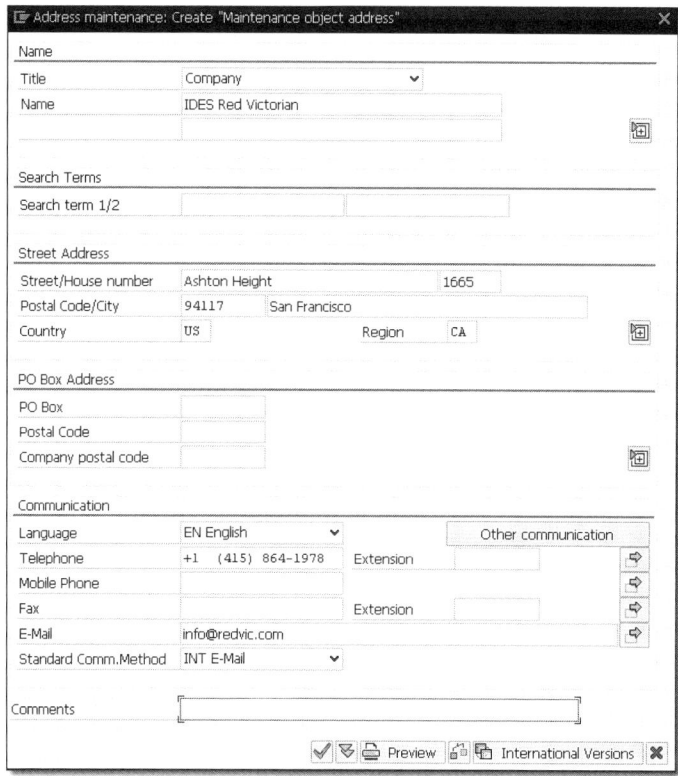

Figure 4.72 Address of a Technical Object

[+] **Using Address Management**

If you deploy typical plant maintenance and the postal addresses of the objects are identical to the plant address, you do not have to define any object addresses.

However, if your objects are spread across and throughout regions (for example, electric utilities, water utilities, gas utilities, telecommunications, or infrastructure), I recommend that you transfer the address information to the relevant technicians and external companies.

Warranties

Definition

A warranty is a commitment from the manufacturer, supplier, or seller to a customer to provide services that are not billed for, or only partially billed for, during a defined period of time. A warranty always refers to a technical object (functional location, equipment, or serial number). You can cover the following warranties (see Figure 4.73):

- Manufacturer and vendor warranty (warrantee, inbound)
- Customer warranty (warrantor, outbound)

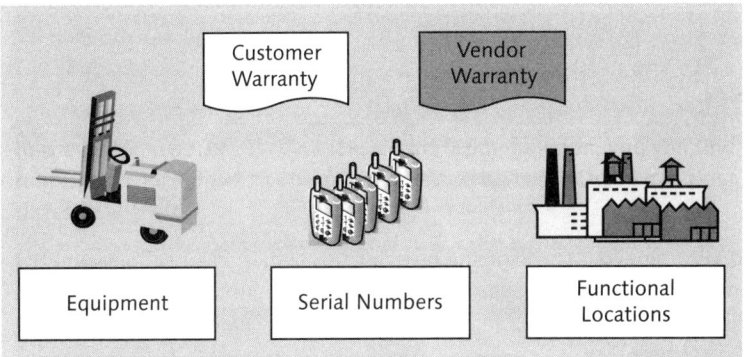

Figure 4.73 Warranties

> **[+] Do You Require Only a Vendor Warranty?**
>
> If you, yourself, are not a warrantor and thus require only a vendor warranty, which is mostly the case in maintenance, you hide the customer warranty by deleting the entry WARRANTY TYPE 1 = CUSTOMER WARRANTY in the Customizing function CHANGE WARRANTY TYPES.

Prerequisite for warranties

To be able to manage warranties for a technical object, you must assign the WARRANTIES screen group in the view profile (Customizing function SET VIEW PROFILES FOR TECHNICAL OBJECTS).

Time-based Warranty

There are usually time-based warranties (see Figure 4.74). The CHECK STATUS indicates that there is a warranty claim.

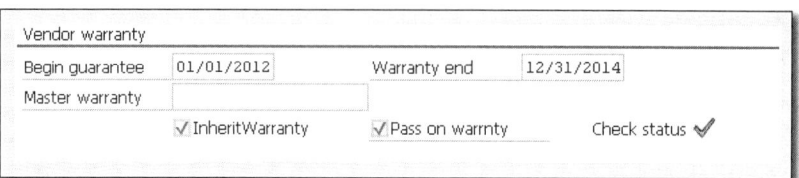

Figure 4.74 Time-based Warranty

Performance-based warranty

Your warranty may also depend on a certain level of performance (for example, kms, or hours of operation). There are time-based and performance-based warranty counters defined in master warranties. You maintain master warranties using Transactions BGM1 to BGM3 (see Figure 4.75).

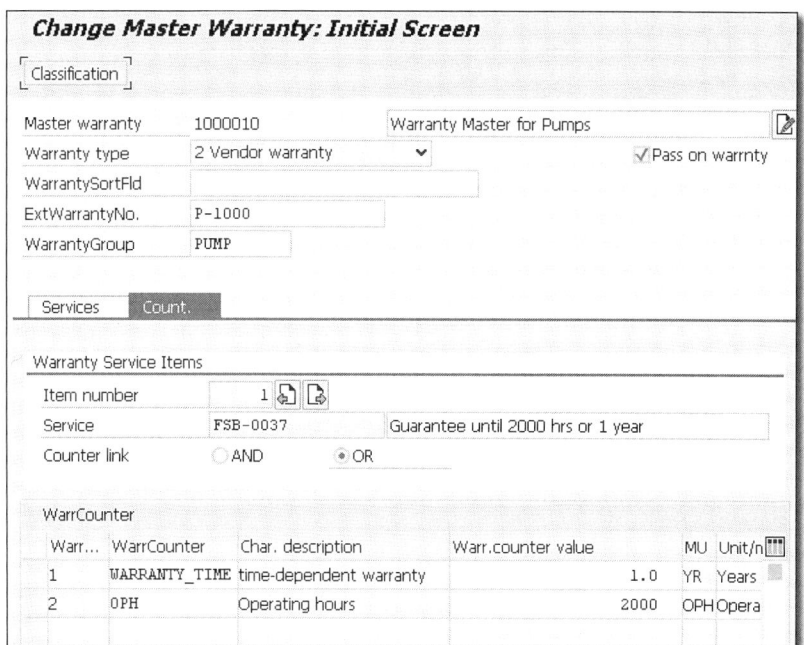

Figure 4.75 Warranty Counters

Time-based and performance-based warranty counters differ as follows:

- **Time-based warranty counters**
  For a time-based warranty counter, you must create a characteristic in the class system, which has a unit of the *time* dimension. The system

can use the warranty start date to determine whether the counter is still valid on the key date of the check.

- **Performance-based warranty counters**
  When using a performance-based warranty counter, the relevant technical object must have a counter (for example, kilometer counter, operating hours counter). Furthermore, the counter reading must have been recorded for this counter at the start of the warranty.

Figure 4.76 shows you a vendor warranty that has been defined for a technical object; this vendor warranty references a master warranty. The CHECK STATUS indicates that there is no longer a warranty claim.

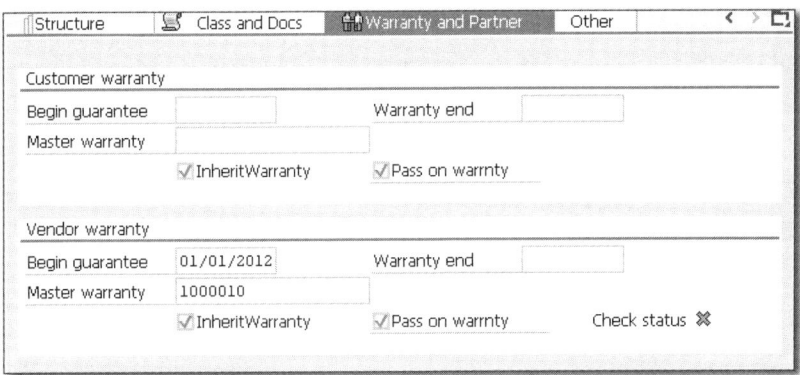

Figure 4.76 Warranty for the Technical Object

Warranties for the Technical Object [+]

You can define a warranty for a technical object and perform a warranty check based on the defined warranty. You can use the warranty check to determine whether the technical object is still under warranty. Furthermore, warranty inheritance enables you to view the warranty data of the superior technical object.

Partners

SAP knows by default only a few organizational objects you can assign to a technical object. Essentially, these are the maintenance planner group and the main work center.

Definition By defining partners, you can considerably expand these areas and people responsible and also specify them in more detail. You can assign any number of partners to a technical object. A partner (business partner) is either an internal or external organizational unit, as follows:

- **Internal partners**
  Internal partners can be, for example, departments, cost centers, or persons involved in processing maintenance tasks.
- **External partners**
  External partners can be, for example, vendors, manufacturers, or service providers that play an important role for a technical object.

A partner can be a natural or legal entity.

You must be able to distinguish among the following terms (see Figure 4.77):

- **Partner Type**
  Partner types are predefined by SAP and always contain a database table (customer, contact person, vendor, user, personnel number, organizational unit, and position).
- **Partner Function**
  You can freely define partner functions with reference to a partner type in Customizing (DEFINE PARTNER DETERMINATION PROCEDURE AND PARTNER FUNCTION). For example, you can define partner functions such as the manufacturer, plant vendor, and service provider and refer all functions to the *Vendor* database table.
- **Partner Determination Procedure**
  You can freely define a partner determination procedure. This is a grouping of partner functions that specifies which partner functions are permitted or must always be specified. For example, you can determine that manufacturer and vendor must always be specified for a piece of equipment but that the service provider is an optional specification.

To make this assignment to a technical object, you use the Customizing functions ASSIGN PARTNER DETERMINATION PROCEDURE TO EQUIPMENT CATEGORY or DEFINE CATEGORY OF FUNCTIONAL LOCATIONS.

4.2 SAP Elements for Structuring Technical Systems and How to Use Them

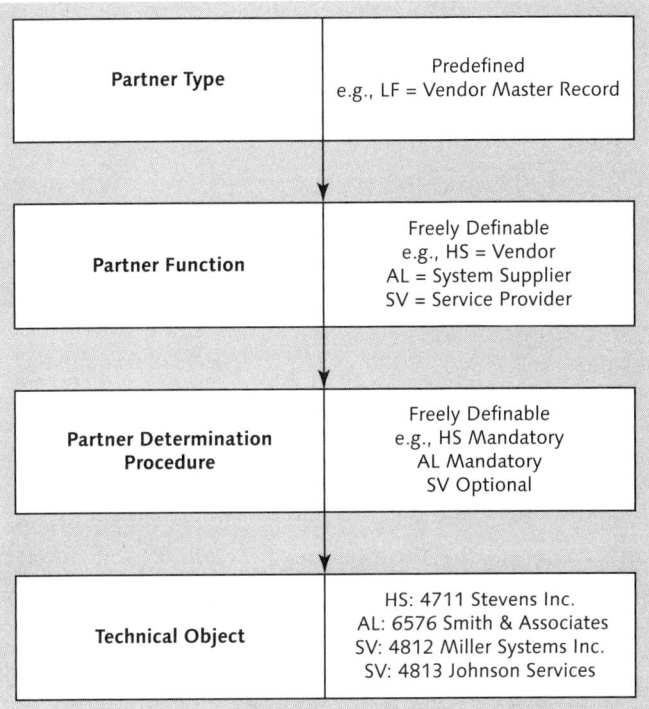

Figure 4.77 Partners

Figure 4.78 shows you potential functions that can be assigned to a technical object.

Partners				
Funct		Partner	Name	A Address
AB Department res...	✓	50001682	Production Unit 8	$1B Prod 8, , ,
VN Vendor	✓	3818	Atlanta Electronics Sup...	Atlanta Electronics Suppl
VW Person Respons...	✓	108255	Matt Toomey	Toomey, 2152845525, ,

Figure 4.78 Partners in the Technical Object

Permit

For some technical objects, there are certain regulations or conditions that must be taken into account when using them or performing

Definition

maintenance work. You can define these regulations for a technical object as permits. Important permits in plant maintenance include the following:

- Fire permits
- Notifications of environmental protection
- Welding permits
- Drivers' licenses
- Fire protection permits
- Vat access permits
- Activation authorizations
- Technical inspection certificates
- Explosion protection zones

Defining permits

To define permits, you use the Customizing function DEFINE PERMIT CATEGORIES and then assign the technical object via GOTO • PERMITS (see Figure 4.79).

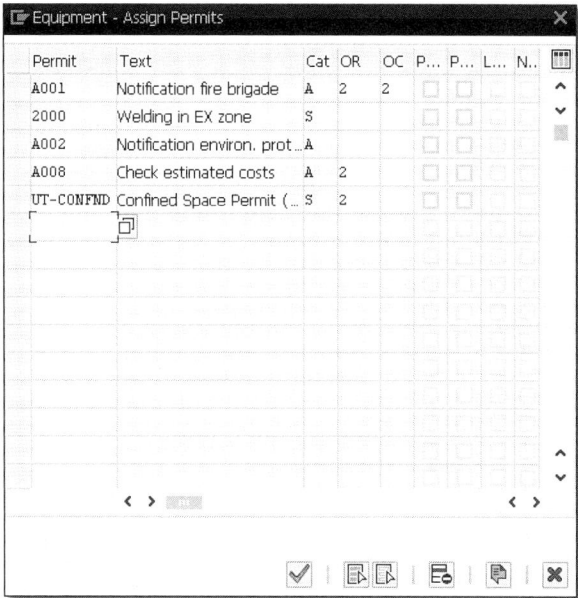

Figure 4.79 Permits

When you assign permits for the technical objects, you also define whether an order is to be placed, must be placed, or must not be placed when an order is released (column OR) or when an order is technically complete (column OC).

Furthermore, you can define whether the relevant permits is to be printed on the order paper (PRINT column) and whether the permit is to be transferred to the processing data (for example, order and notification) (SUGGESTION column).

> **Permits as Option** [+]
>
> You can use permits to determine that an order is not released or technically complete until authorized users have added their electronic signatures.

System Status and User Status

The technical objects and the complete processing with notification and order are linked to SAP's general status management. Here, you have to distinguish between the system status and the user status.

For certain business processes, the system sets the system statuses internally and automatically as part of its general status management. Typical system statuses for technical objects include the following:

System status

- CRTE: created
- AVLB: available
- INAC: inactive
- DLFL: deletion flag set
- EFRE: Equipment free (not installed)
- INST: equipment installed
- ASEQ: equipment in hierarchy
- ESTO: placed in storage

The business processes you can execute for each of these object statuses is also defined in status management. If, for example, you set a piece of equipment to inactive, then you inform the business processes which of them are still permitted (green traffic light), which will trigger a warning message (yellow traffic light), and which are prohibited (red traffic light) (see Figure 4.80).

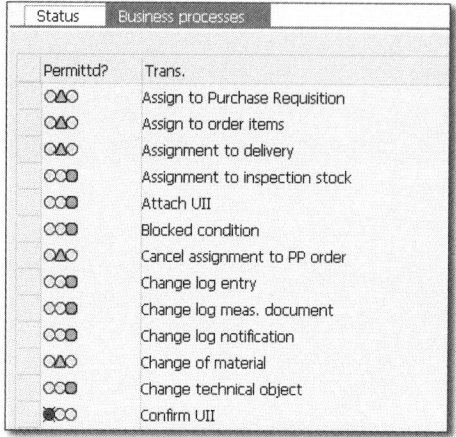

Figure 4.80 Business Transactions

Since you cannot change the system statuses directly (they are automatically set by the system), you can only display them.

User status   In addition to the predefined system statuses, you can freely define user statuses that fulfill your requirements.

Requirements   To be able to assign a user status to a technical object, you must fulfill the following requirements:

- You define a status profile with the necessary status.
- You assign the status profile to the equipment category or functional location category.

To define a status profile with the necessary status, you use the Customizing function DEFINE USER STATUS. You can define any number of statuses within the status profile (see Figure 4.81).

To assign your status profile to an equipment category or functional location category, you use the Customizing functions ASSIGN USER STATUS PROFILE TO EQUIPMENT CATEGORY or DEFINE CATEGORY FOR FUNCTIONAL LOCATIONS.

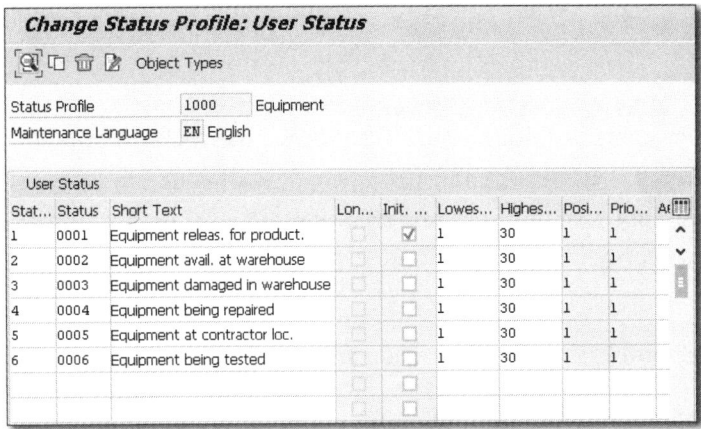

Figure 4.81 Status Profile

> **Using the User Status Efficiently** [+]
>
> You can use the user status to control, in detail, which business processes should be permitted or prohibited for your technical objects.

If these prerequisites are fulfilled, you can choose the ![] button to navigate to the status within the technical objects and set the status you require (see Figure 4.82).

Assigning status

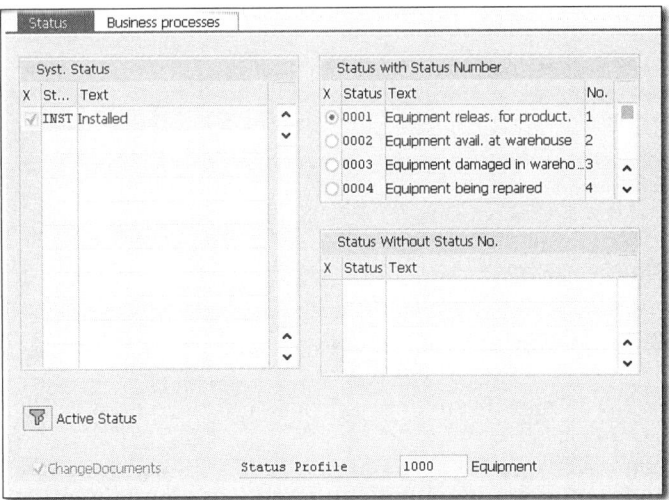

Figure 4.82 User Status

Several statuses If there are several system statuses and user statuses, the following sequence generally applies for determining which business processes are permitted:

- If only one status prohibits a business process, then it is prohibited.
- If none of the statuses prohibits the business process, but at least one permits it while issuing a warning message, then it is permitted with a warning message.
- The business process is permitted only if all of the statuses permit it.

You can check this using the transaction analysis (see Figure 4.83).

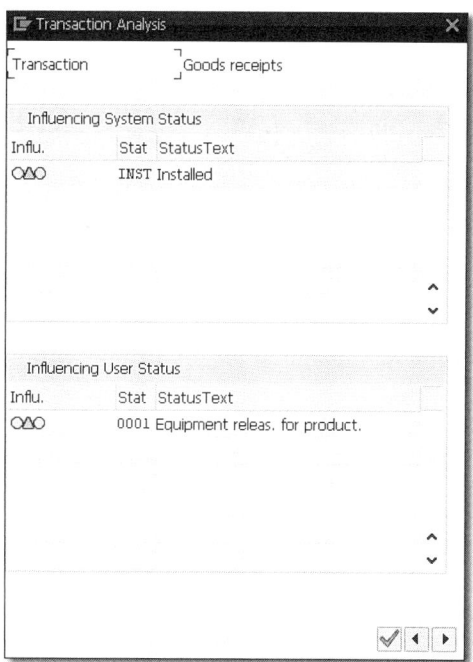

Figure 4.83 Transaction Analysis

[+] **Automating the Status Assignment**

You can set up the user status in Customizing in such a way that it is automatically set or deleted when the system status is changed. This enables you to further restrict the permitted business transactions of a system status in a clever way, without the user having to carry out additional data maintenance.

This chapter forms the core of this book: it shows you how you can map and implement typical business processes of plant maintenance. Since the business processes in particular differ in every company, you have to find your own method of designing them, and this chapter helps you to do so.

5 Business Processes

This chapter deals with the core business of plant maintenance: business processes. After having already seen many companies from the inside, I can, in good conscience, state that each company has its own idea about what business processes in plant maintenance should be like and how they must be mapped in the SAP system. This means that you—like all other user companies before you—must consider how you can map your day-to-day activities in EAM and how EAM will support you in accomplishing tasks. No book on earth can do this work for you; however, I believe you will find this chapter helpful.

How do you now arrive at your business processes? The following section will use reference processes to show you the options of EAM you can use and provide you with many tips on how you can adapt it to meet your own requirements. The following reference processes have been selected for you:

Reference processes

- Processing planned repair tasks
- Processing immediate repair tasks, such as troubleshooting measures
- Entering maintenance activities that have already been performed (after-event recording)
- Shift Notes and Shift Reports
- Outsourcing maintenance tasks
- Subcontracting—that is, subcontracting for service and repair

- Processing preventive maintenance measures, based on time and performance
- Processing condition-based maintenance
- Processing refurbishment measures
- Processing test equipment calibrations
- Implementing maintenance projects

Before we look at these processes in detail, the next section gives you a few tips about what you should do before you map the processes in EAM.

5.1 What You Should Do before You Map Your Business Processes in the SAP System

As with the structuring of technical systems, the following principle should also apply in your search for all answers for business processes: as much as is necessary, but as little as possible.

You will quickly notice that EAM knows a great deal of functions that you can use within the business processes. Find out what your business and technical requirements are and look for the easiest way to map these requirements in EAM. In this chapter, I will show you numerous examples of how you can implement this principle.

Question 1: Which Functions Should You Use?

Appendix B includes an overview of EAM functions that you can use to process your business processes. The chapter will discuss in detail specifically what the keywords mean later on. I have included three columns in Appendix B to indicate priority. Decide for yourself and assess the relevant functions according to their significance in your company.

[+] **Have Courage in Relation to Gaps: Omit What Is Unnecessary**

The full functionality of the SAP system does not have to be, and should not be, implemented all at once.

What You Should Do before You Map Your Business Processes in the SAP System | 5.1

> **Prioritize the Functions** [+]
>
> In principle, you should provide users with solutions where they are needed the most. I recommend a three-tier prioritization, as follows:
>
> - Priority A: absolutely necessary; must be implemented immediately in the first expansion phase
> - Priority B: could have additional benefits; could be implemented in a subsequent expansion phase
> - Priority C: is not implemented
>
> First and foremost, deal with the functions with Priority A. Remove the functions with Priority C from the list and banish them from your thoughts.

Question 2: Should You Use a Notification and/or an Order?

You can and must decide which of the following objects you want to use to support your business processes:

- Only the notification
- Only the order
- Both

The answer to this question generally depends on the functions and information that the individual objects have to offer and how important these functions are to you.

Notification

What are the basic differences between a notification and an order?

Notification vs. order

- **Purpose**
  A notification is used to request and document a maintenance activity, whereas an order is used to plan and implement a maintenance task.

- **Information therein**
  A notification, therefore, contains mainly technical information, while an order contains, essentially, processing information.

- **Integration points**
  A notification has practically no integration points with other SAP applications and therefore does not contain information about any costs, whereas the order, as a highly-integrative object, has many links to applications, such as Warehouse Management, Purchasing, or Controlling.

This quite different orientation is reflected in different functions (see Appendix B) and different information of both objects.

A notification has the following characteristics:

- **Header data**
  Each notification has header data, which includes information used to identify and manage the notification. The header data applies to the complete notification.

- **Notification item**
  You enter and maintain the data in a notification item for the purpose of identifying in more detail the problem or damage that occurred, or the executed action. A notification can have several items. However, most notifications, in practice, consist of only one item, which is created automatically when you record a damage code or a cause of the damage.

- **Activitiess**
  Activities document the work performed for a notification. They are particularly important in inspections to provide evidence of the work performed and the established results. Activities can relate to either the header or an item of the notification.

- **Task data**
  Task data describes activities that still have to be performed and may only have resulted from implementing the maintenance activity (for example, creating a report). Tasks can relate either to the header or to an item of the notification.

Figure 5.1 shows an overview of the structure of a notification with the relevant information.

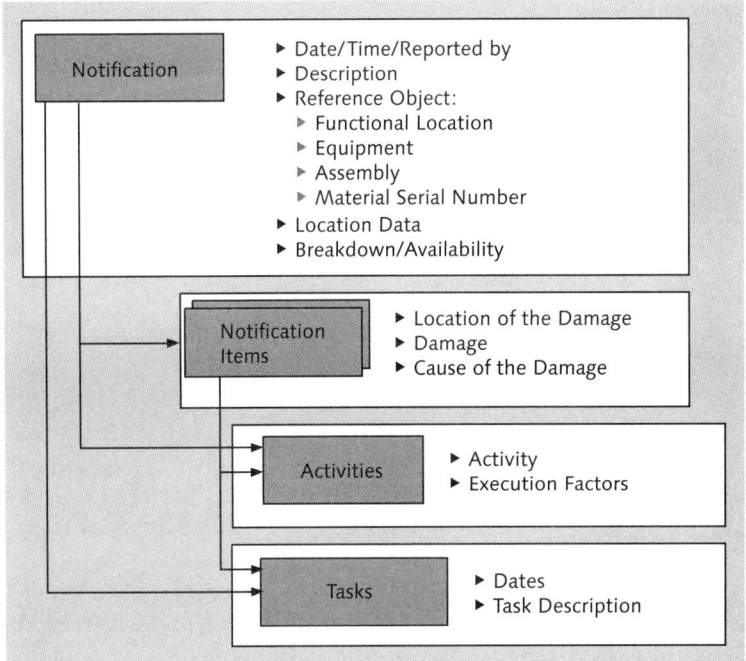

Figure 5.1 Structure and Content of a Notification

Order

The order has a different structure from the notification:

- **Header data**
  Header data is information that is used to identify and manage the order; it applies to the complete order.

- **Object list**
  If the order involves several objects (for example, for an inspection round), you can enter these objects in the object list. The object list contains the objects on which the order is executed (functional locations, equipment, assemblies, notifications).

- **Operations**
  You can use operations to describe the work you want to be performed when the order is being implemented. Operations are performed by either your own employees or external companies.

- **Material list**
  The material list contains spare parts that are required and used when the order is being implemented. This is either stock material for which a reservation is generated, or non-stock material for which a purchase requisition is created.

- **Production resources/tools**
  Production resources/tools (for example, tools, protective clothing, and pallet trucks) are also required for implementing an order. However, unlike a material, they are not consumed.

- **Settlement rule**
  In the settlement rule, you specify the cost unit (for example, cost center), to which the costs must be charged. Either the settlement rule applies to the complete order, or you assign different assignments to the operations.

- **Cost data**
  Cost data informs you about how high the estimated, planned, and actual costs are in the value categories for this order, which cost elements are relevant for the order, which key figures of the Plant Maintenance Information System are updated using the value categories, and how these key figures are updated by the actual costs of the order. You obtain the cost information both for individual operations and as a total for the complete order.

Figure 5.2 shows an overview of the structure of an order with the relevant information.

[+] **Deciding on an Order or Notification**

Decide as early as possible whether you want to use a notification and/or an order. If you make the same decision as the majority of approximately 80% of SAP user companies, you will use the notification and the order. The rest only use the order. In some individual cases (mainly in the initial phase), companies opt to use the notification only.

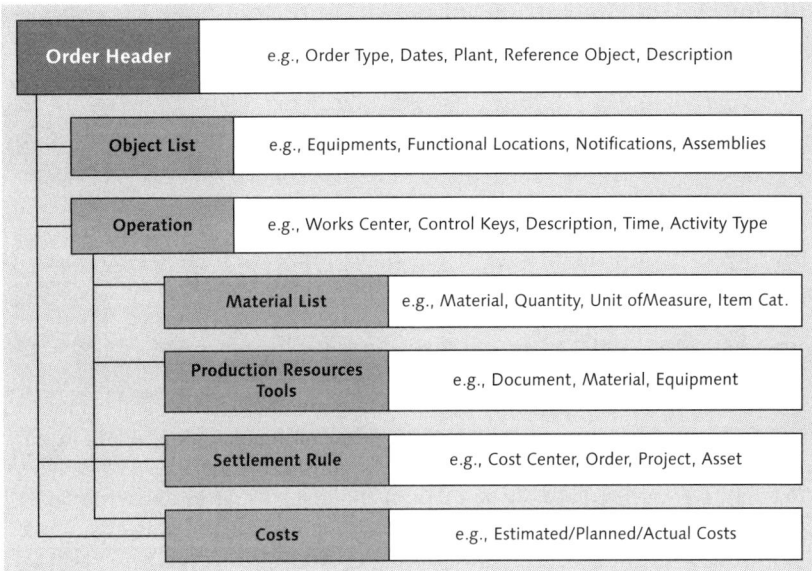

Figure 5.2 Structure and Content of an Order

Question 3: Which Information Should You Store?

The third question applies to the following types of business information that you store in the system:

▸ Information you absolutely must store in order to be able to process a notification or an order (for example, reference object)
▸ Information you reasonably want to store in EAM (for example, the cost center)

As Much as Necessary, but as Little as Possible [+]
The principle "as much as necessary, but as little as possible" must also apply to the stored information. A data graveyard, which is created only for its own sake and is of no interest to anyone, is not seen or analyzed by anyone, and signifies only time and effort in terms of entering and maintaining data, makes no sense. Thus, enter only data that is also information for you.

The SAP system also enables you to configure notifications and orders flexibly, as follows:

- You can define the layout of screen templates yourself based on the notification or order type (number, sequence, and name and content of tabs).
- The field selection option enables you to differentiate important information from unimportant information or hide fields that you do not require.

Business function   The LOG_EAM_SIMP business function must be activated in order for you to use a flexible screen layout for orders.

[+] **Design Your Own Layouts**

Actively use this option to define the appearance of the notification and order yourself and design your own layouts: for example, place the most important information on the first tab and hide unimportant fields. You will find the explanations about how to do this in Section 5.2.1 and Section 5.2.2.

Question 4: How Can You Ensure that the Users Accept the System?

Although this question also applies essentially to the structuring of technical systems, the topics *user acceptance* and *usability* are much more important in relation to maintenance processing because work is performed in these areas on a daily basis.

There is no guarantee that the system will be accepted by the users or considered user friendly. However, you can increase the likelihood by reading Chapter 9 and implementing the suggestions made there.

Question 5: What Role Does Business Process Modeling Play?

Actual and planned processes   Business Process Modeling (BPM) plays a very important role when SAP systems are being implemented—regardless of the application. Proper analysis and documentation of the previous maintenance processes (actual analyses) and a detailed planned concept of the business processes indicating how they must subsequently be performed with the support of the SAP system are basic prerequisites for the implementation and are the basis for customizing EAM.

The time and effort required to complete a full and correct business process modeling will definitely be worth it. You will find further information on this topic in the book *Configuring SAP Plant Maintenance*, which will be published by SAP PRESS in 2014.

Question 6: When Should You Include the Other User Departments?

You should include other user departments in the company as soon as possible. If you choose order processing, this raises numerous questions that affect the business processes and require permits. This applies particularly if you want to integrate Warehouse Management, Purchasing, and Controlling. In this context, for example, you must answer the following questions:

- What information must the automatically generated purchase requisitions contain?
- Who creates the purchase order?
- Where is the acceptance of services performed entered?
- How is the notification made for goods receipts?
- Is the material delivered to or collected from the warehouse?
- Who calculates the final costing, and when?
- Are the orders settled automatically?
- What does the costing sheet look like for maintenance orders?

Experience shows that such permit processes with the relevant user departments take longer than you would initially think.

Double the Planned Time [+]

Rule of thumb: if you double the time planned for approval with the relevant user departments, you will be more or less on the right track. Specify the approval process as early as possible. Specifically, define who must look after which aspect and when, and who must make which decisions, and, finally, check the "homework" in terms of sustainability.

We will now look at the business processes in detail. Let's begin with the process of a planned repair task because this is the most comprehensive business process. This will make it easier to describe other business processes, such as breakdown maintenance or follow-up entries, using abstracts based on this process.

5.2 Planned Repairs Business Process

Can be planned but not predicted — The business process for a planned repair task is characterized by the fact that the required resources (work centers, materials, external companies, and so on) can be planned, but are only identified when the need arises. This business process occurs, for example, in the following cases:

- If the casing on a pump has to be resealed
- If the lift chain on a fork lift truck has to be replaced
- If a door in a building has to be replaced
- If a pressure control valve in the process plant has to be changed
- If test equipment has to be recalibrated.

The process for a planned repair, thus, differs from an immediate repair (refer to Section 5.3) in terms of the ability to schedule it—you can react to malfunctions, but not plan them—and from preventive maintenance (refer to Section 5.8) in terms of the prescribed schedule—maintenance and inspection tasks have regular cycles and, consequently, recurring deadlines.

The process for a planned repair could be performed in the following five steps (see Figure 5.3):

1. **Notification**
   In Step ❶, you enter the notification of specific damage, or any other request (such as a request for a modification).

2. **Planning**
   In Step ❷, the order is created and planned from the notification. Typical planning tasks include creating operations, reserving spare parts, assigning external companies, or planning operating times. The defining of posting rules is also included within this step.

3. **Controlling**

   In Step ❸, you transfer the order to Controlling. There, you check the corresponding availability (particularly the material availability), provide the required capacities, and print out the order papers.

4. **Implementation**

   The processing phase (Step ❹) involves the withdrawal of the spare parts from the warehouse and the actual processing of the order.

5. **Completion**

   After you complete the tasks, the required actual times are confirmed in the completion in Step ❺; technical completion confirmations about how the damage was processed, as well as the status of the technical system, are also entered here. The order is finally settled by Controlling. The information is updated in the history.

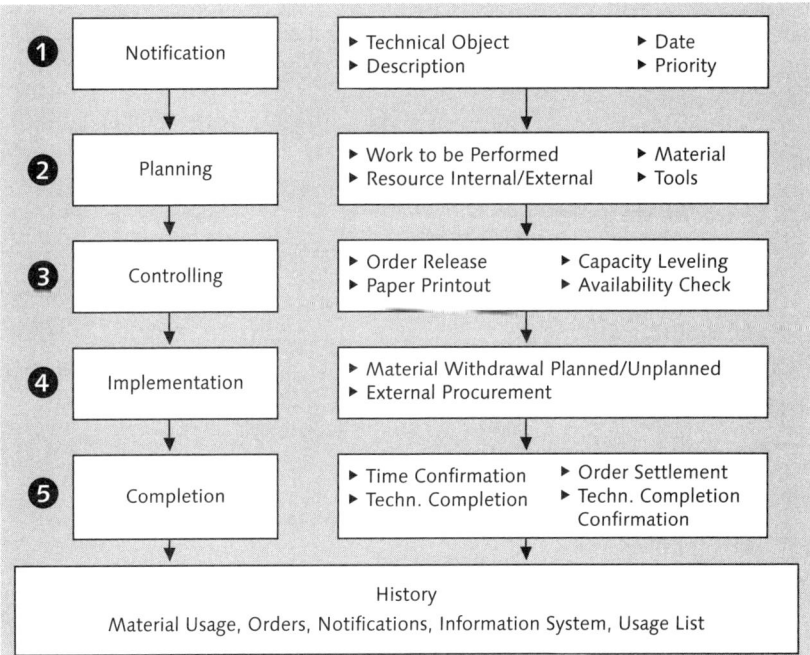

Figure 5.3 Planned Repairs Business Process

The following sections go through these five specified steps and, in doing so, explain the functions that the SAP system offers.

5.2.1 Notification

Why use notifications?

Notifications are the maintenance processing tool that you use in exceptional operational situations to perform the following activities:

- Describe the technical emergency situation of an object
- Request a required task in the maintenance processing
- Document the work performed

Notifications thus document maintenance tasks and make them available for analysis in the long term.

Opening Notifications

Who enters notifications?

The notifications are either entered directly by the relevant requester (for example, a production employee) or transferred to plant maintenance using the usual means of communication (for example, by telephone or form) and entered there.

How are the notifications entered?

There are different ways you can create notifications in the SAP system, as follows:

- **SAP dialog transactions**
  You can use the SAP dialog transactions (IW21, IW24–26), which are directly available in EAM.

- **Easy Web Transaction**
  You use the Easy Web Transaction—that is, a web transaction that contains a simple HTML form (see Section 8.3).

- **Your own web transactions**
  In addition, you can develop your own web transactions, the data of which is transferred by BAPIs to the SAP system (see Section 9.5).

- **Upstream systems**
  Procedures are used in which the notification data is created in upstream systems (such as geographic information systems [GIS], process control systems, and diagnostic systems). This is then transferred to EAM via an interface (for example, PM-PCS interface) and creates the notification there (see Section 6.4.1).

In this section, I first focus on entering notifications in EAM itself.

Notification Types

In earlier releases, SAP predefined three notification types in the standard system:

- **Activity report**
  For documenting performed actions
- **Malfunction report**
  For information about malfunctions and problems that occur
- **Maintenance request**
  For requesting tasks to be performed

You can now define notification types as you wish according to your own requirements. You should define the notification types based on the functions in which the notification types differ in Customizing. You can define, for example, the following settings for each notification type in Customizing:

Defining notification types as you wish

- Number range
- Partner determination procedure
- Print control
- Status profile

One of the most important functions, however, is the option to define your own screen layout for each notification type. The structure displayed in Figure 5.1 containing all the data of a notification is reflected in the layout of the M1 notification type delivered by SAP (see Figure 5.4).

Screen layout

This notification type consists of eight tabs, whereby individual tabs still have sub-tabs. Thus, for example, the ITEMS tab still contains sub-tabs for items, causes of damage, tasks, and actions. Each tab has up to five field groups.

However, this type of screen layout would be overly complex for a production employee, for example, who merely wants to report damage.

> **Design Your Own Layouts for Notifications** [+]
>
> Design suitable screen layouts for your notification types. Adapted and simplified screen layouts increase user acceptability. Use the Customizing function SCREEN STRUCTURE FOR EXTENDED VIEW or SCREEN STRUCTURE FOR SIMPLIFIED VIEW for this purpose.

5 | Business Processes

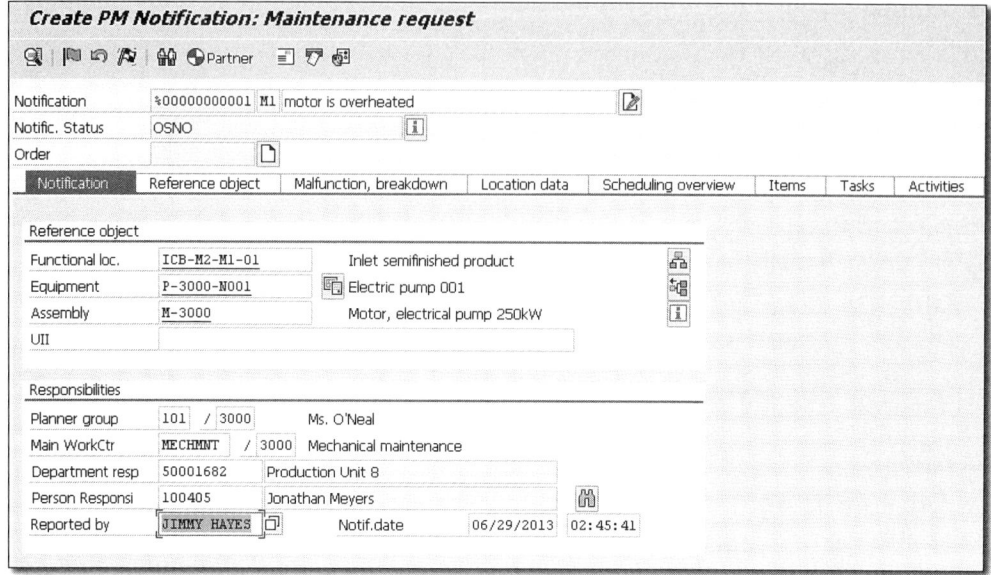

Figure 5.4 Notification Type M1

An entry screen could look like the one configured for you as notification type 00 (see Figure 5.5).

[+] **Different Layouts for Entering and Changing**

You can even set up the screen layout in such a way that a different layout appears when you change data compared to when you enter data. In this case, use the activity type for the screen structure in the Customizing function.

When do you need this option? You need it, for example, when you want to provide a production employee with a screen that is as basic as possible for entering a notification. If the maintenance employee calls the same message at a later point, however, he or she must be able to add further necessary information.

If the same notification is called in change mode, for example, it could then have tabs and field groups like those shown in Figure 5.6.

5.2 Planned Repairs Business Process

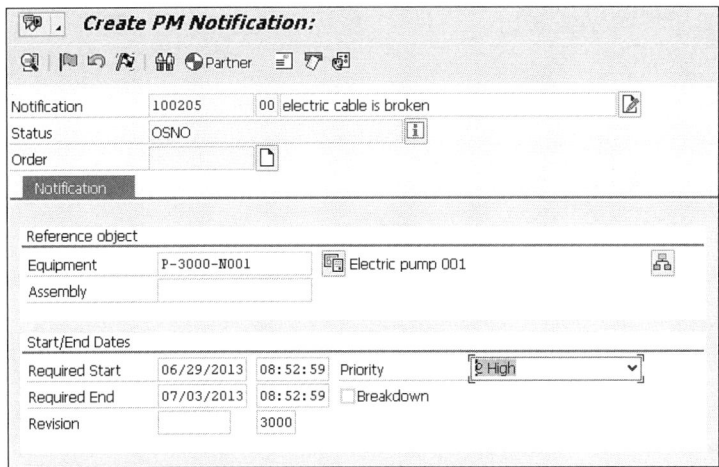

Figure 5.5 Notification Type 00

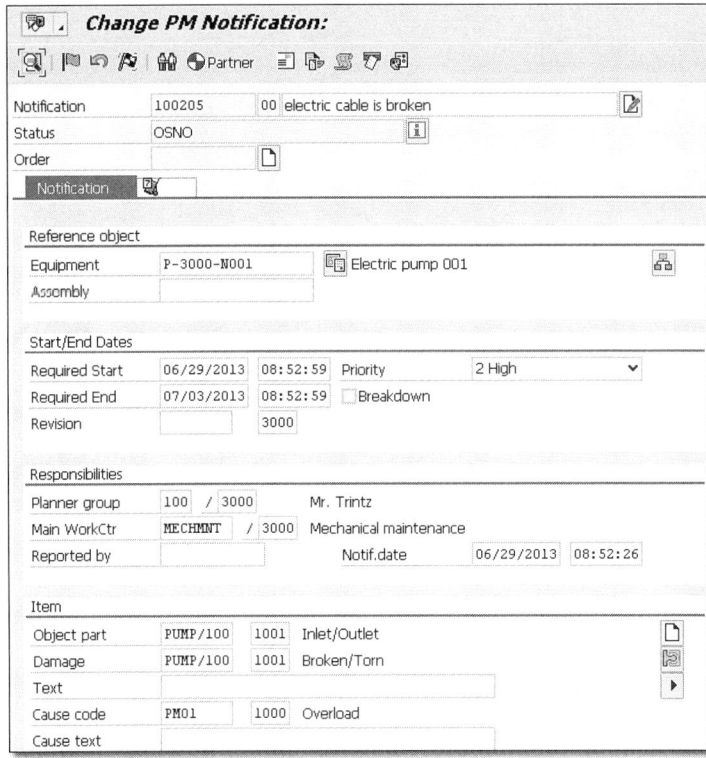

Figure 5.6 Notification Type 00 in Change Mode

Notification Content

Screen groups The following screen groups or tabs are available as possible notification content:

- Reference object (for example, equipment, functional location, assembly, material serial number)
- Responsibilities (for example, planner group, main work center)
- Item and cause (for example, damage, cause of damage, object part)
- System availability (for example, system availability before, after)
- Malfunction data (for example, breakdown, start, end, duration of breakdown)
- Start/end dates (for example, priority, required start, and required end)
- Item overview (for example, assembly, text)
- Activities for notification header and notification item
- Tasks for notification header and notification item
- Causes for notification header and notification item
- Notification and object address
- Partner overview (for example, partner role, partner, address)
- Warranty (for example, start, end of warranty)
- Location (for example, maintenance plant, cost center, business area)
- Scheduling overview (for example, date of notification, completion, technical control)
- Maintenance plan (for example, maintenance task list, maintenance plan)

Important information in the notification is the object in question, the reference object.

Flexible Reference Object

You can enter notifications as reference objects for all technical objects: functional locations, pieces of equipment, assemblies, or material serial numbers. If you assign a lower-level object to a notification, the higher-level objects are also entered automatically. Thus, if you enter an assembly, for example, the equipment and functional location are also automatically included in the notification.

You can also enter notifications without specifying a technical object, for example, in the following cases:

- If a malfunction report refers to an object that is not listed under a number in the system
- If the faulty object cannot be located precisely yet
- If a notification refers to a new object to be provided as part of an investment measure.

You have the following options to specify the type of technical object to be entered:

Type of technical object

- For a notification type: in Customizing, using the function SCREEN AREAS IN NOTIFICATION HEADER
- For a user: within the notification by selecting EXTRAS • SETTING • DEFAULT VALUES
- For an individual notification: within the notification, by selecting EXTRAS • SETTING • REFERENCE OBJECT

When you receive a new notification from the requester and have to decide whether the maintenance task is to be performed, it is very useful to find out concise information about the object. You use the object information, which you will learn about in the next section, for this purpose.

Object Information

You can display concise information relating to the reference object—that is, object information—in a dialog box (see Figure 5.7).

This involves the following information:

- Structure data (for example, object hierarchy)
- Technical characteristics of classification
- Previous cases of damage and number of processing days

- Previous notifications and/or orders, or ones that are still open, which were created or completed for the object
- Maintenance plans and documents
- Warnings when limits are exceeded

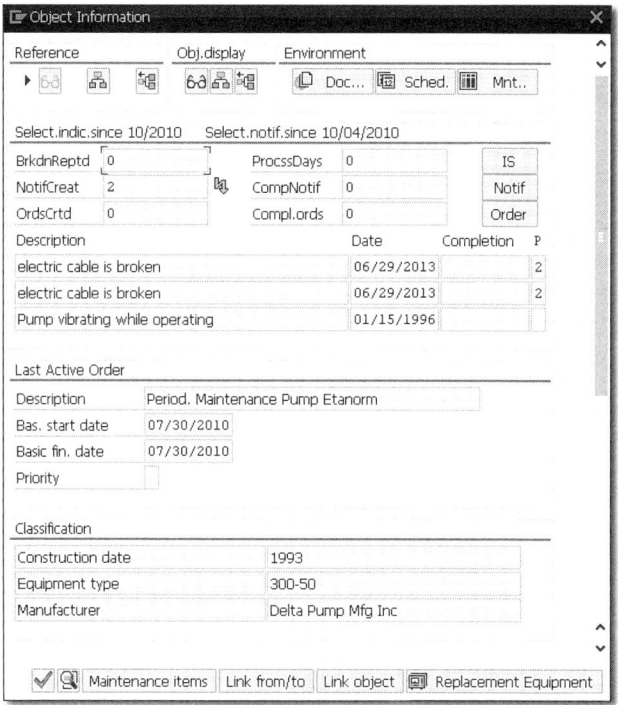

Figure 5.7 Object Information

You can call more detailed data, such as an individual notification, for example, for all this information from the dialog box. You can also go to the information system to compile statistics and reports.

[+] **Object Information Provides a Concise Overview**

Object information gives you concise information about the reference object and contributes to your decision about whether and when a task must be performed. You define the content of the object information in Customizing using the function DEFINE OBJECT INFORMATION KEY and assign the object information to your notification type using the Customizing function ASSIGN OBJECT INFORMATION KEYS TO NOTIFICATION TYPES.

Notification Item

You would generally be able to use notification items to specify the information of the notification header in more detail—for example, specifying several locations of damage where damage has occurred (notification header: forklift truck; notification items: lifting frame, brake system, and operator's compartment, see Figure 5.1).

However, since the items are not subsequently transferred when an order is created, user companies rarely use this option. This is also reflected in empirical studies: a survey among members of the "Maintenance and Service Management" DSAG working group (German-speaking SAP user group) showed that the average number of items is less than 1.1. If you now consider that an item is generated automatically when you record a damage code or a cause of the damage, the reverse scenario here means that not even every tenth notification has manually created items.

> **Notification Items Are Hardly Used** [!]
>
> Notification items are rarely used in practice. Damage and requests are usually specified in the long text or using catalogs.

Catalogs and Catalog Profiles

In addition to organizational information (such as deadlines, responsibilities, or cost centers), you can also store technical information about problems, malfunctions, damage, causes, and solutions or troubleshooting in a notification. This information is part of the notification and is included in the history. The special feature here compared to all other information is that you can formalize this information in catalogs and, therefore, make it available for analysis.

You generally use a maximum of five catalogs, as follows, in plant maintenance (see Figure 5.8): *Catalogs*

- Damages
- Causes of damage
- Object parts

- Tasks
- Actions

Code and code groups

Each catalog has a three-tier structure: catalog → code groups → codes. There is a code for every defect found, and the codes are categorized into code groups based on certain factors.

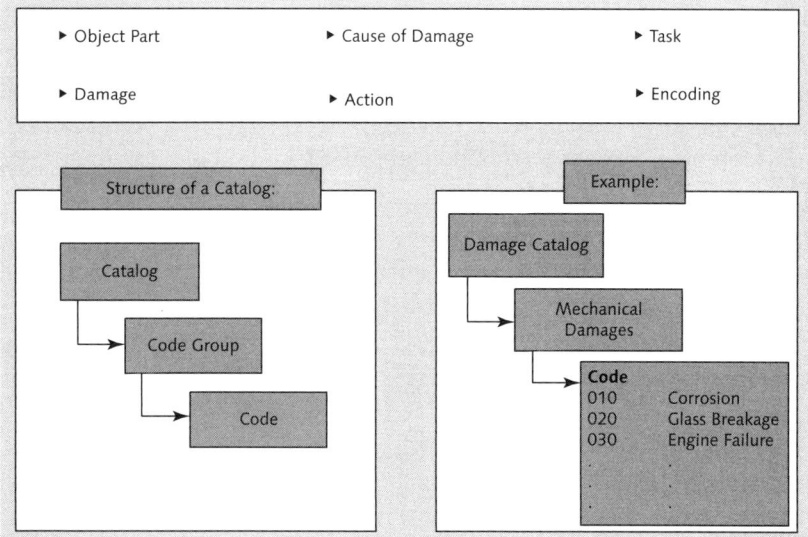

Figure 5.8 Catalogs

[!] **Categorization Criteria for Catalogs**

User companies normally use the following as categorization criteria for code groups in catalogs:

- Functional criteria (for example, mechanical damage, electrical causes of damage, or hydraulic object parts)
- Object-related criteria (for example, damage to engines, causes of damage to pumps, or object parts for forklifts)

You maintain catalogs in Customizing using the function MAINTAIN CATALOGS or via Transaction QS41.

You see in Figure 5.9, for example, what the codes for forklifts might look like in the catalogs for *damage*, *causes of damage*, and *object parts*.

5.2 | Planned Repairs Business Process

> **Catalog Groups Should Contain 25 Entries at Most** [+]
>
> Arrange the damage, cause, and object part codes clearly. The user should not be able to select more than approximately 25 codes; otherwise, the search for codes will be too time-consuming for employees, which means that the quality of the data and acceptance of the system will suffer. Therefore, the principle "as much as necessary, but as little as possible" applies here, also.

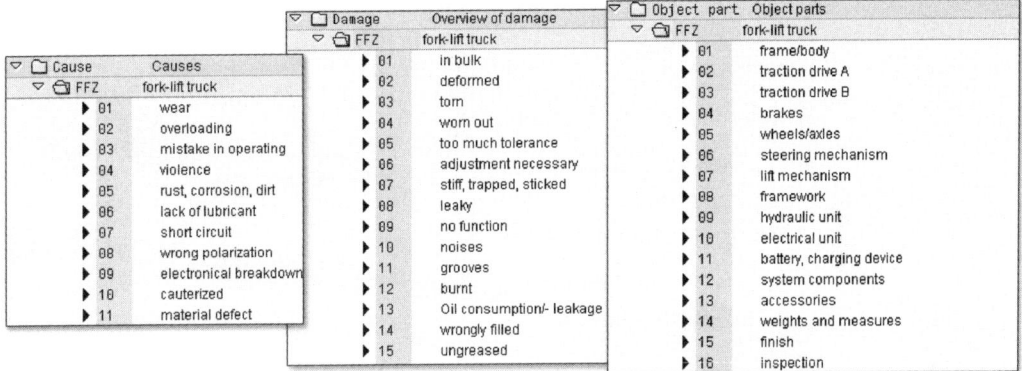

Figure 5.9 Code Groups for Forklifts

In the catalog profile (see Figure 5.10), you can, on the basis of functional factors, specify which code groups must be used for a certain reference object or notification type.

Catalog profile

You can assign a catalog profile to the following objects:

- Equipment in the RESPONSIBILITIES screen group (see Figure 5.11)
- A functional location, also in the RESPONSIBILITIES screen group
- A notification type in Customizing via the Customizing function CHANGE CATALOGS AND CATALOG PROFILE FOR NOTIFICATION TYPE

If you have now entered a catalog profile for the technical objects and notification type, the following sequence applies: equipment → functional location → notification type. Irrespective of this sequence, you can individually change or assign the catalog profile in a notification by selecting EXTRAS • SETTINGS • CATALOG PROFILE • SELECTION.

169

5 | Business Processes

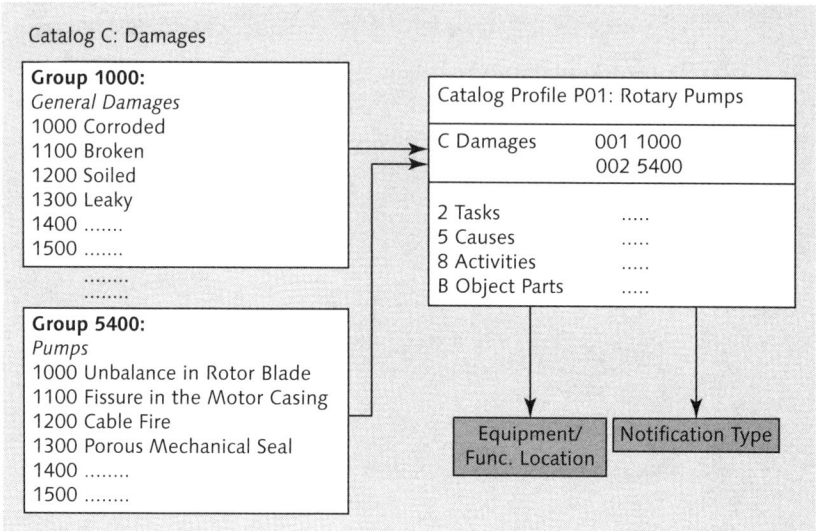

Figure 5.10 Catalog Profile

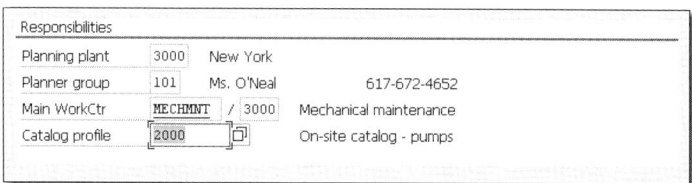

Figure 5.11 "Responsibilities" Screen Group

[+] **Use the Catalog Profile**

You use a catalog profile to make a basic amount of codes available that are useful for the reference object; all other codes are "sorted." This increases accuracy and user acceptance.

Classification

In the section about notification content, you saw the varied options you can use to store information in a notification. If this is not sufficient or you require different information, you can also classify notifications.

Planned Repairs Business Process | **5.2**

In Section 4.2.7, I already explained the basic principles of classification. What must you now do to be able to classify notifications?

Prerequisites

- You require characteristics.
- You need classes with Class Type 015 (error records).
- You use the Customizing function CHANGE CATALOGS AND CATALOG PROFILE FOR NOTIFICATION TYPE to activate the ACTIVE CLASS switch and assign a catalog profile.
- You assign a classification to the catalog profile, in turn, using the Customizing function DEFINE CATALOG PROFILE and set the CLASSIFICATION SCREEN switch.

When you have fulfilled these prerequisites, you can classify the notification on the item detail screen (see Figure 5.12).

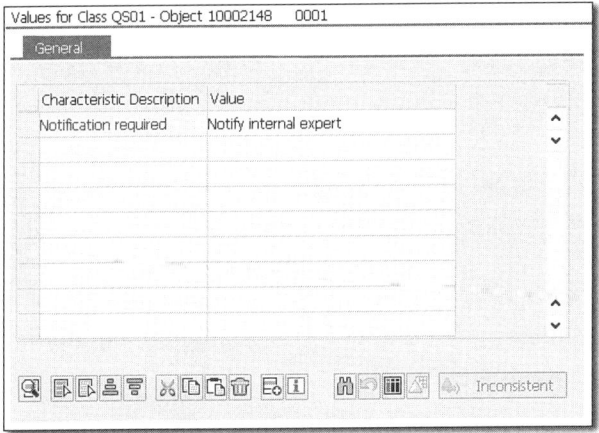

Figure 5.12 Notification Classification

| **Additional Information by Classifying a Notification** | **[+]** |

You can use the classification to add additional information to your notifications without any programming or modifications. In this case, however, you must define classes of Class Type 015 (error records) and their assignment in the Customizing for the catalog profile.

Partners

The same process that is described for the master data in Section 4.2.9 also applies for notifications. You can assign and define as many partners as freely as you wish to a notification. For example, these could include the following:

- Contact person at the plant
- Service company
- Organizational unit responsible
- Vendor
- Person responsible in Controlling
- Technician
- Maintenance supervisor's office

You must create a partner determination procedure for this (Customizing function DEFINE PARTNER DETERMINATION PROCEDURE) and assign it to the notification type (Customizing function ASSIGN PARTNER DETERMINATION PROCEDURE TO NOTIFICATION TYPE).

Partner transfer

If you now create a notification and enter a reference object, both of which are assigned to the partner, the system tries to transfer the partners from the reference object. If the partner roles in the partner determination procedure of the reference object and partner determination procedure of the notification are identical, the partner is transferred from the reference object to the notification.

Thus, for example, a vendor (Partner Determination Procedure YEQ, Partner Role LI, Vendor Number 1000) is assigned to the equipment. This vendor is now transferred to the notification if the partner determination procedure of the notification (for example, YMD) also contains the LI partner role. Incidentally, the same also applies for the partner transfer from the reference object to the order and from the notification to the order (see Figure 5.13).

[+] **Additional Responsibilities Due to the Partner Roles**

By default, the SAP system knows only a few organizational units that you can assign to a maintenance task: these are, basically, the planner group and the work center responsible. By defining partners, you can considerably expand these areas and people responsible and specify them in more detail. To do this, you must define partner roles and partner determination procedures and their assignment to the notification type.

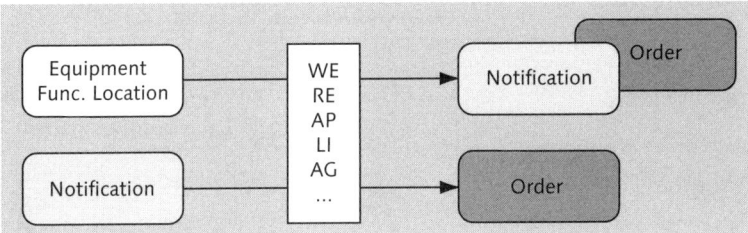

Figure 5.13 Partner Transfer

Address

If you have stored an address for the reference object, this address is transferred to the notification. However, if the notification processing does not take place at this address (i.e., because the reference object was brought to a central workshop), you can change this address and store an individual notification address (see Figure 5.14).

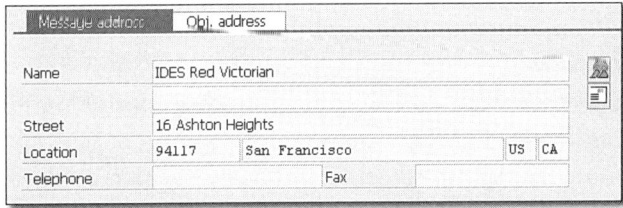

Figure 5.14 Address

Documents

You can assign related documents during the processing of maintenance notifications (see Figure 5.15). You can create new documents, assign existing documents, and change or cancel document assignments. You can navigate to the view of the respective document info records and call the original files of the assigned documents.

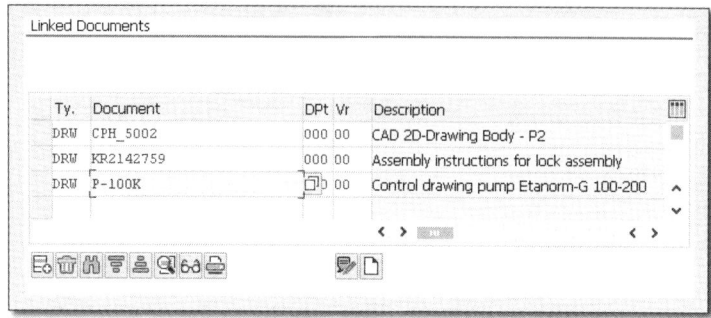

Figure 5.15 Documents in the Notification

To be able to assign documents to a notification, you need to define the relevant document types using the Customizing function DEFINE DOCUMENT TYPES for the PMQMEL object and use the Customizing function SET SCREEN TEMPLATES FOR NOTIFICATION TYPE to assign the screen 092 DMS LINKS to the notification type.

Printing

The SAP system enables you to output notifications on different media in different layouts. The following notification papers, for example, can be printed:

- **Notification overview**
  The notification overview is a complete printout of a notification to enable the parties involved (technicians, employees of work scheduling and production, and so on) to get an overview of the respective notification.

- **Activity report**
  You could use the activity report as the basis for the work. It contains a list with possible activities, tasks, and so on. The person who corrects the malfunction can only confirm the work he or she has performed by checking it off in this list.

- **Breakdown analysis**
  The breakdown analysis could be a printout of the specifications about the breakdown duration and system availability.

> **You Have a Choice when Printing** [+]
>
> It is up to you to decide how many and which notification papers you want to print, the layout you want these notification papers to have, and which notification papers are to be output on which output medium.

The following media are relevant as output media: *Output media*

- Local printers
- Network printer
- Fax machines
- Email
- PC downloads

> **Notification Printing and/or Shop Paper Printing** [!]
>
> However, shop papers, rather than notification papers, are printed. Notification papers are normally used only to enhance the shop papers, or if the sales order processing is not active.

Section 5.2.3, will, therefore, discuss the other details about the topic of *printing* (prerequisites, functions, Customizing) in conjunction with the order.

System Status and User Status

For notifications, it also applies that you can assign user status to them and that the system status is set by the system, depending on the functions performed. Thus, the process described for the master data in Section 4.2.9 applies.

You must have defined a status profile for the *notification* object type (Customizing function DEFINE USER STATUS FOR NOTIFICATIONS) and assigned it to the notification type (ASSIGN USER STATUS TO NOTIFICATION TYPES). *Prerequisites*

In the notification itself, you then set a status by going to the status using the ⓘ button and setting the required status there (see Figure 5.16). *Setting a status*

5 | Business Processes

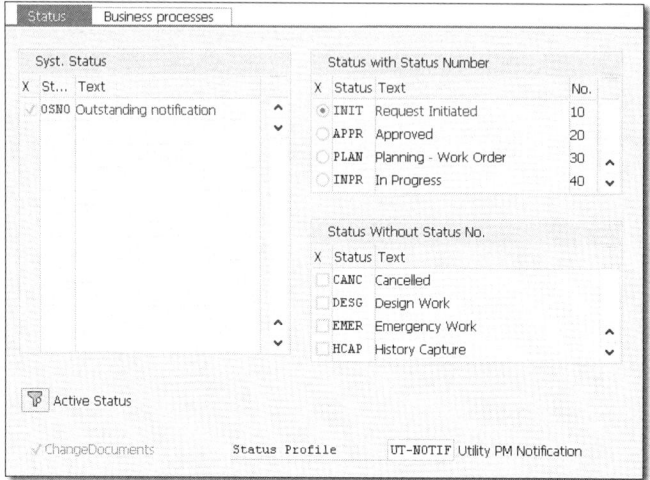

Figure 5.16 Status of a Notification

[+] **Permitting or Prohibiting Functions with User Status**

You can use user statuses to explicitly control which business transactions will be permitted or prohibited in your notifications.

You can set up the user status in Customizing in such a way that it is automatically set or deleted when the system status is changed. This enables you to further restrict the permitted business transactions of a system status in a clever way, without the user having to carry out additional data maintenance.

I have, thus, explained the most important functions of the notification, and we can conclude the notification phase. We now come to the planning phase, which represents the transition to the order, and the commissioning of the maintenance workshops.

5.2.2 Planning

Many functions we learned about for the notifications (refer to Section 5.2.1) are also available for processing orders.

Flexible reference object

You can also assign technical objects flexibly in the order, either as a default value per order type via Customizing (using the function SET UP

ORDER TYPES) or user-specifically (within the order via EXTRAS • SETTINGS • REFERENCE OBJECT).

In the order, you can also use the object information to obtain concise information about the object environment if you have created object information keys in Customizing and assigned them to the order type (Customizing functions DEFINE OBJECT INFORMATION KEY AND ASSIGN OBJECT INFORMATION KEY TO ORDER TYPES).

Object information

The order also contains system statuses that are automatically assigned by the system when business functions are executed (for example, REL = Released, MACM = Material availability confirmed), and you can also assign user statuses manually in the order if you have defined a status profile for the *order* object type (Customizing function DEFINE USER STATUS PROFILE FOR ORDERS) and assigned this to the order type (ASSIGN USER STATUS TO ORDER TYPES).

System status and user status

You can also assign partners in the order if you have defined a partner determination procedure and assigned it to the order type (Customizing functions DEFINE PARTNER DETERMINATION PROCEDURE or ASSIGN PARTNER DETERMINATION PROCEDURE TO THE ORDER). In the order, the same rules apply for transferring partners as those that are described for the notification.

Partners

If you have stored an address for the reference object and/or in the notification, this address is copied to the order as the object address or as the order address. However, you can change the order address or manually create an order address if one has not yet been created automatically.

Address

The following section will now focus on the order functions that are not available in the notification.

Creating an Order

There are six options you can use to create an order (see Figure 5.17):

- **Automatic generation of an order from a maintenance plan**
  You have defined a maintenance plan, and this automatically generates an order at periodic intervals on the basis of the information stored there (for example, reference object, order type, maintenance task list) ❶. Section 5.8 discusses this in more detail.

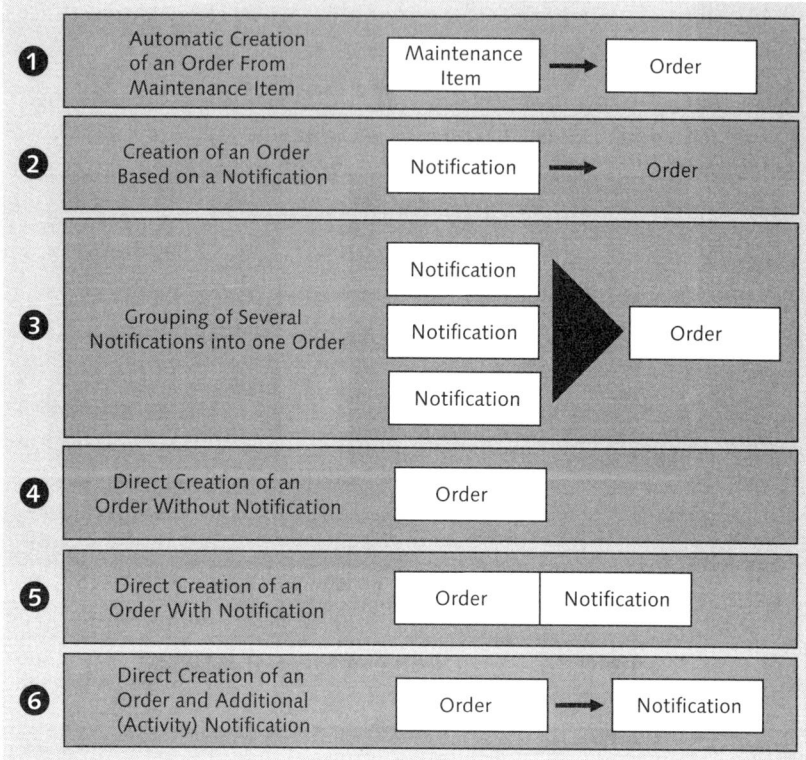

Figure 5.17 Creating an Order

- **Creation of an order based on a notification**
  You have an individual notification that you received from a requester (for example, from production); you now create an order from the notification ❷. In Figure 5.18, you see a notification from which you can now create an order using the 🗋 button.

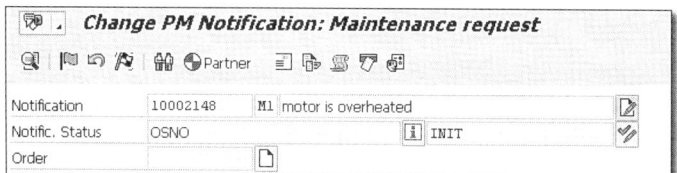

Figure 5.18 Order From Notification

▶ **Combining several notifications into one order**
You receive several notifications that must be processed within a single order (i.e., several malfunction notifications that refer to the same technical system) and have the option of creating an order from the notification list (Transaction IW28; see Figure 5.19) ❸; the notifications are entered automatically in the object list.

S	Notification	Req. start	Req. End	Description	Equipment	Functional Location
	10001948	12/17/2009	12/24/2009	Emission Exceedance		RFN-01
	10001967	01/12/2010		needs to install noise reduction kit	10006656	ICS-MC-001-CU-ABS-B
	10002017	05/24/2011		pump repair	10006691	UT-NPG-01-CIR-P11
	10002027	11/11/2011		Pump Leaking water	10006757	SU-SC-AU-OP
	10002037	04/13/2012	04/13/2012	install new speed limit signs through...		SU-SC
	10002047	07/11/2012	07/11/2012	Quarterly Maintenance of Pump	10006757	SU-SC-AU-OP
	10002048	07/31/2012	07/31/2012	Quarterly Maintenance of Boiler	10006739	SU-SC-AU-OP
	10002049	06/01/2012	06/15/2012	Preventive Maintenance of Boiler	10006739	SU-SC-AU-OP
	10002050	06/01/2012	06/15/2012	Preventive Maintenance of Pump	10006757	SU-SC-AU-OP
	10002070	10/29/2012	10/29/2012	Quarterly Maintenance of Boiler	10006739	SU-SC-AU-OP
	10002071	01/27/2013	01/27/2013	Quarterly Maintenance of Boiler	10006739	SU-SC-AU-OP
	10002072	04/27/2013	04/27/2013	Quarterly Maintenance of Boiler	10006739	SU-SC-AU-OP
	10002073	10/09/2012	10/09/2012	Quarterly Maintenance of Pump	10006757	SU-SC-AU-OP
	10002074	01/07/2013	01/07/2013	Quarterly Maintenance of Pump	10006757	SU-SC-AU-OP
	10002075	04/07/2013	04/07/2013	Quarterly Maintenance of Pump	10006757	SU-SC-AU-OP
	10002076	07/01/2012	07/15/2012	Preventive Maintenance of Pump	10006757	SU-SC-AU-OP
	10002077	07/28/2012	08/11/2012	Preventive Maintenance of Pump	10006757	SU-SC-AU-OP

Figure 5.19 Notification List

Here, there are four notifications for a forklift. You select these and combine them into a single order by selecting NOTIFICATION • CREATE ORDER.

▶ **Direct creation of an order without notification**
You want to create an order directly without a notification. You use Transaction IW31 ❹ for this purpose. The order header contains similar information to that of a notification (see Figure 5.20): description, reference object, dates, and people responsible.

▶ **Direct creation of an order including notification**
As with the previous option, you want to create an order directly, but you would like to add information such as damage, cause of damage, or breakdown to it ❺. For more detailed information about this, refer to Section 5.3.

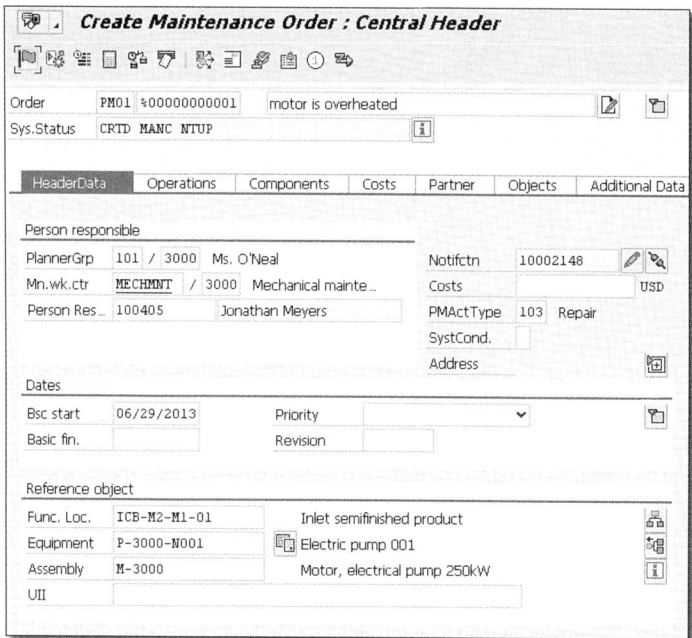

Figure 5.20 Order Header

- **Direct creation of an order with subsequent notification**
  You have created an order without a notification ❹, but when completing the order, you realize that you also want to enter technical confirmation data of a notification in addition to time confirmation data. If a notification is not yet assigned to an order, you can create a new notification for the order at any time from the order using the Notifctn button ❻.

Order Types

You can define order types as you wish to meet your own requirements. You should define the order types based on the functions where they differ in Customizing. You can define settings for each order type in Customizing, such as the following:

Decision-making criteria
- Number range
- Default values (for example, for external processing or for using maintenance task lists)

- Priorities
- Costing and order settlement
- Availability check
- Scheduling
- Print Control
- Interface for Internet catalogs
- Confirmation procedure
- Object information
- Partner determination procedure
- Status Profile
- Screen layout (for more information, refer to Section 5.3)

If you want to access different number ranges, or require different screen layouts, or want to settle the orders differently, for example, you have to set up different order types.

Order Types in Plant Maintenance	[+]
Experience has shown that you normally require at least the following order types: - An order type for repairs - An order type for preventive maintenance - An order type for calibrations (if used) - An order type for investment measures	

Order Types Must Be Agreed Upon with Other Areas	[+]
When you define your order types, you must consult with your colleagues from Controlling (CO internal orders), Production (PP production orders), Service Management (CS service orders), and Project Management (PS networks) because they use the same order tables.	

Content of Orders

You define the layout of the orders in Customizing using the Customizing function DEFINE VIEW PROFILES or ASSIGN VIEW PROFILES TO ORDER TYPES.

5 | Business Processes

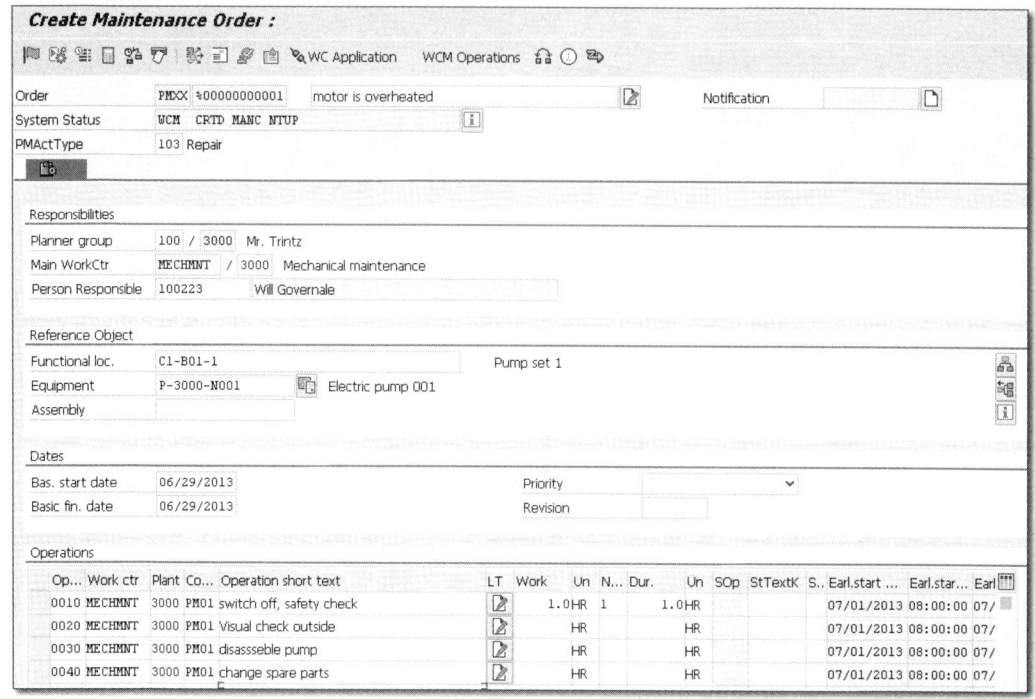

Figure 5.21 Reduced Order

[+] **Design Your Own Layouts for Orders**

Design suitable screen layouts for your order types; you can also base these on the type of activity (adding, changing, displaying). Adapted and simplified screen layouts increase user acceptability.

Figure 5.21 displays an adapted order layout that consists of only one tab with a few field groups. Using the 🔒 button, you can always switch between the adapted layout and the standard layout defined by SAP.

Order Operations

Why operations? In the order operations (see Figure 5.22), you describe the maintenance activities to be performed. If the short text is not sufficient for your description, a separate long text is available for every operation. In addition to the description, the operation contains the standard time, work center, number of people involved, and other control information.

Op...	Work ctr	Plant	Co...	Operation short text	LT	Work	Un	N...	Dur.	Un
0010	MECHMNT	3000	PM01	switch off, safety check			30MIN			30MIN
0020	MECHMNT	3000	PM01	Visual check outside for leaks, rust eg			30MIN			30MIN
0030	MECHMNT	3000	PM01	visual check inside			60MIN			60MIN
0040	MECHMNT	3000	PM01	disassemble pump shaft and clean			120MIN			120MIN
0050	MECHMNT	3000	PM01	measure bearing tolerance			30MIN			30MIN
0060	MECHMNT	3000	PM01	change sealings of gearbox cover			100MIN			100MIN
0070	MECHMNT	3000	PM01	safety check running pump			30MIN			30MIN
0080	MECHMNT	3000	PM01				HR			HR
0090	MECHMNT	3000	PM01				HR			HR

Figure 5.22 Order Operations

You must differentiate between the columns WORK and DURATION for the standard times. The WORK column represents the scope of work; in other words, the volume of work to be completed per operation. The values entered therein are included in the costing and capacity requirements planning. In contrast, the DURATION column represents the lead time of the individual operations; the relevant values are included, in turn, in the scheduling.

Work and duration

Another important control element is the control key. This is suggested as the default value from the performing work center, but you can change it. Section 3.2 has already discussed the control key in detail.

Control keys

Responsibilities

You can use the following options to define the people responsible at both the header level (see Figure 5.23) and operation level in the order:

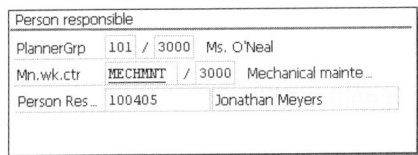

Figure 5.23 People Responsible in the Order Header

- **Planner group**

  You can define a planner group at the order header level (PLANNER GROUP field). This is either an individual person or a group (for example, work scheduling) responsible for planning the relevant order.

- **Main work center**

  You must define a main work center at the order header level (MAIN-WRKCTR. field). Here, you specify the workshop that holds the primary responsibility for implementing the order.

- **Person responsible**

  You can also name a person responsible (RESPONS field). This is usually a person from the responsible work center who serves as the central contact person during execution of the order. That person would answer any questions that arise, for example. You must have used the Customizing function ASSIGN PARTNER DETERMINATION PROCEDURE TO ORDER to define an *order* role.

- **Work center**

  You assign a work center to each operation (WKCTR/PLT field), thus the workshop executing the operation. You can involve several workshops in an order in this way.

- **Processor**

  You can also assign each procedure to a person who should perform it (see Figure 5.24). This is usually a person from the work center.

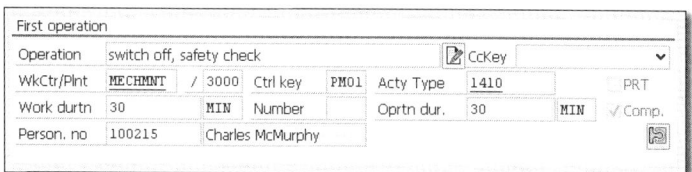

Figure 5.24 Work Center and Person

- **Several persons**

  You can also assign several persons to a procedure if the procedure involves several technicians. You enter the number of persons involved, which you indicate for the requirements assignments (see Figure 5.25). However, you must have used the Customizing function ASSIGN PARTNER DETERMINATION PROCEDURE TO ORDER to define a

split creation function role and assigned a control key to the relevant operation, for which, in turn, the function DETERMINE CAPACITY REQUIREMENTS has been activated.

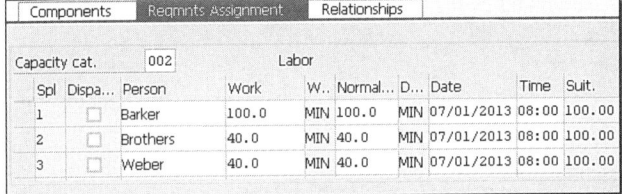

Figure 5.25 Requirements Assignments

| Responsibilities for the Order | [+] |

As the person responsible, you can assign a planner group, main work center, and person responsible to the order at the header level. You can assign the latter if this person is assigned to the order type as a partner in Customizing.

As the person responsible for executing the order, you can assign a work center, person, or several people at the order level, the latter if *splits* is assigned to the order type as the role in Customizing.

You can also assign any number of other people responsible to the order using partner determination procedures.

Scheduling

Scheduling involves calculating the scheduled dates at the operation and header level, based on the basic dates manually defined in the order and taking into account the durations at the operation level.

Definition

| Scheduling Does Not Always Make Sense | [+] |

Scheduling in the SAP system makes sense only if you have saved standard times. If you do not have these, you should not activate the scheduling initially at all. You can ensure this by using a control key for which the SCHEDULE option is not activated.

The SAP system basically supports two different types of scheduling: lead time scheduling and network scheduling (see Table 5.1).

Scheduling types

5 | Business Processes

Lead Time Scheduling	Network Scheduling
Carries out either forward or backward scheduling	Carries out forward and backward scheduling
Assumes sequential processing of the order	Can take into account sequential processing and dependencies ▸ Relationships ▸ Network structure
Determines dates of the order	Determines the earliest and latest dates of an order ▸ Buffer

Table 5.1 Scheduling Types

Lead time scheduling Lead time scheduling is executed as either forward scheduling or backward scheduling. Based on the basic start date and by adding the operation durations, forward scheduling involves calculating the earliest scheduled start and end dates at both the header and operation level. In contrast, backward scheduling involves calculating the latest scheduled start and end dates at the header and operation level based on the basic end date and by subtracting the operation durations.

Network scheduling Both forward and backward scheduling are executed for network scheduling, taking relationships into account, in particular; the basic start date is used as the basis for calculating the earliest scheduled dates, while the latest scheduled dates are calculated based on the basic end date. The difference between the earliest and latest date results in the buffer is shown for each operation and at the header level.

Prerequisites To be able to execute scheduling, you must fulfill the following prerequisites:

▸ Enter the respective duration in the operations.

▸ Assign the operation a control key for which the SCHEDULING option is active.

▸ Assign an *internal processing duration* to the work center. This must point to the DAUNO field—that is, the duration from the operation. By default, this is the SAP004 formula.

- If you want to execute lead time scheduling, you use the Customizing function SET SCHEDULING PARAMETERS to assign the scheduling type (forward, backward) to the order type in the plant.
- If you want to execute network scheduling, you define a graphics profile in Customizing using the function SAP NETWEAVER • APPLICATION SERVER • FRONTEND SERVICES • BAR CHART • DEFINE GRAPHICS PROFILES, which you make available, in turn, for maintenance orders using the Customizing function CREATE DEFAULT VALUE PROFILES FOR GENERAL ORDER DATA and assign to the PLANT/ORDER TYPE combination using the Customizing function DEFAULT VALUES FOR MAINTENANCE TASK LIST DATA AND *Profile Assignments*.

> **Do Not Adjust Basic Dates** [+]
>
> In the SET SCHEDULING PARAMETERS Customizing function, you will find a setting option for adjusting the basic dates. Set this to DO NOT ADJUST BASIC DATES.
>
> Otherwise, the basic dates you entered manually are overwritten by the SCHEDULED DATES during scheduling; in other words, they are lost, and you cannot restore them again.

Based on these prerequisites, the system first calculates the scheduled dates as the lead time scheduling at the header level (see Figure 5.26) and for the individual operations.

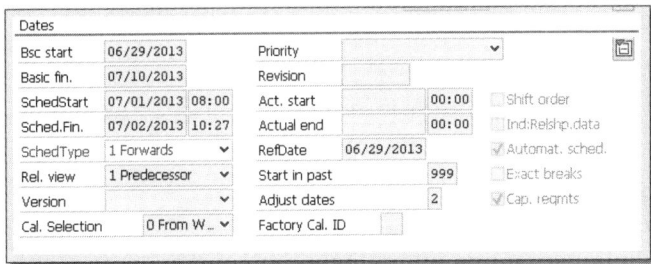

Figure 5.26 Scheduling Data

> **Forward Scheduling as the Normal Case** [!]
>
> Forward scheduling is the normal case for lead time scheduling in plant maintenance.

5 | Business Processes

Relationships   You switch from lead time scheduling to network scheduling by maintaining the relationships. To do so, choose GOTO • GRAPHICS • NETWORK STRUCTURE in the order and navigate to the network structure table. There, you activate the LINK mode using the 🔲 button. You can then maintain different types of relationships (see Figure 5.27).

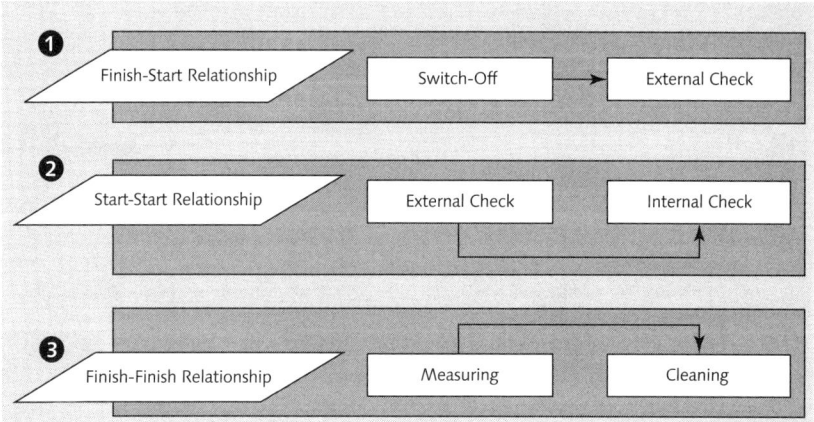

Figure 5.27 Relationships

❶ Finish-start relationship

You use a finish-start relationship to connect the end of an operation with the start of a follow-on operation. Since you can define finish-start relationships for several follow-on operations, namely from one operation, this consequently means that you can process the follow-on operations in parallel.

❷ Start-start relationship

You use a start-start relationship to connect the start of two operations to each other; these operations, thus, must start simultaneously.

❸ Finish-finish relationship

You use a finish-finish relationship to connect the end of two operations to each other; these operations, thus, must end simultaneously.

[+] **Creating Finish-Start Relationships Automatically**

In the order, you can automatically create finish-start relationships in the system for all operations by selecting ORDER • FUNCTIONS • DATES • CREATE RELATIONSHIPS. This means that you create a graphical network structure (see Figure 5.28).

Planned Repairs Business Process | 5.2

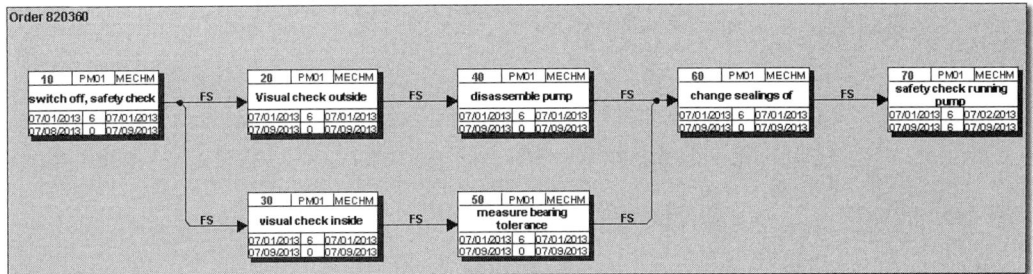

Figure 5.28 Network Graphic

A network graphic illustrates the logical dependency of the individual operations. In contrast, a bar chart (called in the order by selecting GOTO • GRAPHIC • BAR CHART) displays the dates and duration of the operations (see Figure 5.29).

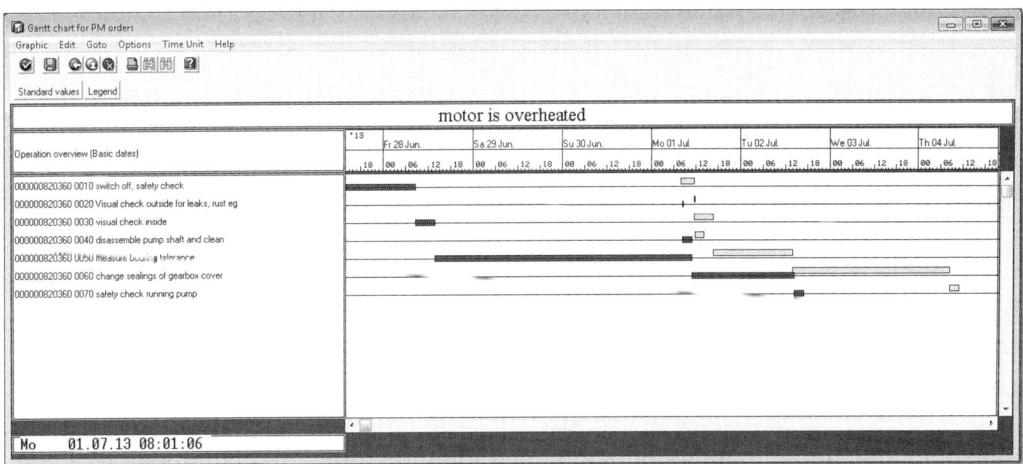

Figure 5.29 Bar Chart

Material Planning

When planning the required material, you must determine whether it is stock material or non-stock material.

The planning process for the stock material takes place as follows (see Figure 5.30):

Stock material-process

The stock materials (Item Category L) that you schedule for the order are reserved in storage ❷. For each order type, you determine in Customizing whether the material reservation must become effective immediately or only when the order is released ❸ (Customizing path DEFINE • CHANGE DOCUMENTS • COLLECTIVE PURCHASE REQUISITIONS MRP RELEVANCE and activate the RESERVATION/PURCHASE REQUISITION option). However, you can change the relevant indicator in the material item of the order when you process the order.

[!] **Creating Reservations Automatically**

Note that you cannot suppress the activation of a reservation for stock material; material reservations are, thus, created in any case. With the Customizing function DEFINE • CHANGE DOCUMENTS • COLLECTIVE PURCHASE REQUISITIONS MRP RELEVANCE, and by activating the RESERVATION/PURCHASE REQUISITION option, you can control when the reservation becomes effective, either immediately or when the order is released.

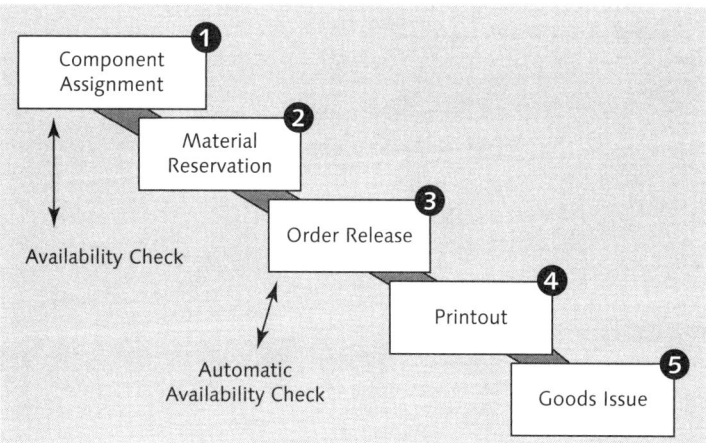

Figure 5.30 Process when Using Stock Material

[+] **No Separation between Reservation and Purchase Requisition**

It is also important that you cannot create any separation between a reservation for stock material and a purchase requisition for non-stock material. Therefore, if you activate the RESERVATION/PURCHASE REQUISITION option via the Customizing path DEFINE • CHANGE DOCUMENTS • COLLECTIVE PURCHASE

REQUISITIONS MRP RELEVANCE and set the IMMEDIATE option, the reservations become effective immediately, and purchase requisitions are created. Thus, you cannot, for example, create purchase requisitions immediately and let the reservations become effective only when the order is released. This is possible only if you manually change this in each case in the order.

1. **Component assignment**
   The component assignment ❶ in the order enables you to perform an availability check straight away.

2. **Order release**
   When you release the order ❸, the system automatically performs an availability check.

3. **Print**
   When you print the shop papers ❹, you can also print out corresponding documents for the workshop and warehouse (for example, a material pick list and material issue slips).

4. **Goods issue**
   You enter planned goods issues with a reference to the reservation and unplanned goods issues by entering the order number ❺.

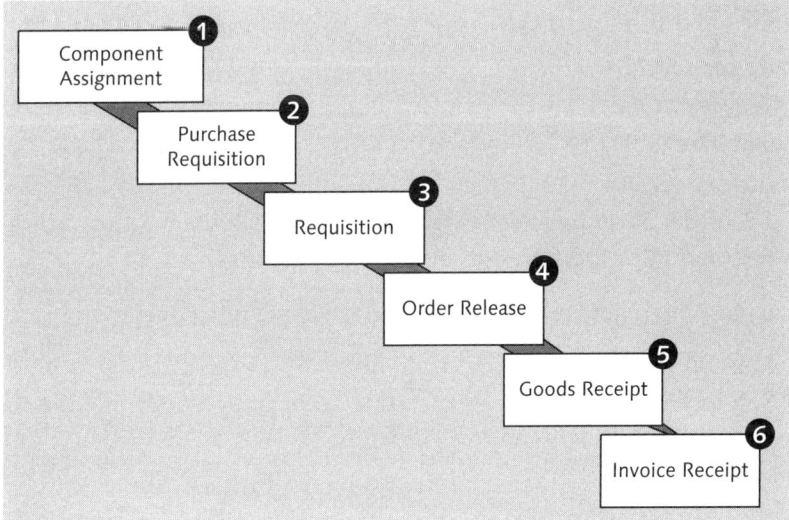

Figure 5.31 Process when Using Non-Stock Material

Non-stock material: process

The planning process for non-stock material is done in the following six steps (see Figure 5.31):

1. **Component assignment**
   The component assignment ❶ in the order (item category N) enables you to specify additional purchasing information. The component that you assign can, but does not have to, have a material number. In the latter case, you describe the material by manually entering a short text.

2. **Purchase Requisition**
   The system creates a purchase requisition ❷ based on this information, either directly when you save the order or when you release it (by activating the RESERVATION/PURCHASE REQUISITION option via the Customizing path DEFINE CHANGE DOCUMENTS • COLLECTIVE PURCHASE REQUISITIONS MRP RELEVANCE).

3. **Purchase order**
   In Purchasing, purchase orders ❸ are created from the purchase requisitions. The purchase order items are assigned to the order in this case.

4. **Order release**
   Goods receipts with reference to the order can be entered as soon as the order is released ❹.

5. **Goods receipt**
   When you enter the goods receipts ❺, the purchase order value is debited on the order when the goods receipt is valuated.

6. **Invoice receipt**
   The order is automatically debited or credited when an invoice is received ❻ or if differences occur in the invoices.

Material planning options

You have the following options for the actual planning operation:

- **Manual entry**
  You can manually assign a material to an operation from the general material list.

- **Structure list**
  You can select spare parts from the structure list of the reference object (List button). If you assign the order a functional location,

equipment, and an assembly, all direct and indirect bills of material (if available) are displayed in the structure list.

- **Maintenance task list**
  If you use a maintenance task list in the order and spare parts are assigned to the maintenance task list, these are transferred to the order.

- **Material where-used list**
  If you process orders for the reference objects in the past and used spare parts in this case, you can display these using the material where-used list (via the Material Where-Used button) and transfer items from this into the existing order.

Material Where-Used List for Material Planning	[+]
The longer equipment or a functional location is already in use, the more meaningful the history of the exchanged spare parts is, and therefore the more helpful the material where-used list for component planning is.	

Figure 5.32 shows an overview of these options.

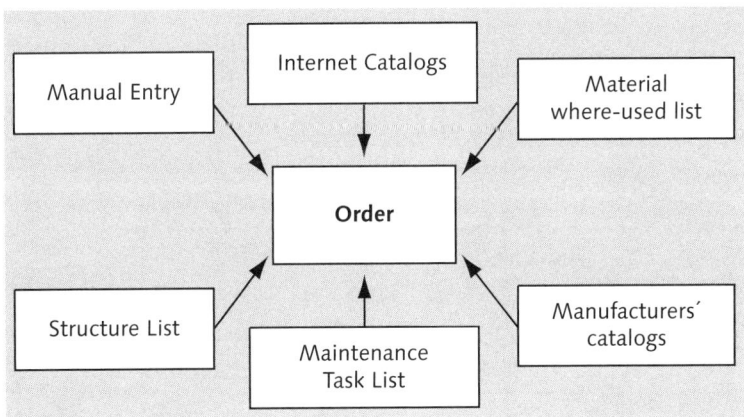

Figure 5.32 Material Planning Options

You can also use Internet and manufacturers' catalogs for material planning. For more information, refer to Section 8.2.

Requirement date of material components

In Customizing, choose SET SCHEDULING PARAMETERS and use the ADJUST DATES indicator to specify the following for each plant and order type:

- Whether all material components are required on the start date of the order
- Whether individual material components are required on the start date of the individual operation

[+] **Do Not Adjust Basic Dates, Requirements Dates at the Operation Level**

Set the parameter ADJUST DATES to DO NOT ADJUST BASIC DATES, DEPENDENT REQUIREMENTS ON OPERATION DATES. The section on Scheduling has already explained why you should not adjust the basic dates. You should schedule the dependent requirement at the operation level because all materials are otherwise made available at the start of the order processing, which would increase warehouse stocks unnecessarily.

Alternatively, you can assign a requirement date to each component manually (see Figure 5.33). If the component is a non-stock material, the requirement date is simultaneously the required delivery date, which is communicated to the supplier.

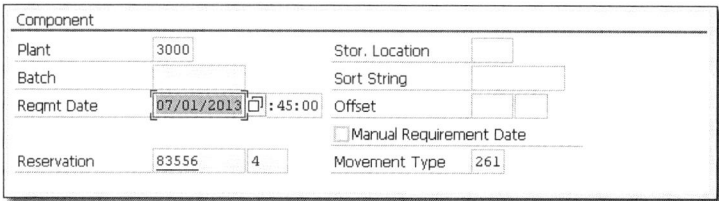

Figure 5.33 Requirement Date of a Material Component

Business function

The LOG_EAM_CI_3 business function must be activated in order for you to assign a requirement date manually. Figure 5.34 displays a fully planned material list.

The components are used (like lubricants, for example) or integrated (like assemblies, for example) during the processing of the order.

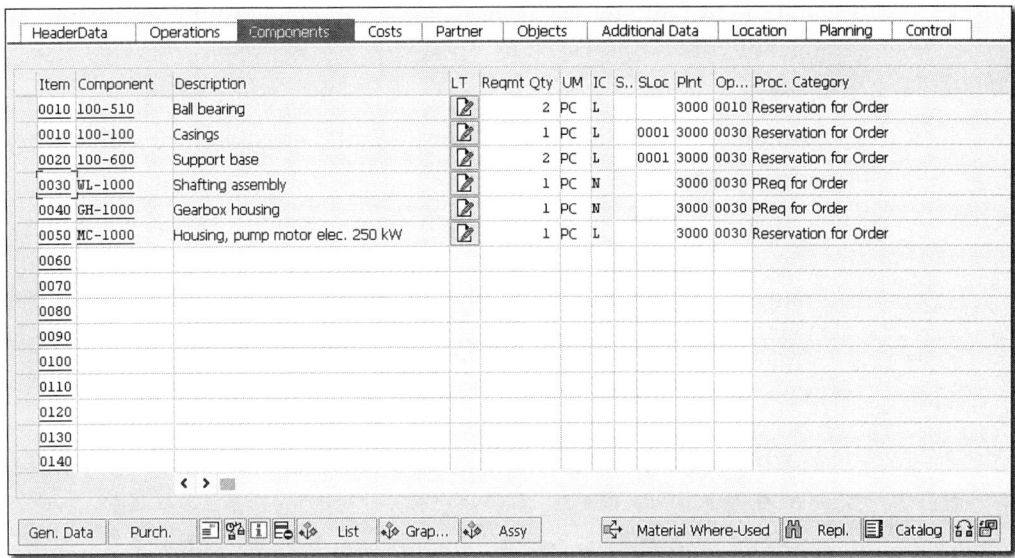

Figure 5.34 Component List

SAP ERP 6.0 with Enhancement Package 6 offers yet another welcome innovation: the operation overview and the component overview previously included only a selection of fields predefined by SAP. The purchasing data, in particular, was sorely missed. This has now changed: you can maintain all purchasing data with EHP 6 in the two aforementioned table controls (for example, vendor, material group, goods recipient, unloading point, or purchasing group; see Section 9.5.7).

New in EHP 6

To be able to maintain the purchasing data in the operation overview and component overview, the activation of the LOG_EAM_CI_5 business function is required.

In addition to the components, you may also need production resources/tools.

Production Resources/Tools

In contrast to components, production resources/tools (PRT), like protective clothing, hand pallet trucks, drawings, and so on, are not used when the order is being executed, but are instead required for processing the order and are returned again (to the stock) at the end.

Why use PRTs?

Types You can assign three different types of production resources/tools to an operation (see Figure 5.35):

- **Material**
  If the required production resource/tool is listed as a material number
- **Document**
  If it is a document and this is stored as a document master record
- **Equipment**
  If the required production resource/tool is listed as an equipment master record

It is called via the button.

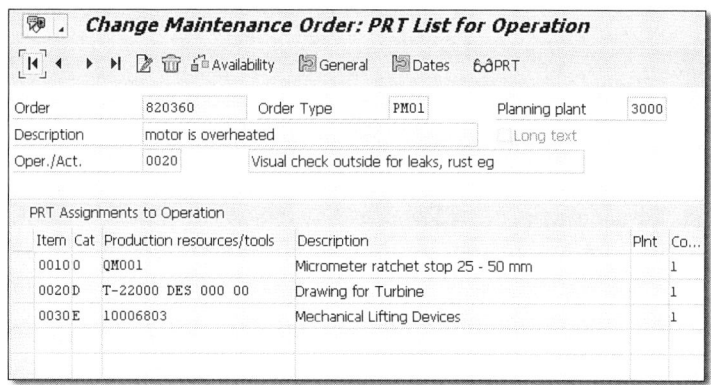

Figure 5.35 PRT List

Documents

You can assign related documents during the processing of maintenance notifications (see Figure 5.36), as follows:

Object Description	Op.	Type	Document	Description	File Name	Description of Original Doc.	Object key
Equipment Master	0020	SP	STB-VALVE	Valve	Valve Assembly Repair Procedure.rh		STB-VALVE
		VI	STB-VALVE-ASSEMBEL	Valve assembly procedure	Valve_Assembly_visual_Instruction.rh		STB-VALVE
		VI	STB-VALVE-DISMANTEL	Valve Dismatel procedure	Valve_dismantel_Visual_Instruction.rh		STB-VALVE
	0050	VI	VI-STB1-EQ-ID1	Document assigned to Equi	pump.rh	Pump	STB1-FL-MAT-ID
		VI	VI-STB1-EQ-ID2	Document 2assigned to Equi	tube.rh	Tube Removal	STB1-FL-MAT-ID
Functional Location		VI	VI-STB1-FL-ID1	Document assigned to FL	burner.rh	Burner change	STB1-0001-ID
		VI	VI-STB1-FL-ID2	Document 2 assigned to FL	coil.rh	Coil Transport	STB1-0001-ID
Maintenance Order		DRW	PUMP	Pump service operation	Pump Service Operation v1.6.rh		000004005001
Material Master	0060	VI	VI-STB1-EQ-MAT-I	Document EQUI Const type Item	pistol.rh	Pistol	STB1-EQ-MAT-I

Figure 5.36 Documents in the Order

- You can create new documents, assign existing documents, and change or cancel document assignments.
- You can navigate to the view of the respective document info records and call the original files of the assigned documents.
- You can also show the assigned documents for the maintenance notifications and the reference objects *equipment*, *functional location*, and *assembly*.
- Functions for filtering, searching, and sorting are available within the document list.

You must activate the LOG_EAM_CI_6 business function in advance in order to be able to assign documents to an order or order process.   **Business function**

You must also use the Customizing function DEFINE DOCUMENT TYPES to define the relevant document types for the object PMAUFK (order) or PMAFVC (operation).

Object List

You must perform certain activities not only on one object, but on a whole range of objects (i.e., an inspection round), or you may have several notifications that you want to process as part of a single order. You can use the object list in the order for these cases.   **Why use an object list?**

You can add the following objects to an object list (see Figure 5.37):

- Functional location
- Equipment
- Material serial number
- Notification

> **Costs for Object List**   [+]
>
> The accruing costs are updated by default on the reference object in the order header, and the relevant cost center is debited in the order settlement. If you want to settle the costs proportionally on all affected cost centers, use the customer exit CREATE CUSTOMER-SPECIFIC SETTLEMENT RULE (IWO10027).
>
> Unfortunately, there is no default option to distribute the costs in the history.

5 Business Processes

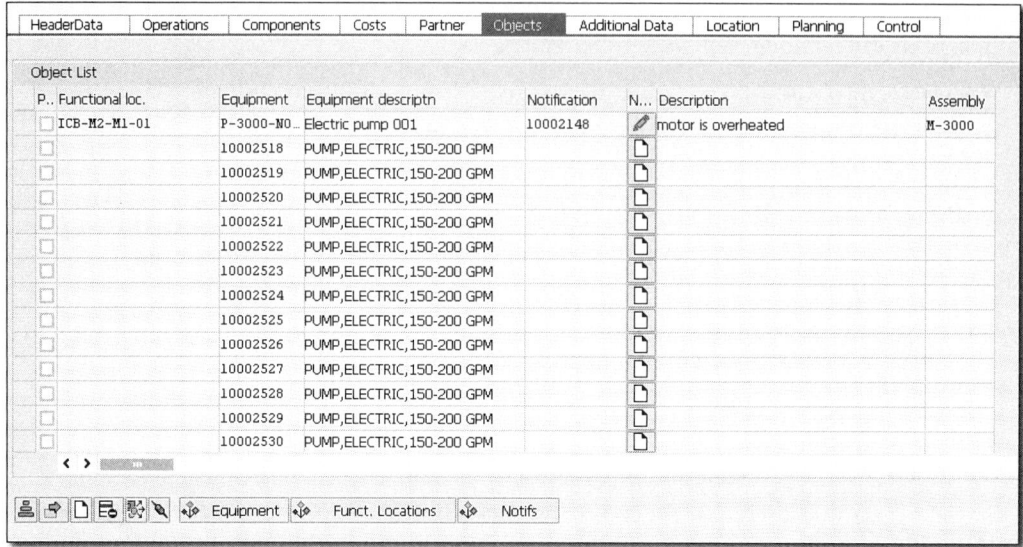

Figure 5.37 Object List

Costing and Estimated Costs

Definition — In the costing, the costs are automatically calculated based on the allocation records you stored in the system and on the amounts specified in the resource planning. The planned costs (as well as the actual costs that subsequently accrue) are not planned manually.

Displaying costs — The planning of resources leads to the accrual of planned costs on the order. You can display the costs there via two different methods (see Figure 5.38):

- **According to the cost elements**
  The costs displayed according to the costs elements show all cost elements included in the costing. This is more like a controlling-oriented view. It displays a comparison of planned and actual costs.

- **According to the value categories**
  The costs displayed according to the value categories summarize several cost elements into value categories. This is normally the display that is more clearly laid out for maintenance purposes; it displays a comparison of estimated, planned, and actual costs.

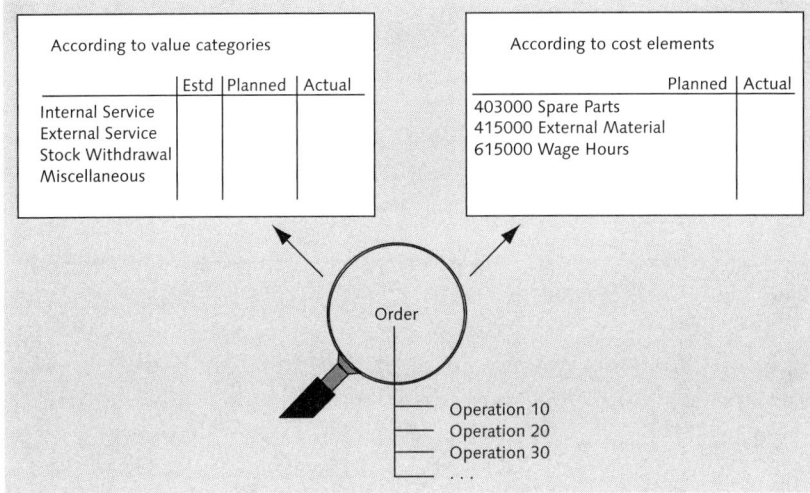

Figure 5.38 Displaying Costs in the Order

The costs of an order are calculated at two summarization levels, at which you can also display the costs:

Level of costs

- **At the operation level**
  The costs displayed at the operation level show all costs involved in the respective operation, either on the basis of cost elements as a planned/actual comparison, or on the basis of maintenance categories as a comparison of estimated/planned and actual costs (see Figure 5.39). To display the costs at the operation level, activate the Customizing function COSTS AT OPERATION LEVEL per plant and order type. Orders, the costs of which are displayed at the operation level, are given the status ACAS; thus, you can select the relevant orders via this status.

- **At the header level**
  The costs displayed at the header level summarize all costs at the operation level and show all costs involved in the order, on the basis of either cost elements as a planned/actual comparison or maintenance categories as a comparison of estimated/planned and actual costs. The costs at the header level are always indicated, regardless of whether you have activated the costs at the operation level.

5 | Business Processes

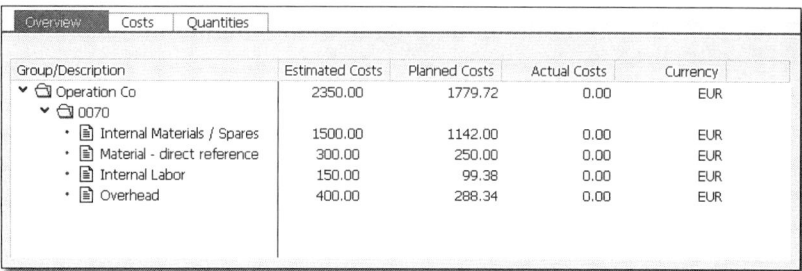

Figure 5.39 Costs at the Operation Level

Prerequisites To ensure that the system can determine the costs based on your resource planning, you must meet the following prerequisites in advance:

- Assign a control key with the COST function to the operations you want to be included in the costing.
- Assign work to the operations you want to be included in the costing.
- Use Transaction KP26 to define a fixed price (option FIXED PRICE) and/or variable price (option VARIABLE PRICE) for the version you use, fiscal year, cost center, and activity type.

[!] **Fixed or Variable Prices**

Since the costing is based on full costs in plant maintenance, it does not matter if you split the price at a fixed and variable price or not.

- Use the Customizing functions of Controlling to maintain the costing variant, valuation variant, and costing sheet (for more information, refer to Section 6.2.8).
- Use the Customizing function ASSIGN COSTING PARAMETERS AND RESULTS ANALYSIS KEYS to assign a Planned Costing Variant and an Actual Costing Variant to the order type for each plant.
- In the work center, maintain the following data on the COSTING TAB: cost center, activity type, and formula key.
- The formula key must point to the ARBEI field—that is, the work from the operation. By default, this is the SAP008 formula.

Planned Repairs Business Process | 5.2

- The materials to be calculated must have an activity price— either a standard price or a moving average price.
- You enter a value for non-stock materials and external activities.
- To display the costs at the operation level, you activate the Customizing function COSTS AT OPERATION LEVEL per plant and order type.
- If you have subsequently activated the costs at operation level, you have used Transaction OLI5N to run the report RIPMCO01 to rebuild existing order costs.

Preliminary costing of an order occurs automatically when you save or is triggered during order processing when you click on the 🖩 button manually.

Procedure

Figure 5.40 shows the costs displayed at the cost element level—you can display these costs by selecting the COSTS tab and executing the PLANNED/ACTUAL REPORT function.

If the order was costed, the system sets the status of the order to PRC (pre-costed). If there are also costs at the operation level, the system sets the status to ACAS (activity account assignment).

Statuses

Change Maintenance Order 819568: Cost Overview

Plan Version 0 Plan/actual version

Cumulative Data
Legal Valuation
Company Code Currency/Object Currency

Cost Elem.	Cost Element (Text)	Σ	Total plan costs Σ	Total act.costs Σ	Plan/actual variance	P/A var(%)	Currency
415000	External procurement costs		250.00	0.00	250.00-	100.00-	EUR
415000	**External procurement costs**	■	250.00 ■	0.00 ■	250.00-		EUR
615000	Dir.Int.Activity Alloc. Repair Hours		1,325.02	0.00	1,325.02-	100.00-	EUR
615000	**Dir.Int.Activity Alloc. Repair Hours**	■	1,325.02 ■	0.00 ■	1,325.02-		EUR
655901	Overhead Repair, Maintenance		410.91	0.00	410.91-	100.00-	EUR
655901	**Overhead Repair, Maintenance**	■	410.91 ■	0.00 ■	410.91-		EUR
890000	Consumption of semifinished product		1,142.00	0.00	1,142.00-	100.00-	EUR
890000	**Consumption of semifinished product**	■	1,142.00 ■	0.00 ■	1,142.00-		EUR
		■■	3,127.93 ■■	0.00 ■■	3,127.93-		EUR

Figure 5.40 Displaying Costs According to Cost Elements

Figure 5.41 shows the costs displayed according to value categories.

5 | Business Processes

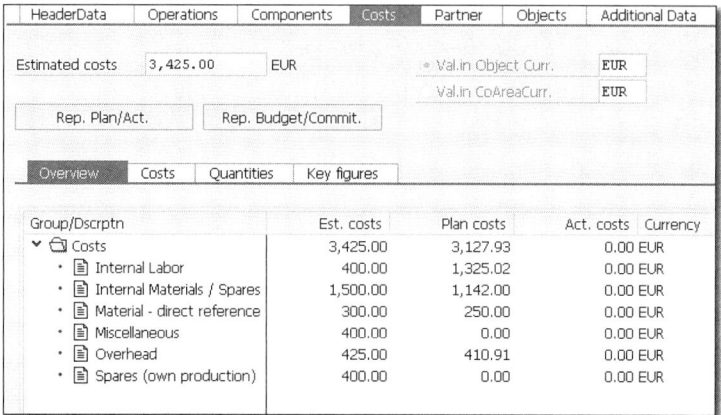

Figure 5.41 Displaying Costs According to Value Categories

Estimated costs
Planned and actual costs are costed automatically. You can also enter estimated costs. However, the estimated costs are not costed, but manually predefined, since estimated costs are based on only the empirical values of an maintenance planner and not planned resources. There are three different methods of entering the estimated costs:

- Differentiated for each value category at the operation level (the total of all operations is then indicated at the header level for each value category and overall)
- Differentiated for each value category at the header level (the total is then created automatically)
- As the total for the whole order

In the following cases, the exclusivity principle applies:

- If you have activated the COSTS function at the operation level, you can perform the cost estimation either at the operation level or as a total for the entire order. However, a cost estimation at the header level for value categories is not possible.
- If you have not activated the COSTS function at the operation level, you can perform the cost estimation either at the header level for the individual value categories or as a total for the entire order; a cost estimation at the operation level is not possible.

Using the ![icon] button, you can copy the planned costs into the estimated costs at any time until the order is released. What economic background, however, lies behind this function? This function is intended for users who want to freeze the planned costs of an order at any given time (often with the order release). Using this function, you can define the planned costs, for example, at the level that exists at the time of the order release; thus, subsequent plans change the planned costs, but not the estimated costs.

> **Estimated Costs Do Not Represent an Upper Value Limit** [+]
>
> Neither determining planned costs nor assigning estimated costs prevents certain value limits from being exceeded. If you want to prevent the exceeding of value limits, assign an order budget. If you have then activated the availability check in Customizing, warning or error messages appear when you reach or exceed certain value limits (refer to Section 7.3.1).

Section 4.2.9 explained that you can assign permits to a functional location or equipment. With this assignment, you were able to select the V column (that is, permit proposed for the processing) and also force the permit to be granted either when the order was released (OR column) or when it was technically completed (OC column). If this is the case, you must now grant these permits within the order processing before the order can be released or completed (see the OR and OC columns in Figure 5.42).

Permits

In addition to the permits that are proposed automatically from the object master record, you can also manually assign additional necessary permits for this order only.

You grant permits via the ![icon] button; you can undo the granted permits via the ![icon] button. In the overview, the system shows who granted the permit and when.

> **Using Permits Where It Makes Sense** [+]
>
> You can use permits to ensure that an order is not released or technically completed until the required permits have been granted according to the dual-control or multiple-control principle.
>
> You can use the SAP authorization concept to ensure that different people grant permits and release or technically complete the order.

5 | Business Processes

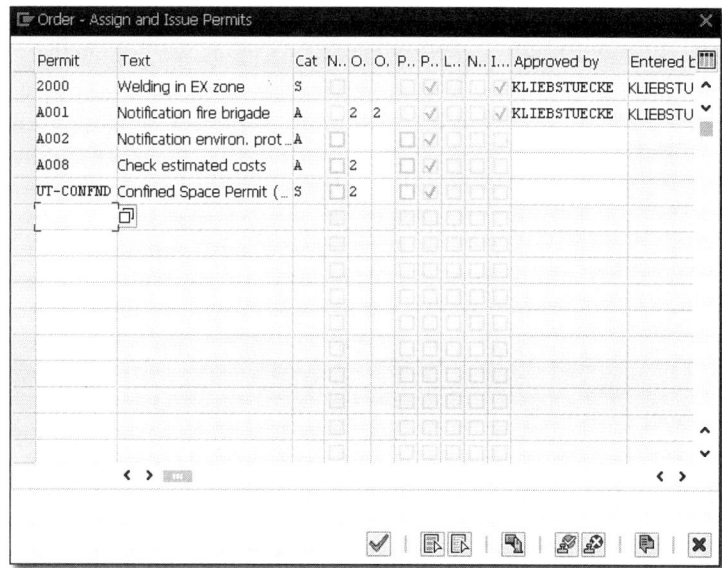

Figure 5.42 Granting Permits

Order Hierarchy

Definition — When one or more suborders are created for an order, this is referred to as an *order hierarchy*. An order hierarchy is a multilevel structure of orders and suborders to separate comprehensive orders or combine several orders.

Procedure — You create a suborder for a superior order in Transaction IW36 (see Figure 5.43).

Suborder or operation? — In practice, the creation of suborders rivals the creation of operations. As you saw above, you can perform certain planning operations on operations, as in the following operations, for example:

- Work specifications and work centers
- Materials
- Production resources/tools
- Scheduling

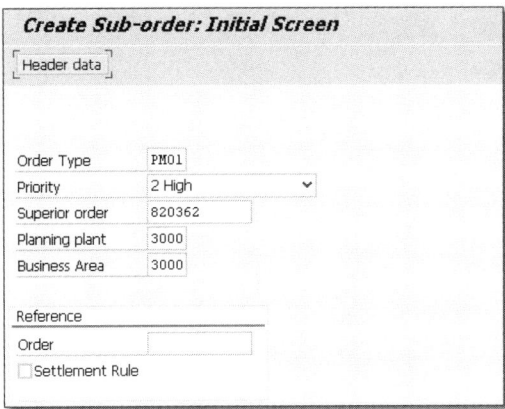

Figure 5.43 Creating a Suborder

However, the operations are bound by the specifications of the order header. The suborder, in contrast, is planned completely separately, which means that the following:

- You can assign an independent reference object to a suborder.
- The suborder can be budgeted independently.
- The suborder can be approved independently.

All these functions exceed the functions of an operation.

Sometimes Suborders Are Useful	[+]
You should create suborders rather than operations within order processing if you have tasks that require the following: - A separate reference object - A separate order budget - Independent approval	

In the main order, you can view the order structure (by choosing EX- TRAS • SUBORDERS • OVERVIEW) and the cost summarization (by choosing EXTRAS • SUBORDERS • COST OVERVIEW) using special reports. Figure 5.44 displays the incrementally summarized cost overview.

Reports

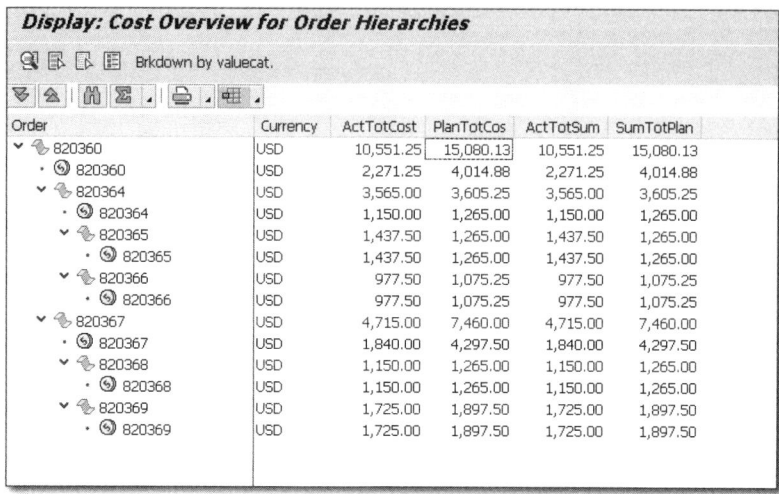

Figure 5.44 Order Hierarchy Cost Overview

Object Services

In Section 4.2.9, I explained the options available as part of object services when discussing the special functions for technical objects.

Of course, object services are also available for orders. However, note the following aspect of object services that applies to orders only: if you have assigned the *attachment* object service to an order and the order therefore has a list of attachments, this is clearly indicated by the button in the order header (see Figure 5.45). When you call the relevant order, you can immediately tell whether an attachment list has been assigned to it. To display the attachment list, click this button.

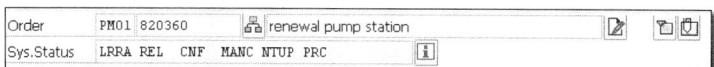

Figure 5.45 Order with Attachment List

[!] **Attachment List Button**

The ATTACHMENT LIST button in the order header indicates directly whether documents have been assigned to an order using the object service.

The LOG_EAM_CI_3 business function must be activated in order for you to display the ATTACHMENT LIST button.

Business function

We can leave the subject of planning the order and now move on to options of the SAP system that you normally use when the actual order processing is immediately imminent: controlling.

5.2.3 Controlling

Controlling comprises the functions MASS CHANGE, AVAILABILITY CHECK (material, production resources/tools, staff), CAPACITY REQUIREMENTS PLANNING, ORDER RELEASE, and SHOP PAPER PRINTING.

Mass Change

As part of your daily business, you are certain to frequently encounter scenarios in which you need to assign the same information to several orders. This is necessary, for example, in the following cases:

- You want to draw up a weekly timetable and need to schedule several orders on the same dates.
- You are down several employees in one workshop and need to shift orders to another workshop.
- Controlling has created new settlement orders to which several plant maintenance orders are to be assigned.
- You have hired a new planner to whom you want to assign a new worklist.

In these or similar scenarios, proceed as follows:

- Start Transaction IW38 to execute a list change for orders, and then restrict the worklist (for example, by order type or date).
- In the displayed list, select the orders you want to change simultaneously.
- Choose ORDER • PERFORM MASS CHANGE.
- Enter the relevant new information (for example, the main work center or date), and then implement the changes (see Figure 5.46).

5 | Business Processes

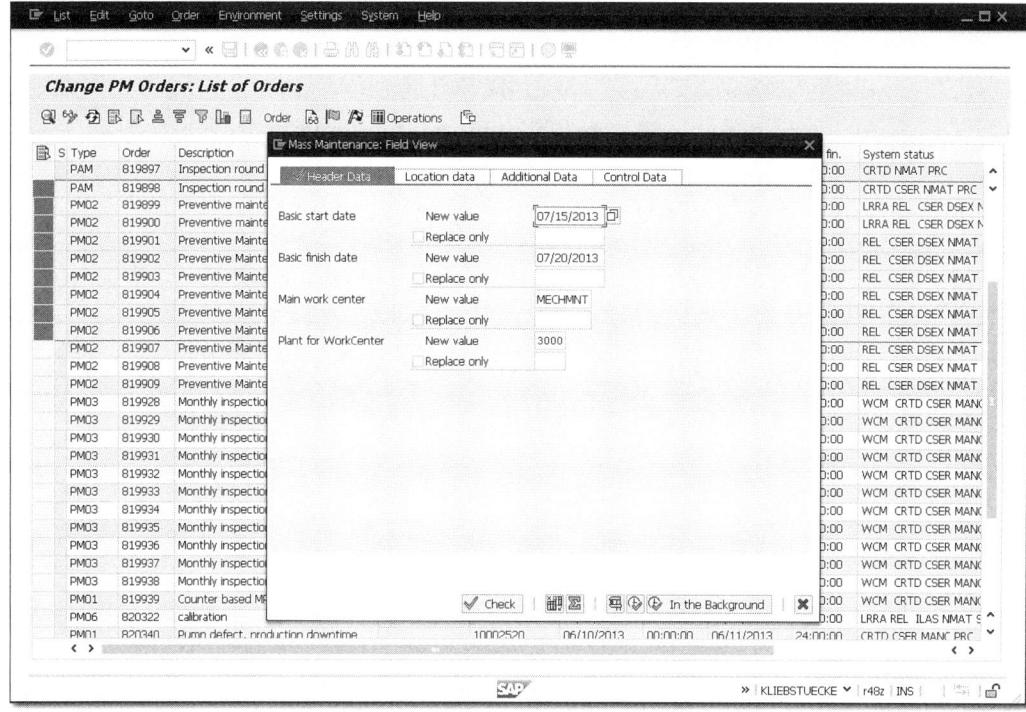

Figure 5.46 Mass Change of Orders

[+] **Mass Changes Reduce Maintenance Effort**

The MASS CHANGE function provides an easy, reliable, and fast way of changing the field contents in several orders simultaneously.

Capacity Requirements Planning

In capacity requirements planning, you compare the available capacity with the capacity requirement. You maintain the available capacity in the work center (see Section 3.2), and the capacity requirement is determined by the standard times of the operations in the order. However, capacity requirements planning does not always make sense.

> **First, Check whether Capacity Requirements Planning Makes Any Sense.** [+]
> Capacity requirements planning basically only makes sense if the plannedorder volume is sufficiently large and the standard times are reasonably exact. Unlike in production, these prerequisites are frequently not fulfilled in plant maintenance: there are either no exact specifications for the standard times or you have a large number of unplanned orders.

In most production departments, inexact standard times are not normally a problem since similar production orders always recur. In plant maintenance, however, this mainly applies only to the areas of preventive maintenance and inspection. All other tasks more or less occur only once, and the estimates concerning the required time are correspondingly inexact.

Exact standard times?

This prerequisite also does not present a problem in the majority of production departments, with the exception of rush orders. In plant maintenance, however, we encounter the problem of emergency maintenance and short-term repairs, and we cannot plan in advance when and how often they will occur. Only the periods of the preventive maintenance, as well as the longer-term repairs, are known and can, thus, be planned.

Planned orders?

> **Capacity Requirements Planning for Plannable Volumes of More Than 60%** [+]
> If you have a planned order volume of less than 60% due to unplanned repairs and emergency maintenance and can only enter inexact details for the standard time, simply deactivate the capacity requirements planning. You can ensure this by using a control key for which the DETERMINE CAPACITY REQUIREMENTS function is not activated.

However, if you have exact standard times, the proportion of planned orders is high, and you think capacity requirements planning could help you, this always consists of three levels (see Figure 5.47):

Levels of capacity requirements planning

1. **Capacity requirement**
   The capacity requirement ❶ specifies the capacity required for individual orders at any given time. Capacity requirements are determined during the lead time scheduling and scheduled at the work centers.

2. **Capacity leveling**
Now, compare these requirements with the available capacity and then carry out a capacity leveling ❷—that is, a leveling of overloads and underloads—by taking corresponding tasks, such as shifting the date of an order.

3. **Available capacity**
Available capacity ❸ has already been described in detail in Section 3.2.

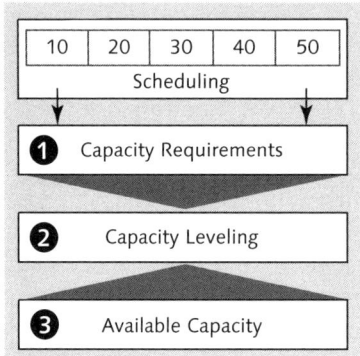

Figure 5.47 Capacity Requirements Planning

Prerequisites for capacity requirements

Capacity requirements are created based on orders—more specifically, specifications in the operations in the WORK field. To ensure that capacity requirements are created, you must fulfill the following prerequisites:

- Enter a formula for calculating the capacity requirements of internal processing in the work center. This formula must point to the ARBEI field—that is, the work from the operation. By default, this is the SAP008 formula.

- Use a control key, for which the CAPACITY REQUIREMENTS DETERMINATION function is active, for the operations.

- Schedule the order (see the section on Scheduling within Section 4.2.2).

Capacity overviews

You can use capacity overviews (for example, Transaction CM01) to view a comparison of available capacity and capacity requirements, either in table format or, as shown in Figure 5.48, as a graph.

Planned Repairs Business Process | **5.2**

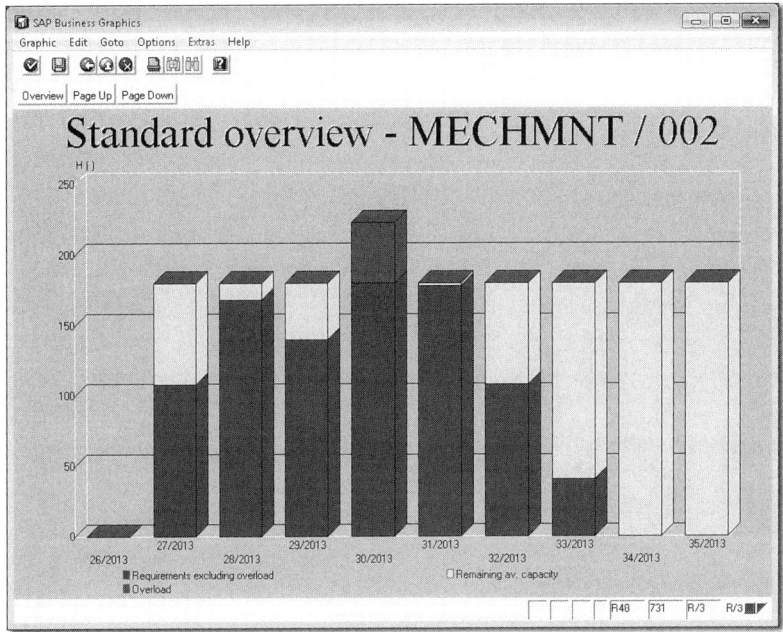

Figure 5.48 Capacity Overview

You can obtain the following information, in particular, from the capacity overviews:

- Current available capacity
- Amounts of capacity loads
- Overload situation
- Available capacity

When it is clear from the capacity overview that the available capacity is not sufficient, you must take capacity leveling measures (see Figure 5.49), as follows:

Capacity leveling

- You increase (temporarily or permanently) the available capacity by scheduling additional shifts, workdays, or manual workers.
- You can reschedule individual orders at other work centers if these still have remaining available capacities.
- You can move the date of individual orders forward or backward.
- You assign individual orders to external companies.

211

5 | Business Processes

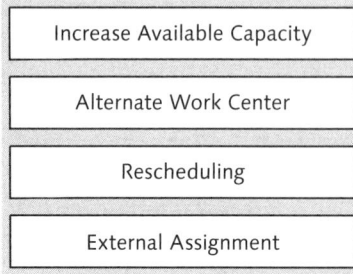

Figure 5.49 Capacity Leveling Options

[+] **First Choice: Postpone Orders**

The most common and, thus, least complicated procedure used to level capacity overloads or underloads in plant maintenance involves postponing orders or bringing them forward.

General Availability Checks

Definition — An *availability check* means that you let the system check whether the resources you plan for the requirements date are available in sufficient quantities or numbers.

You can perform an availability check for materials, available capacities, and production resources/tools. You control this for each plant and order type using the Customizing function AVAILABILITY CHECK FOR MATERIALS, PRTS AND CAPACITIES.

Availability and release — You can use all three availability checks, as follows, to determine how the system should behave if the requested resource is not available in sufficient quantities or numbers:

- Release based on a user decision
- Automatic release despite insufficient availability
- No release

[+] **User Should Decide**

When performing an availability check, always let the user decide what should happen when a resource is not available.

Prerequisites for the performance of an availability check are an active availability check and the definition of an overall profile that controls how the capacity requirements planning is to be performed. The overall profile consists of several individual profiles, such as a control profile, time profile, and evaluation profile. You set up the profiles in Customizing using the detail functions under PRODUCTION • CAPACITY REQUIREMENTS PLANNING • CAPACITY LEVELING AND ENHANCED EVALUATION.

Availability of capacities

If you have not yet checked the capacity availability, the order is given the CANC status (capacity availability not checked); if the capacity check is unsuccessful, the system sets the status in the order to MSCP (capacity shortage).

Statuses

Where a check of production resources/tools is concerned, you can control whether only the status, or also the inventory, is checked. However, you can check the latter only if you list the production resources/tools as material master, but not for equipment or documents. However, I will not discuss these aspects in more detail here because this check is seldom used.

Availability of production resources/tools

If the check for the availability of production resources/tools is performed, but unsuccessful, the system sets the status of the order to MSPR (PRT availability shortage).

Statuses

Material Availability Check

There are basically three different types of availability checks: static, dynamic, and global availability checks.

During the static availability check, the system checks whether the relevant material is available in sufficient quantities at the plant on the current date (today). This type of check is not suitable for a modern material availability check.

Static availability check

A dynamic availability check checks whether the required material is sufficiently available in the plant for the requirements date (that is, when the order is being implemented). Figure 5.50 illustrates how the current warehouse stock (based on the current date and taking into account safety stocks) is likely to change until the requirements date due to stock movements (planned goods receipts, planned goods issues,

Dynamic availability check

planned stock transfers). The Available-to-Promise (ATP) quantity is determined for the requirements date. This type of availability check is used by EAM.

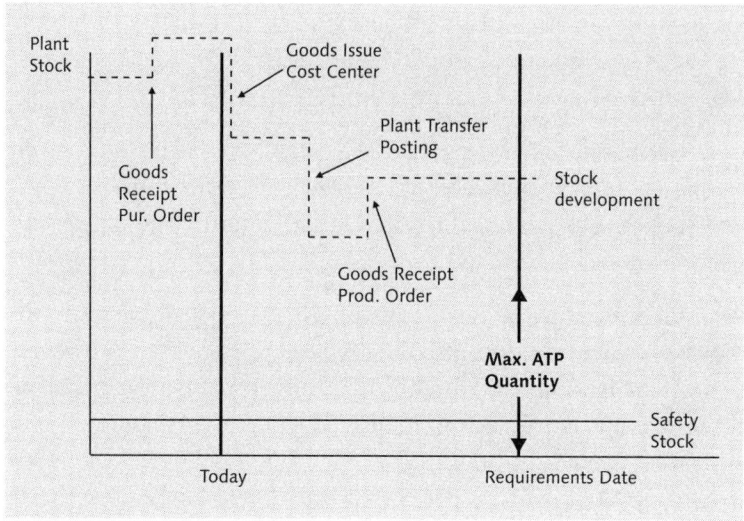

Figure 5.50 ATP Availability Check

Global availability check

A dynamic availability check is initially performed for a global availability check. If the result of this check is negative, you can use alternative strategies. You can check, for example, whether the material is available in another plant, spare material is available, or the required material can be delivered at short notice by potential vendors. This type of availability check is used in SAP SCM with the SAP APO component (SAP Advanced Planning & Optimization).

However, since we are dealing with SAP ERP here, the section below will discuss only the procedure used for the dynamic availability check.

Prerequisites

To be able to perform a material availability check, you must first fulfill the following prerequisites:

- First, you enter a checking group on the MRP 3 tab in the material master—for example, 02 (Individual requirements). From the perspective of plant maintenance, this checking group is simply a combination of several materials for a group that must be checked according to the same procedure, but does not have any effect for the time being. You maintain the checking group using the Customizing function DEFINE CHECKING GROUP.

- You then define a checking rule (for example, PM Plant Maintenance) using the Customizing function DEFINE CHECKING RULES. This checking rule also has no initial effect, but, rather, merely represents a grouping of procedures.
- You define the actual scope of the check from the combination of checking group and checking rule using the Customizing function DEFINE SCOPE OF CHECK. Here, you define, for example, which stock types and planned goods receipts and issues must be taken into account for the check.
- Finally, you define the actual checking control for each plant and order type using the Customizing function DEFINE CHECKING CONTROL.

When you have fulfilled all of these prerequisites, you can check whether the materials you planned are available for the requirements date. You can do this at different levels:

Execution

- You check the availability of an individual material within an individual order (Transaction IW32, [icon] button at the material level).
- You check the availability of all materials within an individual order (Transaction IW32, [icon] button at the header level).
- When you release the order (see the section on Releasing Orders), the system automatically triggers an availability check again. If all materials are available, the order is released. If all materials are not available, the system response is based on your setting for the MATERIAL RELEASE option in the Customizing function DEFINE CHECKING CONTROL: the order is either implemented or rejected, or you determine whether the order should be released.

You can now display the results of a material availability check as follows:

Result

- You can display the result for an individual order within Transaction IW32 by choosing ORDER • FUNCTIONS • AVAILABILITY • AVAILABILITY LIST.
- In Transaction IW38, you can display the result of several orders by choosing GOTO • LIST OF AVAILABLE MATERIAL (see Figure 5.51).

5 | Business Processes

Availability list for materials for operations											
Exce.	Order	Op	Erl. start	Latest start	Item	GR	Purchase o	Material	Material Description	Σ Reqmt Qty Σ	Withdrawal Qty Σ
○○●	820340		0010 07/10/2013	07/10/2013	0010	⊟	Not ordered	GS-1000	Planetary gear mounting	1	0
○○●	820340									1	0
●○○	820360		0010 06/29/2013	06/29/2013	0010			100-510	Ball bearing	2	0
●○○			0030 06/29/2013	06/29/2013	0010			100-100	Casings	1	0
●○○			0030 06/29/2013	06/29/2013	0020			100-600	Support base	2	0
●○○			0030 06/29/2013	06/29/2013	0030	⊟	Not ordered	WL-1000	Shafting assembly	1	0
●○○			0030 06/29/2013	06/29/2013	0040	⊟	Not ordered	GH-1000	Gearbox housing	1	0
●○○			0030 06/29/2013	06/29/2013	0050			MC-1000	Housing, pump motor elec. 250 kW	1	0
●○○	820360									8	0
●○○	820367		0010 06/29/2013	06/29/2013	0010			100-100	Casings	1	0
●○○			0010 06/29/2013	06/29/2013	0020			100-400	Electronic	1	0
●○○			0010 06/29/2013	06/29/2013	0030			DG-1000	Rubber Seal	1	0
●○○			0010 06/29/2013	06/29/2013	0040			100-600	Support base	2	0
●○○			0010 06/29/2013	06/29/2013	0050			100-431	Mains adaptor 100 - 240 V	4	0
●○○			0010 06/29/2013	06/29/2013	0060			KR117185	Distance plate	5	0
●○○			0010 06/29/2013	06/29/2013	0070	⊟	Not ordered	WL-1000	Shafting assembly	1	0
●○○			0010 06/29/2013	06/29/2013	0080			G-1000	Gears, electrical pump	4	0
●○○			0010 06/29/2013	06/29/2013	0090			M-3000	Motor, electrical pump 250kW	1	0
●○○	820367									20	0
●○○										29	0

Figure 5.51 Availability List for Materials

Statuses   If you have not yet performed the availability check, the order has a status of material availability not checked (MANC). If the availability check is performed with the result that the material is available, the system sets the status of material committed (MACM) in the order. If the availability check is performed with the result that the material is unavailable, the status is set to material shortage (MSPT).

Order Release

As long as the order still has the Created (CRTD) status, you cannot print shop papers, withdraw material, or confirm times. You cannot post a goods receipt for ordered spare parts, either. This changes when the order is released; you can then perform the following activities:

- The reservation is effective, and you can withdraw the material.
- You can print shop papers.
- You can confirm the order.
- You can move goods.

When you release an order, the system checks whether the required materials and production resources/tools are available and whether the required permits are granted. At the latest when the order is released, the material reservations are relevant for materials planning and can be withdrawn, and the purchase requisitions are created.

Also note that you can no longer change the cost estimation after the order is released.

You can use various options to release orders:

Execution

- releaseRelease an individual order (Transaction IW32, 🚩 button).
- Use the PUT IN PROCESS function (Transaction IW32, button); the order is released, and the shop papers are simultaneously printed.
- Simultaneously release several orders from list processing (Transaction IW38; select the orders and 🚩 button).

You can also release orders immediately when they are created. This option is available when the system creates orders automatically—that is, for orders generated using a maintenance plan (see Section 5.8) or that you create from a notification.

Automatic release

Releasing Orders Automatically [+]

To ensure that orders that result from maintenance plans or notifications are immediately released when they are created, use the Customizing function CONFIGURE ORDER TYPES to set the RELEASE IMMEDIATELY indicator for the required order types.

When the orders are released, the system sets the status in the order to REL.

Statuses

Shop Paper Printing

When notifications and orders are being used, the order is normally printed.

Freedom of Choice in Shop Paper Printing [+]

You have considerable freedom of choice with regard to the following content:

- The number of shop papers you print
- Which shop papers you print

- What you call the shop papers
- Which layout these shop papers should have
- Which shop paper should be output on which output media

Document types

You could print the following documents as shop papers, for example (see Figure 5.52):

- **Operation control ticket**
  An operation control ticket provides the maintenance engineer responsible with a complete overview of the maintenance order. You could also print the permit details here.

- **Job ticket**
  A job ticket, which accompanies the order, provides the manual worker performing the task with a complete overview of the order.

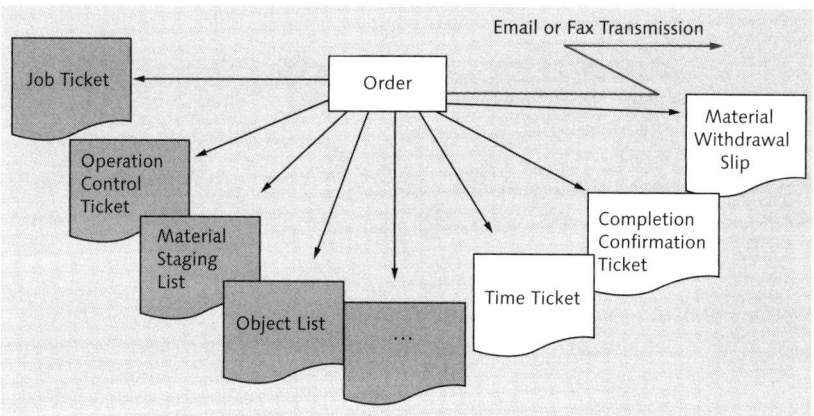

Figure 5.52 Order Documents

- **Material pick list**
  A Material pick list shows the warehouse clerk which materials for this order have been scheduled for each operation. This list, for example, could be printed directly in the warehouse.

- **Material issue slip**
  The material issue slip authorizes the manual worker to retrieve the materials required for the order from the warehouse. A material issue slip is printed for each material component.

Planned Repairs Business Process | **5.2**

- **Time tickets and completion confirmation tickets**
  Time tickets and completion confirmation tickets are printed out only for those operations for which this is specified by their control keys. The number of time/completion confirmation tickets specified there is printed out for each operation for each manual worker involved in processing an order. The manual worker enters the time he or she needs to perform the relevant operation.
- **Object list**
  An object list contains all functional locations, equipment, notifications, and so on, involved in the order if an object list is to be processed in the order (for an inspection round, for example).

Shop Paper Printing with Documents	[+]
Documents are frequently stored for the technical objects (refer to Section 4.2.9), which must be printed out completely or partially together with the shop papers. Unfortunately, SAP does not provide a standard solution for this. However, some manufacturers have started to develop and distribute a fee-based add-on for this purpose—for example, SEAL Systems (*http://www.sealsystems.com*) and the Prometheus Group (*http://www.prometheusgroup.us*).	

The following output media are available: Output media

- Local printers
- Network printer
- Fax machines
- Email
- PC downloads

Which prerequisites must you fulfill to be able to print shop papers?   Prerequisites

- First, use the Customizing function DEFINE SHOP PAPERS to define which shop papers should be used in general. You refer to an output program, form routine and form; these elements are where you define the layout and output control.
- In the Customizing function DEFINE SHOP PAPERS FOR ORDER TYPE, you then define which shop paper you want to be printed for which order type.

- In the Customizing function USER-SPECIFIC PRINT CONTROL, you finally define the printer on which the shop paper you choose should be printed for a particular user.

[+] **Recommendations for Printing**

Use the Customizing function USER-SPECIFIC PRINT CONTROL to activate the OUTPUT IMMEDIATELY option because otherwise, the shop papers will be set only in the spool file, and you will have to trigger the printing separately from there.

In the same Customizing function, you should also immediately print out the papers for the warehouse on the warehouse printer to ensure that the warehouse employees can schedule their pick tasks on time.

Printing procedure

You have the following options when printing documents:

- You can trigger the order printing for an individual order while processing the order by choosing the function ORDER • PRINT • ORDER or choosing the 🖨 button (see Figure 5.53)

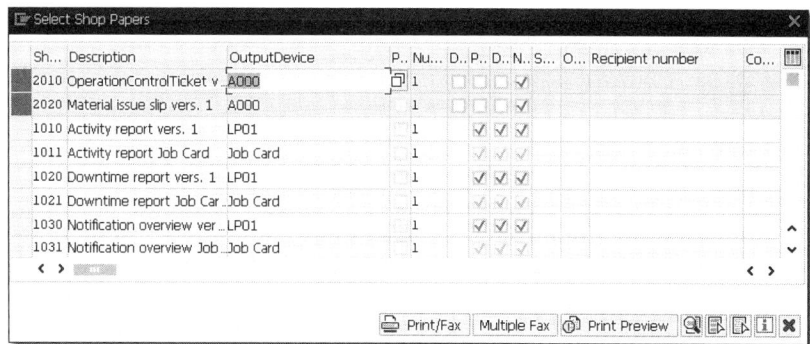

Figure 5.53 Dialog Box for Shop Paper Printing

- For authorization reasons, there is a separate Transaction IW3D for printing individual orders.
- You can use the order list (Transaction IW38) to print several orders simultaneously by selecting the relevant orders and choosing the function ORDER • PRINT ORDER.
- If you want to send shop papers by fax instead of printing them, enter a recipient number in the relevant column.

- If you want to print only the changes to the order since the last print operation, select the column D DELTA PRINT.
- If you want to send the shop papers by e-mail, refer to SAP Notes 317851 and 513352.

The system sets the status of the order to PRT for the print operation. | Statuses

Simplifying Print Operation	[+]
If you find the dialog box for printing the orders a nuisance because you always want to print the predefined shop papers anyway, you can prevent the appearance of this box as follows: within the order, choose EXTRAS • SETTINGS • DEFAULT VALUES to call the CONTROL tab, and then activate the PRINT WITHOUT DIALOG option.	

You have now completed all the preparatory work for implementing the order and can begin actually processing the order.

5.2.4 Processing

During the processing phase, you need to enter only the withdrawn materials in the system.

For you to be able to enter material issue slips in the system, the order must already be released. You can make a material issue slips as either a planned material issue slip or an unplanned material withdrawal. | Prerequisites

A planned material issue occurs when you have already performed material planning (see the section on Material Planning) and, therefore, created a reservation. | Planned material issue

The standard transaction for a material withdrawal is MIGO (see Figure 5.54); you enter a planned material withdrawal using the function GOODS ISSUE • ORDER.

However, since all required spare parts are rarely known before an order is started in plant maintenance, the option of an unplanned material issue is at least as important as a planned material issue. You also perform an unplanned material issue using Transaction MIGO, but via the menu path GOODS ISSUE • OTHER • MOVEMENT TYPE 261. | Unplanned material issue

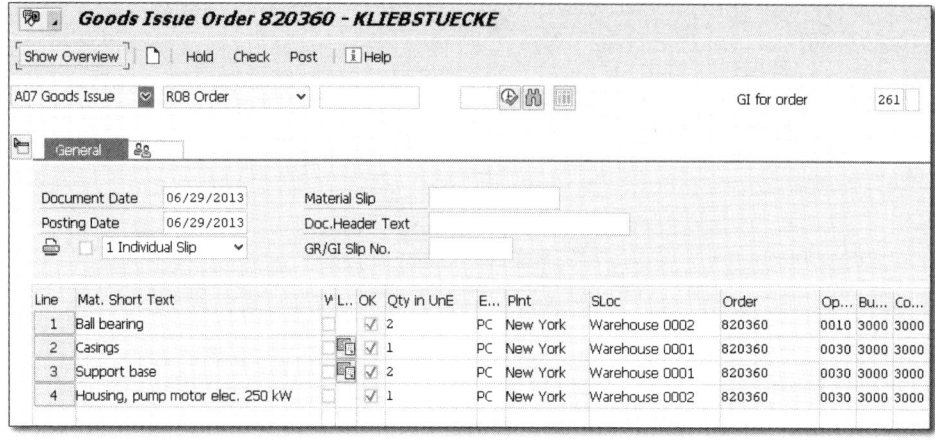

Figure 5.54 Goods Issue

For activity-assigned orders, enter the order number and operation number as a posting rule (see Figure 5.55), and only the order number for all other orders.

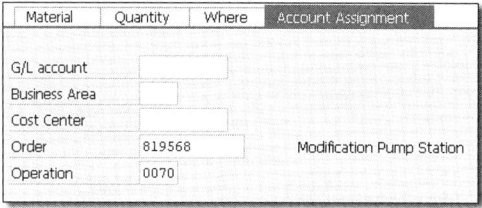

Figure 5.55 Material Withdrawal on Order and Operation

Documentation of goods movements

Both the planned and unplanned goods movements are documented in the order. You can display the list of goods movements by choosing EXTRAS • DOCUMENTS FOR ORDER • GOODS MOVEMENTS (see Figure 5.56).

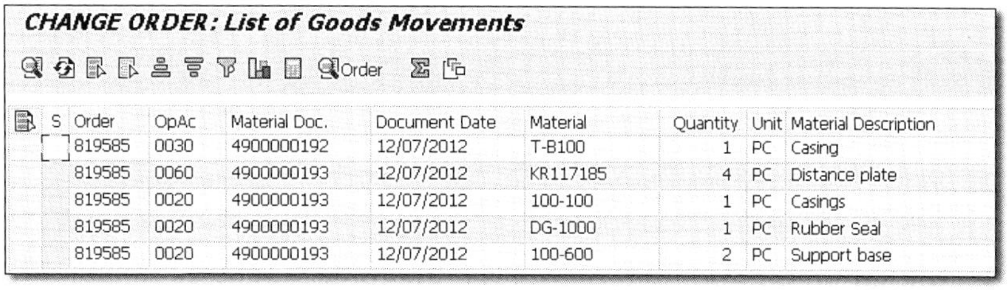

Figure 5.56 Goods Movements

After processing the order, you must enter the accumulated data in EAM.

5.2.5 Completion

Now, enter the times that were required for processing the order and then store the technical information, such as the causes of damage, or activities. After you enter this information, settle the order, which must still be technically and commercially completed.

Confirmations

You basically perform time confirmations at the operation level in EAM.

> **Simplifying Confirmation** [+]
>
> If you find it too laborious or time-consuming to confirm each operation individually, create a final *completion confirmation* operation in the order. You assign a control key only to this operation via the function CONFIRMATION PROVIDED; you assign a control key to all others that contain either the function CONFIRMATION NOT POSSIBLE or the function CONFIRMATION POSSIBLE, BUT NOT NECESSARY.

To ensure that you can enter time confirmations, you must fulfill two prerequisites: *Prerequisites*

- Release the orders to be confirmed.
- In Customizing, use the function DEFINE CONTROL PARAMETERS FOR CONFIRMATIONS to define how to perform the time confirmations for each plant and order type. There, for example, you define whether default values should appear or whether deviations should be allowed.

> **Take Care with "Clear Open Reservs"** [!]
>
> Do not set the two indicators FINAL CONFIRMATION and CLEAR OPEN RESERVS. at the same time because, when you perform a final confirmation, the CLEAR OPEN RESERVS. option deletes the reservations that are not yet issued. The FINAL CONFIRMATION option automatically performs a final confirmation on the operation for a time confirmation that is greater than the planned time. If

you do not now enter the material withdrawal promptly, but you do enter the confirmation without delay, the open reservations are deleted, even though they are issued.

Different transactions are available for entering the actual times.

Individual time confirmation

You use the individual time confirmation (Transaction IW41; Figure 5.57) to enter exactly one completion confirmation for an operation. If you want to enter other completion confirmations for the same operation or a different operation of the same order, you start this transaction several times in succession.

From the individual time confirmation, you can skip to entering other data (for example, goods issue, or measurement documents).

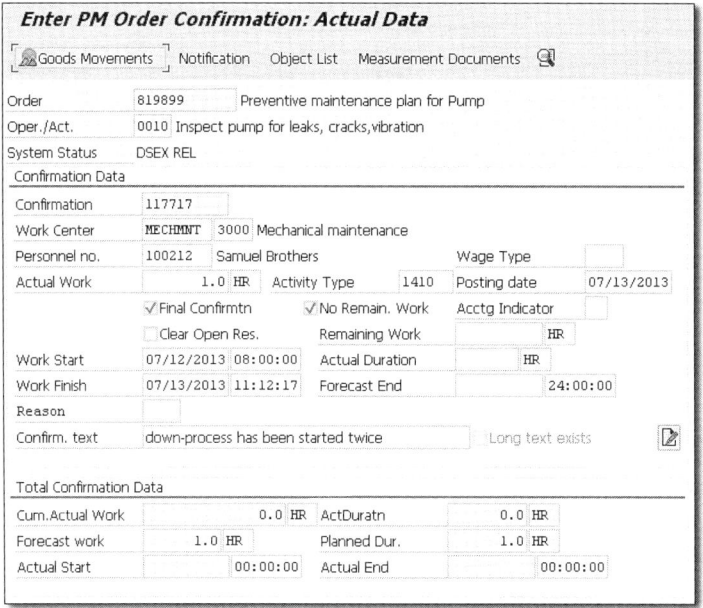

Figure 5.57 Single Entry

Collective time confirmation

You can use the collective time confirmation (see Figure 5.58) to confirm times for several operations and orders. The collective time confirmation is available with a preceding selection option (Transaction IW48) or without a preceding selection option (Transaction IW44).

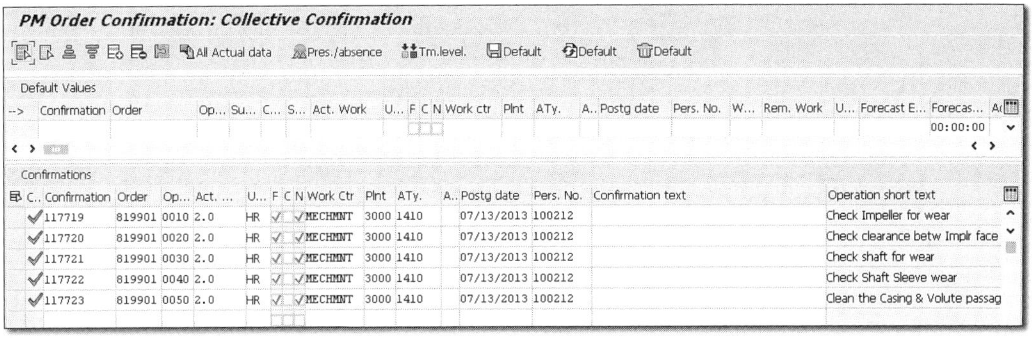

5.2 Planned Repairs Business Process

Figure 5.58 Collective Time Confirmation

Cross Application Time Sheet (CATS) is an application you can use to enter several person-related actual times. This application is available not only in Plant Maintenance, but also in other application areas, such as Human Resources or Production.

CATS

As a prerequisite for using this function, you must define data entry profiles, which you set via the Customizing function SET UP DATA ENTRY PROFILES. In the data entry profiles, you define whether the actual times recorded need to be released and permitted separately, for how many periods the times can be recorded simultaneously, or whether, as in our case (see Figure 5.59), totals rows should be displayed for each operation and day.

The CATS process consists of the following steps:

1. Time data recording in the data entry sheet (Transaction CAT2)
2. Release of time data (optional, Transaction CAT2, depends on the data entry profile)
3. Approval of time data (optional, Transaction CATS_APPR_LITE, depends on the data entry profile)
4. Transfer of CATS data to the target application and, therefore, in our case, to plant maintenance (Transaction CAT9)

You use overall completion confirmation (Transaction IW42) to enter not only times for several operations of an order, but also goods issue, counter readings, causes of damage, measurement readings, and notification items (see Figure 5.60).

Overall completion confirmation

225

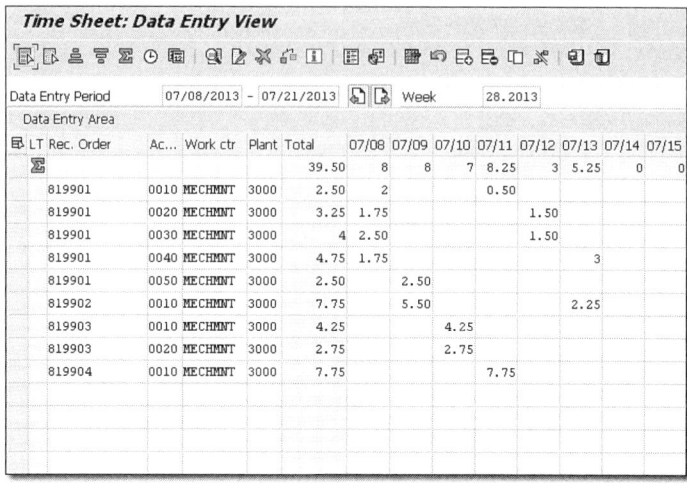

Figure 5.59 Cross-Application Time Sheet (CATS)

Figure 5.60 Overall Completion Confirmation

As a prerequisite for performing the overall completion confirmation, you must define data entry profiles using the Customizing Function SET SCREEN TEMPLATES FOR THE COMPLETION CONFIRMATION and assign a data entry profile (Transaction IW42, function EXTRAS • SETTINGS).

> **Advantage of Overall Completion Confirmation** [+]
>
> A particular advantage, compared to the other confirmation procedures, that has emerged in practice for the overall completion confirmation (Transaction IW42) is that, in addition to entering the actual data, you can also technically complete the order at the same time.

The recording of notification items and causes of damage was already the transition from the pure time confirmation to the technical completion confirmation.

Technical Completion Confirmations

You perform technical completion confirmations at the notification level and enter information such as the damage code, cause of damage, downtimes, actions, tasks, or system availability. *Definition*

Figure 5.61 displays an overview of the options you can use to record a technical completion confirmation. *Recording*

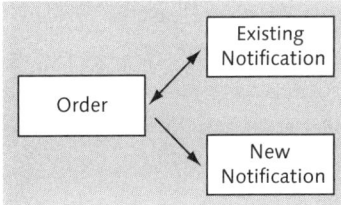

Figure 5.61 Technical Completion Confirmation

Specifically, this means the following:

- If the order already contains a notification—for example, because it emerged from this notification—you can go directly from the order (Transaction IW32, Notifctn button) to the notification and enter the information there.

- When you use the overall completion confirmation (Transaction IW42), you can use or define a corresponding data entry profile there to enter notification data there.
- You can also enter the information directly in the notification (Transaction IW22).
- If the order does not yet have a notification, you can create a new notification from the order, either at the header level using the `Notifctn` button or for each entry in the object list using the button.

Technical Completion

Consequences of technical completion

When you have processed the order, you technically complete it. This results in the following consequences:

- The status of the order is set to TECO (technically completed).
- Purchase requisitions that were not yet converted into purchase orders get the deletion indicator.
- You can still process purchase orders and enter goods receipts or invoice receipts.
- You can still enter time confirmations.
- Reservations that have not been issued are deleted.
- Open capacity loads are reduced, or capacities are released.

[+] **Completing Order and Notification Together**

You can also complete the notifications when you technically complete the order. If you do not do this, you will have to complete the notifications separately.

Procedure

There are several options you can use to technically complete orders:

- When you use the overall completion confirmation (Transaction IW42), you can technically complete the order and time confirmation at the same time from there using the `Tech.completion` button.
- Otherwise, you can technically complete an individual order (Transaction IW32) using the button.

Planned Repairs Business Process | 5.2

- You can also technically complete several orders simultaneously from the list processing (Transaction IW38) by selecting the orders and then choosing ORDER • COMPLETION • COMPLETE TECHNICALLY or by using the 🚩 button.

> **Simplifying Technical Completion** [+]
>
> If you find the dialog box for the technical completion a nuisance because you want to complete the order anyway without having to enter more data, you can suppress this as follows: within the order, choose EXTRAS • SETTINGS • DEFAULT VALUES to call the CONTROL tab, and then activate the NO DIALOG COMPL. option.

If you complete an order by mistake, you can also cancel the technical completion: within the order, call Transaction IW32 — the function ORDER • FUNCTIONS • COMPLETE • CANCEL TECHNICAL COMPLETION, in this case.

Canceling a technical completion

The order is, thus, set to the exact status it had before the technical completion:

- Deletion indicators in the purchase requisition are canceled.
- Capacity loads are increased again.
- Reservations become active again.
- The order has RELEASED status.

If you also complete notification(s) when you technically complete the order, these remain unaffected by the cancellation of the order completion. Although the notifications remain completed, you can set them separately to the IN PROCESS status again.

If the order is technically completed and all associated cost postings are entered in the order, you can also perform a business completion of the order.

Business Completion

As with the technical completion, business completion takes place when you set a status to CLSD ("closed"). When you perform the business completion, no further costs can be posted to the order.

Definition

Prerequisites The following prerequisites must be met so that a business completion of an order can occur:

- The order must be technically completed (TECO status).
- The order is settled and has the actual cost balance 0.
- The order no longer has an open purchase order.
- No further costs are otherwise expected to be posted to the order.

Procedure To perform the business completion, you have the following options:

- Complete an individual order within order processing (Transaction IW32) using the Complete (business) button
- Perform completions of several orders simultaneously from the list processing (Transaction IW38) by selecting the orders and choosing ORDER • COMPLETE • COMPLETE BUSINESS FUNCTION

Canceling a business completion If you inadvertently perform a business completion for an order or need to enter a subsequent debit (for example, an invoice), you can also cancel the business completion. Within the order, call Transaction IW32 — the function ORDER • FUNCTIONS • COMPLETE • CANCEL BUSINESS COMPLETION, in this case. You can, thus, post to the order again and enter the subsequent debit.

Document flow The document flow is an important tool that users like to use. The document flow shows you all documents that were created during notification and order processing (see Figure 5.62):

- Notifications
- Purchase requisitions
- Purchase orders
- Material withdrawals
- Confirmations
- Goods receipts
- Invoice receipts

You can call the document flow at any time via the button. You can also use the field selection to define which fields you would like to display for which documents.

Planned Repairs Business Process | 5.2

- To display a document in detail, select the document number and choose the `Display document` button.

- To be able to use this enhanced document flow, Enhancement Package 6 and the activation of the business function LOG_EAM_CI_6 are required.

Prerequisites

- If you do not fulfill these prerequisites, the simplified document flow is available, without invoice receipts or field selection.

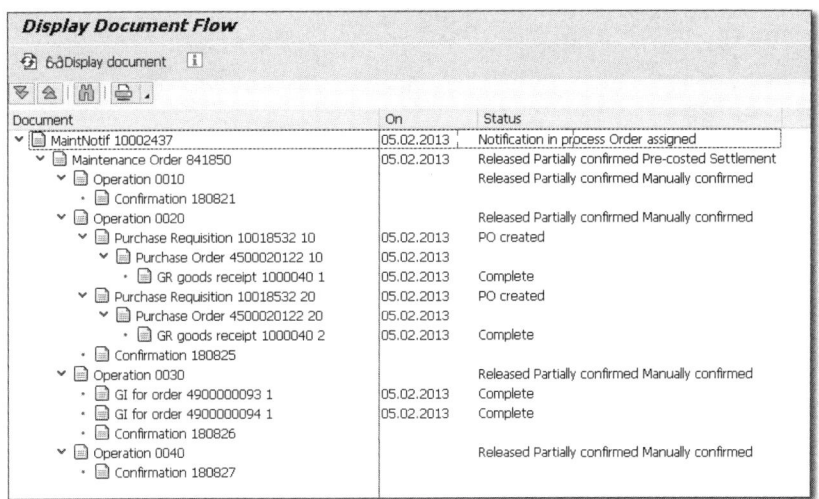

Figure 5.62 Document Flow

Another function that users really like to use is the action log. You can use the action log to display all changes (see Figure 5.63) that you have made to the following objects:

Action log

- Order header
- Statuses
- Operations
- Materials
- Production resources/tools

You define the objects for which you want to generate change documents using the Customizing function DEFINE CHANGE DOCUMENTS, COLLECTIVE PURCHASE REQUISITIONS MRP RELEVANCE. You call the action

231

log via the menu within the order (EXTRAS • DOCUMENTS FOR ORDER • ACTION LOG).

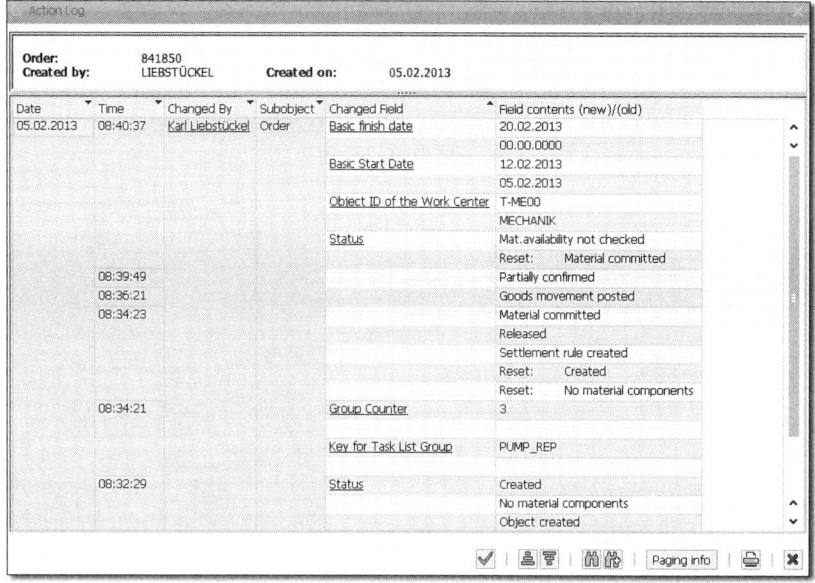

Figure 5.63 Action Log

Thus, I have explained the most important functions provided by the SAP system for the handling and processing of orders.

5.3 Immediate Repairs Business Process

Cannot be planned or predicted

The business process for an immediate repair is characterized by the facts that it is not known in advance, and the resources (work centers, materials, external companies, and so on) cannot be planned. You can and must react as quickly as possible to a business transaction, such as a malfunction, for example. An immediate repairs business process occurs, for example, in the following cases:

- A pump fails.
- A forklift breaks down in transit.
- An elevator in a building gets stuck.

- A closed valve cannot be opened.
- Measuring equipment, such as a scale, for example, displays nothing.
- A robotic arm no longer extends.

The process for an immediate repair differs from a planned repair in terms of the ability to plan for it—you can only react to malfunctions, but not plan them—and from preventive maintenance in terms of the prescribed schedule—maintenance and inspection tasks have regular cycles and, consequently, recurring deadlines.

Accruals/Deferrals

Figure 5.64 shows how the process for an immediate repair could proceed. The five-step cycle of a plannable maintenance process is summarized into a three-step cycle for an immediate repair.

Flow

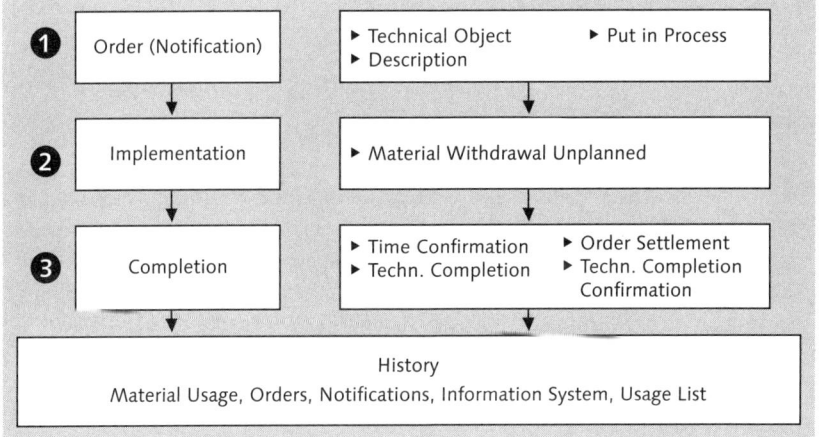

Figure 5.64 Immediate Repairs

1. **Order creation**
   The starting point in the first step is formed by the creation of an order ❶ (possibly with data about the notification) for damage or a malfunction. This order is not planned, but released immediately for processing, and shop papers that may be required are printed out.

2. **Processing**
   The processing phase ❷ involves the withdrawal of the spare parts from the warehouse and the actual processing of the order.

3. **Completion**

    After you complete the tasks, the required actual times are confirmed in the order completion in Step ❸; technical completion confirmations about how the damage was processed and the status of the technical system are also entered here. The order is finally settled by Controlling.

Creating Order (with Notification)

It is important that you set up the repair order and print out the required shop papers as quickly as possible for this business process to enable the technician to begin the repair work.

Simple order view

The structure with all the order data displayed in Figure 5.2 at the start of the chapter is reflected in the layout of a fully detailed order type, like the one shown in Figure 5.20. The order type consists of ten tabs with up to four screen elements on one tab. This is too much detail and too confusing for entering an order quickly.

[+] **Defining a Simple Order Layout**

One of the most important functions in terms of an immediate repair involves defining a separate screen layout for each order type—in this case, one that is as basic as possible, preferably with only one single tab containing a few input fields. You achieve this via the Customizing function SIMPLE ORDER VIEW.

There, you can use the Customizing function DEFINE VIEW PROFILES to arrange the tabs according to your own requirements and assign them to your order types via the Customizing function ASSIGN VIEW PROFILES TO ORDER TYPES.

Integrating notifications and orders

You can also create a notification at the same time as setting up an order, provided that you activate the integrated entry of order and notification data for an order type in Customizing. You do so via the Customizing function DEFINE NOTIFICATION AND ORDER INTEGRATION.

[!] **Entering Notification and Order Data in Only One Screen**

You can use the Customizing function DEFINE NOTIFICATION AND ORDER INTEGRATION to enable you to enter order and notification data on only one screen.

A suitable reduced layout for an immediate repair could, thus, look like the one displayed in Figure 5.65. The tab with the order header data simultaneously contains notification data and the option to assign spare parts.

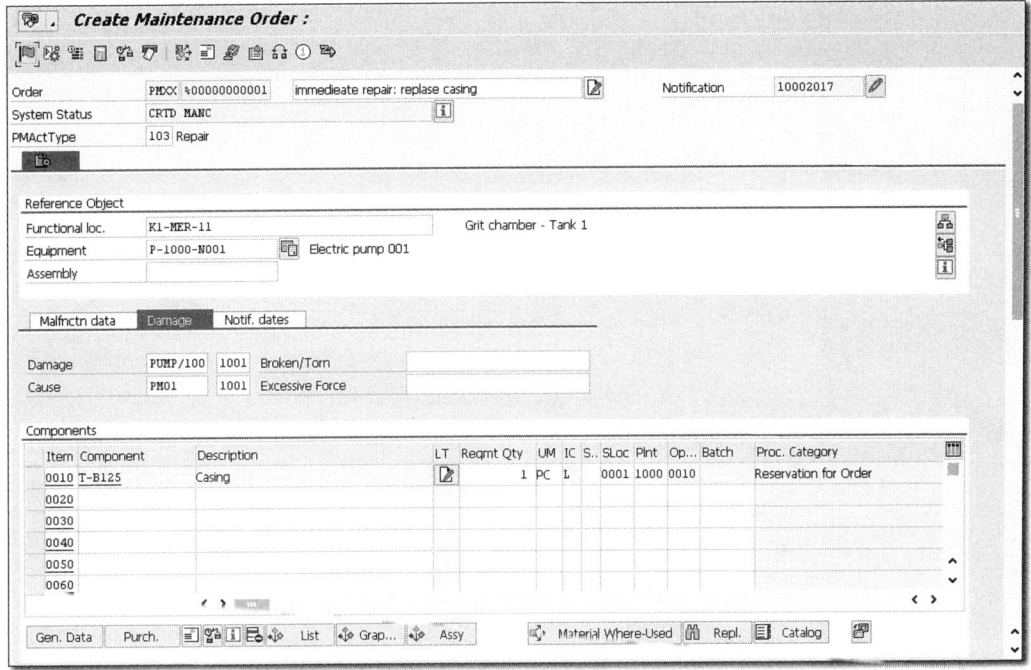

Figure 5.65 Order with Notification and Components

You complete entering the order using the PUT IN PROCESS function (button) because this means that you immediately Acceptance the order and generate the shop papers.

Completion

I recommend the overall completion confirmation (see Figure 5.66) for completing an order for an immediate repair because you can enter not only the actual times here, but also the unplanned material issues and technical data. You can also immediately complete the order and notification from there.

5 | Business Processes

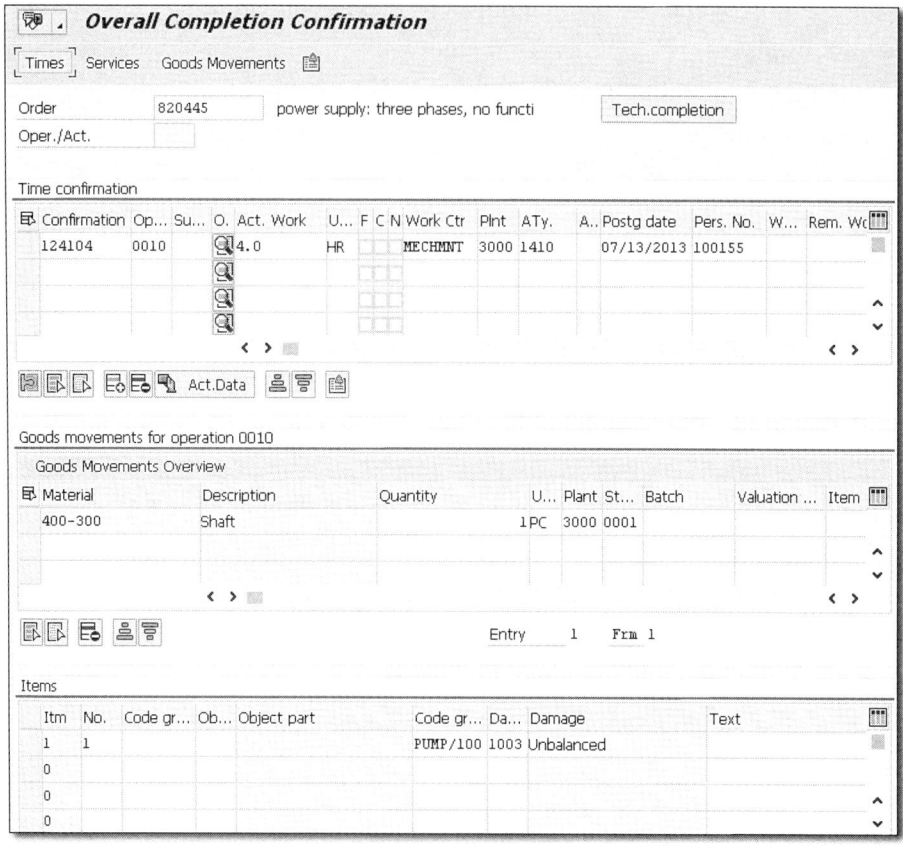

Figure 5.66 Overall Completion Confirmation

You must now also perform the functions for the order settlement and business completion.

This completes the business process for an immediate repair, and the information is entered into the SAP system in just two steps (order creation, completion), which does not require much time.

Special Case: "After-Event Recording"

Not planned, not foreseen, already performed

The *after-event recording* business process is a modification of the *immediate repair* business process. This is characterized by the fact that, at the time when you enter the order in the SAP system, the order processing has already taken place. You have this type of business process, for example, in the following cases:

- A pump was put into operation again.
- A broken-down forklift truck was repaired.
- The backup of control elements was replaced in a process plant.
- A jammed sliding door in a building was made accessible.
- An unscheduled adjustment had to be made to test equipment.

The difference between the after-event recording process and an immediate repair process is that the repair work was already completed when you entered the order, and thus, it is entered into the SAP system later on. Figure 5.67 shows the schematic diagram of after-event recording.

Work already completed

SAP provides a standard solution for the after-event recording process. However, this is not available within SAP ERP ECC, but only via the SAP NetWeaver Portal (for more detailed information, refer to Section 8.1.3) and via SAP NetWeaver Business Client (for more detailed information, refer to Section 8.6.3).

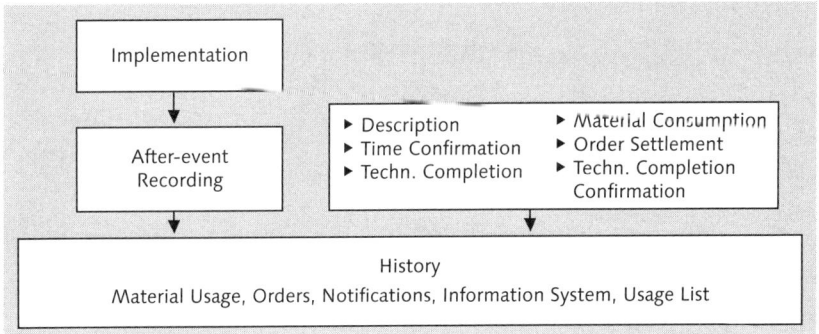

Figure 5.67 After-Event Recording

There Is No Standard Transaction for After-Event Recording [+]

What do you do if you require after-event recording but are not yet using SAP NetWeaver Portal and SAP NetWeaver Business Client?

- Option 1: You enter the data as described in Section 5.3 for an immediate repair, only you do this in immediate succession; that is, you enter the order in Transaction IW31 and then immediately confirm it in Transaction IW42 (including the technical completion).

- Option 2: You enter the data using Transaction IW61 (historical order). However, this transaction does not have any integration with the other SAP components. Thus, if you want to allocate the actual times entered there to the asset cost center, you have to write a batch program in advance that would carry out this transfer posting.

5.4 Shift Notes and Shift Reports

Definition You use shift notes and reports to document events that occur during a shift. In a shift note, you enter information about an event, such as comments, times, or objects.

A shift report is a PDF generated at the end of a shift by the person responsible for the shift. It comprises the shift notes that have been recorded and other documents, such as confirmations, material issues, counter readings, and so on. A digital signature can be used to sign a shift report, if necessary.

Shift note Shift notes can, for example, contain the following information:

- General notes (for example, shift interruptions, power outages)
- Malfunction documentation (for example, turning machine breakdown from/to)
- Suggestions for improvement (for example, "Reduce machine speed by 10% because ...")
- Notes on employees (for example, "Mr. Huber finished one hour early because...")
- Notes on material usage (for example, "Casing should be clamped with a maximum pressure of 10 bar")
- Comments on use of tools (for example, "Hand brace 9700 is not suitable for material T-B400")

You create shift notes using the following transactions:

▶ Transaction ISHR1, if you want to start by creating a reference to a technical object (functional location, equipment)

▶ Transaction SHN1, if you want to start by creating a reference to a work center (see Figure 5.68)

Creating shift notes

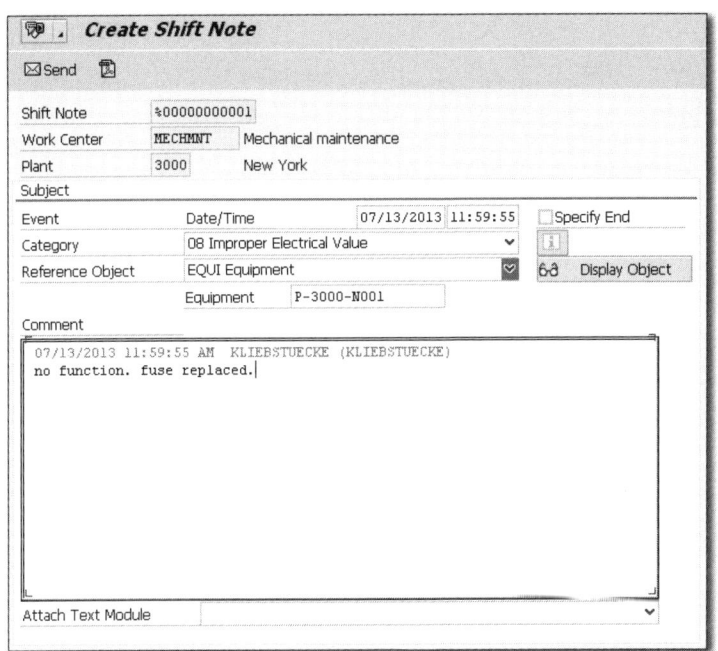

Figure 5.68 Shift Note for a Work Center

You enter information about the work center, the date and time (from/to), and text in a shift note.

You can also assign a CATEGORY to the shift note. The category indicates whether the shift note is a general note, malfunction notification, note on employees, or similar. You can define the categories in Customizing and select them using the F4 help.

Category

In Customizing, you can also specify the reference objects to which you want your shift notes to refer. The following reference objects can be selected:

Reference object

- Equipment
- Functional location
- Materials
- Production order
- Process order
- Maintenance notification
- Quality notification
- Other objects

Additional functions

Shift notes also offer the following functions:

- If you choose the [Send] button, you can send the shift note to a recipient by email.
- You can send alerts automatically; alerts are notifications such as SMS or email that are triggered when a particular event occurs. Thus, it can be specified, for example, that the production manager is to receive an SMS with a notification and the material number if a shift note of the material category is triggered.
- If you choose the [ ] button, you can output the shift note as a PDF.
- The [Display Object] button displays the shift note's reference object (for example, the production order or equipment).
- The [ ] object service allows you to attach documents to the shift note.
- If you want to display or change shift notes, you can select a full-text search and fuzzy mode in the [F4] help.
- You can display a list of shift notes in Transaction SHN4 or ISHN4.
- You can use Transaction SHN5 to display a shift note monitor with which you can monitor several work centers simultaneously (see Figure 5.69).

Prerequisites

To use shift notes as described above, you must ensure that certain prerequisites are met in relation to the Customizing settings for the work center and technical object (functional location, equipment).

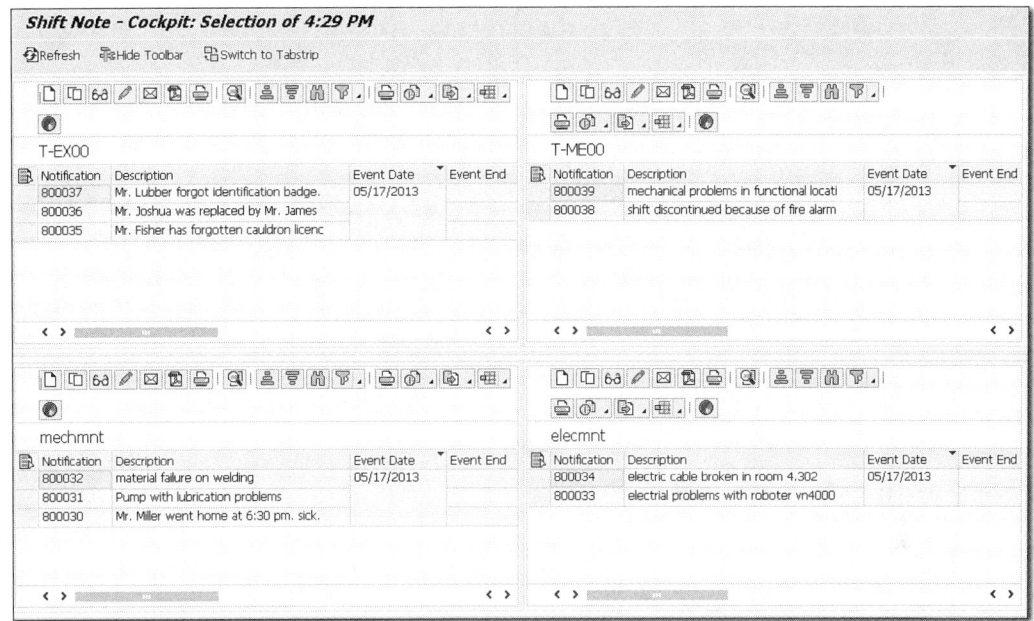

Figure 5.69 Shift Note Monitor

You must first perform the following steps in Customizing:

Customizing

- Create a new notification type (for example, SN). To this end, choose the Customizing function DEFINE NOTIFICATION TYPES.
- Assign a separate screen layout to the notification type using the Customizing function DEFINE SCREEN TEMPLATES. As a minimum, assign the value 130 SHIFT NOTE in the SCREEN AREA field.
- Make specific settings for the shift note notification type using the Customizing function MAKE SETTINGS FOR SHIFT NOTE TYPE. There, you can assign the category and reference objects, among other things.

In each work center and technical object (functional location, equipment) in the GENERAL DATA screen group, you must also enter the shift note type in the NOTE TYPE field and the shift report type in the REPORT TYPE field (see Figure 5.70).

Work center and technical object

Figure 5.70 Shift Note and Shift Report in Technical Object and in Work Center

[+] **Using Shift Notes**

Shift notes provide an easy option for documenting specific details for a technical object or work center.

Shift report
A shift report is a PDF generated at the end of a shift by the person responsible for the shift, which is intended to facilitate the handover to the next shift.

Contents
A shift report may include the following elements:

- Shift notes
- Production activities
- Confirmations
- Goods movements
- Maintenance notifications
- Quality notifications
- Maintenance orders
- Measurement documents
- Graphical analyses

Creating shift reports
You create shift reports using the following transactions:

- Transaction ISHR1, if you want to start by creating a reference to a technical object (functional location, equipment)
- Transaction SHR1, if you want to start by creating a reference to a work center (see Figure 5.71)

Displaying a Shift Report
A specific shift report is generated on the basis of the selection criteria entered and the layout settings you defined in Customizing (see Figure 5.72).

5.4 Shift Notes and Shift Reports

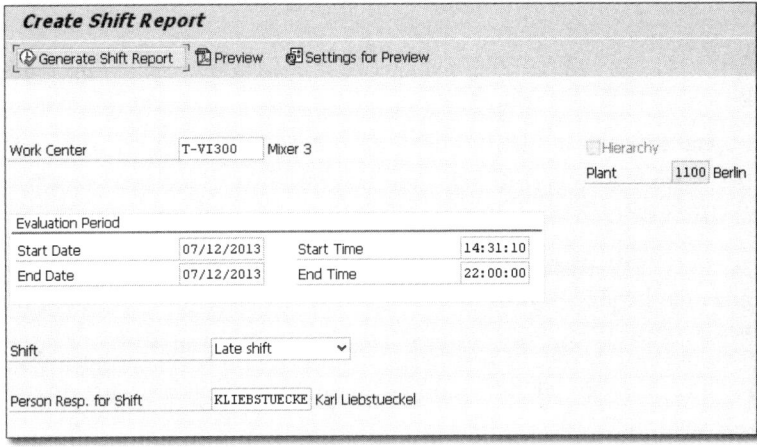

Figure 5.71 Creating a Shift Report

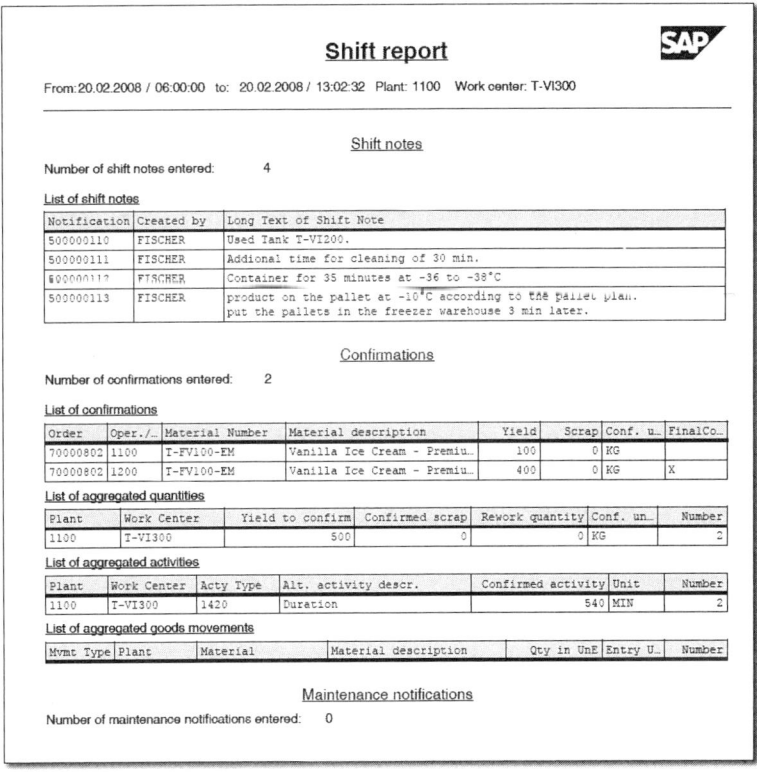

Figure 5.72 Displaying a Shift Report

Additional functions	Shift reports also offer the following functions:

- To use a digital signature, check the shift report and then sign it by clicking the [Sign] button.
- If you want to delete a shift report, click the [Discard] button. The shift report is then assigned the DISCARDED status. You can then create a new shift report for the relevant shift.
- You can use the [Send] button to send a shift report. The SAP system then sends the shift report as a link.
- To print a shift report, open it and click the 🖨 button in the PDF.
- You can create a list of shift reports that have already been generated in Transaction SHR4 or ISHR4.
- You can run a full-text search in a list of generated shift reports. |
| Prerequisites | To use shift notes as described above, you must ensure that certain prerequisites are met in relation to the Customizing settings for the work center and technical object (functional location, equipment). |
| Customizing | You must perform the following steps in Customizing:

- Create a shift report type (for example, SR) via the Customizing function DEFINE SHIFT REPORT TYPES. Here, you can specify, for example, whether the sequence of shift reports is to be continuous (with no gaps), you use a signature, or you send the shift reports by email. You also need to assign a layout to the shift report.
- The layout is defined by a form. SAP delivers the COCF_SR_PDF_LAYOUT form for shift reports as standard. If you require a separate form, you can define one in Transaction SFP.
- If you require an electronic signature, you can configure this using the Customizing functions DEFINE AUTHORIZATION GROUPS FOR SIGNATURE IN SHIFT REPORT, DEFINE INDIVIDUAL SIGNATURES, and DEFINE SIGNATURE STRATEGIES. |
| Technical objects and work center | In addition, you are required to enter the shift report type in each work center and technical object (functional location, equipment). |
| Business functions | The business functions LOG_PP_SRN_CONF and LOG_PP_SRN_02 must be activated in order for you to use shift notes and shift reports. |

> **Shift Reports Are Clear and Concise** [+]
> Shift reports provide a clear and concise overview of all events occurring during a shift. Their layout can be adapted flexibly to suit your needs.

5.5 External Processing

External processing means that external companies are used or orders are assigned externally for processing pending maintenance activities.

5.5.1 Basic Principles of External Processing Assignment

External processing is extremely important in plant maintenance—considerably more so than in production, for example. A non-representative short survey of SAP user companies that are organized in the German-speaking SAP user group showed that, on average, approximately half of their maintenance costs result from external processings. Thus, some companies have no maintenance workshops of their own, only coordination points (for example, work scheduling, planner) that are responsible for planning, monitoring, and accepting external services.

Reasons for External Processing

Why has there always been external processing in plant maintenance, and why is this trend increasing even further in the course of national and international division of labor and globalization? Many reasons can be given for this fact (see Figure 5.73).

- **Lack of qualifications**
  A company cannot employ separate technicians who are qualified for every type of work that arises in plant maintenance; instead, work is often awarded specifically to external companies that specialize in a particular field (for example, elevator service, air conditioning, electronic controls, robot maintenance, and so on).

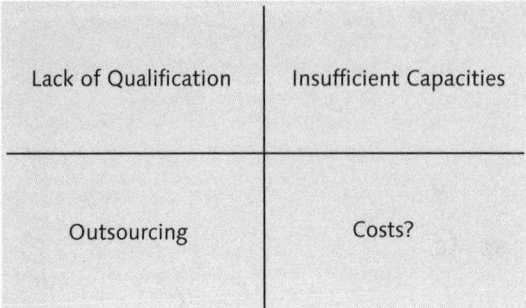

Figure 5.73 Reasons for External Processing of Maintenance Orders

- **Lack of capacity**
  External companies can support internal maintenance departments in covering peak capacity times (for example, for revisions, shutdowns, work required for the year-end, and so on).

- **Possibly lower costs by using external companies**
  The argument about whether external companies are really more economical than your own workshops is often only one-sided, when you compare an allocation record X of your own manual workers to a lower allocation record Y of the external company.

  For a cost comparison, you must not only use the primary costs (invoice amount) of the external processing, but also take into account the secondary costs associated with the external processing as internal administration and control effort (for example, order planning, purchase order, Acceptance of services performed, invoice verification, and so on). You must also consider that an internal award "only" concerns costs, whereas an external award involves expenditure and payment.

- **Outsourcing**
  During restructuring, departments are often outsourced, and independent companies are established. A department that is often affected by such outsourcing is plant maintenance, which is established as "Maintenance Inc." in such cases. Although the colleagues still sit across the hall from each other, they now work for a different company. Since a separate company code has to be set up in the SAP system for this company, this is an external processing in purely legal terms.

Initiating the External Processing

You initiate an external processing using the control key. You use different control keys (see Figure 5.74) depending on how you want the assignment and processing to occur.

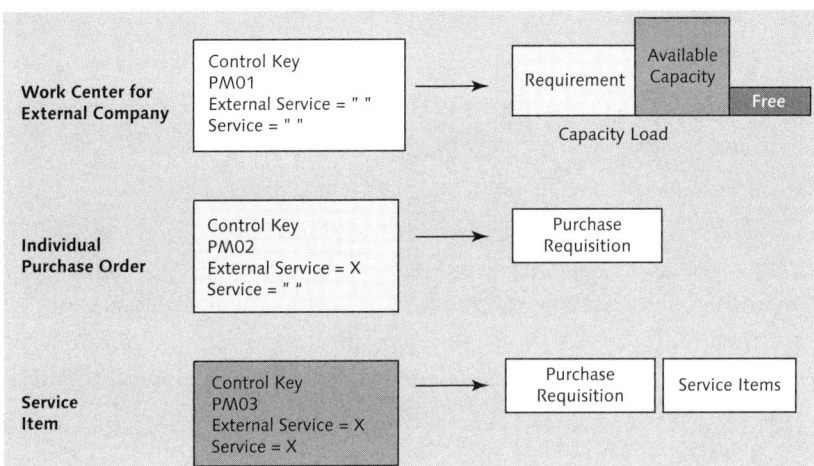

Figure 5.74 Control Key for External Processing

The specification of the control key in this case controls the type of external processing.

If you have set up a work center for the external company and want to execute the external processing using an internal order in the same way as for your own work centers (see Section 5.5.3), you can initiate this type of external processing using a CONTROL KEY (PM01, or similar), for which the EXTERNAL PROCESSING option is set to INTERNALLY PROCESSED OPERATION and the SERVICE option is not selected.

Work center for external company

If you want to execute the external processing using a purchase requisition and an individual standard purchase order (see Section 5.5.2), you can initiate this type of external processing using a control key (PM02, or similar), for which the EXTERNAL PROCESSING option is set to EXTERNALLY PROCESSED OPERATION and the SERVICE option is not selected.

Individual purchase order

If you want to execute the external processing using service items or service specifications and a subsequent service entry sheet (see Section 5.5.4), you initiate this type of external processing using a CONTROL KEY

Service specifications

(PM03, or similar), for which the EXTERNAL PROCESSING option is set to EXTERNALLY PROCESSED OPERATION and the SERVICE option is selected.

5.5.2 External Services as an Individual Purchase Order

If you want to assign external services as an individual purchase order, the procedure is something like the following (see Figure 5.75):

1. When you plan external services in an order, a purchase requisition is automatically triggered in the background.
2. The Purchasing department (or Maintenance planners) converts the purchase requisition into a purchase order.
3. After the external company has rendered the services, you enter them in the system. However, you do not confirm external services like normal time confirmations; instead, you enter a service confirmation as a goods receipt for the purchase order. If the goods receipt is valuated (option on the item in the purchase order), the actual costs are posted to the order at this point.
4. The invoice receipt concludes this process. If the invoice amount differs from the amount on the purchase order, a correction automatically takes place, and the order shows the net costs of the invoice.

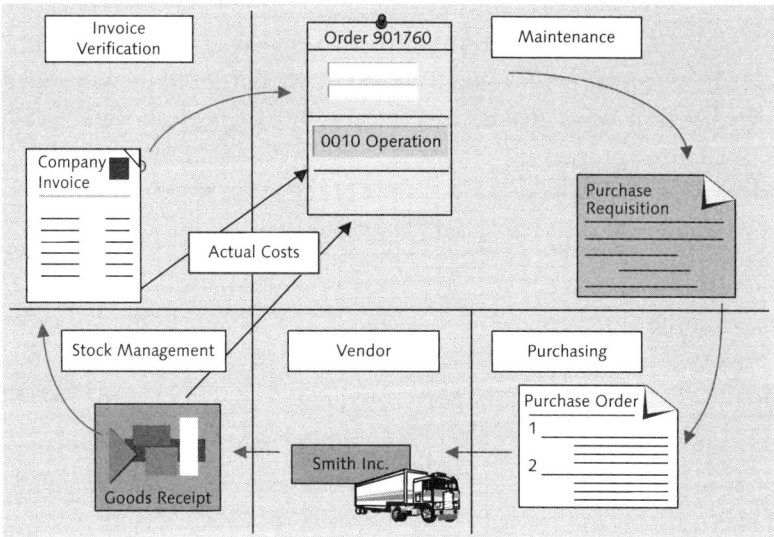

Figure 5.75 External Processing Process Flow

You plan the external service at the level of an order operation. You cannot assign an external company using notifications or order header data.

Setting up the order

> **Separate Order Type for External processing** [+]
>
> A separate order type is often set up for external processing. This has several advantages: you can specifically set default values—for example, whereby the PM02 control key (external processing) is always used for the PM02 order type (external processing). You can also search for and summarize data more selectively in lists and reports.

To process the external processing further, you need control and organizational information in the purchase requisition and purchase order (see Figure 5.76), such as the following:

- Material group
- Cost element
- Purchasing group
- Purchasing organization
- Ship-to-party
- Unloading point

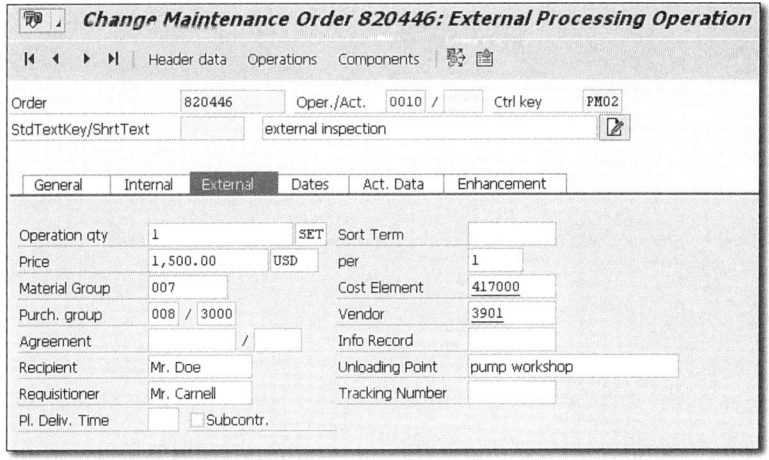

Figure 5.76 External Operation

5 | Business Processes

[+] **Default Values Simplify External Processing Assignment**

Since the information required by Purchasing remains as constant as possible, you should use the option to store default values to ensure that they do not always have to be entered again in each order.

- You can store the default values using the Customizing function CREATE DEFAULT VALUES FOR EXTERNAL PROCUREMENT in order to then assign them to the order type for each plant in the EXTERNAL PROFILE field using the Customizing function DEFAULT VALUES FOR MAINTENANCE TASK LIST DATA AND PROFILE ASSIGNMENTS.
- The same also applies for external material: the assignment here is made using the MATERIAL PROFILE field.
- However, you can also store the default values based on users by calling EXTRAS • SETTINGS • DEFAULT VALUES within an order and storing the data on the EXTERNAL PROCESSING tab (see Figure 5.77).
- The same applies for external material: you fill the EXTERNAL PROCUREMENT tab here.
- If both default values and user-based default values are stored in Customizing, the user-based default values have priority.

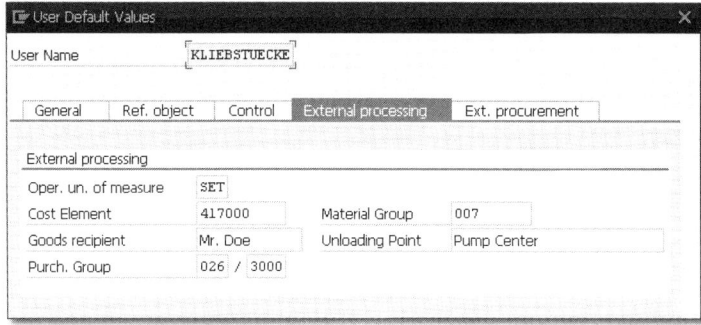

Figure 5.77 Default Values for External Processing

Purchase requisition and purchase order

A purchase requisition is automatically generated in the background on the basis of the external processing operation. You can display the number of the purchase requisition on the ACTUAL DATA tab and also go directly to the purchase requisition from there. The information from the order has been transferred identically to the purchase requisition (see Figure 5.78).

5.5 External Processing

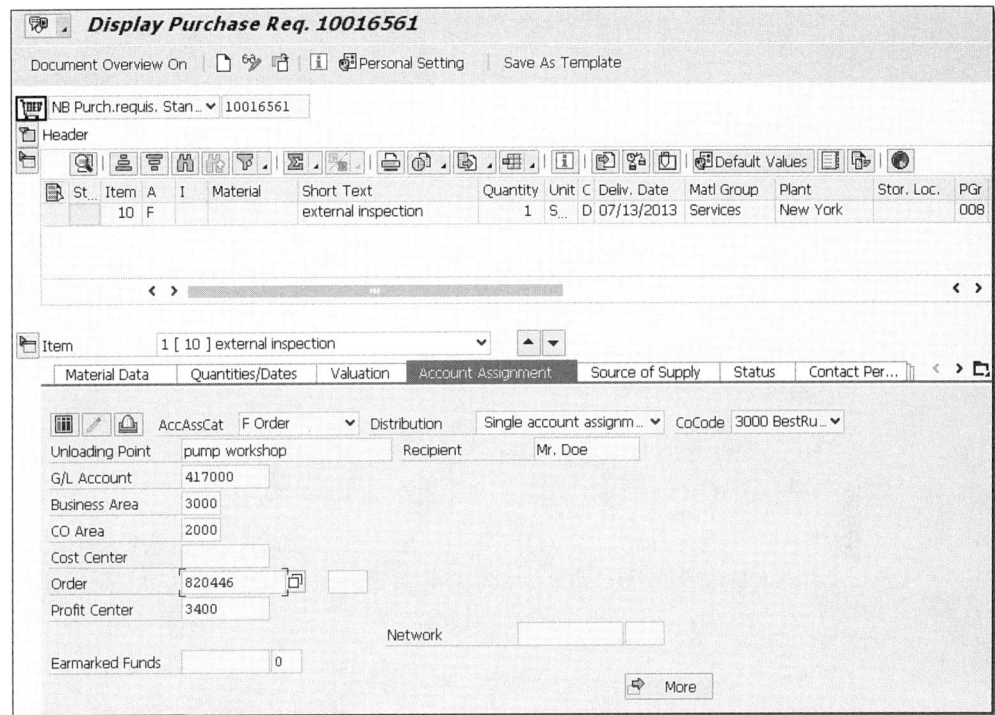

Figure 5.78 Purchase Order Requisition

Depending on the organizational responsibility, the purchase requisition is converted into a purchase order by either Purchasing or the Technical Department itself. When specifying an outline agreement number, you can also execute a call from an outline agreement in the same way.

The purchase requisition is automatically assigned to the order, and this assignment cannot be changed.

You do not confirm external services like internal services; instead, you enter a goods receipt (Transaction MIGO, GOODS RECEIPT FOR PURCHASE ORDER function). If you order a general performance unit of measurement, also known as a service unit (SU), as a unit, you can only confirm or not confirm the service. If you trigger the purchase order on an hourly basis, you can accept the effective hours; these can be more or fewer hours than ordered (see Figure 5.79).

Goods receipt and invoice receipt

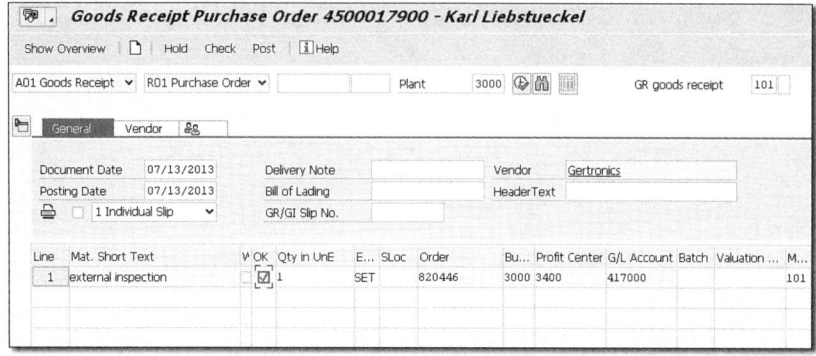

Figure 5.79 Goods Receipt

To ensure that the goods receipt can be entered, you must release the order, but not yet perform a business completion for it.

If you set the GOODS RECEIPT VALUATED indicator in the purchase order, the purchase order value is debited on the order at this point; the offsetting entry is made on a clearing account.

Figure 5.80 Invoice Receipt

When the invoice is received (see Figure 5.80; Transaction MIRO) the value is automatically cleared again on the clearing account. Any differences between the purchase order value and the invoice value are subsequently debited or credited.

5.5.3 External Services with External Work Centers

In many companies, there are service companies that you work with permanently (for smaller tasks, also)—external companies that provide staff and perhaps even have their own office on the premises, companies that then work "on call" and process many tasks in the course of a day, week, or month in this way.

Initial situation

Do you also work with such companies? If you were now to commission these companies according to the above model, you would have the following cycle for each individual task: order → purchase requisition → purchase order → goods receipt → invoice receipt. For you, this would signify a level of administrative effort that would no longer be justified.

So, what can you do to reduce the administrative effort? The following section will describe the model for external services with work centers, which is now being used in many companies and which may also help you to work with these external companies without a high level of administrative effort.

To be able to use this model, you fulfill the necessary prerequisites in advance. Figure 5.81 provides an overview in this case.

Prerequisites

- **Cost center**
  You require a cost center where the external services are cleared. You have three options in terms of the cost center: you use your own maintenance cost center, set up a new cost center (for all external companies in total), or set up several new cost centers—one for each external company.
- **Standard purchase order**
  You set up a standard purchase order. This is assigned to the above-mentioned cost center, has a runtime (month, quarter, year), and contains the hourly rate of the external company. You can also open purchase orders with several items—for example, if you have agreed to

different allocation records with the external company (for example, technicians, assistants, trainees).

- **Activity planning**
  In Transaction KP26, you perform activity type planning whereby you store prices for the periods, cost centers, and activity types.

- **Work center**
  You set up a work center for each external company. On the COSTING tab, you assign a cost center, the *internal processing* activity type, and the formula key for the internal processing (for example, SAP008) to this work center.

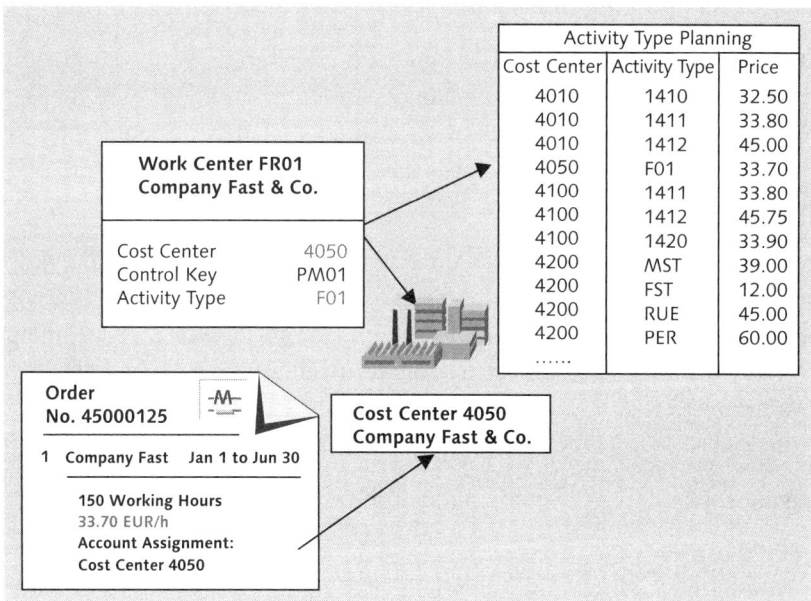

Figure 5.81 Prerequisites for an External Work Center

[+] **External Work Centers like Internal Work Centers**

The settings for this work center do not differ from your own work center settings. Therefore, if you enter a control key on the DEFAULT VALUES tab, for example, this is a control key for the internal processing (for example, PM01).

Processing

The processing of maintenance tasks that you perform with this work center barely differs from the processing described in Section 5.2 and Section 5.3 for processing with internal work centers.

- You set up your orders with the external work center as the performing work center. It does not matter whether you also enter it as the main work center.
- You print the shop papers.
- You confirm the orders using the same transactions that you also use for the internal orders (Transactions IW41, IW42, IW44, and IW48).
- You settle these orders exactly like the internal orders. This credits the cost center entered in the work center and debits the asset cost center.

Shop Papers for External Work Centers [+]

To be able to differentiate them on a purely visual basis, the shop papers for external companies should look different from internal shop papers. After the order is completed, you should sign the shop papers and give a copy of them to the external company.

Invoice receipt

Some special features arise in relation to invoicing (see Figure 5.82):

- You receive an invoice periodically (for example, monthly), rather than for each individual service.
- The invoice total contains the value of all services performed since the last invoice was issued.

Checking Invoicing [+]

Where invoicing is concerned, you should make sure that the list of executed orders is also specified on the invoice as additional information. You may also, perhaps, ask the external company to attach copies of the shop papers. Otherwise, you cannot verify the orders to which the issued invoice refers.

- Due to the account assignment of the purchase order, the invoice amount is debited to the external company cost center (not to the individual orders).

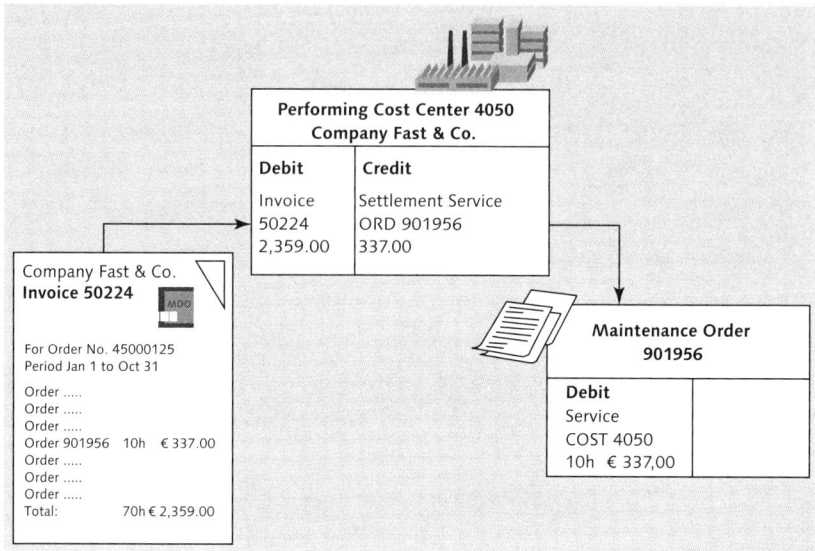

Figure 5.82 Invoice Receipt

- The external company cost center must clear in the medium term; in other words, the total credits via orders and the total debits via invoices must be equally high. If they are not, you can simultaneously use the cost center as a Controlling instrument that shows that the external company invoiced amounts for services other than those that were rendered.

The savings relating to the administrative cost, compared to the processing with individual purchase orders illustrated in Section 5.5.2, are obvious:

- There are no purchase requisitions.
- You have only one purchase order, rather than a number of purchase orders.
- You have a confirmation, rather than a goods receipt.
- There is only one invoice per period, rather than an invoice for each purchase order.

External Companies Reduce Administrative Effort   [+]

Compared to individual purchase orders, you can save a considerable portion of the administrative cost with external companies, with which you regularly work, by processing with external work centers.

5.5.4 External Services with Service Specifications

The *external services with service specifications* business process differs from the *external services with individual purchase order* business process in that the services to be rendered by the external company do not occur inclusively via a verbal description in the short and long text of the purchase order item, but rather, the services are specifically rendered individually using a services specification. The following differences result in the process (see Figure 5.83):

Special features

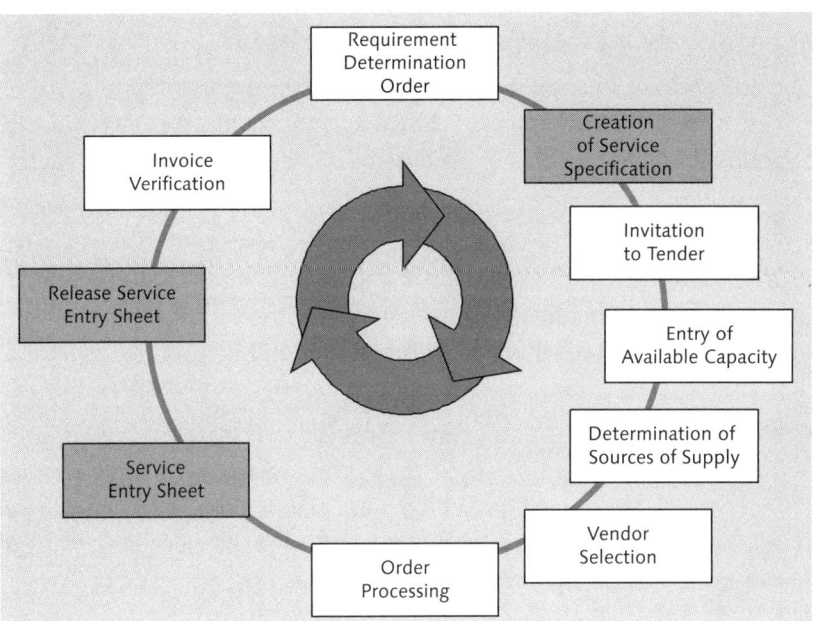

Figure 5.83 Process with Service Specifications

- You perform the planning in the order using a service specification.
- You can store limits for planned and unplanned services in the order planning.
- You enter a service entry sheet, rather than a goods receipt. This can also be carried out by the vendor.
- Unlike the goods receipt, the service entry sheet enables you to add unplanned items.
- You must release the services entered using an acceptance of services performed (dual-control principle) to ensure that an invoice can be issued.

Planning the services

You can use the following options to plan the services to be assigned externally within the order:

- You plan the services manually—that is, without using any default values.
- You plan the services using service master records. You use Transaction AC03 to maintain service master records.
- You plan the services using service specifications from other documents (such as an outline agreement, purchase order, order, and so on).
- You plan the services using model service specifications (see Figure 5.84). You can store service lines and an outline in a model service specification. You can also specify a purchasing organization, vendor, and contract as default values. You maintain model service specifications via Transactions ML10-12.
- You can define prices and conditions of service master records either inclusively (Transaction ML45), for vendors without a plant (Transaction ML39), or for vendors with a plant (Transaction ML33). Defined prices and conditions are included as default values in the order service specification and can be changed there.

The general data of the external operation is no different from that of an external service as an individual purchase order.

External Processing | **5.5**

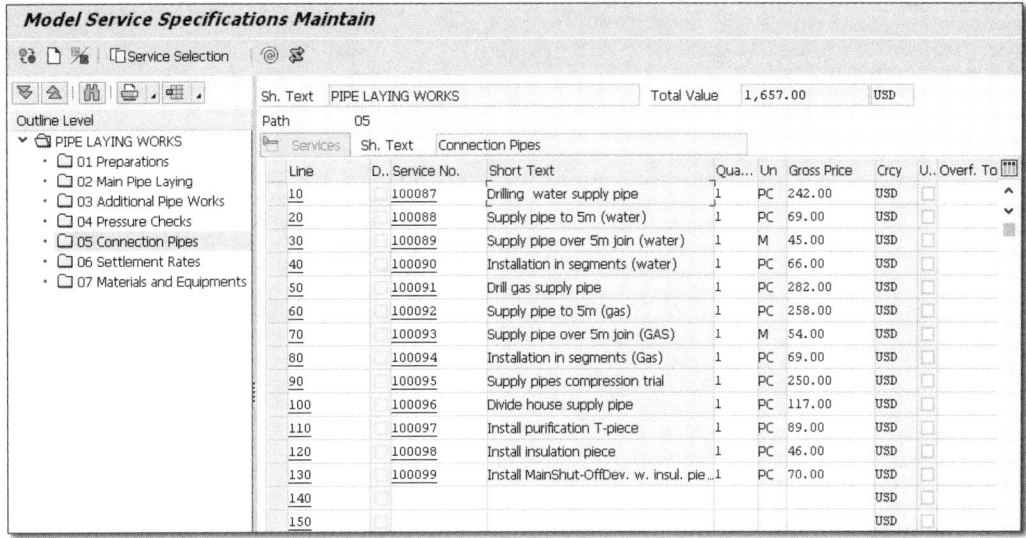

Figure 5.84 Model Service Specification

In addition, you can enter the following specific data for External Services Management if you navigate via the [icon] button from the original display to the full screen (see Figure 5.85):

- You can enter service lines with or without a service number, price, cost element, quantity, and so on.
- You can enter limits. The overall limit represents the upper limit for unplanned additional services. Thus, the expected value must be less than or equal to the overall limit and is entered in the standard costing and in the purchase order commitment.

> **Found Location for Service Specifications** [+]
>
> There are professional providers of service specifications, such as Beuth Verlag (http://www.beuth.de) or the German Joint Committee for Electronics in Construction (http://www.gaeb.de), from which you can acquire pre-fabricated standard and model service specifications in digital format, which you can then import into your system using SAP tools.

The values of the individual services are shown as the total for the complete service specification.

5 | Business Processes

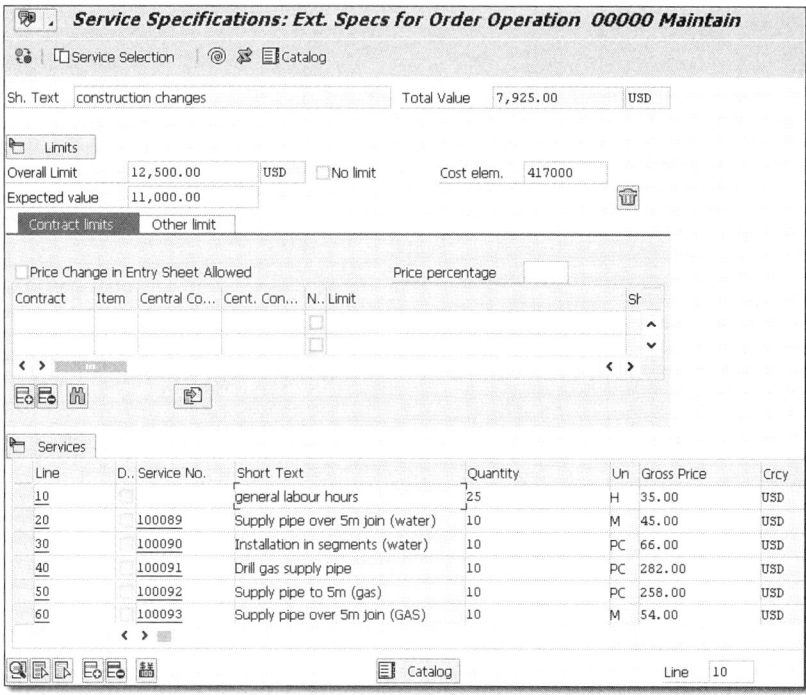

Figure 5.85 Order Service Specification

Purchase requisition and purchase order

A purchase requisition is automatically generated in the background on the basis of the external processing operation. You can display the number of the purchase requisition on the ACTUAL DATA tab and go directly to the purchase requisition from there. The service specification of the order is transferred identically to the purchase requisition.

Depending on the organizational responsibility, Purchasing or the technical department itself converts the purchase requisition into a purchase order; the purchase order adopts the service specification from the purchase requisition in this case. The purchase order is then transferred to the service company.

Entry and Acceptance of services performed

If you have ordered external services on the basis of a service specification, you do not enter the rendering of the services with a goods receipt, but rather with an entry of services performed, using service entry sheets (see Figure 5.86). You use either Transaction ML81N or Internet Application Component MEW10 for this.

5.5 External Processing

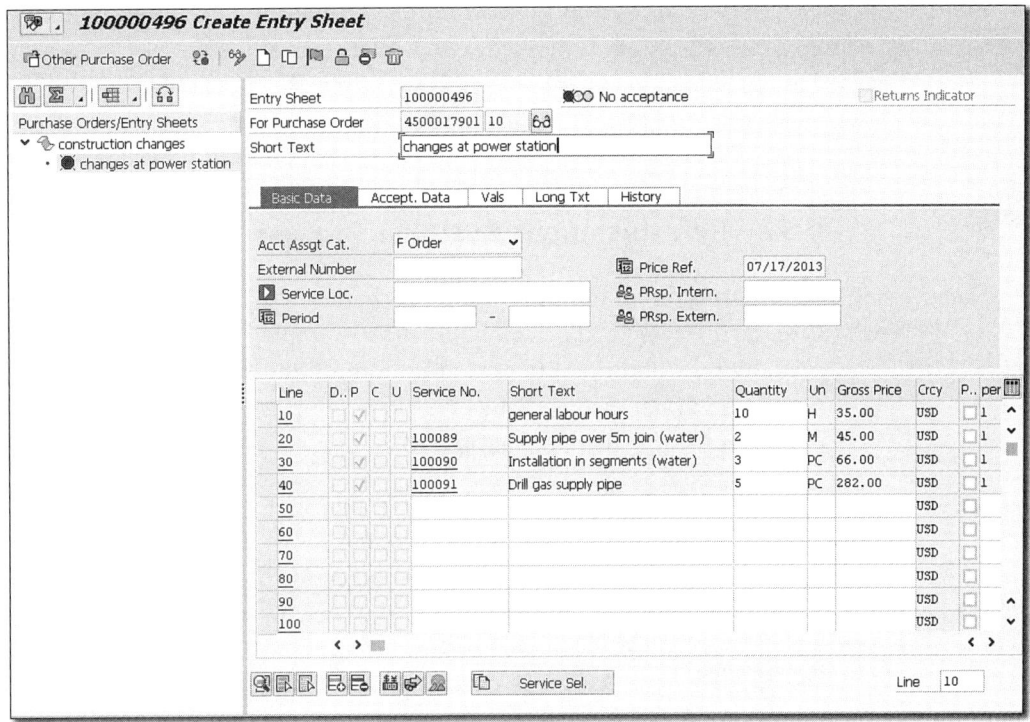

Figure 5.86 Entry of Services Performed

We differentiate between the entry of services performed and the release of services performed in the SAP system. These two functions can (if the authorizations exist) be performed by the same person. However, you could also distribute responsibility to several people using the dual-control principle.

> **Entry by External Persons, Release by Internal Persons** [+]
>
> In practice, the service entry is often performed on the Internet by the service provider (for example, using an Internet Application Component (IAC); see Section 6.4.3), and the service is released by the people responsible in your own company.[1]

---

[1] In this case, for example, see Anschütz, O.; Junior, J.: Die Fremdleistungsbeschaffung beim Großkraftwerk (*External Service Procurement at a Large Power Station*), Mannheim, Frankfurt: DSAG-Arbeitskreis 2003. (DSAG working group).

Invoice receipt The released service entry sheet represents the basis for the invoice verification. The order is debited with actual costs at the time of release. A goods receipt document is generated when the service entry sheet is release.

5.6 Refurbishment Business Process

Refurbishment: definition The refurbishment business process is characterized by spare parts being held as reserves in the warehouse (for example, for ensuring system availability). There are different statuses for the spare parts (for example, new, operational, faulty). Faulty parts are refurbished by your own staff or external staff—that is, relegated to an operational status.

You must manage the spare parts with different accounting values in the warehouse: when you refurbish a spare part, it has a higher value than it would have in a faulty status. The spare parts are managed either only as material or as individual units (i.e., material serial number).

[+] **Multiple Prices for the Same Material**

With the refurbishment process, you can ensure that the refurbished material or individual unit subsequently has a higher value than it had before.

Flow You process the management of spare parts with the processing of refurbishment orders, as follows (see Figure 5.87):

1. **Procurement of spare parts**
   You store spare parts for certain critical and high-value components that are used in a technical system, to be able to replace the components immediately if a breakdown occurs ❶.

2. **Withdrawal of functional spare parts and return of faulty spare parts**
   If a material (single unit) managed as a spare part in a technical system is faulty, you replace it with a functional spare part ❷. To do this, you remove the faulty spare part from the technical system and return it to the warehouse, whereas you withdraw a functional spare part from the warehouse and install it in the technical system.

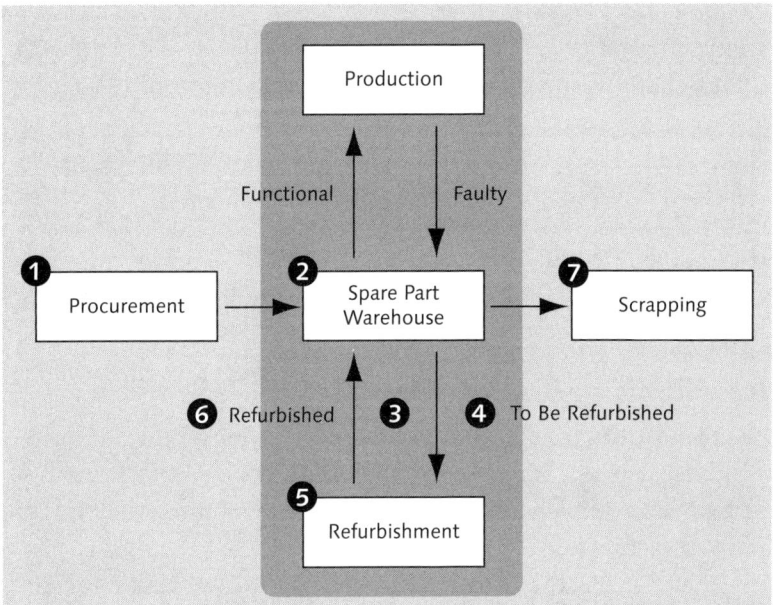

Figure 5.87 Refurbishment Process Flow

3. **Creation and release of a refurbishment order**
   As soon as the number of faulty repairable parts has reached a certain amount in the warehouse, you create a refurbishment order ❸. You schedule all required operations, materials, tools, and so on, for the refurbishment. All the options described in Section 5.2 are available for this purpose.

4. **Withdrawal from the warehouse**
   The employees responsible for the refurbishment withdraw the faulty spare parts from the warehouse, including all other materials scheduled in the order that they need for the refurbishment ❹.

5. **Performance of refurbishment**
   You perform the refurbishment. You can post confirmations for internal services, goods receipts, or service entries for external material or external services ❺.

6. **Return to warehouse**
   You return the refurbished spare parts to the warehouse per goods receipt ❻. For spare parts that are not to be refurbished, you cancel the reservation and post a scrapping.

7. **Scrapping**
   If faulty spare parts can no longer be refurbished, you scrap them ❼. Do not forget to also post a goods issue for this situation.

> [+] **Notification of Refurbishment**
>
> In order to document in full the history of a technical object, it is recommended that you enter a notification for a faulty spare part, which serves as a request for refurbishment.

Prerequisites To enable you to initiate and process the business process for refurbishing spare parts, you must first fulfill the following prerequisites.

Order type You need your own order type. In Customizing, you set this up for the refurbishment process using INDICATE ORDER TYPES FOR REFURBISHMENT PROCESSING. You implement this setting at the client level; thus, it applies to all plants.

> [+] **Separate Notification Type**
>
> If you want to request refurbishment services using a notification, it is advisable, for various reasons (such as selection or screen control), to define a separate notification type.

> [+] **Separate Order Type**
>
> You need a separate order type for the refurbishment business process. However, you cannot use an order type that you selected for the refurbishment for "normal" maintenance processes. You can define your own notification type, but you are not required to do so.

Split valuation For the spare parts, you need a material master that has a split valuation. You create the basis for a split valuation in Customizing using the function CONFIGURE SPLIT VALUATION by defining a valuation category C (status) and several valuation types C1 (as new), C2 (refurbished), and C3 (to be refurbished) there.

> **Two to Three Valuation Types** [+]
>
> You should use two or three valuation types for the refurbishment; fewer valuation types would not make any sense, and more valuation types would no longer be manageable.

You can perform the refurbishment process at either the material level or the serial number level (that is, equipment). If you want a separation with serial numbers, the material master must have a serial number profile that enables you to store and remove equipment in the warehouse (for more information, refer to Section 4.2.2).

Serial numbers

Spare Part

To be able to use the material master of the spare part for the refurbishment, you define the valuation category (for example, C for condition) in the accounting data at the plant level and then create several valuation types for the valuation category (see Figure 5.88).

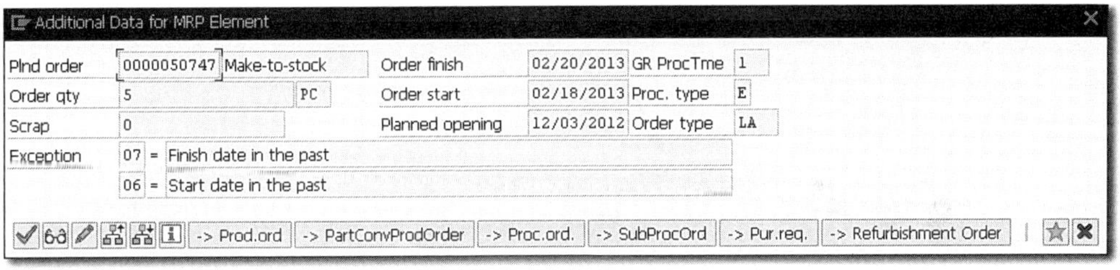

Additional Data for MRP Element						
Plnd order	0000050747 Make-to-stock		Order finish	02/20/2013	GR ProcTme	1
Order qty	5	PC	Order start	02/18/2013	Proc. type	E
Scrap	0		Planned opening	12/03/2012	Order type	LA
Exception	07 = Finish date in the past					
	06 = Start date in the past					

✓ 6∂ ✎ ⛿ ⛿ i -> Prod.ord   -> PartConvProdOrder   -> Proc.ord.   -> SubProcOrd   -> Pur.req.   -> Refurbishment Order

Figure 5.88 Valuation Category and Valuation Type

Figure 5.89 shows the accounting data of a material master for which the valuation category C was set in the ACCOUNTING view, and a price was defined for the valuation type C3.

Figure 5.90 shows a notification, which can be used to request a refurbishment. The notification has its own notification type (here, M4) and, as an object type, has been assigned a material number, serial number, and equipment number.

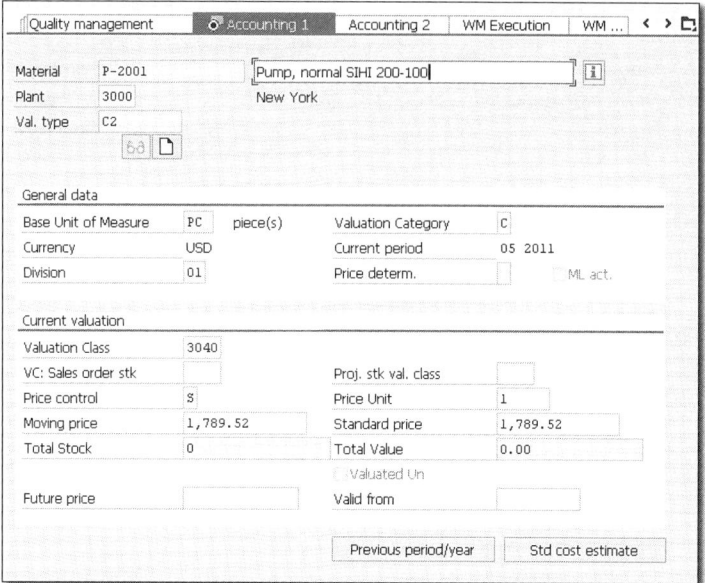

Figure 5.89 Condition-Based Valuated Material Master

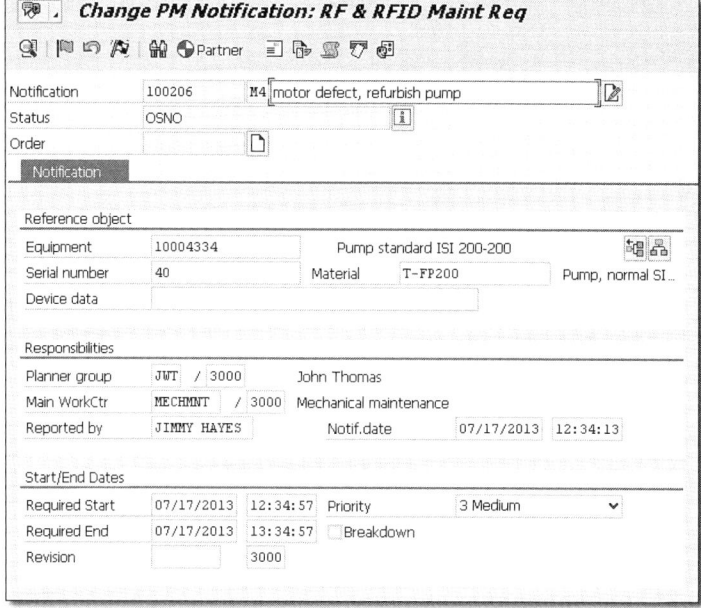

Figure 5.90 Request for Refurbishment Based on a Notification

You now have several options for ensuring the assignment of notifications and refurbishment orders:

Order from notification

- You generate a refurbishment order from a notification.
- You generate a refurbishment order and assign the relevant notification to it later.
- You can merge several notifications for a refurbishment using the object list.

The LOG_EAM_ROTSUB, LOG_EAM_ROTSUB_2, and LOG_MM_SERNO business functions must be activated, and DIMP 6.0 must be installed in order for you to be able to use a notification for a refurbishment order.

Business functions

You can now also generate refurbishment orders in material requirements planning, specifically, in the stock/requirements list (Transaction MD04).

Refurbishment orders based on material requirements planning

The business logic behind this function is that, whenever the quantity of functional parts drops below the reorder point but non-functional parts are in stock, material requirements planning should automatically generate planned orders. Previously, it was possible to convert planned orders only into purchase requisitions for purchasing, production orders in discrete manufacturing, or process orders in process manufacturing. Now, however, you can also convert the automatically generated planned orders into refurbishment orders to ensure that you always have the required quantity of functional parts.

In order to convert planned orders into refurbishment orders, you must first assign a Spare Part Class Code on the BASIC DATA 2 screen in the field of the same name in the material master and define it as either a repairable spare with a CMM (code 2) or as a repairable spare without a CMM (code 6) (see Figure 5.91).

Prerequisites

SPEC 2000: Class Code for Spare Parts and Extra Long Parts No.	
Spare Part Class Code and Overlength Part Number:	
Spare Part Class Code	2
Overlength Part Number	

Figure 5.91 Spare Part Class Code

When you choose the -> Refurbishment Order button (see Figure 5.92, you can enter additional details for the refurbishment order on the next screen displayed (see Figure 5.93).

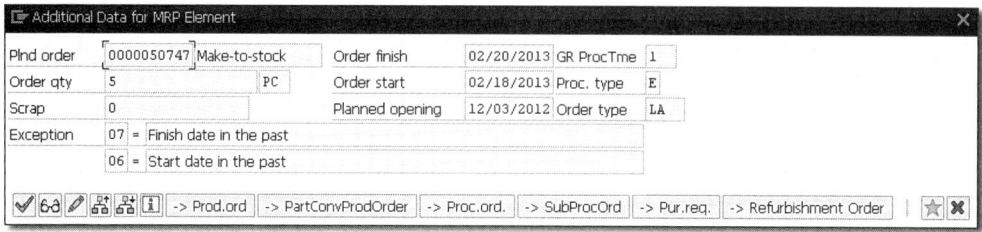

Figure 5.92 Stock/Requirements List

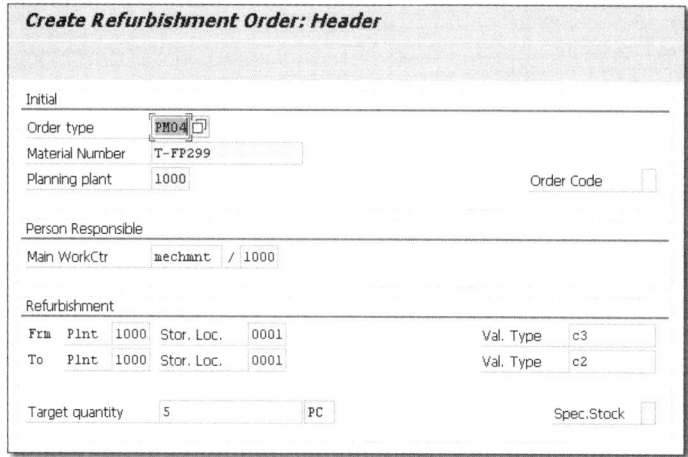

Figure 5.93 Refurbishment Order from MRP

[!] **Refurbishment Integrated in Material Requirements Planning**

Refurbishment has now been integrated into material requirements planning, which means that you can generate a refurbishment order from a planned order.

Business functions　The LOG_EAM_ROTSUB, LOG_EAM_ROTSUB_2, and LOG_MM_SERNO business functions must be activated, and DIMP 6.0 must be installed in order for you to convert a planned order into a refurbishment order.

The setup of a refurbishment order differs from the setup of a "standard" maintenance order in the following points (see Figure 5.94):

Manual setup of a refurbishment order

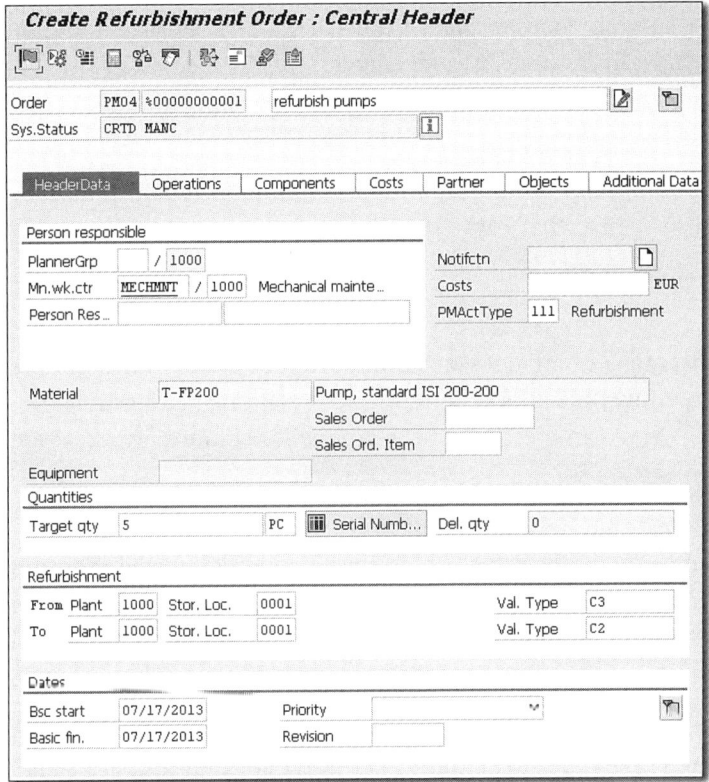

Figure 5.94 Refurbishment Order

- You use the specific Transaction IW81.
- You use a specific order type (for example, PM04).
- You always specify a *From* material number.
- You can also specify a *To* material number if a new material number should result from the refurbishment process.
- If you want personalized refurbishment processing, you add the objects of the serial numbers to the material number.
- You cannot specify a reference object—in other words, no functional location or equipment.

- The system generates a MAT settlement rule with the material number as the receiving object.
- You always specify an amount; this can be greater than 1.
- You always specify a *From* plant from which the material should be withdrawn, storage location, and valuation type.
- The SAP system automatically creates a reservation for the goods issue.
- You always specify a *To* plant to which the material should be returned, as well as the storage location and valuation type.
- The SAP system automatically creates a reservation for the goods receipt.

The refurbishment order does not differ from a normal maintenance order in other functions (operations, material planning, cost estimation, and so on). You can perform all planning operations as they are described in Section 5.2.

Goods issue When you create the refurbishment order, a reservation for the withdrawal of materials to be refurbished is automatically created. You can then book this out using Transaction MIGO (movement type 261) with reference to the order. Note that the withdrawal occurs from the special stock *valuation type* (here: C3) (see Figure 5.95).

If you have set up the refurbishment order for personalized processing, also specify the serial numbers to be withdrawn for thematerial issue.

Goods receipt When you create the refurbishment order, a reservation for the goods receipt of materials to be refurbished is automatically created. You can then book this in using standard Transaction MIGO (movement type 101) with reference to the order or with the special refurbishment Transaction IW8W, including any potential change of material. Note that the booking in is performed in the special stock *valuation type* (here: C2) (see Figure 5.96).

If you have set up the refurbishment order for personalized processing, also specify the serial numbers to be placed in storage for the goods receipt.

5.6 Refurbishment Business Process

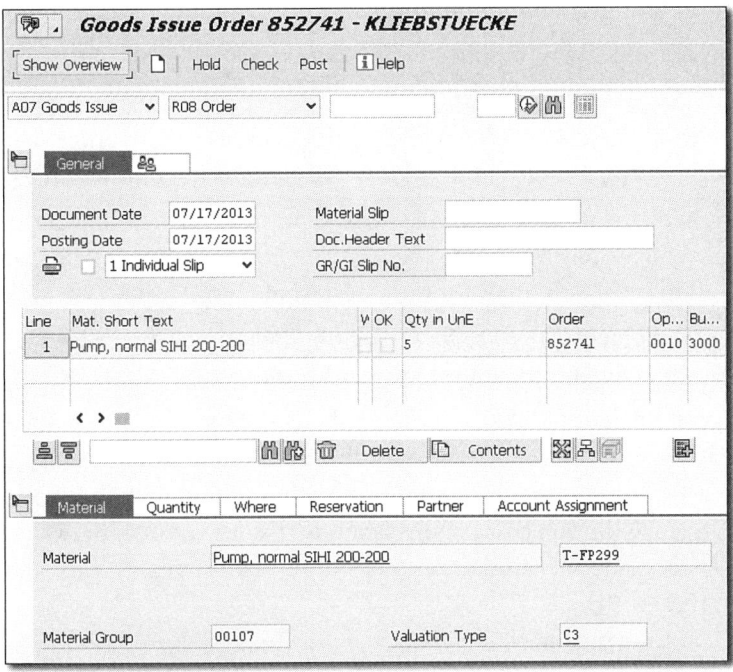

Figure 5.95 Material Withdrawal for Refurbishment

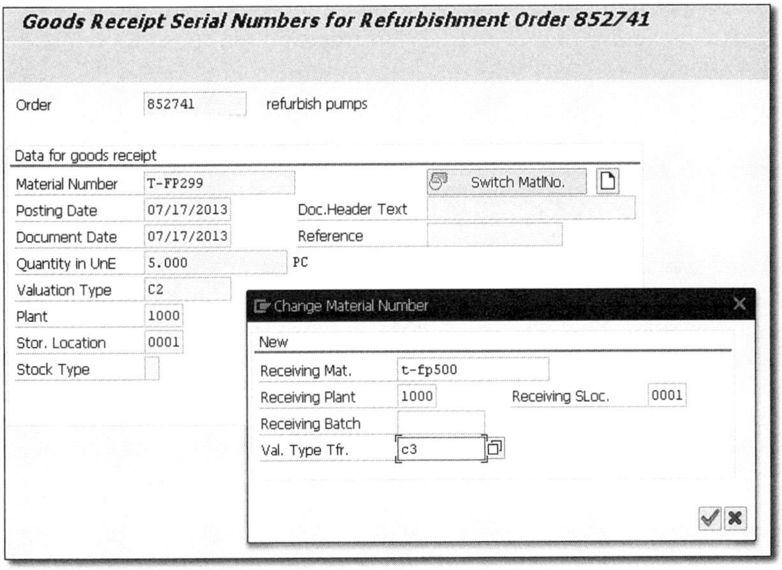

Figure 5.96 Goods Receipt of Refurbished Material

5 | Business Processes

Final costing

After you enter the goods issues, time confirmations, and goods receipts and after you settle the order, the cost situation of the refurbishment order is now represented as follows (see Figure 5.97):

- with cost element 404000 represents the debiting of the order that has occurred due to the goods issue of the parts to be refurbished ❸.
- with cost elements 400000 and 890000 represents the debiting of the order that has occurred due to the goods issue of other materials that were additionally required for the refurbishment ❹.
- with cost element 615000 represents the debiting of the order that has occurred due to the time confirmations ❺.
- with cost element 895000 represents the crediting of the order that occurred due to the goods receipt of the refurbished parts. The moving average price of the material was initially adjusted with the goods receipt. Since the value of a refurbished part is higher than the value of a faulty part, the moving average price also increases with the goods receipt ❷.
- with cost element 895000 represents the value of the order settlement. The values are normally settled on the stock assets, or to be more specific, on the material number, and thus change the moving average price of the material again. In our case, the refurbishment costs were lower than the value that was credited to the C2 valuation type by the goods receipt; thus, the moving average price decreases again ❶.

Cost Elem.	Cost Element (Text)		Σ Tot. plan costs	Σ Total act.costs	Σ	Plan/act. var.	Currency
895000	Factory Output of Production Orders ❶		0.00	7,118.20		7,118.20	USD
Settlement			0.00 ▪	7,118.20 ▪		7,118.20	USD
895000	Factory Output of Production Orders ❷		12,500.00-	12,500.00-		0.00	USD
Delivery			12,500.00- ▪	12,500.00- ▪		0.00	USD
404000	Consumables consumed	❸	2,500.00	2,500.00		0.00	USD
890000	Credit Stock change	❹	0.00	1,545.80		1,545.80	USD
615000	Dir.Int.Activity Alloc. Repair Hours	❺	1,043.75	1,336.00		292.25	USD
655110	Overhead Surcharge - Other Materials		604.38	0.00		604.38-	USD
Debit			4,148.13 ▪	5,381.80 ▪		1,233.67	USD
			8,351.87- ▪▪	0.00 ▪▪		8,351.87	USD

Figure 5.97 Costs of a Refurbishment Order

> **Prompt Settlement of the Refurbishment Order** [+]
>
> Settle the order as quickly as possible after the goods receipt you used to post the final delivery. If the refurbished material is already withdrawn from the warehouse before the settlement, the costs can be allocated only to an allocation cost center, not to the material.

5.7   Subcontracting Business Process

The *subcontracting* business process, also known as *subcontracting for MRO* (maintenance, repair, and overhaul) processes, describes the process used when having a piece of equipment (that is, a material serial number) repaired by a service provider. This means that here, in contrast to the processes used for external processing (see Section 5.5, External processing), the object to be repaired or maintained is sent to the service provider, processed, and then returned.

Definition

> **Subcontracting = Refurbishment + External Service** [+]
>
> Since the subcontracting operation may also be associated with refurbishment, this business process can be viewed as the link between the external service and refurbishment processes.

The subcontracting process flow comprises the following steps (see Figure 5.98):

Flow

① You have a faulty part that requires maintenance or repair and is to be processed by a service provider. You therefore create a maintenance order with a subcontracting operation.

② The SAP system then uses the maintenance order to generate a purchase requisition for the external repair or maintenance service, with a subcontracting item (item category L) and the material serial number.

③ You convert the purchase requisition into a purchase order for the external repair or maintenance service. The purchase order item is indicated as a subcontracting item (item category L) and assigned the part to be returned following repair (material serial number).

5 | Business Processes

❹ You send the part to be repaired to the subcontractor using an outbound delivery.

❺ The provided parts are managed as stock provided to vendors (subcontracting stock). The provision represents a transfer posting from unrestricted-use stock to stock provided to vendors (subcontracting stock).

❻ The subcontractor repairs, modifies, replaces, or exchanges the faulty part and returns the serviceable part.

❼ You create a goods receipt posting for the part delivered, which refers to the subcontracting item in the purchase order.

❽ A goods issue is posted from the subcontracting stock for the components.

❾ You receive an invoice for the service provided by the subcontractor.

❿ You complete the maintenance order.

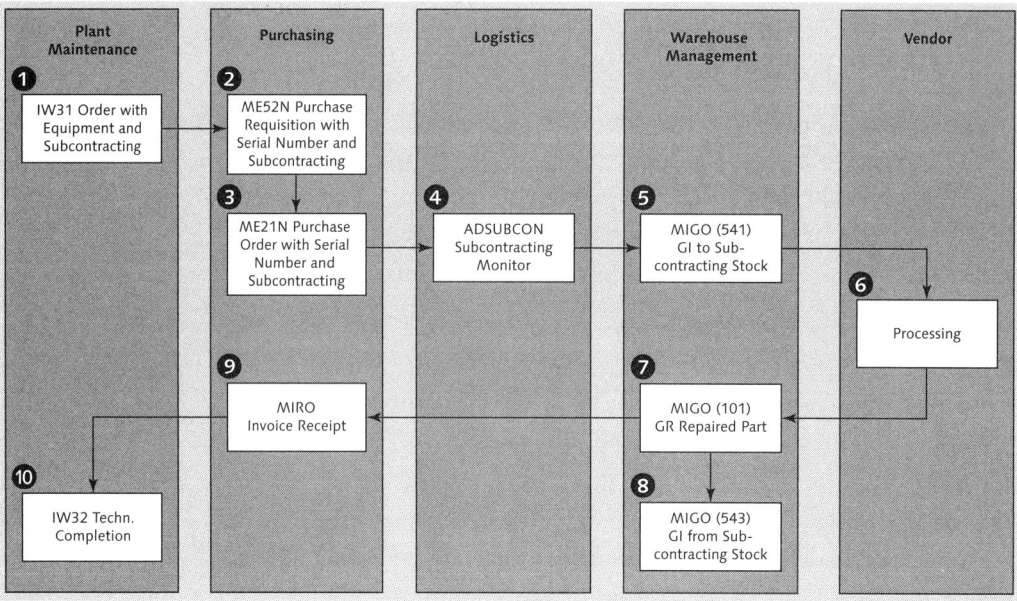

Figure 5.98 Subcontracting Process Flow

274

You create a maintenance order using Transaction IW31. Note the following differences between this order and a "standard" maintenance order.

Order with subcontracting

You set up an external processing operation in which you select the SUBCONTR. (Subcontracting) indicator; see Figure 5.99.

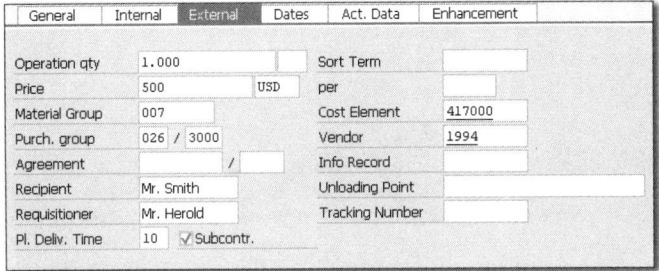

Figure 5.99 Subcontracting—External Processing Operation

In addition, you schedule the material number of the serial number for the operation and select the material provision indicator S (i.e., refurbishment material) field for the material item, as shown in Figure 5.100. When you set this indicator, the same material number is expected both at goods issue to the vendor and at goods receipt from this vendor.

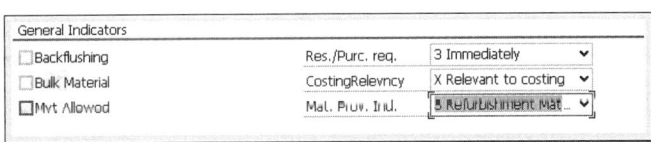

Figure 5.100 Subcontracting—Material Item in the Order

[!] Do Not Forget the Indicator

When creating the subcontracting order, ensure that the SUBCONTR. indicator is set on the EXTERNAL tab (external processing operation) and that the value S is selected in the Mat. Prov. Ind. (material provided indicator) field for the material components.

A purchase requisition is automatically generated in the background when you save the order. It differs from a "standard" purchase requisition in the following ways (see Figure 5.101):

Purchase requisition

- The purchase requisition item contains the material components instead of the external service.
- The item has item category L (i.e., subcontracting).
- The item contains a serial number, which belongs to the equipment and which you can check via the 🗈 button.

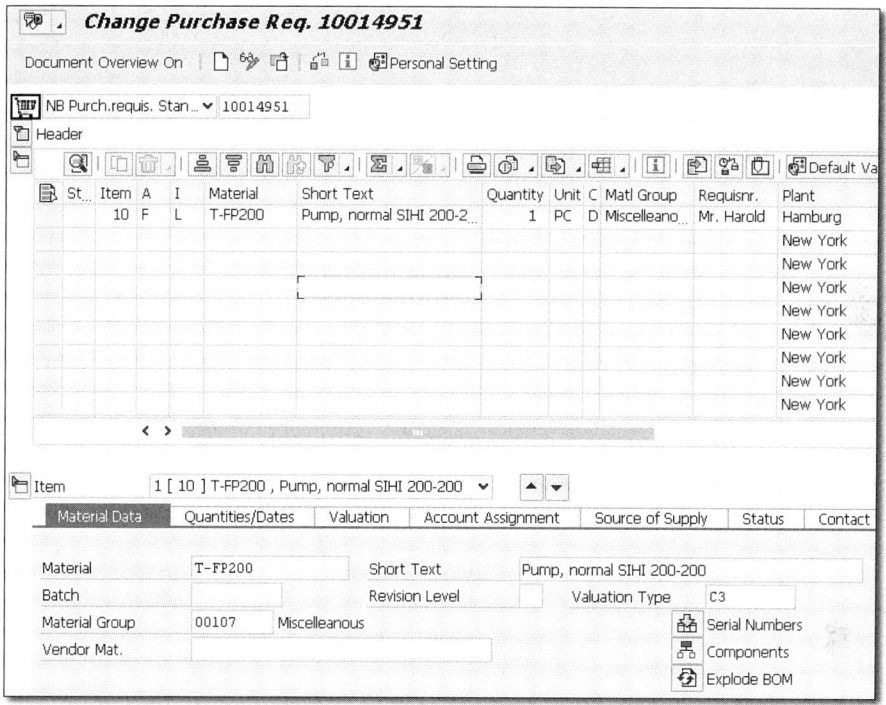

Figure 5.101 Subcontracting—Purchase Requisition

Subcontracting monitor

You can execute steps 3, 4, 5, 7, and 8 in the subcontracting monitor (Transaction ADSUBCON). You can use the monitor to create an overview of all subcontracting items or perform targeted searches for specific documents (for example, by vendor or material number).

[+] **Subcontracting Monitor**

The subcontracting monitor not only provides an overview of the current status of the subcontracting processes, but also supports you in executing them.

You then convert the purchase requisition into a purchase order (see Figure 5.102) using the function CREATE PO VIA PR (`Create PO via PR` button). The purchase order also contains a material item with item category L (i.e., subcontracting) and the serial number of the equipment.

PurchaseOrder

You can then create an outbound delivery for the purchase order for the component using the `Delivery for PO` button and provide the component via the function POST GOOD ISSUE FOR PURCHASE ORDER or using the ⇨ button. This function executes a transfer posting from your own stock to the subcontracting stock. The reference to the serial number of the equipment is retained here, also. The stock overview shows the defective part provided to the subcontractor in the *Stock Provided to Vendor* special stock, as well as the functional part you expect to be returned in the on-order stock (see Figure 5.103).

Material provision

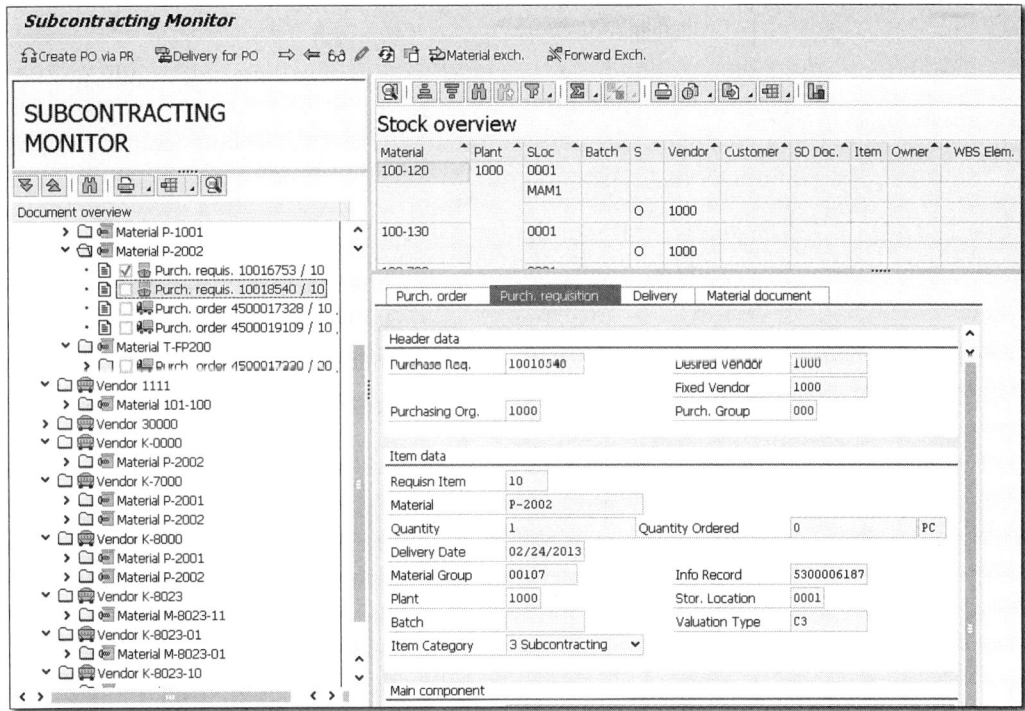

Figure 5.102 Subcontracting Monitor (Transaction ADSUBCON)

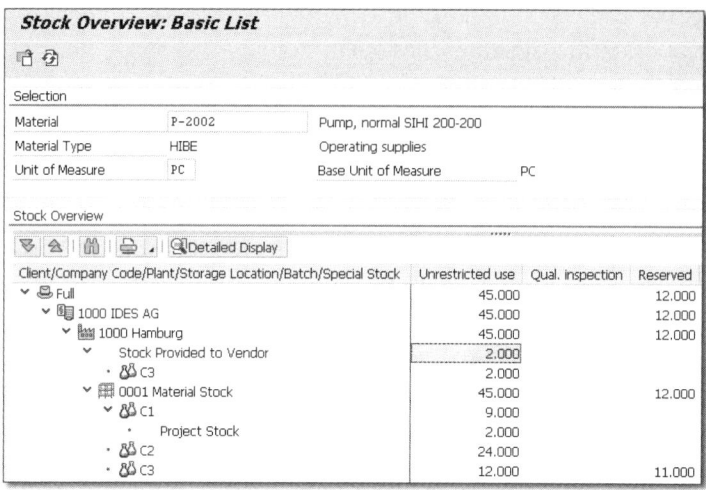

Figure 5.103 Subcontracting—Stock Overview

Goods receipt
You can also enter the goods receipt of the functional part in the subcontracting monitor with the function POST GOODS RECEIPT FOR PURCHASE ORDER or using the ⇐ button. This function simultaneously triggers two functions in the background:

- The goods receipt of the functional part is executed.
- The goods issue of the defective part from the *Stock Provided to Vendor* special stock is triggered, and this special stock is canceled.

The material's reference to the serial number, and therefore to the equipment, is preserved in both postings.

If the purchase order is then completed, it is no longer displayed in the subcontracting monitor.

Prerequisites
In order for the process to work as described above, you must fulfill the following prerequisites:

- Before you can use serial numbers in purchasing documents, you must assign a serial number profile to the material master in the view GENERAL PLANT DATA/STORAGE 2.
- You must also assign a serial number profile to the document types of the purchase order and the purchase requisition in the Customizing settings for Purchasing.

You maintain serial number profiles using the Customizing function DEFINE SERIAL NUMBER PROFILES. There, you must assign, in particular, PRSL (serial numbers in purchase requisitions) and POSL (serial numbers in purchase orders) to the MMSL serialization procedures (maintain goods receipt and issue document).

On the ITEMS DETAILS screen, you can then click the 🔘 button on the MATERIAL DATA tab in the purchase requisition or the DELIVERY SCHEDULE tab in the purchase order to maintain the serial numbers (see Figure 5.104).

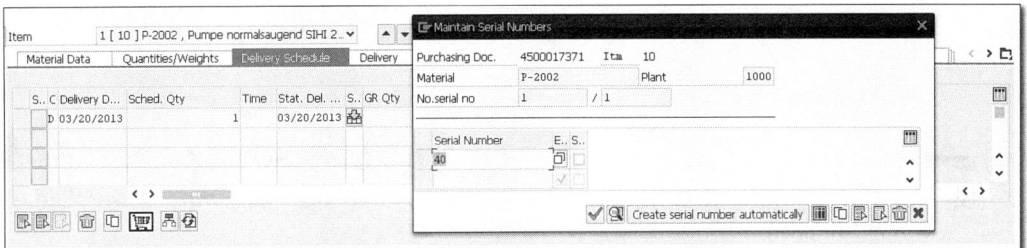

Figure 5.104 Serial Numbers in the Purchase Order

The scenario described above is known as *recursive repair*, and it is undoubtedly the subcontracting scenario that is most frequently encountered in practice. Table 5.2 provides an overview of all scenarios. It explains what the individual scenarios involve and indicates how each scenario affects the material provision indicator in the order or the subcontracting type in the purchasing documents.

Enhancing the scenario

Scenario	Definition	Material Provision Indicator in Order	Subcontracting Type in the Purchase Order
Recursive repair	Same physical part, same material number A, same serial number 1	Material A with S (refurbishment to subcontractor)	1 (refurbishment; material number unchanged)
Unit exchange	Different physical part, same material number A, different serial number 2	Material A with S (refurbishment to subcontractor)	1 (refurbishment; material number unchanged)

Table 5.2 Scenarios in Subcontracting

Scenario	Definition	Material Provision Indicator in Order	Subcontracting Type in the Purchase Order
Modification	Same physical part, different material number B, same serial number 1	2 materials: material A with S (refurbishment to subcontractor); Material B with S (refurbishment from subcontractor)	2 (refurbishment; material number changed)
Replacement	Different physical part, different material number B, different serial number 2	2 materials: material A with S (refurbishment to subcontractor); Material B with S (refurbishment from subcontractor)	3 (replacement)

Table 5.2 Scenarios in Subcontracting (Cont.)

Business functions — The LOG_EAM_ROTSUB, LOG_EAM_ROTSUB2, and LOG_MM_SERNO business functions must be activated, and DIMP 6.0 must be installed in order for you to use subcontracting.

5.8 Preventive Maintenance Business Process

Can be planned in respect to content and scheduling — The business process for preventive maintenance is characterized by the fact that you can plan required resources (work centers, materials, external companies, and so on) in advance in respect to content and scheduling. You have this type of business process, for example, in the following cases:

- A pump undergoes a visual and functional inspection every six months, and the mechanical seal has to be changed every twelve months.
- The hydraulic oil on a forklift must be changed regularly after every 1,000 operation hours (OH), and the brake fluid after every 2,000 OH
- The fire extinguisher in the building must be refilled every two years.
- Test equipment must be recalibrated every 120 days.

The preventive maintenance process thus differs from the process for a planned repair (see Section 5.2) in terms of the ability to schedule it.

This is due to the fact that only the content, not the date of a planned repair, can be predetermined.

Preventive maintenance differs, in turn, from an immediate repair (see Section 5.3) in terms of being able to plan it in respect to content and scheduling. You can respond to malfunctions only in the course of an immediate repair, not plan them in advance.

5.8.1 Basic Principles of Preventive Maintenance

Preventive maintenance is always associated with effort only—in both its planning and execution.

Nevertheless, there are many reasons why you must or should perform preventive maintenance in your company:

Why have preventive maintenance?

- **Legal requirements**
  There may be legislation relating to plant safety or industrial health and safety that stipulates that you must inspect or maintain your technical system regularly.
- **Quality assurance**
  The quality of a product depends largely on the condition of the production facility in which it is manufactured.
- **Reduction in frequency of malfunctions**
  One of the most important tasks in maintenance planning is to keep a production facility continuously available in the long term, and effective preventive maintenance ensures that a technical system does not break down and also reduces unnecessary costs that accrue due to repairs, replacing the system, or production downtimes.
- **Environmental protection requirements**
  Effective preventive maintenance can contribute to preventing system breakdowns that can lead to environmental impacts.
- **Recommendations of the manufacturer**
  The manufacturer of your technical system may recommend certain procedures for ensuring that the system always runs optimally.
- **Improved utilization control of capacities**
  The preventive maintenance ensures that you have a work list for uti-

lizing your workshops more consistently (for example, if there are fewer breakdown repair tasks to process).

- **Decrease in maintenance costs**
  It is debatable whether you can decrease your maintenance costs. This depends mainly on whether you have already reached the optimal intensity level of preventive maintenance.

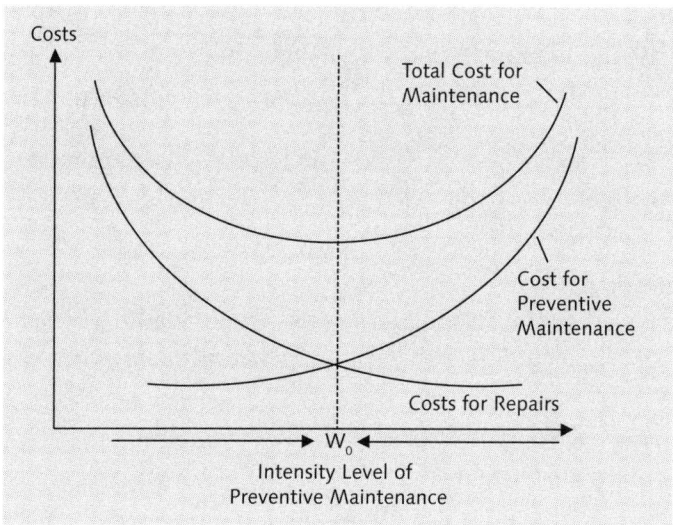

Figure 5.105 Plant Maintenance Costs

Inversely proportionate costs

The cost scheduling for preventive maintenance and repairs are inversely proportionate, and depend specifically on the intensity level of the preventive maintenance (see Figure 5.105).

- The higher the intensity level of preventive maintenance, the higher the costs for preventive maintenance.
- The higher the intensity level of preventive maintenance, the lower the costs for repairs.

There is an optimal intensity level, W0, for which the overall costs of plant maintenance are minimal. Follow-up costs that can be incurred because of inadequate preventive maintenance (for example, Starting costs) are not taken into account for this cost consideration because they are regarded as only opportunity costs.

There are basically three different types of preventive maintenance (see Figure 5.106):

Types of preventive maintenance

- **Time-based maintenance**
  The preventive maintenance task is triggered after a certain period of time has expired (for example, every six months).
- **Performance-based maintenance**
  The preventive maintenance task is triggered upon reaching a certain level of performance (for example, every 10,000 km).
- **Condition-based maintenance**
  The preventive maintenance task is triggered when a certain diagnostic value is not reached or is been exceeded (for example, a pressure lower than 15 bar or temperature higher than 85° C).

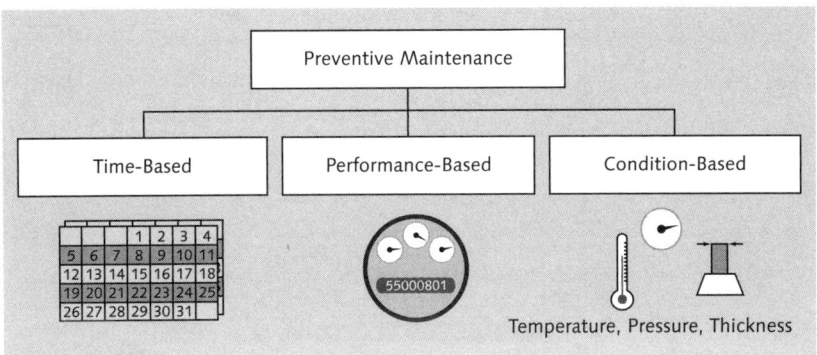

Figure 5.106 Types of Preventive Maintenance

5.8.2 Objects of Preventive Maintenance

To be able to perform the preventive maintenance business processes, several objects are used in EAM whose significance and interrelationships are briefly explained in the following section (see Figure 5.107):

Terms and interrelationships

- **Maintenance strategy**
  A maintenance strategy contains the chronological sequence of maintenance activities (for example, maintenance packages of 3, 6, 12, or 24 months for time-based maintenance, or maintenance packages of 1,000, 2,000, or 5,000 operation hours for performance-based maintenance). The maintenance strategy does not provide any details

about the activity, object, or date, but is only required for strategy-based maintenance plans (see Section 5.8.4 and Section 5.8.5).

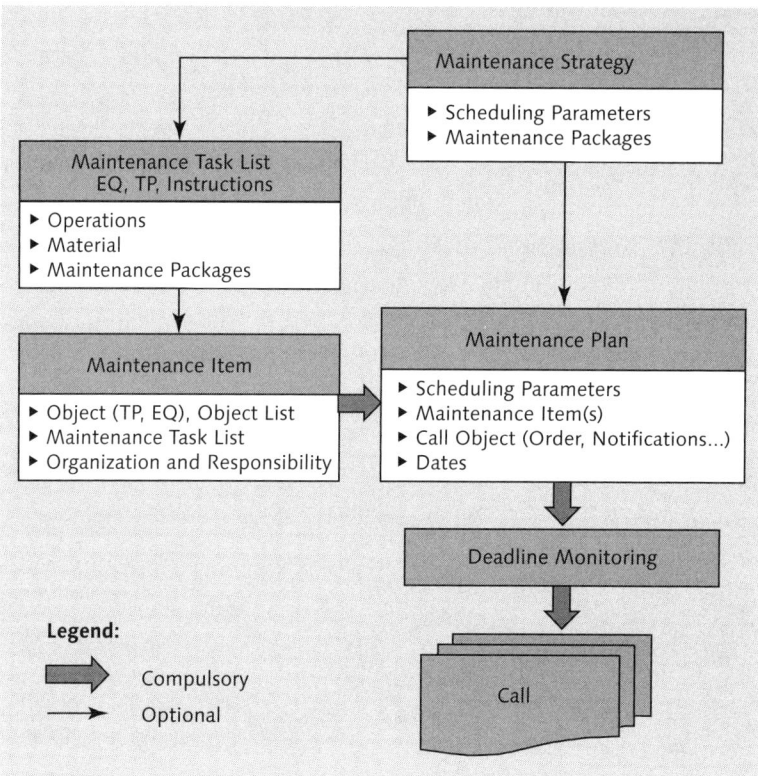

Figure 5.107 Interrelationships of EAM Maintenance Planning

- **Maintenance task list**

    The maintenance task list describes the activities (operations) and contains materials and deadlines (maintenance packages). There are object-specific maintenance task lists (equipment plan, functional location plan) and neutral maintenance task lists (instructions). Strategy-based maintenance plans must, whereas all other maintenance plans can, contain a maintenance task list.

- **Maintenance item**

    The maintenance item describes the activities to be performed, contains the reference object (or also the object list), and has organizational data for subsequent processing purposes.

5.8 Preventive Maintenance Business Process

- **Maintenance plan**
  The maintenance plan contains one or more maintenance items and determines the maintenance dates, as well as the maintenance call object (order, notification, and so on).
- **Deadline monitoring**
  Deadline monitoring (program RISTRA20) runs automatically as a batch job and ensures that the maintenance call objects (for example, the orders) are generated automatically on the due date.

> **[+] Preventive Maintenance in the Second Step of the Implementation**
>
> When Implementing EAM, you should think twice about whether you necessarily have to implement preventive maintenance in the first step because preventive maintenance uses many special functions and requires a high level of acceptance among users.

EAM provides you with maintenance plans to be able to support the preventive maintenance business processes. The following maintenance plan types can be selected (see Figure 5.108):

Categories of Maintenance Plans

- **Single cycle plans**
  You create single cycle plans when you have to perform the same maintenance activities in full at regular intervals (time-based or performance-based). In this case, you can, but do not have to, include a maintenance task list.
- **Maintenance strategies and strategy plans**
  You create maintenance strategies and strategy plans when you have to perform maintenance activities that are based on each other or supersede each other, either as a time-based strategy (for example, every three, six, or twelve months, and so on) or as a performance-based strategy (for example, every 10,000, 20,000, or 40,000 km, and so on). In this case, you must include a maintenance task list, specifically one that has the same strategy as the maintenance plan.
- **Multiple counter plans**
  You create multiple counter plans when fixing the maintenance date depends on several influencing factors (for example, every six months, every 10,000 km, and every 1,000 operation hours). In this case, also, you can, but do not have to, include a maintenance task list.

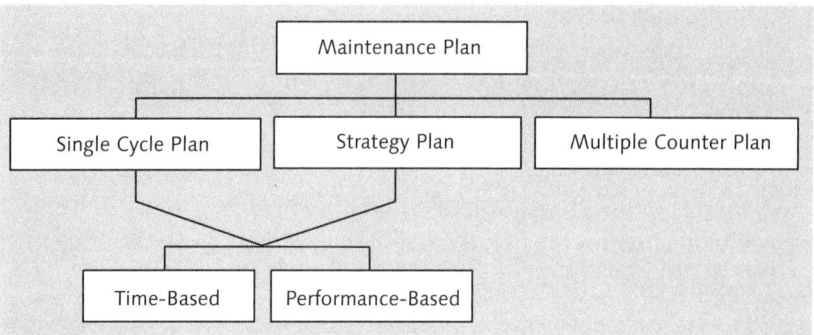

Figure 5.108 Categories of Maintenance Plans

Maintenance plan category

You can use the Customizing function SET MAINTENANCE PLAN CATEGORIES to define which of the following maintenance call objects should be called from the maintenance plan when due:

- You select ORDER as the maintenance call object if you want to perform the specifications of the maintenance plan exactly as given, without further planning.

- You select NOTIFICATION as the maintenance call object if you want to perform other detailed planning when due—for example, if you want to combine several notifications for an order based on the current capacity load utilization. In this case, several maintenance task lists are then copied into the respective order as an operation list.

- You select INSPECTION LOT as the maintenance call object if you want to perform a calibration inspection of test equipment (for more information, refer to Section 5.10).

- You select the SERVICE ENTRY SHEET maintenance call object if you have agreed on an outline agreement about regular services with an external company and want the system to automatically generate the service entry sheets required for acceptance at regular intervals.

Since the ORDER maintenance call object represents the normal situation in preventive maintenance, I will focus on this in the following descriptions, but I will refer to the other maintenance call objects where appropriate.

5.8.3 Maintenance Task Lists

A maintenance task list essentially describes activities (operations) and contains materials that are required during processing of the activities.

Definition

Maintenance task lists are used not only in plant maintenance, but also in the following areas in the SAP system:

- In discrete manufacturing as routings or reference operation sets
- In process manufacturing as a planning recipe
- In project processing as a standard network
- In quality management as an inspection plan

In plant maintenance, maintenance task lists are used primarily for the following two purposes:

Usage in plant maintenance

- **Preventive maintenance**
  In the area of preventive maintenance, in particular, maintenance task lists are widely used to map maintenance and inspection tasks, inspections, legal obligations, and so on.

- **Repairs**
  You can also use maintenance task lists in plant maintenance by predefining standard workflows for repair tasks or defining a complete list of all possible maintenance tasks and then deciding, as the need arises, which of these tasks actually needs to be performed.

From a plant maintenance perspective, we can distinguish among three different types of maintenance task lists:

Maintenance task list types

- **Maintenance task list for equipment**
  You create a maintenance task list for equipment for exactly one piece of equipment (Transaction IA01) if you want to map specific tasks for the equipment. However, you can use this maintenance task list only in connection with this one piece of equipment.

- **Maintenance task list for functional location**
  You create a maintenance task list for a functional location for exactly one functional location (Transaction IA11) if you want to map specific

287

tasks for the functional location. You can also use this maintenance task list only in connection with this one functional location.

- **General maintenance task list**

  A general maintenance task list (Transaction IA05) is not object-specific, which means that it is not assigned to any particular piece of equipment or functional location. However, you can indirectly make a general maintenance task list available for several pieces of equipment and/or functional locations. Here, you use the CONSTRUCTION TYPE field in the master record for the piece of equipment or functional location in the STRUCTURING screen group. This means that all pieces of equipment and functional locations for which a material number is entered in the CONSTRUCTION TYPE field can access general maintenance task lists for which the same material number is entered, in turn, in the ASSEMBLY field in the task list header (see Figure 5.109).

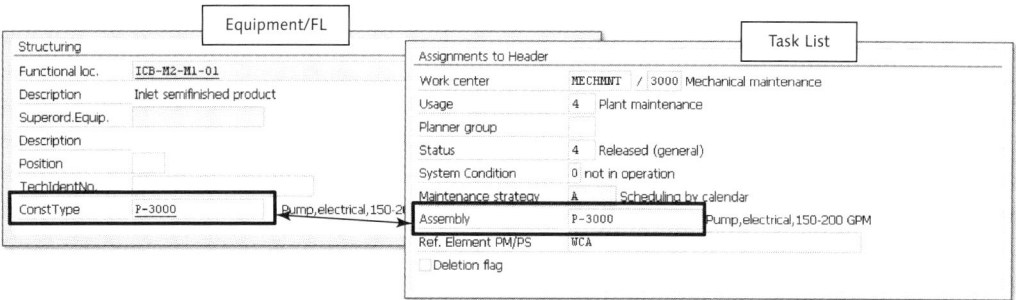

Figure 5.109 Assignment of Equipment/Functional Location to a General Maintenance Task List

[+] **Use General Maintenance Task Lists Whenever Possible**

If you use maintenance task lists in plant maintenance, note the following:

- Equipment and functional locations may have individual maintenance task lists or access general maintenance task lists indirectly.
- You should create general maintenance task lists, if possible. This saves time entering and maintaining data.
- You should create maintenance task lists for equipment or functional locations only if you want to map tasks that are specific to a piece of equipment or functional location.

The numbers for equipment task lists and functional location task lists are assigned internally. When creating an equipment task list or a task list for a functional location, the system informs you of the number under which it saved the maintenance task list. The first maintenance task list you create for a specific piece of equipment or functional location is identified by a task list group number and a group counter. Subsequent task lists for the same piece of equipment are identified only by the sequential group counter within the group.

Numbers and group counters

The numbers for general maintenance task lists can be assigned internally or externally.

> **Meaningful Numbers for General Maintenance Task Lists**
>
> When you create general maintenance task lists, you can use the task list number to indicate the objects for which the individual general maintenance task lists are suitable (for example, B. PUMP_WTG, FFZ_TUEV, MOT_REP). This makes selection easier later.

[+]

A maintenance task list contains the following elements (see Figure 5.110):

Structure of a maintenance task list

- **Header data**
  Header data is information used to identify and manage the maintenance task list. This data is valid for the entire maintenance task list—for example, number, group counter, plant, main work center, and so on.

- **Operations**
  You can use operations to describe the work you want to be performed when the maintenance task list is being implemented.

- **Material list**
  The material list contains spare parts that are required and used when the maintenance task list is being implemented.

- **Production resources/tools**
  Production resources/tools (for example, tools, protective clothing, and hand pallet trucks) are also required for implementing the maintenance task list. However, unlike a material, they are not consumed.

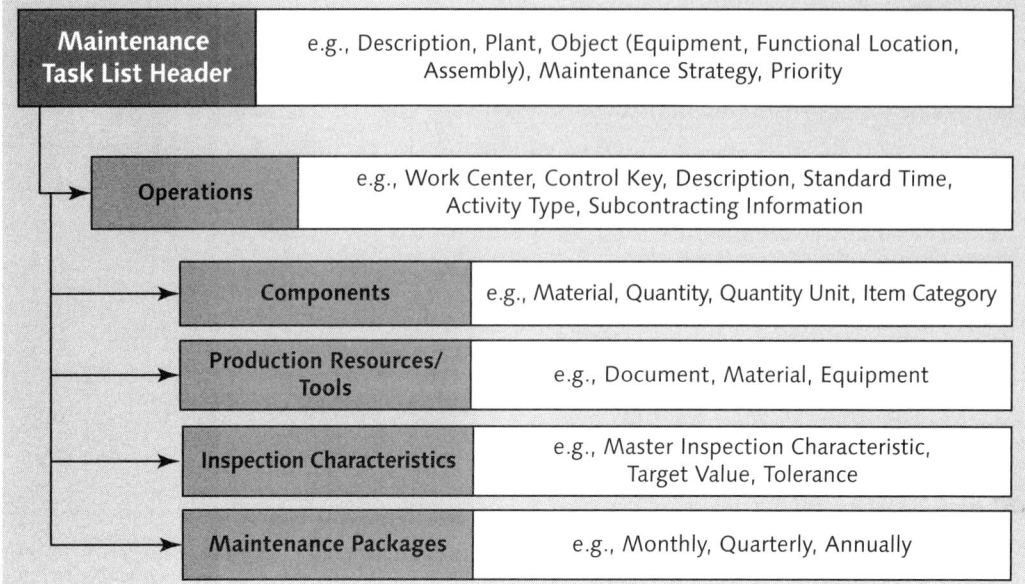

Figure 5.110 Structure of a Maintenance Task List

- **Inspection characteristics**
  If inspections are to be conducted as part of an operation (for example, inspections of length, weight, and function), you can define them as inspection characteristics.

- **Maintenance packages**
  If the maintenance task list is used in a strategy maintenance plan, you use maintenance packages to control the frequency with which the maintenance work is performed—either time based (for example, every three months) or performance based (for example, every 1,200 operating hours).

An example of an operations list in a maintenance task list is provided in Figure 5.111.

General Operation Overview									
Op...	SOp	Work ctr	Plnt	Ctrl	Operation Description	LT	Work	Un.	No. Duration Un.
0010		MECHMNT	3000	PM01	switch off, safety check	✓	30	MIN	30 MIN
0020		MECHMNT	3000	PM01	Visual check outside for leaks, rust eg		30	MIN	30 MIN
0030		MECHMNT	3000	PM01	visual check inside		60	MIN	60 MIN
0040		MECHMNT	3000	PM01	disassemble pump shaft and clean		120	MIN	120 MIN
0050		MECHMNT	3000	PM01	measure bearing tolerance		30	MIN	30 MIN
0060		MECHMNT	3000	PM01	change sealings of gearbox cover	✓	100	MIN	100 MIN
0070		MECHMNT	3000	PM01	safety check running pump		30	MIN	30 MIN

Figure 5.111 Operations in a Maintenance Task List

If you want to assign components to a maintenance task list, you can do this in one of the following ways:

Components in the maintenance task list

- You assign material components from the bill of material of the maintenance object (equipment, functional location, or header assembly) that is assigned to the maintenance task list; in this case, the BOM matches the content of the structure list exactly.

- Alternatively, you assign stock materials that are not in the BOM of the maintenance object to the maintenance task list directly. This is referred to as *free material assignment*. In this case, the materials are assigned by their material numbers. As a prerequisite for using free material assignment, you must specify a BOM usage (usually PLANT MAINTENANCE USAGE) in Customizing. In this case, use the Customizing function DEFINE DEFAULT SETTING FOR FREE MATERIAL ASSIGNMENT. The SAP system, thus, creates an internal BOM in the case of a free assignment. This BOM cannot be edited by the application.

The most common use of maintenance task lists will be discussed later in this chapter: their use, together with maintenance plans, in preventive maintenance. However, you can also use maintenance task lists in connection with maintenance tasks by assigning a maintenance task list to an order directly. The following selection methods are available for assigning a maintenance task list within an order (Transaction IW31/32, menu option EXTRAS • TASK LIST SELECTION):

Order and maintenance task list

- **Direct entry**
  If you know the task list group and group counter, you can use direct entry to select the maintenance task list.

- **General maintenance task lists**

  When using this selection procedure, you can select general maintenance task lists from a list. The selection criteria TASK LIST TYPE (A), PLANT, and STATUS (RELEASED FOR ORDER) are set by default. The individual criteria can still be added.

- **For object structure**

  This option displays all maintenance task lists that were created for the objects that are, in turn, sub-objects of the reference object.

- **For assembly**

  This selection procedure selects all maintenance task lists that have been created for the object entered in the ASSEMBLY field.

- **For reference object**

  This is the simplest of all selection procedures because it allows you to select maintenance task lists on the basis of the reference object. If an equipment with a construction type is specified as the reference object, all equipment task lists for the relevant equipment are displayed, as well as all general maintenance task lists with an assembly in the task list header that corresponds to the construction type of the equipment. The same applies for the functional location.

The system response to your selection of a maintenance task list depends on the personal settings you make under EXTRAS • SETTINGS • DEFAULT VALUES (see Figure 5.112).

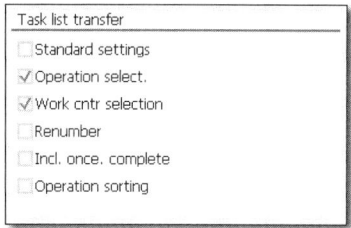

Figure 5.112 Task List Transfer

If you activate the OPERATION SELECT. option, a dialog box appears when the maintenance task list is transferred, in which you can select specific operations. This is useful, for example, if you do not require all the operations in a maintenance task list for a specific scenario (see Figure 5.113).

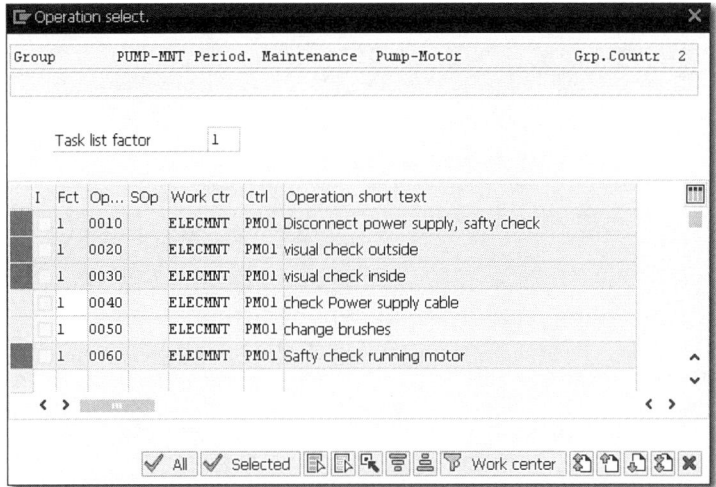

Figure 5.113 Operation Selection

When the OPERATION SELECT. option is activated, you can choose to execute operations multiple times in the dialog box. This may be necessary if, for example, you have added an object list to the relevant order.

> **Activating Operation Selection** [+]
>
> If you select the OPERATION SELECT. option in your personal settings, you have the option of not only selecting specific operations when a maintenance task list is transferred into an order, but also executing individual operations multiple times using the execution factor (for example, if an object list exists).

If you activate the WORK CNTR SELECTION option, you can replace the work centers of the maintenance task list with other work centers in the order (see Figure 5.114). This may be necessary, for example, if the work centers you originally planned to use are already utilized to their maximum capacities.

Change documentation can now be used for maintenance task lists. To use this feature, choose EXTRAS • ACTION LOG in a maintenance task list to display the changes (see Figure 5.115) or start Transaction IA21, where you can display the changes across several maintenance task lists.

Action log and changes

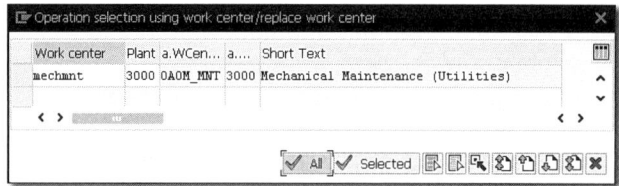

Figure 5.114 Work Center Selection

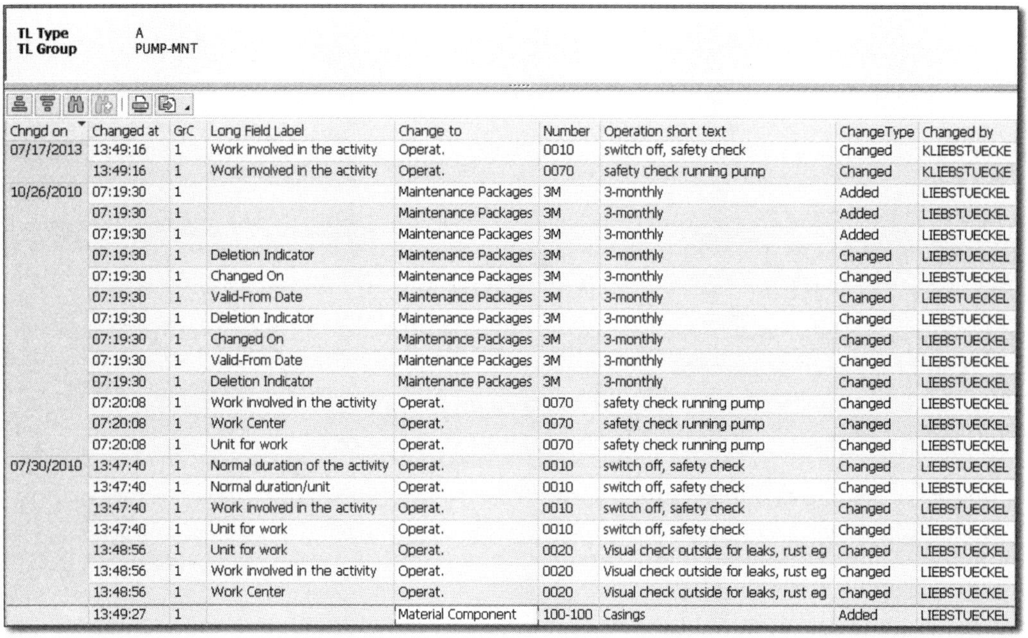

Business function

The LOG_EAM_CI_3 business function must be activated in order for you to use the action log for maintenance task lists.

TL Type A
TL Group PUMP-MNT

Chngd on	Changed at	GrC	Long Field Label	Change to	Number	Operation short text	ChangeType	Changed by
07/17/2013	13:49:16	1	Work involved in the activity	Operat.	0010	switch off, safety check	Changed	KLIEBSTUECKE
	13:49:16	1	Work involved in the activity	Operat.	0070	safety check running pump	Changed	KLIEBSTUECKE
10/26/2010	07:19:30	1		Maintenance Packages	3M	3-monthly	Added	LIEBSTUECKEL
	07:19:30	1		Maintenance Packages	3M	3-monthly	Added	LIEBSTUECKEL
	07:19:30	1		Maintenance Packages	3M	3-monthly	Added	LIEBSTUECKEL
	07:19:30	1	Deletion Indicator	Maintenance Packages	3M	3-monthly	Changed	LIEBSTUECKEL
	07:19:30	1	Changed On	Maintenance Packages	3M	3-monthly	Changed	LIEBSTUECKEL
	07:19:30	1	Valid-From Date	Maintenance Packages	3M	3-monthly	Changed	LIEBSTUECKEL
	07:19:30	1	Deletion Indicator	Maintenance Packages	3M	3-monthly	Changed	LIEBSTUECKEL
	07:19:30	1	Changed On	Maintenance Packages	3M	3-monthly	Changed	LIEBSTUECKEL
	07:19:30	1	Valid-From Date	Maintenance Packages	3M	3-monthly	Changed	LIEBSTUECKEL
	07:19:30	1	Deletion Indicator	Maintenance Packages	3M	3-monthly	Changed	LIEBSTUECKEL
	07:20:08	1	Work involved in the activity	Operat.	0070	safety check running pump	Changed	LIEBSTUECKEL
	07:20:08	1	Work Center	Operat.	0070	safety check running pump	Changed	LIEBSTUECKEL
	07:20:08	1	Unit for work	Operat.	0070	safety check running pump	Changed	LIEBSTUECKEL
07/30/2010	13:47:40	1	Normal duration of the activity	Operat.	0010	switch off, safety check	Changed	LIEBSTUECKEL
	13:47:40	1	Normal duration/unit	Operat.	0010	switch off, safety check	Changed	LIEBSTUECKEL
	13:47:40	1	Work involved in the activity	Operat.	0010	switch off, safety check	Changed	LIEBSTUECKEL
	13:47:40	1	Unit for work	Operat.	0010	switch off, safety check	Changed	LIEBSTUECKEL
	13:48:56	1	Unit for work	Operat.	0020	Visual check outside for leaks, rust eg	Changed	LIEBSTUECKEL
	13:48:56	1	Work involved in the activity	Operat.	0020	Visual check outside for leaks, rust eg	Changed	LIEBSTUECKEL
	13:48:56	1	Work Center	Operat.	0020	Visual check outside for leaks, rust eg	Changed	LIEBSTUECKEL
	13:49:27	1		Material Component	100-100	Casings	Added	LIEBSTUECKEL

Figure 5.115 Action Log of a Maintenance Task List

Costing of maintenance task lists

Using Transaction IA16, you can also perform costings for maintenance task lists without having to create an order. The transaction thus answers the question about what this maintenance task list would cost if executed. The costs are displayed (see Figure 5.116) separately by item type, as follows:

- I = Internal activity
- E = External service

- M = Material
- O = Overhead rates

```
Task List Type        A
Group                 PUMP-MNT
Group Counter         01 Period. Maintenance Pump Etanorm
Plant                 3000 New York
Costing Variant       PM01 Maintenance Order
Costing Version
Costing Date from-to  05/17/2013 - 05/17/2013

Itm  I Resource              Cost Eleme  Σ Total Value  Σ Fixed Value  COCr  Quantity  Un
  1  E 4300    MECHMNT 1410  615000            27.50           27.50  USD     0.500   H
  2  M 3000 100-510          410000             2.00            0.00  USD     2       PC
  3  E 4300    MECHMNT 1410  615000            27.50           27.50  USD     0.500   H
  4  E 4300    MECHMNT 1410  615000            55.00           55.00  USD     1       H
  5  E 4300    MECHMNT 1410  615000           110.00          110.00  USD     2       H
  6  E 4300    MECHMNT 1410  615000            27.50           27.50  USD     0.500   H
  7  E 4300    MECHMNT 1410  615000            91.69           91.69  USD     1.667   H
  8  E 4300    MECHMNT 1410  615000            27.50           27.50  USD     0.500   H
  9  G 4300 655110            655110            36.67           36.67  USD
                                              405.36          403.36  USD
```

Figure 5.116 Costing of a Maintenance Task List

Other potential item types, such as co-product or base planning object, however, are irrelevant for plant maintenance.

There are two transactions you can use to make mass changes to maintenance task lists:

- Transaction CA87 to replace work centers (see Figure 5.117)
- Transaction CA77 to replace production resources/tools

Mass changes

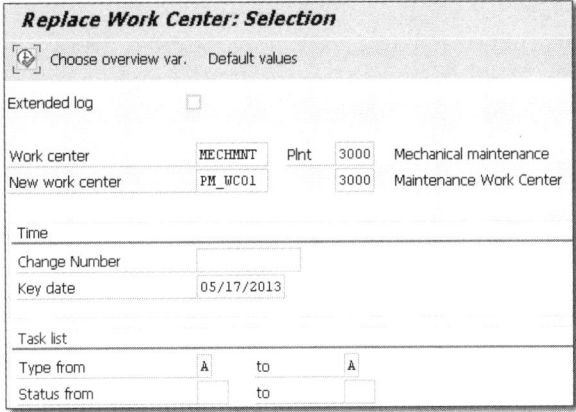

Figure 5.117 Mass Change of Maintenance Task Lists

In both cases, after you execute the selection, the system displays an overview of the maintenance task lists or operations that have been found, from which you now select the maintenance task lists that are to be involved in the replacement.

Next, we will turn our attention to the other elements that are essential to preventive maintenance: the maintenance plans.

5.8.4 Preventive Maintenance, Time-Based

For time-based maintenance, the maintenance dates are calculated solely via the calendar (for example, every six months). Performance-based values (such as, for example, operation hours) have no effect.

Time-Based Single-Cycle plan

You create time-based single-cycle plans if you have to perform the same maintenance activities in full at regular intervals.

Creating the single-cycle plan

You create the single-cycle plan via Transaction IP41. Here, you choose between internal and external number assignment. You specify the cycle where the maintenance is to take place directly in the maintenance plan, just like all other data required for a maintenance task (see Figure 5.118):

- Short description (possibly with a long text)
- Reference object
- Order type and maintenance activity type that the subsequent orders are to receive
- Organizational responsibilities (planner group, work center)
- Maintenance task list, if a maintenance task list is to be executed

[+] **The Simplest Case: Time-Based Single-Cycle Plan**

The time-based single-cycle plan involves the least amount of effort of all maintenance plan types in terms of entering and maintaining data, and experience has shown that this maintenance plan type is used the most. You should, therefore, also try to map as many of your maintenance activities as possible using this maintenance plan type.

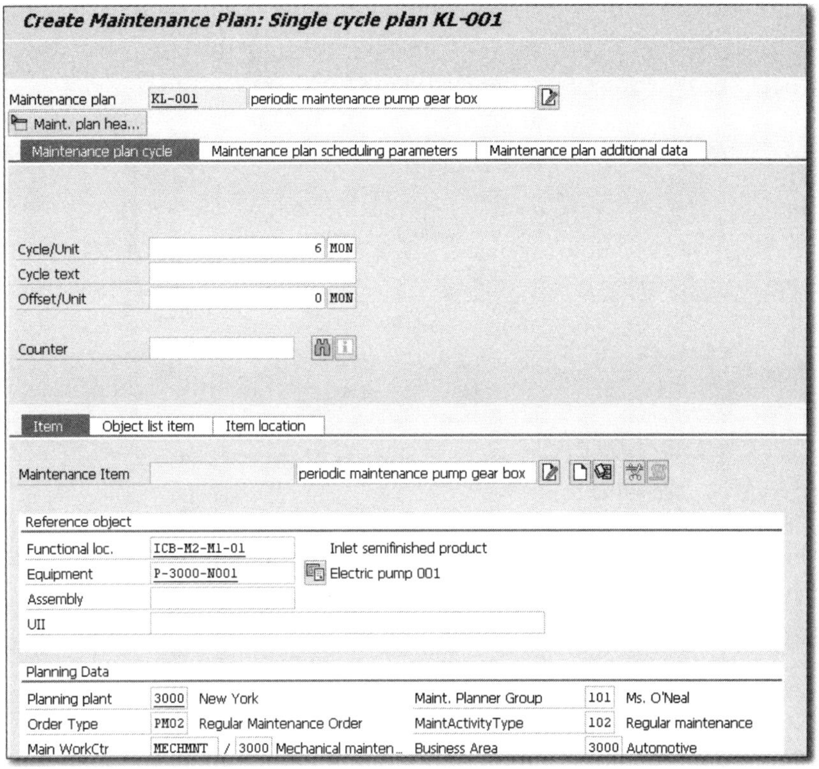

5.8 | Preventive Maintenance Business Process

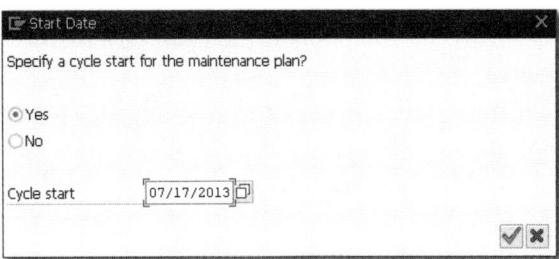

Figure 5.118 The Single-Cycle Plan

Use Transaction IP10 or click the start button to start the maintenance plan and create the first order. The system asks you for a START OF CYCLE DATE (see Figure 5.119). This is the date when you performed the last maintenance.

Starting the maintenance plan

Figure 5.119 Cycle Start Date

The system calculates the first planned date based on the start of cycle and scheduling parameters and creates the first maintenance order when you save your data (see Figure 5.120).

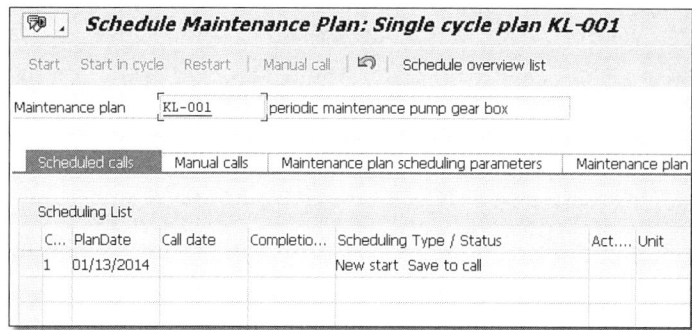

Figure 5.120 Planned Date

Several influencing factors affect the calculation of the planned date, which the following section explains in more detail, as scheduling parameters.

Scheduling Parameters

You also maintain the scheduling parameters for the single-cycle plan directly in the maintenance plan (see Figure 5.121).

Scheduling indicator

You use the scheduling indicator to define the basis for calculating the planned dates:

- **Time**
  The calculation basis for the month is always 30 days; all calendar days are counted. For example, cycle: 3 months; start of cycle: April 01 results in June 30 as the planned date.

- **Time—factory calendar**
  The calculation basis for the month is always 30 days; only the factory calendar days are counted. For example: cycle: 3 months; factory calendar: Saturday/Sunday/public holidays free; start of cycle: April 01 results in a planned date around August 10 (depending on when the public holidays fall).

▶ **Time—key date**

The calculation basis is the effective days of a month. For example, cycle: 3 months; start of cycle: April 01 results in July 01 as the planned date.

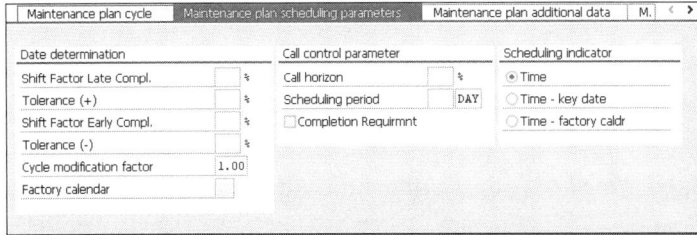

Figure 5.121 Scheduling Parameter

Scheduling Indicator: Key Date	[+]
Of the potential scheduling types, the key date time is the one most frequently used in practice.	

You use the shift factor (SF) to control what percentage of the early completion date (SF EARLY COMPLETION field) or late completion date (SF LATE COMPLETION field) is to be transferred to the next planned date. Take a look at the following examples of this scenario:

▶ Planned date: April 01; completion date: April 10; cycle: 3 months, key date scheduling; shift factor: late completion of 0% results in July 01 as the next planned date.

▶ Planned date: April 01; completion date: April 10; cycle: 3 months, key date scheduling; shift factor: late completion of 50% results in July 06 as the next planned date.

▶ Planned date: April 01; completion date: April 10; cycle: 3 months, key date scheduling; shift factor: late completion of 100% results in July 10 as the next planned date.

Shift factor

Shift Factors: 0% or 100%	[+]
Set the shift factors to either 0% or 100% for time-based maintenance plans, regardless of whether a single-cycle plan or strategy plan is used. In practice, other values are not normally important.	

Tolerance In reality, there are always reasons you cannot accept the calculated planned date, but instead have to shift it by a few days—for example, if the planned date falls on a non-working day, the utilization of workshops needs to be shifted slightly, or Production can only make the technical system available late for the maintenance order. Such small shifts do not normally affect the follow-up dates immediately. You can, therefore, use the tolerance to specify as of which deviation (expressed in percentages of the cycle) the shift factors should take effect. Take a look at the following examples of this scenario:

- Planned date: April 01; completion date: April 10; cycle: 3 months, key date scheduling; shift factor: late completion of 0%; tolerance: 10% results in July 01 as the next planned date.
- Planned date: April 01; completion date: April 05; cycle: 3 months, key date scheduling; shift factor: late completion of 100%; tolerance: 10% results in July 01 as the next planned date (tolerance = 10% of 90 days = 9 days not yet reached; shift factor does not take effect).
- Planned date: April 01; completion date: April 12; cycle: 3 months, key date scheduling; shift factor: late completion of 100%; tolerance: 10% results in July 12 as the next planned date (tolerance = 10% of 90 days = 9 days exceeded; shift factor takes effect).

[+] **Tolerance: ~10%**

Set a tolerance value only if you have activated the shift factors (that is, greater than 0%).

If you set tolerances, note that values around 10% have proved themselves in practice.

Completion requirement Set the COMPLETION REQUIREMENT parameter if you want the system to generate subsequent orders only once the previous order has been completed.

[+] **Completion Requirement: Decide Individually**

Check whether you want to set the completion requirement in individual cases. Both cases occur regularly in practice.

Preventive Maintenance Business Process | 5.8

You can define a scheduling period in the maintenance plan, with which you can create a preview of the pending maintenance dates. The scheduling period specifies the period of the preview in days, months, or years. If you want to have a preview for a maintenance plan for the entire year, for example, set the scheduling period to 365 days, or 12 months.

Scheduling period

Figure 5.122 shows a maintenance plan with a monthly cycle, a start date of December 01, and a scheduling period of one year.

Scheduled calls		Manual calls	Maintenance plan scheduling parameters		Maintenance plan additional data	
Scheduling List						
C...	PlanDate	Call date	Completio...	Scheduling Type / Status	Act....	Unit
1	01/13/2014			New start Called		
2	01/13/2014			New start Save to call		
3	07/12/2014	01/13/2014		Scheduled Hold		
4	01/08/2015	07/12/2014		Scheduled Hold		
5	07/07/2015	01/08/2015		Scheduled Hold		
6	01/03/2016	07/07/2015		Scheduled Hold		
7	07/01/2016	01/03/2016		Scheduled Hold		

Figure 5.122 Maintenance Plan with Scheduling Period

> **Scheduling Period: 6–24 months** [+]
>
> In reality, a scheduling period of 6–24 months is not rare. It allows you a long-term preview of the pending maintenance dates.

You use the call horizon to specify in percentage when an order should be created for a calculated maintenance date—thus, how much time is to elapse between the two planned dates until the order is created in the system. The date as of which the order can then be created is known as the *maintenance call date*.

Call horizon

Take a look at the following example of this scenario:

The maintenance cycle is 12 months; December 01 is specified as both the planned date and the completion date of the predecessor. The call horizon is as follows:

- 0%

  The order can be created immediately if the predecessor order has been completed; the maintenance call date is, thus, December 01.

- 100%

  The order can be called only when the next planned date is reached; the maintenance call date is, thus, December 01 of the following year.

- 75%

  The order can be called if 75% of the time between December 01 of the previous year and December 01 of the following year has elapsed; the maintenance call date is, thus, September 01.

In the last two cases, the scheduling list of the maintenance plan has the HOLD status (see Figure 5.123).

C...	PlanDate	Call date	Completio...	Scheduling Type / Status	Act....	Unit
1	01/13/2014	12/08/2013		New start Hold		

Figure 5.123 Scheduling List

Procedures in practice

In practice, there are different procedures you can use for dealing with the call horizon for time-based preventive maintenance.

You set the call horizon to 100% and then use the period for maintenance call objects (see Figure 5.125) in the deadline monitoring (Transaction IP30 or program RISTRA20) to control how much time before the maintenance call date the order is to be created (for more information, refer to the section on deadline monitoring).

[+] **Calculation Formula for the Call Horizon**

If you want to set a call horizon, you can use the following formula to calculate the initial phase in days, in percentages:

$CH = (C-I) \times 100 / C$

- CH = Call horizon, in percentages
- I = Initial phase, in days
- C = Cycle, in days (for strategy plans, the smallest cycle)

Always round off the result.

If you want the call horizon to control the maintenance call directly, proceed as follows:

- If your cycles are shorter than one year, set the call horizon to 0%. In this case, the subsequent orders can be created as of the date when the predecessor order is completed.
- If your cycles are longer than one year, set the call horizon to a high percentage value (greater than 80%) to ensure that the orders are not created too early and, thus, do not remain in the SAP system too long.

If this calculation of percentages appears too cumbersome or too complicated, you can now also specify in factory or calendar days the number of days before the planned date that the order should be called in the SAP system (see Figure 5.124).

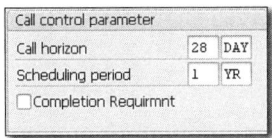

Figure 5.124 Call Horizon as a Percentage or in Days

In order for this function to be available, you must activate the business function LOG_EAM_CI_6 and add the EAM_SFWS_MPLAN_OPEN_HORIZ_DAYS option there.

Business function

Deadline Monitoring

When you start the maintenance plans, it is advisable not to monitor the maintenance plans and create the subsequent orders manually, but let the system monitor the deadlines automatically instead. You can either start this online using Transaction IP30 or schedule an automatic batch job for the RISTRA20 program (see Figure 5.125).

Batch job

> **Automate the Deadline Monitoring** [+]
>
> Schedule a batch job for the RISTRA20 program. This should run regularly, based on the cycles of the maintenance plans:
>
> - Daily for all maintenance plans with cycles up to one month

- Weekly for all maintenance plans with cycles between one month and six months
- Monthly for all maintenance plans with cycles longer than six months

The information here is provided as an orientation aid; it can, of course, differ from the details you use in specific situations.

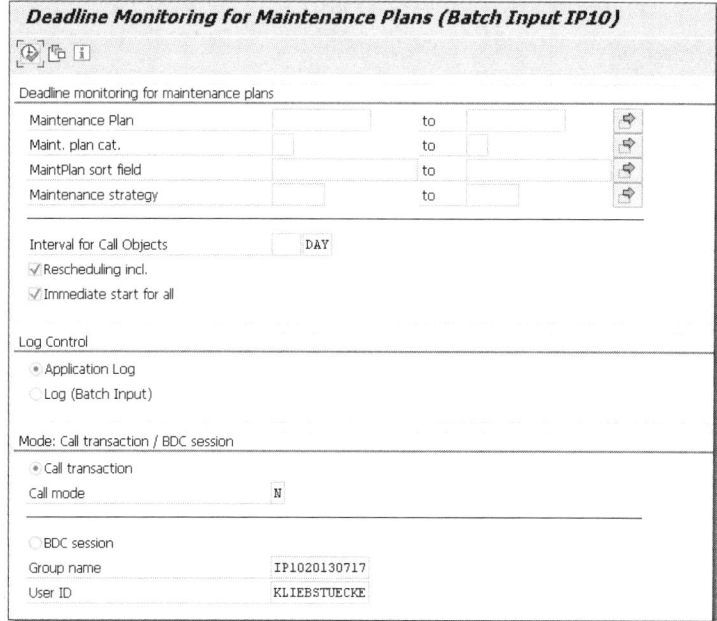

Figure 5.125 Deadline Monitoring

Problem of selection

However, you must solve the problem that RISTRA20 has only very few selection criteria: how can you schedule all maintenance plans with deadlines of between one month and six months once a week?

[+] **Meaningful Numbers or Sort Field**

To ensure that the RISTRA20 program runs specifically for the required maintenance plans, either assign meaningful maintenance plan numbers to group the maintenance plans and to be able to then schedule them together, or use the sort field in the maintenance plan (see Figure 5.126) to be able to schedule all maintenance plans together with the same sort field. You can use the maintenance strategy as a grouping characteristic for strategy plans.

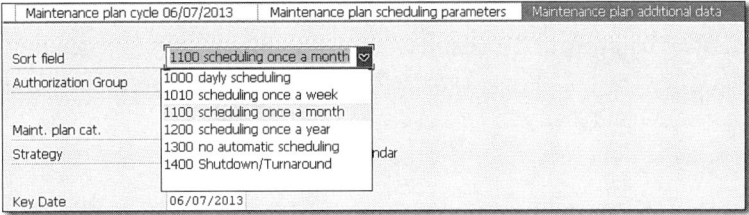

Figure 5.126 Sort Field

Interval for Maintenance Call Objects [+]

You use the interval for call objects for controlling how long before the maintenance call date the order should be created. Particularly, if you have set the call horizons to 100%, this value must be sufficiently high. Otherwise, the orders are created too late.

Each run of the RISTRA20 program generates a scheduling log, which is saved and can be called via Transaction IBIPA (see Figure 5.127).

Scheduling Log

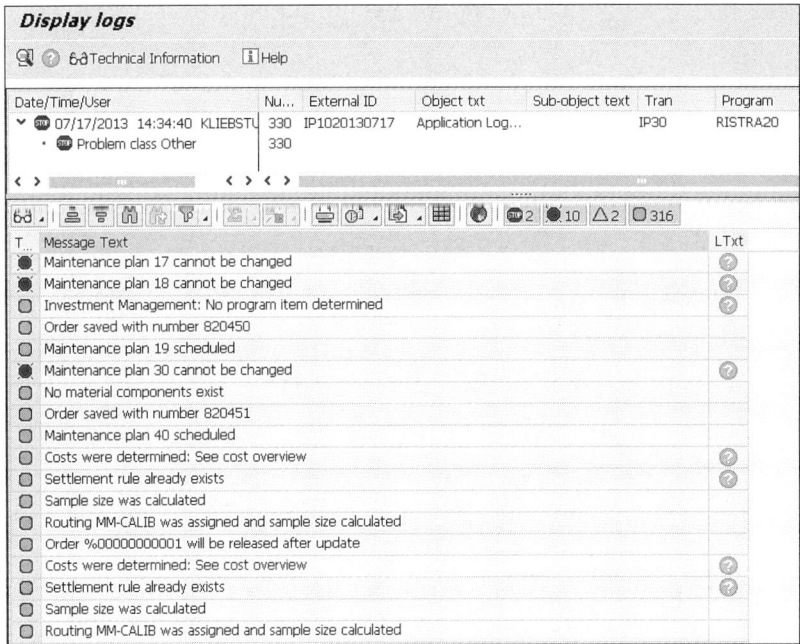

Figure 5.127 Scheduling Log

In addition to the basic functions ENTER and SCHEDULE, there are other functions for maintenance plans that can help you in your maintenance planning. The two functions COST DISPLAY FOR MAINTENANCE PLAN and SCHEDULING OVERVIEW are introduced below.

Cost Display for Maintenance Plan

You can use the cost display for maintenance plan (Transaction IP31) to determine the expected costs of one or more maintenance plans for any period.

Prerequisites The following prerequisites must be fulfilled:

- You schedule the maintenance plans. The cost display for maintenance plan does not work if you have only created, but have not started, the maintenance plan.
- You create orders from the maintenance plan. The cost display for maintenance plan does not work if you call notifications or service entry sheets.
- The maintenance plan does not have the INACTIVE or DELETION FLAG status.
- You specify a maintenance task list in the maintenance plan and store data in the maintenance task list that is relevant for costing for the operations—for example, work center, activity type, standard time, material. You assign prices to the activity type and the materials were valuated.

Functional scope The system determines the expected costs for the specified period as follows (see Figure 5.128):

- It calculates the existing calls (that is, orders).
- It simulates maintenance calls for the next period and determines expected costs.

Itemization			Values inUSD	US Dollar		
Internal activities			Total value	Fixed value	Vbl. value	Quantity
**	5000	5000	838.28	838.28		20 H
**	ELEKTRIK	ELEKTRIK	2,494.04	2,494.04		60 H
**	MACHTECH	MACHTECH				60 H
**	MECHANIK	MECHANIK	5,400.16	5,400.16		129 H
**	MECHMNT	MECHMNT				559 H
**	R_1140	R_1140	123,691.14	111,884.76	11,806.38	2,759 H
***	Internal activities		132,423.62	120,617.24	11,806.38	3,586 H
External services			Total value	Fixed value	Vbl. value	Quantity
*	1011	SKF Americas	28,376.78		28,376.78	37 PC
**	External services		28,376.78		28,376.78	37 PC
Material components			Total value	Fixed value	Vbl. value	Quantity
*	1000 100-100	Casings	135.98	92.94	43.04	1 PC
*	1000 100-600	Support base	81.34		81.34	2 PC
*	1000 DG-1000	Rubber Seal	23.01		23.01	1 PC
*	1000 F-1000	Filter for unit 178				37 PC
*	1000 KR117185	Distance plate	16.32		16.32	16 PC
*	1000 MB-1000	Carbon brushes, elec. Motor	81.76		81.76	16 PC
**	Material components		338.41	92.94	245.47	73 PC

Figure 5.128 Cost Display for Maintenance Plan

Graphic Scheduling Overview

The following functions are available in the graphic scheduling overview (see Figure 5.129), which you reach via Transaction IP19:

- You can display when certain maintenance dates are to be expected for a particular reference object. The system displays the dates that have already been calculated and the dates simulated for the period you specified.
- You can shift maintenance dates.
- You can display the capacity load that results from the maintenance plans (see Figure 5.130) and then shift dates based on the result.

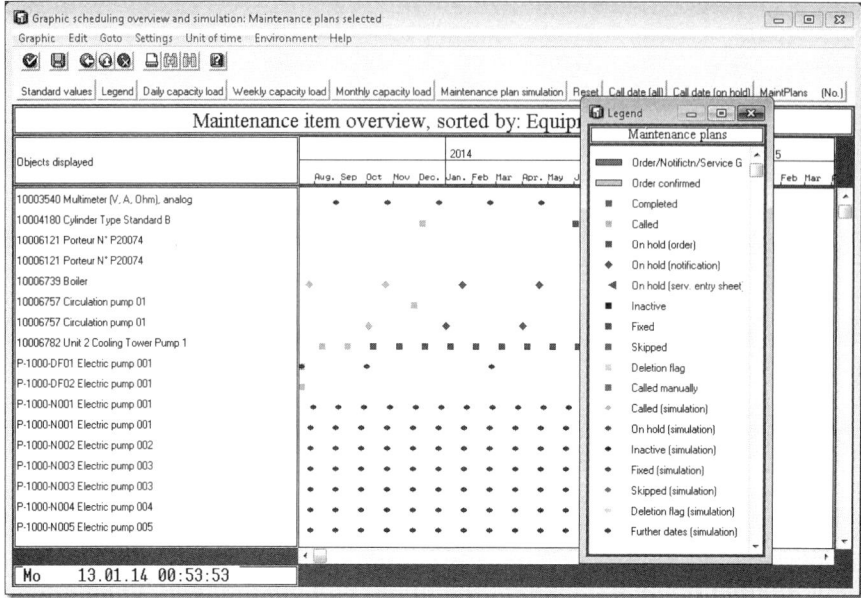

Figure 5.129 Scheduling Overview

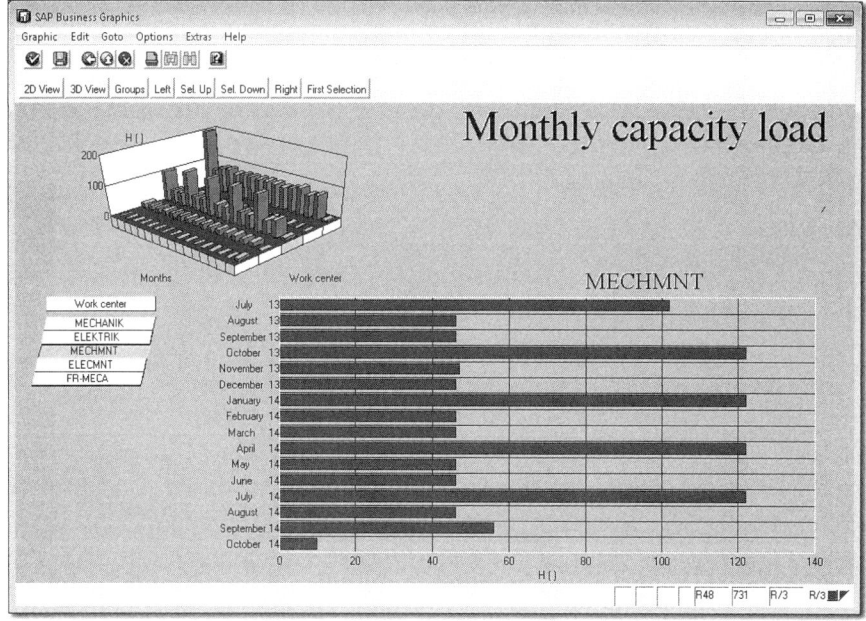

Figure 5.130 Capacity Load

> **Graphic Scheduling Overview Has Many Functions** [+]
>
> You can use the graphic scheduling overview not only to display the next maintenance dates, but also to simulate and display the expected capacity loads.

Time-Based Strategy Plan

You create time-based strategy plans if you have to perform maintenance activities based on each other or that supersede each other—for example, if you have a service manual from the manufacturer that contains activities with different deadlines, such as every three months, every six months, every twelve months, and so on.

Definition

In this case, you must include a maintenance task list, specifically one that has the same strategy as the maintenance plan. You will need a maintenance strategy and suitable maintenance task list to ensure that this type of business process will work.

Prerequisites

You define maintenance strategies using Transaction IP11. A maintenance strategy contains the chronology of maintenance packages (see Figure 5.131).

Maintenance strategy

Name	A							
Description	Scheduling by calendar							
Scheduling indicator	Time				Pack. seq.			

P...	Cycl.length	Unit	Maintenance cycle text	C...	H...	H...	Offset	O...	Initial	Subs...
1	1	MON	monthly	1M	1	H1			2	0
2	3	MON	3-monthly	3M	2	H1			5	0
3	12	MON	yearly	1Y	3	H2			10	0

Figure 5.131 Maintenance Strategy

A maintenance strategy does not contain the following elements:

- Reference object
- Tasks
- Dates

5 | Business Processes

The hierarchy indicators (the offset and initial/subsequent phase) are explained in the section on scheduling parameters within Time-based Single Cycle Plan.

> **[+] Subsequent Items**
>
> If you subsequently discover that you need additional packages, always append these in the consecutive sequence. Otherwise, the maintenance plan will, in the future, fill your orders with incorrect operations from the maintenance task list. If you require a six-month package in the maintenance strategy from Figure 5.131, do not insert it between items 2 and 3, as you might assume because of the cycle duration, but enter it instead as item 4.
>
> Alternatively, you assign item numbers from the outset in increments of ten (10, 20, 30, and so on) to the individual maintenance packages. This enables you to add maintenance packages between the ten positions (10, 15, 20, 30, and so on). However, do not use existing item numbers.

Maintenance task list
To be able to perform strategy-based preventive maintenance, you need a maintenance task list in addition to the maintenance strategy. Then, execute the following steps:

- Assign the same strategy to the maintenance task list at the header level that is to be included in the subsequent maintenance plan.
- Assign the maintenance packages to operations for which they are due (see Figure 5.132).

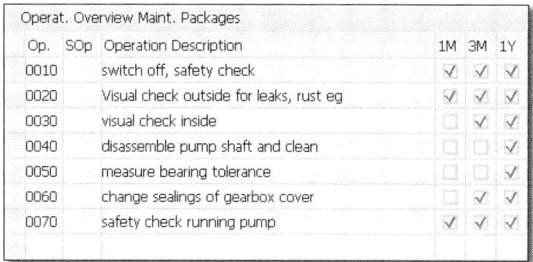

Figure 5.132 Operations with Maintenance Packages

Creating the strategy plan
You create the strategy plan in Transaction IP42. You choose between an internal and external number assignment. Rather than specifying the cycle, where you want the maintenance tasks to take place, you create

the maintenance packages directly in the maintenance plan using the maintenance task list that is to be included (see Figure 5.133).

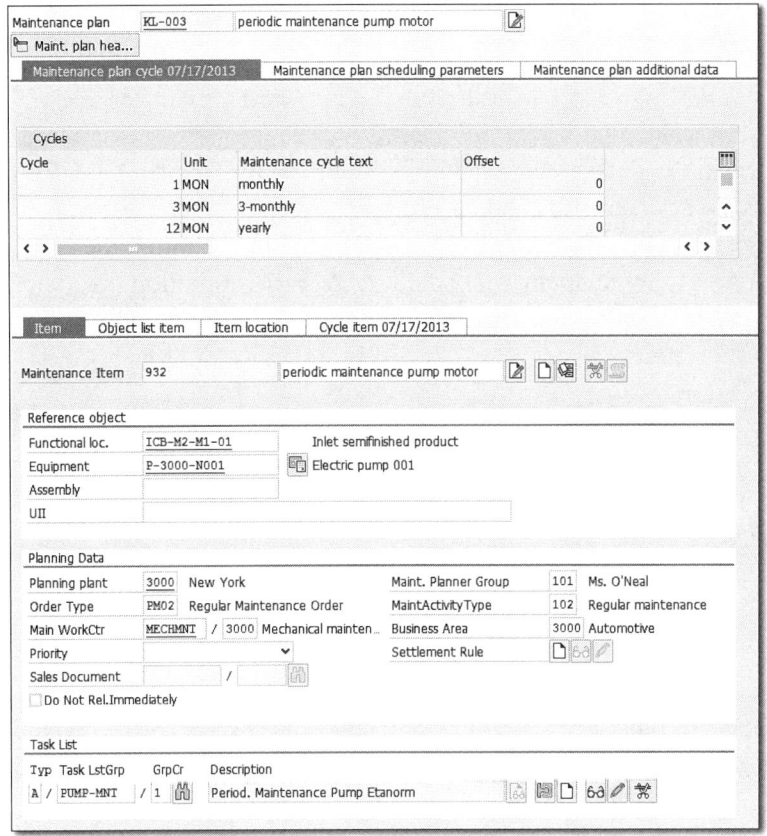

Figure 5.133 Strategy Plan

You already know the majority of scheduling parameters for a strategy plan from the single-cycle plan.

Scheduling parameter

The following values are suggested from the maintenance strategy that you can change in the strategy plan:

- Shift factors
- Tolerances
- Scheduling indicators
- Call horizon

You define the scheduling period and completion requirement individually for each strategy plan.

However, the strategy plan includes some scheduling parameters that either do not exist in the single-cycle plan or are not relevant there.

Cycle modification factor
If you discover in the live system that you have to adapt the maintenance intervals because you perform maintenance either too often or too seldom, you can change the cycle modification factor. The default value is always set at 1.00. When you specify a cycle modification factor (values from 0.01 to 9.99), you can use it to extend or shorten the cycles specified in the maintenance strategy. A cycle modification factor greater than 1 extends the cycle, whereas a cycle modification factor less than 1 shortens it.

[+] **Cycle Modification Factor: Dynamic**

You can use the cycle modification factor to extend or shorten the maintenance cycles individually for each strategy plan and thereby adjust the maintenance intensity, without having to change the maintenance strategy.

In principle, a cycle modification factor also exists in a single-cycle plan. However, it plays a minor role there because you would make a cycle adjustment directly by changing the cycle.

Maintenance package hierarchy
You maintain the hierarchy of the maintenance packages in the maintenance strategy (see Figure 5.131). The hierarchy determines which maintenance packages are executed if several maintenance packages are due at one time:

- **Same hierarchy number**
  If you want to execute the maintenance packages together for this date, they are given the same hierarchy number, for example, if there is an oil change every six months, and also a filter change every twelve months. The SAP system then combines the maintenance packages into one order with several operations.

- **Different hierarchy numbers**
  If you want to execute only specific maintenance packages for this date, these packages must have a higher hierarchy number than the

other packages. The SAP system, thus, always selects only the packages with the highest hierarchy number. If, for example, the spark plugs are cleaned every six months and changed every twelve months, it would not make any sense to first clean the spark plugs after twelve months and then change them: the package with the higher hierarchy (Change) thus replaces the package with the lower hierarchy (Clean).

> **Different Maintenance Package Hierarchies** [+]
>
> You achieve the most sophisticated control of maintenance activities when you assign different hierarchy numbers to all maintenance packages and, if necessary, then make a multiple assignment of maintenance packages in the maintenance task list (as shown in Figure 5.132). You usually assign the hierarchy indicator in ascending order according to the term.

You assign the preliminary and follow-up buffers in the maintenance strategy at the level of the maintenance packages; they are always expressed in days. The SAP system uses the preliminary and follow-up buffers to determine the basic start date and basic end date of the order based on the planned date.

Preliminary and follow-up buffers

Thus, for example, maintenance package 01 with a preliminary buffer of five days, a follow-up buffer of ten days, and a calculated planned date of May 15 results in the basic start date of May 10 and basic end date of May 25 in the order.

What is the business background? Maintenance activities take a certain amount of time, and long-term maintenance activities, in particular, cannot normally be completed in one day. You can, therefore, use the preliminary and follow-up buffers to specify a *from/to* time span from the outset.

> **Setting Follow-Up Buffer to Zero** [+]
>
> Always set at least one of the buffers to 0; otherwise, you will no longer be able to recognize the actual planned date by the basic dates of the order. I recommend that you always set the follow-up buffer to 0 because the required basic end date then corresponds to the planned maintenance date.

Offset An offset ensures a one-off time shift. You assign offsets in the maintenance strategy at the maintenance package level; they are always expressed in the unit of the maintenance package. You use offsets in the following cases:

- The maintenance package is to be executed only once. In this case, set only the OFFSET in the maintenance package.
- The cyclical work is to start only after a certain time. In this case, set a CYCLE DURATION and an OFFSET.

I will explain this using the following example. I received the following request from a former customer a while ago:

There is a requirement in our company for different operations to be performed with a maintenance plan. Although these operations should have the same time interval, they are to be generated at a later point in time than the orders.

Interval due:		1J	2J	3J	4J	5J	6J
Operation1	3Y	X			X		
Operation2	3Y		X			X	
Operation3	3Y			X			X

You implement the customer's requirement using a maintenance strategy with three packages. All three packages include a cycle duration of three years. By setting an offset of one year in the second maintenance package and of two years in the third maintenance package, you achieve the required chronological sequence exactly (see Figure 5.134).

Name			OFF					
Description			offset strategy					
Scheduling indicator			Time				Pack. seq.	
P...	Cycl.length	Unit	Maintenance cycle text	C...	H...	H...	Offset	O... Initial Su...
1	3	YR	3 years w/o offset	30	1	H1		
2	3	YR	3 years w offset 1 year	31	2	H2	1	01
3	3	YR	3 years w offset 2 years	32	3	H3	2	02

Figure 5.134 Maintenance Strategy with Offsets

> **Offset for Offsetting Maintenance Packages** [+]
>
> By setting offsets, you achieve a chronological offsetting of maintenance packages.

When you start a strategy plan, you must decide whether it is a Start (for example, if a new machine is purchased) or a start in the current cycle (for example, an existing machine with maintenance dates already implemented).

Starting the strategy plan

- **Start**
  You use Transaction IP10 (START function) to start the maintenance plan and, thus, create the first order. The system asks you for a START OF CYCLE DATE (see Figure 5.119). This is the date when you put the reference object into operation or have put it into operation shortly before.

- **Start in cycle**
  However, if you already implemented maintenance dates for the reference object in the past, use the START IN CYCLE function in Transaction IP10. The SAP system asks you for not only the Completion date (the date when you performed the last maintenance), but also an offset. Do not confuse this with the offset from the maintenance strategy because, here, you use the offset to determine which maintenance package you executed last. Use the `Select package` function to call the table for selecting packages (see Figure 5.135) and set the START offset there using the `Set start offset` function.

The system calculates the first planned date based on the start of cycle and scheduling parameters and creates the first maintenance order when you save your data.

In further procedures and all other functions, such as DEADLINE MONITORING, SIMULATION, COST DISPLAY FOR MAINTENANCE PLAN, and so on, the strategy plan does not differ from the single-cycle plan.

> **Time-Based Maintenance Plans: Little Administrative Effort** [+]
>
> The system can calculate the planned dates as automatically as possible with the calendar for time-based maintenance plans, regardless of whether these

are single-cycle plans or strategy plans. Ongoing effort is required for performance-based maintenance plans because counter readings are permanently being entered. You should, therefore, stick to the time-based maintenance plans, if possible.

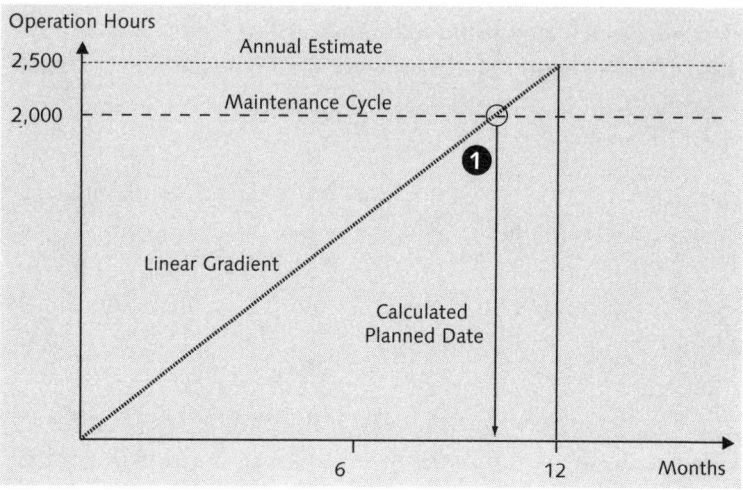

Figure 5.135 Start in Cycle

We now come to the business processes of preventive maintenance in which the calendar alone is no longer sufficient for calculating the maintenance dates, but rather where service indicators and counter readers are required. Thus, the business processes of the performance-based preventive maintenance are involved specifically here.

5.8.5 Preventive Maintenance, Performance-Based

For performance-based maintenance, the maintenance dates are calculated solely via performance-based values (such as operation hours, kilometers, or produced quantities). Calendar cycles (for example, a six-month cycle), however, have no effect.

Performance-Based Single-Cycle Plan

Definition A maintenance plan for a performance-based single cycle-plan has a maintenance cycle (for example, every 2,000 operation hours), and the maintenance dates are called based on counter readings. An order is always created when the counter reading reaches the cycle or is shortly before it.

To be able to implement performance-based maintenance, you must first fulfill some prerequisites.

You assign a counter to the reference object using the MEASURING POINTS/COUNTERS function. To do this, you use the corresponding transactions (for example, Transaction IE02 for equipment or IL02 for functional locations). You define the counter itself as follows (see Figure 5.136):

Counters

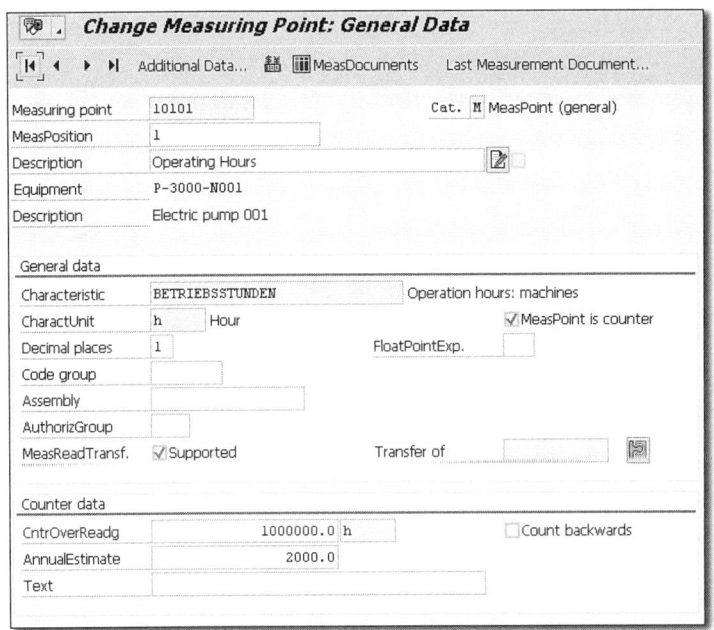

Figure 5.136 Counter for Reference Object

- The counter refers to a characteristic (for example, OPERATION_HOURS_1 here). You maintain this characteristic using Transaction CT04; note here that the characteristic has the *Numeric Format* data type and the relevant unit (for example, h, km, l).
- The COUNTER OVERFLOW READING represents the first value that the counter can no longer display. If you had a five-digit counter, for

example, you would have to enter the value 100,000 here; the system needs this value for scheduling the maintenance plans.

▶ The annual estimate represents a value you estimated about the extent to which the reference object is used each year in relation to the counter. The system also needs this value for the scheduling.

▶ If you have constructed a measuring point hierarchy, activate the MEASUREMENT READING TRANSFER option and define the measuring point/counter from which the value is to be transferred.

▶ A continuously growing counter reading is, without doubt, the normal situation for performance-based maintenance. However, there are also situations (for example, for a decreasing tire diameter) when the counter reading continuously decreases, and the maintenance is initiated when it goes below a limit. You activate the COUNT BACKWARDS option in such cases. However, you must then set up an additional counter that counts forward and for which you activate a measurement reading transfer from the backward-counting counter. You refer the maintenance plan to the forward-counting counter.

Initial counter reading

You enter an initial counter reading for the counter using Transaction IK11 (see Figure 5.137). This represents when the reference object was put into operation with a particular counter reading.

Document data				
MeasurementTime	07/17/2013 / 15:07:43		☐ Documtd after task	
Characteristic	BETRIEBSSTUNDEN		Operation hours: machines	
CharactUnit	h	Hour		
Counter reading		0.0		
Difference		0.0		
TotalCtrReading		0.0		
Valuation code				
Text	initial counter reading			📝 Long text

Figure 5.137 Initial Counter Reading

Creating the single-cycle plan

Like the time-based single cycle plan, you create the performance-based single-cycle plan using Transaction IP41. You specify the counter and the cycle, where you want the maintenance to take place, directly in the maintenance plan (see Figure 5.138). On the basis of the cycle unit, the system makes a suggestion: If multiple counters with the same unit exist, a dialog box is displayed in which you can select the relevant counter. If only one counter with a suitable unit exists, it is entered directly by the SAP system.

Figure 5.138 Performance-Based Single-Cycle Plan

You can use the scheduling parameters for a performance-based single-cycle plan as described in the section there, but with one exception: the significance of the call horizon increases in performance-based maintenance. — Scheduling parameters

> **Call Horizon Greater than 90%** [+]
>
> Set the call horizon to a high value (greater than 90%) for all performance-based maintenance plans. Otherwise, the SAP system creates the maintenance orders too early. More detailed explanations are provided in the next section.

Scheduling

I will now use a specific numerical example to demonstrate how performance-based maintenance is scheduled.

A piece of equipment is equipped with an operation-hour counter with an annual estimate of 2,500 operation hours (OH) per year and contains a single-cycle plan with a maintenance cycle of 2,000 OH and a call horizon of 95%. An initial counter reading was entered for March 01 with 0 OH. — Starting point

The geometric solution (see Figure 5.139) is as follows: — Basic scheduling

If the pieces of equipment were utilized exactly as estimated in the annual estimate, this would result in the counter being linear, and 2,500 OH would be reached after one year. The intersection between the linear gradient and the maintenance cycle would now determine the maintenance date ❶.

The arithmetic solution is as follows:

01.03. + 2,000 / 2,500 × 365 days
= 01.03. (March 01) + 292 days
= 17.12. (December 17)

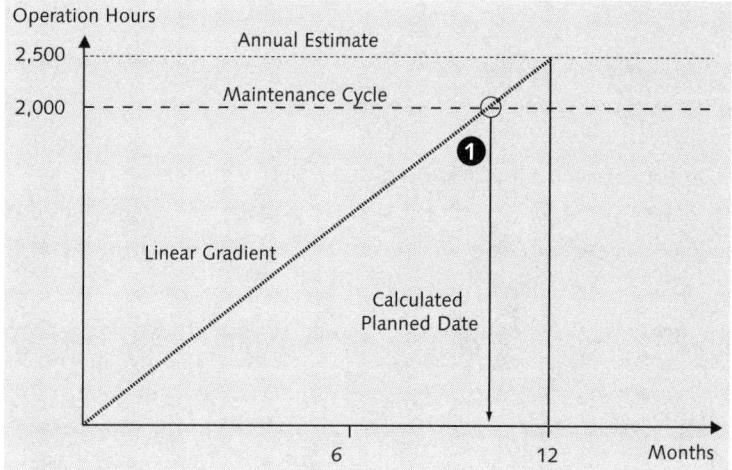

Figure 5.139 Scheduling 1

New measurement document

A counter reading of 500 OH is read on April 01 (the equipment was used more extensively than planned in the annual estimate).

[+] **Date Calculation for Each Entry of Counter Readings**

Every time you enter a measurement document, the system reschedules the maintenance plan and determines a new maintenance date.

The geometric solution looks as follows (see Figure 5.140).

An equivalent to the annual estimate is drawn from the measurement document, and the intersection with the maintenance cycle determines the new maintenance date ❷.

The arithmetic solution is as follows:

01.04. + (2,000 − 500) / 2,500 × 365 days
= 01.04. (April 01) + 1,500 / 2,500 × 365 days
= 01.04. (April 01) + 219 days
= 06.11. (November 06)

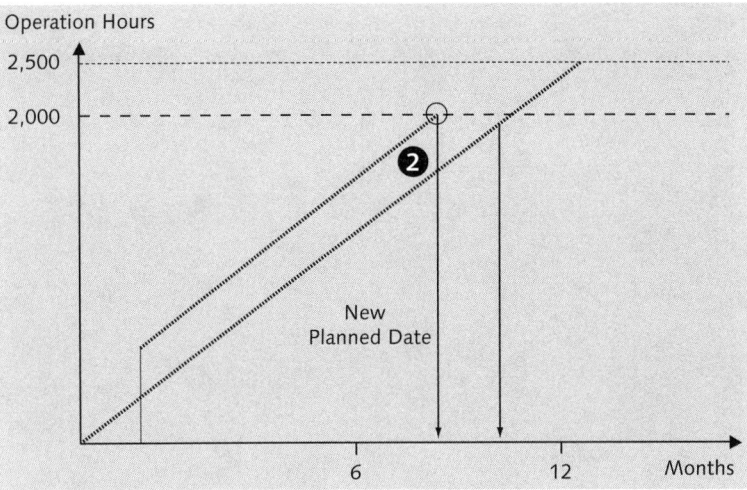

Figure 5.140 Scheduling with a Measurement Document

If you do not set a call horizon, the system immediately creates an order the moment you enter the first measurement document. This is very problematic because you are still far away from the maintenance cycle at the time of the first measurement document. As already recommended above as a practical tip, you should therefore assign a high call horizon to the maintenance plan to ensure that the order is created on time only on the actual planned date. In our case, the call horizon was set to 95%, that is, 1,900 OH.

Scheduling with call horizon

The geometric solution in this case is as follows (see Figure 5.141):

The intersection of the measurement document projection line with the line of the call horizon determines the maintenance call date ❸.

The arithmetic solution looks as follows:

01.04. + (1,900 − 500) / 2,500 × 365 days
= 01.04. (April 01) + 1,400 / 2,500 × 365 days
= 01.04. (April 01) + 204 days
= 22.10. (October 22)

Thus, in the specified combination, the planned date of November 06 would be calculated with a maintenance call date of October 22 in this situation.

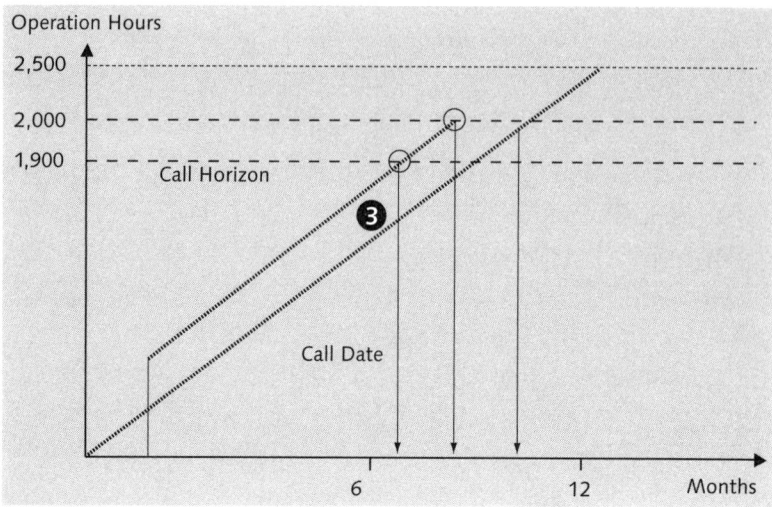

Figure 5.141 Scheduling with Call Horizon

Maintenance call and order

When is an order actually created? If you do not enter another measurement document, the RISTRA20 deadline monitoring creates the maintenance call with an order the first time it runs on or after October 22.

However, this is quite unrealistic. You should, in fact, continuously enter measurement documents for performance-based maintenance. The maintenance call is created with an order the moment you enter a measurement document that is above the call horizon (thus, more than 1,900 OH) and after the deadline monitoring runs for the first time.

[+] **Regular Entry of Counter Readings**

To ensure that performance-based maintenance fulfills its purpose, enter counter readings regularly. Whether you do this daily, weekly, or in a different sequence depends on each particular case.

Practical tip: there should be at least 10 measurement documents between two maintenances. If you perform maintenance, for example, after every 2,000 OH, you should enter the counter reading at least at an interval of 200 BH.

If you do not do this, performance-based maintenance does not fulfill its purpose, and you should preferably switch to time-based maintenance.

> **Entering Counter Readings Even When Out of Operation** [+]
>
> Even if you temporarily take the technical object out of operation, you must continue to enter counter readings. Even though the readings are always the same, they have a more current date each time.

Performance-Based Strategy Plan

You create performance-based strategy plans if you have to perform maintenance activities based on each other or that supersede each other—for example, if you have a service manual from the manufacturer that contains activities with different performance levels, such as every 1,000 OH, every 2,000 OH, every 5,000 OH, and so on. In such cases, you must include a maintenance task list with the same strategy as the maintenance plan. You need a performance-based maintenance strategy and suitable maintenance task list to ensure that this type of business process works.

Definition

You also maintain performance-based strategies using Transaction IP11. The only differences compared to a time-based strategy are the scheduling indicator and unit of measurement (see Figure 5.142):

Maintenance strategy

- You set the Scheduling indicator to performance-based.
- You use a performance unit of measurement (operation hours, kilometers, number of pieces, tons, flow rates, and so on) as the unit of measurement.

All other control options (shift factors, call horizon, hierarchy, offset, and so on) correspond to the time-based maintenance strategy.

Name	EP-P1						
Description	Electric pumps perf. based OPH						
Scheduling indicator	3 Activity			Pack. seq.			

P...	Cycl.length	Unit	Maintenance cycle text	C...	H...	H...	Offset	O...	Initial Su...
1	1000	OPH	Every 1000 operating hours	01	1	H1		1	
5	5000	OPH	Every 5000 operating hours	05	1	H1		3	
10	10000	OPH	Every 10.000 operating hours	10	1	H1		5	

Figure 5.142 Performance-Based Maintenance Strategy

Maintenance task list

The only difference between the maintenance task list for a performance-based strategy plan and a maintenance task list for time-based strategy plans (see the Maintenance Task List section) is that you assign a performance-based strategy to the maintenance task list header and performance-based maintenance packages to the operations.

Creating the strategy plan

The creation of the strategy plan is practically a combination of the time-based strategy plan and performance-based single cycle plan:

- You use Transaction IP42.
- You assign the reference object and a maintenance task list.
- The SAP system proposes a counter, or you assign a counter manually.
- The maintenance packages are automatically entered from the used maintenance packages.

Figure 5.143 displays the result of a completed performance-based strategy plan.

Starting the strategy plan

Starting the strategy plan is also a combination of the time-based strategy plan and performance-based single cycle plan:

- You enter an initial counter reading for the reference object.
- You use Transaction IP10 with the START function when you want to start a new maintenance cycle. In this case, you specify a START COUNTER READING for when the cycle began (for example, 0 operation hours).
- You use Transaction IP10 with the START IN CYCLE function when you want to proceed in an existing maintenance cycle. In this case, you specify a COMPLETION COUNTER READING for when the last maintenance was performed and select the last executed package (see Figure 5.144).

The SAP system then calculates the next Packages due, next Planned Date, and the associated Call date based on the maintenance strategy, current counter reading, annual estimate, completion counter reading, and start counter reading (see the relevant columns in Figure 5.145).

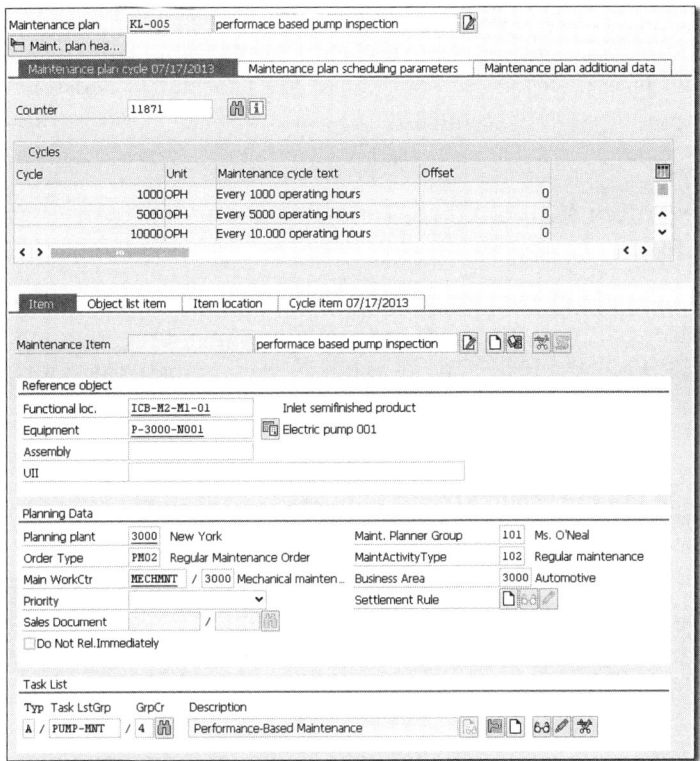

Figure 5.143 Performance-Based Strategy Plan

Figure 5.144 Completion Counter Reading

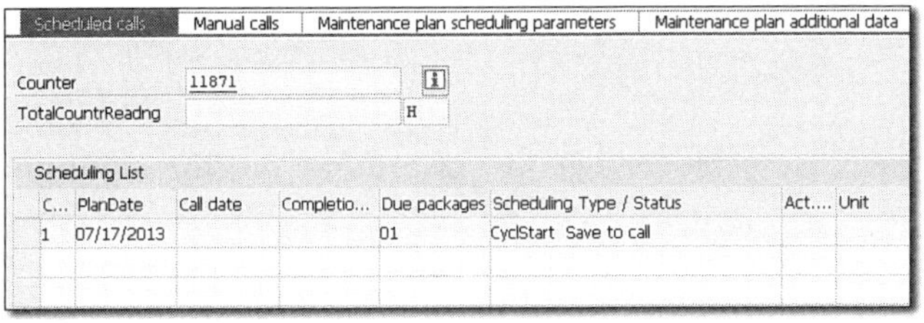

Figure 5.145 Started Performance-Based Strategy Plan

The other procedures (such as processing orders, monitoring deadlines, and so on) and other functions (such as cost display for maintenance plan, scheduling overviews) are identical to the procedures and functions for all other maintenance plans.

5.8.6 Preventive Maintenance, Time-Based and Performance-Based

For time-based and performance-based maintenance, the maintenance dates are calculated both via the calendar (for example, in a six-month cycle) and on the basis of performance (for example, operation hours, kilometers, or produced quantities).

Basic Multiple Counter Plan

Definition   You define maintenance cycles with different dimensions when using multiple counter plans. Multiple counter plans enable you to integrate performance and time dimensions into a maintenance plan—that is, every 1,000 operation hours, every 5,000 kilometers, and every 12 months (see Figure 5.146).

Figure 5.146 Object with Several Counters

Cycle sets   You can create cycle sets to reduce the effort of entering multiple counter plans. These are similar to maintenance strategies but are not a mandatory prerequisite for basic multiple counter plans.

You create cycle sets using Transaction IP11Z. Figure 5.147 shows the cycle set for the above example.

5.8 Preventive Maintenance Business Process

Name	FORK				
Description	fork lifters				
P...	Cycl.length	Unit	Maintenance cycle text	C...	Offset	O...
10	5000	KM	every 5000 km	5K	
20	12	MON	every 12 months	12	
30	2000	H	every 2000 operating hrs	20	

Figure 5.147 Cycle Sets for the Basic Multiple Counter Plan

If you now create a basic multiple counter plan (Transaction IP43), you create the cycles directly in the maintenance plan itself or refer to an existing cycle set when you open it (see Figure 5.148).

Creating a multiple counter plan

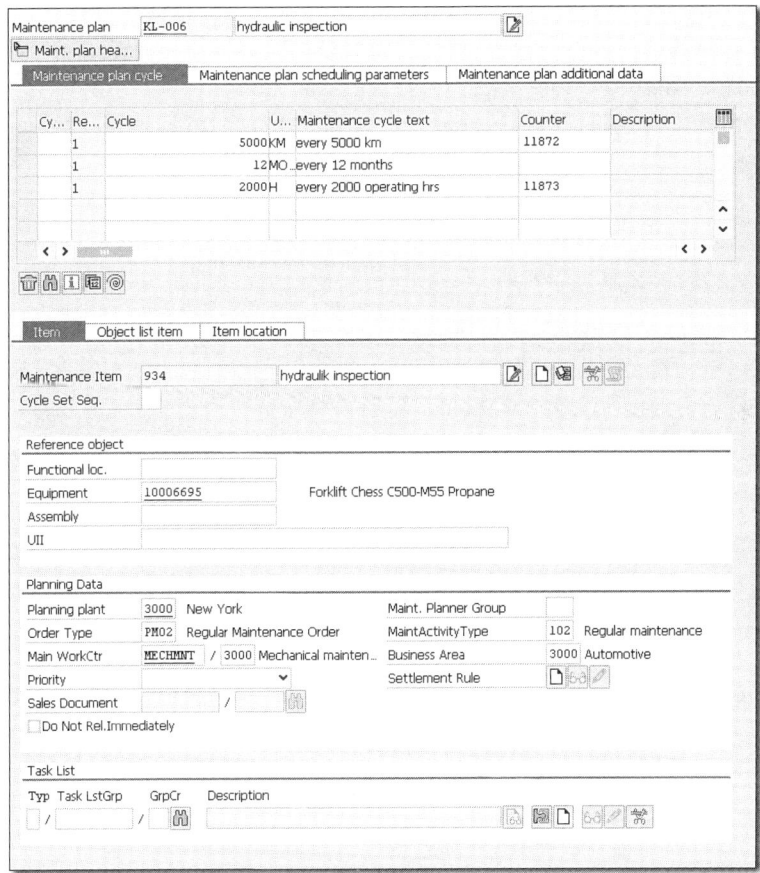

Figure 5.148 Multiple Counter Plan

Due to the units specified there, the SAP system searches for suitable counters and suggests them for the relevant units. If the SAP system does not suggest a counter, or if it suggests an incorrect one, you can also change this manually.

Scheduling parameters

You are already familiar with most of the valid scheduling parameters in a multiple counter plan. However, two new parameters have been added: the OPERATION TYPE parameter and the LEAD FLOAT parameter (see Figure 5.149):

- A selected OR link means that an order is created for the earliest planned date. The case that occurs first is crucial. This is surely the standard case in performance-based maintenance with several dimensions.

- A selected AND link means that an order is created for the last planned date. The case that occurs last is crucial. This is surely the exceptional case in performance-based maintenance with several dimensions.

- The LEAD FLOAT specifies how many days before the planned date the basic start date of the order should be. The basic end date of the order is always created using the planned date.

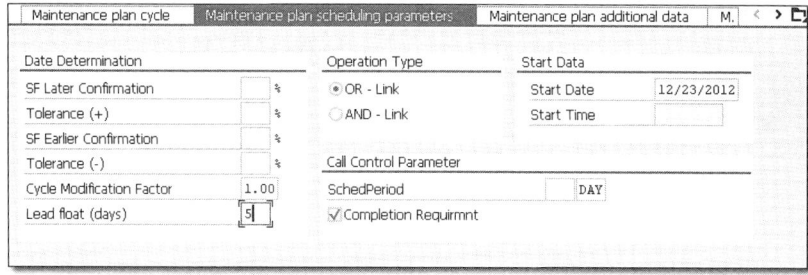

Figure 5.149 Scheduling Parameters for Multiple Counter Plan

Starting the basic multiple counter plan

Starting the basic multiple counter plan is a combination of the time-based single-cycle plan and performance-based single cycle plan, as follows:

- You have entered the initial counter readings in the reference object.
- You use Transaction IP10 with the START function when you want to start a new maintenance cycle. In this case, you specify a start date when the cycle began.
- The SAP system then calculates the various planning data based on the current counter readings, relevant annual estimate, and start date.
- If you select the OR link, the system suggests the first planned date as the planned date; if you selected an AND link, it suggests the last planned date as the planned date of the order (see Figure 5.150).

Note that you must not set a call horizon for multiple counter plans. Instead, the SAP system sets a maintenance call date identical to the planned date, which results in the deadline monitoring generating the order.

Figure 5.150 Started Basic Multiple Counter Plan

The other procedures (such as monitoring deadlines, processing orders, and so on) and other functions (such as cost display for maintenance plan, scheduling overviews) are identical to the procedures and functions for all other maintenance plans.

Enhanced Multiple Counter Plan

Definition Unlike the basic multiple counter plan, enhanced multiple counter plans enable you to define several cycles based on each other, as the following examples show:

- Cycle set 1: every 1,000 OH, every 5,000 km, or every twelve months
- Cycle set 2: every 3,000 OH, every 15,000 km, or every 36 months

To put it another way: the enhanced multiple counter plan is a combination of a performance-based strategy plan and a time-based strategy plan.

Prerequisites To be able to use the enhanced multiple counter plan, you must fulfill the following prerequisites:

- In the Customizing function SET SPECIAL FUNCTIONS FOR MAINTENANCE PLANNING, set the ENHANCED MULTIPLE COUNTER PLAN option. Caution: when you have activated the option once, you can no longer cancel it.
- You define the two cycle sets using Transaction IP11Z (see Figure 5.151).

Name			FORK			
Description			fork lifters			

P...	Cycl.length	Unit	Maintenance cycle text	Cycle ...	Offset	O...
10	5000	KM	every 5000 km	5K		
20	12	MON	every 12 months	12		
30	2000	H	every 2000 operating hrs	20		

Figure 5.151 Cycle Sets

- You need two different maintenance task lists, one of which must be executed on the date when cycle set 1 is due, and the other on the date when cycle set 2 is due. Unlike the strategy maintenance plan, the maintenance task list header is not assigned the cycle set, and the operations are not assigned maintenance packages.

Figure 5.152 displays the basic structure and the effect for scheduling.

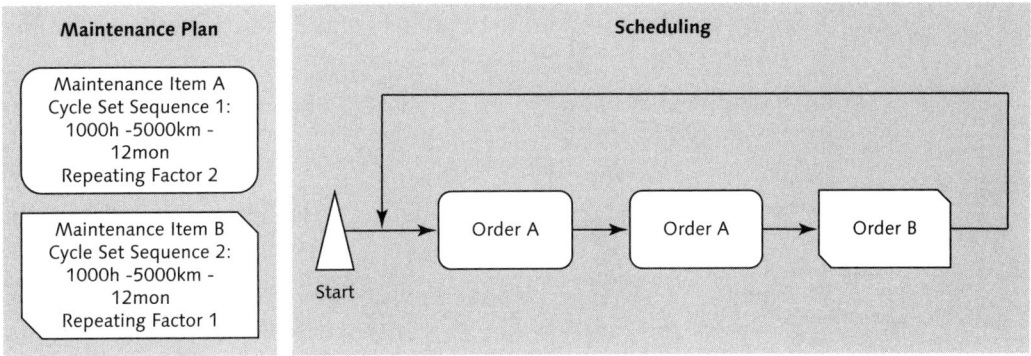

Figure 5.152 Structure of an Enhanced Multiple Counter Plan

Proceed as follows to define an enhanced multiple counter plan (see Figure 5.153):

1. You create a multiple counter plan using Transaction IP43.
2. You assign the required cycles from cycle sets 1 and 2 to the maintenance plan.

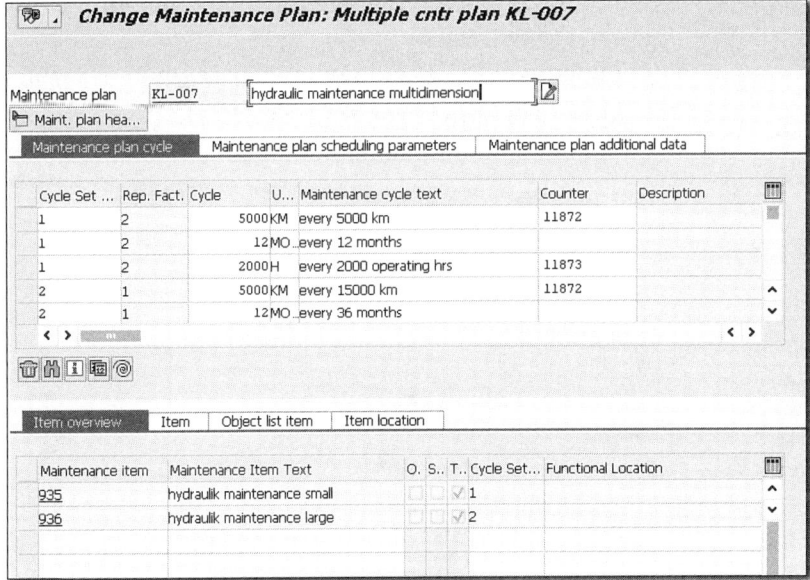

Figure 5.153 Enhanced Multiple Counter Plan

3. You assign cycle set sequence 1 to the cycles from cycle set 1 and cycle set sequence 2 for cycle set 2. You then create two items. You assign cycle set sequence 1 to the first item and cycle set sequence 2 to the second item.

4. You use the 🔘 button to change the repetition factors. You set the repetition factor to 2 for the cycle set sequence, and you set the repetition factor to 1 for the cycle set sequence. Thus, the first item is first performed twice, then the second item once, and then the first position twice again, and so on.

5. Due to the units specified there, the SAP system searches for suitable counters and suggests them for the relevant units. If the SAP system does not suggest a counter, or if it suggests an incorrect one, you can also change this manually.

6. The scheduling parameters (for example, AND/OR link) are identical to the scheduling parameters of the basic multiple counter plan.

Starting the enhanced multiple counter plan is a combination of the time-based strategy plan and performance-based strategy plan:

- You use Transaction IP10 with the START function when you want to start a new maintenance cycle. In this case, you specify a START DATE when the cycle begins.

- You use Transaction IP10 with the START IN CYCLE function when you want to proceed in an existing maintenance cycle. Here, you specify the CYCLE SET SEQUENCE and COMPLETION DATE, for which the last maintenance was performed (see Figure 5.154).

Figure 5.154 Start in Cycle Multiple Counter Plan

- The system then calculates the various planning data based on the current counter readings, relevant annual estimate, and start date.

- If you select the OR link, the system suggests the first planned date as the planned date; if you selected an AND link, it suggests the last planned date as the planned date of the order. It is also clear which cycle set sequence is the next one due (see Figure 5.155).

Scheduled calls	Maintenance plan scheduling parameters	Maintenance plan additional data				
Scheduling List						
C... PlanDate	Call date	Completio...	Cycl...	Scheduling Type / Status	Act....	Unit
1 07/13/2014	07/13/2014		2	CyclStart Hold		

Figure 5.155 Started Enhanced Multiple Counter Plan

Note that you must not set a call horizon for multiple counter plans. Instead, the SAP system sets a maintenance call date identical to the planned date, which results in the deadline monitoring generating the order.

The other procedures (monitoring deadlines, processing orders, and so on) and other functions (cost display for maintenance plan, scheduling overviews, and so on) are identical to the procedures and functions for all other maintenance plans.

You must activate the business function LOG_EAM_SHIFTFACTORS in order to be able to use the multiple counter plans in the displayed form.

Business function

5.8.7 Inspection Rounds

How do the functions for inspection rounds differ from those for maintenance planning described above? Maintenance planning usually involves a single object for which a series of activities, some very complex, is to be executed. The reverse is the case when it comes to inspection rounds. With an inspection round, you want to process a large number of objects, executing the same activities on each object. These activities are not usually very complex and require the same tools, spare parts, and qualifications. These include such activities as the following:

Definition

- Lubrication services
- Visual checks
- Counter readings

- Oil level checks
- Minor part replacements

There are two different ways to map inspection rounds in the SAP system:

- Inspection rounds using an object list (basic inspection rounds)
- Inspection rounds using maintenance task list (advanced inspection rounds)

Basic Inspection Rounds Using the Object List

If you always perform the same activities on the objects on the inspection round (for example, the lubrication condition of all objects must be checked and re-lubricated, if necessary), use the following (see Figure 5.156):

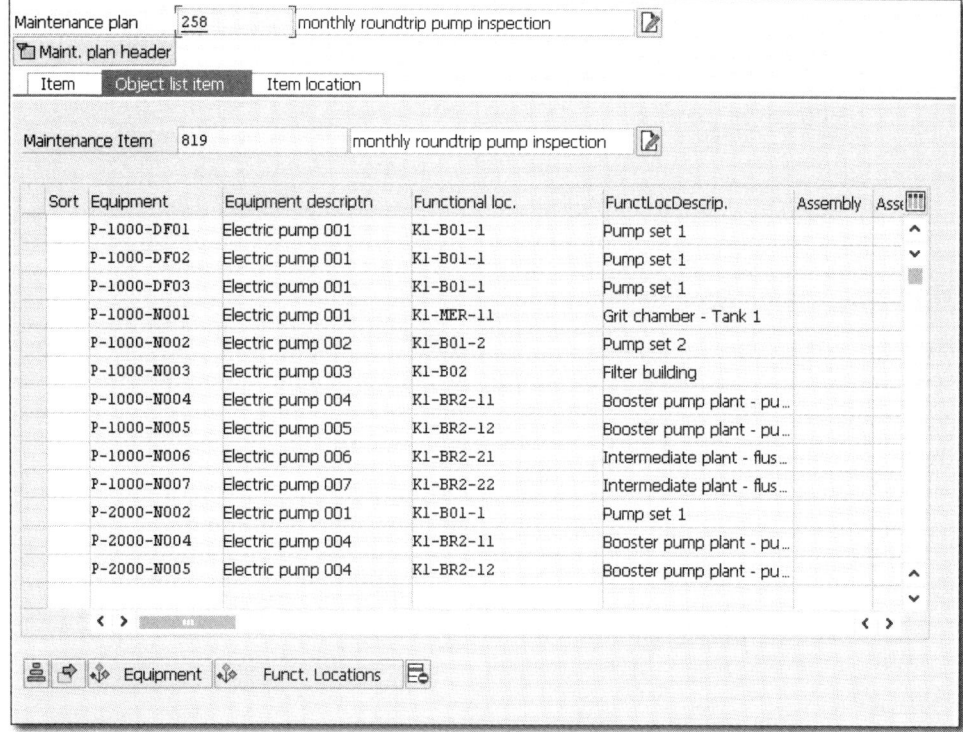

Figure 5.156 Basic Inspection Rounds—Maintenance Plan

- A single-cycle plan to store the organizational data (such as plant, order type, and so on) and to describe the content as maintenance plan text or maintenance plan item text
- The object list to define the technical objects to be inspected on the inspection round

When you start the maintenance plan, it generates an order that usually contains an operation and an object list (see Figure 5.157).

Basic inspection rounds—orders

Figure 5.157 Basic Inspection Rounds—Order

To confirm the basic inspection round, it is best to use Transaction IW42 for the overall completion confirmation. You can first report the times there. Using the ENVIRONMENT • OBJECT LIST, you then navigate to the confirmation of the object list (see Figure 5.158). There, you select in column B (i.e., processing indicator) the objects you have processed.

Basic inspection rounds— confirmation

Figure 5.158 Basic Inspection Rounds—Confirmation

Advanced Inspection Rounds Using the Maintenance Task List

You use the advanced inspection round via a maintenance task list if you perform different activities on the objects of the inspection round; these could include, for example:

- Object 1: Check lubrication condition
- Object 2: Record noise levels
- Object 3: Read counter reading
- Object 4: ....

[!] **Advanced Inspection Rounds—Elements**

You map the advanced planning and execution of inspection rounds in the SAP system as follows:

- You define the content of inspection rounds in maintenance task lists.
- You define the frequency of inspection rounds in a maintenance plan.
- You control the execution of inspection rounds using orders generated by the maintenance plan.
- The best way to document the confirmation of inspection rounds is with the overall completion confirmation.

Maintenance tasks lists used for advanced inspection rounds differ from other maintenance tasks lists in the following ways (see Figure 5.159):

Advanced inspection rounds—maintenance task list

- You use the sequence of operations to define the sequence of stations and individual steps that make up the inspection round.
- You assign the technical object to be inspected to the operations (functional location, equipment and, if necessary, an assembly).
- You can also assign any measuring points/counters, documents, lubricants, or test equipment to that operation.
- If the inspection round is to be executed on a regular basis (daily, weekly, or monthly), this can be specified in a maintenance plan.
- You can execute the inspection round if certain events occur (for example, before/after a production start, before/after a shutdown). In this case, you execute the maintenance task list using a manual order (Transaction IW31).

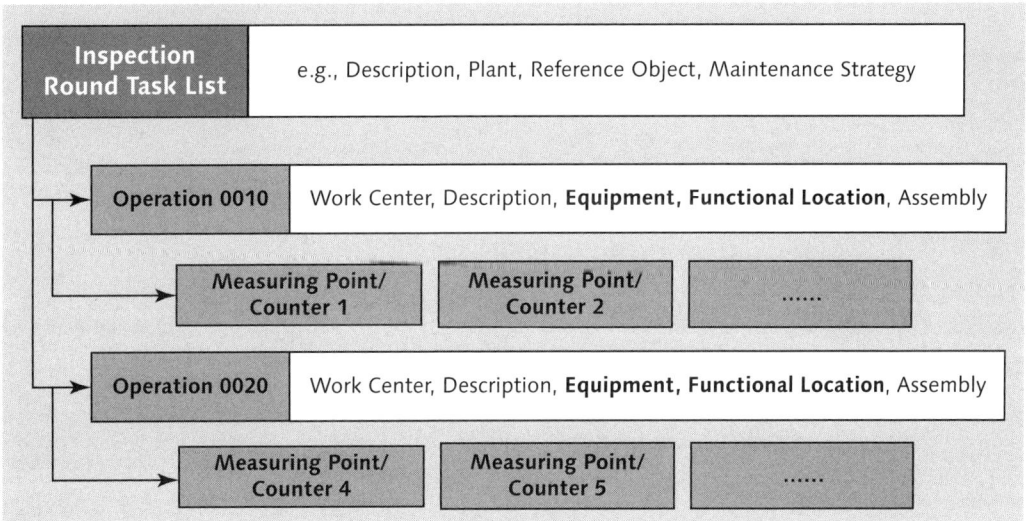

Figure 5.159 Advanced Inspection Rounds—Structure

Figure 5.160 shows technical objects for which lubrication services are to be executed and counter readings taken.

Group		PUMP_RDG Round tour planning pump stations			Grp.Countr 2		
General Operation Overview							
Op...	SOp	Work ctr	Plnt	Ctrl	Operation Description	LT Equipment	Functional loc.
0010		MECHMNT	3000	PM01	counter reading	P-3000-N001	C1-B01-1
0020		MECHMNT	3000	PM01	lubrication check, refill where needed	P-3000-N002	C1-B01-2
0030		MECHMNT	3000	PM01	lubrication check, refill where needed	P-3000-N003	C1-B02
0040		MECHMNT	3000	PM01	lubrication check, refill where needed	P-3000-N004	C1-BR2-11
0050		MECHMNT	3000	PM01	counter reading	P-3000-N005	C1-BR2-12
0060		MECHMNT	3000	PM01	counter reading	P-3000-N006	C1-BR2-21
0070		MECHMNT	3000	PM01	lubrication check, refill where needed	P-3000-N007	C1-BR2-22
0080		MECHMNT	3000	PM01	lubrication check, refill where needed	P-3000-N008	
0090		MECHMNT	3000	PM01			

Figure 5.160 Advanced Inspection Rounds—Maintenance Task List

You define the counters as PRTs for the operation (see Figure 5.161).

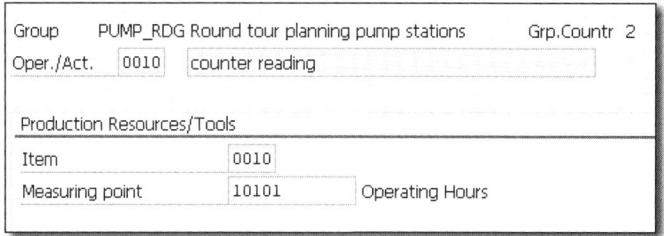

Figure 5.161 Advanced Inspection Rounds—Measuring Point

[+] **Advanced Inspection Round: Which Maintenance Plan Category?**

You use a maintenance plan to define the frequency with which the inspection round task list is to be executed:

▶ You use the time-based, single-cycle plan if you want the entire inspection round to be executed at defined intervals.

▶ You use the time-based strategy plan if the inspection of individual stations takes place in different cycles.

▶ In contrast, performance-based maintenance plan categories are not relevant for inspection rounds because you want to inspect several objects with differing counter readings.

Figure 5.162 shows a single-cycle plan that executes the inspection round task list created above on a weekly basis.

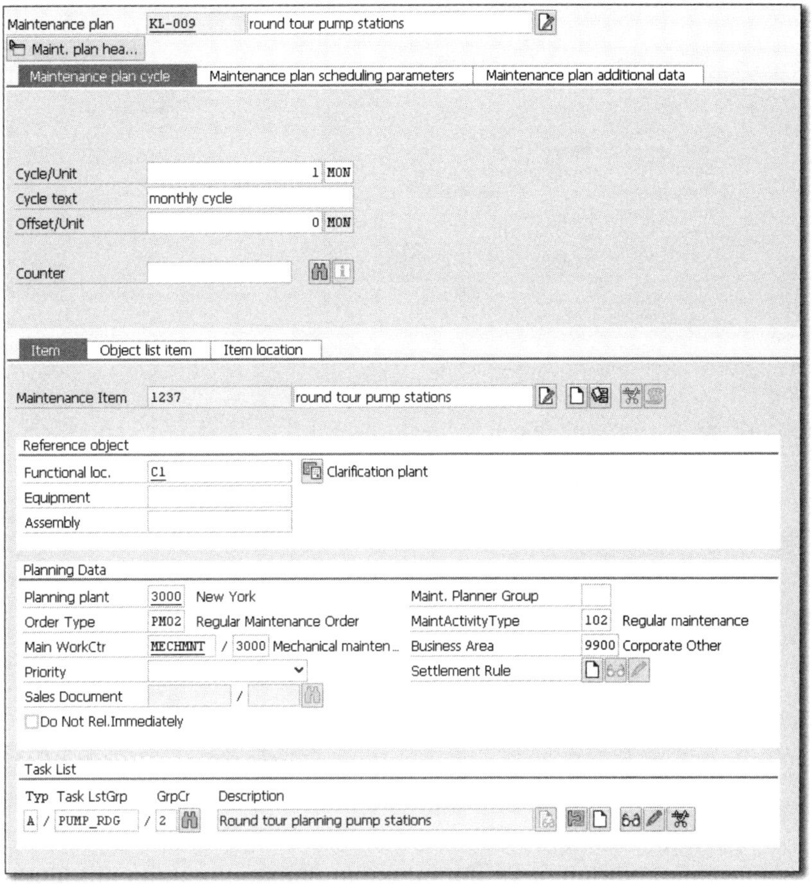

Figure 5.162 Advanced Inspection Rounds—Maintenance Plan

When you start the maintenance plan, it generates an order, which contains the technical objects (functional locations, equipment) and measuring points as PRTs at the operation level (see Figure 5.163).

Advanced inspection rounds—orders

In order for this to work, you must make the following setting: choose the Customizing function DEFINE NOTIFICATION AND ORDER INTEGRATION and deactivate the ASSIGNMENT OF OPERATIONS TO OBJECT LIST ENTRIES option for the ENHANCED OBJECT LIST indicator for the relevant order type.

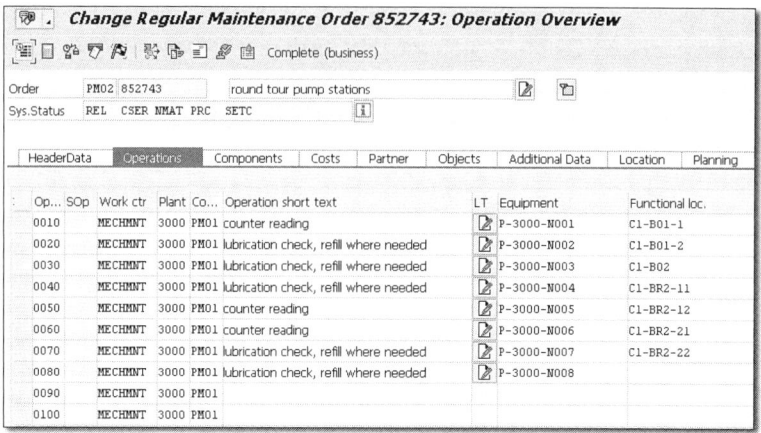

Figure 5.163 Inspection Rounds—Order

To confirm the order for the inspection round, it is recommended that you use Transaction IW42 (Overall Completion Confirmation) because it allows you to record measurement/counter readings, as well as confirm operations (see Figure 5.164). Furthermore, you can directly create a new notification for technical confirmation for every operation to which an object is assigned from the overall completion confirmation.

[Advanced inspection rounds— confirmation]

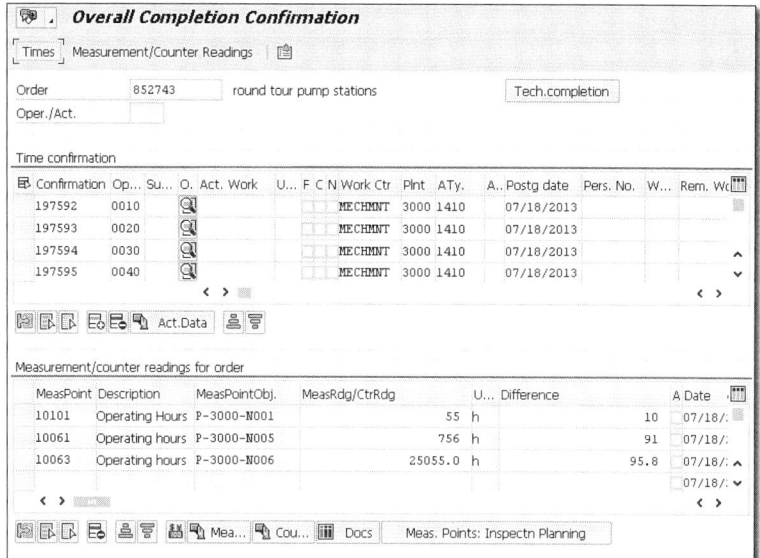

Figure 5.164 Confirming Inspection Rounds

As a prerequisite, you must define data entry profiles using the Customizing function SET SCREEN TEMPLATES FOR THE COMPLETION CONFIRMATION and assign a data entry profile (function EXTRAS • SETTINGS in Transaction IW42). When you define screen templates, you must activate the MEASUREMENT/COUNTER READINGS screen area.

The LOG_EAM_CI_3 and LOG_EAM_CI_4 business functions must be activated in order for you to be able to use inspection rounds completely.

Business function

> **Overall Completion Confirmation with Layout for Advanced Inspection Rounds** [+]
>
> Define a screen layout for the overall completion confirmation of orders for advanced inspection rounds, which contains the operations and measuring points/counter readings and allows you to confirm all information relating to inspection rounds from a single screen template.

5.9 Condition-Based Maintenance Business Process

Condition-based maintenance is defined as a maintenance strategy for which a maintenance task is triggered by a difference in the actual condition of a technical system or part of a technical system compared to the target condition.

Definition

As explained in Section 4.2.9, the following applies:

Counters are the tools you can use in the SAP system to represent the wear and tear of an object, consumption, or the reduction of an object's useful life—for example, an odometer, operation hours counter, numbers of pieces, or output in tons. Counters have a continuous (increasing or decreasing) counter reading.

Counters

Measuring points in the SAP system are used to indicate locations where the current condition of a technical system is described—for example, temperature, number of revolutions, pressure, level of contamination, and viscosity. You can specify target values and upper/lower limits on measuring points. Measuring readings have a discontinuous progression.

Measuring points

While we learned that counters are the basis for performance-based maintenance, measuring points and measurement readings form the basis for condition-based maintenance.

Prerequisites You must fulfill the following prerequisites to be able to perform condition-based maintenance:

- First, define the target conditions of the technical systems and parts of a technical system.
- Monitor the technical system and parts of it regularly or permanently in terms of the target conditions.
- You are not required to define any maintenance plans.

Examples While a maintenance task for time-based maintenance is triggered when a certain date is reached or for performance-based maintenance when a specific counter reading is achieved, tasks for condition-based maintenance are triggered, for example, by the following events:

- The temperature has risen too high or fallen too low.
- The flow rate is too quick or too slow.
- The oil shows too high a level of pollution.
- The voltage has dropped too low or built up too far.
- The viscosity of the lubricant is too high or too low.

Comparing strategies Table 5.3 contains an overview of the differences among time-based, performance-based, and condition-based maintenance.

	Time-Based Maintenance	Performance-Based Maintenance	Condition-Based Maintenance
Basis	Calendar	Counters	Measuring point
Readings	–	Sporadic to regular	Regular to permanent
Run chart	–	Continuous increase or decrease	Discontinuous

Table 5.3 Maintenance Strategies

5.9 Condition-Based Maintenance Business Process

	Time-Based Maintenance	Performance-Based Maintenance	Condition-Based Maintenance
Maintenance plan	Yes	Yes	No
Task is triggered	When a date is reached	When a counter reading is reached	When target values have been exceeded or not reached

Table 5.3 Maintenance Strategies (Cont.)

How does condition-based maintenance work in the SAP system? An overview of this is provided in Figure 5.165.

How it works

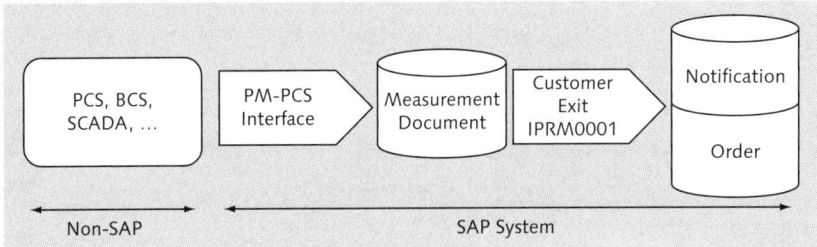

Figure 5.165 How Condition-Based Maintenance Works

You use an upstream system to obtain current data regularly or permanently about the condition of the technical system. Such systems can be the following:

- Process Control Systems (PCS)
- Building Control Systems (BCS)
- Supervisory Control and Data Acquisition (SCADA) systems
- Electronic control stations
- Network monitoring systems
- Systems for plant data collection and machine data acquisition (PDC/MDA systems)
- Warehouse computers
- Systems for sound or vibration analyses

- Diagnostic systems
- Mobile data entry systems

For more information about the way these systems work and how data is transferred to EAM, refer to Section 6.4.1.

You can use the PM-PCS interface to transfer measurement readings from these upstream systems to EAM. The data is saved in measurement documents and can be further processed.

In customer exits, you define what the further processing should look like. Customer exit IMRC0001 is particularly important in this context because it can automatically trigger activities in EAM if certain thresholds are exceeded (see Figure 5.166). You can define a target value and measurement range limits for each technical object—that is, a value range within which the measurement results must be.

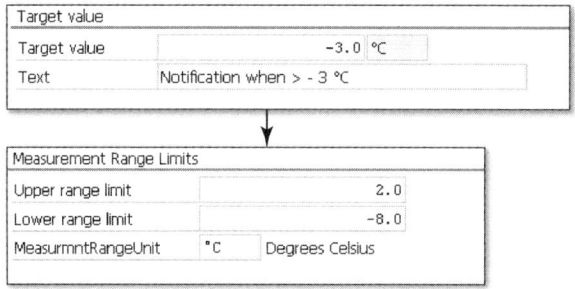

Figure 5.166 Target Value and Measurement Range Limits

You can use the Customizing function DEFINE MEASURING POINT CATEGORIES to specify that the SAP system must issue a warning or an error message if measurement ranges are exceeded or not reached. You can also define that a malfunction report is automatically triggered when a certain threshold is exceeded. Other tasks can be triggered through customer exits in the report (for example, orders can be created).

5.10 Calibration of Test Equipment Business Process

Scenario   In many companies, test equipment such as scales, gauges, calipers, or similar, is used for quality inspections in the intermediate and final checking of products and for checking equipment. To ensure that the test equipment being used always meets the specified performance criteria, it is regularly checked and calibrated. You can use the functions of test equipment management to perform the following actions:

- Manage equipment
- Plan and schedule inspections
- Execute orders and inspection lots for processing calibration inspections on equipment.

Figure 5.167 provides an overview of the objects and the process of test equipment management.

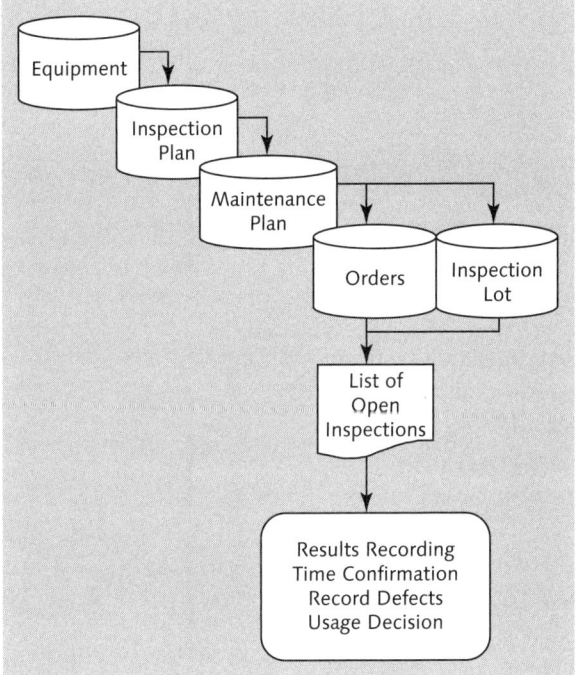

Figure 5.167 Overview of Test Equipment Management

- An inspection plan is created for the test equipment.
- Here, the master inspection characteristics describe the properties to be measured (such as visual inspections and length measurements).
- The inspection plan is included in a maintenance plan.

- The maintenance plan generates an order and an inspection lot.
- The processes in inspection lot management (results recording, error recording, and usage decision) and the processes of order management (time confirmation and technical confirmation) run for each test.

Equipment You manage the test equipment itself as equipment master records (see Figure 5.168). Test equipment has its own tab on which the specific data relating to the production resources/tools is to be maintained. The task list usage is important here so that the relevant test equipment can be used in maintenance-specific task lists.

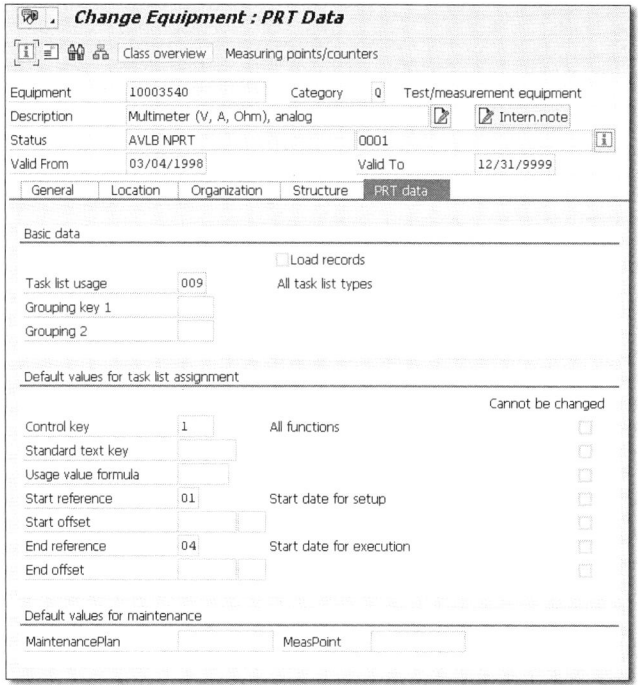

Figure 5.168 Equipment Master Record for Test Equipment

[!] **Separate Equipment Category for Test Equipment**

You need a separate equipment category for test equipment. In this case, use the Customizing function MAINTAIN EQUIPMENT CATEGORY to create an equipment category that is referred to as a PRODUCTION RESOURCE/TOOL REFERENCE

CATEGORY. In the Customizing function DEFINE ADDITIONAL BUSINESS VIEWS FOR EQUIPMENT CATEGORIES, you must also activate the PRT FLAG option.

If inspection characteristics are often required, you can record them as master records and then use them in inspection plans. Master inspection characteristics are managed by means of Transactions QS21–23 (see Figure 5.169).

Master inspection characteristics

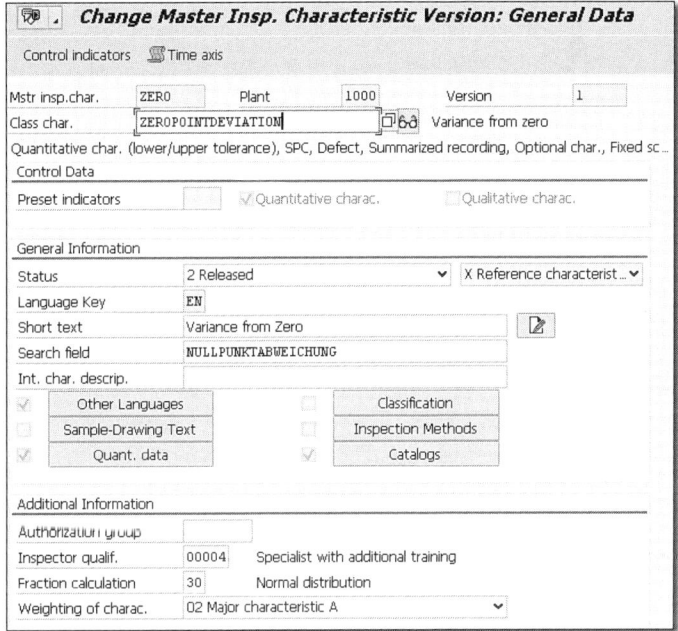

Figure 5.169 Master Inspection Characteristic

In a maintenance task list, you describe the inspections to be subsequently carried out. You can create this as either a general task list (Transaction IA05) or an equipment task list (Transaction IA01).

Inspection plan

| Inspection Point for the Inspection Plan | [+] |

To be able to use your maintenance task list at a later stage as an inspection plan for equipment, you must define an Inspection Point for Equipment in Customizing using the function DEFINE INSPECTION POINTS and then assign it to the header data of the maintenance task list (see Figure 5.170).

5 | Business Processes

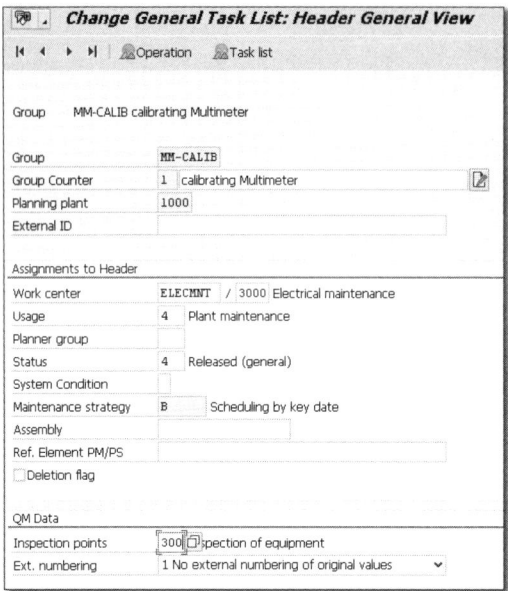

Figure 5.170 Inspection Point for Equipment

The inspection plan must now contain at least one operation that is indicated as requiring inspection, even if it is only a single operation that is merely used as an anchor for the actual inspections (see Figure 5.171). You do this by using a control key provided for this purpose.

Group	74	Calibration Multimeter				Grp.Countr	1				
General Operation Overview											
Op...	SOp	Work ctr	Plnt	Ctrl	Operation Description		LT	Work	Un.	No. Duration	Un.
0010		ELEKTRIK	1000	PM01	Functional test			15	MIN	0.5	H
0020		ELEKTRIK	1000	QM01	Check before calib.			15	MIN	0.5	H
0030		ELEKTRIK	1000	PM01	Calibration			30	MIN	1	H
0040		ELEKTRIK	1000	QM01	Linearity check			15	MIN	0.5	H
0050		ELECMNT	3000	PM01							
0060		ELECMNT	3000	PM01							

Figure 5.171 Inspection Operation

[+] **Separate Control Key for Inspection Operations**

You use the Customizing function DEFINE CONTROL KEY FOR INSPECTION OPERATION to define a control key for which the INSPECTION CHARACTERISTIC EXPECTED indicator is activated.

Due to the control key, you can now use the [Insp.Char] button to assign inspection characteristics in which the actual inspections are contained (see Figure 5.172):

- Description
- Identification as qualitative (QL indicator) or quantitative (QN indicator)
- For quantitative inspection characteristics, the unit of measurement and inspection specifications (target value, upper limits, and lower limits) via the [Quan. Data] button (see Figure 5.173)
- Sampling procedures: Sampling procedures are created using Transaction QDV1. You need a sampling procedure for quantitative characteristics and a sampling procedure for qualitative characteristics.

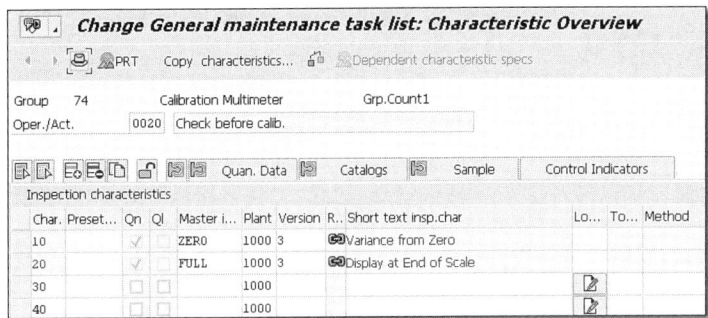

Figure 5.172 Inspections in the Inspection Plan

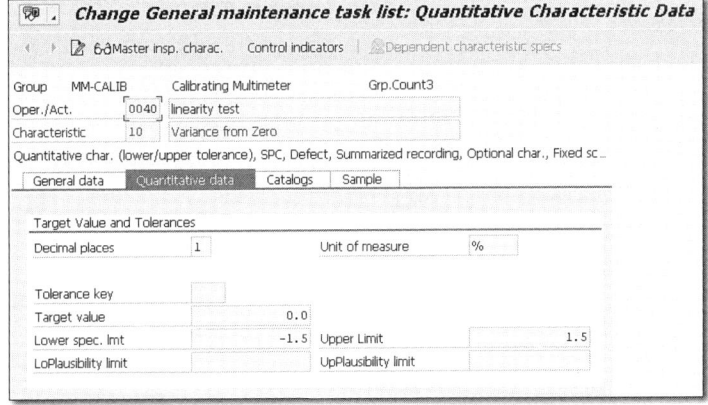

Figure 5.173 Quantitative Data in the Inspection Plan

You also create the relevant control indicator for each inspection characteristic using the `Control Indicators` button (see Figure 5.174).

The control indicators contain the following information:

- Whether upper and lower limits should be measured for a quantitative characteristic
- How the results confirmation is to be performed (for example, summarily, i.e., only entering one number, or individual entry, *i.e.*, the measurement of each individual item, and so on)
- Whether a mandatory or optional characteristic is involved
- Whether the sample size is unrestricted or fixed
- Whether result documentation is required

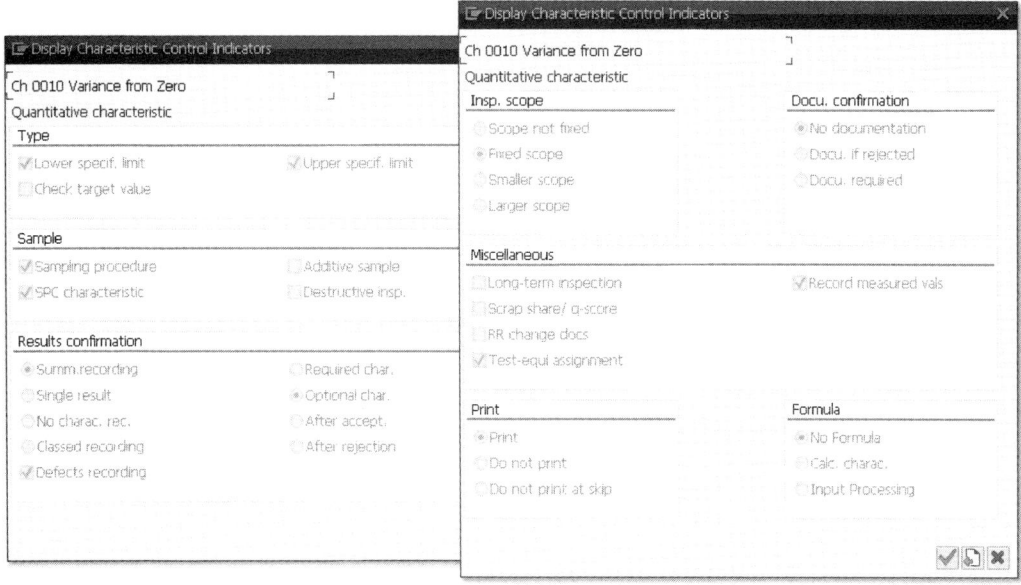

Figure 5.174 Control Indicator in the Inspection Plan

Maintenance plan   You now include the inspection plan in a maintenance plan (for example, as a single-cycle plan) and define the frequency of the inspections in the form of the cycle (see Figure 5.175).

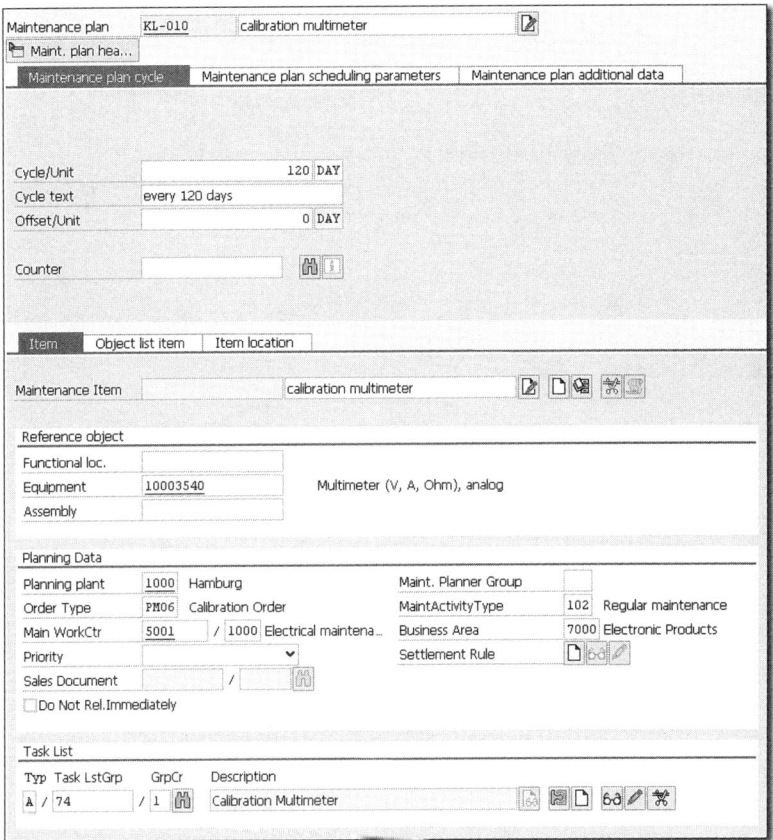

Figure 5.175 Maintenance Plan for Test Equipment

The details you enter in the maintenance plan include the order type, which should receive an order created from this maintenance plan. This must be a separate order type because you cannot use any order type that you have set up for normal maintenance or repair work.

If you have now set up a maintenance plan for your test equipment in this way, not only will an order be created, but also an inspection lot, when a maintenance call occurs. In quality management, the inspection lot corresponds to an order and is a request to perform a quality inspection on a certain quantity of a material, in this case, on test equipment.

Order and inspection lot

> [!] **Separate Order Type for Test Equipment Management**
>
> To ensure that you can map the business process for calibrating test equipment in the SAP system, you need a separate order type.
>
> In addition to the usual basic settings, you assign an inspection type (corresponds to an order type in quality management) to this order type using the Customizing function ASSIGN INSPECTION TYPES TO MAINTENANCE AND SERVICE ORDER TYPES.

The created calibration order differs from "normal" maintenance orders in only two areas (see Figure 5.176):

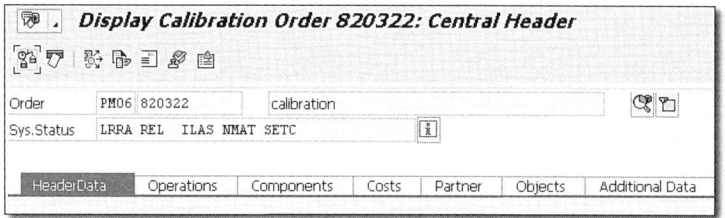

Figure 5.176 Order for Test Equipment Inspection

- The calibration order has the status ILAS (inspection lot assigned); thus you can select according to this status, for example.
- The calibration order contains the additional button in its header. This enables you to go directly to the display of the inspection lot with usage decision (see Figure 5.177).

Results recording — You can now either enter the recorded results in Transaction QE17 for a single inspection lot (see Figure 5.178) or enter all results in Transaction QE51N for several inspection lots. If the entered results are within the tolerance limits or qualified as good, the system performs a positive valuation (✓).

If the entered results are not within the tolerance limits or are qualified as bad, the system performs a negative valuation (✗).

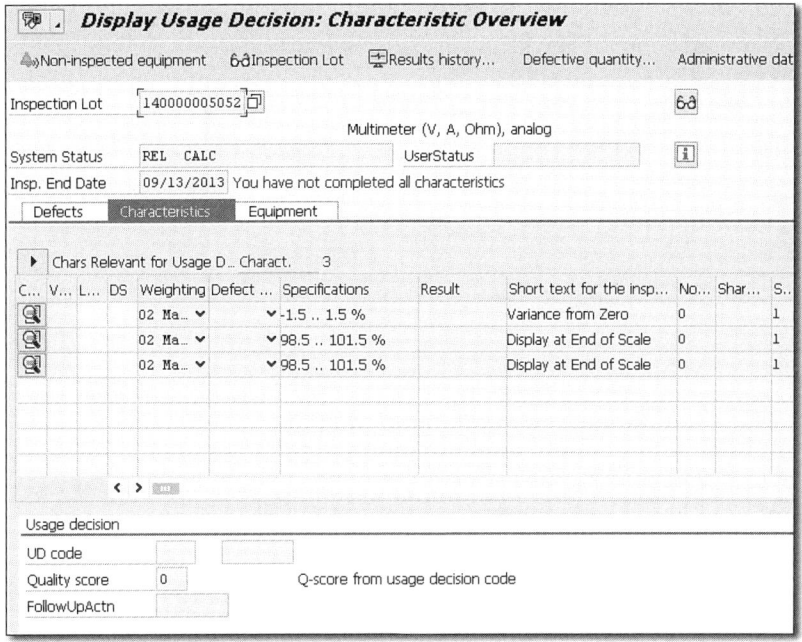

Figure 5.177 Display of Inspection Lot with Usage Decision

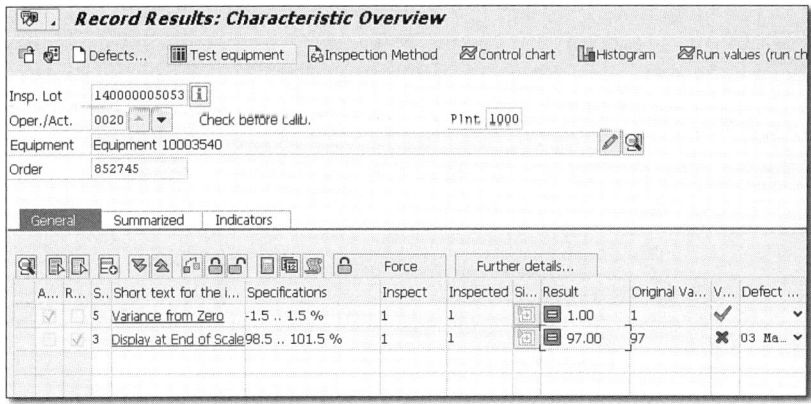

Figure 5.178 Results Recording

Time confirmation   When you save the recorded results, you can also immediately specify the required time for the inspection (see Figure 5.179).

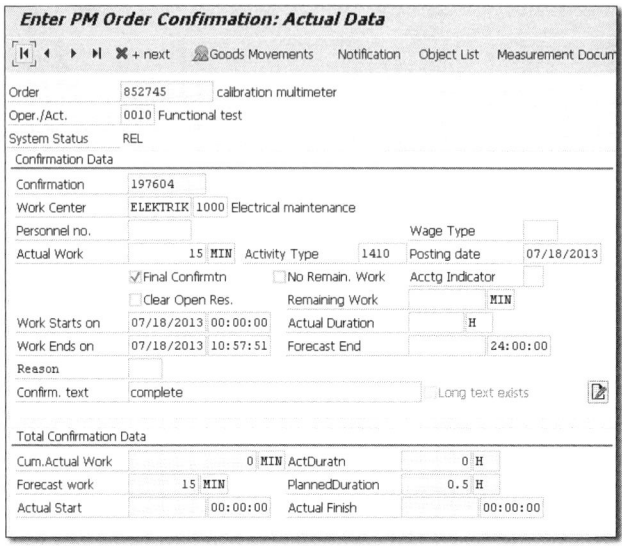

Figure 5.179 Time Confirmation for Inspection

Usage decision   When you save the recorded results, you can also make a usage decision at the same time. Alternatively, however, you can use the special Transaction QA11 for this purpose. The window for the usage decision is shown in Figure 5.180.

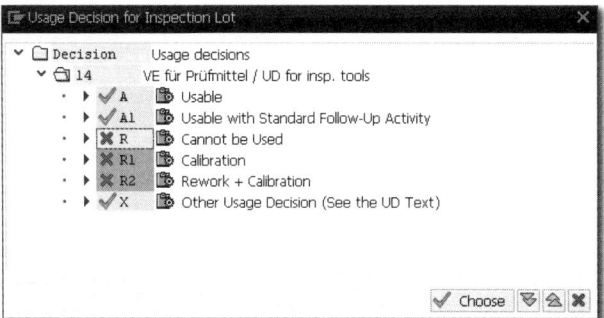

Figure 5.180 Usage Decision

Follow-up actions   You can have follow-up actions automatically triggered with the usage decision, as follows:

- Indicating equipment as no longer ready for use
- Technical completion of the order
- Changing the cycle modification factor in the maintenance plan

You define them using the Customizing function DEFINE FOLLOW-UP ACTION.

If you have set the follow-up action for locking the equipment, you are asked when you make the usage decision to accept the suggestion for the lock or change it manually (see Figure 5.181). You can also change the cycle modification factor for the maintenance plan in the same window.

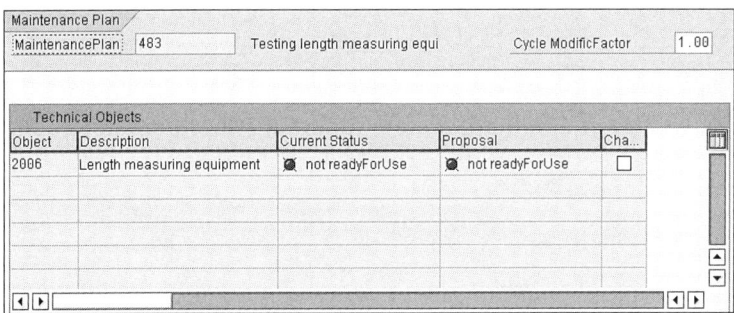

Figure 5.181 Locking a Piece of Equipment

The NPRT status (PRT not ready for use) is thus set in the equipment master, thereby locking the equipment for further use (see Figure 5.182). However, you can use a maintenance task, for example, to set the equipment to an operational status again and reset the status again.

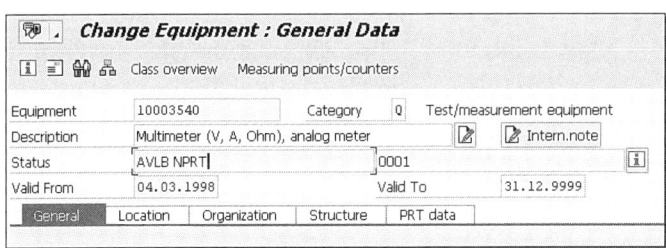

Figure 5.182 Equipment Not Ready For Use

The maintenance plan creates the next order with an inspection lot on the next due date.

5.11 Pool Asset Management Business Process

You can use pool asset management to manage objects that are contained in a pool, from which they can be borrowed for a certain time. Examples of such objects include the following:

- Vehicles
- IT equipment (notebooks, projectors, and so on)
- Cell phones
- Tools
- Other objects

These objects are returned to the pool after they are borrowed and the cost unit (for example, cost center) is charged for the service. Figure 5.183 shows the complete process flow of pool asset management, using the example of a car pool. Pool asset management works the same way for other types of pools, also.

Here, pool asset management comprises the following steps:

❶ **Request**
An employee enters a demand for a vehicle in the system.

❷ **Vehicle scheduling**
A vehicle scheduler assigns a vehicle to the demand.

❸ **Confirmation of reservation**
The employee receives an automatic email to confirm that the vehicle is reserved.

❹ **Vehicle issue**
A kilometer reading is taken for the vehicle, and the time at which it is required is recorded. The vehicle is then issued to the employee.

❺ **Vehicle return**
The employee returns the vehicle, another kilometer reading is taken, and the date is recorded.

❻ **Cost allocation**
The costs of the employee's use of the vehicle are calculated and allocated to the account assignment object.

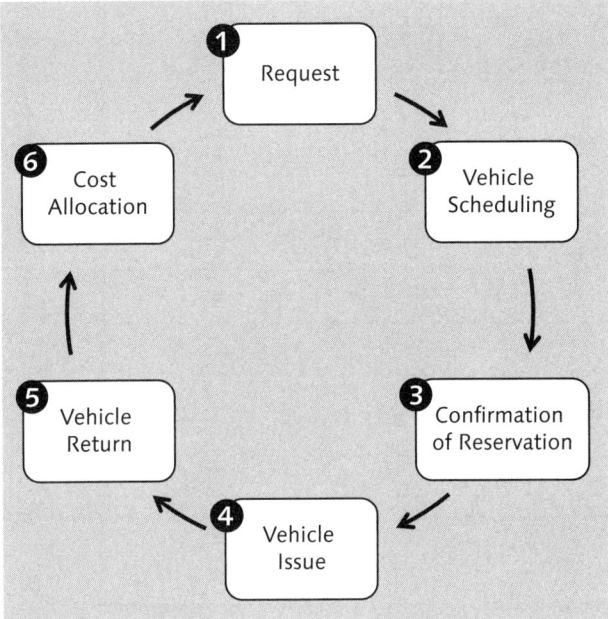

Figure 5.183 Pool Asset Management—Process Flow

As with any other maintenance notification, you use Transaction IW21 to create a requirement notification for a pool asset (see Figure 5.184).

Requirement notification

> **Separate Notification Type for Pool Asset Management** [+]
>
> It makes sense to use a separate notification type for pool asset management requirement notifications so that they have a layout that is specific to pool asset management. You maintain this using the Customizing function SCREEN LAYOUT FOR EXTENDED VIEW. Assign the notification type 10\TAB23 POOL ASSET MANAGEMENT.

In addition to the trip data, you can specify the following information:

- Information about the persons (requester, driver, and so on)
- Information about account assignment (cost center, internal order)
- Information about the vehicle equipment (see Figure 5.185), where you can freely define the equipment characteristics using the class system.

5 | Business Processes

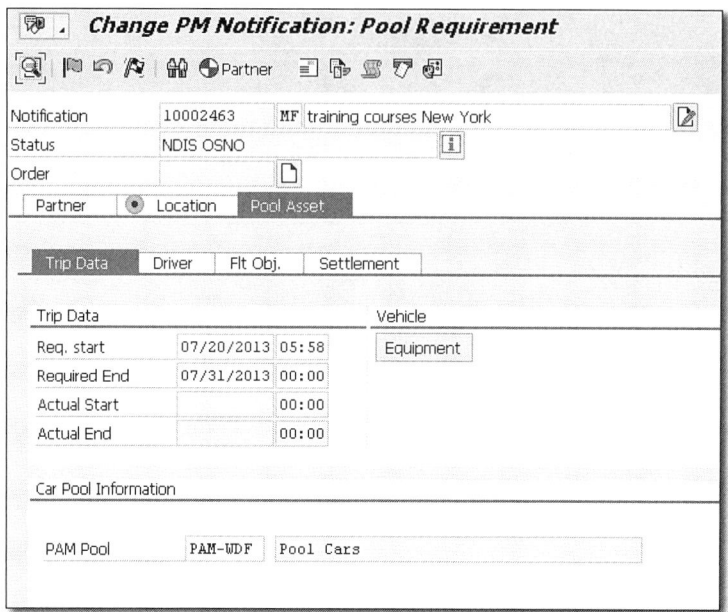

Figure 5.184 Pool Asset Management—Requirement Notification

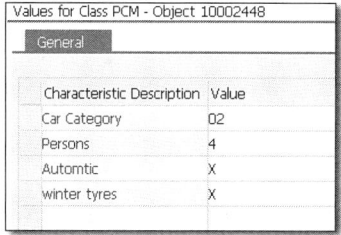

Figure 5.185 Equipment Characteristics

Vehicle scheduling

Requirement notifications are sent to the planning board for pool asset management (Transaction PAM03). Here, the vehicle scheduler can use drag and drop to assign the requirements to vehicles (see Figure 5.186).

The various colors used for the vehicles have the following meanings:

- Yellow: Outstanding demand.
- Red: Reserved—in other words, the pool asset has been assigned.
- Green: Issued.

358

- Gray: Returned.
- Blue: Settled.

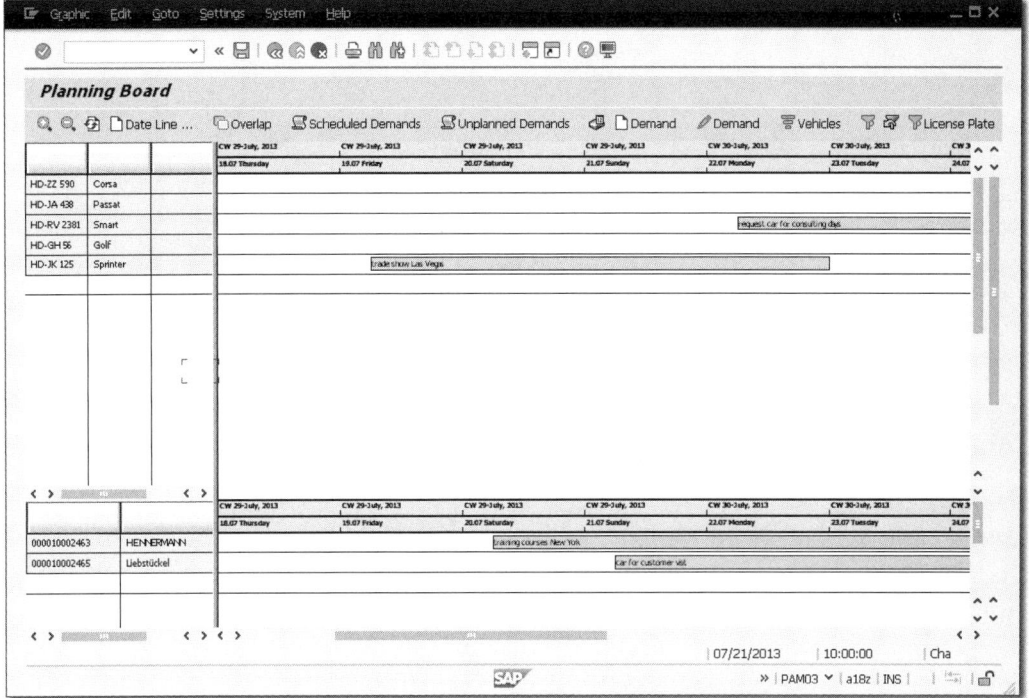

Figure 5.186 Pool Asset Management—Planning Board

All assets belonging to the PAM pool selected on the initial screen of the planning board are displayed here.

Functions of the Planning Board [!]

In addition to providing an overview of the current situation with regard to reservations, the planning board for pool asset management helps you execute the business transactivities RESERVE, ISSUE, RETURN, and SETTLE the assets.

To reserve a vehicle, double-click on one of the scheduled bars. A dialog box is then displayed, in which you can make the reservation using the Reserve button (see Figure 5.187).

5 | Business Processes

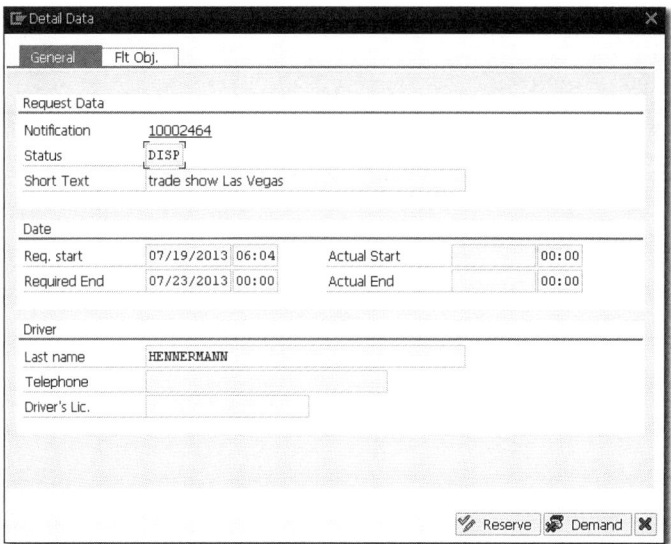

Figure 5.187 Pool Asset Management—Reservation

Confirmation of reservation

Due to the reservation, email is automatically sent to the employee who requested the vehicle to confirm that it has been reserved (see Figure 5.188).

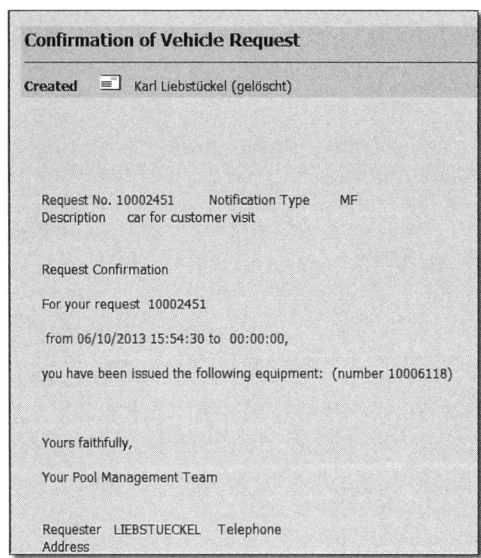

Figure 5.188 Pool Asset Management—Confirmation

If you double-click the bar that indicates a reserved asset and then press the Issue button, the vehicle is shown in the dialog box that is displayed, with the current counter reading and the date recorded (see Figure 5.189).

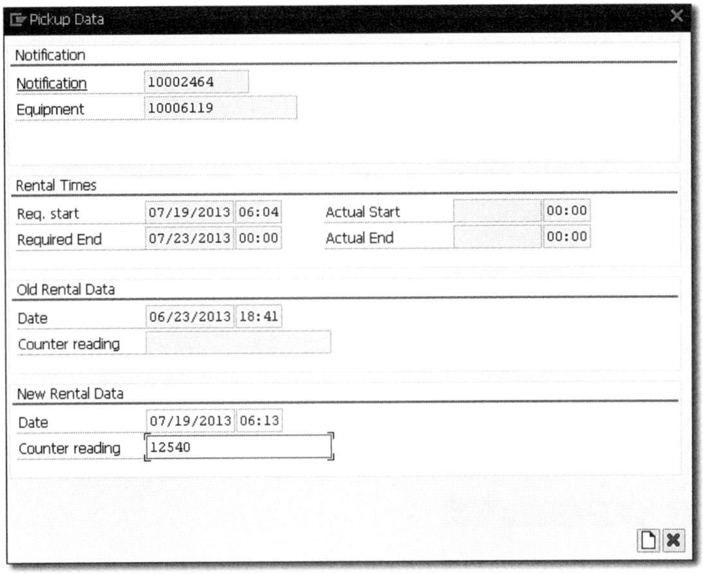

Issue

Figure 5.189 Pool Asset Management—Issue

Similarly, you can double-click the relevant bar and, in the dialog box that opens, click the Return button to enter the return of the vehicle, together with the current data (date of return, current counter reading) in the planning board (see Figure 5.190).

Return

Based on the current data (number of days, number of kilometers driven, free kilometers), the costs are settled to the cost center or a settlement order. To execute the settlement function, click again on the relevant bar and click the Settle button. The system now displays the settlement information—for example, how many days or how many kilometers are settled (see Figure 5.191).

Settlement

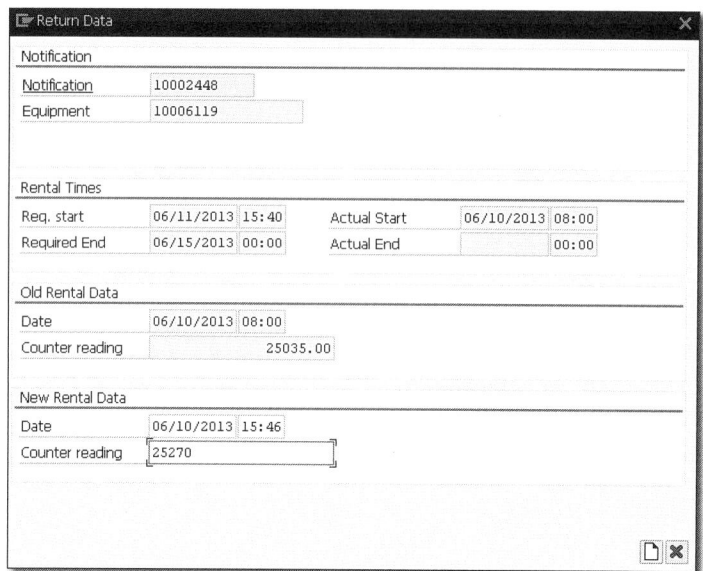

Figure 5.190 Pool Asset Management—Return

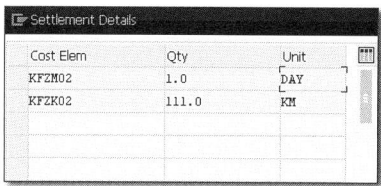

Figure 5.191 Settlement Details

Prerequisites To use the *pool asset management* business process as described above, you must ensure that certain prerequisites are met:

- First, choose BASIC SETTINGS FOR POOL ASSET MANAGEMENT to implement basic settings—for example, a confirmation text or the class for requirement notifications.

- You maintain the categories of your vehicles by choosing DEFINE POOL CATEGORIES (for example, small car, medium-class car, station wagon, delivery vehicle, and so on).

- Choose DEFINE SERVICE TYPES FOR POOL CATEGORIES to maintain the service types required for settlement for each pool category (for example, daily flat rates, price per kilometer, or free kilometers).

- The allocation rates themselves can be maintained via Transaction KP26.
- You create at least one PAM pool using Transaction PAM01 or PAM02. A PAM pool is merely a functional location incorporating a list of equipment (see Figure 5.192).

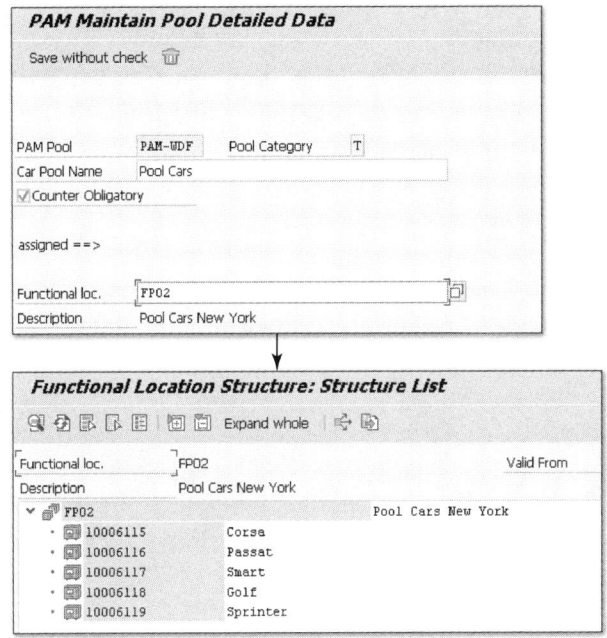

Figure 5.192 Pool Asset Management—PAM Pool

The LOG_EAM_PAM business function must be activated in order for you to use pool asset management.

Business function

5.12 Project-Based Maintenance Business Process

One of the following two situations occurs in many companies. Individual maintenance tasks accumulate within the framework of a higher-level project (for example, this situation occurs for new constructions of technical systems or relocations), or the maintenance task itself reaches such a scale that it can be referred to as a project. This situation occurs, for example, when maintaining aircraft or during shutdowns in refineries or the revision of power plants.

There are two tools you can use in SAP ERP for project-based maintenance:

- **SAP Project System**
  With SAP Project System (PS), you can plan both of the aforementioned project types.
- **Maintenance Event Builder**
  With the Maintenance Event Builder (MEB), you can plan small to medium-sized projects of the latter project type. The former project type cannot be mapped in this manner.

5.12.1 SAP Project System

Scenario
When you use the SAP Project System[2] (PS) for project-based maintenance, you perform the higher-level planning in PS and the order planning in EAM.

PS Objects

Project
A project is a one-off task, limited in duration and function, for solving a complex plan involving various user departments. It is used to control and check this task in relation to dates, resources, capacities, costs, revenues, and funds. A project is divided (as shown in Figure 5.193) into different phases for this purpose. You create projects, for example, using Transaction CJ06.

WBS elements
You use work breakdown structure elements (WBS elements) as elements of the project system to define the planning, organization, and structure of a project and break down the project into individual, hierarchically arranged, multilevel structural elements. You thereby describe detailed tasks. WBS elements have functions such as time scheduling, budget allocation, progress analysis, and so on. You create WBS elements, for example, using Transaction CJ11.

Network
You use a network to plan the workflow of your processes and arrange the elements in a chronological sequence. In project processing, you use

---

2 For detailed information on the capabilities of SAP Project System, you are referred here to such special literature as Franz, M. *Project Management with SAP Project System*, 3rd edition, Boston: SAP PRESS, 2012.

networks as the initial basis for planning, controlling, and monitoring dates, costs, and resources. You have similar functions available in networks for planning materials, machines, and people as you do in planning EAM orders. You maintain networks using Transaction CN21.

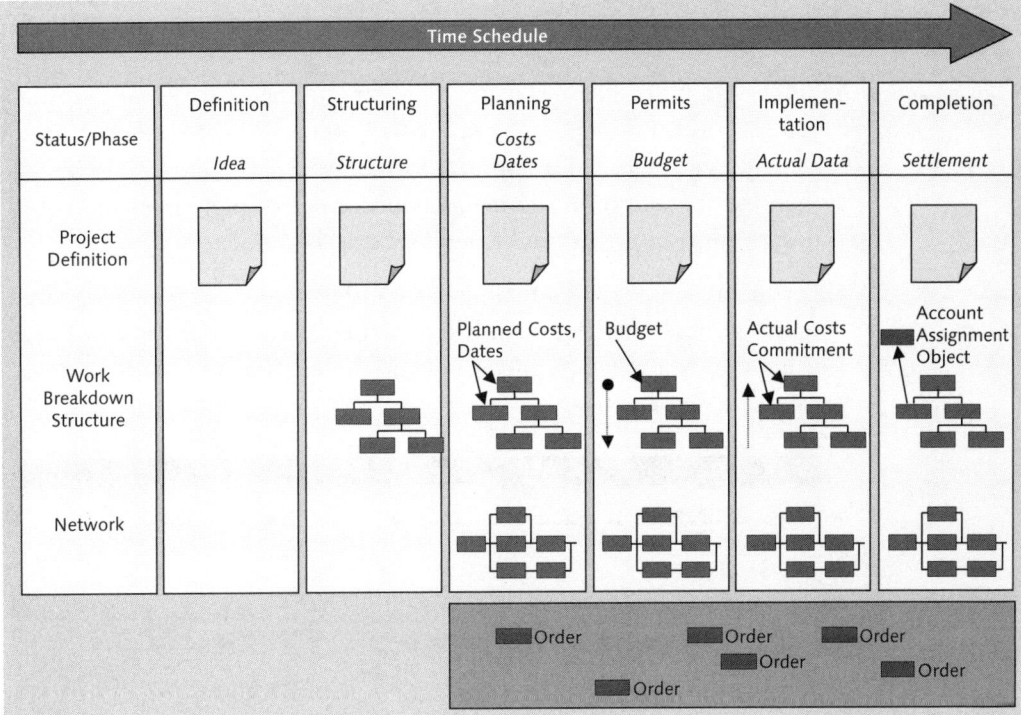

Figure 5.193 Projects and Orders

Manual Assignment

You can now assign your orders to PS objects manually, or this can be done automatically. When you manually assign your orders, you link them to either WBS elements or projects:

You assign individual orders to a WBS element on the ADDITIONAL DATA TAB using Transaction IW32 (see Figure 5.194). You use this option if the maintenance area has taken over individual orders within a project, and a network was not created for the activity.

Assigning an order to a WBS element

5 | Business Processes

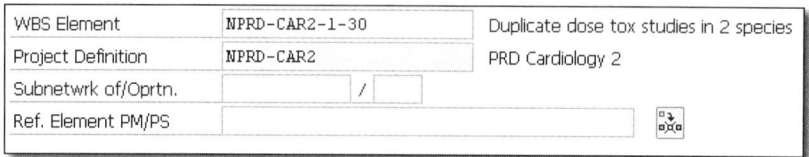

Figure 5.194 Assigning an Order to a WBS Element

Assigning an order to a network

You assign individual orders to a network on the ADDITIONAL DATA tab using Transaction IW32. You can thereby transfer WBS elements, profit centers, and other information into the order (see Figure 5.195). You then use this option if the maintenance area has taken over individual orders within a project and a network exists for the activity.

For the assignment of a maintenance order to a network to work, you must establish an assignment between the network type and order type using the Customizing function of the Project System DEFINE PARAMETERS FOR SUBNETWORKS.

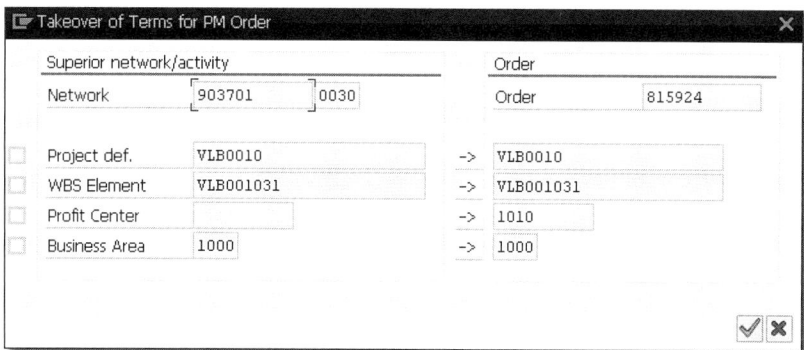

Figure 5.195 Assignment from Order to Network

Automatic Assignment

You use Transaction ADPMPS for the automatic assignment of orders to WBS elements. The idea behind this process is that there are extensive maintenance tasks in the maintenance area that are repeated at regular intervals. You can use this automatic assignment option to avoid having to manually assign the orders to WBS elements every time.

You must fulfill three prerequisites for this purpose: **Prerequisites**

- First, you maintain fields, which will subsequently create the cross connection, using the Customizing function DEFINE FIELD VALUES FOR PM/PS REFERENCE ELEMENT.
- You assign the PM/PS reference element to a maintenance task list (see Figure 5.196) or maintenance item. When you create a maintenance item with a maintenance task list, the reference element is automatically transferred to the maintenance item (see Figure 5.198).

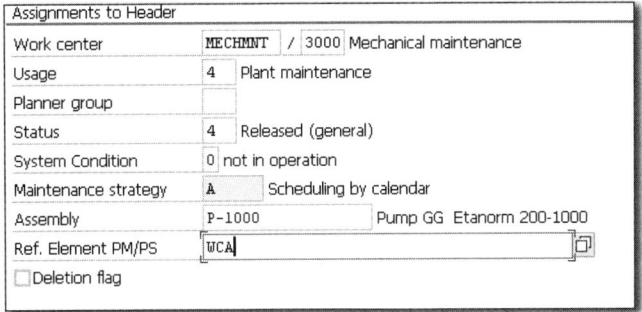

Figure 5.196 PM/PS Reference Element in the Maintenance Task List

- You assign the PM/PS reference element to either standard objects (standard WBS, standard network) or operational objects (WBS element, network; see Figure 5.197).

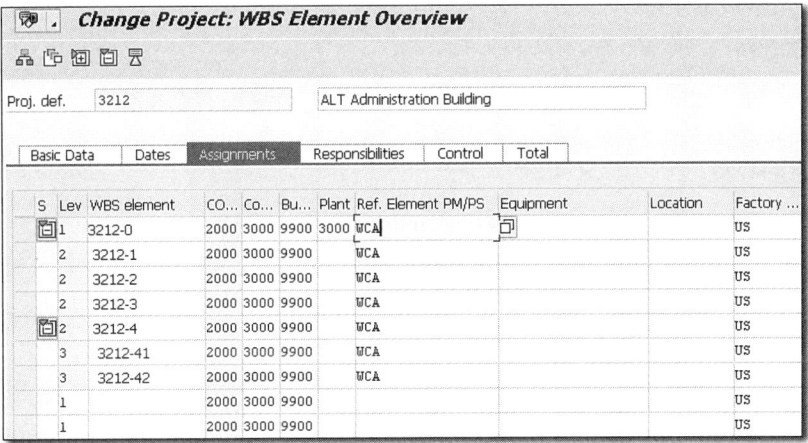

Figure 5.197 PM/PS Reference Element in the WBS Element

5 | Business Processes

When you create a project relating to a standard project or network or work breakdown structure relating to a standard network or standard WBS, the field values are transferred from the referenced object for the reference element (see Figure 5.198).

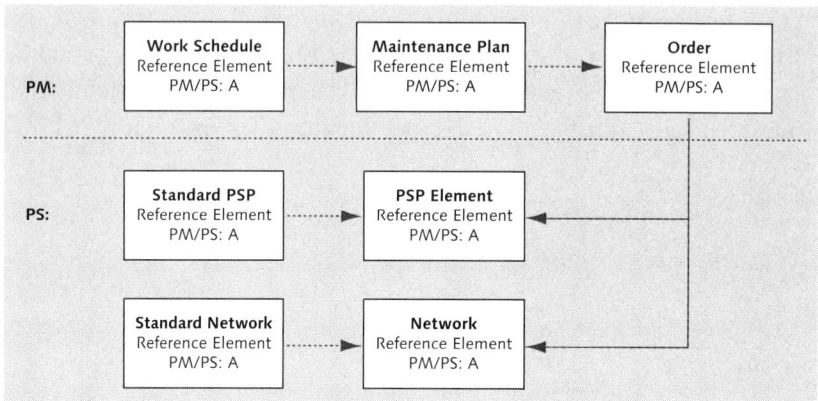

Figure 5.198 Assigning the PM/PS Reference Element

Semi-automatic assignment

To make a semi-automatic assignment, perform the following steps in Transaction ADPMPS:

1. Select the orders to be assigned.
2. Select the WBS elements to be assigned.
3. In the left-hand area of the screen, select the orders to be assigned (see Figure 5.199).
4. In the right-hand area of the screen, select the WBS element, to which you want to assign the orders (see Figure 5.199).
5. You start the assignment manually in the foreground using the button.

Automatic assignment

To now make an automatic assignment, perform the following steps in Transaction ADPMPS:

1. Select the orders to be assigned.
2. Select the WBS elements to be assigned.
3. In the left-hand area of the orders, select the PM/PS REFERENCE ELEMENT column.

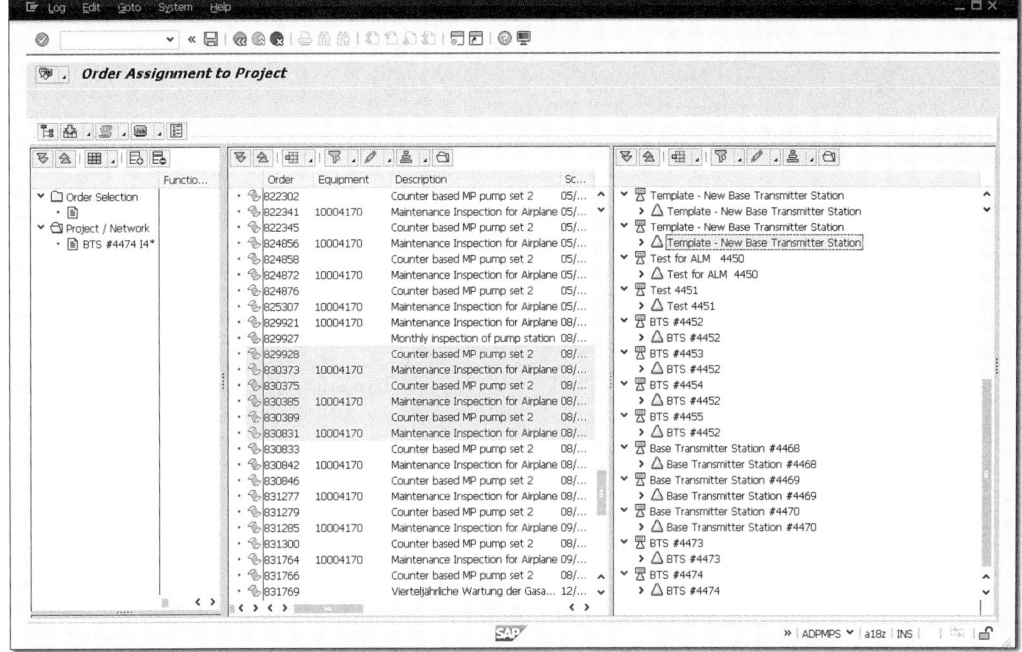

Figure 5.199 ADPMPS Workbench

4. Also select the PM/PS REFERENCE ELEMENT column in the right-hand area of the projects.

5. To start the automatic assignment in the foreground, then select the [icon] button (Automatic Assignment).

Integration Functions

Which functions now become available from assigning orders to PS objects?

- You can combine the order dates with the project dates—that is, a shift in the project will automatically result in a shift in the order.
- You can use active availability control to check whether there is still sufficient budget available for performing the task. For more information, refer to Section 7.3.4.

- You can valuate the projects, including all assigned orders, together in the Project System.

Summary of SAP Project System

The following points summarize project-based maintenance based on SAP Project System:

- You can use the operational objects of the project system (WBS elements, networks) in connection with orders to plan and control bigger maintenance projects.
- You can also assign individual orders to WBS elements or networks if plant maintenance carries out work within a different project.
- You make the assignment either individually or using Transaction ADPMPS.
- The assignment makes available integration functions such as budget availability control, commitment to deadlines, and so on.

> [+] **External Project Tools**
>
> To plan and process maintenance projects, you can also use the interface for shutdown planning with external project systems. This interface connects SAP ERP to external project systems (for example, Primavera P3 or MS Project). You can use the interface with EAM and/or PS.

5.12.2 Maintenance Event Builder

What is the MEB?

The Maintenance Event Builder (MEB) was initially a component of the SAP for Aerospace and Defense industry solution and was made available for all user companies in SAP ERP 6.0 with Enhancement Package 2. You can use the MEB to plan smaller maintenance projects in the form of individual work packages. You start the Maintenance Event Builder using Transaction WPS1. The MEB is technically a workbench that supports you when you perform the following tasks:

- Check the work list of notifications (backlog).
- Bundle the notifications for revisions.
- Create orders from the notifications.
- Assign the orders.

- Display various information, such as open work requirements, due dates, orders, and so on.
- Check the availability situation of resources.

You then process the work packages in up to five steps (see Figure 5.200).

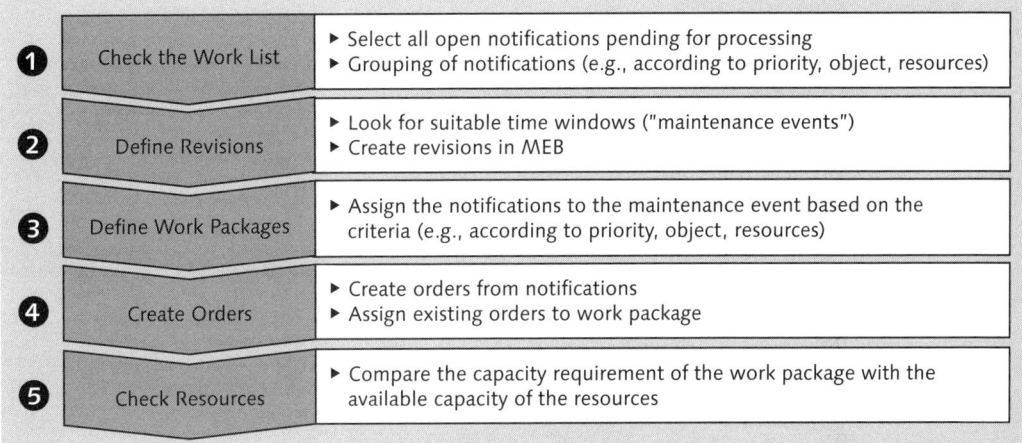

Figure 5.200 Process Flow in the Maintenance Event Builder

The MEB enables you to select the pending notifications and group them according to different criteria, such as priority, reference object, and work center responsible ❶. The notifications may, but do not have to, be already assigned to a revision at this point.

Together with those responsible for the technical system from Production (for example, the operations engineer, production supervisor, and person responsible for work scheduling), you look for suitable time slots (maintenance events) when the technical system can be released for maintenance tasks. You create revisions for these time slots in the MEB in the REVISION WORK AREA section using the 🗋 button ❷. Revisions have start and end dates and status management (for example, created, released, assignments exist, and so on) (see Figure 5.201).

5 | Business Processes

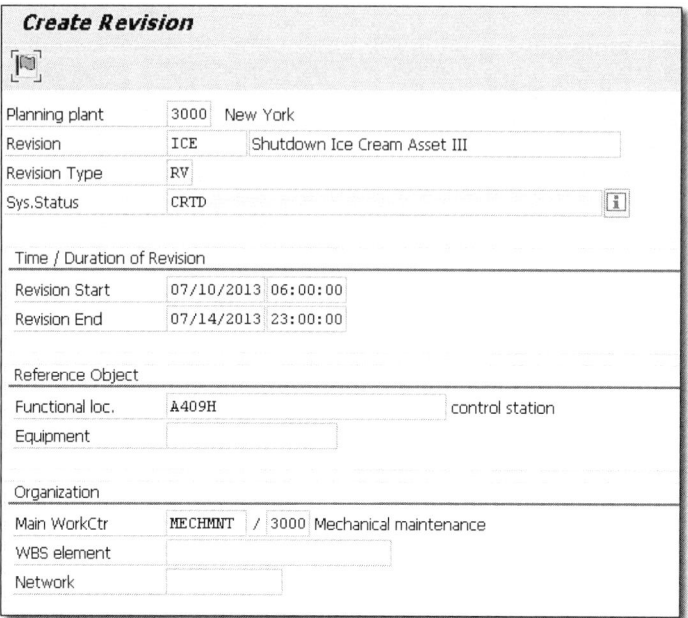

Figure 5.201 Revisions

You can display different views in the MEB Workbench: Figure 5.202 shows the notification view in the upper part of the list and the revision view in the lower part of the list. Other views can be, for example, the work center view, order view, or object view.

Defining work packages

You now create work packages by assigning, from the work list, the notifications to be processed to a revision using drag and drop ❸. At this point, you could then create simulation orders to check the capacity load, for example.

Creating orders

You then create the orders ❹. If an assigned notification already had an order, this is also assigned to the work package. For all others, the MEB enables you to create orders all at once from all notifications assigned to a work package using the 🔄 button (see Figure 5.203). These orders receive an MEB status to enable you to differentiate them from the other orders. When you remove a notification from a work package again, the automatically created orders receive a deletion flag (status DLFL).

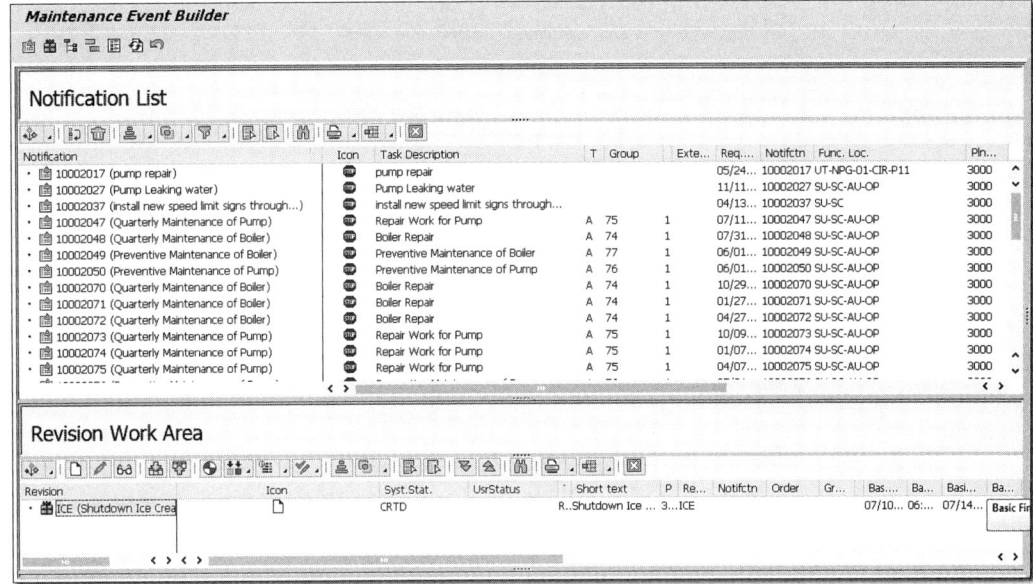

Figure 5.202 MEB Workbench with Revisions

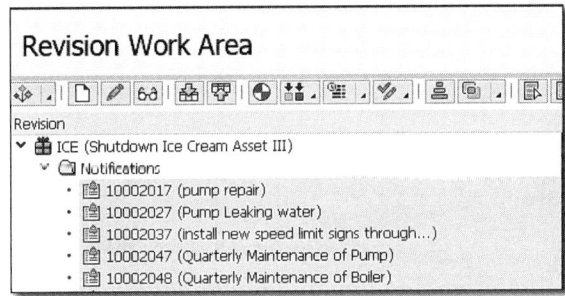

Figure 5.203 Creating Orders for a Work Package

You could, at this point, also assign the orders to the operational objects of the project system (WBS elements, networks) using the button. This is useful, for example, if you have budget restrictions or want to synchronize dates.

Integration with PS

The resource view of the MEB gives you a quick overview of the capacity situation of the work centers involved (see Figure 5.204): are the work centers already working to full capacity in the period of a work package, or is there still free capacity available for other orders ❺?

Checking resources

373

5 | Business Processes

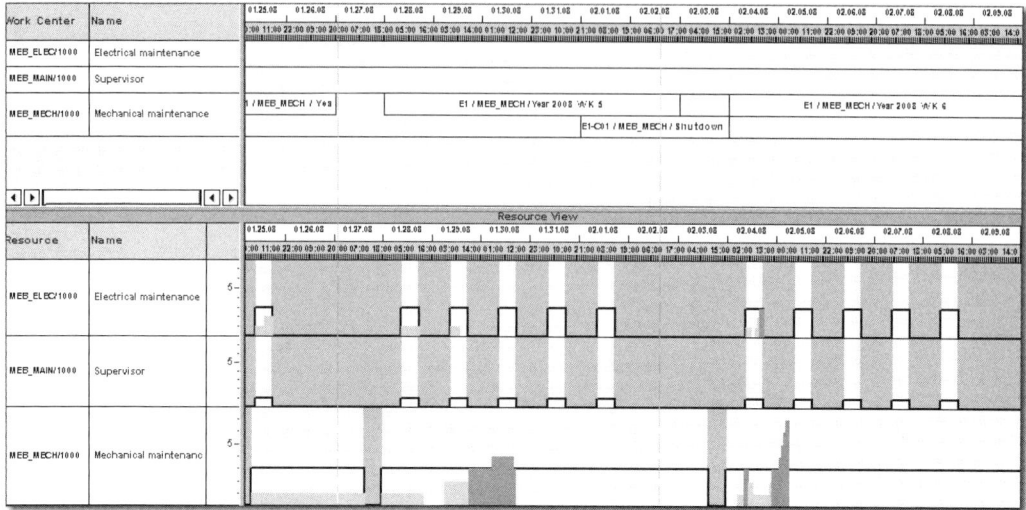

Figure 5.204 Resource View of MEB

Business function — The LOG_EAM_POM and LOG_EAM_POM_2 business functions must be activated in order for you to use the Maintenance Event Builder.

Summary of the Maintenance Event Builder — What is so special about the MEB?

- The MEB enables you to plan smaller maintenance projects (maintenance events).

- You can use the MEB to perform the majority of required planning steps from one single transaction.

- In agreement with the system operators and on the basis of the planning in the MEB, you can, to some extent, ensure that the maintenance tasks are performed and prevent the system from having to be shut down several times.

- You can link the orders created from the MEB to WBS elements and networks.

Plant maintenance is constantly exchanging data with other departments in the company. The SAP system reflects that situation in the broad and deep integration of plant maintenance with applications used by other departments. This chapter illustrates the integration of EAM with other applications within the SAP ERP system, with other SAP systems, and with non-SAP systems.

6   Integrating Applications from Other Departments

Plant maintenance is a service area of your company and, thus, works closely with the other departments of the company in handling your business processes. These business processes do not stop at departmental boundaries or system boundaries. To provide the required services, there must be a permanent exchange of information between the applications and systems that other departments use. Information must flow in both directions—between plant maintenance and other departments in your company.

6.1   How Other Departments Are Involved

Several questions must be answered when you have to integrate the applications of other departments with EAM:

Questions relating to integration

- Which departments may potentially require an exchange of information with plant maintenance?
- How are these departments involved in the business processes of plant maintenance?
- What information must be exchanged?

- In which direction does the information flow? Does the information flow from plant maintenance to another department, does plant maintenance require information from other departments, or must information be exchanged mutually?
- Which systems are used to exchange information? Does it involve integration within SAP ERP, or is data required from another SAP system or a non-SAP system?

Appendix B.3 contains a table that provides a detailed overview of the interrelationships of EAM with the different departments, which does not claim to be exhaustive.

> **[!] Very Diverse Integration**
>
> The experience of numerous companies has shown that the business processes are too different and the system landscapes in use too complex for you to be able to create a list of all points of contact and systems involved.

Nevertheless, the aforementioned table gives you some idea of the differentiated and complex interaction of plant maintenance with other departments.

I discuss below, in detail, the implementation of integration of EAM:

- Integration of EAM within SAP ERP
- Integration of EAM with other SAP systems
- Integration of EAM with non-SAP systems

6.2 Integration within SAP ERP

SAP ERP is a highly integrated system. Just like the pieces of a puzzle, the individual parts of SAP ERP fit together exactly to create a whole (see Figure 6.1).

This section discusses the most important integration points of EAM within SAP ERP. I will show you what this integration looks like and how it can be organized.

Integration within SAP ERP | **6.2**

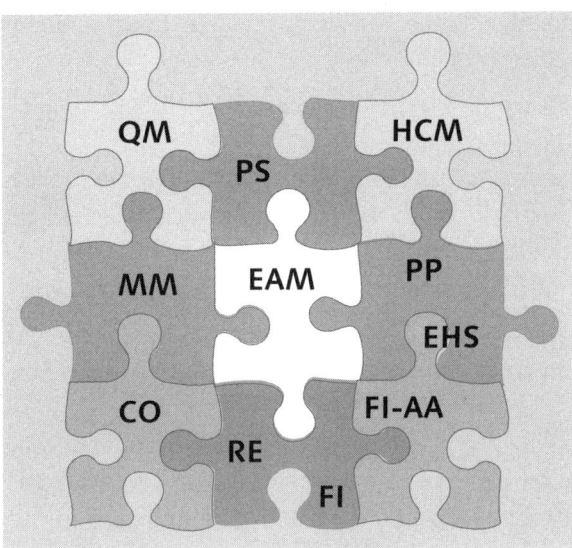

Figure 6.1 Integration of SAP ERP Modules

> **Focus on: CO and MM** [!]
>
> First things first: the integration of EAM with Controlling (CO) and Materials Management (MM) is most important for plant maintenance.

Let's start with one of the most important aspects: the integration of EAM in materials management.

6.2.1 Materials Management

I have already presented the following points of contact of EAM and MM in previous chapters, and I thus intend only to recapitulate them briefly at this point:

- **Reservations**
  Section 5.2.2 illustrated how a reservation is automatically triggered when you schedule a stock material or component with item type L in your order.

- **Purchase requisitions from non-stock material**
  The same section showed how a purchase requisition is automatically

generated when you schedule a non-stock material or component with item type N in your order.

- **Purchase requisition from external services as an individual purchase order**
  In Section 5.5.2 services as an individual purchase order, I also explained how a purchase requisition is automatically generated when an external service is scheduled as an individual order in your order if you use a control key (for example, PM02) with the appropriate properties.

- **Purchase requisition from external service with service specifications**
  Section 5.5.4 discussed how a purchase requisition is automatically generated when you schedule an external service with a service specification, use a control key (example: PM03) with the appropriate properties, and then schedule the required services.

- **Availability check**
  Section 5.2.3 explained how you can perform a dynamic availability check for your scheduled stock materials. This enables you to determine whether your order is feasible on the scheduled date.

[+] **Unique Differentiator: Availability Check**

A dynamic availability check is a unique differentiator of an integrated system like SAP ERP compared to non-SAP plant maintenance systems. This is because it requires information about the existence of MRP elements for the scheduled material, such as the following:

- Planned goods issues from reservations (also reservation for non-maintenance orders, like production orders and reservations for cost centers)
- Planned goods issues from sales requirements
- Planned goods issues from dependent requirement
- Planned goods receipts from purchase orders
- Planned goods receipts from purchase requisitions
- Planned goods receipts from planned orders
- Planned goods receipts from production orders
- Planned goods receipts from shipping notifications

> This involves information from inventory management, purchasing, production, sales, project management, and other areas that require the same material. Only an integrated system can provide such a function.
>
> Stand-alone IPS systems like DIVA, Maximo, or other systems may have an interface to SAP ERP, but only batch interfaces are involved here, which are simply capable of sending information in a delayed one-way manner (for example, transferring a reservation to SAP ERP).

- **Actual costs from the release of services performed**
  Section 5.5.4 showed that actual costs are stated on the order when releasing services performed via service entry forms.

- **Actual costs from goods receipts for external services**
  Section 5.5.2 showed that, when you enter the goods receipt for a purchase order for external services, the actual costs are stated on the order when the GOODS RECEIPT VALUATED flag is set with the purchase order.

- **Actual costs from incoming invoices for external services**
  In Section 5.5.2, you learned that when entering the incoming invoice for a purchase order, the goods receipt/invoice receipt clearing account (GR/IR clearing account) is reversed again, and the order is then debited with the actual costs invoiced.

- **Goods receipts and invoice receipts for external material**
  Here, the same applies as in the previous point.

- **Actual costs from material issues**
  Section 5.2.4 showed how you can withdraw planned and unplanned materials from an order. These withdrawals trigger related actual costs in the relevant order.

- **Inventory management of equipments**
  In Section 4.2.2, I showed how you can use material serial numbers to manage inventory for equipment and the required preconditions in the equipment and material master data.

- **Refurbishment of spare parts**
  Section 5.6 explained how you can use the refurbishment process to repair faulty spare parts. The withdrawal of faulty spare parts, return

of operational spare parts, and management of separate inventories were covered.

▶ **Subcontracting**
Section 5.7 showed how you can use the subcontracting process to repair faulty spare parts with the help of service providers and illustrated, among other things, the shipping of faulty spare parts and the goods receipt of operational spare parts.

> [+] **MM Transactions Are Only the Second-Best Solution**
>
> You can also use purchasing documents (purchase requisitions or purchase orders) with the material management transactions (for example, ME51N or ME21N) and assign them to the order. However, the costs that arise are initially visible as actual costs in the orders. With this approach, you avoid any required budget checks. Thus, you should always create procurement transactions from orders.

I will now discuss some more aspects of the integration of EAM with MM. I will start with *the* central element of logistics: the material master.

The Material Master

Spare parts management

Users have often asked me whether EAM has its own spare parts management or uses the same parts as MM. The answer is yes and no. The material masters managed in SAP ERP are used by all areas of logistics: inventory management, purchasing, production, sales, project management, and even plant management. Individual spare parts management is usually desired because of the internal organization of a company. The control of the material master is in the hands of the warehouse or purchasing department, for example. Here, you can offer some assistance.

> [+] **Separate Material Type for Spare Parts**
>
> To work with spare parts management, create a separate material type—for example, ERSA (spare parts) and MAZE (machine equipment and spare parts) in Customizing and transfer responsibility for the material master of this material type to plant maintenance.

The creation of a separate material type provides, among other things, the following benefits:

- You can assign separate authorizations.
- You can use a specific number range.
- You can define your own screen layout.
- You can define the field selection.
- You can activate special stock and consumption accounts.
- You can define your own quantity and value update.
- You can select according to your own material type.

Figure 6.2 shows how a separate material type is represented in the SAP system.

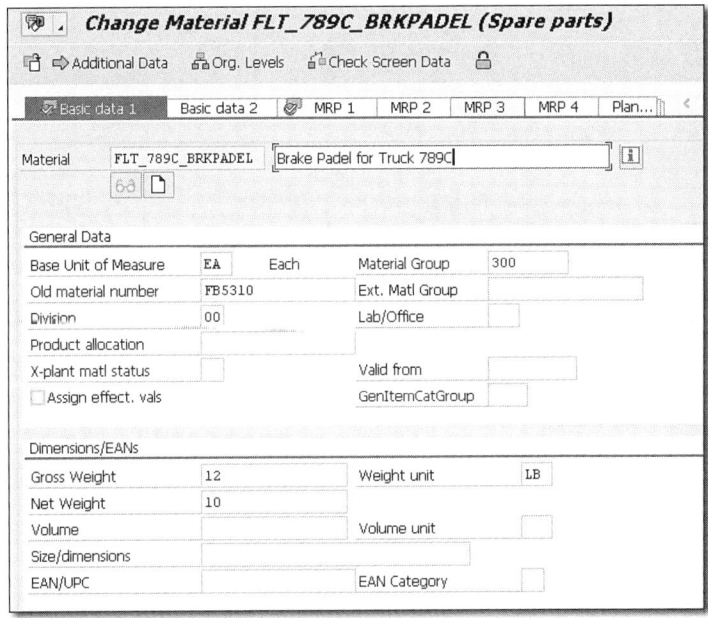

Figure 6.2 Material Type for Spare Parts

Material Requirements Planning

The most common procedure for material requirements planning (MRP) of spare parts is reorder point planning (see Figure 6.3).

Reorder point planning

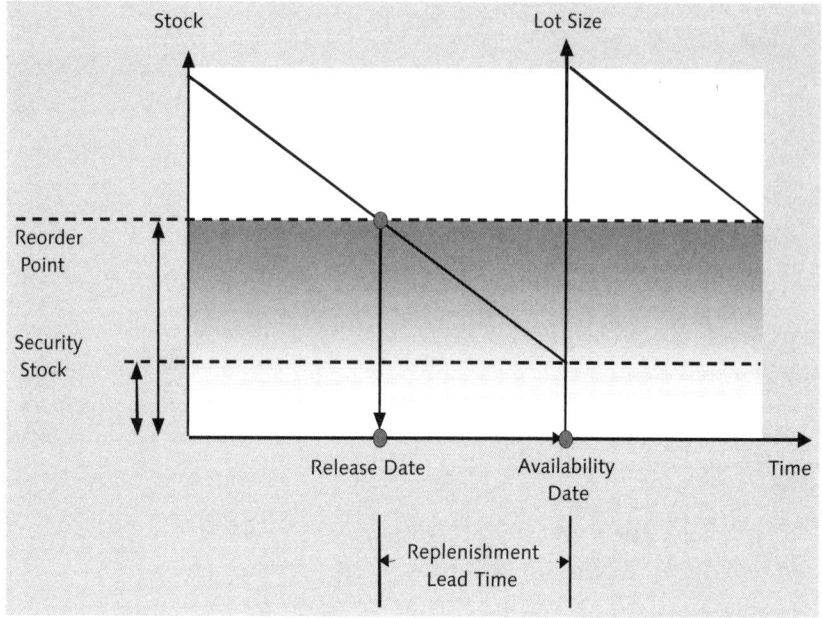

Figure 6.3 Reorder Point Planning

The basis of reorder point planning is the comparison of available stock and the defined receipts with the reorder point. If the available stock is smaller than the reorder point, procurement is triggered.

The level of the reorder point is based on the expected average material requirements during the replenishment lead time, as well as the safety stock. Accordingly, the following values must be considered when defining the reorder point:

- Safety stock
- Previous use and expected future requirements
- Replenishment lead time

The safety stock covers unplanned material use during the replenishment lead time and additional requirements during delivery delays.

MRP type VB

The standard version of SAP ERP contains MRP type VB (i.e., manual reorder point planning) for this purpose. A disadvantage of using this

Integration within SAP ERP | **6.2**

MRP characteristic, however, is that it performs only a comparison of the actual warehouse stock and reorder point. That means that the SAP system triggers replenishment only if you remove a material, and its stock falls below the reorder point. However, nothing happens if the stock falls below the reorder point because of a reservation in the future, as no procurement transaction is triggered. As a result, there may not be enough stock there when you want to remove the part from the warehouse.

> **Separate MRP Type for Maintenance** [+]
>
> Create your own MRP type (for example, V1 = manual reorder point planning with regard to external requirements) and assign it to the material type *Spare Parts*. This MRP type ensures that MRP considers your reservations from maintenance orders and triggers procurement transactions on time.

You maintain MRP types using the Customizing function DEFINE MRP TYPES (see Figure 6.4). Set INCLUDE EXT. REQMTS to 2 (external requirements within the replenishment lead time) and activate the PM/NTWORK RESERV setting.

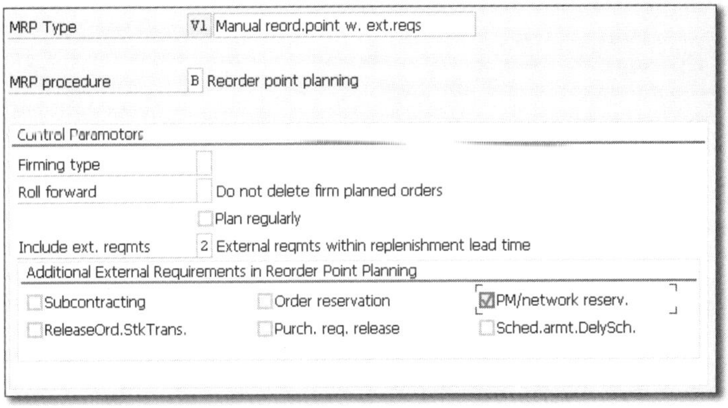

Customizing

Figure 6.4 MRP Type

Then, perform the assignment per plant in the material master in the MRP PROCEDURE screen group (see Figure 6.5).

Material master

383

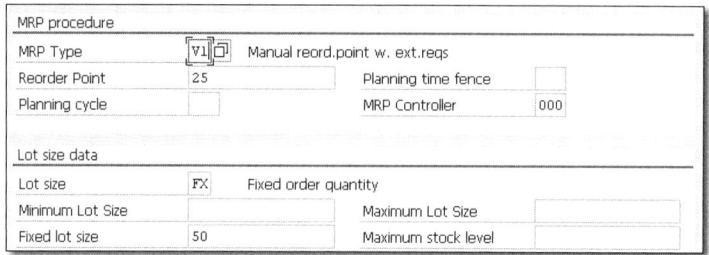

Figure 6.5 "Material Requirements Planning 1" View in the Material Master

Handling Unit Management

Definition

A *handling unit* is a physical unit of packaging and the material contained on or in it. A handling unit has a unique identification number that can be called with the data on the handling unit. The packaging material consists of loading equipment (pallets, wire baskets, crates, trucks, and so on) and packaging itself (cartons, wrap, and so on) (see Figure 6.6). Handling units can be nested, which means that you can build a new handling unit from several handing units as often as desired.

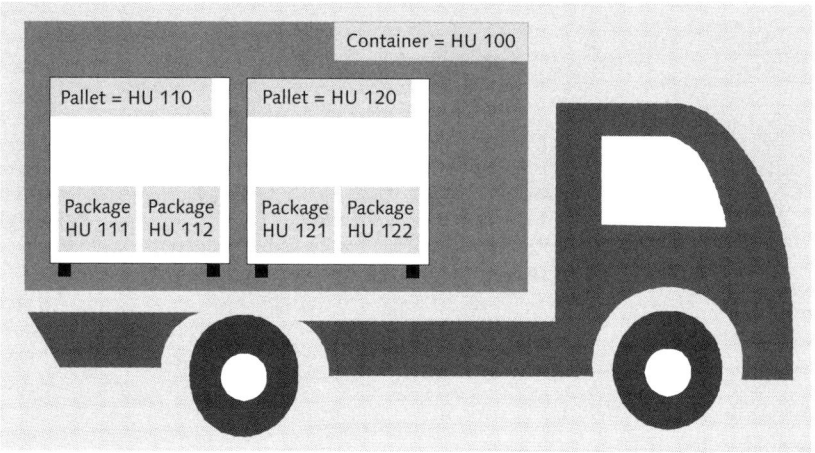

Figure 6.6 Handling Unit

Business processes

Handling unit management looks at handling units rather than individual materials. The common unit for the flow of materials and information is the handling unit. A business process for a handing unit implies related business transactions in the background for the materials and packaging contained in the handling unit. A business transaction, thus, replaces individual entry of multiple material movements.

You can manage serial numbers in handling units or assign a serial number to a handling unit. When you create handling units, you can specify materials with serial numbers in the items of the handling unit (see Figure 6.7).

Serial numbers

At any given time, a serial number can be found in a maximum of one handling unit. When you assign a serial number to a handling unit, the system sets the status to HUAS in the master record. The serial number can then be processed only in business processes with handling units.

Figure 6.7 Serial Numbers in Handling Units

To be able to use serial numbers in handling units, you must use the function DEFINE SERIAL NUMBER PROFILES to create a serial number profile to which you assign the serialization procedure HUSL in Customizing. You enter the serial number profile in the material master record of the serial number.

Prerequisites

6 | Integrating Applications from Other Departments

Goods issue — When you post a goods issue of a handling unit, the serial numbers of the handling unit are copied to the material document, and the SAP system resets the system status of the serial numbers to HUAS in the master record. In the serial number history, you can see the handling unit used to post the goods issue.

Goods receipt — When you post the goods receipt of a handling unit to a storage location that requires a handling unit, the serial numbers of the handling unit are also copied to the material document. The SAP system sets the system status of the serial numbers to HUAS in the master record. In the serial number history, you can see the handling unit used to post the goods receipt.

[+] **Handling Units Can Include Serial Numbers**

You can manage serial numbers on handling units and assign a serial number to a handling unit. A business transaction with handling units (examples: goods issue and goods receipts), therefore, replaces individual entry of several material movements.

Now, let's look at another integration aspect of logistics: the integration with Production Planning and Control (PP).

6.2.2 Production Planning and Control

The integration of EAM with PP involves four elements:

- You can use the master data of technical objects to create a cross-reference to the work center as a PP resource.
- You can make scheduled EAM orders in the PP planning board visible.
- You can use PP orders to create your own spare parts.
- You can make the EAM work center aware of specific procedures or suborders in the context of PP orders.

The Work Center

In the master data of a technical object—be it a functional location or equipment—you will find the WORK CENTER field in the LOCATION DATA field group (see Figure 6.8). This work center is often confused with the work center responsible for maintenance activities. However, this is incorrect because you use the MAIN WORK CENTER field in the RESPONSIBILITIES field group for this purpose. In contrast, the WORK CENTER field is intended as a cross-reference. It answers the question of which PP work center, and thus which capacity resource on the part of production, corresponds to this functional location or equipment.

> **Not All Work Centers Are Created Equal** [+]
>
> By assigning a technical object to the work center, you create a cross-connection to the PP component. The main work center is the workshop responsible for maintenance activities. A 1:N relationship exists here: several technical objects can be assigned to a PP work center.

> **No Automatic Calculation of Available Capacity** [+]
>
> The number of individual capacities of the PP work center, which represent an essential factor in determining the capacity that PP can offer, is not calculated by the number of assigned technical objects.

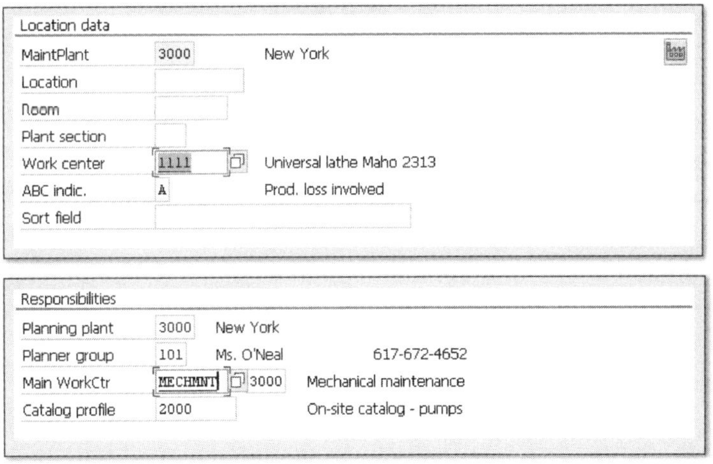

Figure 6.8 Work Center and Main Work Center

Pure assignment of a technical object to a work center is initially only a cross-reference that does not create any reservations, capacity loads, and so on when a maintenance order for the related technical object is pending.

Maintenance Orders in the PP Planning Board

Prerequisites

If you want the maintenance tasks to influence production planning, however, you must first fulfill the following prerequisites:

- Assign the technical object to a work center (see Figure 6.8).
- Use the function CREATE SYSTEM CONDITIONS OR OPERATING CONDITION to define an operating condition in Customizing for which the RESERVATION BY PM option is activated (see Figure 6.9).

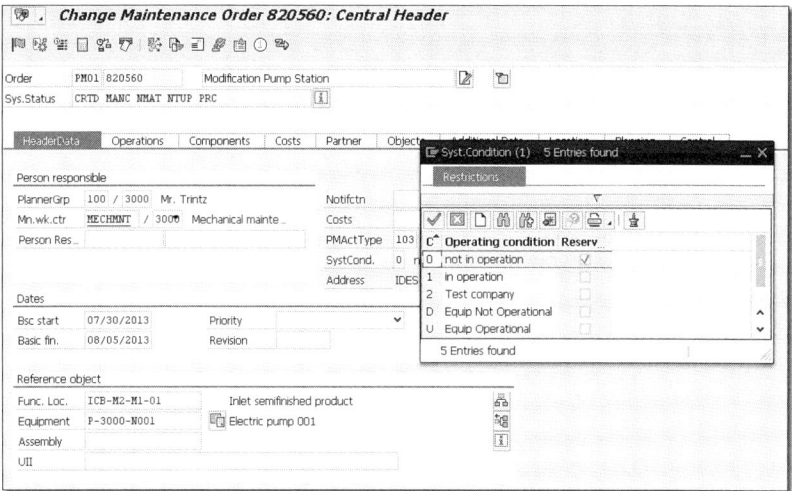

Figure 6.9 Operating Condition Indicator

EAM order

If you want to make your EAM order visible in production planning, enter an appropriate value in the SYSTCOND field of the order header, as shown in Figure 6.9.

PP planning board

The upper part of the PP planning board (Transaction CM21) now displays the maintenance orders scheduled for this resource by plant maintenance, including the production orders of the resource (see Figure 6.10). However, you will see only the maintenance orders that require machine downtime—that is, those for which the system condition indicator is set to RESERVATION. The planning board does not display maintenance orders that can be performed during production and for which you have not set the system condition indicator.

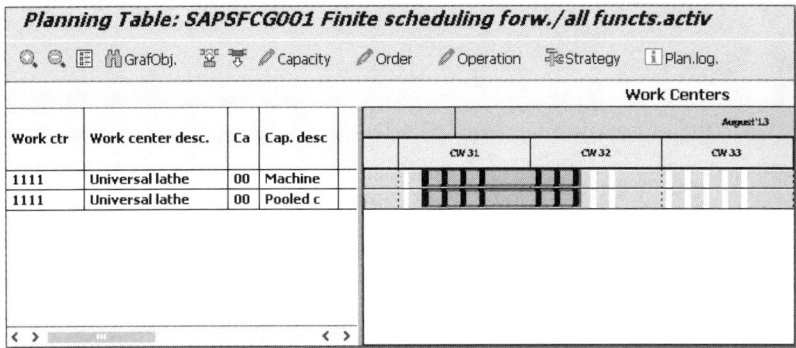

Figure 6.10 PP Planning Board

However, the production scheduler cannot change the EAM order from the PP planning board. The scheduler cannot reschedule it, for example, if production cannot release the resource on that date for maintenance tasks.

Showing EAM Orders in the Planning Table	[+]
Showing EAM orders in the PP planning board serves only as an indication to production that plant maintenance has scheduled an order on the date. No automatic load or block of the PP resource occurs. If the date cannot be met from the production perspective, manual communication must occur between production and plant maintenance.	

In-House Production of Spare Parts

A maintenance order requires spare parts that can or should not be procured externally. They must be manufactured in house by plant maintenance or production.   *Starting point*

You create a production order (Transaction CO01) for the spare part. In addition to the general transaction and material planning information, you enter the EAM order as the settlement rule (see Figure 6.11).   *Procedure*

After the spare part is finished, you settle the PP order to the EAM order (Transaction KO88).

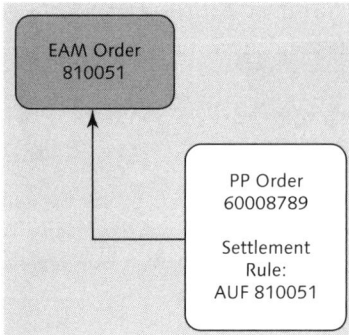

Figure 6.11 Settling a PP Order to an EAM Order

[+] **Assigning a PP Order to an EAM Order**

When you manufacture your own spare parts, you create a PP order. The costs generated by the PP order are visible in the EAM order. The costs are settled to the EAM order and indicated in the history of the technical object.

Maintenance Services for Production

Initial situation   More or less the opposite situation would occur when plant maintenance performs services as part of production orders, such as retooling procedures, rebuilding, and so on.

Procedure   You schedule an EAM order and enter the PP order as the settlement rule (see Figure 6.12).

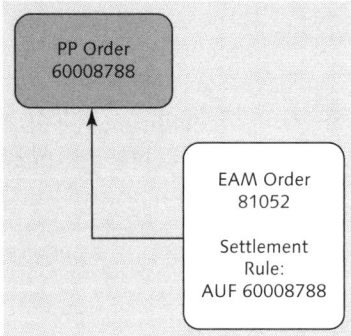

Figure 6.12 Settling an EAM Order to a PP Order

> **Assigning an EAM Order to a PP Order** [!]
>
> When plant maintenance performs services in the context of production, you create an EAM order that you then settle to a PP order. After settlement of the EAM order, the costs incurred in plant maintenance are visible in the PP order and become part of follow-up calculations for the product.

> **Always Settle Suborders First** [!]
>
> Make sure that the subordinate order is always settled and closed first from an organizational and technical perspective.

After encountering the topic of *in-house production of spare parts* in the course of several projects and having had to find a solution to it, allow me to digress at this point. This involves, specifically, answering the question of which order type you should use in the SAP system if spare parts are to be produced for stock.

6.2.3 Digression: In-house Production of Spare Parts for Stock

For the implementation of in-house production of spare parts in stock, there are two completely different approaches:

- Production order
- Refurbishment order

These two options will be discussed next.

Spare Part Production Using a Production Order

The spare part production process using production orders occurs as follows:

- **Material master**
  A material master is required (for example, the material type ERSA). It has the special features moving average price and MRP type PD to plan the spare part automatically and the procurement type E or X so that the part can be produced by a production order.

- **Material BOM**
  A material BOM is required (Transaction CS01), which contains the components that are required for the production of the spare part. It has the special feature of usage 1 (production).
- **Routing**
  A routing is required (Transaction CA01), which contains the steps for the production of the spare part. It has the following special feature: number of routing = material number and usage 1 (production)
- **Production order**
  A production order is set up (Transaction CO01). The order type is, for example, PP01. Only the end date must be filled out by hand in the order header; all other data is set automatically (see Figure 6.13).

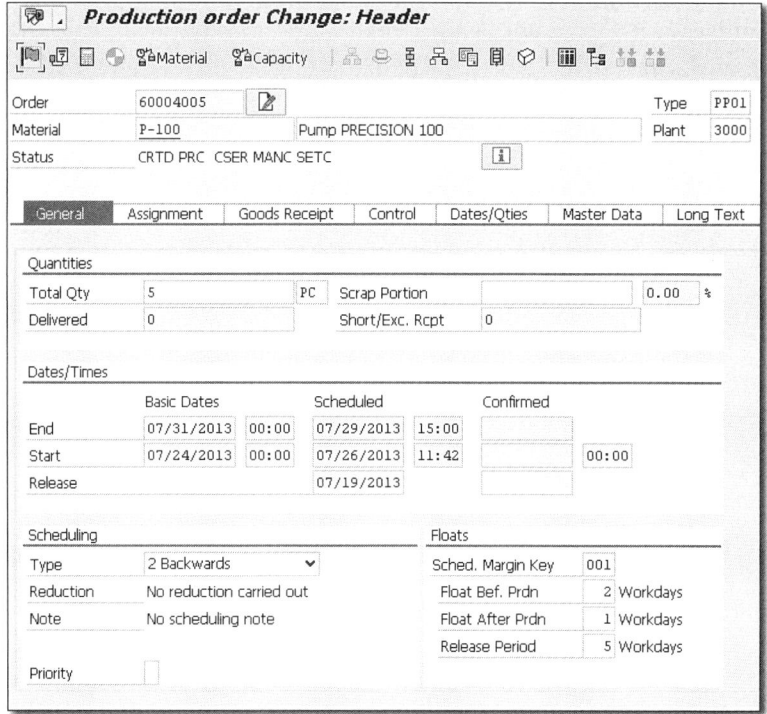

Figure 6.13 Production Order

- **Automatic routing explosion**
  The operations are generated using an automatic routing explosion.

- **Automatic BOM explosion**
  The component list is generated using an automatic BOM explosion. The required quantities are automatically calculated on the basis of the lot size of the order.
- **Material issue**
  The material issue is performed as usual via Transaction MIGO.
- **Confirmation**
  The confirmation is performed using a production transaction—for example, Transaction CO1F (progress confirmation) or Transaction CO15 (confirmation of the order).
- **Goods receipt**
  The goods receipt of the produced spare part is performed using Transaction MIGO.
- **Order settlement**
  The order settlement of the production order is the material. A new moving average price ensues for the spare part after the order settlement (Transaction KO88).

Spare Part Production Using a Refurbishment Order

The spare part production process using refurbishment orders occurs as follows:

- **Material master without split valuation**
  A material master is required (for example, the material type ERSA). Special features: moving average price. You do not require any split valuation here as with normal materials to be refurbished.
- **Material BOM**
  A material BOM is required (Transaction CS01), which contains the components that are required for the production of the spare part. It has the following special feature: usage 4 (maintenance).
- **General maintenance task list**
  A general maintenance task list is required (Transaction IA06), which contains the steps for the production of the spare part. It has the following special features: internal or external number assignment, usage 4 (maintenance), and assembly = material number of spare part.

- **Refurbishment order**
  A refurbishment order is set up (Transaction IW81), for example, with the order type PM04. You do not enter any *From* or *To* valuation type as with normal refurbishment orders (see Figure 6.14). The system now displays a window with a warning message because the refurbishment order was originally developed for a different purpose.
- **Data in the order header**
  All data in the order header must be filled out manually.
- **Manual selection of general maintenance task list**
  The operations must be generated via a manual selection of the general maintenance task list. You control the quantity of the spare part to be produced via the execution factor.

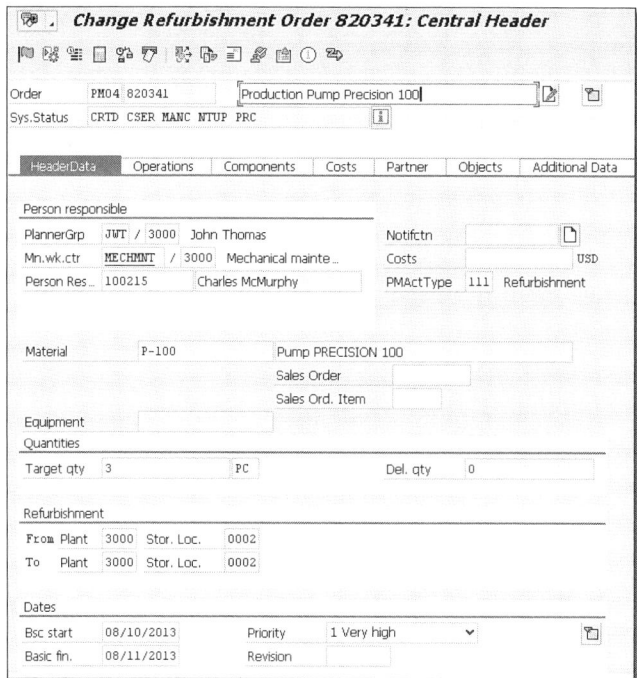

Figure 6.14 Refurbishment Order

- **No automatic BOM explosion**
  There is no automatic BOM explosion, but the BOM must be exploded manually and the components manually selected. The execution

factor ensures that the correct quantities are reserved. An automatic reservation is also created for the spare part to be produced, which is necessary from the production perspective.

- **Material issue**

  The unnecessary reservation is also displayed for the material issue (Transaction MIGO) and may not be withdrawn.

- **Confirmation**

  The confirmation is performed using a maintenance transaction (for example, Transaction IW42).

- **Goods receipt**

  The goods receipt of the produced spare part is also performed using a maintenance transaction (IW8W).

- **Order settlement**

  The order settlement of the refurbishment order is the material. A new moving average price ensues for the spare part after the order settlement (Transaction KO88).

A summary comparison of refurbishment orders and production orders can be found in Table 6.1.

	Refurbishment Order	Production Order
Bill of Material	Maintenance BOM	Production BOM
Maintenance Task List	General maintenance task list with manual assignment of material number	Routing with direct reference to material number
MRP	Possible with automatic generation of planned orders	Possible with automatic generation of planned orders
Order	Maintenance transaction	Production transaction
Routing Explosion	Manual assignment of general maintenance task list with dialog boxes	Automatic
BOM Explosion	Manual selection of components, unnecessary reservation	Automatic

Table 6.1 Comparison of Refurbishment and Production Order

	Refurbishment Order	**Production Order**
Confirmation	Maintenance Transaction IW41 et seq.	Production Transaction CO11 et seq.
Goods Receipt	Maintenance Transaction IW8W	Transaction MIGO
Settlement	In stock	In stock

Table 6.1 Comparison of Refurbishment and Production Order (Cont.)

And what is the conclusion? You will find the answer in the following two boxes.

[!] **Advantage of the Production Order**

The production order has a functional advantage over the refurbishment order. You have to accept a few functional restrictions in the refurbishment order.

[!] **Advantage of the Refurbishment Order**

If you are working with the refurbishment order, you do not need to implement an additional module (PP). Furthermore, you can remain in your usual EAM interface when processing the business processes and do not need to change interfaces for your daily work.

This is the reason the aforementioned user companies have opted for the refurbishment order.

6.2.4 Quality Management

In terms of quality management (SAP QM module), the following issues are important:

- You can manage the test and measurement equipment used in QM as equipment master records.
- The inspections performed with this test and measurement equipment are entered in an EAM maintenance task list, as either a general maintenance task list or an equipment task list.

- A maintenance plan for the equipment takes care of controlling the inspection dates for you.
- To perform the inspection, the maintenance plan generates both an EAM order and a QM inspection lot that are uniquely assigned to each other.
- In the context of inspection lot processing, results recording, and the usage decision, ensure that the equipment is set to the correct status (blocked or available).

Section 5.10 described the business process and required prerequisites (in Customizing, for example) in detail, so I will not discuss them any further here.

The final aspect of integration into ERP logistics is the interaction with the SAP application for environment, health, and safety—thus, with SAP Environment, Health, and Safety Management (EHS Management).

6.2.5 Environment, Health, and Safety

The SAP Environment, Health, and Safety Management (SAP EHS Management) solution has the following main functions:

- **Product safety**
  Product safety contains functions required for hazardous substance management in the company, even in a company that produces hazardous substances.
- **Hazardous substance management**
  Hazardous substance management contains functions required for hazardous substance management in the company, even in a company that uses hazardous substances.
- **Dangerous goods management**
  With dangerous goods management, dangerous goods master records can be managed, dangerous goods checks performed, and dangerous goods papers created.
- **Waste management**
  You can use waste management to develop waste disposal processes, which create reports necessary for transport and disposal, and distribute resulting costs in a usage-related manner within the company.

- **Occupational Health**
  With Occupational Health, health surveillance protocols can be planned and performed in your company, and occupational health questionnaires created and managed.
- **Occupational health and safety**
  With the occupational health and safety functions, health and safety in the company can be organized, and loads that arise can be managed. In addition, events with or without personal injury can be handled, and reports such as operating instructions and accident notifications can be created.

As of Release SAP ERP 6.0 EHP 6, a business function is available for the area *Occupational Health and Safety* with which plant maintenance tasks and the EHS tools can be integrated. These functions are intended to assist you in creating a safe work environment; the most important tools are the safety measure list and safety plan.

Safety measure list — Using the safety measure list (see Figure 6.15), you can classify standard objects as safety measures—for example, documents, permits, maintenance task lists, and PRTs. Thus, you can create a list of safety-relevant objects from all available objects. By assigning these safety-relevant objects in maintenance orders and maintenance task lists, you can provide safety information during the planning and performance of maintenance tasks that are critical to safety.

Safety plan — With the safety plan (see Figure 6.16), you support the safety aspects in plant maintenance planning and implementation. By using the safety plan, the person responsible for maintenance planning can ensure that all safety measures necessary to reduce identified risks are assigned in maintenance orders and maintenance task lists. All information contained in the safety plan can be issued as part of the shop papers. Thus, the maintenance workers responsible for the implementation of maintenance are informed of the safety risks and can ensure that they take all necessary safety measures into account.

Integration within SAP ERP | 6.2

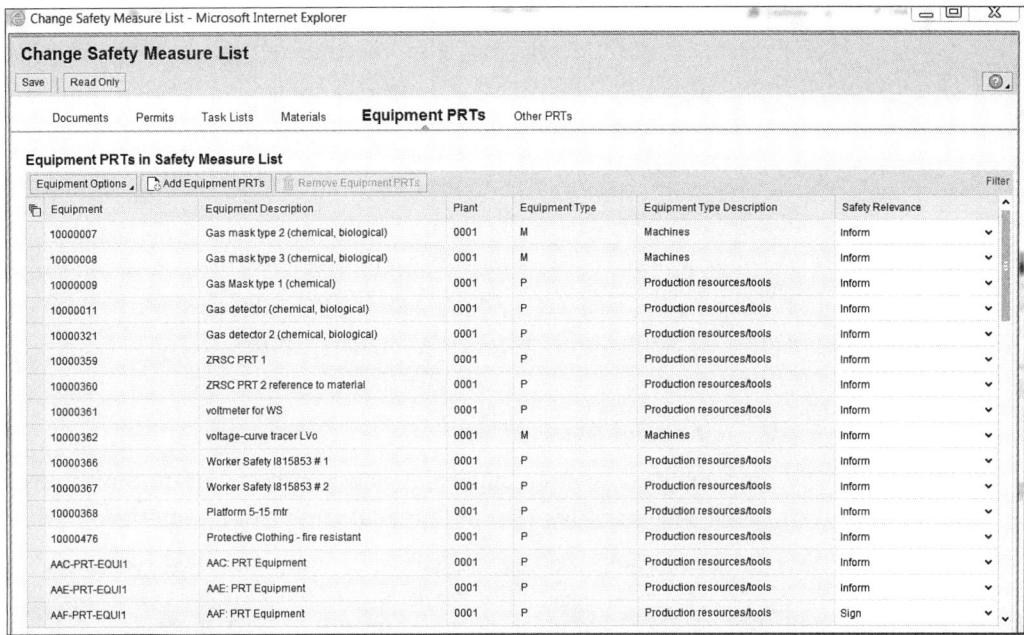

Figure 6.15 Safety Measure List

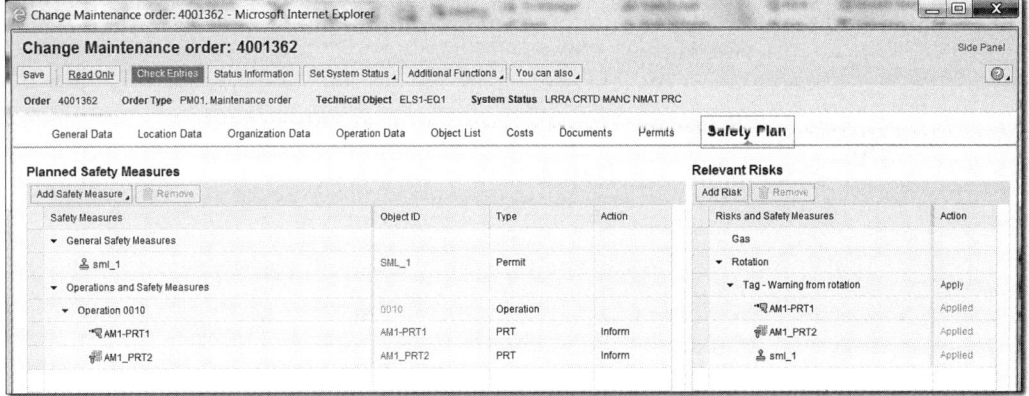

Figure 6.16 Safety Plan

6   Integrating Applications from Other Departments

Prerequisites
To be able to use the functions of the safety measures and safety plan, you must first fulfill the following prerequisites:

- Make all required settings for health and safety using the Customizing function HEALTH AND SAFETY IN PLANT MAINTENANCE.
- Activate the business functions /EAMPLM/LOG_EAM_WS, LOG_EAM_SIMPLICITY_2, and /PLMU/WEB_UI.
- Use SAP NetWeaver Business Client with the PFCG roles *Maintenance Worker* (SAP_COCKPIT_EAMS_MAINT_WORKER2) and *General EAM Functions* (SAP_COCKPIT_EAMS_GENERIC_FUNC2).

6.2.6   Financial Accounting

We now come to another important aspect of integration: the connection between accounting (SAP FI module) and plant maintenance.

[!] **General Ledger (G/L) Accounts as the Basis of All Business Processes**

The integration of EAM with FI is fundamental because the general ledger accounts, on which all business processes in SAP ERP are based, are maintained in FI.

General ledger accounts
For example, if you take another look at the cost report for a normal maintenance order (see Figure 6.17), you see general ledger (G/L) accounts based on the following business transactions:

- Consumption of spare parts (account categories 4 and 8)
- External procurement of spare parts (account category 4)
- External procurement of services (account category 4)
- For a refurbishment order, postings to the stock assets (account category 3) can be added to these rows.

Invoice receipt
Section 5.5.2 covered invoice receipts related to goods receipts, which refer to a purchase order. But what happens when there's no order? If the vendor had delivered something "as required" and now sends an invoice?

Integration within SAP ERP | 6.2

Cost Elem.	Cost Element (Text)	Σ	Total plan costs Σ	Total act.costs Σ	Plan/actual variance	P/A var(%)	Currency
415000	External procurement costs		2,000.00	1,750.00	250.00-	12.50-	USD
417000	Purchased Services		2,735.00	2,345.00	390.00-	14.26-	USD
615000	Dir.Int.Activity Alloc. Repair Hours		2,300.00	1,840.00	460.00-	20.00-	USD
655110	Overhead Surcharge - Other Materials		1,177.00	819.00	358.00-	30.42-	USD
Debit		∎	8,212.00 ∎	6,754.00 ∎	1,458.00-		USD
650000	Order settlement		0.00	819.00-	819.00-		USD
651000	Order settlement - Material Costs		0.00	4,095.00-	4,095.00-		USD
Settlement		∎	0.00 ∎	4,914.00- ∎	4,914.00-		USD
		∎∎	8,212.00 ∎∎	1,840.00 ∎∎	6,372.00-		USD

Figure 6.17 Displaying Costs of a Maintenance Order

You would use the general function for invoice entry (Transactions FB60 or F-43) and assign the amount to the order (see Figure 6.18).

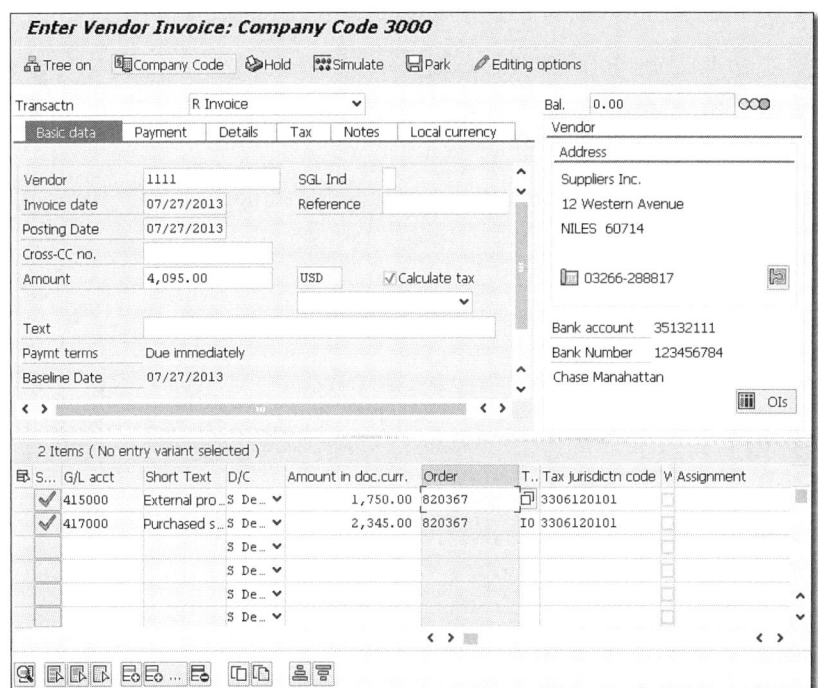

Figure 6.18 Vendor Invoice

Invoice without Purchase Order [+]

You can also post an invoice that does not relate to a purchase order. You assign the invoice to the EAM order; the costs are available in the history.

6.2.7 Asset Accounting

Integration points with FI-AA

EAM has the following integration points with asset accounting (SAP FI-AA module):

- You can assign an asset master record to your technical objects.
- You can automatically generate equipment when you create asset master records.
- You can automatically change equipment master records when you change asset master records.
- You can automatically generate asset master records when you create equipment master records.
- You can automatically change asset master records when you change equipment master records.
- You can activate your maintenance services and settle them to an *Asset under Construction* account.

Asset number

You can have your equipment and/or functional location refer to an asset number in the ACCOUNT ASSIGNMENT screen group (see Figure 6.19).

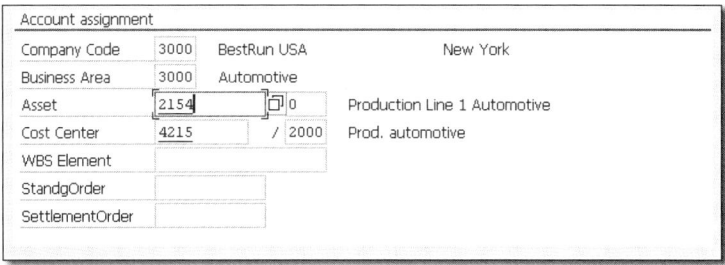

Figure 6.19 Asset Number in Equipment Master

The reference involves a 1:n link. This means that you can assign several technical objects to a single asset number but cannot assign one technical object to several asset numbers.

When you display the asset master record, you can navigate from there to the assigned technical objects (Transaction AS03, ENVIRONMENT • EQUIPMENT and ENVIRONMENT • FUNCTIONAL LOCATIONS).

Synchronizing Equipment and Asset

Many users are unaware of the option to match equipment master records and asset master records to each other. However, it is possible.

> **Synchronizing Asset and Equipment Is Possible** [!]
>
> SAP ERP offers you a synchronization mechanism that you can use to generate equipment when you create asset master records, and vice versa. The synchronization mechanism also works for the change service.

For example, when you change the cost center for the asset, you can set the system to change the cost center of the equipment automatically in the background.

> **Synchronizing Asset and Functional Location Is Not Possible** [!]
>
> The standard delivery of SAP ERP does not include a synchronization mechanism to match assets and functional locations.

What do you have to do to be able to use synchronization? — Prerequisites

- In Customizing, use FINANCIAL ACCOUNTING (NEW) • ASSET ACCOUNTING • MASTER DATA • AUTOMATIC CREATION OF EQUIPMENT MASTER RECORDS • SPECIFY CONDITIONS FOR SYNCHRONIZATION OF MASTER DATA to define the direction of synchronization based on the asset class and equipment type (asset equipment and/or equipment asset).
- You use the same function to define whether synchronization should occur immediately, a workflow should be triggered, or both.
- In Customizing, use AUTOMATIC CREATION OF EQUIPMENT MASTER RECORDS • ASSIGN MASTER DATA FIELDS OF ASSETS AND EQUIPMENT to define the fields to be synchronized.

If you then create an asset (Transaction AS01) and have defined in Customizing that an equipment master is to be generated immediately, the equipment number is displayed directly in the asset master record (see Figure 6.20). You can use the CREATE button to generate additional equipment that is also assigned to this asset. — Procedure

6 | Integrating Applications from Other Departments

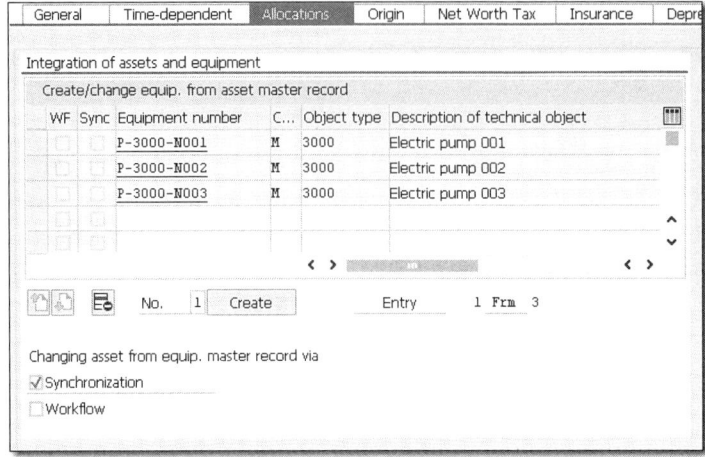

Figure 6.20 Asset-Equipment Synchronization

Activating Maintenance Services

Initial situation Certain services in maintenance departments require activation or can be activated. Especially when value-added orders are involved, for example, cases of modernization, rebuilding, installing additional components, and so on, these tasks should not be settled to the cost center and, thus, posted to the expenses. In such cases, the values should be activated.

Procedure You create an order and enter FXA (i.e., asset) as the account assignment category in the settlement rule and the asset number as the account assignment object. When the order is completed, you settle it (Transaction KO88).

Result The values generated in plant maintenance are assigned to the asset master record as an acquisition from SETTLEMENT OF CO TO ASSETS, the acquisition cost is increased, and the depreciation amounts are adjusted (see Figure 6.21).

[!] **Consultation with Asset Accounting Required**

Consult closely with asset accounting, especially regarding the activation of internal activities.

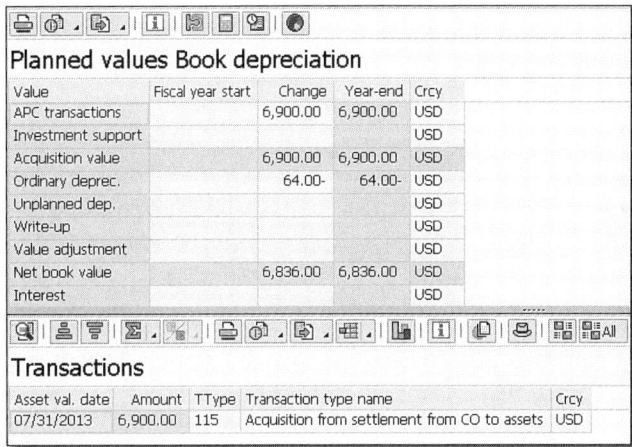

Figure 6.21 Asset Values

We now come to a very wide-ranging and deep and, along with materials management, the most important integration: the integration of plant maintenance with controlling.

6.2.8 Controlling

The following factors influence the integration of plant maintenance with controlling (SAP CO module):

Overview

- To enable integration of EAM and CO, make sure that the required cost elements are available in the chart of accounts.
- Assign a cost center (as a receiving cost center) to the functional locations and/or equipment as a possible cost object.
- Assign a cost center (as a performing cost center) to the work center.
- Define the activity types and, based on those, the allocation rates (prices) of plant maintenance.
- In CO Customizing, define how you want to cost your orders.
- Define a settlement rule in the order and settle the order there.
- Determine the overhead rates for your orders (if necessary).
- You can use the tools of controlling (examples: cost center reports or order reports) to analyze your maintenance activities.

Cost Elements

Information is always exchanged between EAM and CO using cost elements.

[+] **Completing Cost Elements**

When you implement EAM, make sure that you have all the required cost elements for costing and settling orders. You may have to supplement the existing chart of accounts.

The following cost elements are required to cost and settle EAM orders (see Figure 6.17):

- Cost elements for the consumption of spare parts (account category 4, cost element type 1 = primary costs)
- Cost elements for the external procurement of spare parts (account category 4, cost element type 1 = primary costs)
- Cost elements for the external procurement of services (account category 4, cost element type 1 = primary costs)
- Cost elements for the entry of maintenance services (account category 6, cost element type 43 = internal activity allocation)
- Cost elements for the overhead rates (account category 6, cost element type 41 = overhead rates)
- Cost elements for the order settlement (account category 6, cost element type 21 = internal settlement)

Cost Centers

To ensure that internal activity allocation (IAA) can charge maintenance services to the asset cost centers, you must perform the following activities:

- Assign a cost center as a performing cost center to the work centers of plant maintenance.
- Assign a cost center to the functional locations and/or equipment as the receiving cost center.

| Cost Center in the Technical Object | [!] |

In 90% of cases, maintenance services are settled to the asset cost center. Thus, you should assign a cost center to your technical objects so that they can be transferred automatically to the order as a settlement rule.

Activity Types and Prices

You need activity types for the performing cost center. An activity type is a unit within a controlling area that classifies the services of a cost center and that you can use to differentiate the charge rates of the cost center. You define activity types with Transaction KL01.

If there is only one charge rate for each maintenance cost center, one activity type is sufficient. If you have differentiated cost rates for each maintenance cost center, however, you need more activity types. What are the likely reasons for differentiated charging rates? You differentiate maintenance services, for example, according to the following criteria:

Overall or differentiated?

- **Urgency**
  (Rush orders, normal orders, worklist)
- **Time of occurrence**
  (Normal shift, night shift, weekend)
- **Qualification**
  (Foreman, technician, extra hours, trainees)
- **Type of activity**
  (Normal hours, hazardous bonus, dirty work bonus)
- **Type of tools used**
  (Work with special machines, use of trucks, and so on)

Activity types can be used to differentiate the charge rates of plant maintenance. Thus, you can avoid differentiating by urgency, for example, by having the contracting entities give every order a priority of 1.

You set the charge rates once a year for each cost center and activity type with Transaction KP26 (scheduling activities/prices): see Figure 6.22.

6 | Integrating Applications from Other Departments

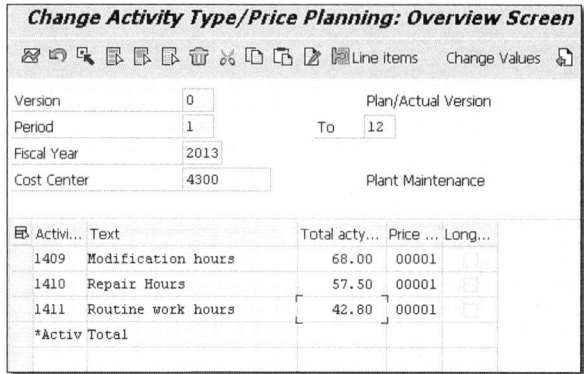

Figure 6.22 Planning Activities and Prices

Costing

Customizing

You control costing (planned and actual) via the Customizing function COSTING DATA FOR MAINTENANCE AND SERVICE ORDERS. The tables involved here build on each other. Thus you should proceed in the following sequence (see Figure 6.23):

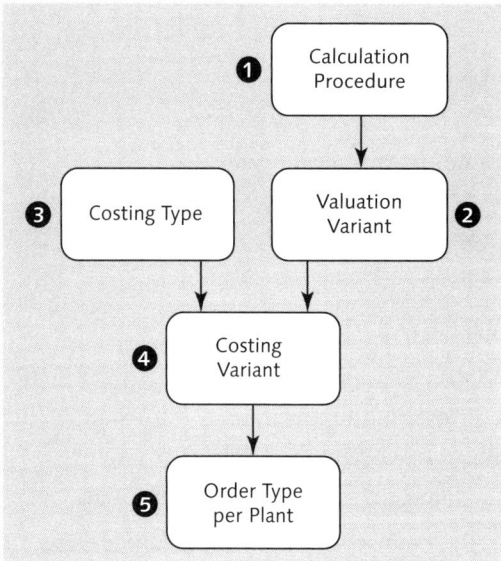

Figure 6.23 Customizing Order Costing

408

1. **Maintain costing sheet**
   You first use the Customizing function MAINTAIN COSTING SHEET ❶ to define which cost elements should be used as the BASIS for the costing, how high the percentage or absolute overhead rate should be, and which cost center serves as the credit for the relevant amounts.

2. **Define valuation variant and define costing type**
   You use the Customizing function DEFINE VALUATION VARIANTS ❷ to define how the material valuation should occur (normal case: valuation according to price control in the material master), how the activity types are to be valuated (normally the planned price of the period) and which Costing Sheet ❸ should be used.

3. **Maintain costing variants**
   Use the Customizing function MAINTAIN COSTING VARIANTS ❹ to combine the COSTING TYPE and the VALUATION VARIANT.

4. **Define costing parameter and results analysis key**
   Use the Customizing function ASSIGN COSTING PARAMETER AND RESULTS ANALYSIS KEY ❺ to define for each plant and type of order the costing variant that should be used in the preliminary costing and final costing (which are normally identical).

Preliminary costing of an order occurs automatically when you save or when you click the 🗒 button manually during order processing. The actual costing of an order also occurs automatically when you perform cost postings (material withdrawals, confirmations, and so on).

Allocation of Overhead Costs

When you cost an order, overhead rates are calculated automatically within the standard cost estimate and assigned to the planned costs if they have been defined in the costing sheet.   *Standard costing*

This does not occur automatically during actual costing. Overhead costs are not automatically surcharged to the actual costs (goods movements, time confirmations, invoices, and so on).   *Actual costing*

Overhead costs are calculated and surcharged to actual costs in the following manner:

- Final costing of an order using Transaction KGI2
- Final costing of a group of orders using Transaction KGI4

[!] **No Automatic Determination of Overhead Rates in the Actual Costing**

Because the overhead rates are automatically charged in preliminary costing but not in final costing, you must re-cost the orders. For safety's sake, schedule a batch job in background processing to perform final costing at short intervals.

Order Settlement

Definition What does order settlement mean? During processing of the order, the entry activities trigger actual costs on the order. Because the order cannot be a permanent cost object, even as an internal order, the costs must be settled periodically (for example, once a week) or after completion (for example, when it is technically completed) to the actual target account assignment and re-debited (see Figure 6.24). During the order settlement, the debit cost elements are transformed into settlement cost elements, and the costs redirected to the target account assignment via the settlement cost elements.

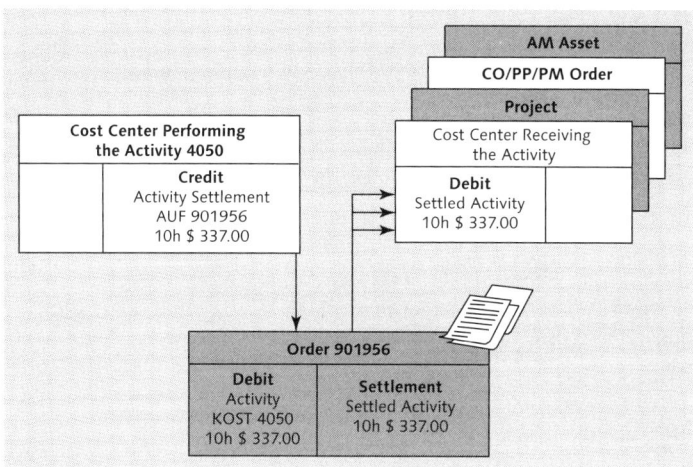

Figure 6.24 Order Settlement

The following prerequisites must be met so that you can settle an order: **Prerequisites**

- Maintain a settlement profile using the Customizing function MAINTAIN SETTLEMENT PROFILE. Set the permitted receivers there.
- Also, assign a settlement profile to the order type in Customizing by choosing CONFIGURE ORDER TYPES.
- Use the Customizing function SETTLEMENT RULE: DEFINE TIME AND CREATION OF THE DISTRIBUTION RULE to define order release or technical completion as the time for creating the settlement rule for the order type.

> **Time for Creating the Settlement Rule** [+]
>
> The best time to select as the time for creating the settlement rule is the order release. Otherwise, you cannot settle the order if it lasts longer than the cycle of your periodic order settlement.

- The order has a settlement rule: you can tell if it does from the status SETC (settlement rule created).
- If you work with overhead rates in the actual costing, you have determined the actual cost surcharges with either Transaction KGI2 for an individual order or Transaction KGI4 for a group of orders.

Who are the possible receivers? In most cases, the cost center serves as the receiver of order settlement in plant maintenance. However, you can also settle your orders to asset numbers, WBS elements, or another order. **Receivers**

> **Default Account Assignment CTR = Cost Center** [+]
>
> In 90% of cases, the cost center of the technical object is the target account assignment of the maintenance orders. In Customizing, enter CTR as the default account assignment for the settlement profile. Then, the cost center of the reference object is automatically transferred to the order as the account assignment; you do not have to maintain it manually.

How does a settlement rule look in the order? Figure 6.25 shows a typical settlement rule for maintenance orders. The order is settled 100% to an asset cost center. **Settlement rule**

6 | Integrating Applications from Other Departments

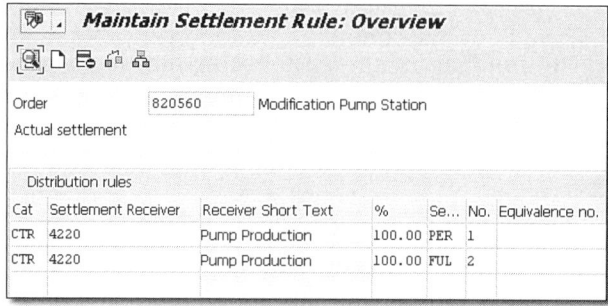

Figure 6.25 Settlement Rule

If you have a settlement rule created automatically, the SAP system generates two entries for the settlement type:

- **PER (periodic settlement)**
  For the monthly settlement, the system considers here only the costs that arise in the specified period.
- **FUL (full settlement)**
  Here, the system considers all the costs that arise up to the time of settlement.

When PER settlement rules are present, they are applied ahead of FUL settlement.

[+] **Period Accruals in the Order Settlement**

You also have the option to use period accruals (*From* period and *To* period) to settle costs over time to different target account assignments.

[!] **Do Not Forget FUL Settlement Rule**

Make sure that a FUL settlement rule is present in your order as the settlement rule. Otherwise, not all costs might be settled to the target account assignment.

Settlement by amount

You also have the option to settle a fixed amount. You need it, for example, when you have agreed on a fixed price with the contracting entity. In such a case, enter a settlement rule as indicated in Figure 6.26:

- **Amount**

  You create a settlement rule with the amount. This means the relevant amount is settled to the specified settlement rule (for example, asset cost center).

- **Amount rule category**

  Do not forget to specify the amount rule category in the ARULCAT column. Set the amount rule category to 1 if you want the amount to be settled once. Leave the amount rule category empty if the amount is to be settled in each period.

- **Percentage rate settlement**

  You can create one or more percentage rate settlements. This means the effective actual costs are settled to this account assignment rule (usually the maintenance cost center).

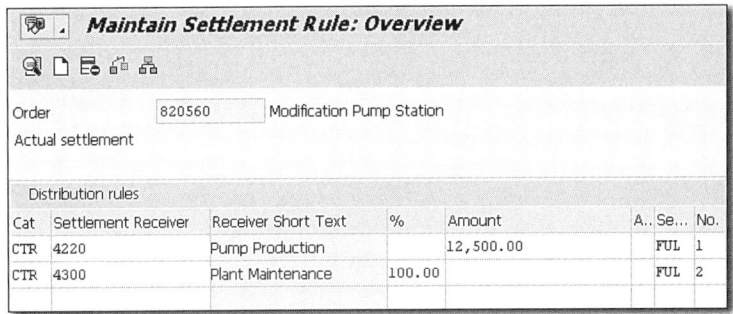

Figure 6.26 Settlement by Amount

To perform a settlement by amount, select the SETTLEMENT AMOUNT option (Customizing function MAINTAIN SETTLEMENT PROFILE).

Prerequisites

Settlement at a Fixed Price [+]

You can also settle your orders at a fixed price. You simply activate settlement by amount in the settlement rule. Then, enter the first settlement rule with the amount for target account assignment and a second settlement rule with 100% assigned to the performing cost center.

6 | Integrating Applications from Other Departments

Settlement procedure
How do you settle orders? You have two options in this case:

- Use Transaction KO88 (individual settlement) and settle an individual order.
- Use Transaction KO8G (collective settlement)—a batch program is the best approach—and settle all orders that can be settled at the end of a period (month-end, for example) with the actual costs that have arisen during that time.

Result
How can you tell whether an order has been settled or what the result of an order settlement is?

Settlement re-debits all debits of the order to the target account assignment; thus, the report on individual costs shows zero (0) as the overall total of actual costs (see Figure 6.27).

Cost Elem.	Cost Element (Text)	Σ	Total plan costs Σ	Total act.costs Σ	Plan/actual variance	P/A var(%)	Currency
415000	External procurement costs		2,000.00	1,750.00	250.00-	12.50-	USD
417000	Purchased Services		2,735.00	2,345.00	390.00-	14.26-	USD
615000	Dir.Int.Activity Alloc. Repair Hours		2,300.00	1,840.00	460.00-	20.00-	USD
655110	Overhead Surcharge - Other Materials		1,177.00	819.00	358.00-	30.42-	USD
Debit		■	8,212.00 ■	6,754.00 ■	1,458.00-		USD
650000	Order settlement		0.00	819.00-	819.00-		USD
651000	Order settlement - Material Costs		0.00	4,095.00-	4,095.00-		USD
652000	Order settlement - Internal Activities		0.00	1,840.00-	1,840.00-		USD
Settlement		■	0.00 ■	6,754.00- ■	6,754.00-		USD
		■ ■	8,212.00 ■ ■	0.00 ■ ■	8,212.00-		USD

Figure 6.27 Settled Order

Controlling Information System

You can see the total of services and costs incurred by the order in cost center reports, such as the report created with Transaction S_ALR_87013611 (cost centers: actual/plan deviation).

Figure 6.28 illustrates a typical result for a performing cost center: the cost center is credited with the cost elements of internal activity allocation (615000, in this example).

Figure 6.29, however, shows a typical receiving cost center: the cost center is debited with the cost elements of order settlement (here, for example, 650000 et seq.).

Cost elements		Act.costs	Plan costs	Abs. var.
400000	Raw Materials 1	28.500,00		28.500,00
403000	Operating Supplies	2.000,00		2.000,00
420000	Direct labor costs		59.624,56	59.624,56-
430000	Salaries		47.652,04	47.652,04-
435000	Annual Bonus		8.823,36	8.823,36-
440000	Legal social expens		25.911,90	25.911,90-
449000	Other pers. costs		1.276,20	1.276,20-
476000	Office supplies		719,36	719,36-
481000	Cost-acctg deprec.	3.443,00	8.127,00	4.684,00-
483000	Imputed interest	1.250,00	6.156,96	4.906,96-
617000	DAA Energy		27.985,68	27.985,68-
618000	DAA IT Development		3.804,49	3.804,49-
619000	DAA Production	1.499,94		1.499,94
651000	ORS Material	1.460,00		1.460,00
652000	ORS Int. Activities	2.264,99		2.264,99
699900	0000699900	1.125,00		1.125,00
890000	Cons.semifin.produc	800,00		800,00
* Debit		43.899,93	190.081,55	146.181,62-
615000	DAA Repair Hours	51.711,27-	263.895,38-	212.184,11
655901	Overhead Rep. Maint	520,77-		520,77-
* Credit		52.232,04-	263.895,38-	211.663,34
** Over/underabsorption		8.332,11-	73.813,83-	65.481,72

Figure 6.28 Cost Center Report for a Performing Cost Center

Cost elements		Act.costs	Plan costs
211100	0000211100	625.188,00	
211200	0000211200	41.997,00	
261000	0000261000	799.298,00-	
417000	Purchased services		18.305,08
420000	Direct labor costs		126.716,52
430000	Salaries		
431900	Holiday premium		
435000	Annual Bonus		10.096,99
440000	Legal social expens		30.680,87
449000	Other pers. costs		1.435,68
459000	Other maint. costs		
466000	Insurance expenses		9.608,96
476900	Miscellaneous costs		
481000	Cost-acctg deprec.	799.298,00	12.709,20
483000	Imputed interest	354.591,00	7.076,84
617000	DAA Energy		6.996,40
618000	DAA IT Development		2.282,69
630000	Assessment General		1.946,00-
650000	Order settlement	29.521,02	
651000	ORS Material	55.820,56	
652000	ORS Int. Activities	145.772,37	
* Debit		1.252.889,95	223.963,23

Figure 6.29 Cost Center Report for a Receiving Cost Center

6.2.9 Real Estate Management

SAP Real Estate Management (RE) and the newer flexible real estate management component (RE-FX) offer functions you need when managing real estate, for example, the following:

Overview

- Management of various types of real estate objects: business entity, property, building, rental units, rental space, and rental rooms
- Management of real estate contracts: renting to and from contracts, service contracts, and maintenance contracts
- Area management: size and equipment
- Business processes related to real estate: new construction, order processing, and activity allocations

Real Estate Objects and Functional Locations

Utilization view

At every level in the utilization view, you can assign a functional location to a real estate object, as follows:

- To a business unit, if it involves real estate holdings that are related to each other (in an industrial park, for example)
- To a building, if it involves an object that creates the basis for renting space (apartments, warehouses, and businesses). A building is a component of a business unit.
- To a rental object, such as an area pool, rental space, or rental unit

Figure 6.30 illustrates the assignment of a functional location to a real estate object from the perspective of the object—a building, in this case.

[+] **Creating Functional Locations Automatically**

You can use the Customizing function FLEXIBLE REAL ESTATE MANAGEMENT (RE-FX) • GENERAL SETTINGS FOR MASTER DATA AND CONTRACTS ASSIGNMENT OF OBJECTS FROM OTHER COMPONENTS • PM INTEGRATION • PM INTEGRATION: DEFINE SETTINGS PER OBJECT TYPE to define per company code and type of object whether a functional location should be generated automatically when you create a real estate object.

You can also display the assignment from the perspective of the functional location (Transaction IL03): all functional locations that are assigned to a real estate object have a REAL ESTATE tab, where the assignment is automatically entered (see Figure 6.31).

6.2 Integration within SAP ERP

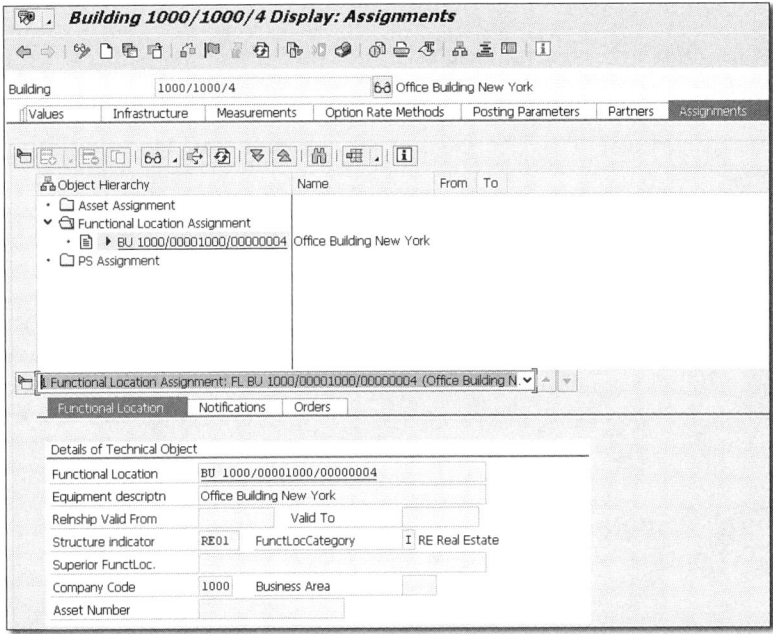

Figure 6.30 Assignment of Functional Location to Real Estate Object

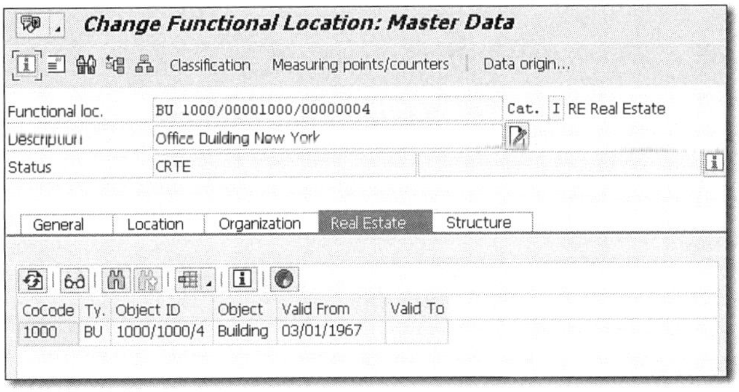

Figure 6.31 Functional Location—Real Estate

In the architectural view, you can also manually assign a functional location to a real estate object. In Customizing, you can also use FLEXIBLE REAL ESTATE MANAGEMENT (RE-FX) • MASTER DATA • ARCHITECTURAL VIEW • PM INTEGRATION • DEFINE SETTINGS PER ARCHITECTURAL OBJECT TYPE to define whether or not a functional location is automatically created for the architectural object type (area, building, property, and so on).

Architectural view

Subsequent Processes

If you have assigned the real estate object and functional location, you can initiate the following processes:

- You can create or assign notifications for the functional location from the real estate object.
- You can also create orders for the functional location from the real estate object or from IW31 and assign them to the real estate object.
- Settlement of the order can occur on real estate objects, such as a rental unit, settlement unit, or usage object. The costs are then stated for each real estate object and can be used later on in service charge settlement (see Figure 6.32). To this end, use Transaction REIS-COLIBD (real estate objects actual line items).

Document	Cost element name	Cost Ele	OTy	Object	CO object name	Σ	Val/COArea Crcy	P	Year	PTy	PartnerObj
600059068	ORS Order Settlement	650000	BE	1000	Areal / Locality		8,403.36	12	20...	ORD	819630
600059068	Cons.semifin.product	890000			Areal / Locality		1,359.80		20...	ORD	819630
600059068	Cons.semifin.product	890000			Areal / Locality		799.40		20...	ORD	819630
			BE		Areal / Locality	.	10,562.56				
				1000	Areal / Locality	..	10,562.56				
						...	10,562.56	1			
						....	10,562.56				

Figure 6.32 Settled Costs in a Real Estate Object

6.2.10 Human Capital Management

The application SAP ERP Human Capital Management (SAP ERP HCM, formerly: HR) offers functions related to human resources, as follows:

- Personnel management
 (recruitment, remuneration, vacation, organization, personnel development, retirement provisions, and so on)
- Payroll accounting
 (gross, net, reduced-hours workers, pensions, and so on)
- Time management
 (schedules, time entry, incentive wages, and so on)

- Event management
(events, speakers, room management, registration, and so on)
- Continuing education and training

Integration of SAP ERP HCM and EAM is always active when you assign a personnel number to objects or business processes of plant maintenance.

Work Center and Personnel Number

The assignment of persons to the work center is the starting point for the use of persons in the business processes of plant maintenance. You can assign a person as shown in Figure 6.33, either directly or indirectly using positions. You link the two using transactions for maintaining a work center (IR01 and IR02) or via Human Capital Management transactions.

Assignment	Name	Name	Object Period
MECHANICS	Mechanical maintenance	A 50000132	11/21/1994 - 12/31/9999
Person			
· Kelly	Kevin Kelly	P 00100288	07/01/1997 - 12/31/9999
Position			
PM technics	Maintenance technician	S 50010227	01/01/1996 - 12/31/9999
· Miller	Helen Miller	P 00001602	01/01/1996 - 12/31/9999
PM technics	Maintenance technician	S 50011049	01/01/1996 - 12/31/9999
PM technics	Maintenance technician	S 50011050	01/01/1996 - 12/31/9999
PM Mechanic	Plant Maintenance Mechanic (1)	S 50011055	01/01/1994 - 12/31/9999
· O'Malley	Linda O'Malley	P 00100105	07/01/1996 - 12/31/9999
PM Mechanic	Plant Maintenance Mechanic (2)	S 50011056	01/01/1994 - 12/31/9999
· Gregson	Mark Gregson	P 00100106	07/01/1996 - 12/31/9999
· Weldin	Joe Weldin	P 00100236	01/01/1999 - 12/31/9999
· Sibley	Mary Sibley	P 00100314	04/01/1998 - 12/31/9999
PM Service	Plant Maintenance Service Tech	S 50012287	01/01/1997 - 12/31/9999
PM Mecchanic	Plant Maintenance Mechanic	S 50012292	01/01/1997 - 12/31/9999
PM Mecchanic	Plant Maintenance Mechanic	S 50012293	01/01/1997 - 12/31/9999
· Knittle	Janet Knittle	P 00100155	01/01/1997 - 12/31/9999
Mechanic	Mechanic	S 50013175	01/01/1994 - 12/31/9999
· Weber	Frank Weber	P 00001603	01/01/1997 - 12/31/9999
Mechanic	Mechanic	S 50013176	01/01/1994 - 12/31/9999

Figure 6.33 Work Center and Persons

Technical Objects and Personnel Number

User firms often want to store named contact persons in the master data records of technical objects—for example, the addressee in the event of further questions.

> [!] **Person Assignment in the Technical Object Using Partner Determination Procedure**
>
> You can always assign equipment and functional locations to a person if you have assigned a partner determination procedure, which includes a partner role that refers to partner type PE (HR master record), to the equipment type or functional location type.

See Section 4.2.9 for details about defining and assigning partners.

Figure 6.34 shows, for example, the assignment of equipment to two partner roles of type PE.

Partner Overview		
Funct	Partner	Name
KO Coordinator	70234	Mrs Jordan Kelly
VW Person Responsible	100405	Mr. Jonathan Meyers

Figure 6.34 Technical Object and Person

Notifications and Personnel Number

When you want to assign a contact person by name to a notification, the procedure is similar to that for master data records.

> [!] **Person Assignment in the Notification Using Partner Determination Procedure**
>
> You can always assign persons to a notification if you have assigned a partner determination procedure, which has partner roles that refer, in turn, to partner type PE (personnel master data), to the notification type. If the same partner role is present in the type of the technical object, the relevant person is transferred to the notification.

Order and Personnel Number

Section 5.2.2 explained that you can assign a personnel number to several levels of an order.

You can name a responsible person in the order header. This is usually a person from the responsible work center who serves as the central contact person during performance of the order—for example, the person who would answer any questions that arise (see Figure 6.35).

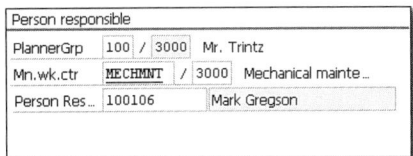

Figure 6.35 Person Responsible in the Order Header

You can also assign an operation to the person who should perform it. This is usually a person from the work center (see Figure 6.36).

First operation									
Operation	Pump defect, production downtime					CcKey	1 Calculate duration		
WkCtr/Plnt	MECHMNT	/ 3000	Ctrl key	PM01	Acty Type	1410			PRT
Work durtn	8.0	HR	Number	1	Oprtn dur.	8.0	HR		Comp.
Person. no	100223		Will Governale						

Figure 6.36 Person Responsible for Executing Operation

You can also assign several persons to an operation if it involves several technicians. You enter the number of persons involved and then indicate the persons for the requirements specifications (see Figure 6.37).

Components	Reqmnts Assignment		Relationships					
Capacity cat.	002		Labor					
Spl	Dispa...	Person	Work	W..	Normal...	D...	Date	Time	Suit.
1	☐	Governale	3.0	HR	3.0	HR	06/10/2013	08:00	100.00
2	☐	Knittle	3.0	HR	3.0	HR	06/10/2013	08:00	100.00
3	☐	Sibley	2.0	HR	2.0	HR	06/10/2013	08:00	100.00

Figure 6.37 Several Persons Responsible for Executing Operation

Confirmation and Personnel Number

In all confirmation transactions, you have the option of entering a personnel number along with the confirmation. During confirmation with maintenance Transactions IW41, IW42, IW44, and IW48, you can enter a personnel number, and during confirmation via the SAP application Cross-Application Time Sheet (CATS; Transaction CAT2), you must specify a personnel number.

> [!] **Observe Local and National Laws for Confirmation with Personnel Number**
>
> When you execute a confirmation with a personnel number, please consider local and national laws. In Germany, for example, you can do this only if you have given your employee representatives a written company agreement in which, among other things, you state that the information will not be used to compare employee performance.

How can you reasonably work with confirmations at the level of the personnel number? You can check to see whether all the attendance time was settled to orders. An example of this is shown in Figure 6.38.

Postg date	S	Pers.No. Σ	Actual work	Un. W	Order	Op	Equipment	Functional Location
12/28/2...			135.0	HR	819579	0010	P-1000-N001	K1-MER-11
12/07/20...			30	MIN	819585	0010	TEQ-00	00-B02
12/15/20...			2.5	HR	819600	0010	TEQ-00	00-B02
12/29/20...			45.0	HR	819630	0010		BU 1000/00001000/00000004
		▪	30	MIN				
			182.5	HR				
12/27/20...		258	1.0	HR	818962	0010	TEQ-00	00-B02
12/27/20...			6.0	HR	819270	0020		K1
12/28/20...			8.0	HR	819565	0010	P-1000-N005	K1-BR2-12
12/29/20...			7.0	HR	819565	0100	P-1000-N005	K1-BR2-12
		258 ▪	22.0	HR				
12/26/20...		1200	2.5	HR	819134	0010	P-1000-DF01	K1-B01-1
12/26/20...			5.0	HR	819135	0030	P-1000-DF02	K1-B01-1
12/27/20...			5.0	HR	819136	0020	PP-FHME	
12/27/20...			3.0	HR	819137	0010	PP-FHME	
12/28/20...			5.0	HR	819138	0020	PP-FHME	
12/28/20...			3.0	HR	819139	0010	PP-FHME	
12/29/20...			4.0	HR	819139	0020	PP-FHME	
		1200 ▪	27.5	HR				
		▪▪	30	MIN				
			232.0	HR				

Figure 6.38 Confirmation List by Personnel Number

Ensure that the Confirmations Are Complete [!]

Based on person-related times, you can evaluate whether the relevant person entered the time spent on the orders or, for example, confirmations were forgotten. If you do not enter all attendance times in orders, the allocation record of the workshops tends to increase in the next period.

A similar evaluation exists in time management using time leveling (Transaction PW61; see Figure 6.39). The time leveling shows the planned attendance times and the time accounted to orders.

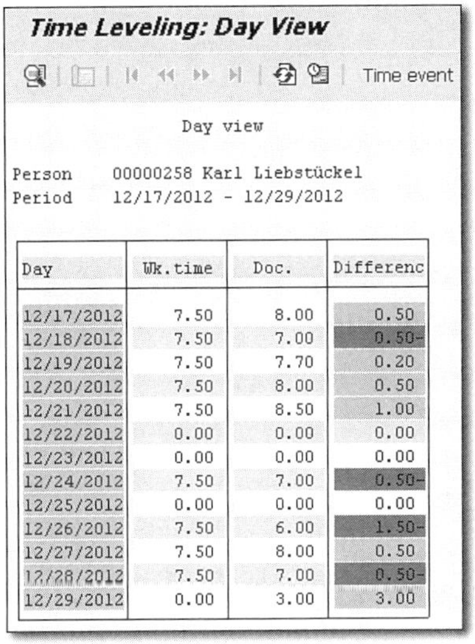
Time Leveling: Day View

Time event

Day view

Person 00000258 Karl Liebstückel
Period 12/17/2012 - 12/29/2012

Day	Wk.time	Doc.	Differenc
12/17/2012	7.50	8.00	0.50
12/18/2012	7.50	7.00	0.50-
12/19/2012	7.50	7.70	0.20
12/20/2012	7.50	8.00	0.50
12/21/2012	7.50	8.50	1.00
12/22/2012	0.00	0.00	0.00
12/23/2012	0.00	0.00	0.00
12/24/2012	7.50	7.00	0.50-
12/25/2012	0.00	0.00	0.00
12/26/2012	7.50	6.00	1.50-
12/27/2012	7.50	8.00	0.50
12/28/2012	7.50	7.00	0.50-
12/29/2012	0.00	3.00	3.00

Figure 6.39 Time Leveling

6.2.11 Service and Sales

Distinctive customer service?

If you have distinctive customer service, I recommend that you implement the SAP Customer Service (CS) module. It is a sister component of EAM that has functions and business processes oriented to customer service. These are, in particular, the following (see Figure 6.40):

- Structuring and maintenance of service objects using functional locations, equipment, and installations
- Warranty management with warranty claim processing
- Management of service contracts and service level agreements

- Creation of quotations for service offerings
- Returns processing
- Advance shipment of spare parts
- Customer Interaction Center
- Service processing with service notification, service orders, and sales orders
- Solution database
- Billing of services provided
- Monitoring of notifications with reaction times and availability times
- Connection between service objects and business partners

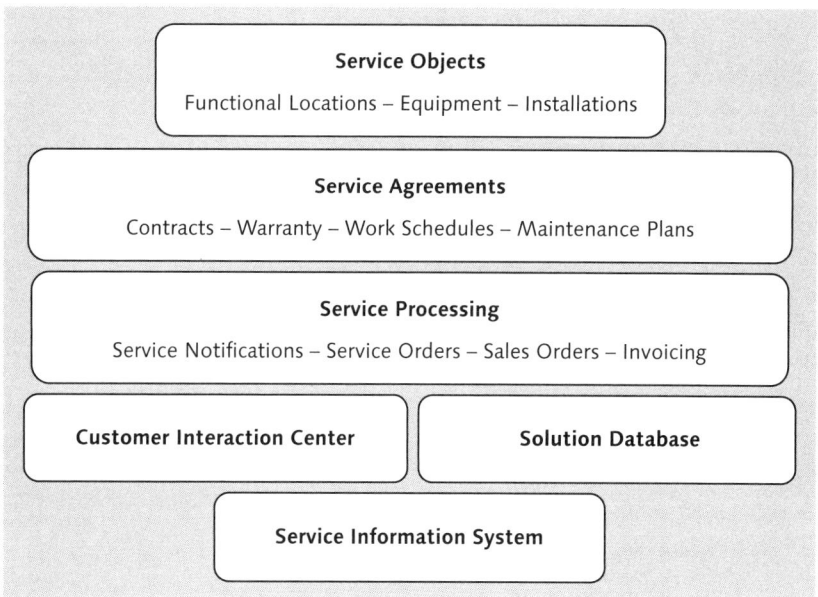

Figure 6.40 Customer Service in SAP ERP

Plant Maintenance in the Context of Sales Orders

Even if you do not have distinctive customer service but simply provide services in the context of sales orders at irregular intervals, you can also benefit from integration with sales. For example, the following services could be involved:

- A technician undertakes an assembly at a customer site.
- A customer returns a device that is then repaired in the workshop.
- A technician repairs a machine at a customer site.
- A technician briefs an employee at a customer site as part of the sales order.

What do you have to do to be able to map these business processes in your system without having to implement a complete CS system?

- You have a regular sales order.
- You create a maintenance order when one of the previously noted cases occurs.
- You can assign the maintenance order to a sales order item (see Figure 6.41). The requirement here is that the sales order is entered as a VALID RECEIVER in the settlement profile.

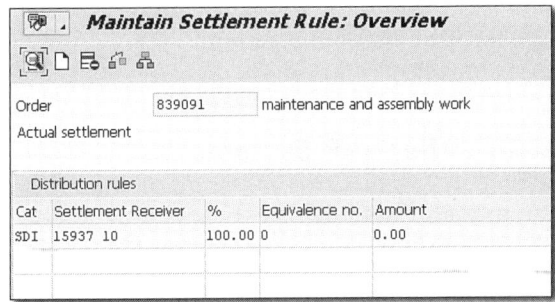

Figure 6.41 Sales Order as Settlement Rule

- You perform the maintenance order as normal.
- You settle the maintenance order to the sales order.

The sales order states the settled costs (see Figure 6.42); you can invoice these and reduce the profit expected from the sales order.

[+] **Assigned EAM Order versus CS Order**

If you have distinctive customer service, I recommend that you implement CS. If you perform services related to sales at irregular intervals, you could benefit from integration with sales and settle the maintenance order to the sales order.

Change Standard Order 15937: Overview				
Sales Document/Item 15937/ 10				
Cost Elem.	Cost Element (Text)	Origin	Σ Total plan costs	Σ Total actual costs
800000	Sales revenues - domestic		13,000.00-	13,000.00-
			▪ 13,000.00- ▪	13,000.00-
650000	Order settlement	ORD Undefined	0.00	1,684.64
			▪ 0.00 ▪	1,684.64
650000	Order settlement		0.00	1,864.30
			▪ 0.00 ▪	1,864.30
			▪▪ 13,000.00- ▪▪	9,451.06-

Figure 6.42 Cost Analysis of a Sales Order

This integration is one of the most important that exists between plant maintenance and other departments that use SAP ERP components. However, because SAP offers other systems beyond the SAP ERP environment that other departments may use and that affect plant maintenance, the next section will focus on these integration issues.

6.3 Integration with Other SAP Systems

In addition to the integration points described in the previous sections within SAP ERP, functions of SAP NetWeaver Master Data Management (SAP NetWeaver MDM) and SAP Supplier Relationship Management (SAP SRM) are used essentially in plant maintenance.

6.3.1 Integration with SAP NetWeaver MDM

Initial situation and objectives

Many companies use not only an integrated system like SAP ERP, but also possibly many others that handle business processes and manage master data. As a result, master data is distributed across various systems, applications, and tables, and this leads, almost by necessity, to inconsistencies and conflicts.

This is illustrated by the following example: a spare part is purchased from various suppliers in different plants. Each supplier uses a different part number, and each plant uses its own material number for the spare part in its system. The spare part is never scheduled in common, and its availability is never made known to the other plants, which inevitably leads to increased inventory. You can now use SAP NetWeaver MDM to identify duplicates and to consolidate, synchronize, distribute, and centrally manage master data objects from various IT systems.

SAP NetWeaver MDM attempts to achieve these goals at various levels (see Figure 6.43):

Levels of SAP NetWeaver MDM

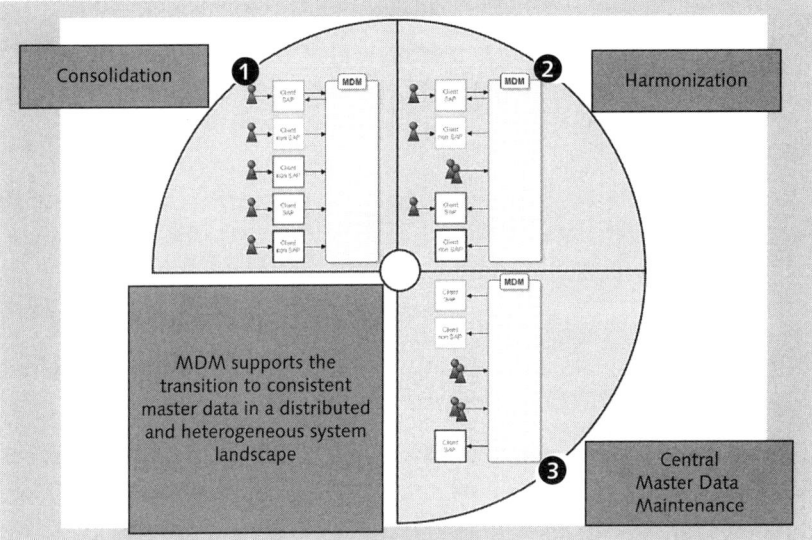

Figure 6.43 SAP NetWeaver Master Data Management (SAP NetWeaver MDM)

- **Master data consolidation**
  Master data consolidation ❶ seeks to identify identical master data from various systems, compare the master data objects centrally in SAP NetWeaver MDM, and supply decentralized systems with mapping information. To this end, data is loaded into SAP NetWeaver MDM and consolidated there. Any required corrections occur in the decentralized systems, which can be SAP or non-SAP systems.

- **Master data harmonization**
  With master data harmonization ❷, data is also maintained in decentralized SAP and non-SAP systems, loaded into SAP NetWeaver MDM, and harmonized there. In this case, the master data is distributed to SAP and non-SAP systems, where it is updated or recreated.

427

- **Central master data maintenance**
  With central master data maintenance ❸, the master data is centrally maintained and stored on the SAP NetWeaver MDM server. Distribution mechanisms are used to distribute the data to the SAP and non-SAP systems to be addressed. The difference between this approach and master data harmonization is that the data is centrally maintained in SAP NetWeaver MDM and distributed from there, rather than being loaded and consolidated from the decentralized systems.

Objects

Which objects that are relevant from a plant maintenance perspective can be processed by SAP NetWeaver MDM? The most important objects include the following:

- Materials
- BOMs
- Vendors
- Personnel

Other master data objects (such as retail materials or customers) do not play any role from a plant maintenance perspective.

This issue won't be discussed in any more detail here. If SAP NetWeaver MDM seems to be a reasonable approach to your master data management, please refer to more detailed literature[1] on the technology, architecture, and solution landscape of SAP NetWeaver MDM.

6.3.2 Integration with SAP SRM

Overview

SAP SRM is a new purchasing system from SAP that can be used instead of or parallel to the purchasing component in SAP ERP. SAP SRM includes the following functions:

- **Self-service procurement**
  Employees can use this function to make purchasing easier and to create and manage their own order processes to accelerate procurement transactions.

---

[1] For example, Heilig, L.; Karch, St.; Böttcher, O.; Hofmann, C.; Pfennig, R.: *SAP NetWeaver Master Data Management*, Bonn: SAP PRESS, 2007.

- **Service procurement**
  This function is used for the procurement of services.
- **Plan-driven procurement**
  Plan-driven procurement is used to cover requirements that are reported from other systems.
- **Spend analysis**
  This function is used to analyze procurement expenses in the company.
- **Strategic sourcing**
  Strategic sourcing is used to manage sources of supply.
- **Catalog content management**
  Catalog content management is used to manage sales catalogs.
- **Contract management**
  This function is used to manage contracts and delivery schedules.

From a plant maintenance perspective, *Plan-driven Procurement* is the most interesting component. It deals with the procurement of material and service requirements that originate in external planning systems. For plant maintenance in particular, SAP SRM supports a scenario for *Plan-driven Procurement with Plant Maintenance*.

Plan-driven Procurement with Plant Maintenance

Two variations of the scenario exist:

- Classic scenario (see Figure 6.44)
- Enhanced classic scenario (see Figure 6.45)

In the classic scenario, SAP ERP generates a purchase requisition and sends it as an external requirement to SAP SRM via an open XML interface.

Classic scenario

SAP SRM executes sourcing for the required product. Purchasing agents can use functions to create contracts for the requirements or trigger bid invitations.

SAP SRM generates one or more purchase orders that it transfers to SAP ERP for subsequent processing of the purchase order.

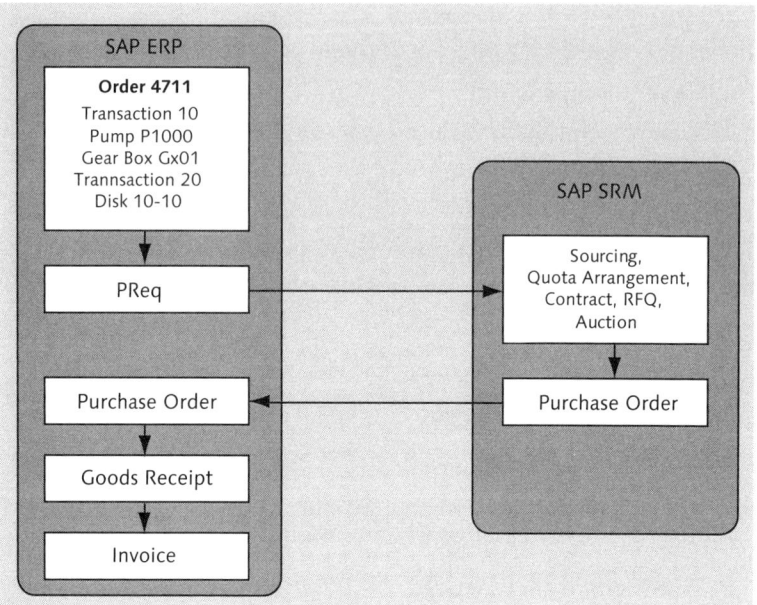

Figure 6.44 The Classic Scenario of SRM Integration

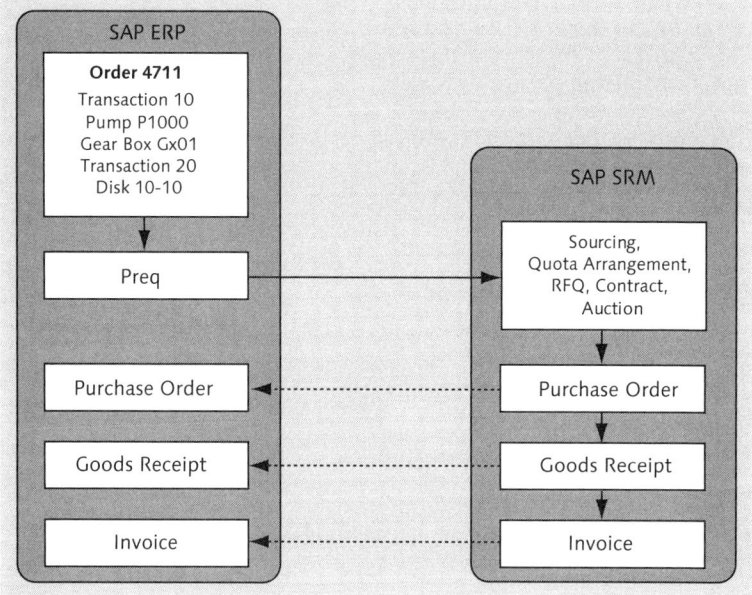

Figure 6.45 The Enhanced Classic Scenario of SRM Integration

In the enhanced classic scenario, the subsequent processing occurs in SAP SRM, but the documents arising from goods receipts and invoice receipts are still stored in SAP ERP.

Enhanced classic scenario

> **[!] Setting Classic or Enhanced Scenario?**
> You make the decision to process materials according to the classic scenario or enhanced classic scenario in Customizing of SAP ERP using the Customizing function INTEGRATION WITH OTHER SAP COMPONENTS • SUPPLIER RELATIONSHIP MANAGEMENT • MAINTAIN PROFILE FOR EXTERNAL PROCUREMENT or CONTROL EXTERNAL PROCUREMENT, with the help of which you can direct the procurement process to a system other than the ERP system, depending on product group and purchasing group.

These are likely to be the most important of the SAP systems that are used by other departments and interact with EAM.

When you implement EAM, however, you generally deal with other systems that are used by other departments and with which you must or want to exchange data. Such cases are the subject of the next section.

6.4 Integration with Non-SAP Systems

The implementation of EAM often leads to situations in which existing non-SAP systems (for example, from the area of plant data collection, construction, and building services) must be coupled with EAM. These non-SAP systems can be different categories of systems that are organized as follows for further discussion:

- **Operations monitoring systems**
  Like process control systems, network monitoring systems, building control systems, and diagnostic systems
- **Operations information systems**
  Like CAD systems, GIS systems, and network information systems
- **Systems for entry of services performed**
  For example, systems for entry of measurement quantities

6.4.1 Operations Monitoring Systems

Definition Operations monitoring systems monitor, control, regulate, and optimize operations events online and in near-real time. Depending on the industry and purpose, the following systems are used:

- **Process control systems**
  Process control systems are used in process industries like chemicals, pharmaceuticals, and food. They help monitor, control, regulate, and optimize a technical process. Examples include refrigeration in a plant that produces ice cream and the throughput speed of a unit to dry powder.

- **MES systems**
  Manufacturing execution systems (MES) are used in discrete manufacturing and differ from production planning systems in SAP ERP because of their direct connection to automated production in real time. They thereby enable control of production in real time. These include electronic control stations and traditional data entry, such as production data acquisition, machine data acquisition, and entry of personnel data.

- **Building control systems**
  Building control systems are used in building management. They are used to monitor, regulate, and optimize a technical process within a building, such as air conditioning or ventilation.

- **Network monitoring systems**
  Network monitoring systems are used in the energy industry and by major energy consumers. They help monitor, control, regulate, and optimize the production and distribution of electricity. Another form of network monitoring systems is used in telecommunications to monitor, control, and optimize telecommunications networks.

- **Diagnostic assemblies**
  In addition to the complete systems previously noted, diagnostic assemblies exist for individual units like robots, flexible manufacturing cells, vehicles, or elevators. The assemblies can recognize, diagnose, and register errors automatically. Examples include the lack of hydraulic pressure in an elevator, a slowing down of the

rotational speed of a robot, and the lack of pressure in a vehicle's braking system.

Operations monitoring systems provide a variety of data related to a process, building, assembly, or infrastructure. You have two ways of transmitting the information from your operations monitoring systems to an SAP system:

- **RFC connection**
  With the first option, there is a direct Remote Function Call (RFC) connection between the operations monitoring system and the SAP system (see Figure 6.46).

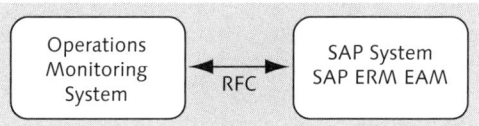

Figure 6.46 Direct Connection to the SAP System

- **SCADA systems**
  An indirect connection is established using Supervisory Control and Data Acquisition (SCADA) systems. They perform a filtering function. They filter out data relevant to maintenance and thereby protect the SAP system from being flooded with data. SCADA systems also establish communication between one or more process control systems and the SAP system (see Figure 6.47).

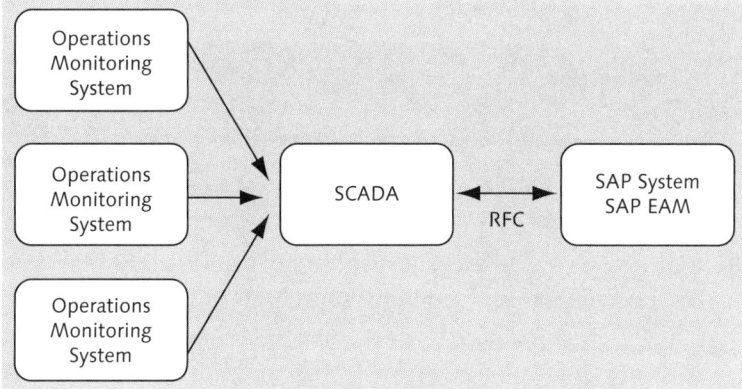

Figure 6.47 Indirect Connection to the SAP System via SCADA

PM-PCS Interface

What is the PM-PCS interface? The PM-PCS interface (PCS stands for Production Control System) is a basic element of EAM for recording data from external systems. This includes not only data from operations monitoring systems, but also data that was captured with mobile devices (laptops and barcode readers). Using this interface, you can transfer measurements and counter readings from upstream systems to the SAP system.

How can you use the PM-PCS interface with EAM in SAP ERP?

- **Performance-based maintenance planning**
  The PM-PCS interface supports performance-based maintenance planning, for which a recalculation of the next maintenance date takes place based on the transferred counter readings (see Section 5.8.5 and Section 5.8.6).

- **Condition-based maintenance**
  The PM-PCS interface enables you to work with condition-based maintenance, whereby a malfunction message is issued on the basis of the transferred measurements (see Section 5.9).

- **Documentation**
  The measurement documents that are created form the basis for documentation of the actual situation for reports on asset security, work safety, and environmental protection (see Section 4.2.9).

- **Consumption billing**
  The measurement documents can be used as the basis for consumption billing when managing real estate (see Section 6.2.9).

> [!] **Data Transfer with the PM-PCS Interface**
>
> The PM-PCS interface is a flexible instrument for transferring measurements and counter readings from upstream systems to EAM and processing them further there.

In addition to systems that intervene directly in operations, systems that support the construction and building of operating facilities are also important to plant maintenance.

6.4.2 Operations Information Systems

Essentially, operations information systems involve computer-aided design (CAD) systems and geographical information systems (GIS).

CAD systems are used, for example, in the following areas: **CAD systems**

- In asset construction as diagrams for piping and instrumentation (P & I diagrams, see Figure 6.48)
- In facility management as building plans, room specifications, and surface usage
- In construction for developing complex devices (such as industrial robots and aircraft, for example)

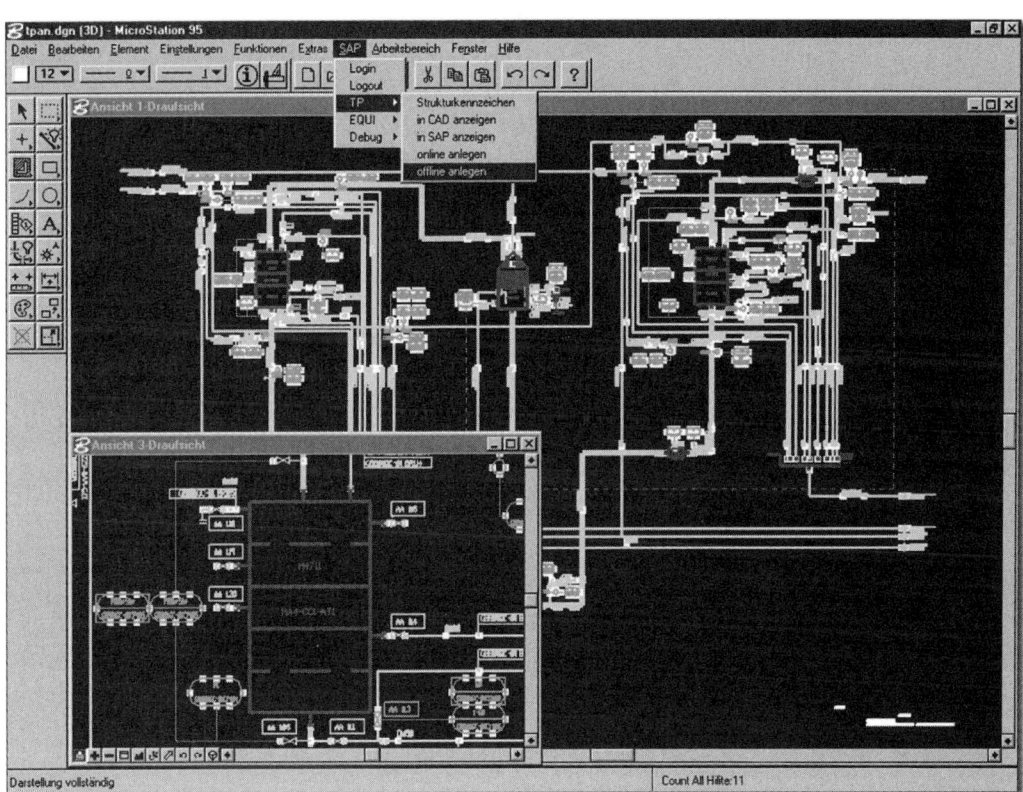

Figure 6.48 CAD System

Common CAD systems like AutoCAD, MicroStation, and CATIA have certified interfaces to the SAP system.

> **Certified CAD Interface to the SAP System**
>
> If you want to know whether the CAD system you are using has a certified interface to the SAP system, visit *http://www.sap.com/partners/directories/SearchSolution.epx*. Search under CERTIFICATION CATEGORY with the keywords CAD and COMPUTER AIDED DESIGN.

GIS systems

GIS systems exist in different forms: as country information systems, land information systems, environmental information systems, and other systems. From a plant maintenance perspective and your connection to SAP systems, the most important GIS systems are network information systems (NIS). The NIS system is an instrument for capturing, managing, analyzing, and presenting data on operating resources from network topology. Utilities and waste disposal companies work with these kinds of GIS. The primary use is for geometric and graphic documentation of connections (see Figure 6.49).

Familiar GIS manufacturers like GE Smallworld, Bentley, Intergraph, ESRI, and others have had SAP certify their GIS interfaces.

> **Certified GIS Interface to the SAP System**
>
> If you want to know whether the GIS system you are using has a certified interface to the SAP system, visit *http://www.sap.com/partners/directories/SearchSolution.epx*. Search under CERTIFICATION CATEGORY with the keyword GEOGRAPHICAL INFORMATION SYSTEMS.

Functional scope

What do these CAD and GIS interfaces do? The functional scope varies from manufacturer to manufacturer, but here are some of the options:

- Create, change, search, and display equipment
- Create, change, search, and display functional locations
- Create, change, search, and display materials
- Create, change, search, and display BOMs

- Synchronize classification data
- Create, change, search, and display a notification or order and visualize the status of the notification or order

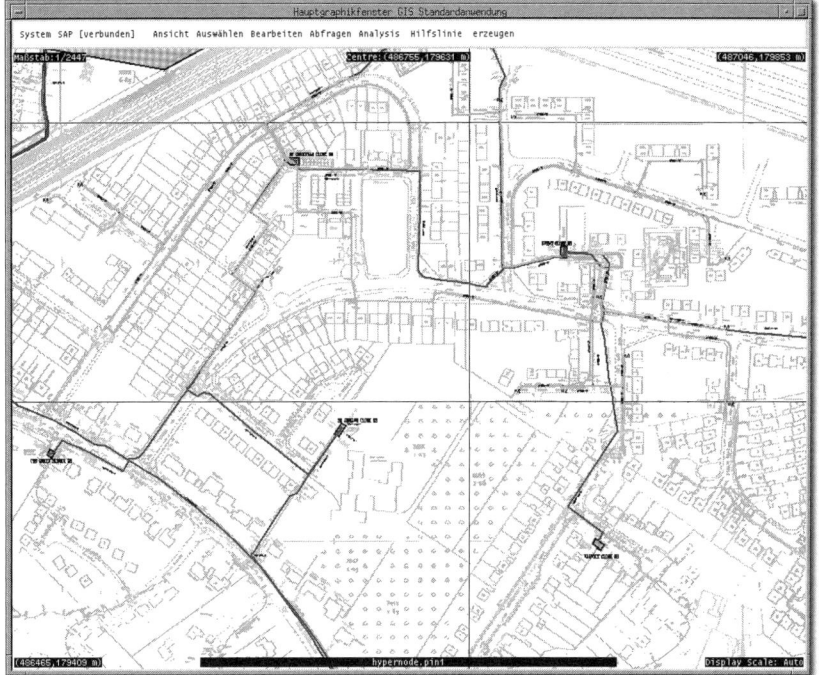

Figure 6.49 GIS System

The interfaces can use different approaches to technical implementation:

Technical implementation

- You are working in your CAD or GIS application and want to see the data in the SAP system for a graphical object you have selected in the CAD or GIS system. You start a query on the SAP application server and see the result in an SAP window and in the CAD or GIS application.
- You see the result in a CAD or GIS window.
- You are working in your SAP system and want to see the CAD or GIS drawings for a highlighted technical object (equipment or functional

location). You start a query on the SAP application server: the CAD or GIS application loads the drawing.

- You can use the business connector, the GIS business connector, or SAP NetWeaver Process Integration (SAP NetWeaver PI) for the technical implementation.

[+] **Functional Scopes Are Extremely Different**

Because the functional scope of your CAD or GIS system and technical realization can vary quite considerably, ask the manufacturer for more detailed information.

6.4.3 Service Specifications and Entry of Services Performed

When you deal with business processes on the basis of service specifications with vendors (see Section 5.5.4), you have two ways of exchanging data with your vendors.

Exchanging Data via Interfaces

SAP offers interfaces that you can use to transfer data to your vendors or receive data from vendors and record it in the SAP system. You can also use the interfaces to import predefined, standard service specifications to storage devices in the SAP system.

You can exchange the following data with the service providers (see Figure 6.50):

- Requests for quotations and quotations
- Service master data, contracts (purchase orders), and service entry sheets

The following media are available for exchanging data:

- File Transfer Protocol (FTP)
- SAP email and Internet email
- Storage media such as CDs or USB sticks

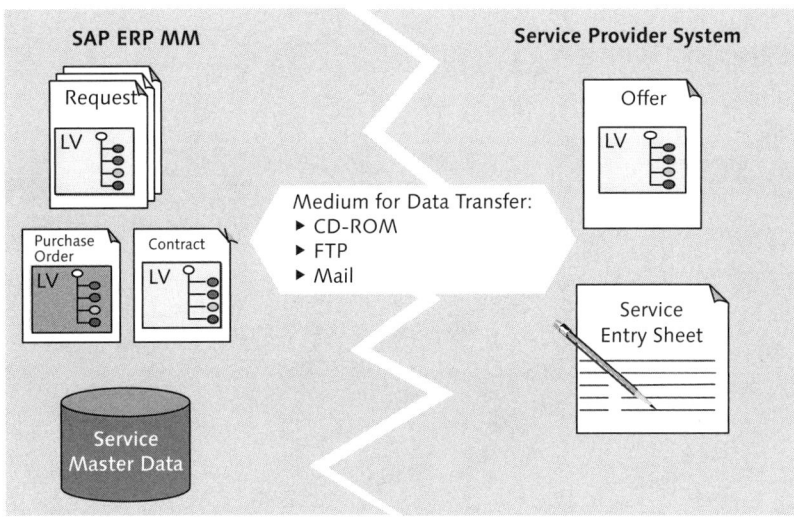

Figure 6.50 Exchanging Data with Vendors

Exchanging data with vendors enables you to simplify and accelerate the business processes for entry of services performed. Data is exchanged via the following steps:

1. You send vendors the service specifications as purchase orders, contracts, or service master records (for example, by email).
2. After the services are performed, the vendor creates a service entry sheet and sends it to you, for example, by File Transfer Protocol (FTP).
3. You record the service entry sheet in the SAP system.
4. You then perform a formal acceptance of the services.

Little Expense for Entry of Services Performed	[!]
If you use data exchange with vendors, the greatest advantage is that you incur no expenses for entering the services performed.	

Entry of Services Performed via the Internet

You can also connect your vendors via the Internet. The other option for transferring the expenses for entry of services performed to your vendors, besides electronic data storage media, is to use the Internet

Internet Application Component

Application Component (IAC) from SAP for a browser-based entry of services (see Figure 6.51).

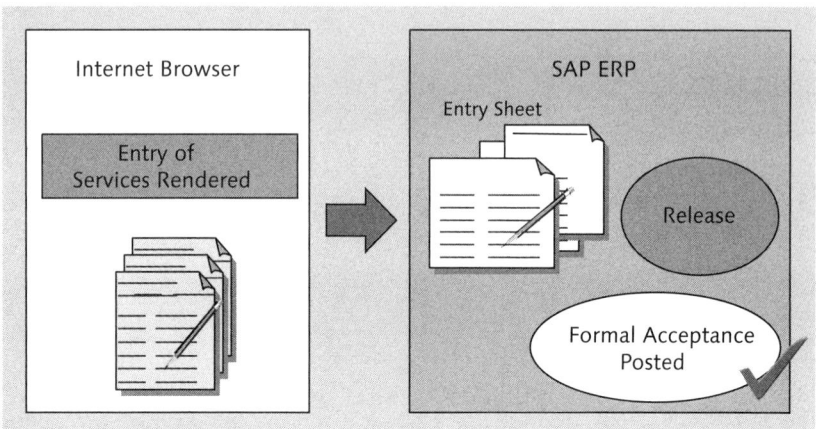

Figure 6.51 Internet Application Component for Activity Recording

The data entered on the Intranet or Internet is transferred to SAP ERP via the BAPI ENTRY SHEET.CREATE. A simplified Transaction MEW10 was also created with Dynpros for the IAC.

Controlling can be understood in several different, more or less literal senses. Operational controlling is used to control current business processes, whereas analytical controlling is intended to support tactical and strategic decision making. This chapter looks first at the active control of plant maintenance tasks and then also considers the options and limits of the tools SAP provides for reporting.

7   Plant Maintenance Controlling

The English term *to control* is often translated in a very limited manner in German as *kontrollieren* (to control/check) and, thus, controlling tends to be unfairly discredited as purely controlling and monitoring. However, the term *to control* is much more complex and multifaceted. Depending on the application and purpose, it can be taken to mean to *control, guide, influence, manage, check,* or *regulate*. It is in this broader sense that the term *plant maintenance controlling* is meant: as instruments for guiding and controlling the plant maintenance processes.

7.1   What Plant Maintenance Controlling Involves

Depending on the time period and scope involved, different instances of plant maintenance controlling may differ (see Figure 7.1):[1]

Types of plant maintenance controlling

- **Operational controlling ❸**
  Operational plant maintenance controlling is a short-term approach thus focused on daily business (for example, third-party outsourcing

---

[1] For the following discussions, see also Liebstückel, K.: Technisches Controlling liefert konkrete Entscheidungsgrundlagen, in: ("Technical controlling delivers specific decisions", in:) Die Industrie – Fachzeitschrift für Wirtschaft und Technik 48 (2002). *Die Industrie – Journal of Economics and Technology* 48 (2002).

of plant maintenance contracts, damage analysis of machines, and utilization of workshops).

- **Tactical controlling** ❷
  Tactical controlling has a medium-term focus and relates to business processes (for example, change of business processes, negotiation, and preparation of contracts with service companies).
- **Strategic controlling** ❶
  The long-term goals are the subject of strategic controlling; it is used to ensure the survival of the company (for example, outsourcing the service department or attracting new markets).

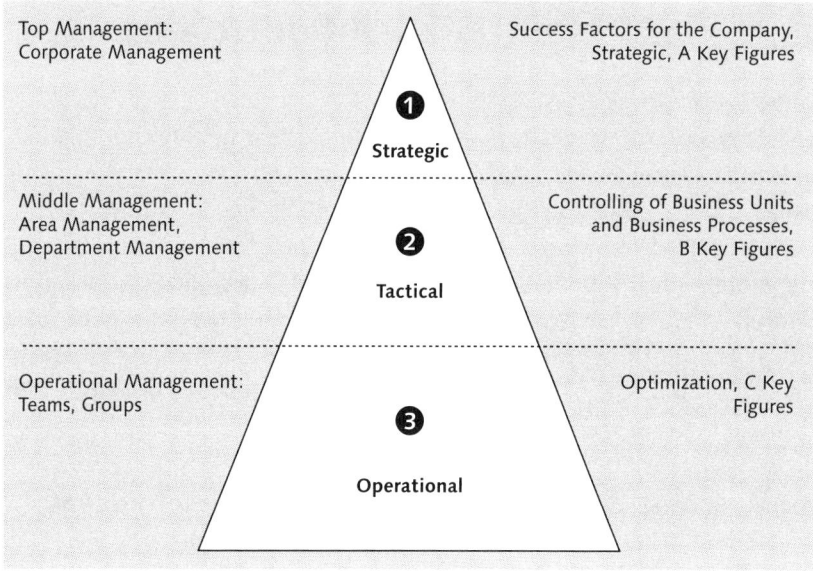

Figure 7.1 Types of Controlling

Commercial and technical controlling

You know the term *Controlling* from the commercial sector. There, Controlling is a central organizational unit with a critical business function. In the technical area, controlling is not usually established in its own organizational unit, but has a central corporate function. If we compare commercial controlling with technical controlling, there are a few major differences (see Table 7.1).

Commercial Controlling	Technical Controlling
Oriented toward commercial organizational structures (for example, company code, controlling area, cost centers, profit centers)	Oriented toward technical organizational structures (for example, machines, work centers, tools, materials)
Evaluates commercial posting objects (for example, general ledger accounts and cost elements)	Evaluates technical processing objects (for example, orders, damage notifications, and purchase orders)
Determines solely cost values/key figures	Determines technical and cost values/key figures

Table 7.1 Comparison of Commercial and Technical Controlling

Commercial controlling is oriented toward commercial organizational structures; accordingly, the focus of the perspective is on organizational units like the company code, controlling area, cost center, and profit center. On the other hand, technical controlling is oriented toward the technical conditions and evaluates units like machines, systems, materials, and work centers.

In commercial controlling, commercial posting objects like general ledger accounts and cost elements are evaluated, while technical controlling focuses on technical processing objects like notifications, orders, confirmations, purchase orders, goods movements, and deliveries.

Finally, only costs, expenses, revenue, income, and other business key figures are calculated in the context of commercial controlling, whereas cost figures and technical figures are the focus of technical controlling.

We can distinguish among the following topics depending on the view level of plant maintenance controlling:

View levels

- **Measure-based controlling**
  Here, the focus is on either a single measure (for example, recalculating an order) or a group of measures (for example, analyzing a revision).

- **Object-based controlling**
  The focus here is on a technical object (for example, the ranking list of equipment by actual costs or damage analysis of functional locations).
- **Period-based controlling**
  Here, the focus is on analyses over a certain time period (for example, use of replacement parts per month or planned costs per week).

Aggregation levels — The information calculated and provided in the context of plant maintenance controlling is at different aggregation levels:

- **Lists**
  For example, list of open notifications, list of pending maintenance plan orders, or list of blocked equipment
- **Reports**
  For example, the total plant maintenance costs per functional location, number of malfunction reports per month
- **Key figures**
  For example, relation between planned and actual costs, mean time between failures (MTBF), average time per order

Cycle — Depending on the informational need, information must be available and/or provided in different cycles:

- Daily (for example, list of open malfunction reports)
- Weekly (for example, weekly schedule of maintenance plan orders)
- Monthly (for example, total costs incurred)
- Annually (for example, comparison of budget with actual costs)

Media — Depending on the role of an employee in the company and his technical possibilities, information must be available or distributed in different media:

- **Paper**
  If access to online data is not desired, not possible, or not necessary, the information must be provided as a printout.
- **SAP system**
  The information can be called online in SAP ERP or SAP NetWeaver BW (for short, BW) or also via SAP NetWeaver Portal if it is needed promptly and if direct access to it should be possible.

▶ **Email or workflow**
The information is sent via email or using a workflow if information is desired online, but there is no access to the SAP system.

▶ **Mobile devices**
External sales technicians must be able to access the desired information via mobile devices, for example.

Figure 7.2 shows an overview of the tasks of plant maintenance controlling.

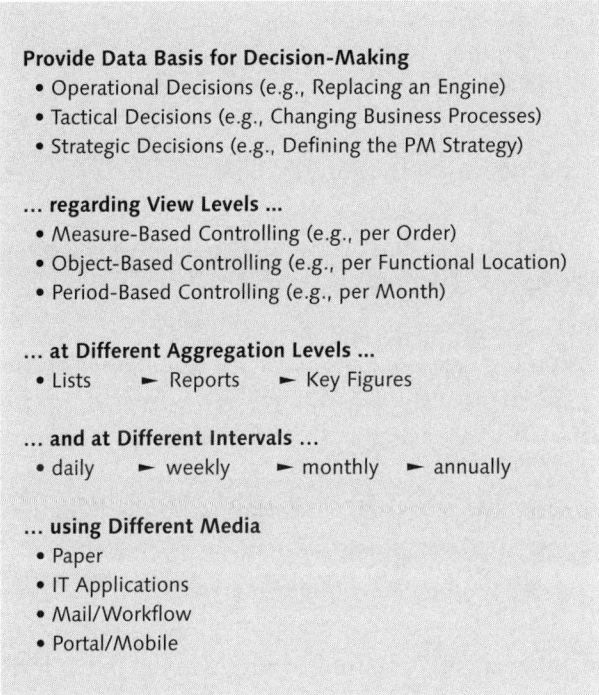

Figure 7.2 Tasks for Plant Maintenance Controlling

The following questions are, thus, the focus of the following two sections, respectively:

▶ What tools does SAP offer you for obtaining information, and how do you use them?

▶ What tools does SAP offer you for budgeting, and how do you use them?

7.2 SAP Tools for Obtaining Information and How to Use Them

Types of decision

The tools listed in this section do not affect business processes and their mapping in the SAP system. Their task is, rather, to provide you with the necessary information so that you can make organizational decisions on that basis—every day there are plenty of decisions to be made, which refer, in turn, to a different time horizon:

- **Operational decisions**
  In operational plant maintenance controlling, for example, decisions are made about the composition of a weekly schedule, external assignment of an order, or tasks for capacity leveling.

- **Tactical decisions**
  In tacticalplant maintenance controlling, for example, decisions are made about tasks due to expiration of warranties, scrapping a machine, tasks to avoid errors, the conclusion of service agreements and decisions for or against a particular type of machine.

- **Strategic decisions**
  In the course of operational plant maintenance controlling, for example, decisions are made about the outsourcing or reintegration of a task area or about structural changes.

[!] **An IT System Does Not Make Any Decisions**

You need to make the right decisions yourself, but the IT system can provide you with the necessary information.

As tools for obtaining information, I'll briefly introduce you in the next section to the SAP List Viewer, SAP Queries and Quick Views, the Logistics Information System (LIS) of SAP ERP, and SAP NetWeaver BW.

7.2.1 SAP List Viewer

Flexibility

SAP List Viewer does not present information to you as a rigid list, but makes it possible to adapt the list flexibly to your own information requirements. All EAM lists were converted to this technology.

The following lists are available in EAM: EAM lists

- List of *Functional Locations* (Transaction IL05, Transaction IL06, Transaction IH06)
- List of *Reference Functional Locations* (Transaction IL15, Transaction IH07)
- List of *Equipment* (Transaction IE05, Transaction IH08)
- List of *Vehicles* (Transaction IE36, Transaction IE37)
- List of *Object Links and Object Network* (Transaction IN15, Transaction IN16, Transaction IN18, Transaction IN19)
- List of *Measurement Documents* (Transaction IK17, Transaction IK18)
- List of *Material Serial Numbers* (Transaction IQ08)
- List of *Materials* (Transaction IH09)
- List of *Measuring Points* (Transaction IK07, Transaction IK08)
- List of *Reference Measuring Points* (Transaction IK07, Transaction IK08)
- List of *Notifications* (Transaction IW28, Transaction IW29)
- List of *Tasks* (Transaction IW66, Transaction IW67)
- List of *Actions* (Transaction IW64, Transaction IW65)
- List of *Notification Items* (Transaction IW68, Transaction IW69)
- List of *Orders* (Transaction IW38, Transaction IW39)
- List of *Order Operations* (Transaction IW37, Transaction IW49)
- Combined Order/Operation List (Transaction IW37N, Transaction IW49N)
- List of *Components* (Transaction IW3K, Transaction IW3L)
- List of *Permits* (Transaction IPM2, Transaction IPM3)
- List of *Confirmations* (Transaction IW47)
- List of *Goods Movements* (Transaction IW3M)
- List of *Maintenance Plans* (Transaction IP15, Transaction IP16)
- List of *Maintenance Items* (Transaction IP17, Transaction IP18)
- Scheduling Overview list (Transaction IP24)
- List of *Maintenance Task Lists* (Transaction IA08, Transaction IA09)

7 | Plant Maintenance Controlling

- List of *Shift Notes* (Transaction SHN4 or Transaction ISHN4)
- List of *Shift Reports* (Transaction SHR4 or Transaction ISHR4)

Flow   When you use the SAP List Viewer, processing always takes place in the following sequence: selection → basic list → further processing (see Figure 7.3).

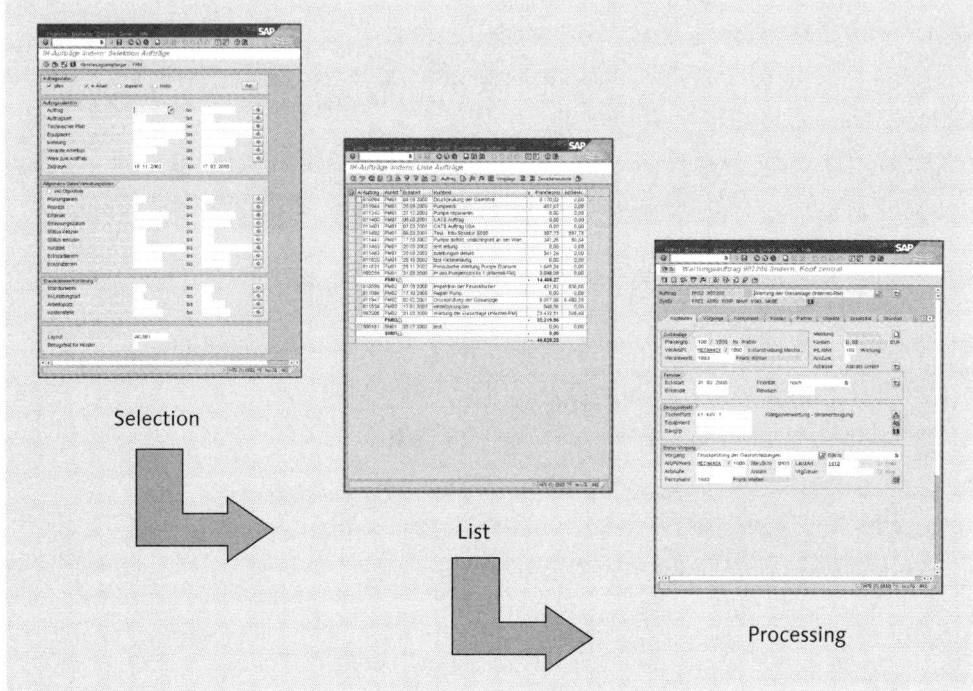

Figure 7.3 Processing Sequence in the SAP List Viewer

I will present the SAP List Viewer to you using an example of the order list (Transaction IW38). However, these remarks apply equally for each of the aforementioned lists.

Selection

When you call up a list, you see a selection screen containing all the selection options, extending over two to four pages, depending on the list and screen resolution. Experience shows us that you rarely need any page other than the first. Thus, you should create a selection variant first.

> **Creating Selection Variants** [+]
>
> Create a selection variant that contains one page of selection conditions, at most. You should also follow this basic rule when creating selection variants in the future.

You create a selection variant by saving the selection screen upon clicking the 💾 button and then making active and purposeful use of the option of hiding selection criteria on the following screen (see Figure 7.4).

Selection variant

Field name	Type	Protect field	Hide field
Priority	S	☐	☐
Entered by	S	☐	☐
Created on	S	☐	✓
Status inclusive	S	☐	☐
Status exclusive	S	☐	☐
Description	S	☐	✓
Last changed by	S	☐	✓
Change date for order master	S	☐	✓
Available to date	S	☐	✓
Basic Start Date	S	☐	☐
Basic finish date	S	☐	☐
Maintenance Plan	S	☐	✓
Maintenance item	S	☐	✓
Revision	S	☐	✓
WBS Element Order Header	S	☐	✓

Figure 7.4 Hiding a Field

Because list variants can make a significant contribution to increasing usability and user acceptance (there are details on this in Section 9.4), you are sure to subsequently create other selection variants.

You call your list variants by clicking on the 📋 button, which is to be found on the initial screen of every list. You can display a list of selection variants in this manner and select the desired variant. Since this list can become quite extensive over time, here is your next practical tip.

> **Default Variant U_USERNAME** [+]
>
> The selection variants you use most often should be named as U_ followed by your SAP user name (see Figure 7.5); these selection variants are now shown automatically when the list is called.

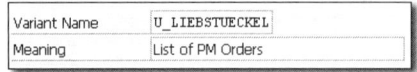

Figure 7.5 Variant Name

Selection options For each selection field, you can use the following selection options:

- **Single value**
  You can search for a single value (for example, order type PM01) or multiple single values (for example, order types PM01, PM05, and PM10).

- **Interval**
  You can search for an interval (for example, order type PM01 to PM05) or multiple intervals.

- **Wildcard search**
  You can do a wildcard search (for example, order type PM* selects all order types that start with PM).

- **Exclusion of elements**
  You can exclude values and intervals (for example, not order types PM03 or PM05-08).

- **Clipboard**
  You can paste in search values from the Windows Clipboard.

It is particularly useful that you can define selection variables for dynamic date calculation, where, depending on the current date, the FROM/TO date selection is dynamically calculated based on the chosen selection option (see Figure 7.6).

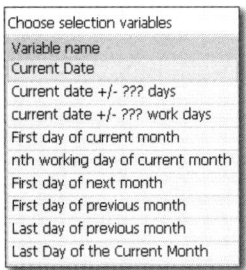

Figure 7.6 Date Variable

Take a look at the following example of this scenario: on September 01, you set the list with the selection *Start date equal to current date in 180 days and +60 days*. Thus, on September 01, you would be selecting the dates from March 04 to October 31.

Example

Dynamic Data Calculation [+]

By using the DYNAMIC DATE CALCULATION selection variables, you can determine the selection date of the list dynamically.

Activate Monitor if Possible [+]

Some lists (not all) allow the activation of a monitor. Depending on the parameters selected (for example, the basic date), the list entries are then red, yellow, or green (for example, red for overdue orders, yellow if the starting date has been reached but the ending date has not, and green for future orders).

The List Display

If you now start the list, you will see the initial list according to the selections and settings made (see Figure 7.7).

Monitor	S	Type	Order	Description	FunctLoc.	Equipment	Bas. start date	Basic fin. date	Σ ActTotCost Σ	PlanTotCos
		PM01	852742	external refurbishment service partner	C1-B01-1	P-3000-N001	07/17/2013	07/17/2013	0.00	600.00
		PM01	852753	Maintenance Inspection for Airplane		10004170	07/21/2013	07/21/2013	0.00	0.00
		PM01	852766	Counter based MP pump set 2	C1-B01-2		07/18/2013	07/24/2013	0.00	0.00
		PM01	853212	Maintenance Inspection for Airplane		10004170	07/21/2013	07/21/2013	0.00	0.00
		PM01	853214	Counter based MP pump set 2	C1-B01-2		07/18/2013	07/24/2013	0.00	0.00
		PM01	853221	Maintenance Inspection for Airplane		10004170	07/28/2013	07/28/2013	0.00	25.08
		PM01	853239	Counter based MP pump set 2	C1-B01-2		07/25/2013	07/31/2013	0.00	125.40
		PM							0.00	750.48
		PM03	825776	quarterly PM gas station	C1-KGV		08/01/2013	08/10/2013	684.00	12,683.82
		PM03	843671	quarterly PM gas station	C1-KGV		05/30/2013	06/04/2013	0.00	7,904.05
		PM03	849540	semi-annual PM gas station 2	C1-KGV		08/28/2013	09/02/2013	0.00	7,560.46
		PM03	852762	Monthly inspection of pump station	C1-B01		04/02/2013	04/04/2013	0.00	0.00
		PM03	852763	Monthly inspection of pump station	C1-B01		05/02/2013	05/04/2013	0.00	0.00
		PM03	852764	Monthly inspection of pump station	C1-B01		06/01/2013	06/03/2013	0.00	0.00
		PM03	852765	Monthly inspection of pump station	C1-B01		07/01/2013	07/03/2013	0.00	0.00
		PM							684.00	28,148.33
									684.00	28,898.81

Figure 7.7 List in the SAP List Viewer

List options You now have the following options for adapting the layout of the list to your own needs:

- **Showing and hiding fields**
  You can show additional fields or hide the visible fields; almost all fields of the object to be evaluated are available. For functional locations and equipment, you can also show fields from their classifications.

- **Sorting**
  You can sort by a criterion (for example, by date) or several criteria (for example, by cost center and date within each cost center).

- **Calculating totals**
  For value and quantity fields (for example, actual costs), you can calculate totals and display subtotals (for example, for each order type).

- **Changing column width**
  You can optimize the column width.

- **Searching**
  You can search within a list for a particular term (for example, leaks). This is an especially useful function for large lists.

- **Filtering**
  You can filter a displayed list (for example, display only entries with system status REL).

- **Performing ABC analysis**
  You can perform an ABC analysis based on a key figure (for example, an ABC analysis of orders relative to actual costs).

- **Graphical representation**
  You can generate a graphical representation (for example, a bar chart with the number of orders for each order type).

- **Using display variants**
  You can save your settings as a display variant.

[+] **Default Setting for Display Variant**

The most frequently used display variant should be marked as a default setting.

Further Processing

If you now have the list in the desired form, the following options for further processing are available to you:

- **Details**
  You can select a certain line and call the database object (for example, a certain order, in order to change the date.)

- **Mass processing**
  You can select several lines and perform the same function in each selected line (for example, print all selected orders or assign the same date to all selected orders).

- **Mass change**
  With regard to list editing, there is a MASS CHANGE function for orders and notifications with which you can change practically any field in all selected objects in one step.

- **Sending**
  You can send the list via SAP internal mail or via Email.

Is no Email Button Available?	[+]
If you cannot find a button for sending a list (for example, ▥), use the function LIST • SAVE • OFFICE.	

- **Download**
  You can save the list in any current Office format and work with it there (for example, download the order list to Excel in order to display it there using pivot functions).

Scheduling Lists as Periodic Jobs	[+]
You can also schedule lists as periodic jobs, which then run automatically at regular intervals and perform certain follow-up functions (for instance, an email can be sent to the production manager, which contains the maintenance orders for the coming week).	

The lists in the SAP List Viewer are predefined in EAM for certain database objects. As a result, SAP List Viewer reaches its limits: on the one hand, in cases in which you require information or fields that are not

Limits

defined in SAP List Viewer, there is a *Material* list, but it is not possible to show the storage bin where each material is stored.

On the other hand, it is not possible to display information or fields for different database objects in a single list. Thus, it is not possible to display notification information (for example, damage codes) and order information together in a single-level list.

Here is a tool that is easy to use and that gives you more flexibility: SAP Quick Viewer.

7.2.2 SAP Quick Viewer

Applications

SAP Quick Viewer (Transaction SQVI or menu path SYSTEM • SERVICES • QUICK VIEWER) starts where SAP List Viewer reaches its limits and provides options for exceeding those limits:

- SAP Quick Viewer makes it possible for you to display any database field in a list. Thus, you can, for example, create a list of materials with their storage bins.
- You can use SAP Quick Viewer to link database tables. For instance, you could show notification and request information together in a single list.
- SAP Quick Viewer makes it possible to answer ad hoc questions that cannot be answered using SAP List Viewer—for example, which equipment has no maintenance plan or which functional location can access which general maintenance task list via the construction type.

Example

Let's look at SAP Quick Viewer based on a specific example: one of my customers wanted to know how many man hours he was using for each damage code and each repair shop. This requirement could not be met using the techniques of the SAP List Viewer because information was needed for this purpose from the notification, order, and confirmations. The creation of a Quick View helped in this case.

Database table

If you now create a Quick View, you are asked for the names of the database tables. The determination of the relevant database tables is the most difficult part when you create a Quick View; there are several options for searching by the desired table:

- You can navigate via the application hierarchy ([F4] help in the field TABLE • SAP APPLICATIONS) and work through the hierarchy to the desired database table.
- You can navigate via the information system ([F4] help in the field TABLE • INFO SYSTEM) of the SAP Quick Viewer and search for a keyword.

> **[!] Keyword Search in the Information System**
>
> The keyword search in the information system of the SAP Quick Viewer is case sensitive; that is, it distinguishes between upper case and lower case letters. Thus, if you are looking for the table of time confirmations in plant maintenance and are unsure of the name of the table in the short text, it is safer to search for *onfirmation* (see Figure 7.8).

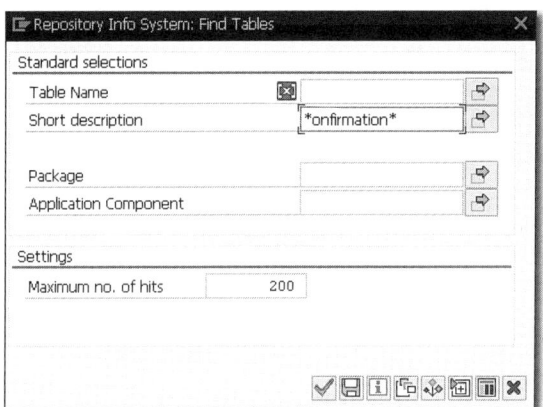

Figure 7.8 SAP Quick Viewer Info System

- Or—and this seems to me the simplest and safest way to go—you can call the original transaction (for example, Transaction IW41 for time confirmations) and use the [F1] help • TECHNICAL INFO (see Figure 7.9).

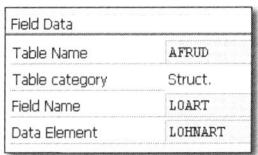

Figure 7.9 Technical Information

In our specific example, the tables QMEL (notification), QMFE (notification items), and AFRU (order confirmations) would be relevant. These tables are now linked via a table join (see Figure 7.10).

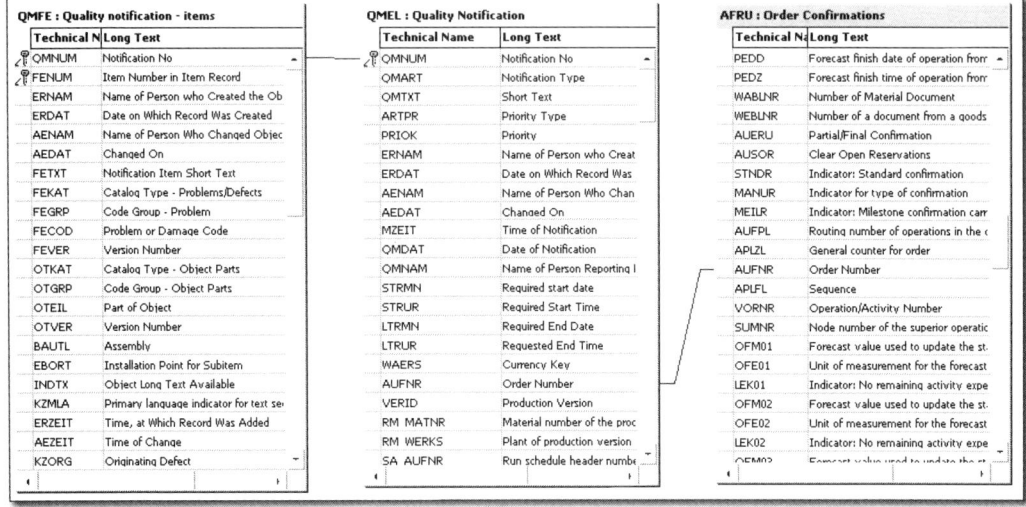

Figure 7.10 Table Join

Functions The SAP Quick Viewer provides you with various options for list layout and list processing:

- **Selecting fields**

  You can select lists by any fields (for example, by damage code or period of time).

  You have the same options as for the SAP List Viewer (single, multiple, range selections, exclusion).

- **Displaying fields**

  You can display any fields (for example, damage code, notification number, order number, work center, date, or actual time).

- **Calculating totals**

  You can calculate totals for value and quantity fields (for example, actual time).

- **Sorting and forming subtotals**

  You can sort and form subtotals based on one or more criteria (for example, damage code and work center) and then display individual lines or the totals lines only.

▶ **Output formats**
You have various output options (for example, output as SAP List Viewer or download to an Office format).

▶ **Graphical representation**
You can format the results as a graphic.

▶ **Sending the list**
You can send the list as an SAP mail or as an email.

Possible results of an SAP Quick Viewer are shown in Figure 7.11 and Figure 7.12.

Actual Times per Damage Code					
Notification	Dam.	Order	Σ	Act.work	Un.
	1		▪	7.0	HR
	1000		▪	2,709.7	HR
	1001		▪	762.5	HR
	1002		▪	34.0	HR
	1003		▪	94.0	HR
	1004		▪	36.5	HR
	1005		▪	26.0	HR
	1006		▪	56.5	HR
10000489	1007	810241		1.0	HR
10000489		810241		2.0	HR
10000727		811300		5.0	HR
10002251		820348		5.0	HR
10002251		820348		1.0	HR
10002251		820348		10.0	HR
	1007		▪	24.0	HR
	1008		▪	5.5	HR
	13		▪	1.0	HR
100013	15	817861		45.0	HR
	15		▪	45.0	HR
			▪▪	3,801.7	HR

Figure 7.11 List Output in SAP Quick Viewer

However, SAP Quick Viewer also has its limits, as already indicated:

Limits of SAP Quick Viewer

▶ You cannot call the operational database object from the list of SAP Quick Viewer; thus, you would not be able to view the individual confirmation directly in our example.

▶ The SAP Quick Viewer itself is user dependent; that is, only the user who created a Quick View can execute it.

7 | Plant Maintenance Controlling

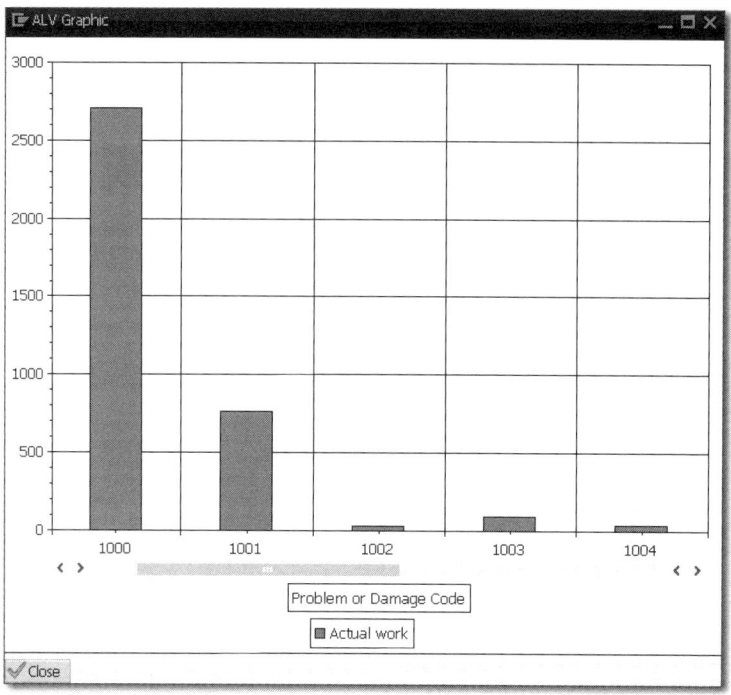

Figure 7.12 Graphic in SAP Quick Viewer

- The SAP Quick Viewer does not have an authorization concept; that is, anybody who can create Quick Views can view all company data.
- Using SAP Quick Viewer, you cannot perform any arithmetic operations—for example, calculating totals, differences or ratios.
- A Quick View cannot be connected to the SAP Transport System. This means that you cannot create it in a development system and then transport it to your production system after a successful testing phase.

Overcoming the limits

These restrictions should not mean that SAP Quick Viewer is unsuitable, in principle, for you. There are various ways to overcome these limits:

- **ABAP program**
  The SAP Quick Viewer generates an ABAP program in the background. If you want to insert authorization checks, mathematical calculations, or other functions, you can do it directly in this program. Similarly, the ABAP program can be transported to another system.

The ABAP program generated has a name similar to the following: AQTGSYSTQV000033QKL001=======. AQ is fixed, as is SYSTQV; TG is the alphabetical code for the client account, and 000033 stands for the 33rd user to create a Quick View. QKL001 is the name the user gave the Quick View and ====== are fill characters.

- **Calling by different users**
  To make a Quick View accessible for multiple users, you can convert it to an SAP Query. To do so, start Transaction SQ01, and call the function QUERY • CONVERT QUICK VIEW (see Figure 7.13).

- **Transporting to the production system**
  Both the SAP Queries and the generated programs are connected to the SAP transport system and can, thus, be transported to the production system.

- **Authorization check**
  In addition, you can create a transaction with an authorization check for SAP Query or SAP Quick Viewer via Transaction SE93. This is also connected to the transport system.

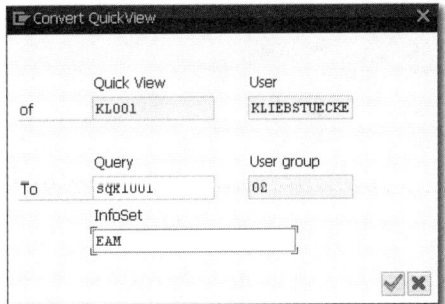

Figure 7.13 Converting Quick View into a Query

Now, let's look at another tool provided by SAP ERP for obtaining and presenting information: the Logistics Information System (LIS).

7.2.3 SAP ERP Logistics Information System

The Logistics Information System (LIS) is used for logistics applications in SAP ERP and has specific variant names like the purchase information system, inventory control, etc. In plant maintenance, the PM-IS plant maintenance information system is used. All logistics information systems have the same structure (see Figure 7.14).

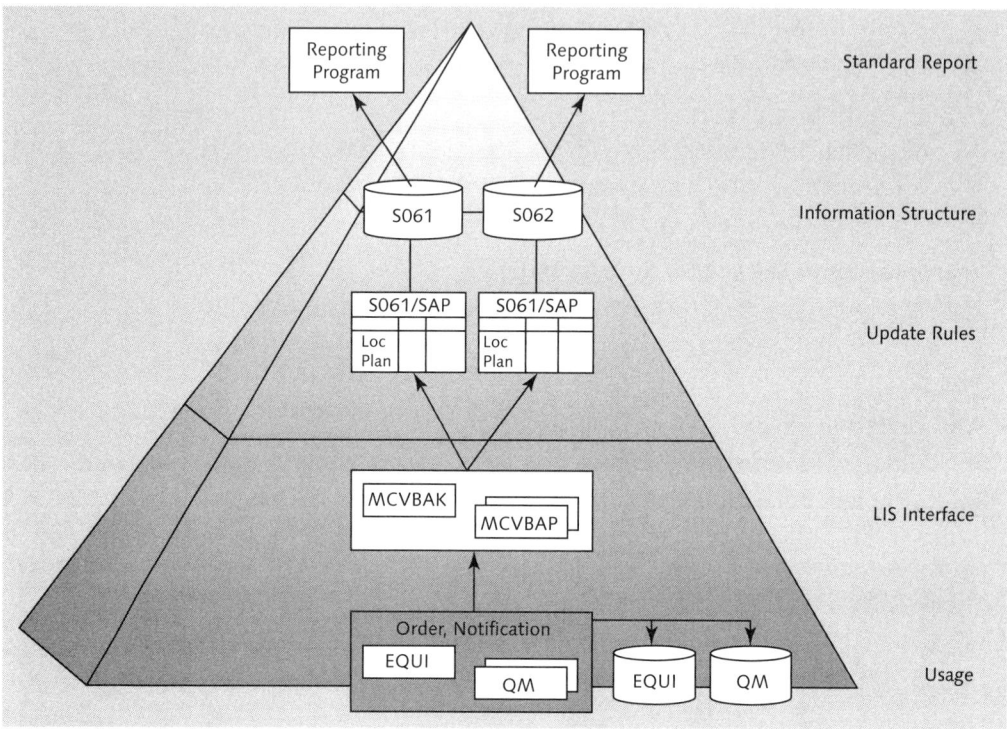

Figure 7.14 Structure of the Logistics Information System

From the applications, information structures are filled on the basis of update rules using transfer programs. These information structures are stand-alone databases, separate from the operational databases. LIS makes the transition from an OLTP to an OLAP system.[2]

[!] **LIS Is an OLAP system**

By nature, the logistics information system is an OLAP system. As a result, reports from the LIS are significantly more efficient than reports from operational databases.

---

2 Online Transaction Processing (OLTP) system: system in which business processes are handled. Online Analytical Processing (OLAP) system: system in which only evaluations and analyses are carried out.

LIS is supplied with information via the LIS interface.

> **Synchronous or Asynchronous?** [!]
>
> Using the Customizing function LOGISTICS INFORMATION SYSTEM (LIS) • LOGISTICS DATA WAREHOUSE • UPDATING • UPDATING CONTROL • ACTIVATE UPDATE • PLANT MAINTENANCE, you can control whether an information structure should be supplied synchronously (that is, in parallel with posting to the operational database) or asynchronously.

The Information Structure

The information structures are the focus of LIS. An information structure consists of the following three elements (see Figure 7.15):

- **Key figure**
  A key figure is the value to be aggregated (for example, the number of orders, actual costs, breakdown duration, or number of notifications).

- **Characteristic**
  A characteristic is a value used to aggregate data (for example, per plant, piece of equipment, order type, or cost center.)

- **Period**
  A period specifies the rhythm of aggregation (the normal case is monthly, but daily or weekly periods are also conceivable, for example).

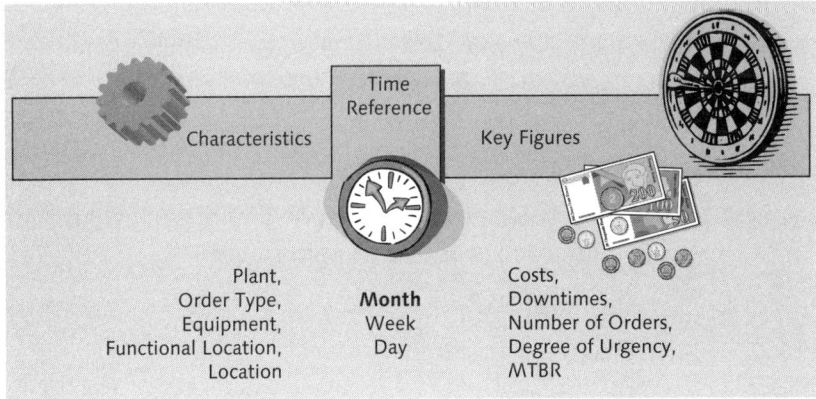

Figure 7.15 Information Structure

Based on these three components of an information structure, a virtual multidimensional information cube results (see Figure 7.16):

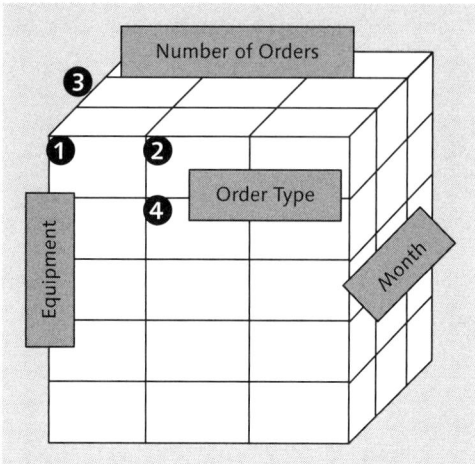

Figure 7.16 Multidimensional Information Cube

- Drawer ❶ contains the key figure *Number of orders for equipment 1,000 of order type PM01 in the month of January*.
- Drawer ❷ contains the key figure *Number of orders for equipment 1,000 of order type PM02 in the month of January*.
- Drawer ❸ contains the key figure *Number of orders for equipment 1,000 of order type PM01 in the month of February*.
- Drawer ❹ contains the key figure *Number of orders for equipment 1,001 of order type PM01 in the month of January*.

Standard Reports of PM-IS

Standard reports are provided by SAP. SAP provides the following standard reports and transaction codes for plant maintenance:

- MCI1: Object class analysis
- MCI2 – Manufacturer analysis
- MCI3 – Location analysis
- MCI4 – Planning group analysis
- MCI5 – Damage analysisMCI6: Object statistics

- MCI7: Failure analysis
- MCI8: Cost analysis
- MCIZ: Vehicle consumption analysis

You can find more details in Appendix B: a list there indicates which standard analysis is based on which information structure, and which characteristics and key figures are in each information structure.

I'll show you the workings and options of PM-IS below, based on a cost analysis (information structure S115; Transaction MCI8).

Functions

The list in Figure 7.17 shows you the estimated, planned, and actual costs for each order type for a selected time period.

Cost Analysis: Basic List

No. of Order Type: 9

Order Type	OrdsCrtd	EstTotalCosts	TotalPlnndCosts	Total act.costs
Total	37,273	307,049.91 USD	16,919,380.75 USD	1,560,975.55 USD
PM00 Maintenance Order	13	26,000.00 USD	27,292.51 USD	13,285.30 USD
PM01 Maintenance Order	2,442	272,209.91 USD	1,713,928.57 USD	1,057,223.84 USD
PM02 Regular Maintenance Order	33,836	0.00 USD	13,525,674.92 USD	304,943.34 USD
PM03 Preventive Maintenance	721	0.00 USD	1,469,541.65 USD	258,436.13 USD
PM04 Refurbishment Order	50	5,850.00 USD	147,086.75 USD	75,480.21- USD
PM05 Order (Incl. Notification)	12	0.00 USD	1,008.36 USD	91.75 USD
PM06 Calibration Order	195	0.00 USD	32,632.35 USD	2,475.40 USD
PM09 Maintenance Order w. Component	2	0.00 USD	0.00 USD	0.00 USD
PMXX Maintenance Order	2	2,990.00 USD	2,215.64 USD	0.00 USD

Figure 7.17 Cost Analysis

You can change the displayed basic list online (that is, without starting any other report and without restarting the present report) using the following functions:

- **Selecting key figures**
  You can display other key figures from a predefined list of figures (for example, completed orders).
- **Switching drill-down options**
  You can switch drill-down—that is, show the list according to a different characteristic (for example, not by order type, but by equipment.)
- **Sorting**
  You can sort the list according to any key figure (for example, sort equipment by actual costs in descending order to obtain a hit list).

- **Inserting comparison values**
  You can compare the values in the list against comparison values (for example, from the previous year) and calculate percent deviations.

- **Displaying as a time series**
  You can show the list as a tabular time series (for example, to see how many orders were made in each month).

- **Using statistical functions**
  You can use the list to calculate statistical functions like ABC analyses, correlations, or segmentations (see Figure 7.18).

- **View by new characteristics**
  You can view by a different characteristic (for example, from the total value for each order type, you can display which equipment is affected).

- **Further processing list**
  You can print, save, or email the list.

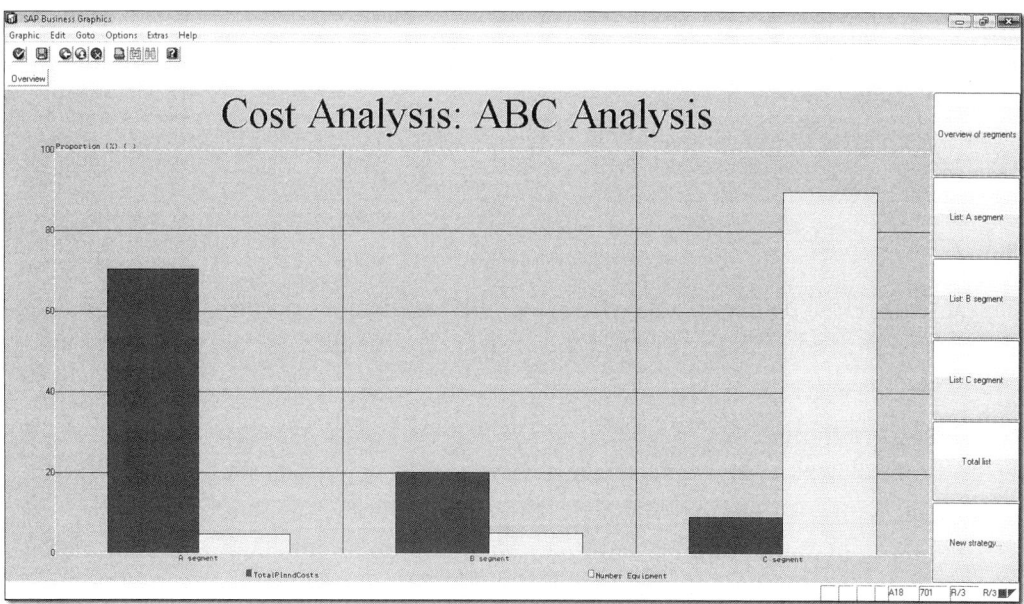

Figure 7.18 ABC Analysis of Equipment by Actual Cost

The standard reports in LIS have their limits: Limits of LIS

- **Unappealing layout**
  The presentation of results does not have an up-to-date layout (for example, the SAP List Viewer is not used here).

- **Rigid information structures**
  The information structures are rigid and cannot be changed.

- **Deficits in technical reports**
  The PM-IS plant maintenance information system has weaknesses in terms of technical reports.

- **No calling of operational database objects**
  You cannot call the operational database objects from the total values. Thus, if you have found an unusual cost value, you cannot directly display the order that led to it.

- **No cross-application key figures**
  The key figures do not apply to all applications. Thus, you cannot calculate the maintenance rates because the actual costs and replacement values come from the EAM and FI-AA applications.

- **No arithmetic operations**
  You cannot perform any arithmetic operations in LIS—for example, calculating totals, differences or ratios.

Flexible Analysis

The restriction of being unable to perform arithmetic operations can be avoided if you define flexible reports. Here, you define your own evaluation structure on the basis of either an operational database table (for example, orders) or an information structure (for example, cost analysis) (see Figure 7.19).

Based on this report structure, you can define reports, within which, in turn, you can define your own key figures. For example, the key figures *Actual Costs* and *Number of Orders* are predefined, and based on them, you can then define the key figure *Average Order Costs* as their ratio.

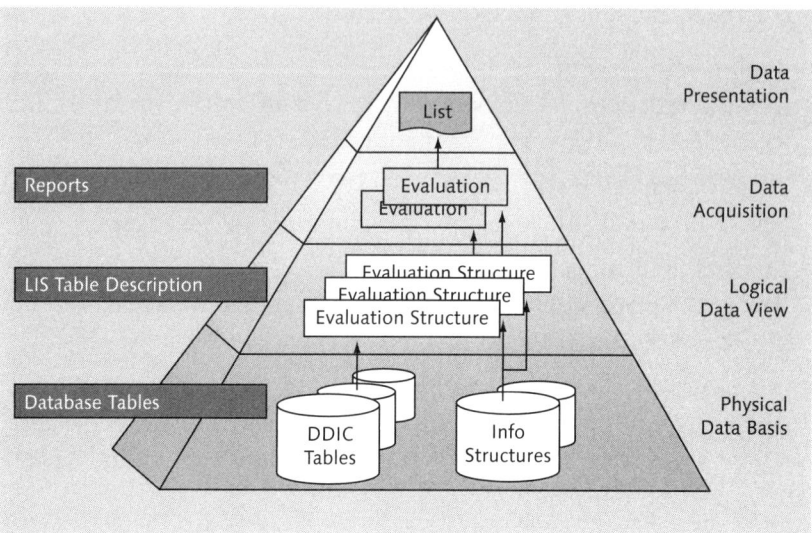

Figure 7.19 Flexible Analysis

[+] **Defining Your Own analysis**

Using flexible analysis, you can evaluate any DDIC tables and information structures. This allows you to define and calculate your own key figures.

Figure 7.20 shows you this example, output as an Excel table.

Characteristics	Orders created	Average	Total act.costs
≈ PM01..PM07	26.015	1,70	44.188,63 EUR
* Maintenance Order	475	113,54	53.929,33 EUR
07/2012	83	494,64	41.055,03 EUR
08/2012	41	7,69	315,24 EUR
09/2012	52		
10/2012	49	10,43	510,84 EUR
11/2012	51		
12/2012	56	137,18	7.682,24 EUR
01/2013	18		
02/2013	32	17,73	567,25 EUR
03/2013	24		
04/2013	14	159,95	2.239,23 EUR
05/2013	11		
06/2013	23	67,80	1.559,50 EUR
07/2013	21		
* Regular Maintenance Order	25.421	0,05	1.186,24 EUR
* Preventive Maintenance	80	6,58	526,15 EUR
* Refurbishment Order	7	1.642,86-	11.500,00- EUR
* Order (Incl. Notification	1		
* Calibration Order	31	1,51	46,91 EUR

Figure 7.20 Example of a Flexible Report

The Early Warning System

The early warning system SAP EarlyWatch is integrated in LIS. LIS provides the data that is analyzed by SAP EarlyWatch. SAP EarlyWatch can be used in any information system in logistics, including PM-IS. The early warning system is based on the information structures; information that can be updated in structures can be analyzed with SAP EarlyWatch. You can use SAP EarlyWatch both to display defined alarm situations and to highlight specific data in a population.

What is SAP EarlyWatch?

You can use the early warning system interactively in standard reports or run it periodically in the background (see Figure 7.21). When used interactively, the warning situations are highlighted in color in the reports or filtered, which allows you to detect alarm situations at an early stage. In periodic analysis, a list of exception data is automatically sent to the desired recipients by fax, email, or a workflow.

Interactive or periodic

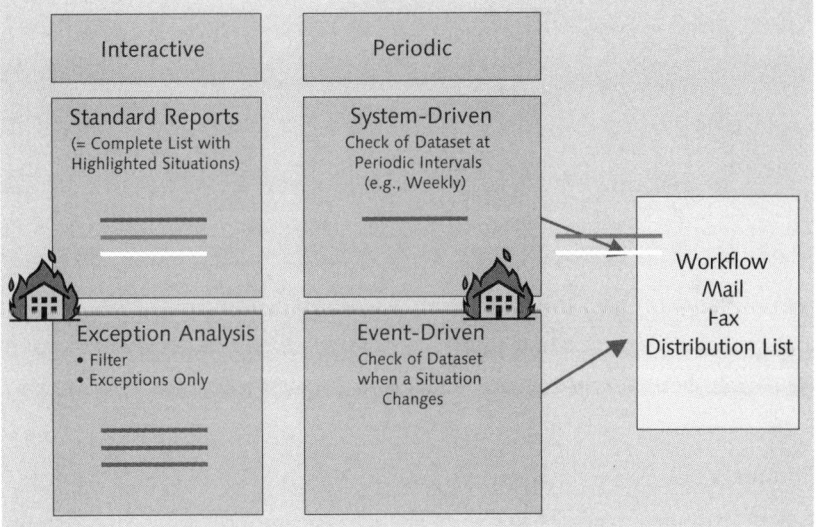

Figure 7.21 The Early Warning System

> **Proactive instead of Reactive** [+]
>
> Using the early warning system, you can turn the PM-IS—if used correctly—into a proactive system. The early warning system allows searches for exception situations, thus helping to detect and correct threatening errors early.

Example   You would like to be notified by email if the actual costs per month for a piece of equipment exceed a threshold of $10,000. To this end, you use Transaction MC=E to create an *Exception*, which contains the characteristics *Equipment* and *Month*. It also includes the key figure *Total actual costs*. You define a threshold value of $10,000, and subsequent processing is email notification, which you schedule as a daily job using Transaction MC=N. The result is shown in Figure 7.22.

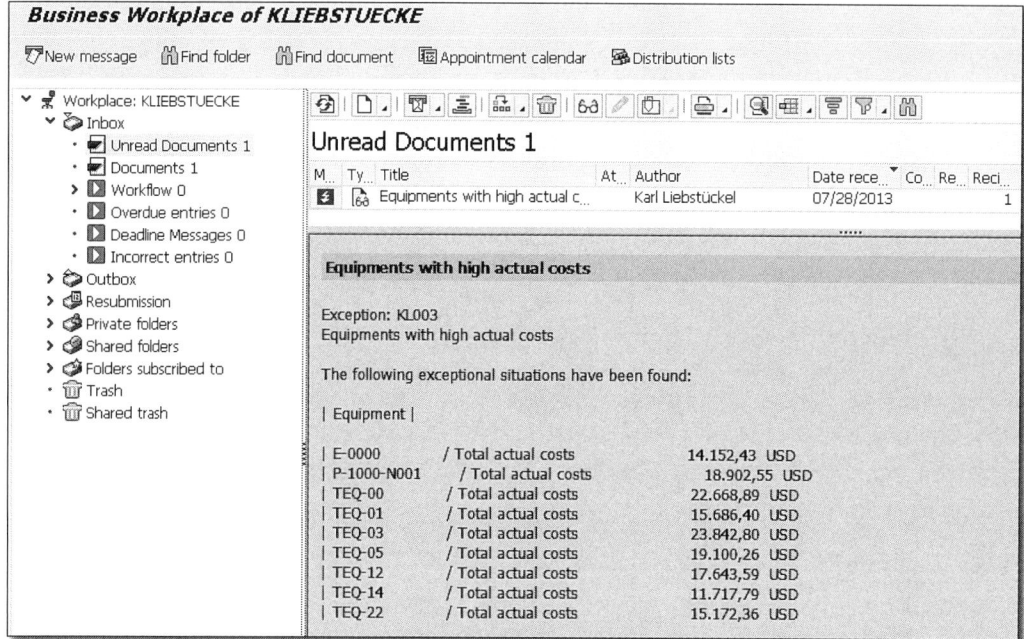

Figure 7.22 Email with an Exception Notification

Summary

PM-IS provides a whole series of frequently underestimated possibilities, but it also has some serious disadvantages. The main disadvantages of PM-IS are its inflexibility and the fact that SAP is no longer developing it. A more detailed list of strengths and weaknesses can be found in Section 7.2.5, in a comparative view with the system SAP has built as a strategic system for the entire analytical area: SAP NetWeaver BW.

7.2.4 SAP NetWeaver BW

In the first sections of this chapter, you have learned of some tools that you can use to provide maintenance-specific information. Why do we need BW as another technical platform for information provision? There are various reasons for this:

- Reporting with BW relieves SAP ERP.
- There are standardized reporting tools available in BW for company-wide data.
- BW works closely with Microsoft Excel.[3]
- You can evaluate across applications in BW.
- BW is *the* strategic analysis product from SAP.

You will discover further advantages of BW compared to the ERP SAP reporting tools in the course of this section. However, BW can and should supplement the "old" SAP ERP world, rather than replacing it. Many basic ideas and concepts from LIS have been incorporated in BW. In contrast to the LIS, however, BW allows reporting on data not just from operational ERP applications, but also from other business applications. Moreover, data can be extracted from external sources like databases, online services, and the Internet, and analyzed.

Concept and Basic Terms of SAP NetWeaver BW

The components and basic terms of BW can be seen in Figure 7.23.

BW provides a wide variety of extraction, transformation, and loading (ETL) functionality, which supports data transfers at the application and file level. This allows you to load data from practically any source. Source systems can be the following:

ETL

- SAP systems (and other BW systems)
- Flat files in which the metadata is maintained manually, and data is sent to BW via a data interface

---

[3] See Brück, U.: Praxishandbuch SAP-Controlling, 4. Aufl., Bonn: SAP PRESS 2011.

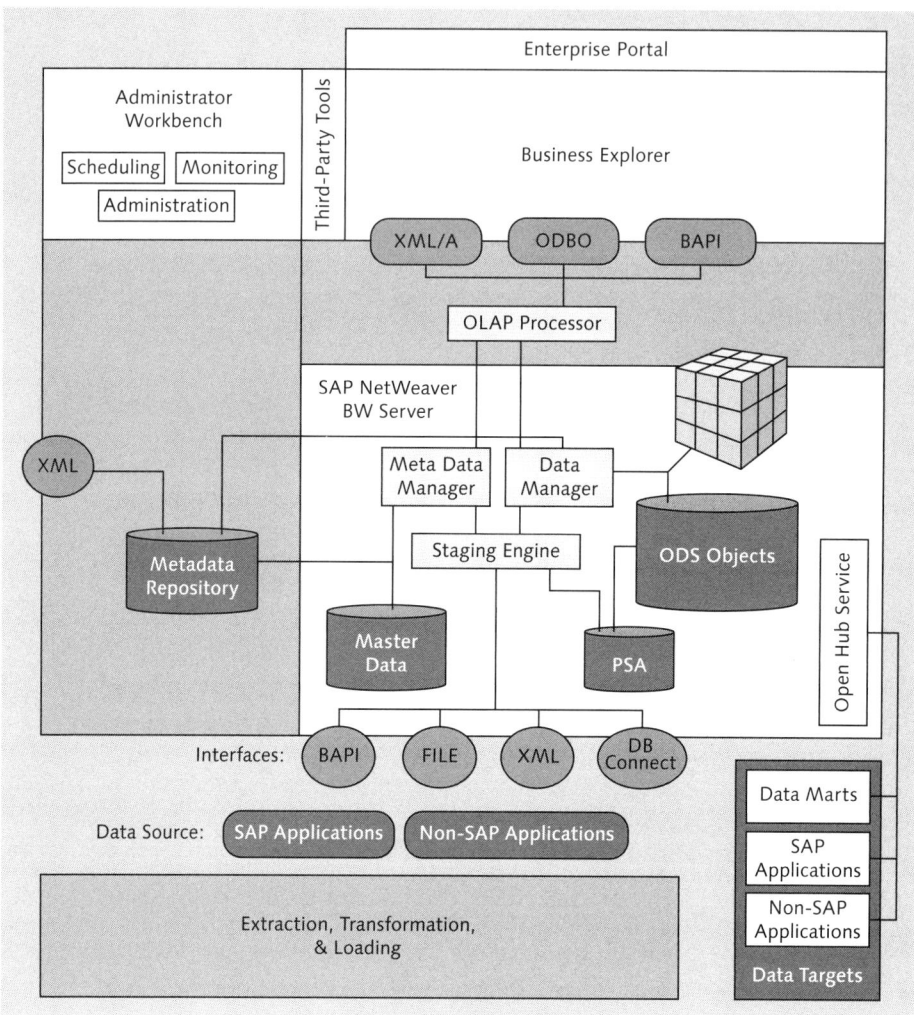

Figure 7.23 Basic Structure of SAP NetWeaver BW

- Database management systems from which the data can be loaded without using an external extraction program, but via DB Connect from a database supported by SAP
- External systems in which the data transfer works through BAPIs[4]

---
4 See Kessler, T. et al: Reporting mit SAP NetWeaver BW und SAP BusinessObjects, Bonn: SAP PRESS, 2012.

PSA

The Persistent Staging Area (PSA) is the physical input buffer for data from the source systems in BW. The transferred data remains unchanged and is initially stored in the source system.

DSO

A DataStore object (DSO) is a data store in which the data is stored at the document level. This is generally used for cleansing and consolidation of data inventories because data inventories often originate from different source systems.

Data Warehousing Workbench

The Data Warehousing Workbench is the work environment for the administrator. Using the functions of the Data Warehousing Workbench, BW can be configured, controlled, and administrated.

InfoCubes

The central data containers on which reports and analyses are based in BW are called InfoCubes. For example, in plant maintenance, the following InfoCubes may be defined:

- Orders
- Notifications
- Measurement results
- Equipment and functional locations

Characteristics and key figures

Like the logistics information system, BW works with key figures and characteristics. Typical key figures in plant maintenance are, for example, the number of orders, the number of breakdown, Mean Time Between Failures (MTBF) or the actual costs. Typical characteristics in plant maintenance are, for example, cost centers, order types, equipment, or planner groups.

Business Explorer (BEx)

The Business Explorer (BEx) is the component of BW that provides reporting and analysis tools, for example, to define queries. BEx enables access to the information in BW in different ways:

- Using SAP NetWeaver Portal (for example, via an iView)
- Using the intranet or Internet (Web Application Design)
- Using mobile devices such as smartphones or tablets

Recommended reading

It would be too long-winded at this point to go into the details of data procurement, modeling, and evaluation in BW. I will leave these topics to others, who understand them better.[5]

Business Content

Under the term *Business Content*, BW provides preconfigured objects that support the department because they provide predefined solutions.

Business content includes the following objects:

- **Extractors**
  Extractors are part of the SAP system and determine the range of data to be supplied to BW.

- **InfoObjects**
  The InfoObjects comprise characteristics and key figures.

- **InfoCubes**
  The determined key figures and characteristics are stored in the InfoCubes.

- **Queries**
  Queries generate reports and views of the InfoCube.

- **Web templates**
  The analyzed data for web applications is provided in web templates.

- **Roles**
  The exact reports needed by the user for his or her work are provided using roles.

InfoCubes

To give you an overview of what goes into business content, Table 7.2 has an excerpt of a list of important InfoCubes with their characteristics and key figures from the business content in EAM.

---

[5] Such as Heilig, L. et al.: (*SAP NetWeaver BW and SAP BusinessObjects*, 2nd edition, Bonn): SAP PRESS, 2013 and other publications by SAP PRESS on data retrieval, data modeling and reporting and analysis.

InfoCube	Examples of Characteristics	Examples of Key Figures
Equipment installation in functional locations	Equipment, Functional location	Duration of installation, Number of installations
Notifications	Material, Plant, Functional location, Equipment, and so on	Number of notifications, Number of notifications on time, Number of measures, Processing time, Downtime, Number of downtimes
Notifications with linear asset management data	Starting point, End point	Number of notifications, Number of notifications on time, Number of measures, Processing time, Downtime, Number of downtimes
Notification items	Plant, Functional location, Equipment, Damage code, Object parts, and so on	Frequency, Total
Notification causes	Equipment, Functional location, Assembly	Number of causes
Orders	Order type, Equipment, Functional location, Maintenance activity type, Planner group, Plant	Processing time, Number of orders, Completed orders, Planned orders, Unplanned orders and so on
Order costs	Order, Partner object, Cost element, Controlling area, and so on	Amount, Quantity, Currency

Table 7.2 Examples of InfoCubes with Key Figures and Characteristics

InfoCube	Examples of Characteristics	Examples of Key Figures
Order operations	Order type, Equipment, Functional location, Maintenance activity type, Planner group, Work center, Plant and so on	Planned work, Actual work, Unit
Order scheduling	Order type, Calendar year, Equipment, Functional location	Planned work, Actual work, Number of orders, completed on time, Processing time
Measurement results	Equipment, Functional location, Assembly	Counter reading, Measurement reading
Vehicle consumption data	Vehicle, Calendar year	Distance traveled, Fuel volume, Actual costs

Table 7.2 Examples of InfoCubes with Key Figures and Characteristics (Cont.)

The following are additional InfoCubes:

- Notification actions
- Notification measures
- Notification response time
- Notification items with linear asset management data
- Notification costs with linear asset management data
- Orders with commitment line item
- Backlog/stock shortfall
- Degree of completion of order operations
- Reworking of orders and notifications
- Maintenance task list simulated costs

- Maintenance plan simulated costs
- Work centers, available capacities, and capacity requirements
- Budgeting data (see Section 7.3.5)

> **[!] InfoCubes from the Business Content as Templates for Your Own Content**
> SAP delivers InfoCubes with the most important key figures and characteristics as business content. You can also create your own InfoCubes.

Based on the InfoCubes included in the business content, the following queries are also delivered:

Queries

- Equipment installation and removal
- Notification report
- Damage report
- Cause report
- Measure report
- Action report
- Failure report
- Object errors
- Orders
- Order operations
- Planned/actual cost deviation
- Mean Time To Repair (MTTR)
- Mean Time Between Repair (MTBR)
- Pending work
- Overdue work
- Planned maintenance work
- Schedule fulfillment
- Measurement results
- Vehicle costs per kilometer
- System availability
- Stock shortfall

- Capacity load utilization
- Degree of completion
- Rework
- Budget proposal
- Budget comparison
- Budgetary control
- Equipment failure

> [!] **Queries from the Business Content as Templates for Your Own Content**
> SAP delivers current queries as business content. However, you can also create your own queries.

Additional business content

Other business content is provided for the following:

- Roles (for example, plant maintenance technician; see Section 8.1.1)
- Web templates (for example, special queries)
- DataSources (for example, hierarchy and functional locations)

Functions

If you start a query, BW creates a basic list for you (see Figure 7.24). You can change the displayed basic list using the following functions without starting any other report and without restarting the present report:

- **Adding other key figures**
  You can display other key figures from a predefined list of key figures (for example, number of notifications).

- **Switching drill-down**
  You can switch drill-down—that is, show the list according to a different characteristic (for example, not by functional location, but by work center).

- **Sorting**
  You can sort the list according to any key figure (for example, sort equipment by number of malfunctions in descending order to obtain a hit list).

- **Including comparison values**
  You can compare the values in the list against comparison values (for example, from the previous year) and calculate percent deviations.

Installation and Dismantling of Equipment				
Plant				
Functional Location				
Functional location category				
Maintenance Plant / Functional Location				
Location / FuncLoc				
Equipment Type				
Maintenance Plant / Equipment				
Equipment Location				
Installation Location				
Calendar Year				
Key Figures				
Equipment				

Equipment			Dismantled	Installation Duration	Average Installation Time
10000498			2	286 DAY	143,0 DAY
100005	Back to Start		2	265 DAY	132,5 DAY
100006			3	1.074 DAY	358,0 DAY
100006	Keep Filter Value		3	1.072 DAY	357,3 DAY
100009	Filter and drilldown according to ▶		1	1.568 DAY	1.568,0 DAY
100010	Add Drilldown According to ▶		1	1.039 DAY	1.039,0 DAY
100010			1	1.039 DAY	1.039,0 DAY
100013	Swap Equipment with ▶	Calendar Year	1	879 DAY	879,0 DAY
100034	Sort ▶	Equipment Location	1	39 DAY	39,0 DAY
100035	Goto ▶	Equipment Type	1	39 DAY	39,0 DAY
100035		Functional Location	1	39 DAY	39,0 DAY
100039	Equipment ▶	Functional location category	1	0 DAY	0,0 DAY
100041	All Characteristics ▶	Installation Location	3	1.598 DAY	532,7 DAY
100061	Properties ...	Key Figures	2	0 DAY	0,0 DAY
100061		Location / FuncLoc	2	6 DAY	3,0 DAY
10006116		Maintenance Plant / Equipment	1	0 DAY	0,0 DAY
BEF4		Maintenance Plant / Functional Location	2	247 DAY	123,5 DAY
EQ1BEF		Plant	1	1 DAY	1,0 DAY
M-1000-N051			5	4.383 DAY	876,6 DAY
M-1000-N052			1	1.594 DAY	1.594,0 DAY
M-1000-N053			1	1.594 DAY	1.594,0 DAY
M-1000-N054			1	1.594 DAY	1.594,0 DAY
M-1000-N055			2	1.594 DAY	797,0 DAY
M-1000-N056			1	1.602 DAY	1.602,0 DAY

Figure 7.24 Malfunction Report[6]

▶ **Displaying graphical time series**
You can show the list as a graphical time series (for example, to see how many malfunctions or orders have accrued in which month, see Figure 7.25).

▶ **Creating statistics**
You can use the list to calculate statistical functions like ABC analyses, correlations, or segmentations.

▶ **Performing drilldown**
You can use the drilldown technique to view by a different characteristic (for example, from the total value for each functional location, you can display which equipment is affected).

---

6 Cited from Krämer, J.: Vorbeugende Instandhaltung mit SAP R/3 PM, in: ("Preventive Maintenance with SAP R/3 PM", in:) Workshop Instandhaltung mit SAP, Berlin 2006. (*Workshop Plant Maintenance with SAP*, Berlin, 2006).

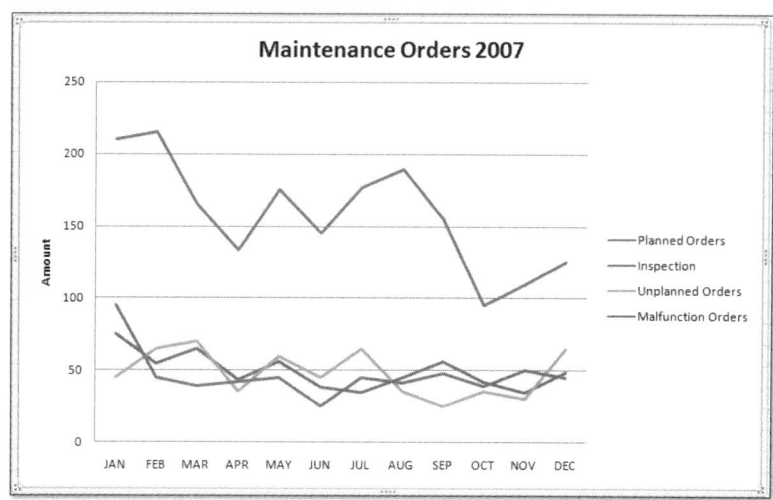

Figure 7.25 Time Series[7]

- **GEO data**
  Using extended navigation options (geographical drilldown), you can highlight regional relationships (for example, the information for an energy provider about the states or cities in which malfunctions are occurring). An example of this kind of BEx Map is shown in Figure 7.26.

- **Access to EAM data**
  Using a RemoteCube, you can access original data in EAM from BW.

- **Exceptions**
  By defining exceptions, you can use BW as an early warning system.

- **Various display options**
  You can present the data based on MS Excel with the BEx Analyzer, on the web in BEx Web Applications, or on mobile devices using BEx Mobile Intelligence.

- **Alert Monitor/Ticker**
  On the web, you have other functions available—for example, the Alert Monitor or the Ticker.

---

7 Cited from Krämer, J.: Vorbeugende Instandhaltung mit SAP R/3 PM, in: ("Preventive Maintenance with SAP R/3 PM", in:) Workshop Instandhaltung mit SAP, Berlin 2006. (*Workshop Plant Maintenance with SAP*, Berlin, 2006).

SAP Tools for Obtaining Information and How to Use Them | 7.2

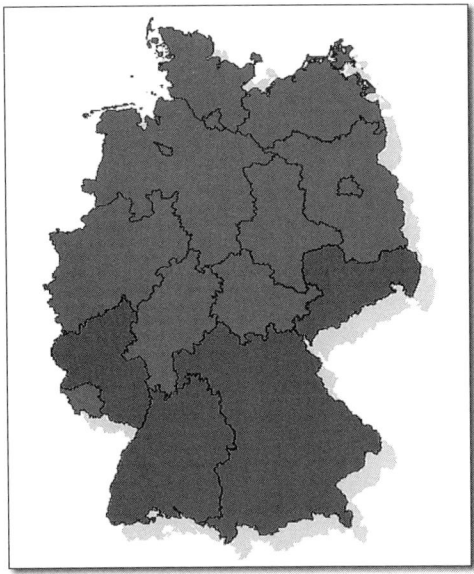

Figure 7.26 BEx Map[8]

These are, by far, not all the options that BW has to offer. However, to list all the possibilities would go beyond the scope of this book.

Now, the question of whether you should use BW or LIS is interesting. I will help you answer that question in the next section, in the form of a direct comparison of the two tools.

7.2.5 Comparison of LIS and SAP NetWeaver BW

The LIS is integrated into SAP ERP, while BW needs a separate system, which you have to administrate.

System administration

It is mentioned in the documentation and flyers that you can also import data from an external system into LIS, but I have never actually done this in practice. On the other hand, it is a necessity that data from different systems can be imported and aggregated in BW as a company-wide Business Intelligence product.

Non-SAP systems

---

[8] Cited from Schneider, H.-J.: Visuelles Lifecycle Management, in: (*Visual Lifestyle Management*, in DSAG-Arbeitskreis 2003. (DSAG working group, Berlin: 2003.)

479

Price list	Both solutions are in the SAP ERP or BW price list and are available without any additional licensing fees.
Project	The introduction and use of PM-IS is generally a decision of the department. Thus, the use of PM-IS can be designed and defined within a normal EAM introduction project.
	On the other hand, introduction and use of BW is a company-wide decision. An overall design must be created, ranging from system operations to use by all the business departments involved.
Development	The LIS and, thus, PM-IS are no longer being developed, but BW is the strategic product from SAP for the entire analysis area.
Interface	PM-IS uses the normal SAP GUI interface. Most reports are tabular and character oriented. On the other hand, in BW, you either work with an Excel interface or in a Web environment, or you access data with a mobile device. BW also uses many graphical elements (speedometer, curves, columns, maps, and so on).
Functionality	Even though the application possibilities are often somewhat underestimated, the functional scope of PM-IS is, in fact, very limited, while the features of BW seem entirely limitless.
Business content and flexibility	The PM-IS is very rigid in its structure. It provides certain standard reports, but extension possibilities can be realized only with difficulty. For instance, key figures can be calculated only if their data refers to objects in EAM.
	BW not only provides a broadly defined business content that is continually being further developed, but it is also very flexible and extensible with respect to your own reporting needs. Thus, you can determine key figures across applications.
Drillthrough	From the aggregated results from PM-IS (for example, number of orders), you cannot call functions to get more details. On the other hand, you can call a list of details directly from BW.

Table 7.3 shows a clear comparison of LIS and BW.

LIS	SAP NetWeaver BW
(+) integrated into SAP ERP	(–) separate system, separate installation
(–) data from SAP ERP only	(+) import of data from external sources
(+) project at the departmental level	(–) company-wide project
(–) not being further developed	(+) strategic Business Intelligence product from SAP
(–) SAP GUI interface	(+) Excel, web, mobile interface
(–) restricted functionality	(+) broad, deep functionality
(–) rigid structure	(+) very flexible (for example, cross-application reports)
(–) no navigation to original document	(+) Drillthrough
(+) free of charge	(+) included in the SAP ERP license

Table 7.3 Comparison of LIS and SAP NetWeaver BW

Now, I would like to introduce important plant maintenance controlling techniques that enable budgeting.

7.3　SAP Tools for Budgeting and How to Use Them

Depending on which functions and applications are active in your company, you have various options for managing budgets for your plant maintenance tasks. In particular, these are order budgeting, cost center budgeting, budgeting for investment management, budgeting in the project system, and maintenance cost budgeting.

7.3.1　Order Budgeting

The simplest, but at the same time most limited, type of budgeting is order budgeting, with which you can assign a budget to a single order. An order budget is assigned with Transaction KO22, either as a total budget or distributed over several years (see Figure 7.27).

How it works

7 | Plant Maintenance Controlling

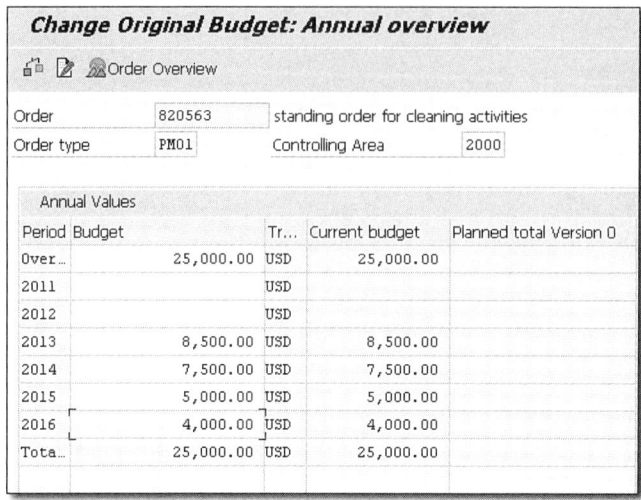

Figure 7.27 Order Budget

Availability control For each actual posting (for example, time confirmations or goods issue), the system checks whether the order budget is sufficient. Depending on the settings in the budget profile, a warning or error message is output.

[!] **Active Availability Control Prevents Budget Overruns**

The activation of the availability control prevents the order budget from being overrun by actual posts. The planned costs have no effect on the order budget; that is, while planning the order, the order budget is not checked.

Areas of application Order budgeting supports you in controlling for an individual order. From my perspective, therefore, the following areas of application are possible:

- Larger plant maintenance tasks (like moves or renovations)
- Standing orders or long-term orders

Budgeting for all plant maintenance activity would mean that you would have to assign an order budget to each and every order. However, this is too time consuming and not normally done.

The prerequisite for an order budget is the assignment of a budget profile to the order type using the Customizing function CONFIGURE ORDER TYPES. The budget profile itself and the control of checks on availability (availability control) are set up using the Customizing function MAINTAIN BUDGET PROFILES and DETERMINE TOLERANCE LIMITS FOR AVAILABILITY CONTROL.

Prerequisites

The settings shown in Figure 7.28 would have the following effects in controlling area 1000 with budget profile 00001:

- When 95% of the order budget is exceeded, a warning message would be issued.
- When 105% is exceeded, an email would also be sent to the responsible parties.
- When 115% is exceeded, an error message would be issued, which means that the budget could be exceeded by 15% at most.

Order Availability Control: Tolerance Limits						
COAr	Prof.	Text	Tr.Grp	Act.	Usag...	Abs.variance
1000	000001	General Budget Profile	++	1		95.00
1000	000001	General Budget Profile	++	2		105.00
1000	000001	General Budget Profile	++	3		115.00

Figure 7.28 Availability Control

> **Order Budgeting Is a Simple, but Limited Resource** [!]
>
> In all, order budgeting is a simple, but very limited, instrument for budgeting. The budget check for orders can be activated only when the order is not assigned to a budgeting WBS element or IM program.

7.3.2 Cost Center Budgeting

Planned values can be created for activity types (Transaction KP26), cost elements (Transaction KP06), and statistical key figures (Transaction KP46). There are also so-called cost center budgets with the option of distributing a budget at the cost center level, with no restriction to certain cost or activity types (Transaction KPZ2).

How it works

7 | Plant Maintenance Controlling

> [!] **Cost Center Budgeting Is Actually Cost Center Planning**
>
> A quick note right at the start: cost center budgeting does not involve budgets with the option of active availability control. Rather, it is cost center planning with the assignment of planned values; a check as to whether the budget has been exceeded or observed is done via reporting tools

Figure 7.29 shows the planning for a receiving cost center at the cost element level. This displays the cost elements with which the cost center is debited by settling plant maintenance orders.

Change Cost Element/Activity Input Planning			
Version	0		Plan/Actual Version
Period	1	To	12
Fiscal Year	2013		
Cost Center	4110		Technical Facilities

Cost elem...	Text	Total planned co...	Dis...	L..
650000	Order settlement	35,000.00	2	
651000	Ord.settmt -Material	22,000.00	2	
652000	Ord.settmt - Int.Act	45,000.00	2	
*Cost elem Total		102,000.00		

Figure 7.29 Planning for a Receiving Cost Center

Monitoring for adherence to this planned data is done in the context of normal reporting at the cost center level. Figure 7.30 (Transaction S_ALR_87013611) shows a section from such a cost center report, particularly with the listing of how cost centers have been debited by order settlement from plant maintenance.

Areas of application

You can create planned values for the performing cost center and planned values for the receiving cost center. Thus, you can assign planned values both for the performance of the service by the performing (plant maintenance) cost centers and the consumption by the receiving (installation) cost centers. The assignment of planned values thus includes the entire plant maintenance activity.

1SIP		Cost Centers: Actual/Plan/Variance			
Date:		07/28/2013			
Requested by:		KLIEBSTUECKE			
Controlling Area		2000	CO N. America		
Fiscal Year		2013			
From Period		1			
To Period		12			
Plan Version		0			
Cost Center Group		*			
Cost Element Group		*	Cost Element Group		

Cost elements	Act.costs	Plan costs	Abs. var.	Var.(%)
481000 Depreciation Expens	910.945,00		910.945,00	
650000 Order settlement	819,00	35.000,00	34.181,00-	97,66-
651000 Ord.settmt -Materia	4.095,00	22.000,00	17.905,00-	81,39-
652000 Ord.settmt - Int.Ac	1.840,00	45.000,00	43.160,00-	95,91-
* Debit	917.699,00	102.000,00	815.699,00	799,70

Figure 7.30 Cost Center Report

The prerequisite for the possibility of cost center planning is the planner profile, which is created in controlling Customizing under DEFINE USER-DEFINED PLANNER PROFILES. Planner profiles are planning layouts containing data entry forms for different planning options. For example, you can define whether you want to plan at the yearly or monthly level, or whether Excel integration is active.

Prerequisites

7.3.3 Budgeting with IM Programs

Investment management (IM) is an application within SAP ERP that supports you in carrying out investments in the true sense (purchase of assets and investments in research and development), but also in plant maintenance programs. The term *investment* is, thus, understood both in the sense of accounting and in the sense of any measure that results in costs and should, therefore, be monitored (for example, plant maintenance projects.)

Investment Management

To budget your investments, projects, and measures, investment programs are available to you (Transaction IM01). An investment program shows the planned or budgeted costs in the form of a hierarchical structure as so-called program items (Transaction IM11). This structure can be arbitrarily defined and is independent of other organizational concepts in the SAP system (for example, business areas, plants, etc.) Within the hierarchy of the investment program, it is possible to plan budgets

Investment program and program items

either bottom-up or top-down (Transaction IM32). Finally, the lowest program items in the hierarchy can be assigned to individual tasks: internal orders, WBS elements (see Section 7.3.4), and plant maintenance orders.

Connecting EAM and IM

The relationship between investment programs and plant maintenance orders is shown in Figure 7.31. Plant maintenance orders, like WBS elements or CO internal orders, can be assigned to an IM program item and, thus, to the underlying budget.

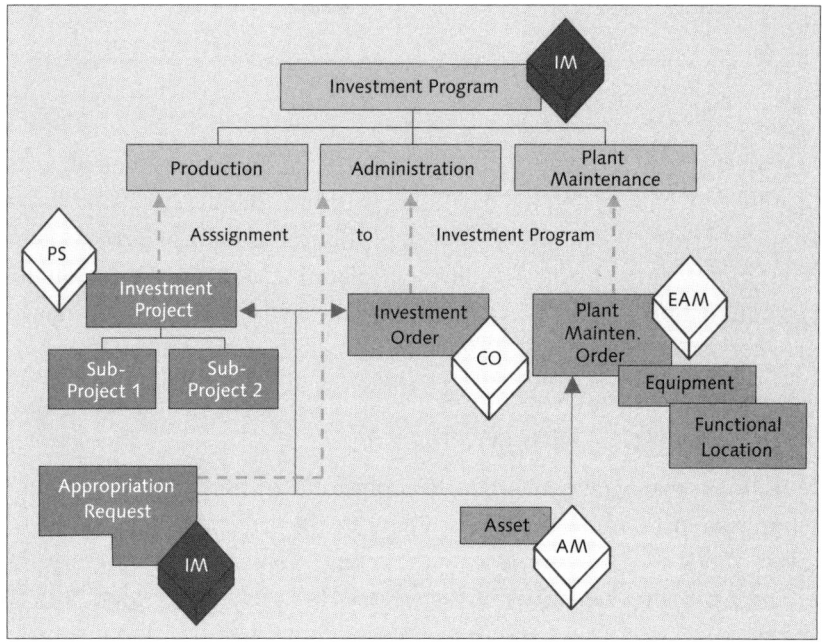

Figure 7.31 Relationship between IM and EAM

The assignment of a plant maintenance order to an item is carried out manually within an order (Transaction IW31, menu path GOTO • INVESTMENT PROGRAM, see Figure 7.32). However, it can also be done automatically using an assignment key. You maintain the assignment key in Customizing.

Availability control

Costs charged to the order then appear in the budget overview for each program item.

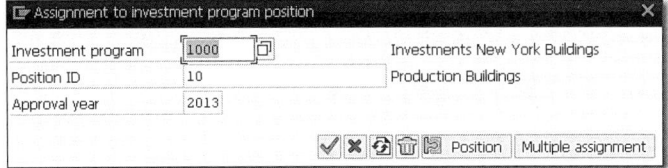

Figure 7.32 EAM Order and Program Item

Figure 7.33 (Transaction S_ALR_87012824) shows an investment program with three program items with assigned budgets. The ongoing plant maintenance tasks are then reflected in the allotted resources or in the remaining availabilities.

				Budg.prog.--...	Assigned--Total	Available--Total	Assign. %--T...	Budg.prog.--...
Navigation	Object							
Object	1000/2013		Investments New York	5,390,000	2,978	5,387,022	0.06	1,414,000
	10		Production Buildings	2,100,000	2,978	2,097,022	0.14	532,000
		ORD 819634	renewal pump station	0	2,978	2,978-	x/o	0
	20		Adminstration Buildi	1,680,000	0	1,680,000	0.00	420,000
	30		Stock Buildings	980,000	0	980,000	0.00	294,000
	40			630,000	0	630,000	0.00	168,000

Figure 7.33 Budget Availability in Investment Management

This means that, even in the budgeting process with IM budgets, monitoring for adherence to budgets is carried out in the context of normal reporting at the program item level. This is not active availability control.

Behind the program items, a "real" investment measure can exist that generates an asset under construction. However, this does not have to be the case. You can also create program items simply for statistical reasons in budgeting. From a plant maintenance perspective, you could use the program items for real investment measures, but you could also set them up to manage your plant maintenance budget. Thus, you could budget all your plant maintenance activities together here.

Areas of application

Prerequisites To enable you to budget your plant maintenance tasks using IM program items, you must execute the following functions in Customizing.

With the Customizing function DEFINE TRANSFER OF PROJECT OR INVESTMENT PROGRAM, you can control for each order type whether you want to budget with WBS elements or investment programs; you cannot do both at the same time.

With the Customizing functions DEFINE RELEVANT FIELDS FOR ASSIGNMENT OF IM PROGRAM and ASSIGN IM ASSIGNMENT KEYS TO ORDER TYPES, you can define, for example, whether the cost center of the reference object or the responsible work center should be used for the automatic determination of the program item.

[!] **Passive Availability Control Using Investment Programs**
Program items can be used as a simple tool for budget monitoring. Here, you must note that this is only a passive budgetary control. Passive budgetary control means that the system will not warn you when the budget is exceeded. You must check adherence to the budget yourself via reporting.

The situation looks different for the other option: budgeting using work breakdown structures, or WBS elements, for short.

7.3.4 Budgeting Using WBS Elements

I have already shown you WBS elements in the context of project-oriented plant maintenance (see Section 5.12.1) as components of the Project System (PS). WBS elements are normally used to define the construction planning, organization, and control of a project. You can also use WBS elements to carry out pure budget planning and control; we will look at them here from that perspective.

How it works To do this, use Transaction CJ01 to define a project (for example, plant maintenance budgeting) and then use Transaction CJ11 to create several levels of WBS elements as a basis for a budgetary structure. The following are possible criteria you can use for orientation:

- **Asset-related**
  For example, each top-level functional location is given a budget

- **Maintenance group–related**
  For example, mechanical workshop, electrical workshop
- **Activity-related**
  For example, for maintenance, repairs, overhaul

Budget planning is then normally done in a top-down manner and assigned to the WBS elements of each budget on an annual basis using Transaction CJ30 (see Figure 7.34).

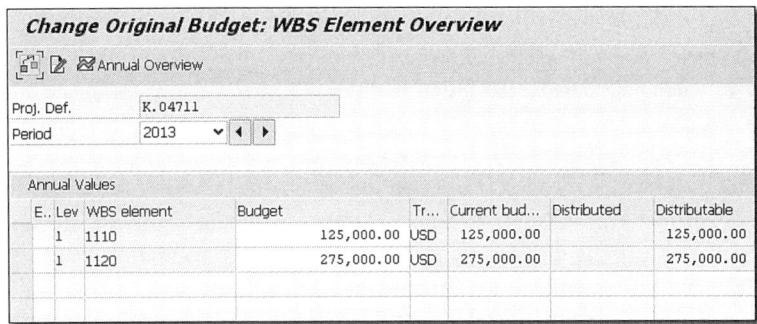

Figure 7.34 Budgets of WBS Elements

If you want to distribute budgets on a system basis, you should then enter the WBS element responsible for the budget into the master record of the technical object (see Figure 7.35).

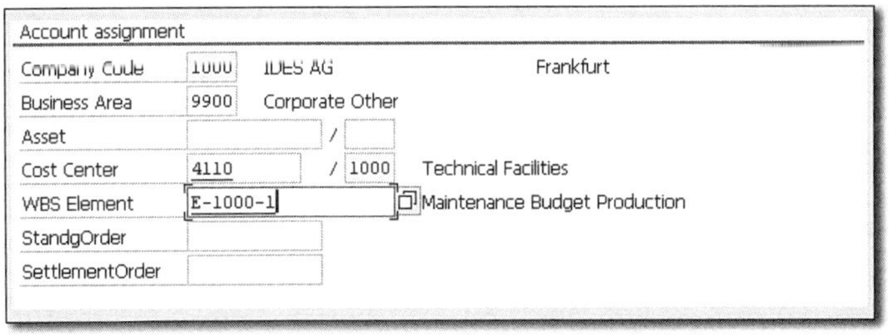

Connecting EAM and PS

Figure 7.35 WBS Element in the Functional Location

Once you complete this and set up Customizing accordingly, the WBS element is automatically transferred to the order, and, thus, the order is assigned to the WBS element. The assignment can be seen in the order on the ADDITIONAL DATA tab (see Figure 7.36); there, you can also perform a manual assignment or change an existing one.

7 | Plant Maintenance Controlling

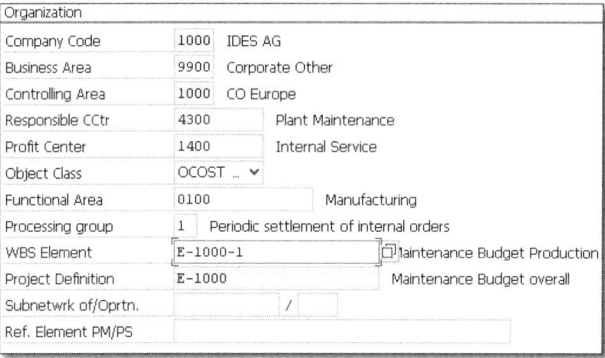

Figure 7.36 Additional Data for the Order

[+] **Changing WBS Assignments Automatically**

You can custom automate the assignment of orders to WBS elements using user exit IWO10010 with a custom assignment routine. Depending on the technical object, for example, you can find the right WBS element here for the order type and maintenance activity type. This saves the user time-consuming manual assignment, increasing acceptance.

Availability control

The budget availability control of WBS elements involves both an active and a passive availability control:

- **Active availability control**
  Active availability control means that for each actual posting (for example, time confirmation, goods issue), the system checks whether the WBS budget is sufficient. Depending on the settings in the budget profile, a warning or error message is issued.

- **Passive availability control**
  Passive availability control means that the system provides you with sufficient reporting options to check your budgets. Costs charged to the order then appear in the budget overview for each WBS element.

Figure 7.37 (Transaction S_ALR_87013557) shows a work breakdown structure with three WBS elements to which budgets were assigned. Ongoing plant maintenance tasks are then shown in the actual costs and/or the remaining availabilities.

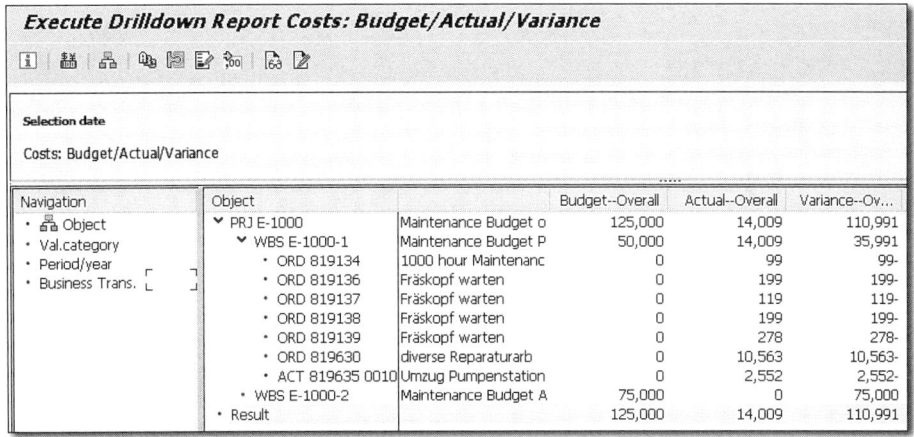

Figure 7.37 Budget Availability in the WBS Element

Behind the WBS elements, either there is an actual plant maintenance project, or you can use them for purely budgeting purposes in order to manage the ongoing budget. Thus, from a plant maintenance perspective, you can budget all plant maintenance activity using WBS elements.

Areas of application

To budget with WBS elements, the following prerequisites must be satisfied:

Prerequisites

- Assign your technical objects (equipment, functional locations) a WBS element in the master record.
- Use the Customizing function DEFINE TRANSFER OF PROJECT OR INVESTMENT PROGRAM for each order type with an assignment with an "X" to ensure that the WBS elements are transferred from the master record into the order.
- Use the Customizing function of the Project System MAINTAIN BUDGET PROFILE to create a budget profile and assign your WBS elements.
- Use the Customizing function of the Project System DEFINE TOLERANCE LIMITS to define the limits for your controlling area and your budget profile at which warning messages and error messages are generated, thus activating the active availability control.

491

7 | Plant Maintenance Controlling

[+] **Active Availability Control with WBS Elements**

WBS elements can be used as a tool for budget monitoring because you have an active availability control, the activation of which prevents the order budget from being exceeded due to actual postings.

With the reporting tools, you also have the option of passive availability control.

We now come to the final option for managing a plant maintenance budget: Maintenance Cost Budgeting (MCB), a process that was developed especially for plant maintenance.

7.3.5 Maintenance Cost Budgeting

What is MCB? Maintenance Cost Budgeting (MCB) is a process developed by SAP for Release Version SAP ERP 5.0 especially for plant maintenance and its budgeting requirements. However, it was not integrated into EAM, but instead uses the platform BW-BPS (BPS stands for Business Planning and Simulation; see Figure 7.38).

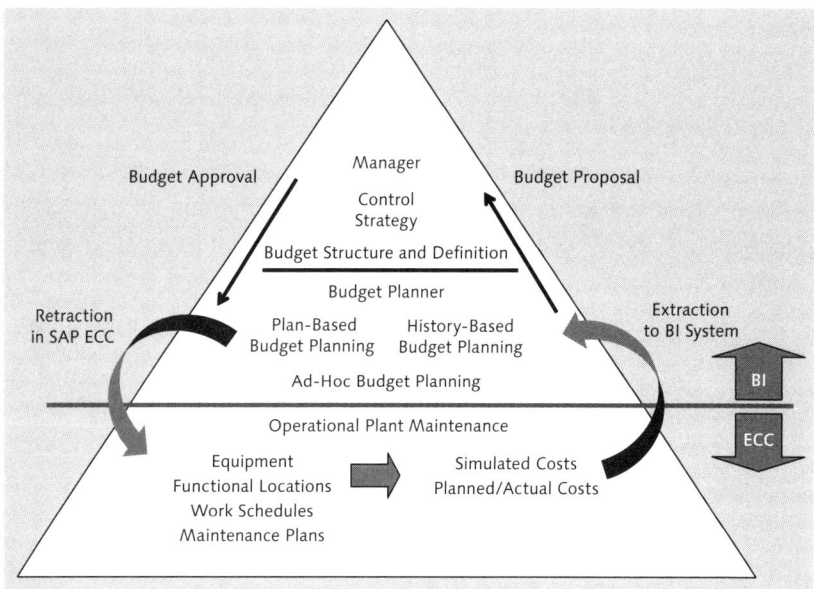

Figure 7.38 Structure of MCB

> **MCB Is Not Integrated in SAP ERP** [!]
>
> You can use MCB only if you have installed BW and configured BW-BPS. You cannot use it with the pure core component EAM.

MCB provides two processes for budget planning, namely a history-based and a planned data–based budgeting process. In both processes, there are different planning scenarios that primarily involve the type of data provision.

Budgeting process

- **History-based budgeting process**
  For the history-based budgeting processes, there is the history-based scenario for which you can use the actual historical costs of previous periods as the basis for planning, and there is also an ad-hoc scenario in which you can use freely entered data for budgeting. In the latter scenario, the determination of the data as a basis for planning takes place outside the SAP system (e.g., in Excel tables).

- **Planning data–based budgeting process**
  In the case of a planning data–based budgeting process, we distinguish between a maintenance task list scenario, a maintenance plan scenario, and an ad-hoc scenario. The ad-hoc scenario, as in the history-based process, is used for free entry of data. Here, too, the determination of the data as a basis for planning takes place outside the SAP system (for example, in Excel tables). The maintenance task list and maintenance plan scenarios, on the other hand, are based on cost simulation from maintenance task lists or maintenance plans stored in EAM.

In Customizing, you can set up which of the budgeting processes may be used. Scenarios can also be used in combination.

> **Actual Costs and Simulated Costs Could Be Transferred Automatically** [+]
>
> MCB supports you in your budget planning by providing history-based actual costs and simulated costs from maintenance task lists and maintenance plans.

The MCB supports both top-down budgeting and bottom-up budgeting (see Figure 7.38). The manager plans the strategic budget for the area and sends a budget draft to the responsible budget planner (top-down

Top-down and bottom-up budgeting process

budgeting process). The planner plans the budget based on historical or simulated data, then sends it back to the manager for approval (bottom-up budgeting process).

The definition is carried out using report and budgeting groups, with which you create a hierarchy within plant maintenance budgeting that makes it possible for you to map the desired process of budget planning and approval.

[+] **Predefined Report and Budgeting Groups Simplify Budgeting**

Using the definition of report and budgeting groups, therefore, MCB supports you in the budgeting process (for example, reporting and approval paths).

The budgeting itself then takes place in a special web user interface (see Figure 7.39). Depending on authorization, budget planners and managers can plan or even approve the budget for their areas.

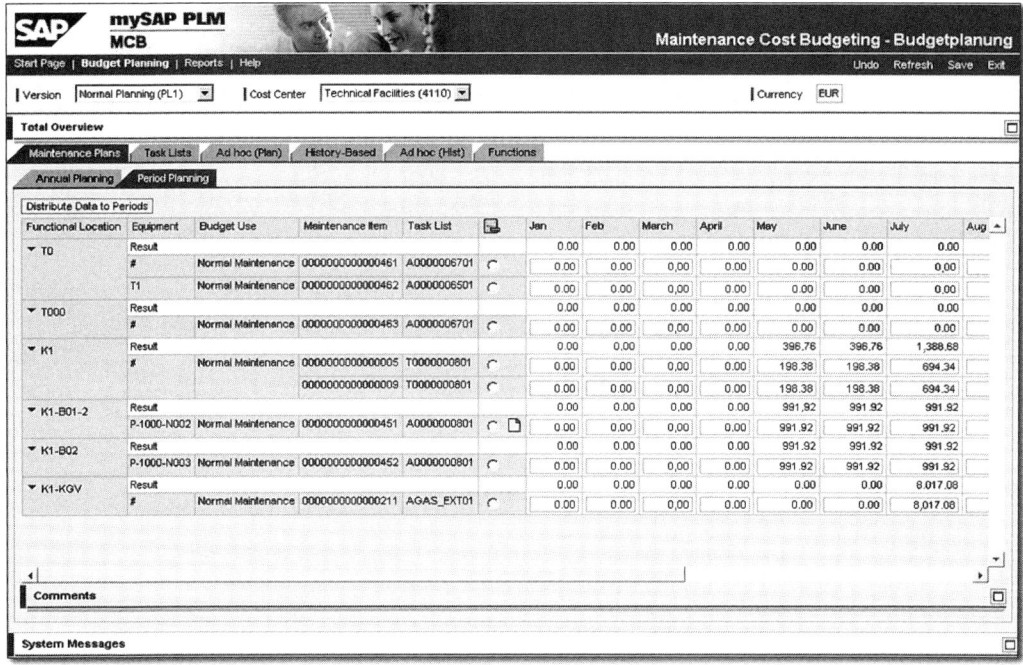

Figure 7.39 MCB Planning Table

The MCB also provides the option of breaking down the budget into categories or by use; a budget category is the differentiation of the budget relative to the planning of plant maintenance tasks. In the standard configuration of budget planning, a budget proposal is broken down into three budget categories, which are shown separately:

Budget categories

- **Preventive**
  Costs from regularly recurring plant maintenance tasks planned based on maintenance plans
- **Planned**
  Costs from irregularly recurring plant maintenance tasks that are planned using maintenance task lists or individually in orders
- **Unplanned**
  Costs resulting from an unplanned plant maintenance task—for example, from repairs during machine downtime due to damage

> **Budgets Can Be Represented by Budget Categories** [+]
>
> Budget categories can be adapted in Customizing to your company-specific needs. Depending on the settings, you can then automatically determine and assign them based on common properties (for example, maintenance activity type or order type) during the data extraction.

The categorization by budget use, on the other hand, concerns the business side of a plant maintenance task. Differentiating by budget use involves the classification of the budget relative to the business process to which a plant maintenance task belongs. In addition to the budget category, this enables further grouping of the budget proposal by the type of activity, such as the following:

Budget use

- Repairs
- Cleaning tasks
- Inspection or maintenance tasks
- Overhauls
- Downtimes

7 | Plant Maintenance Controlling

[+] **Budgets Can Be Represented by Budget Use**

Budget uses can be adapted in Customizing to your enterprise-specific needs. Depending on the settings, you can then automatically determine and assign them based on common properties (for example, WBS elements or cost center) during the data extraction.

Business content

As already mentioned at the start, BW-BPS is the technical platform for MCB. As specified in Section 7.2.4 InfoCubes and queries are needed for this purpose. As for all the other functionality of BW, SAP also provides the business content needed for MCB.

Table 7.4 lists the InfoCubes delivered by SAP.

Name	Description
Simulated plant maintenance costs 0PM_C05	This InfoCube provides data for simulated plant maintenance costs. The calculation of maintenance plans and plant maintenance task lists takes place during the transfer.
Budget data for plant maintenance 0PM_C06	This InfoCube is used to plan the plant maintenance budget. The data is loaded from the InfoCubes MAINTENANCE ORDERS: COSTS AND SETTLEMENTS (0PM_C01) and SIMULATED MAINTENANCE COSTS (0PM_C05).
Budget data for plant maintenance 0PM_MC01	This MultiProvider unites data from the InfoCube MAINTENANCE ORDERS: COSTS AND SETTLEMENTS (0PM_C01) and BUDGET DATA FOR MAINTENANCE (0PM_C06). This makes it possible, for example, to compare current budget planning with historical actual costs.
Budget for maintenance 0PM_C25	This InfoCube is used as an InfoProvider to provide budget data.

Table 7.4 InfoCubes for MCB

Based on these InfoCubes, the queries listed in Table 7.5 are delivered in the MCB business content.

Name	Description
Budget proposal by budget category	You can use this query to display your budget proposal broken down by budget categories.
Budget proposal (periodic)	You can use this query to display your budget proposal broken down by periods.
Budget proposal (objects)	You can use this query to display your budget proposal broken down by your technical objects.
Budget proposal (simulated costs)	You can use this query to compare your budget proposal with simulated costs.
Budget comparison (actual costs)	You can use this query to compare your budget proposal with actual historical costs.
Budget comparison (planned costs)	You can use this query to compare your budget proposal with historical planned costs.
Budgetary control (budget)	You can use this query to carry out budgetary control. The budget proposal is compared with the actual costs incurred in the current period and the remaining budget.
Budgetary control (planned costs)	You can use this query to carry out budgetary control. The budget proposal is compared with the actual costs incurred in the current period and the remaining planned costs.
Actual cost comparison (plan data–based)	You can use this query to compare your budget proposal for the planned data–based budgeting process with historical actual costs.
Actual cost comparison (history-based)	You can use this query to compare your budget proposal for the history-based budgeting process with historical actual costs.

Table 7.5 Queries for MCB

Since SAP ERP 6.0 EHP 5, you have the option of performing a quasi-active availability control. In the order, you find the new ⊙ button, with which you can check the assigned budget for maintenance costs online in MCB. A dialog box shows the result of the check (see Figure 7.40).

Availability control

7 | Plant Maintenance Controlling

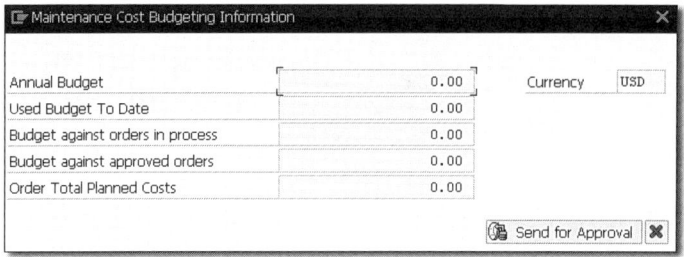

Figure 7.40 Budget Information from MCB

Areas of application

Due to the flexible options to classify your budgets using budget categories and budget use according to your own needs, you can budget all your plant maintenance activity using MCB.

Prerequisites

You must satisfy the following prerequisites to be able to work with MCB:

- Install at least the following technical components: SAP ERP ECC 5.00, SAP R/3 Plug-in 2004.1_500, and BW-BPS 3.52.
- In Customizing for BW-BPS, use the function SAP NETWEAVER • BUSINESS INTELLIGENCE • SETTINGS FOR BI CONTENT • PLANNING CONTENT • PRODUCT LIFECYCLE MANAGEMENT • BUDGET PLANNING FOR PLANT MAINTENANCE AND CUSTOMER SERVICE to make settings for the central attributes of budget planning, budgeting process, and individual planning application.
- In the BW content, create the report and budgeting groups.
- Define the variables for budget planning (for example, planning scenario, budget category, budget use).
- Set whether you want to work on the basis of equipment and/or functional locations.
- Determine the content of the start page.
- Activate the business function LOG_EAM_CI_4 for SAP ERP.
- Use the Customizing function DEFINE BUDGET CHECK FOR ORDER TYPES to define for each plant and order type that a budget check using MCB is permitted.

I have presented to you the different options for budgeting here. Table 7.6 summarizes the processes with their most important properties.

	Budgeting by Order	Budgeting by Cost Center	Budgeting by IM Item	Budgeting by WBS Element	Budgeting with MCB
Integrated into SAP ERP	Yes	Yes	Yes	Yes	No
Application Area	Individual order	Planning for cost center	Investments, ongoing plant maintenance	Plant maintenance projects, ongoing plant maintenance	All plant maintenance plans
Active Availability control	Yes	No	No	Yes	Yes
Flexibility of the Budgeting Object	None	None	In certain cases	In certain cases	Flexibly adjustable
Top-Down and Bottom-Up	No	No	Yes	Yes	Yes

Table 7.6 Comparing Budgeting Processes

As with every chapter, I have once again gathered the most important information about *plant maintenance controlling* and all relevant tips and tricks that I wish to pass on to you.

Modern communication technologies, such as the Internet, mobile solutions, and service-oriented architectures, have become established in plant maintenance, as in almost every other area. This chapter describes the prerequisites, options, and limitations associated with these and other technologies when deployed in plant maintenance.

8 New Information Technologies in Plant Maintenance

For a long time now, the Internet, along with modern information and communications technologies (ICT), has defined everyday communication within a company. While the new technologies have been rather neglected in plant maintenance for a long time, the trend now extends into this area, also.

Therefore, this chapter describes the options available to you in SAP applications, how you can use them, the prerequisites associated with them, and how processes change under their influence. The chapter will focus primarily on SAP NetWeaver Portal, the SAP NetWeaver Business Client, and mobile solutions, but will also briefly introduce the new SAP database technology, SAP HANA, and Service-Oriented Architecture (SOA).

In the meantime, users in plant maintenance can use three user interfaces that enable them to access their SAP functions: User interfaces

- The classic SAP Graphical User Interface (GUI), which is accessed via SAP Logon
- SAP NetWeaver Portal
- SAP NetWeaver Business Client

Table 8.1 shows, in a concise comparison, the platforms for which these three user interfaces are suitable, their main characteristics, and for which typical application cases they are best used.

	SAP GUI	SAP NetWeaver Portal	SAP NetWeaver Business Client
Platform	Windows, Linux, Browser	Browser	Windows, Browser
Attributes	▶ Classic transactions ▶ Menu-based access ▶ Desktop integration	▶ Integrated SAP GUI ▶ Application launcher ▶ Integration on client and server sides ▶ Role-based access ▶ Content management	▶ Integrated SAP GUI ▶ Integrated browser ▶ Application launcher ▶ Integration on client side ▶ Role-based access ▶ Desktop integration
Application cases	▶ ABAP environment ▶ Focus on dynpro ▶ Transactions ▶ Access to multiple systems	▶ ABAP and Java environment ▶ Various user interface technologies ▶ Access to multiple systems	▶ ABAP environment ▶ Various user interface technologies ▶ Access to one system

Table 8.1 Comparison of SAP GUI, SAP NetWeaver Portal, and SAP NetWeaver Business Client

You have already learned about SAP GUI in the previous chapters. I will now discuss the two other user interfaces, SAP NetWeaver Portal and SAP NetWeaver Business Client, more closely in the following sections.

8.1 SAP NetWeaver Portal

The technological basis for the web interface is SAP NetWeaver Portal, the content design of which is based on predefined SAP roles that both bring existing functions to the web and comprise new functions.

8.1.1 Role Concept

SAP differentiates between single roles and composite roles.

SAP currently (as of February 2013) delivers approximately 50 single roles for plant maintenance, for example, for the following:

Single roles

- Work centers
- Data transfers
- Functional locations
- Equipment
- Serial numbers
- BOMs
- Notifications
- Orders
- Resource planning
- Confirmations
- Maintenance task lists
- Maintenance plans
- PM-IS

As in SAP ERP ECC, you can either use the composite roles in SAP NetWeaver Portal, which are based on individual roles and delivered by SAP, or compile your own composite roles. SAP currently delivers the following composite roles for plant maintenance:

Composite roles

- The role *maintenance worker* (Business Package for Maintenance Worker 1.61, technical name SAP_COCKPIT_EAMS_MAINT_WORKER), with functions such as DISPLAY TASKS, PRINT JOB CARD, EXECUTE PLANT MAINTENANCE TASKS, RECORD CURRENT DATA, or CREATE NOTIFICATIONS

- The role *general EAM functions* (technical name SAP_COCKPIT_EAMS_GENERIC_FUNC), with functions such as EDIT TECHNICAL OBJECTS, CREATE MAINTENANCE PLANS, EDIT LINEAR OBJECTS, or MAINTAIN MAINTENANCE TASK LISTS

8.1.2 Service Maps, Overviews, and Reports

Service maps and overviews form the starting point when you call SAP NetWeaver Portal. They comprise a menu-like collection of functions that are assigned to a single or composite role (see Figure 8.1).

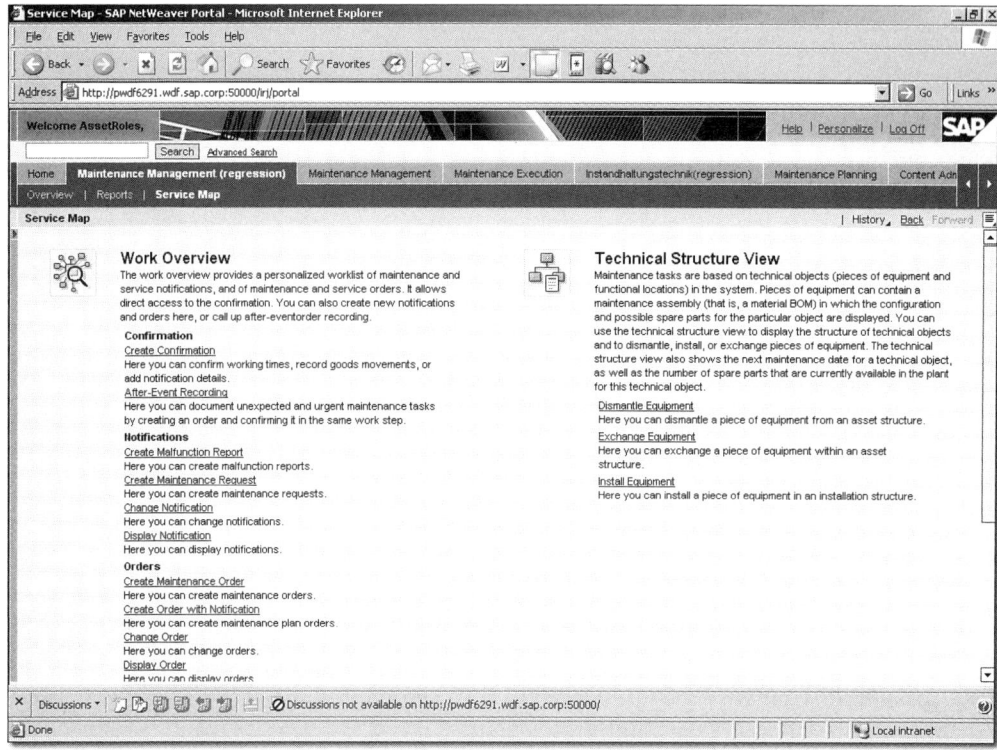

Figure 8.1 Service Map

[+] **Generating Service Maps and Overviews**

Tools are available to enable you to convert your SAP ERP roles into service maps and overviews (see Figure 8.2).

The reports are other role elements. You can execute the following reports (see Chapter 7):

- Queries from BW
- Web templates from BW

- Report writer lists
- List transactions (for example, IW38, IW28, and IW37N)

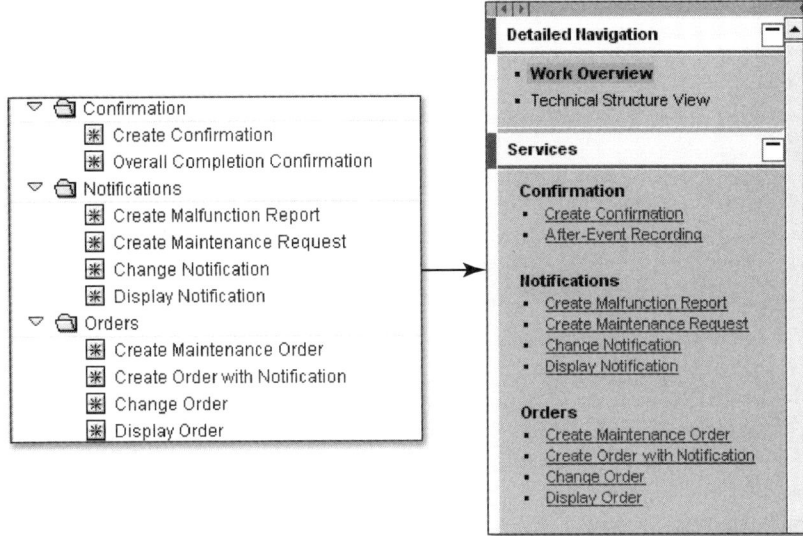

Figure 8.2 Converting a Menu to an Overview

To be able to use the service maps, the business functions LOG_EAM_SIMP, LOG_EAM_SIMPLICITY, and LOG_EAM_SIMPLICITY_2 must be activated.

Business functions

[+] **Defining Your Own Reports**
You use the Customizing function SET UP LAUNCHPAD to define your own report bundle, which can then be selected in the portal.

If you now call one of the functions defined in SAP NetWeaver Portal (for example, a transaction), one of the following two dynpros opens:

Web Dynpro and WebGUI Dynpro

- A Web Dynpro that is similar to the original SAP GUI Dynpro in terms of its functions, structure, and content (see Figure 8.3)
- A WebGUI Dynpro—that is, the original dynpro is displayed in a WebGUI layout (see Figure 8.4)

8 | New Information Technologies in Plant Maintenance

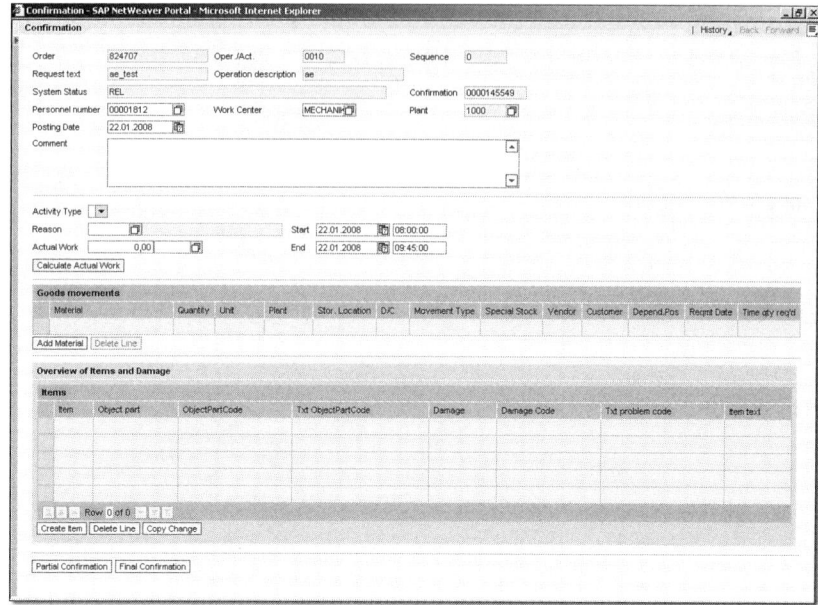

Figure 8.3 Web Dynpro

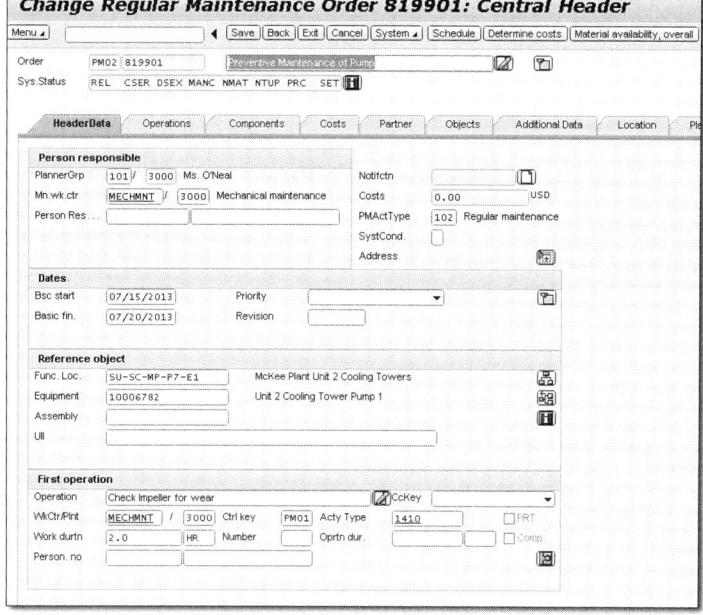

Figure 8.4 WebGUI Dynpro

However, the roles in SAP NetWeaver Portal not only represent known functions from SAP ERP and BW in a new interface, but also provide additional functions that were developed solely for the roles and their use for SAP NetWeaver Portal and SAP NetWeaver Business Client.

> **[!] There Are Only Some Functions in NetWeaver Portal or in SAP NetWeaver Business Client**
>
> You can use some functions—and they will be on the increase in future releases—only via the role concept in SAP NetWeaver Portal or in SAP NetWeaver Business Client; they are not available in SAP ERP.

The following section outlines some of these functions.

8.1.3 After-Event Recording

SAP ERP does not have proper after-event recording functions. This means that there is no standard transaction with which you can retroactively record tasks already performed, including material issue and cost allocation (see also Section 5.3). SAP NetWeaver Portal provides this option using the *Guided Procedures* technology.

In principle, Guided Procedures are workflow modeling tools that enable you to model and manage workflows. Step-by-step instructions guide you through a business process.

Guided Procedures

You are familiar with Guided Procedures from the many Internet sites from which you can order something, for example, choose item → enter customer data → enter bank details → check order → submit order. Even if you book a trip, a Guided Procedure generally processes your booking.

A similar Guided Procedure will guide you through the process of after-event recording (see Figure 8.5):

1. **Order/confirmation data**
   You create an order and enter order data such as the reference object, activity, execution date, and working times. If you define an order type with a notification in Customizing, you can also enter notification data.

2. **Goods movement**
   If a material has been consumed, you can also enter this information here.

3. **Equipment inst./dismant.**
   If a piece of equipment on a functional location has been replaced as part of a maintenance task, you can enter installation/dismantling data here.

4. **Check and save**
   If necessary, you can correct any incorrect data by returning to the relevant step.

5. **Completed**
   The data is transferred, and the after-event recording is completed successfully.

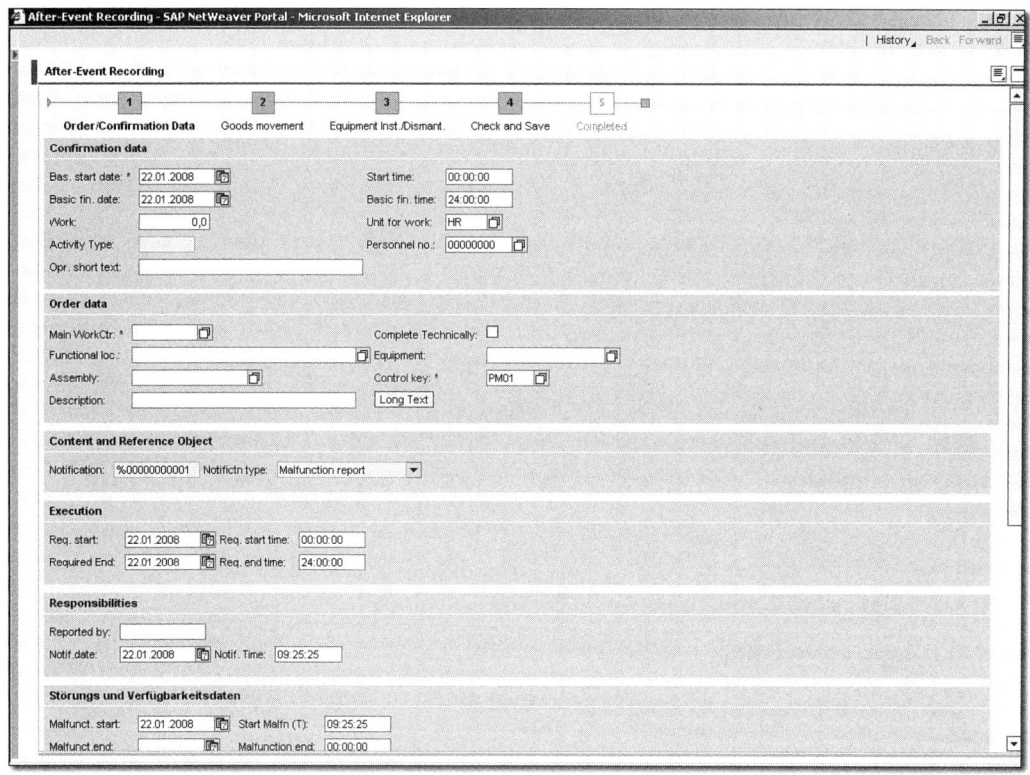

Figure 8.5 After-Event Recording

Once a Guided Procedure is complete, the following technical steps occur in the background:

- An order is opened and released.
- A confirmation is recorded for the actual times entered, and the order receives a final confirmation.
- If necessary, a material issue is posted to the order.
- The order is technically complete.
- If necessary, the equipment is installed at another functional location, or the piece of equipment at the functional location is replaced with another piece of equipment.

You still have to perform a business completion and order settlement.

To be able to use after-event recording comprehensively, you should first activate the business functions LOG_EAM_SIMP, LOG_EAM_SIMPLICITY, and LOG_EAM_SIMPLICITY_2.

Business functions

> **Using After-Event Recording in NetWeaver Portal** [+]
>
> The Guided Procedure for after-event recording is a simple instrument for documenting maintenance tasks retroactively (including spare parts used) and settling the accrued costs.

8.1.4 Technical Structure View

The enhanced technical structure view is another function that you can use only with the role concept in SAP NetWeaver Portal. You can use the technical structure view in SAP ERP (Transactions IH01/03) to display asset structures, but without additional information.

SAP NetWeaver Portal provides an enhanced technical structure view that you can use to display additional information other than the pure asset structure, such as the following:

- Whether document links exist
- The number of notifications (open and/or closed)
- The number of orders (historic, closed, or open)

- The availability of the material
- The next preventative maintenance date
- Whether measuring points and counters exist

Figure 8.6 shows an example of a technical structure view.

From the technical structure view, you can interactively execute specific functions for a technical object, as follows:

- You can create a notification or order.
- You can display information about the object.
- You can install, dismantle, or modify a piece of equipment.

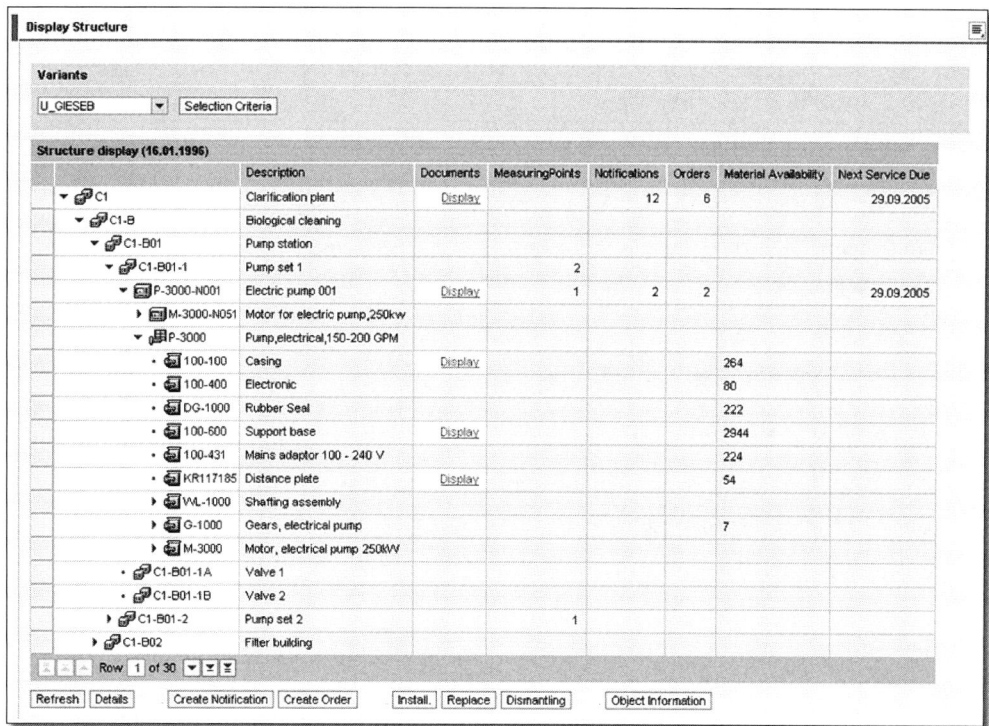

Figure 8.6 Technical Structure View

Business functions   To be able to use the technical structure view comprehensively, you should activate the business functions LOG_EAM_SIMP, LOG_EAM_SIMPLICITY, and LOG_EAM_SIMPLICITY_2.

> **Technical Structure View in NetWeaver Portal Shows Useful Additional Information** [!]
>
> You can use the technical structure view in SAP NetWeaver Portal to view not only the asset structure, but also any additional information (for example, the next maintenance date, availability of spare parts, and so on).

We will now leave behind the portal and discuss a function that is also available to you without SAP NetWeaver Portal.

8.2 Electronic Parts Catalogs

Section 5.2.2 introduced you to the traditional material planning options for an order, and Section 6.3.2 described how SAP ERP has been integrated with SAP SRM, which enables you to use the catalog technology of SAP SRM to procure spare parts.

> **Connecting Catalogues Directly to SAP ERP** [+]
>
> The option to select spare parts from catalogs is also available as a direct connection to the order.

You can use the direct connection of the order to catalogs if you have satisfied two prerequisites in advance:

- Activate the Enterprise Extension EA-PLM using the Switch Framework (Transaction SFW5).
- In Customizing, assign one or more catalogs to the relevant order types (Customizing function INTERFACE FOR PROCUREMENT USING CATALOGS [OCI] • DEFINE CATALOGS and ASSIGN CATALOG TO THE ORDER TYPE).

Prerequisites

In Transaction IW31/32 on the COMPONENTS tab or in Transaction IW3K, you can use the catalogs for your material planning (Catalog button). If you have assigned several catalogs to the order type in Customizing, a dialog box appears in which you select the catalog. The system then jumps directly to the catalog you have selected. Here, you select the required parts, then use the ADD function to place them in

Procedure

your shopping basket, and finally use the CHECK OUT function to transfer them to your SAP system (see Figure 8.7[1]).

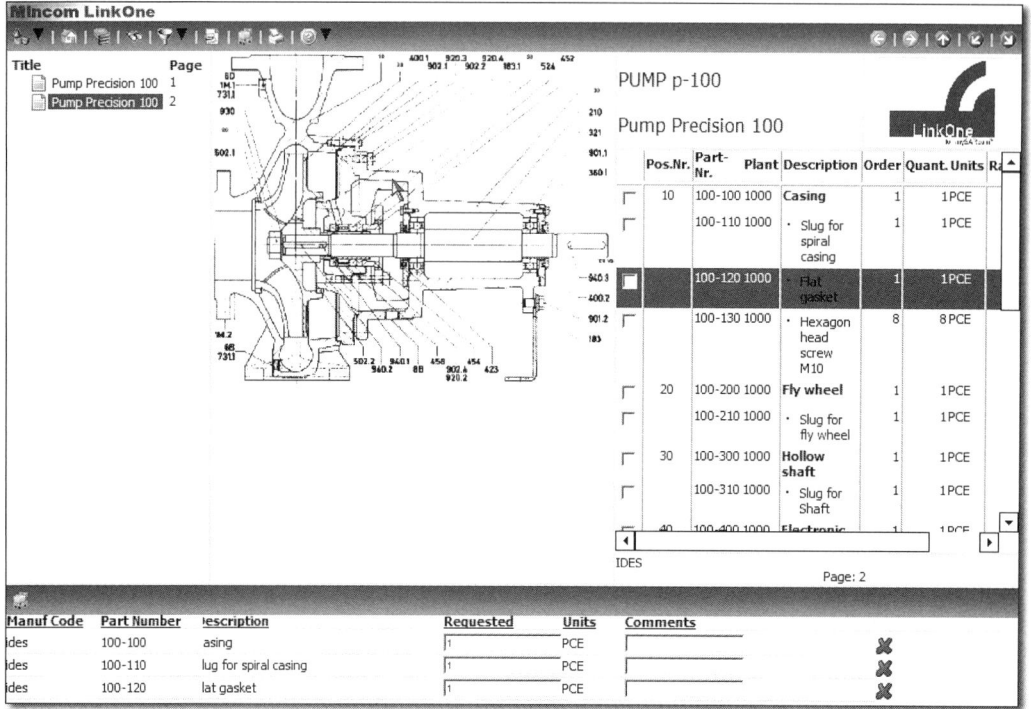

Figure 8.7 Internet Catalog

If you have stored CDs that contain manufacturer catalogs in your network or on your local workstation, you can also use the same technology to select spare parts from these catalogs and transfer them to the order.

[+] **Defining Your Own Checks**

When the shopping basket is transferred to the SAP system, a check is performed to determine whether the selected spare part possibly corresponds to an inventory-managed material number. You can define the type of check performed (for example, a check on the manufacturer material number or on the text) by using the Customizing function DEFINE CONVERSION MODULES. If

---

1 The function names can vary slightly, depending on the selected catalog platform.

the existing conversion modules are unable to perform the check that you want to perform, you can also develop and define your own conversion components.

Catalogs have clear advantages over manual material planning:

- Faster identification of the required spare part
- Prevention of content-related errors as a result of images
- Prevention of data errors as a result of higher data quality
- Fixed definition of materials that can be ordered and sources of supply
- Fewer vendors used for procurement
- Fewer purchase orders never entered in the system as a result of high user acceptance
- More efficient process as a result of easier processing
- Material masters reduced to parts kept in storage[2]

Advantages of Internet catalogs

Catalogs also have a clear advantage over bills of material management. In addition to some of the aforementioned advantages, such as visualization, BOMs do not have to be created or maintained. In particular, engineering change management in many companies is often very fragmented or very laborious.

However, the previous advantages can be achieved only by investing a considerable amount of time and effort into creating, modifying, and using the catalog.

Benefitting from the Advantages of Catalogs [+]

By using catalogs, you avoid effort (for example, of managing material masters and BOMs). The order transactions are less prone to errors (for example, as a result of visualization) and more complete (for example, as a result of a high

---

[2] See also Gertz, W.: E-Commerce, in: *Maintenance 2010, Berlin 2000*, and Deppe, B.: Verknüpfung von PM-Aufträgen mit der Katalogbeschaffung, in: (*Linking PM Orders with Catalog Procurement*) 9. Kongress Instandhaltung und Servicemanagement mit SAP, Berlin 2004. (Congress Plant Maintenance and Service Management with SAP, Berlin 2004.)

> acceptance among users). You can reduce the time and effort required to create and maintain catalogs by insisting that your vendors maintain their items in their catalogs themselves.

8.3 Easy Web Transaction

What is an Easy Web Transaction?

If you do not (yet) use SAP NetWeaver Portal in your company (for example, because of the time and effort required or for licensing reasons), you can also develop an Easy Web Transaction (EWT) for an internal service request so that you can place maintenance notifications.

The EWT for an internal service request enables you to request any service, without having any knowledge of SAP systems on the intranet, by using a simple form or any piece of text that you formulate yourself. The request is automatically forwarded to the person(s) responsible for executing requests and is then displayed, for example, in the list of open notifications (Transaction IW28).

The technology behind EWTs is also used in other applications—for example, in purchasing (as an overview of all materials for a vendor) and in controlling (for displaying internal orders).

The target group for EWTs is always the occasional user. In other words, the EWT is intended for users who do not require or should not be granted direct access to the SAP system, but nevertheless want to execute certain functions from time to time.

Prerequisites

To use this simple option of internal service requests for notification recording, you must first fulfill the following prerequisites:

- Install the Internet Transaction Server (ITS). This fulfills the system requirements for accessing SAP systems over the Internet/intranet.
- In Customizing, define a scenario (Customizing function CROSS-APPLICATION COMPONENTS • NOTIFICATION • NOTIFICATION PROCESSING ON THE INTRANET • DEFINE SCENARIOS). Here, you specify, among other things, whether you want to use the notification transaction, an

Adobe PDF form, or an HTML service to enter the data. Recording a malfunction report and recording a maintenance request are delivered as scenarios for plant maintenance.

▶ Define an HTML form or an Adobe PDF form.
▶ Publish the service and form on the intranet.

Figure 8.8 shows you an example of an internal service request in an HTML form.[3]

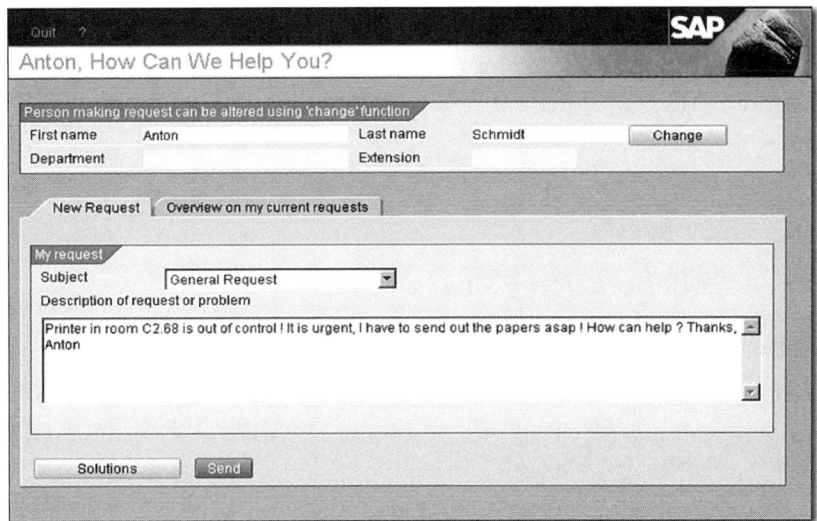

Figure 8.8 Internal Service Request 3

Here, you use the internal service request to enter your notification and describe the problem. Depending on the scenario settings, the service request is then displayed in the SAP Business Workplace (Transaction SBWP, for example, for approval) or directly in the list of open notifications (Transaction IW28).

Flow

---

3 Henneboel, G.: Mobile Lösungen für das technische Anlagenmanagement, in: ("Mobile Solutions for Technical Asset Management", in:) 7. mySAP.com-Instandhaltungs- und Servicemanagement-Kongress, Potsdam 2002, S.18. (1. mySAP.com Plant Maintenance and Service Management Conference, Potsdam 2002, page 18.

[+] You Should, Perhaps, Activate an Approval Process

Since this procedure for entering notifications via the EWT involves people who are less familiar with SAP systems, you should consider whether these notifications should undergo an approval process. To activate the approval process for each notification type, use the Customizing function PARTNER FUNCTIONS, APPROVAL.

[+] Advantages of the Internal Service Request

The internal service request is a simple option that enables occasional users to submit maintenance notifications. Furthermore, the workstations do not require a locally installed SAP GUI, which would be required to generate notifications directly in the SAP system.

8.4 Collaboration Folders

What are cFolders? Collaboration Folders (cFolders) are another resource for exchanging information via the Internet. Collaboration folders are electronic folders published on an Internet platform to facilitate project work in virtual teams. In particular, they were designed for bid scenarios and engineering processes in design and development. However, you can also apply the cFolders technology to the collaborative exchange of information among parties involved in a maintenance process (see Figure 8.9):

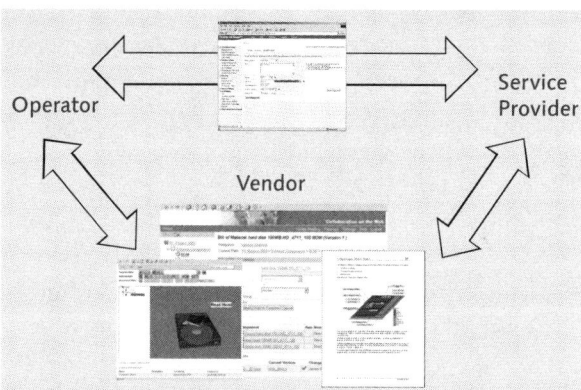

Figure 8.9 cFolders

- You, as the operator
- Your service providers
- The manufacturer of a technical system
- The vendor
- Possible authorities
- Other plants

A folder is a container for a wide range of shared documents that can be accessed by all relevant partners (see Figure 8.10[4]).

Functional scope

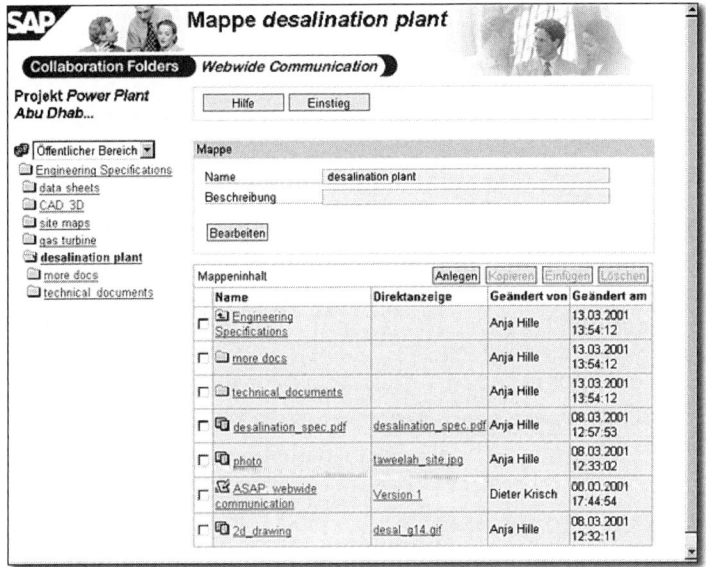

Figure 8.10 Content of a cFolder

A cFolder has the following functions:

- You can store any document type in the cFolder.
- You can assign a status and multiple views to the documents.
- You can make versions of the documents.

---

4 Stengele, H.: mySAP Product Lifecycle Management, DSAG-Arbeitskreis, (DSAG working group) Frankfurt 2004.

- You can store data sheets containing classification data and import data from class systems (for example, eClass).
- You can publish material masters and bills of material.
- You can apply a redlining procedure.
- You can establish discussion forums.

For additional functional information and information about the configuration, project planning, and so on, please refer to some additional reading material.[5]

[+] **cFolders Support Collaboration**

In cFolders, you and your partners can store and maintain shared documents, thus supporting the collaborative exchange of data via the Internet.

8.5 Vision or Reality?

The previous sections provided some approaches to web support in plant maintenance, which are contained in the standard SAP version.

The following section will propose some ideas for using web technologies to support your maintenance processes, most of which can already be implemented using the technologies provided by SAP.

8.5.1 Electronic Data Exchange

You are probably familiar with the following problem: when vendors and service providers communicate with each other, enormous volumes of physical documents are transported, which you initiate and vendors then manually enter, and vice versa. The vendor enters your purchase order again as a sales order; you post the vendor's goods issue again as a goods receipt, and so on. Not only does this duplicate effort occur in many places, but each document carries the risk of transmission errors.

SAP technologies already facilitate a process whereby data is exchanged in electronic form (for example, as an XML document; see Figure 8.11).

---
5 For example, Raap, H.: *SAP Product Lifecycle Management*, Boston: SAP PRESS, 2013.

- The process control system generates a notification via the PM/PCS interface (see Section 6.4.1). Alternatively, a production employee uses the EWT to report a maintenance requirement (see Section 8.3).
- Electronic parts catalogs are used to plan the required spare parts (see Section 8.2), and a purchase requisition is subsequently generated.

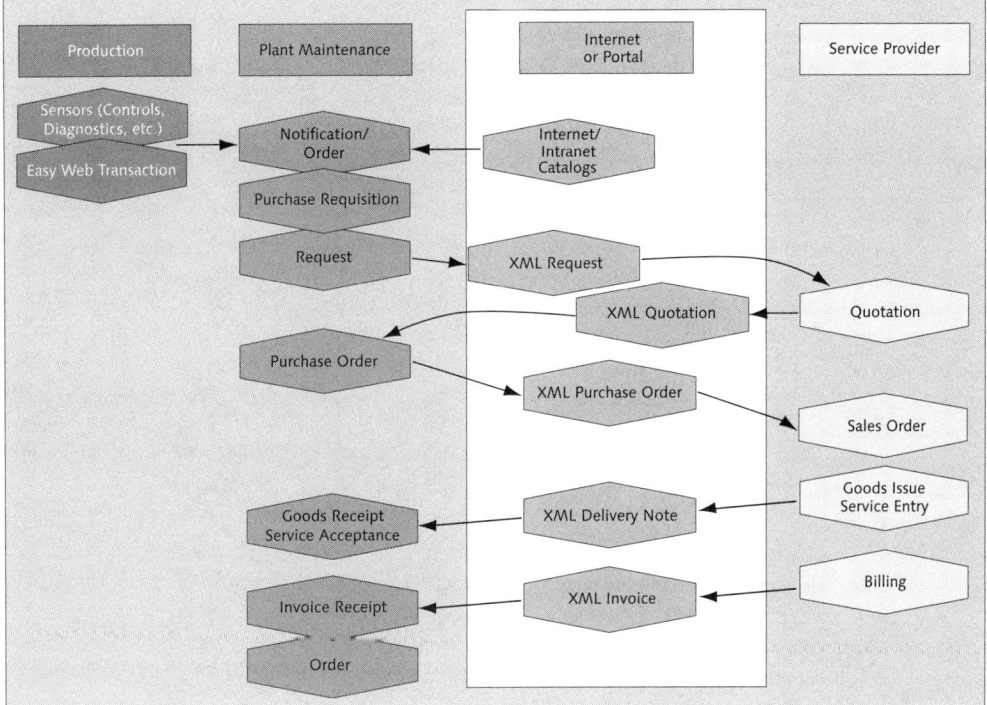

Figure 8.11 Electronic Data Exchange

Additional documents are exchanged electronically with the vendor.

The vendor uses your request to create a quotation. In turn, you transfer the vendor's quotation data to your purchase order and, in turn, to the vendor's invoice, which results in you generating an electronic invoice receipt.

Electronic Data Exchange Saves Time and Prevents Errors	[!]
An electronic data exchange with the vendor not only saves time and effort for both parties, but also reduces the risk of transmission errors.	

In this scenario, you and your vendor operate your own systems. However, a scenario in which you both share one platform would also be conceivable.

8.5.2 Vendor Portal

You could also establish a portal that is accessible by both your employees and your vendors. This portal supports all parties involved in the ordering process for materials and/or services (see Figure 8.12).[6]

- Your purchasers can use the portal to negotiate prices, conclude outline agreements, define service catalogs, and so on.
- Your maintenance planners can, if needed, create contract release orders from the outline agreements and service specifications and place the contract release orders in the portal.
- The vendors can release the purchase orders from the portal, confirm the orders, generate quotations, place goods receipts, enter service entry sheets, and so on.
- Your technical system operators may want to know the current processing status, or they may have to approve the services.

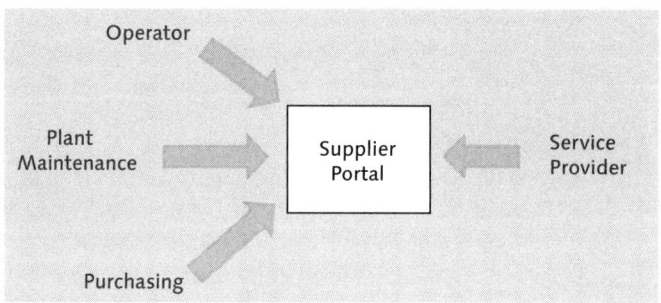

Figure 8.12 Using Vendor Portal

---

6 See also Kaudewitz, R.; Theis, S.: Mobile Instandhaltung und Service Provider Portal, in: ("Mobile Plant Maintenance and Service Provider Portal", in: 11. SAP Conference of Plant Maintenance, Potsdam 2006.

> **Always Up-to-Date with the Vendor Portal** [+]
>
> You use the vendor portal to keep all parties involved up to date and to hand over many of the data entering tasks to your vendors.

8.5.3 Virtual Spare Parts Storage

Everyone can identify with, and has, physical spare parts storage, including stock never recorded in the books. Also, everyone talks about reducing warehouse stock and reducing the tied-up capital, but it is difficult to do anything about it.

What about having virtual spare parts storage? The idea is that not every company keeps every single spare part, but that the companies involved enter a "division of labor" agreement: upon agreement, each company keeps only certain spare parts in physical storage and publishes on the portal those spare parts that can be made available to other companies at short notice. This way, the companies involved can access a virtual warehouse that comprises several physical spare parts storage locations in the background (see Figure 8.13).

What is virtual spare parts storage?

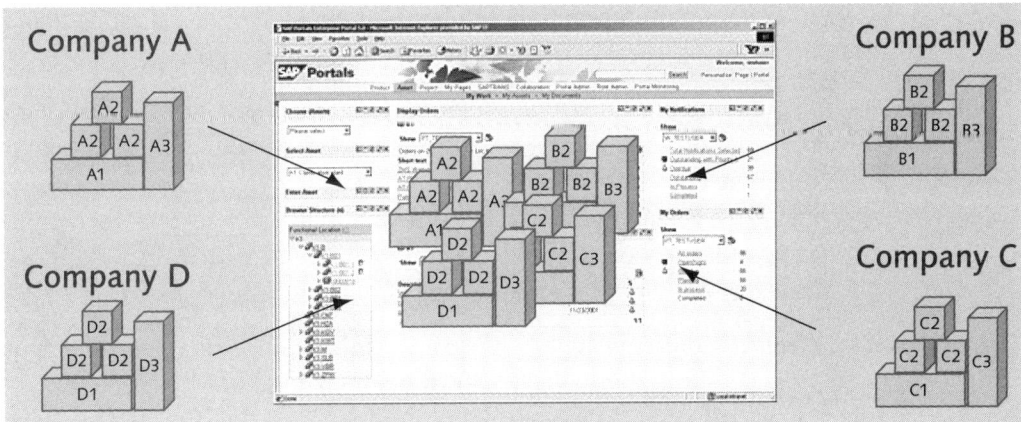

Figure 8.13 Virtual Spare Parts Storage

By far the most important prerequisite for virtual spare parts storage is trustworthy collaboration among all companies involved, and the published warehouse stock must be kept up to date. In addition, the

Prerequisites

companies involved should have a homogeneous composition—that is, belong to the same or similar industries, have the same or similar products and the same or similar machines and technical systems, and so on. Physical proximity is also beneficial. Of course, a technical prerequisite here is the need to establish the necessary infrastructure (portal), which also requires you to clarify the question of the division of costs.

[+] **Virtual Storage Helps to Reduce Your Own Warehouse Stock**

If you can fulfill the necessary prerequisites (for example, trustworthy partnerships); virtual spare parts storage can be an effective way to dramatically reduce the volume of warehouse stock comprising spare parts and the resulting stockholding costs.

8.5.4 Virtual Personnel Capacities

Maintenance capacity utilization varies greatly: sometimes, your capacities are insufficient, and you have to outsource work to external companies (see Sections 3.2 and 5.2.3), and sometimes, you have overcapacities (this is never wanted, but is frequently the reality). What should you do with overcapacities (too many employees) in times of under-utilization? Where can you obtain employees in times of over-utilization if you do not want to outsource work to external companies?

What are virtual personnel capacities?

What about having virtual personnel capacities? Similar to virtual spare parts storage, companies join forces and keep personnel capacities with different skills (for example, company A employs elevator technicians, company B employs refrigeration technicians, and so on). Each company publishes on a portal the time periods in which their skills are available to other companies, along with the available capacity.

Here, the prerequisites are the same as those for virtual spare parts of storage (physical proximity, infrastructure, and so on).

[+] **Virtual Capacities Help to Reduce External Costs**

If you can fulfill the necessary prerequisites, virtual personnel capacities can be an effective way to dramatically reduce your own personnel costs and the costs associated with using external companies.

8.5.5 Sell Rather Than Scrap

What do you do if you no longer require a technical system, parts of a technical system, or spare parts? Throw it away? Scrap it? How about selling it (see Figure 8.14)?

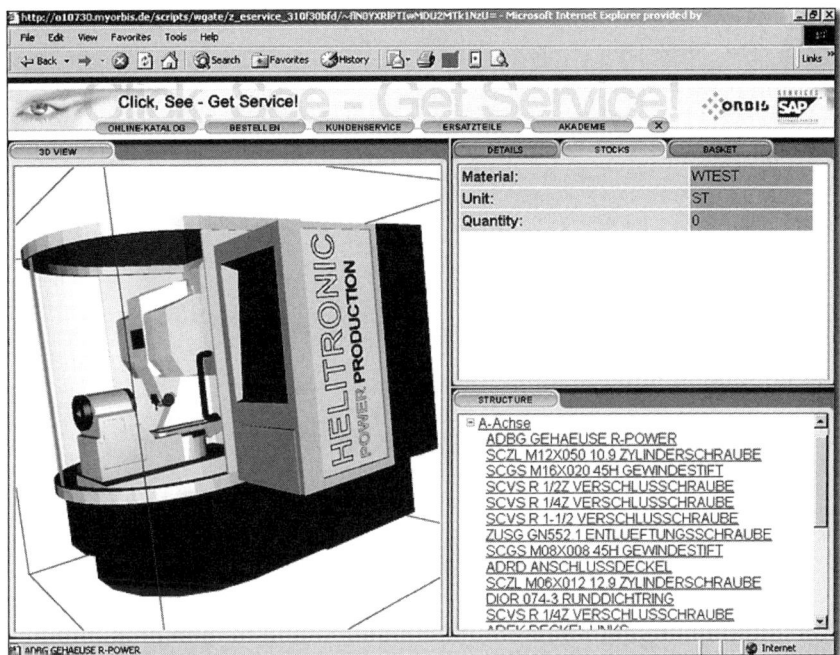

Figure 8.14 E-Selling

SAP provides the option of e-selling with an integrated auction process that allows products to be sold via an auction platform (such as eBay). E-selling covers the entire process, from the creation of an auction through auctions on eBay to payment processing. E-selling is integrated into SAP CRM and SAP ERP.

Sell Rather Than Scrap	[+]
E-selling supports you in selling spare parts, technical systems, and machines you no longer require. E-selling has an interface to the eBay auction platform.	

The intranet and Internet can support you with the previous application cases. As the use of the intranet and Internet is as individual as a company's business processes, however, there are other application cases for your individual business processes, such as the examples below, and many more that cannot be covered in depth here:

- Communication with authorities
- Knowledge exchange with partners
- Shared procurement for bundling demand quantities from several companies
- Remote service and support for your provider
- E-learning with access to test laboratories

We now come to the options that SAP NetWeaver Business Client provides.

8.6 SAP NetWeaver Business Client

What is the Business Client?

SAP NetWeaver Business Client (for short: Business Client) is a rich client. It is a desktop application; that is, at least the Business Client for Windows must be installed like SAP GUI on the desktop. It allows the use of portal services, application content, and tasks directly from the backend.

SAP NetWeaver Business Client is intended to bridge the gap between today's thick clients (such as SAP GUI) and browser access to SAP NetWeaver Portal.

Types of Business Clients

There are two versions of SAP NetWeaver Business Client:

- **SAP NetWeaver Business Client for Windows**
  Here, the Business Client is installed locally on the desktop; it accesses SAP systems with SAP GUI for Windows, and you have a full range of functions. However, this version is available only for Windows platforms.

- **SAP NetWeaver Business Client for HTML**
  Here, no local installation is necessary because you use only one browser (recommendation: Internet Explorer); you access SAP systems with SAP GUI for HTML. SAP NetWeaver Business Client for HTML is available for all major platforms, but with a reduced range of

functions (for example, no search, no dropdown menus, no drag and drop).

Figure 8.15[7] shows the differences between the two SAP NetWeaver Business Client versions.

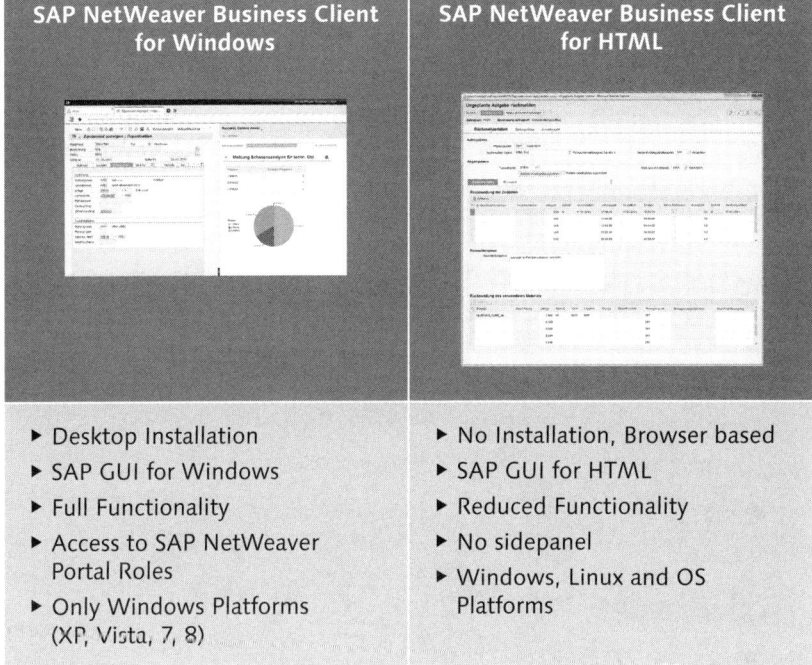

Figure 8.15 Comparison of the Two Versions of SAP NetWeaver Business Client

On the following pages, I will present the most important functions of SAP NetWeaver Business Client for plant maintenance.

8.6.1 General Functions

I will present the general functions of SAP NetWeaver Business Client below.

---

7 In accordance with Jakowski, J.; Binder, C.: SAP NetWeaver Business Client – Einsetzen und Nutzen, DSAG-Webinar am 26.10.2011. ("SAP NetWeaver Business Client – Using and Benefitting", DSAG Webinar on 10.26.2011.

Using Standard SAP Transactions

You can call and execute all standard SAP transactions in SAP NetWeaver Business Client. Figure 8.16 shows Transaction IW31 (Create Order).

Tab pages

As you can see in the top bar in the screenshot from Figure 8.16, SAP NetWeaver Business Client uses a tab technology to display all called functions in a single window. This means that you can access several functions in parallel, without having to open a new window in each case.

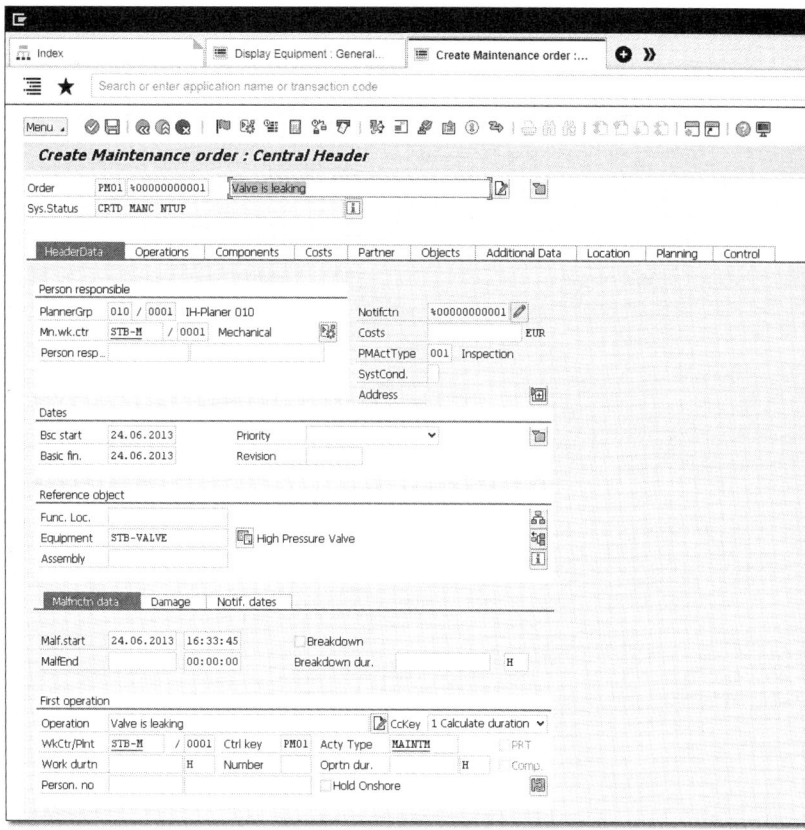

Figure 8.16 Transaction IW31 in SAP NetWeaver Business Client

Search

SAP NetWeaver Business Client has three different search options (bar right below the tabs):

- **Enterprise search**
  Search in company data
- **External search engines and encyclopedias**
  Search via external search engines (such as Google or Yahoo) and encyclopedias (such as Wikipedia)
- **Desktop search**
  Search in the desktop documents

8.6.2 Roles, Task Lists, Overviews, and Reports

SAP NetWeaver Business Client also has access to the portal roles. Thus, task lists and overviews form the initial screen, similar to SAP NetWeaver Portal; they comprise a menu-like collection of functions that are assigned to a single or composite role. Figure 8.17 shows an example of the overview for the role *maintenance worker*.

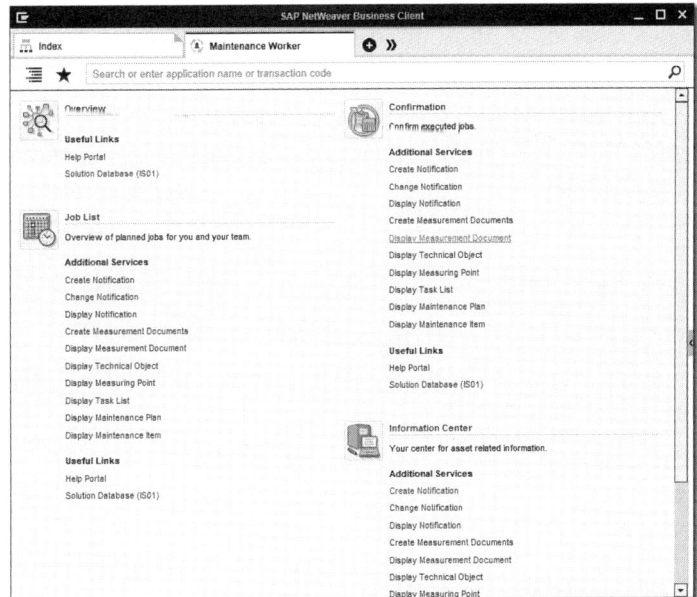

Figure 8.17 Role Menu in SAP NetWeaver Business Client

8.6.3 Confirming Unplanned Jobs

Section 5.3 has already discussed the *immediate Repair* business process, and in Section 8.1.3, I have introduced the option of after-event recording in SAP NetWeaver Portal.

SAP NetWeaver Business Client has a comparable function in the function CONFIRM UNPLANNED JOB. An order can be recorded retroactively here, also.

This function contains the following options (see Figure 8.18):

- **Create order**
  You create an order and enter order data, such as the reference object, activity, execution date, and working times.

- **Enter goods movement**
  If a material has been consumed, you can also enter this information here.

- **Record measurement readings or counter readings**
  If the technical object has measuring points and/or counters, you can record measurement readings and/or counter readings.

- **Create malfunction data**
  You can also record notification data like malfunctions, damage codes, or cause codes.

- **Attach document**
  If a document is created when processing an order (for example, an image or measurement log), you can attach it to the order confirmation.

When you save, the following technical steps occur in the background:

- An order is created with or without a notification and released.
- A confirmation is recorded for the actual times entered, and the order receives a final confirmation.
- If necessary, a material issue is posted to the order.
- If necessary, counter readings and/or measurement readings are stored.
- If necessary, the document is attached.
- The order is technically complete.

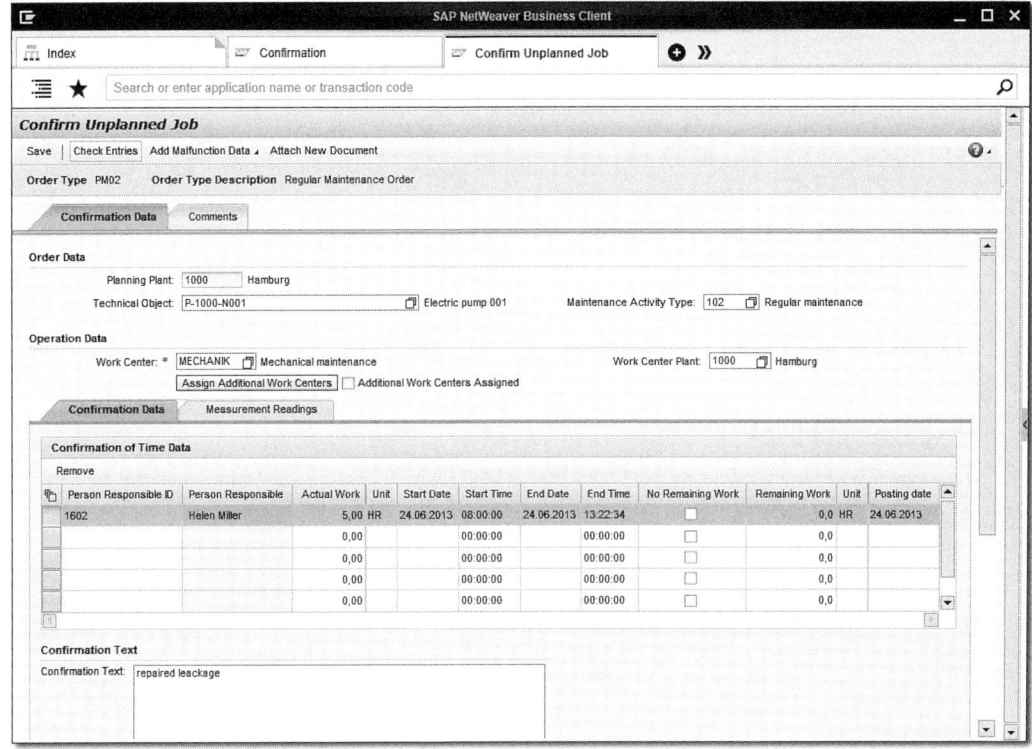

Figure 8.18 Confirming Unplanned Jobs

You still have to perform a business completion and order settlement.

To be able to use an unplanned jobs comprehensively, you should activate the business functions LOG_EAM_SIMP, LOG_EAM_SIMPLICITY, and LOG_EAM_SIMPLICITY_2.

Business functions

8.6.4 Asset Viewer

Section 8.1.4 discussed the "technical structure view" function of SAP NetWeaver Portal. SAP NetWeaver Business Client provides a similar function with the Asset Viewer (see Figure 8.19), with which you can display other information in addition to the pure asset structure, such as the following:

8 | New Information Technologies in Plant Maintenance

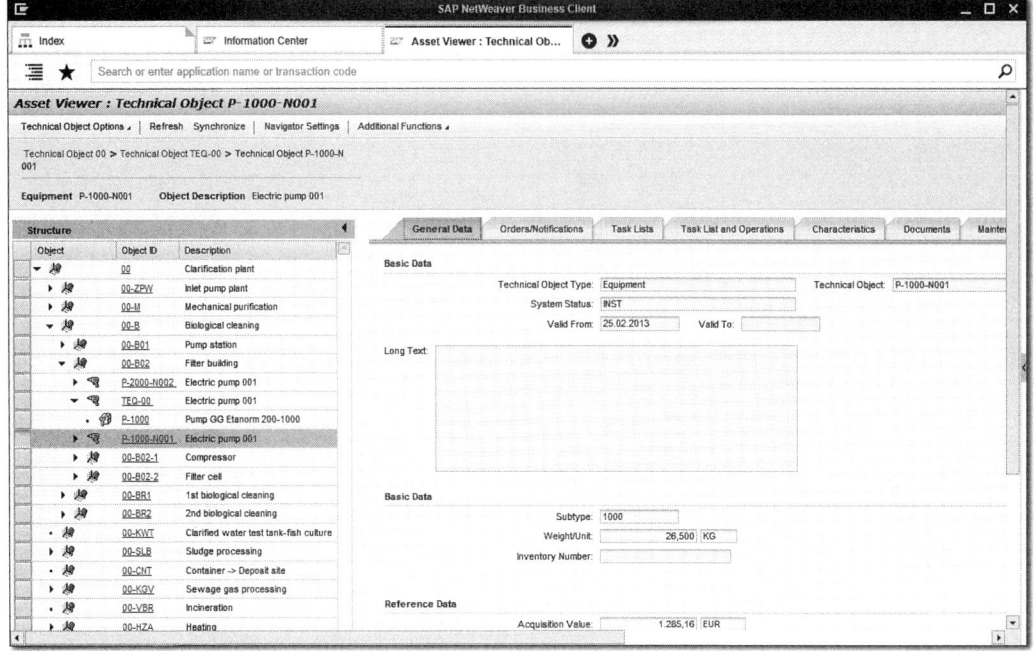

Figure 8.19 Asset Viewer in SAP NetWeaver Business Client

- Whether document links exist
- What notifications exist
- What orders exist
- What maintenance task lists, maintenance items, and maintenance plans were created
- What classes and characteristics are defined
- Whether measuring points and counters exist

From the Asset Viewer, you can interactively execute specific functions for a technical object, as follows:

- You can create a notification or order.
- You can display information about the object.
- You can install, dismantle, or modify a piece of equipment.

To be able to use the technical structure view comprehensively, you should activate the business functions LOG_EAM_SIMP, LOG_EAM_SIMPLICITY, and LOG_EAM_SIMPLICITY_2.

Business functions

[+] **Asset Viewer in SAP NetWeaver Business Client Shows Additional Useful Information**

You can use the Asset Viewer in SAP NetWeaver Business Client to view not only the asset structure, but also any additional information (for example, maintenance plans, orders, and so on).

From the Asset Viewer, you can also create new master data (such as maintenance task lists or maintenance plans) and new transaction data (such as notifications and orders).

8.6.5 Side Panels

An important enhancement of SAP NetWeaver Business Client with respect to SAP GUI is the use of side panels.

Side panels are used to display additional information about an application in a page area. Such information can be, for example, the following:

- Key figures like Mean Time to Repair (MTTR) or Mean Time between Repair (MTBR)
- Damages analyses or cost analyses from BW
- Cost center reporting or internal orders from CO
- Graphics from SAP Visual Enterprise
- Object services

Figure 8.20 shows an example of an equipment master record with the associated damage analysis in relation to damage codes.

To be able to use the side panels comprehensively, you should activate the business functions LOG_EAM_SIMP, LOG_EAM_SIMPLICITY, and LOG_EAM_SIMPLICITY_2.

Business functions

8 | New Information Technologies in Plant Maintenance

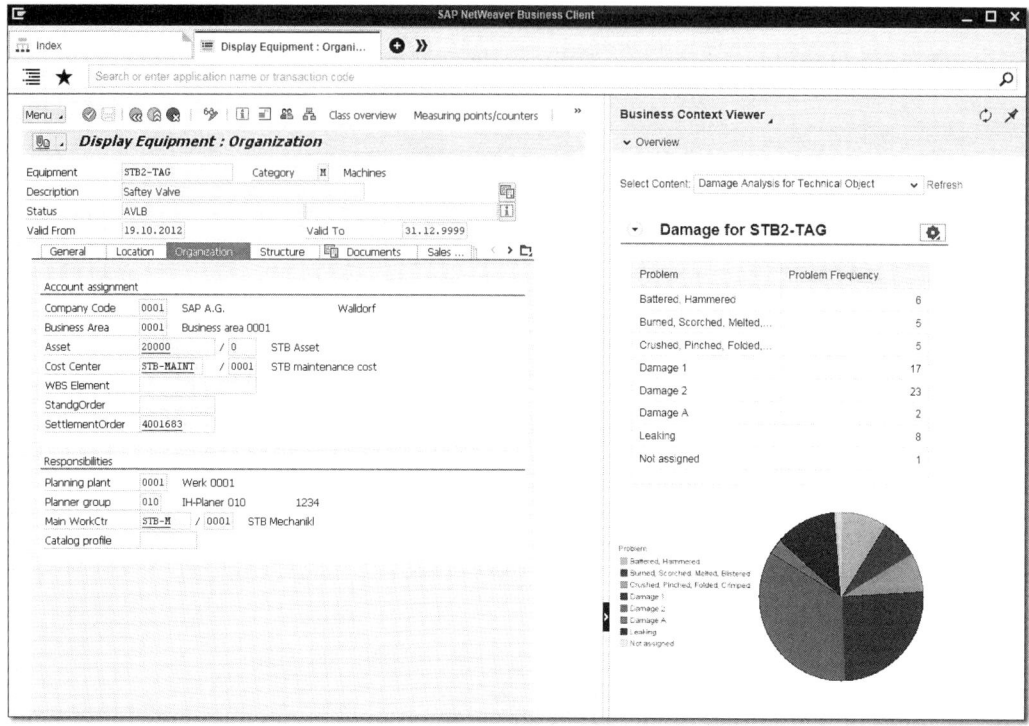

Figure 8.20 Side Panel in SAP NetWeaver Business Client

[+] **Additional Useful Information in the Side Panel of SAP NetWeaver Business Client**

You can use the side panel in SAP NetWeaver Business Client to display additional useful information about the technical object (for example, damage analyses or key figures).

8.6.6 SAP Visual Enterprise Viewer

With the SAP Visual Enterprise Viewer, visualization functions for technical objects, spare parts, and instructions are available in SAP NetWeaver Business Client. Animated scenes and 2-D and 3-D model views support you in tasks such as the provision of spare parts and the execution of maintenance. Only the 2-D images and 3-D scenes, which are published within a company, are available for the display.

SAP NetWeaver Business Client | 8.6

With the integration of SAP Visual Enterprise Viewer in SAP NetWeaver Business Client, you have the following options:

Functional scope

- **Display graphics**
  You can graphically display pieces of equipment and functional locations by calling a 2-D image or a 3-D scene of the technical object from the master data of the technical object (see Figure 8.21).

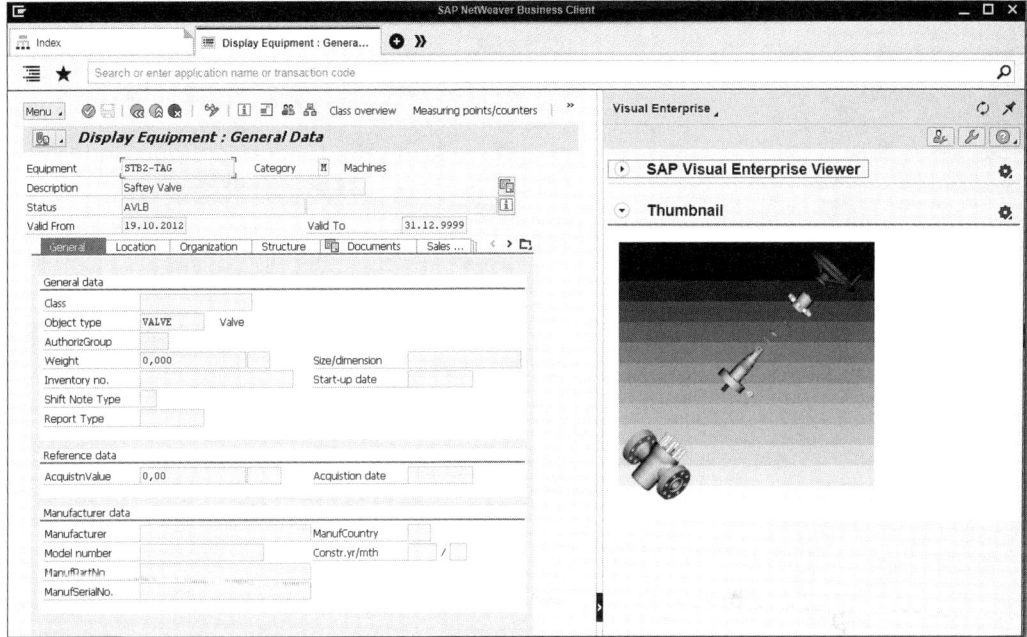

Figure 8.21 3-D Graphic in SAP Visual Enterprise Viewer

- **Select spare parts**
  You can use 2-D or 3-D images to select and determine the required spare parts. The system calls a 2D image or 3D scene of the relevant spare parts in a dialog box. You now have the option of selecting one or more spare parts in the image and transferring them to the spare parts list. The various display functions, such as disassembling or rotating the model, assist you in selecting (see Figure 8.22).

- **Animate maintenance task lists**
  SAP Visual Enterprise Viewer assists you in performing plant maintenance tasks with visual instructions. Visual instructions may be, for

8 | New Information Technologies in Plant Maintenance

example, animated 3-D scenes that visualize the individual steps of the plant maintenance task at the operation level. Figure 8.21 shows an example of how this could look.

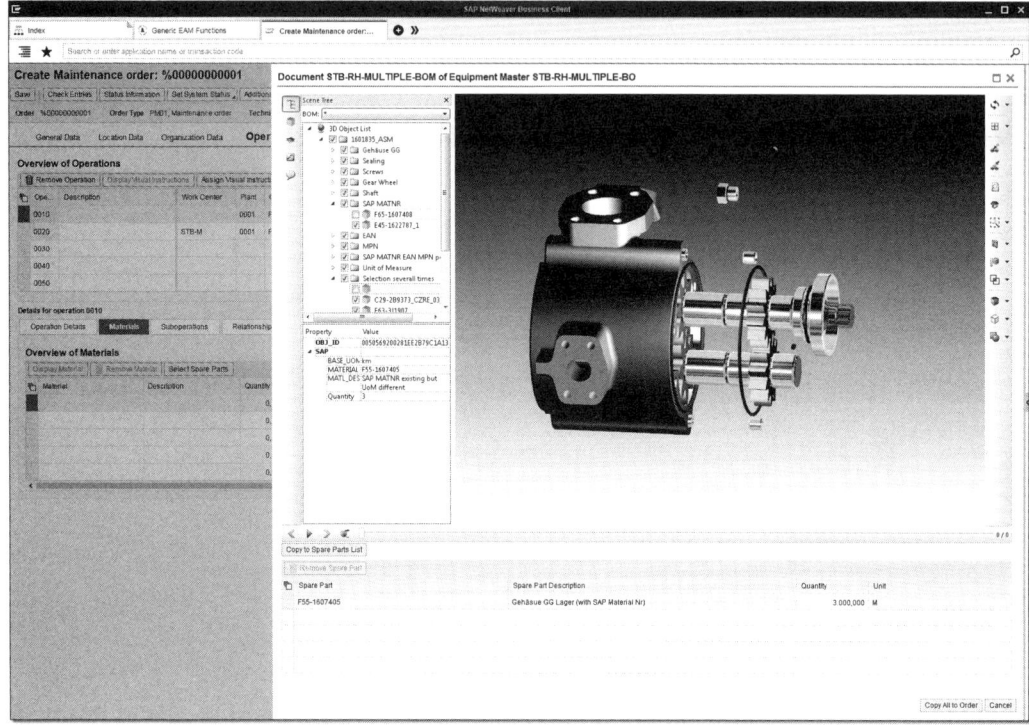

Figure 8.22 Active 3-D Graphic in SAP Visual Enterprise Viewer

Prerequisites To be able to fully utilize the functions described here, you must first fulfill the following prerequisites:

- Install SAP Visual Enterprise Viewer locally.
- Activate the business functions LOG_EAM_SIMPLICITY, LOG_EAM_SIMPLICITY_2, and LOG_EAM_VE_INT.

We will now leave the area of SAP NetWeaver Business Client and turn to a technology that is, together with Internet scenarios, one of the focal points of the SAP setup in plant maintenance and, following some initial reservations, has been successfully implemented in many customer projects: mobile maintenance.

8.7 Mobile Maintenance

Before I introduce the technological characteristics of mobile maintenance at SAP, it is important to first create a basic understanding of the topic of *mobile maintenance*—for example, what actually differentiates a process with mobile maintenance from a process without mobile maintenance, or which scenarios you can implement, and some other aspects.

8.7.1 Fundamentals of Mobile Maintenance

This section presents the fundamentals of mobile maintenance. What does *mobile maintenance* mean, and what do business processes supported in this way look like? It will also provide some application cases and highlight the advantages associated with mobile maintenance.

What Is Mobile Maintenance?

At SAP, *mobile maintenance* means the following:

- In order to perform a maintenance task, a technician requires information stored in the ERP system to be made available to him on site on a mobile device.
- The actual data gathered is entered on site and transferred to the ERP system.

> **[!] Mobility as a Supplement to EAM**
>
> It was not, and is not, SAP's strategy to replace SAP EAM with a mobile version. You won't be able to fully process any business processes with SAP mobile maintenance. SAP regards mobile maintenance as part of a business process and as the technology for supporting maintenance processing.

What Does a Business Process Look Like?

SAP mobile maintenance does not represent an entire process, but rather a sub-process. If you look at a typical maintenance process both with and without mobile support, you see some significant differences (see Figure 8.23[8]).

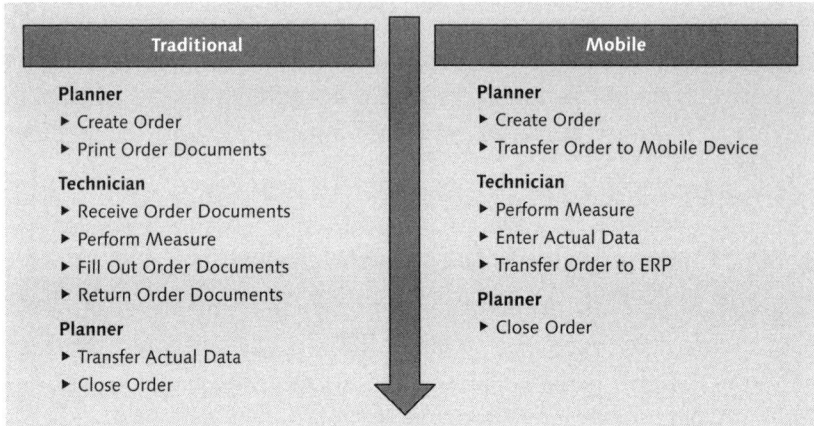

Figure 8.23 Traditional and Mobile Business Processes

The mobile maintenance process differs from the traditional process as follows:

- You do not print any documents.
- You do not transport any documents to or from the maintenance location.
- You do not have to archive any documents.
- You do not separate data entry from the process.
- Instead, the order data is available in electronic form on site.
- You enter the actual data (also in electronic form) shortly after you perform the maintenance task.
- The data is transferred to the backend system (SAP EAM).

---

8 For other similar scenarios, see Müller, F: Mobile Instandhaltungsabwicklung bei Solvay, in: (Mobile Maintenance Management at Solvay, in 11. SAP-Kongress Instandhaltung, Potsdam 2006 (SAP Conference of Plant Maintenance, Potsdam 2006) and Buck, M.: Einsatz mobiler Szenarien mit SAP am Flughafen Frankfurt, in: (Use of Mobile Scenarios with SAP at Frankfurt Airport, in:) Effiziente Instandhaltung mit SAP, Frankfurt 2006. (Efficient Maintenance with SAP).

> **Electronic Data Exchange instead of Gaps in Integration** [!]
>
> The key difference between business processes with mobile support and conventional processing is the continuity of electronic data exchange at the planning and execution stages; there are no gaps in integration.

What Are the Advantages of This?

Irrespective of the details of this process in your company, the general advantages associated with such a working method are evident:[9]

- Less manual effort is required to enter data (the information is not handwritten first and then written in electronic form later, but is in electronic form from the outset).
- Entering data on site in electronic form and transferring it electronically to the ERP system reduces both the risk of transmission errors and the error rate.
- All in all, the data is higher quality.
- Consequently, there should be fewer complaints from sold-to parties as a result of incorrect order settlements.
- Eliminating the need for manual document transports reduces the lead time (technicians do not have to collect or return their order documents).

Which Variants Are Available?

You must distinguish between offline and online scenarios for SAP's mobile solutions (see Figure 8.24, shown here in the context of the SAP NetWeaver platform).

---

[9] See Nettlenbusch, M.: Mobile Lösungen, in: (Mobile Solutions in: Effiziente Instandhaltung mit SAP R/3, Wiesbaden 2004. Efficient Maintenance with SAP R/3) Or Rabeder, H.: Mobile Asset Management bei voestalpine, in: 10. Instandhaltungs- und Servicemanagement-Kongress mit SAP, Berlin 2005.

8 | New Information Technologies in Plant Maintenance

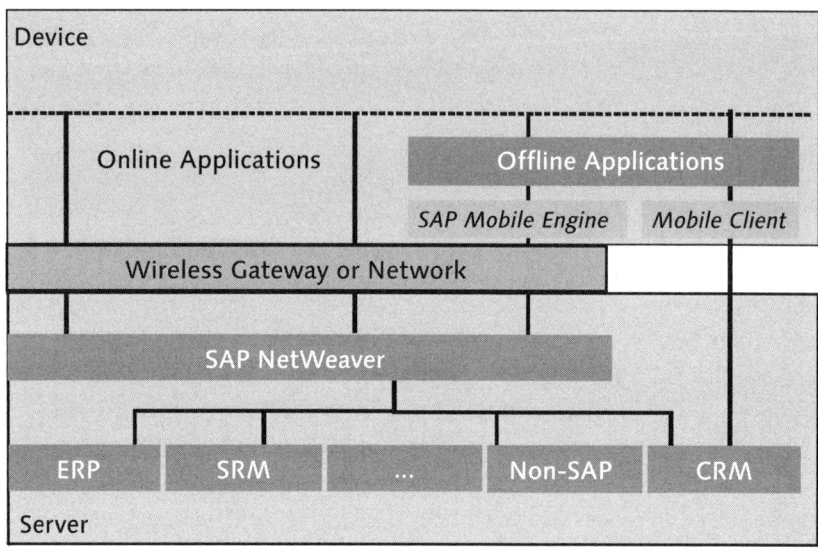

Figure 8.24 Online and Offline Applications

Online scenarios   For online scenarios, you use the mobile device to contact SAP NetWeaver directly and you transfer the data to the backend system immediately (for example, SAP ERP), or vice versa: you send data online from SAP ERP to a mobile device. Typical scenario: paging.

Online scenarios   For offline scenarios, you transfer the data from the backend system to a mobile device. The data is available offline and locally for further processing. Once you have finished entering the data, you transfer the data back to the backend system. Typical scenarios: SAP Mobile Asset Management (MAM) and SAP Work Manager.

Which Application Cases Exist?

Real-life projects have demonstrated a wide range of different application cases in which mobile scenarios were implemented. These include, for example:[10]

- Frankfurt Airport, which inspects its fire shutters (subject to compliance regulations), checks the condition of its parking facilities, monitors

---

10 The relevant references are listed in the bibliography.

its emergency escape routes, and approves the cleaning services of external companies

- RheinEnergie, which supports its metering point operation and network operation, including removal/installation of measuring points and periodic readings of counter readings
- KUKA, which supports its service employees when they perform initial operations, correct malfunctions, and carry out maintenance tasks on robots
- Roche Diagnostics, where safety aspects are a major concern and GMP-relevant maintenance orders are processed
- DB Railion Deutschland, which uses mobile technology for maintenance commissioning and preliminary claims recording for its freight cars
- E.On, which deploys mobile technology for sales order processing, inspection, and meter management (installation, removal, meter reading, collection)
- National Grid, the US utilities company that uses a mobile process for its complete order processing
- Infraserv, which supports its technicians in maintenance and service work in the areas of heating, air conditioning, ventilation, and plumbing
- GWG (the public utility housing enterprise in Wuppertal, Germany), which has implemented mobile property management and mobile apartment inspections
- Voest Alpine, which uses mobile technology to monitor its technical systems and record malfunctions
- The police force in Rhineland-Palatinate, which uses an online mobile scenario to create its electronic logbooks

The list of existing and possible application cases is endless, but this brief list has provided some insight into the many possible uses.

> [!] **Mobile Maintenance Projects Are Very Individual**
>
> Each mobile maintenance project proceeds in a different manner and far more individually than "normal" EAM projects. In particular, the functions and interface design of frontends are usually customized to the needs of the respective company.

Which Devices Are Considered?

Device types
Another question you must clarify in the course of a project for mobile maintenance is the use of mobile devices. The market for suitable mobile devices is very large, very heterogeneous and, in particular, very transparent. Examples of device types include, among others, the following:

- Classic ASCII handheld device
- Graphical handheld device
- Notebook
- Tablets (for example, iPad or Galaxy Note)
- Personal digital assistant (PDA)
- Keyboardless graphical device
- Cellular telephone
- Smartphone (for example, iPhone or Android device)
- Voice picking system

Selection criteria
A wide range of factors determines the best device or device type for you. When choosing a device type, you should answer the following questions, in particular:

- Which processes do you want to support and which functions do you require to do this?
- How much information do you want to process locally (main memory)?
- Do you require online access? Should the device be equipped with a cellular radio or a wireless local radio network (WLAN)?

- Which screen size do you require (from a cellular phone format to the notebook format)?
- Do you require a graphics-enabled device (because, for example, you want to view documents or connect a GIS system)?
- Which equipment must a device have (keyboard, touch screen, barcode reader, RFID scan, stylus, and so on)?
- What are the environmental requirements for the device (dust, impact, ex-protected, humidity)?
- What is a tolerable device weight for your technicians?
- What is your budget?
- Which systems are already available (for example, SAP CRM or mobile devices of a certain format)?

> **[!] Pay Attention when Choosing a Device**
> Several criteria (for example, functions, storage space, and peripheral equipment) are significant when you choose from the wide range of device types available (in particular, tablets, smartphones, notebooks, and tablet PCs).

The following sections present the SAP solutions that are available: one for an online scenario and one for an offline scenario.

8.7.2 Paging

Paging is a typical online scenario. This means that you can use the icon in a notification or order to send short messages to one or more partners. These short messages can be either predefined standard texts or texts you enter directly when sending the notification. You can also enhance predefined standard texts (see Figure 8.25).

What is paging?

Paging supports the following services:

Supported services

- Paging
- Telefax
- Email
- SMS
- SAPoffice mail

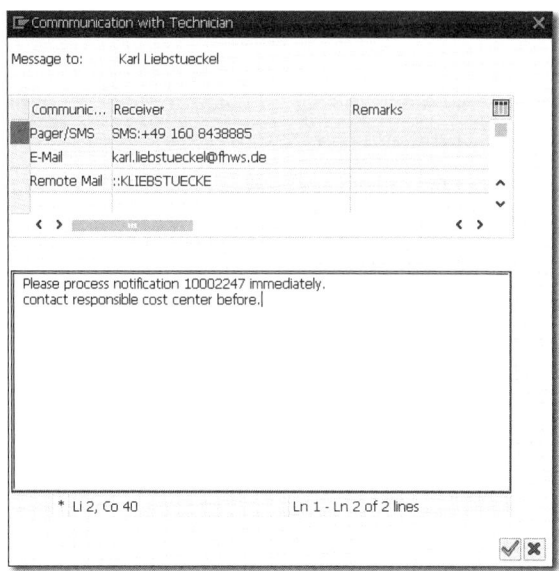

Figure 8.25 Paging

After you send the paging message, the status PAGE is set in the notification.

Prerequisites

The following prerequisites for using this function must be fulfilled:

- The SAPoffice and SAPconnect components are active.
- In Customizing, you have assigned a *paging partner* function to the notification type (Customizing function ASSIGN PARTNER FUNCTIONS TO THE NOTIFICATION TYPE).
- This partner function *paging partner* is filled in the notification (for example, by transferring the contact person from the reference object).
- The person's communication data is maintained in the user master data (Transaction SU01; see Figure 8.26).

[+] **You Can Reach the Technicians Directly with Paging**

You can use the paging function to quickly and easily send short messages to those involved (for example, the technician). This requires you to define a paging partner in the partner function and activate the SAP components SAPoffice and SAPconnect.

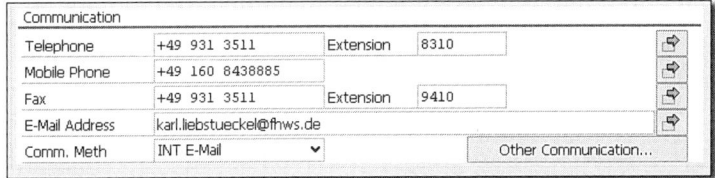

Figure 8.26 Communication Data

Mobile Asset Management (MAM), SAP Work Manager, and SAP Rounds Manager are what SAP means by mobile maintenance, and they correspond to typical offline scenarios. The following section introduces them.

8.7.3 Mobile Asset Management

Mobile Asset Management is one of SAP's mobile application solutions, based on SAP Mobile Infrastructure. In addition to MAM, there are other solutions, such as mobile warehouse management and mobile travel management (see Figure 8.27).

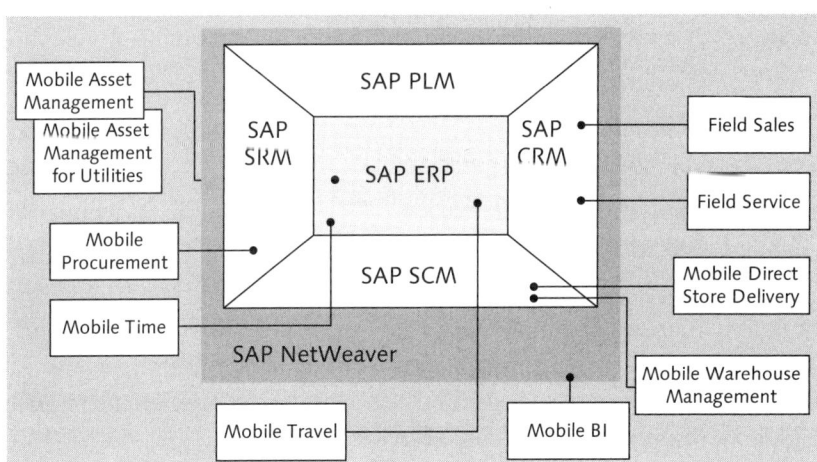

Figure 8.27 SAP Mobile Solutions

Infrastructure of Mobile Solutions

All solutions use SAP Mobile Infrastructure (see Figure 8.28).

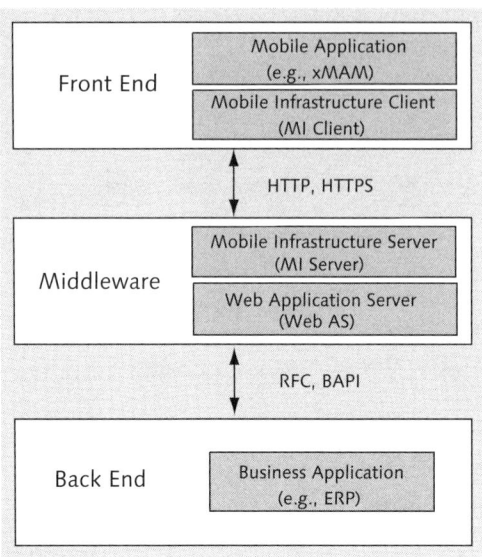

Figure 8.28 Structure of SAP Mobile Infrastructure

Mobile device
: The mobile device contains the mobile application (for example, Mobile Asset Management) and the Mobile Engine Client. The latter is basic software for configuring the device and enabling it to communicate with the middleware. You also require the Java Virtual Machine (JVM) on the mobile device.

Middleware
: The Mobile Engine Server is available as middleware; it is responsible for communicating between the mobile device and the backend. The Mobile Engine Server has a web console that enables you to connect to the devices and monitor communication (see Figure 8.29).

Assigning the user or mobile device
: In the Customizing function SET USER-SPECIFIC DATA, you define the priority procedure according to which the orders or notifications are to be assigned to the technicians or mobile devices. You can assign the following elements to the orders or notifications:

- A user master record
- A personnel number
- A maintenance task list
- A planner group

Mobile Maintenance | **8.7**

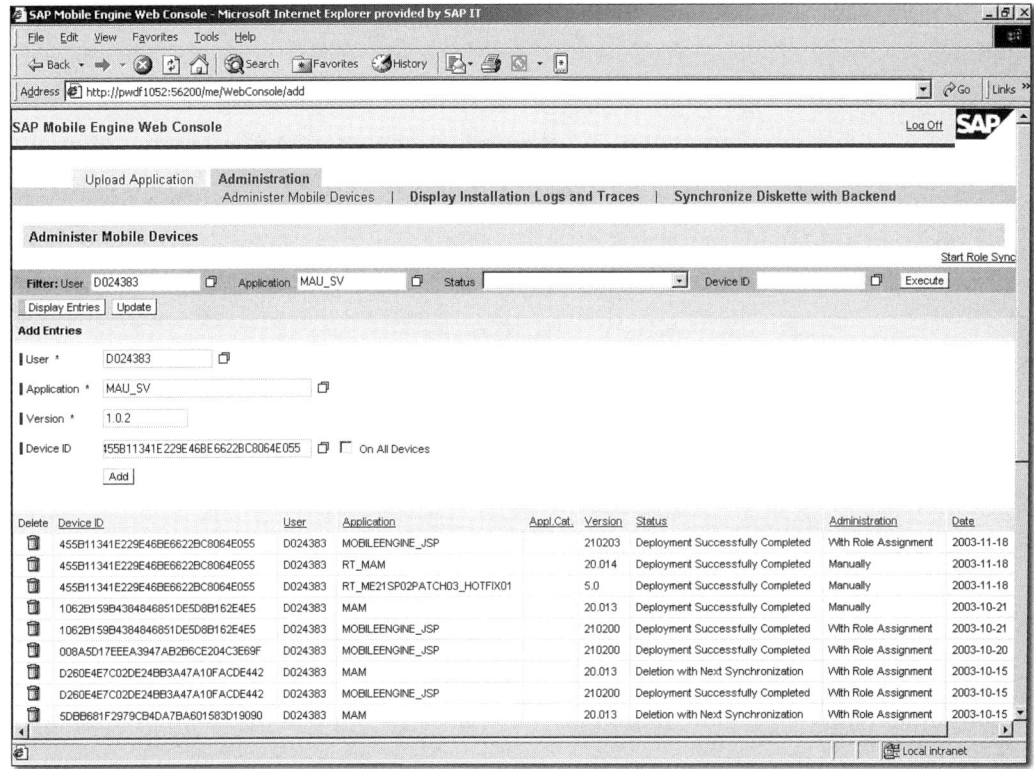

Figure 8.29 Web Console of the Mobile Infrastructure Server

Depending on the priority sequence you have defined, the notification or order is assigned to one of the persons responsible in the order or message header (see Figure 8.30).

Figure 8.30 Persons Responsible in Order and Notification

Local Layout

Depending on whether you use a notebook or PDA as a local device, different layouts are adjusted to the relevant hardware conditions.

Layouts for different device types

545

Figure 8.31 shows an example of an MAM layout on a PDA; an order list is displayed on the left, and after you choose an order, an operation list is displayed on the right.

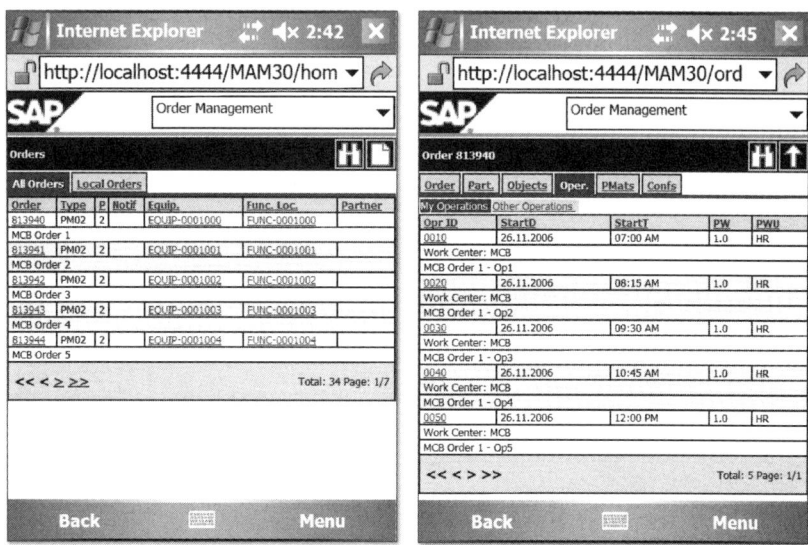

Figure 8.31 MAM Layout on a PDA

In contrast, Figure 8.32 shows the MAM layout on a notebook. Due to its size, you can naturally display more information. In this case, it is a complete order with information about the order header and operation list.

[+] **Adjust the Screen Templates**

In the case of mobile applications, I would strongly advise that you take account of the requirements of your users and then adjust the screen templates accordingly. MAM provides extensive enhancement options for screen templates.

Local Functions

If you have fulfilled the technical prerequisites, the following functions are available, depending on the function activated in the maximum configuration (see Figure 8.33):

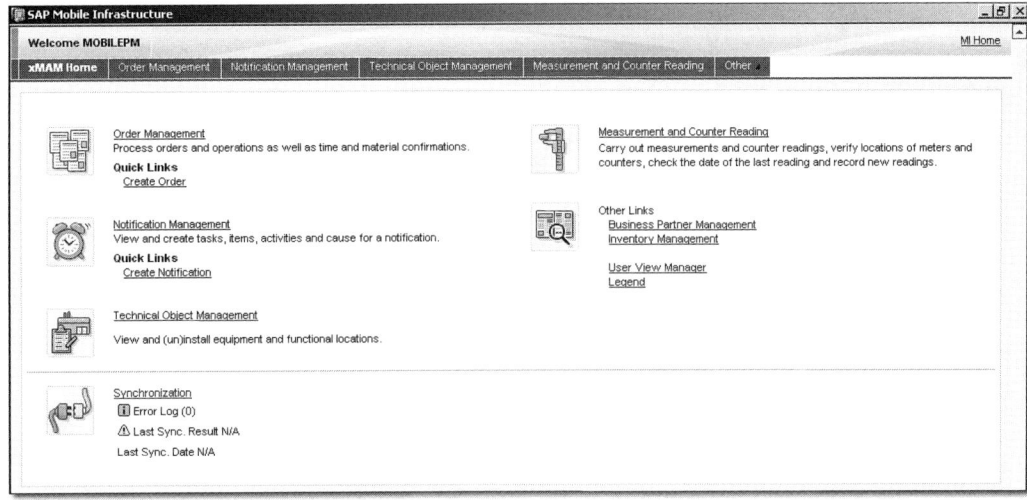

Figure 8.32 MAM Layout on a Notebook

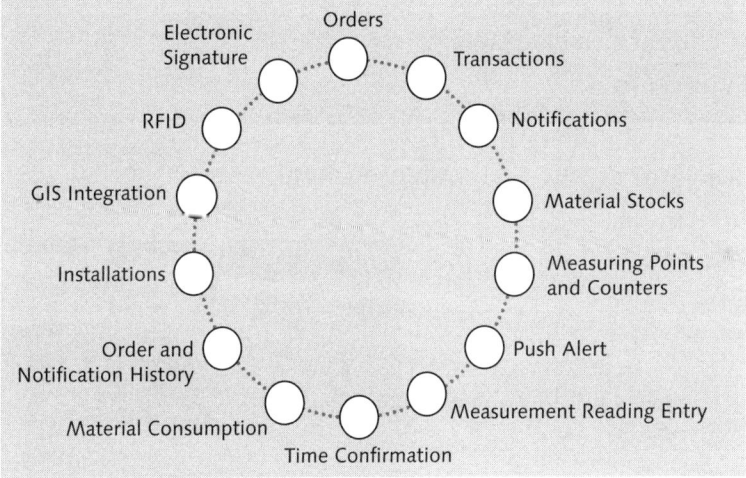

Figure 8.33 Scope of Functions in MAM

- **Order processing**
  - Display order list
  - Display order operations
  - Display object list for the order

- Display notification for the order
- Display partner for the order
- Enter time confirmation
- Enter goods issues
- Change user status
- Create orders
- Change orders

▶ **Notification processing**
- Display notification list
- Display notification
- Create notification
- Change notification

▶ **Measurement reading entry**
- Display measuring points
- Enter measurement readings

▶ **Technical objects**
- Install or dismantle equipment
- Change user status
- Display order history
- Display notification history
- Display classification

In addition to these standard functions, all of which you already know from SAP EAM, Mobile Asset Management for the mobile device has some more special functions.

Mobile push alert — Push messages, which are sent as short electronic messages (SMS) to the mobile device, are used to immediately notify technicians of urgent notifications and orders. This is similar to paging (see Section 8.7.2), but the message can be sent to several technicians simultaneously. The technicians can accept or reject the SMS. In EAM, you can track the time of the alerts and the status.

Once the technician has completed the task, he can ask the sold-to party to (electronically) sign the mobile device, or the technician can sign it. The signatures are entered on a signature pad or directly on the mobile device itself (see Figure 8.34). One or more signatures can be entered for an order. The signatures are sent to the backend and referenced as an object for the order.

Electronic signature

Use the Electronic Signature for Work Subject to Documentation	[+]
The sold-to party can add its electronic signature to accept the service, or the technician can add his electronic signature to confirm that the work for technical systems, which are subject to monitoring and documentation, has been properly executed.	

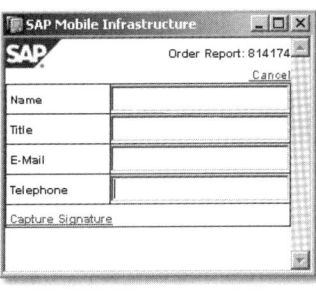

Figure 8.34 Electronic Signature

GIS integration enables your technicians to visualize (in the GIS system) the geographic location of a technical object assigned to a notification or order. The geo-coordinates of a technical object are transferred from the backend to the mobile device. The MAM application transfers the geo-coordinates of a technical object to the GIS system (mobile GIS) installed on the mobile device. You can access the mobile GIS from the MAM application (see Figure 8.35).

GIS integration

Geographic Information Supports Localization	[!]
GIS integration provides the technician with information about route optimization and improves usage flexibility with regard to using technicians who are not familiar with the site.	

Stock processing on the mobile device

You can upload a storage location defined in SAP ERP (for example, a truck) to the mobile device, and the technician can then confirm any material used to this storage location. If the material number on the storage location does not have any stock, the system indicates this fact in a notification. The material stock is updated locally on the mobile device.

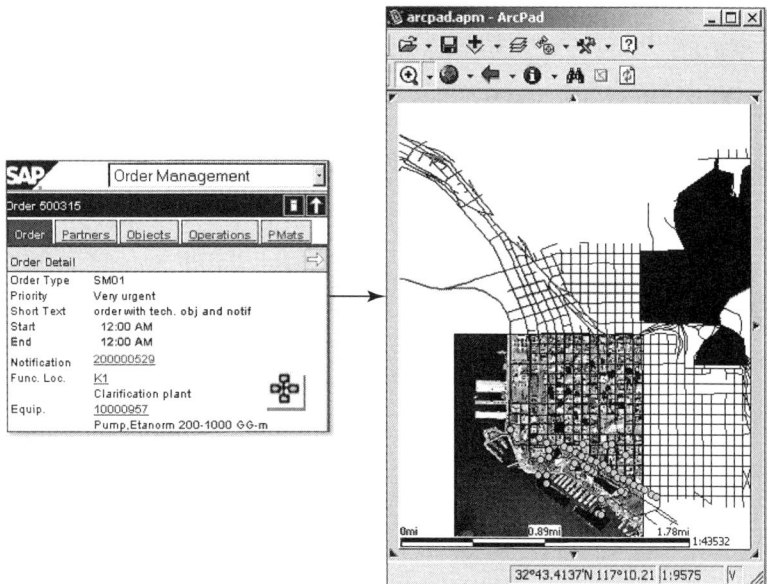

Figure 8.35 GIS Integration in MAM

We now come to the mobile applications that are available due to SAP's acquisition of Syclo.

8.7.4 SAP Work Manager

In 2012, SAP acquired Syclo, a provider of mobile business applications. This acquisition has involved both an additional technology platform and mobile enterprise applications for the following areas:

- Plant maintenance
- Field service
- Materials Management
- Releases within workflows

Two apps are available for plant maintenance:

- SAP Work Manager mobile app
- SAP Rounds Manager app

The following two sections provide more information on these two apps.

Infrastructure of Syclo Solutions

All solutions use the Agentry server to configure and manage communication between mobile devices and SAP systems (see Figure 8.36).

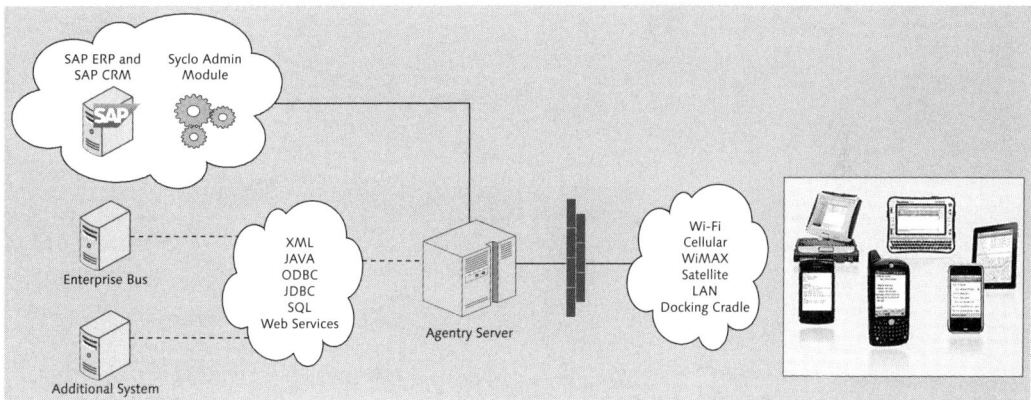

Figure 8.36 Syclo Infrastructure

You install the mobile application on the mobile device (for example, SAP Work Manager app). The technician has permanent access to it in his day-to-day activities.

Mobile device

You install the Agentry server for communication and data exchange with the SAP system; the SMART administration tool is available on the Agentry server (see Figure 8.37).

Agentry server

- **Configuration Panel**
  The Configuration Panel is responsible for the implementation and configuration of mobile applications—for example, to determine which fields are to be transferred to the frontend.

- **System Monitor**
  The System Monitor is a tool for continual implementation monitoring and problem detection. Using the System Monitor, administrators can track who logs on to their mobile application, what kind of work he performs, and what data is transferred between the mobile device and the SAP system.

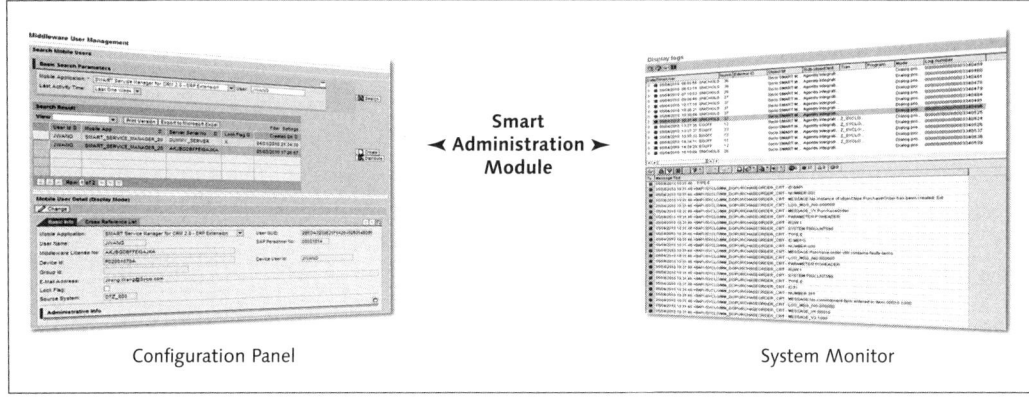

Figure 8.37 SMART Administration Tool

Local Layout

Depending on whether you use a tablet or smartphone as a local device, different layouts are adjusted to the relevant hardware conditions.

Figure 8.38 shows you two screenshots from SAP Work Manager on an iPhone as an example. An order list is displayed on the left, and information on a selected order is displayed on the right.

In contrast, Figure 8.39 shows the layout of SAP Work Manager on an iPad. Due to its size, you can naturally display more information. In this case, an order list is displayed on the left, and a complete order with information on the order header and the notification is displayed on the right.

Figure 8.38 SAP Work Manager on an iPhone

Figure 8.39 SAP Work Manager on an iPad

8 | New Information Technologies in Plant Maintenance

Local Functions

Basic functions | If you have fulfilled the technical prerequisites, the following basic functions are available in the maximum configuration:

- **Order processing**
  - Display order list
  - Display order operations
  - Enter new operations for the order
  - Display object list for the order
  - Material list for the order
  - Display notification for the order
  - Add new components
  - Enter goods issues
  - Technically complete order
  - Create orders
  - Change orders
  - Delete orders that have not yet been transferred
- **Notification processing**
  - Display notification list
  - Display notification
  - Create notification
  - Change notification
  - Delete notifications that have not yet been transferred
  - Complete notification
  - Display, change, and enter tasks
  - Display, change, and enter activities
- **Measuring point management**
  - Create new measuring point
  - Dismantle measuring point
  - Display measuring points

- Repair measuring points
- Record measurement readings and counter readings
▶ **Time recording**
- Add time confirmation
▶ **Equipment and functional locations**
- Display
- Display classification
- Display documents

> **Conclusion 1: Little Difference in the Basic Functions** [+]
>
> In the basic functions that you can expect from a mobile solution for plant maintenance, there is little difference between the two solutions MAM and SAP Work Manager. Both have all the functions that a technician requires in his normal, day-to-day activities.

As shown in Section 8.7.3, MAM has some special functions. The question now arises: what are these functions like in SAP Work Manager? Here are the answers:

Special functions

▶ **Mobile push alert**
Yes, you can also configure SAP Work Manager so that notifications and orders with priority 1 are automatically pushed to the device or devices, and a special message is displayed there.

▶ **Electronic signature**
No, SAP Work Manager does not (yet) have this function.

▶ **Stock processing with availability check**
Although a material withdrawal is integrated in the SAP Work Manager app, there is no complete inventory management. If this is necessary, you have to install the SAP Inventory Manager app, also. It has various availability checks available, as well as a complete inventory management.

▶ **Geographical information**
Yes, SAP Work Manager also has the option of locating and visualizing technical objects or orders on the basis of geographical information in a GIS system (see Figure 8.40).

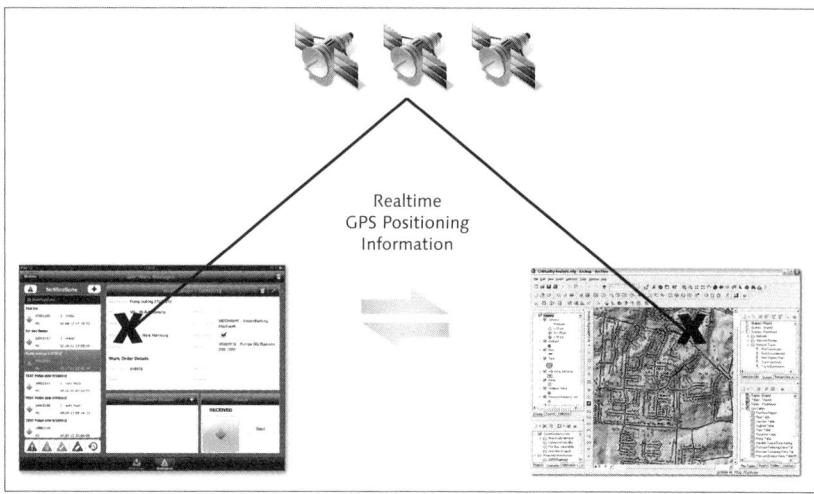

Figure 8.40 GIS Integration of SAP Work Manager

However, the reverse question must now be posed, also: are there special functions in SAP Work Manager that are not in MAM?

Yes, actually a few. They are as follows:

- **Start/Stop function**
  In addition to using the "normal" time confirmation, you also have the option of using the Start/Stop function—that is, that you choose the Start button at the start of the order to let the time run. Using the Hold function (see Figure 8.41), you can interrupt an order and complete it via the TECO function. SAP Work Manager then calculates the required time and creates a relevant time confirmation.

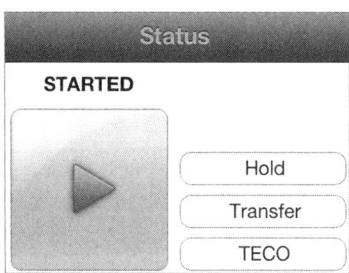

Figure 8.41 Status of SAP Work Manager

- **Transfer function**
  The same window contains the Transfer function, with which you can forward an order that has been allocated from the backend, to a colleague, for example, if you cannot currently process this order due to lack of time.
- **Notes function**
  The Notes function is available for the order (see Figure 8.39), for each operation, each material component, and the notification. The status history is shown in it, on the one hand, and you can enter notes there, on the other hand. In the backend, these are then created either in the long text or as an object service.
- **Timesheet**
  You can not only enter times in the timesheet, but also display the times you have booked in each period according to various selection criteria.

Figure 8.42 shows such a timesheet (together with the initial screen) of SAP Work Manager on an iPhone.

 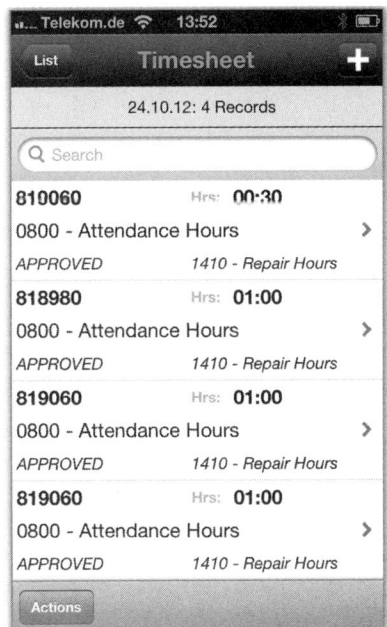

Figure 8.42 Initial Screen and Timesheet of SAP Work Manager

- **Speech recognition with Siri**
  Speech recognition via Siri is an excellent option for avoiding the need to manually enter data and texts in particular (for example, confirmation texts or damage descriptions for new orders to be created), especially for the iPhone, on which entering text is somewhat laborious. However, Siri is available only for iPhone models later than 4S or iPads later than 3 and only for iOS versions greater than 5.0. If you meet these requirements, you can enter your data into SAP Work Manager via speech. I have tried it, and it works!

- **Graphical display**
  Similar to SAP NetWeaver Business Client, SAP Visual Enterprise Viewer is integrated into SAP Work Manager. The options here are exactly the same as I already presented in Section 8.6.6 under the heading "SAP Visual Enterprise Viewer":

  - **Display graphics**
    You can display 2-D images or 3-D scenes for pieces of equipment and functional locations.

  - **Select spare parts**
    You can use 2-D or 3-D images to select and determine the required spare parts. You have the option of selecting one or more spare parts in the image and transferring them to the spare parts list. The various display functions, such as disassembling or rotating the model, assist you in selecting (see Figure 8.43).

  - **Animate maintenance task lists**
    You can visualize instructions, for example, as 3-D scenes, which visualize the individual steps of the plant maintenance task (see Figure 8.44).

Figure 8.43 3-D Model Spare Part Selection in SAP Work Manager

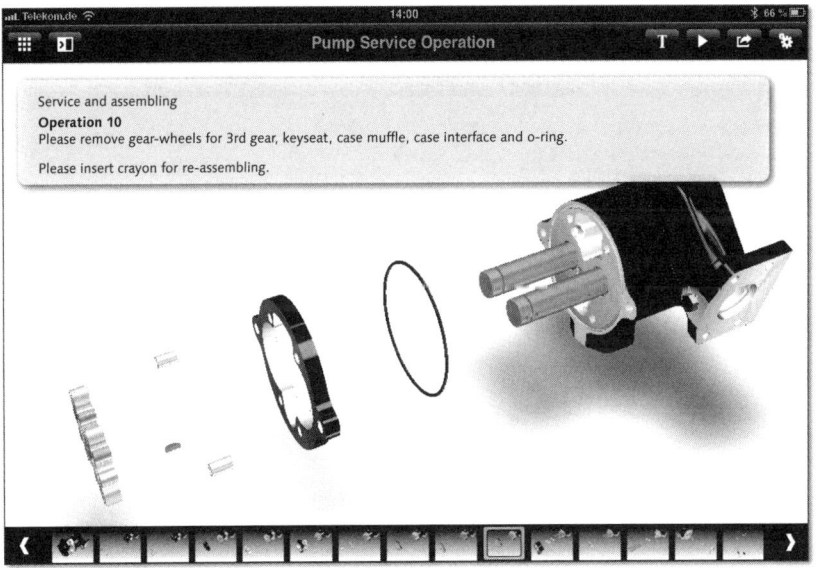

Figure 8.44 Animated Instructions in SAP Work Manager

In addition to SAP Work Manager, yet another app is aligned with the needs of maintenance: SAP Rounds Manager app, which you will learn about in the following section.

8.7.5 SAP Rounds Manager

SAP Rounds Manager is aimed at user companies that operate a performance- and condition-based maintenance (see Section 5.8 and Section 5.9) and want to include the required counters' readings and measurement readings for this purpose. The values can be entered individually or in list form. They are then buffered on your mobile device until the next synchronization takes place.

SAP Rounds Manager app has the following functional scope:

- Displaying a measurement reading entry list (see Figure 8.45)
- Creating a new measurement reading entry list
- Deleting a measurement reading entry list
- Creating a new measuring point (equipment, functional location, neutral)
- Displaying a measuring point
- Recording measurement readings and counter readings

Figure 8.45 Measurement Reading Entry List in SAP Rounds Manager

> **Conclusion 2: Significant Differences in the Additional Functions** [+]
>
> In terms of additional functions, there are significant differences between MAM and the new mobile solutions. In addition to SAP Work Manager, SAP provides not only SAP Rounds Manager, but also integrated pioneering—technological innovations that facilitate the maintenance technician's work on site (for example, speech input) and make it more reliable (for example, by visualizations).

It would be missing the point to focus solely on functional scopes because there are even more non-functional aspects that should be considered, and I would like to introduce them briefly next.

8.7.6 Other Aspects of Mobile Platforms

To make the comparison as clearly and concisely as possible and, thus, as transparent as possible, I have summarized the individual aspects in tabular form (see Table 8.2).[11] For further and more in-depth information, I would like to refer to other sources.[12]

Aspect	MAM	SAP Work Manager
Device independence	☹ Only Windows	☺ iOS, Android, Windows
Adjustment, Configuration	☹ Eclipse, old Java version, no adjustments without special expertise	☺ Eclipse, current Java version, better tools, simple adjustment
Support of partners	☺ Broad partner network	☹ Partner network conceived only during development
Operating concept	☺ Outdated frontend	☺ State-of-the-art frontend

Table 8.2 Comparison of Non-Functional Aspects of Mobile Platforms

---

11 Presentation and statements are essentially based on Wessendorf, M.: Die mobile Plattform muss her, in: SAP.info from 11.6.2012.

12 For example, Beckert, A.; Beckert, S.; Escherich, B.: Mobile Lösungen mit SAP, Bonn: SAP PRESS, 2012.

Aspect	MAM	SAP Work Manager
Maintenance commitment	☺ Through 2020 (discontinuation of maintenance of SAP ERP 6.0)	☹ SAP makes maintenance commitments only through to the next release, currently 2014
Middleware	☺ Somewhat dated middleware, but integrated in SAP NetWeaver	☺ Powerful, but additional middleware (in addition to SAP NetWeaver)
Manageable complexity	☹ Complexity that is difficult to manage	☺ Less effort required for implementation
Pioneering	☹ No	☺ Yes

Table 8.2 Comparison of Non-Functional Aspects of Mobile Platforms (Cont.)

[+] **Conclusion 3: SAP Work Manager Has the Advantage, Even for Non-Functional Aspects**

There are still some aspects that favor MAM (for example, the well-developed network of partners or the long-term maintenance commitment), but otherwise, the advantages lie clearly with SAP Work Manager or SAP Rounds Manager. Both run on all platforms, have a modern frontend, and can be easily implemented and adjusted. The critical points will be qualified over time: the partner network will grow, and it can be assumed that SAP will extend its maintenance commitments.

An additional special function of mobile solutions is of groundbreaking and outstanding significance: the RFID technology, which can support all mobile solutions.

8.7.7 RFID

What is RFID?

RFID stands for *radio frequency identification*. It is a procedure for automatically identifying an object, animal, or person. In addition to the non-contact identification of objects, RFID is also used to automatically enter and save data.

▸ **RFID components**
An RFID system comprises a transponder, which is on or in the object (and known as an RFID tag; see Figure 8.46), and a reader for reading

the transponder ID. In our case, the latter would be the RFID function of the mobile device.

Figure 8.46 RFID tag

- **Storage capacity**

    The storage capacity of an RFID chip ranges from 1 bit to several kilobytes. The volume of data required on the tag (for example, equipment number, maintenance date, and time) will determine what variant you choose.

- **Range**

    Depending on the technical equipment, transponders have a range of between a few centimeters and 10 meters.

Safety Due to Short Distances	[!]
If you use RFID tags with a low range, the data can be read only from a short distance. So, you can be reasonably sure that the technician has completed his work (see Figure 8.47[13]).	

- **Writability**

    There are two types of transponders: non-writable and writable transponders. For writable transponders, you must distinguish between nonvolatile storage (that is, the data is preserved even without a power supply) and volatile storage, which requires a permanent power supply to preserve the data.

---

13 Entnommen aus Psion (Hrsg.): (See also Psion (eds.):) Radio Frequency Identification (RFID) Solutions, London 2012.

Figure 8.47 Short-Range RFID Tag

This book will not discuss RFID technology in any greater detail here. If you want to learn more about RFID technology and some of its general uses, please refer to the extensive reading material on this subject.[14] Instead, it provides some specific examples of when this technology is used in SAP's plant maintenance.

RFID scenarios

In MAM Customizing, you can use the DEFINE SCENARIO function to activate or deactivate the standard RFID scenarios. You can use the following scenarios separately or in combination:

- **Scenario 1 (order processing)**
  When you first activate this scenario, you cannot modify any orders on the mobile device. You cannot process orders or enter confirmations until the reference object's RFID tag has been read. If several orders are assigned to the same reference object, you can select one order from the list.

---

14 For example, Götz, T.: SAP-Logistikprozesse mit RFID und Barcodes, Bonn: SAP PRESS 2010, or Franke, W.; Dangelmaier. W.: RFID-Leitfaden für die Logistik, Wiesbaden 2006 (*RFID Logistics Guide*, Wiesbaden), or Gillert, F.; Hansen, W.: RFID für die Optimierung von Geschäftsprozessen, München 2006. (*RFID for the Optimization of Business Processes*, Munich)

- **Scenario 2 (maintenance history)**
  If this scenario is activated, you can write the confirmation data to the RFID tag of a technical object. So, the confirmation data is available the next time the technical object is processed.
- **Scenario 3 (reference data transfer)**
  If this indicator is selected, you can use the data that was read from the RFID tag of a technical object when you create a notification or order.

If a mobile solution (MAM, in this case) and RFID technology are used in a typical business process, the process may then look as shown in Figure 8.48.

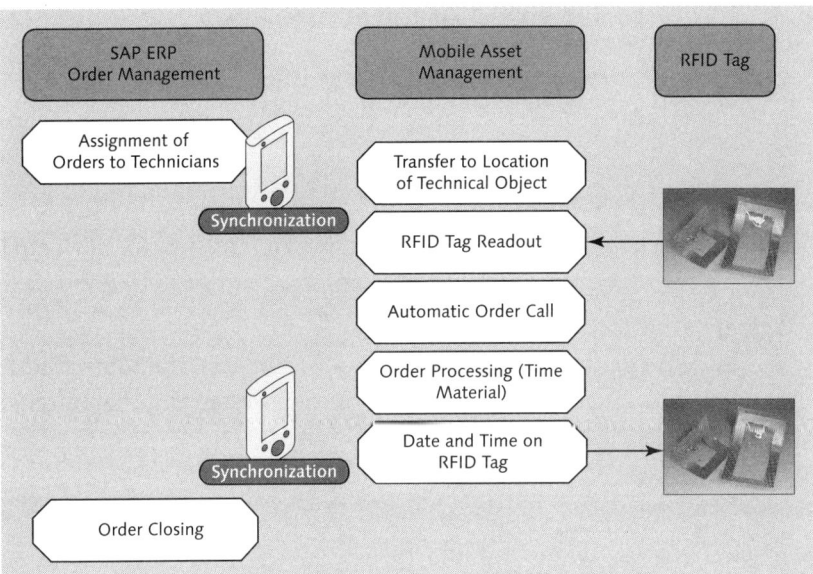

Figure 8.48 Process with MAM and RFID

| Using RFID where It Makes Sense | [!] |

What does the RFID function contribute to mobile maintenance?

- It is used to uniquely identify an object.
- When the RFID tag for a technical object is read, the stored data is displayed.

> ▶ Associated orders are released and displayed; that is, the technician cannot start his work until he has "logged on" to the technical object.
>
> ▶ When you create a notification or order, you read the data from the RFID tag of the technical object, and the new document receives an error-free assignment to the technical object in question.
>
> ▶ For the confirmation, the data is written to the RFID tag and, therefore, considered evidence of having performed the work.

Another concept that may be useful in the future is Service-Oriented Architecture (SOA).

8.8 Service-Oriented Architecture

What Is SOA? The term *service-oriented architecture* (SOA) is primarily a management concept that also requires a system architecture concept (see Figure 8.49[15]):[16]

▶ **Management concept**
The management concept seeks to achieve an infrastructure oriented toward the preferred business processes.

▶ **System architecture concept**
The system architecture concept allows for the provision of technical services and functionalities in the form of services that map atomic process steps.

[!] > **SOA = System + Organization**
>
> It is important to note that the SOA is based on the separation of the business process level and system level.

Unlike other providers of SOA platforms, SAP (with its SAP NetWeaver offering) not only provides the system architecture, but it also delivers the services that can be used to model your business processes:

SOA + enterprise services = service-oriented architecture

---

15 From SAP AG (eds.): Enterprise Services Repository – An Overview, Walldorf 2007.
16 See also the description at *http://www.wikipedia.org/*.

Service-Oriented Architecture | 8.8

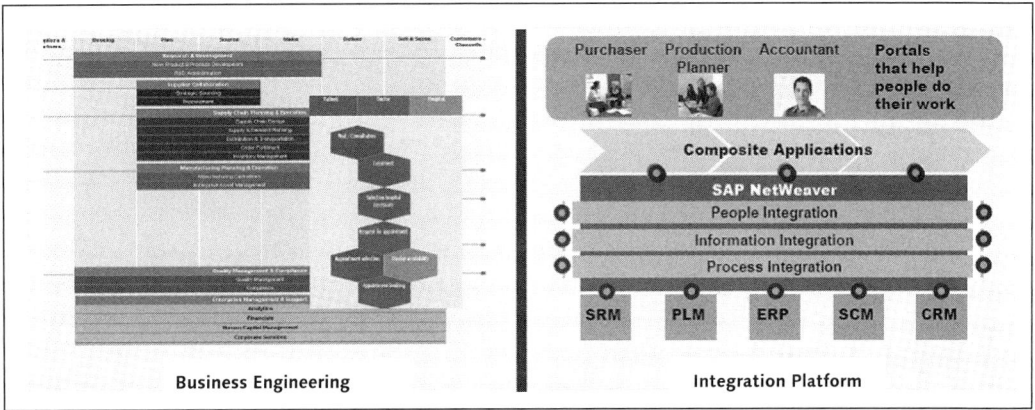

Figure 8.49 Concept of Service-Oriented Architecture

One result of this could be, for example, that you can access several backend systems when processing a business process from a web-based interface, and you can read or write data for these backend systems (see Figure 8.50).

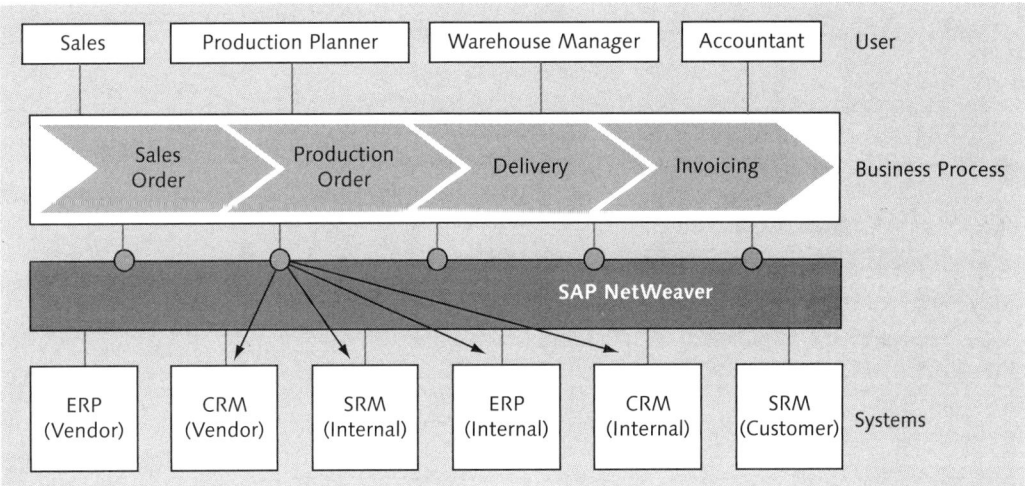

Figure 8.50 Cross-System Business Processes

As part of a business process, a user executes certain functions (for example, the opening and closing of a production order by the production planner) and may trigger a maintenance request when necessary if

What are enterprise services?

567

8 New Information Technologies in Plant Maintenance

there are problems with a machine. In accordance with SAP terminology, each of these functions could be an enterprise service.

What are web services? An enterprise service comprises several detailed functions. For example, the following detailed functions may result from opening a production order: MATERIAL MASTER CHECK, MATERIAL AVAILABILITY CHECK, DATA ENTERED IN A PRODUCTION PROGRAM, SALES NOTIFICATION, EXPLODED BOMs, and many other functions. These could be *web services* within an enterprise service. Technology components such as APIs, RFCs, and so on are used to enable a web service to access the backend systems (see Figure 8.51).

This book will not discuss this concept in further detail, but I refer you to some relevant reading material.[17]

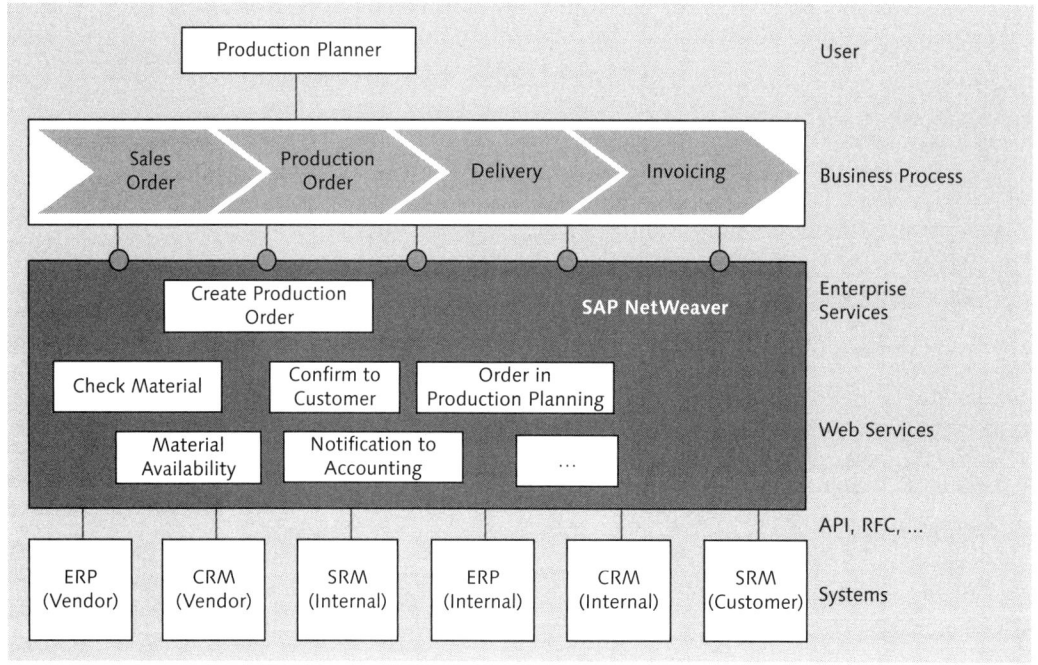

Figure 8.51 Services

---

17 For the management concept, for example, Hack, S.; Lindemann, M.: Enterprise SOA Roadmap, Boston) SAP PRESS, 2007. For the architecture concept, for example, Woods, D. Mattern, T.: *Enterprise SOA – Design IT for Business Innovation*, O'Reilly Media, 2006.

What Does All of This Have To Do with Plant Maintenance?

SAP delivers a maintenance processing enterprise bundle for plant maintenance. Initially, an enterprise bundle is simply a collection of logically related business processes. In this case, the following five sample business processes for maintenance processing are concealed behind this bundle:

- Service bulletin processing
- Warranty monitoring
- Repair or replace decision support
- Maintenance order processing
- Reliability-centered maintenance (based on the partner product RCMO from Meridium Inc.)

Enterprise bundle

Each of these sample business processes comprises a series of enterprise services. For example, the sample business process entitled *maintenance order processing* contains enterprise services such as the following:

Enterprise services in plant maintenance

- Create maintenance request (create notification)
- Read maintenance request (display notification)
- Change maintenance request (change notification)
- Create maintenance order (create order)
- Find employee by work center (assign employee)
- Change maintenance order (change order)
- Read maintenance order (display order)
- Create maintenance confirmation (create confirmation)
- Dismantle individual material (dismantle equipment)
- Install individual material (install equipment)

Each enterprise service contains a BAPI or API. In plant maintenance, these internal program components have extensive functions. For example, the ORDERMAINTAIN BAPI can add object list entries, enter components, form operations, enter partners, and so on. So, the enterprise services in plant maintenance are not subdivided further into several web services.

Web services in plant maintenance

How Can You Use SOA in Plant Maintenance?

Your initial situation and objective will determine whether you will use an SOA for your maintenance processes.

> [!] **SOA in Plant Maintenance Possible Only Under Very Specific Conditions**
>
> Only if one of the following situations applies should you consider employing SOA over other technologies (I am not saying that you should use it):
>
> - You have to integrate other systems into your maintenance processes.
> - You want to swap out individual processes or functions from SAP ERP and make them available on a web user interface.
> - You want to integrate other technologies into your existing processes.

Case 1 occurs, for example, if you process your maintenance processes in EAM:

- But the spare parts are ordered in system X
- But the technical system documents are managed in system Y
- But controlling takes place in system Z

Case 2 applies, for example, if:

- The craftsmen enter their confirmations, but otherwise should not access SAP ERP.
- You want to create an upstream transaction for displaying information from different applications or writing data to these applications.
- Your providers record service entry sheets, but should not access your SAP ERP system.

Case 3 applies, for example, if:

- You want to create a notification or order from a CAD system.
- You want to connect a mobile solution other than SAP MAM.
- You want to transfer the malfunction data from a manufacturing execution system (MES).

In each case, you should check whether there is an alternative technology and whether this would be a better or worse option. If, for example, you require an upstream transaction, an equally good upstream transaction could be developed within SAP ERP. If you want to connect an MES system, you could possibly access the PM-PCS interface (see Section 6.4.1).

> [+] **SOA Normally without Added Value for Plant Maintenance Users**
>
> If none of these situations applies to you, if you process your plant maintenance in the SAP ERP environment only, and if the other technologies available suffice for your maintenance processes, then you will not benefit from SOA at present.

The last new technology I will discuss seems more promising and groundbreaking: SAP HANA.

8.9 SAP HANA

SAP has never marketed a product as much as SAP HANA (HANA stands for high-performance analytic appliance), a database technology SAP introduced in 2010.[18] It involves a combination of hardware and software to enable higher performance by using the in-memory technology compared to the traditional applications. In-memory technology means that the data is not stored on the hard disk, but in the computer's memory; thus, access is much faster. SAP HANA was developed by SAP to enable very large databases (keyword: big data) to be browsed more efficiently.

What is SAP HANA?

SAP HANA combines techniques from the hardware and software sectors. On the software side, SAP HANA constitutes a hybrid of the column-oriented functioning of in-memory databases and row-oriented functioning of relational databases.

How Does SAP HANA Work?

On the hardware side, an attempt is made to move as much as possible from the hardware memory to the CPU cache and from the disk storage to the main memory to take advantage of the faster access speed in each case.

---

18 For example, Neumann, A.: http://www.heise.de/developer/meldung/SAP-liefert-Appliance-fuer-In-Memory-Computing-aus-1145612.html. heise.de, 1.12.2010.

8 | New Information Technologies in Plant Maintenance

SAP Business Suite on HANA

SAP HANA was initially designed for the analytical applications (such as BW or SAP BusinessObjects). Today, SAP focuses increasingly on the use of SAP HANA in applications. On January 10, 2013, SAP announced the availability of core applications of SAP Business Suite on HANA in a press release.[19]

Scenarios

For using SAP HANA, there are two fundamentally different types of scenarios: the side-by-side scenarios (see Figure 8.52[20]) and the integrated scenarios (see Figure 8.53).

- **Side-by-side scenarios**
  In the side-by-side scenarios, only certain data is extracted from the SAP Business Suite, transferred to SAP HANA, processed there, and issued with SAP HANA apps, or the results are returned again to the SAP Business Suite. Another side-by-side scenario would be the extraction of data from SAP Business Suite. The data is then loaded into BW, which runs on an SAP HANA database, and evaluated there.

- **Integrated scenarios**
  For the integrated scenarios, the complete application—that is, both the business processes (transactions)—and the evaluations run on an SAP HANA database.

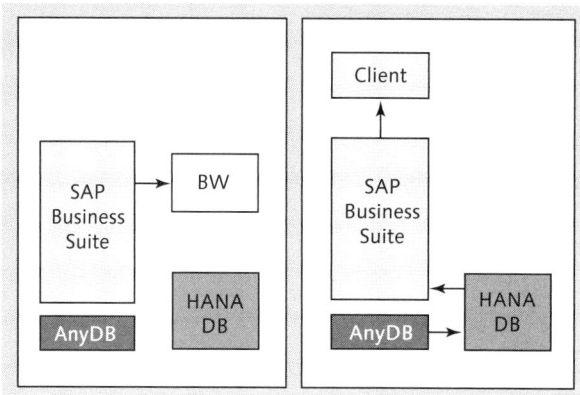

Figure 8.52 Side-by-Side Scenarios

---

19 SAP press release from January 10, 2013.
20 For both figures, see Gerhard Oswald: Keynote auf dem DSAG-Jahreskongress 2012. (Keynote at the DSAG Annual Congress 2012).

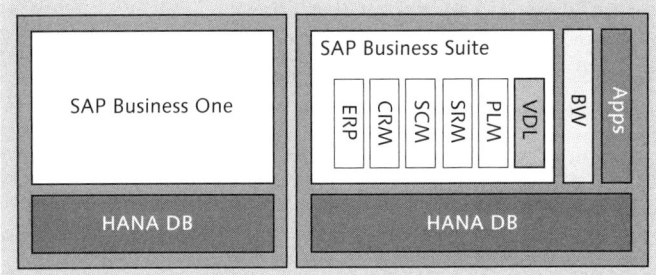

Figure 8.53 Integrated Scenarios

In the aforementioned press release from January 10, 2013, SAP announced that it will provide a Service Pack for customers who want to use certain functions of the SAP Business Suite under SAP HANA (side-by-side scenario). This Service Pack is also included in SAP ERP 6.0 EHP 6 Version for SAP HANA.

For existing customers who want to migrate their databases completely to SAP HANA (integrated scenario), SAP has developed Rapid Deployment Solutions.[21]

SAP HANA and maintenance

You may now wonder what all of this has to do with maintenance. There are two answers to this question.

If your organization should decide to convert the SAP Business Suite completely to an SAP HANA database (that is, to use the integrated scenario), EAM would also be affected. In this case, all transactions you have to complete in your day-to-day activities (notifications, orders, confirmations, maintenance plans, and so on) would be performed in a HANA-based manner. It remains to be seen what improvements in performance can be achieved in this scenario.

Maintenance in the integrated scenario

In the side-by-side scenario, there is also a new function from a maintenance perspective: maintenance plan scheduling.

Maintenance in the side-by-side scenario

---

21 See SAP press release from January 10, 2013.

A new Transaction IP30H is available for the mass scheduling of maintenance plans.

Until now, the maintenance plans were scheduled with the scheduling function DEADLINE MONITORING OF MAINTENANCE PLAN (Transaction IP30). So that the respective runtime would not be too long, you had to select in a targeted manner to avoid scheduling too many maintenance plans at once.

With the new Transaction IP30H, you can now simultaneously schedule *all* maintenance plans that are due within a certain period of time. You do not have to make any parameter restrictions because the system already performs a pre-selection, in which it takes numerous parameters into account (for example, data, maintenance strategies, or counter readings).

On the initial screen (see Figure 8.54), you specify for which advance period of time you want to create the call objects (for example, orders) and how many processes are to be started in parallel.

It is ensured that the system processes *all* due maintenance plans and *only these* maintenance plans. This is particularly important for customers from asset-intensive industries who have to manage a large number of maintenance plans.

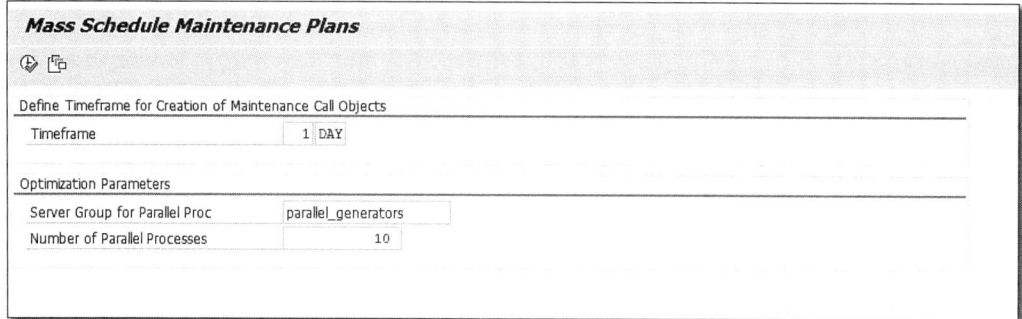

Figure 8.54 Initial Screen of Transaction IP30H

In monitoring (see Figure 8.55), you are informed of the number of objects that have been processed, runtimes that have been achieved, and status of the processes.

According to the initial experience reported by users, the new transaction for maintenance plan scheduling, Transaction IP30H, achieves a 300-fold (!) performance compared to the old Transaction IP30. When Transaction IP30H was repeatedly started, a performance increase by a factor of 1,000 was even measured, which is good news for all users' companies that have to schedule a large number of maintenance plans.

Initial experience

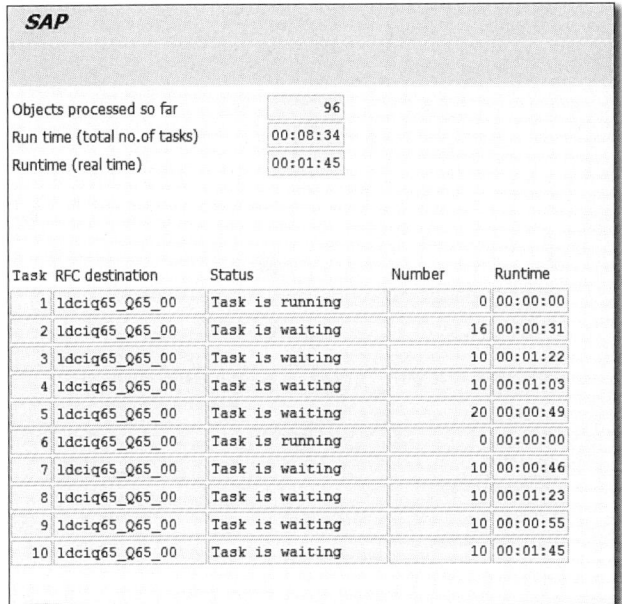

Figure 8.55 Monitoring in Transaction IP30H

As with every chapter, I have once again gathered the most important information about *new technologies* and all relevant tips and tricks I wish to pass on to you.

It is a widespread prejudice that usability is not a major feature of the SAP system. This chapter, therefore, intends to show the possibilities the SAP system offers to improve usability. In an empirical laboratory test, we set up real-world conditions to test whether—and if so how—the time it takes to process business processes can be reduced by improved usability.

9   Usability

There is a reason why this chapter was placed in a prominent position at the end of the book. The subject matter of this chapter is particularly important, and I would like to give it the attention it does not receive in many companies.

It is a common judgment by self-appointed experts and an even more common prejudice among those who know the SAP system only from hearsay that:

- There is not much importance given to usability.
- It takes too long to process business transactions.
- The screens are overloaded with information.
- SAP is not usable at all.

All I can say is: that's right. It is right for the following reasons:

- Many companies use standard settings, screens, and processes when implementing SAP and expect their end users to work with them.
- In my experience, many companies do not pay much attention to this aspect when implementing SAP.
- Many companies do not make ample use of the tuning options the SAP system provides by default—if they even know about them.

It is, therefore, a particular concern of mine to use this final chapter to explore the possibilities for enhancing usability and introduce the results from a laboratory test conducted at my university under real-world conditions.

Perhaps this will help to alleviate the prejudice that the SAP system is not very user friendly.

For a clearer understanding, we have to explore the following four questions:

- What is meant by Usability?
- How can usability be measured?
- Does usability mean the same as user acceptance?
- Why is usability of such importance in plant maintenance?

This chapter will describe the individual tuning measures and point out where and why they can improve usability. Finally, it will introduce the laboratory test and its results, which have been central in answering the following question: by how much can the processing time for a business process be reduced if tuning measures are applied?

9.1 What is Meant by Usability?

Terminology and standards

Usability refers to the user-friendliness that a user experiences when interacting with a system. A system has high usability if its operation is easy and in accordance with the user's requirements and the tasks to be performed.[1]

In a standardization context, this is typically also referred to as the *ergonomics* of a software product. In the DIN EN ISO 9241 standardization series, in Part 110 (Dialogue Principles), this, in turn, is defined as the product of *effectiveness*, *efficiency*, and *user satisfaction*. Whereas hardware ergonomics refers to the adaptation of tools to the movement and perception apparatus of humans (for example, body forces and movement spaces), software ergonomics deals with the adaptation to the cognitive and physical abilities and characteristics of humans, such as their capacity to process information (for example, complexity), as well as software-controlled display features (for example, colors and font sizes).

---

1 See DIN EN ISO 9241, Part 110 (Dialogue Principles).

In DIN EN ISO 9241-110, seven principles have been defined (see boxes below). Because the standardization texts, by themselves, do not provide a lot of information, this chapter contains a few examples to illustrate how the relevant principle could be implemented in an SAP system.

> **Principle 1: Suitability for the Task** [!]
>
> A dialog supports suitability for the task if it supports the user in the effective and efficient completion of the task.

Examples of the suitability for the task in the SAP system include the following:

- A transaction should not require information that has nothing to do with processing the relevant business process.
- In an input screen, the cursor should be placed in the first field to be completed or corrected.
- The sequence of input screens and fields should be designed in a way that is needed for the logical processing of a business process.

> **Principle 2: Self-Descriptiveness** [!]
>
> A dialog supports self-descriptiveness if each dialog step is immediately comprehensible through feedback from the system or explained to the user upon his or her request for the relevant information.

Examples of self-descriptiveness in the SAP system include the following:

- Links are formulated in such a way that their target is clear.
- An application has an online help system providing context-specific information.
- Erroneous entries trigger comprehensible error messages that contain explanatory long texts about how the error can be undone or avoided.

> **Principle 3: Controllability**
>
> A dialog supports controllability if the user is able to maintain direction over the whole course of the interaction until the point at which the goal has been met.

Examples of controllability in the SAP system include the following:

- Transactions contain buttons or menu functions that enable you to navigate directly to any screen of the process.
- Lists contain buttons that enable you to sort the information in any column according to diverse criteria (e.g., date or quantity).
- If a database request takes too long, it can be cancelled.

> **Principle 4: Conformity with User Expectations**
>
> A dialog supports conformity with user expectations if it corresponds to the user's task knowledge, education, and experience, as well as commonly held conventions.

Examples of conformity with user expectations in the SAP system include the following:

- Identical terms should be used to convey identical pieces of information (e.g., a G/L account must always be referred to as a G/L account).
- Identical buttons should be used for identical functions (e.g., the same icon should always be used to enable the deletion of an entry).
- When you press the Tab key, the cursor jumps to the next input field.

> **Principle 5: Error Tolerance**
>
> A dialog supports error tolerance if, despite evident errors in input, the intended results may be achieved with either no or minimal corrective action. Errors should be explained to the user for him to correct them.

Examples of error tolerance in the SAP system include the following:

- Before data is saved, it is automatically checked for plausibility and missing or incomplete information.
- In case of an incorrect data input, the cursor jumps directly to the respective field, which is highlighted in color.
- Error messages are not displayed in technical jargon or as a number, but formulated such that the user understands them.

> **Principle 6: Suitability for Individualization** [!]
>
> A dialog supports suitability for individualization if the dialog system is constructed to allow for modification to the user's individual needs and skills for a given task.

Examples of suitability for individualization in the SAP system include the following:

- In a customized list, the user can determine which information should be displayed, how it should be sorted, and so on.
- The user can define customized default values in order to avoid re-entering standard information, such as plant, company code, and so on.
- The user can set which dialog boxes are to be used in order to support his or her business processes (e.g., warnings prior to saving data).

> **Principle 7: Suitability for Learning** [!]
>
> A dialog supports suitability for learning if it guides the user through the learning stages, minimizing the learning time.

Examples of suitability for learning in the SAP system include the following:

- Users are introduced to the business process in a "guided tour."
- Alternatively, external tools that demonstrate the processing of a business process to the user are provided.
- Before saving, the system allows for simulated executions or test postings.

The following principle applies in all cases: usability is highly inconspicuous because it is meant to serve its assigned function and no other secondary purpose. Usability becomes noticeable only if it is missing.

From a superficial point of view, we could maintain that the SAP system meets all criteria of software ergonomics. In addition to the examples previously listed, there are numerous other examples for each of the seven principles, which could confirm that the software of the SAP system is ergonomic.

Counterexamples in the SAP system

Why then does the SAP system have the reputation of not ranking high in terms of usability? Why do SAP users often have the feeling it is all just too complicated and difficult? The answer is simple: in the standard version, there are also many examples that bear testimony to the opposite:

- The sequence of screens (dialogs, tabs) does not match the workflow of the user.
- The data required for a business process is spread out over several screens.
- Identical fields have different field labels (e.g., vendor and supplier, G/L account and cost element).
- The screens are overloaded with unnecessary information.
- The SAP system still contains a large number of hard-coded lists that cannot be manipulated by the user.
- In addition, the design of these lists is outdated.
- Lists contain many pages of entries even though all the user wants to see is the orders of his cost center, for example.
- The user has to enter data that is not needed for his specific purpose, such as the plant, purchasing organization, business area, or cost element.
- The user has to manually retrieve information from the SAP system, instead of the system presenting information to him.
- In certain circumstances, the user has to call more than five subsequent transactions for a business process.

- Almost never can the user simulate or temporarily store his data before saving it to the database.
- The user repeatedly has to click away pop-up windows.
- The SAP system contains three to four different icons that enable the deletion of entries.
- The pushbutton bar is sometimes positioned in the upper area of the screen and sometimes at the bottom, without any recognizable underlying pattern.
- The user abhors the multilevel SAP menu.

These and similar complaints abound and should not be ignored, but taken seriously.

> **Counteract the Non-Usability Reproach in an Offensive Manner** [+]
>
> During the implementation phase, be attentive to the concerns of your employees regarding the usability of the SAP system. Do not ignore the topic, but address your employees' concerns and try to find a solution by implementing appropriate measures.

9.2 Assessing Usability

To assess the usability of an IT system, we can rely on a qualitative assessment of its users and/or base the assessment on quantitative criteria.

To measure usability by qualitative assessment, different methods, such as surveys, observation, questionnaires, and so on, are used to obtain a subjective evaluation from the users of the system. As you have seen in the previous section, usability and ergonomics involve many subjective aspects. Therefore, user assessment will also be subjective and vary depending on the user and situation.

Qualitative assessment

Results obtained from quantitative methods, for which data can be collected, are much more reliable, objective, and stable.

Quantitative assessment

Processing time key figure After all, everything is reflected in a single key figure: the *processing time key figure*, which represents the time it takes a user to process a business transaction in the system.

Therefore, the main focus is on processing time when you explore the possibilities for improving usability (see Section 9.5), and we will use this key figure in the laboratory test (see Section 9.6).

Control entries key figure In addition to the processing time, another key figure can be used as a measurement of usability: the *control entries* key figure. Control entries are those interactions that are required for controlling the IT system but do not involve data entry. These interactions include the pressing of buttons and [Tab] and [Enter] keys.

Other key figures Other values that allow for assessing usability include the following:

- Number of screens
- Number of mouse clicks
- Time spent looking at a screen
- Length of the mouse trail

You must decide yourself whether collecting this kind of key figure will add value to your company when assessing system usability.

9.3 Why Usability Does Not Mean User Acceptance

Particularly in the IT industry and IT departments, you often encounter the predominant opinion that an improved usability automatically entails an increase in user acceptance. Another assumption is that usability is the only means of achieving the relevant acceptance among users.

In my opinion, both assumptions are wrong; indeed, they are serious mistakes. This is because the actions taken to increase user acceptance must consist of both actions taken to increase usability *and* organizational measures (see Figure 9.1).

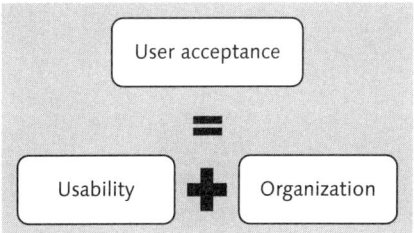

Figure 9.1 User Acceptance

But what organizational measures help you to increase user acceptance? I have run numerous workshops on the subjects of *usability* and *user acceptance*, and in each of these workshops, the participants have developed organizational measures in order to increase user acceptance. Here are some of these measures:

Organizational measures

- Large monitors were used.
- SAPLogon was made available on each computer.
- An intranet help site was set up.
- A small wiki was created.
- Only a small number of options were made available (e.g., for the damage codes).
- Key users were selected from the group of participants.
- Participants trained participants (the so-called "Hey Joe effect").
- A hotline was set up that could be called at any time by the participants (i.e., 24 hours a day), particularly during the early stages.
- Alternatively, a central email address could be set up that automatically responds that a service person calls back within a timeframe to be defined (e.g., no later than 30 minutes).
- During the implementation phase, feedback was collected from the participants and implemented as far as possible.
- Also during the implementation phase, the participants were regularly presented with the latest status of the system.
- The participants were profoundly informed about what was going to happen with the data they had entered.

- The necessity of the respective data entries was emphasized, particularly the correctness of the data.
- Official praise was expressed when, in the preceding year, the number of correct messages exceeded a given figure.
- There was and still is a lot of persuading done, and in particular, the benefits and necessity of using the SAP system are demonstrated.
- End users were intensively involved in the test phase.
- The company representatives are members of user groups (e.g., in the "Plant Maintenance and Service Management" work group of the German SAP User Group or the "User Interface" work group).
- Immediately after the training, the participants were enabled to sift through what they had just learned. For this purpose, they were given a certain amount of time, as well as a test system. In fact, without this possibility of knowledge consolidation, they would quickly have forgotten much of what they had been taught.
- Handouts were created in the language of the technician.
- The business process was visualized by means of a simple event-driven process chain, and SAP transactions were entered.
- Simple operating instructions were created, laminated, and could easily be placed underneath each keyboard.
- The processes were recorded using the relevant tools (such as Datango) and made available to the technician.
- And again and again, it was training, training, training. It was this measure, in particular, that was regarded as extremely important in all discussions.

[+] **Use the Right Approach when Training Your Employees**

When planning and implementing trainings, you should employ the following principles:

- Modularize your trainings. The training of individual modules should take approximately half a day; the absolute maximum is one entire day.
- End-user training should be carried out by employees in your company—ideally, by the representatives of the departments in the project team.

- For the training, use the system environment and examples of the technical objects that the end users will encounter in their work later on.
- Finally, carry out the end-user training close to the time of the go-live; otherwise, the users will forget much of what they learn by the time of the go-live.

The list of measures to increase the user acceptance could be continued endlessly, particularly because each company has its own specific organizational measures. Therefore, you should heed the following advice.

The Organization Is as Important as Usability [+]

Make an informed decision as to which organizational measures are likely to increase the user acceptance in your company.

9.4 The Importance of User Acceptance in Plant Maintenance

The aspects of *usability* and *user acceptance* play an important role in all areas of an organization. However, in the technical areas of a company, which include plant maintenance, their role is substantial.

The reasons the usability and user acceptance of the SAP system are considered more important in Plant Maintenance than in Financial Accounting, Controlling, or Purchasing can be regarded as follows:

- **Number of users**
  The first reason has to do with the number of users involved during implementation. During implementation of commercial applications, the number of users involved is relatively small, whereas you will delve much more deeply into a company's operation and work with a much larger number of users during EAM implementation. This is especially the case if technician need to generate or confirm orders themselves.
- **Level of training and experience**
  The second reason has to do with the level of training and experience

with IT systems. Whereas users from the commercial part of the company already have experience using IT systems and are well trained, in an extreme case, the users you meet during EAM implementation might be sitting in front of a computer for the first time, and even using a mouse and a keyboard might be challenging for them. If users from plant maintenance are slightly more experienced, they might know Office applications or computer-based maintenance systems, but generally, they have no experience using integrated business software such as the SAP ERP system.

▸ **A different approach to handling orders**
Moreover, the approach to handling orders is different from the one employed in Controlling (CO), for example. In Controlling, an internal order is considered more in terms of a cost collector, standing order, annual order, life cycle order, and so on. In plant maintenance, the emphasis is on processing as many activities as possible as measure-related individual orders for assignment and weak-point analysis reasons. As a result, the number of maintenance orders completed in plant maintenance during the course of one year significantly exceeds the number of internal orders, which is why the maintenance orders must be easier to handle than CO internal orders.

▸ **Equipment of work center**
In contrast to employees in many other departments (such as Controlling or Purchasing), employees in plant maintenance often have no assigned work center of their own in which to use the SAP system, for example, in order to print shop papers or display open notification lists. Instead, several employees have to share a work center. For this reason, as the end of a shift approaches and each employee wants to enter their own confirmations, a high level of usability is required to ensure that the system can be used by one employee after another without any unnecessary delays.

▸ **Concrete tasks**
Finally, the concrete tasks assigned to an employee in the company are important: a financial controller posts his items to internal orders or cost centers and analyzes them, an accountant records received invoices and checks balance lists, a purchaser processes his purchase

orders and checks his outline agreements, and every one of them needs an IT system to complete the specific tasks. Every employee enters data into the system and retrieves information from it. However, the tasks assigned to a maintenance engineer basically comprise maintenance and inspection, and not the operation of an IT system, which is why he does not need an IT system to carry out his actual tasks.

The reasons listed above make it an absolute necessity during EAM implementation to apply every effort to increase the usability of the system as much as possible. By default, SAP ERP provides many tools to increase usability. The following section will describe these tools from the point of view of plant maintenance.

> [!] **User Acceptance Is Particularly Important in Plant Maintenance**
>
> For the following reasons, the aspects of *user acceptance* and *usability* play a key role in plant maintenance:
>
> - In plant maintenance, you have a wide variety of users.
> - Many users do not have IT experience or training.
> - Plant maintenance has a different order philosophy than Controlling.
> - The actual job of a maintenance engineer consists of maintenance, which means that he does not need an IT system.

There is no guarantee that the system is accepted by the users or considered user friendly. However, you can improve the probability by remembering the following principles and making them the benchmark in all your decisions regarding system characteristics:

Principles for increased usability

- **Keep the system as simple as possible!**
  This may sound like a commonly used cliché, but experience has shown that user companies do not make use of all options to enhance the usability of the SAP system, either because they do not know about them or because they decide not to use them for other reasons.
- **Apply every effort to increase usability!**
  To achieve this, you have to invest time and effort in the design of your SAP system.

- **It is difficult and requires a lot of effort to provide a simple system. It is easy and requires less effort to provide a complex system.**
  The following comparison may illustrate this: wasn't it easier for you in school to describe a colorful, vivid, and varied painting by van Gogh than an empty inkpot? The same applies to the SAP system. A seemingly perfect system that tries to solve all problems at once, a system that tries to cover all eventualities, is probably so vast and complex that it severely reduces users' willingness to accept it. It is better to forgo some embellishments, to personalize functions, and possibly leave them out altogether to make it easy for users to do their daily jobs.
- **Prioritize!**
  The following statement was made by a speaker at the end of his presentation (and I agree unreservedly):

  It is better to have 80% of the system you want with 100% user acceptance than 100% of the system you want with 20% user acceptance.

9.5 SAP System Options to Improve Usability

This section describes the possibilities for simplifying and accelerating the processing of business transactions in Plant Maintenance.

These options can be divided into three categories, and you should consider employing them in your company in the order shown here.

- **Category 1**
  Options available to the user himself or herself
- **Category 2**
  Options available to the IT department without programming
- **Category 3**
  Options available to the IT department with programming

Table 9.1 provides an overview of the measures related to each of these categories.

Category	Who?	What?
1	Users	▶ General user parameters
		▶ Maintenance-specific user parameters
		▶ Role menus and favorites menus
		▶ List variants
		▶ Personalized input helps
		▶ Table controls
		▶ Buttons and key combinations
		▶ SAP NetWeaver Business Client
2	IT department (without programming)	▶ Transaction variants
		▶ Customizing
		▶ Action box
		▶ GuiXT
3	IT department (with programming)	▶ Upstream transactions
		▶ Web user interface
		▶ Easy Web Transactions
		▶ SAP NetWeaver Portal
		▶ Customer exits
		▶ Business Application Programming Interfaces (BAPIs)
		▶ Classical business add-ins (BAdIs)
		▶ Enhancement points
		▶ Workflows

Table 9.1 Options to Improve Usability

The following section describes the options related to Category 1 in further detail. You will learn not only *what* you can do, but also *how* you should do it. Because the options in Categories 2 and 3 require Customizing and even programming work, only their functions will be described in this book (i.e., the *what*). *How* you should use these options will be described in the book *Configuring SAP Plant Maintenance*, which will be published by SAP PRESS in 2014.

9.5.1 General User Parameters

From a user's point of view, many entries required by the SAP system remain unchanged over a period of time, such as the following data:

- The user is linked to a specific work center.
- The work center, in turn, is assigned to a specific cost center.
- The user works in a specific plant.
- The user is responsible for a specific functional location.

When we look at this in terms of individualization, it helps the user if fields are pre-assigned using user parameters. To pre-assign fields, you can use Transaction SU3 or the SYSTEM • USER PROFILE • OWN DATA menu. Once defined, these fields are populated with the assigned values when business transactions are processed.

Figure 9.2 lists parameter IDs, which are commonly used in Plant Maintenance.

Set/Get parameter ID	Parameter value	Short Description
AAI	pm01	Parameters, order type, maintenance orders
AGR	mechmnt	Work Center
BUK	3000	Company code
EKO	3000	Purchasing organization
EKP	100	Purchasing Group
EQN	P-1000-N003	Equipment number
IFL	K1-B02	PM: Functional Location
IWK	3000	Maintenance planning plant
KOK	2000	Controlling Area
KOS	1000	Cost center
LAG	0001	Storage location
MTA	ROH	Material type
QMR	M1	Notif. type
Q_ALV_GRID_INACTIVE		ALV Grid in QM/PM/SM Inactive
SWK	3000	Maintenance plant
WGR	007	Material group

Figure 9.2 General User Parameters

| Use F1 Help to Find a Parameter ID | [!] |

You can save processing time by pre-assigning fields using parameters. You can view the relevant parameter ID in the Technical Info of the F1 help.

9.5.2 Maintenance-Specific User Parameters

In addition to the general user parameters, there are also maintenance-specific user parameters. From within the notification, you can access them via EXTRAS • SETTINGS • CONTROL/DEFAULT VALUES and from within the order via EXTRAS • SETTINGS • DEFAULT VALUES.

The maintenance-specific user parameters contain the following information:

- **Default values**
  Order type, notification type, functional location, etc. (see Figure 9.3)
- **Control options**
  Suppression of pop-up windows, integration of maintenance task lists, etc. (see Figure 9.4)

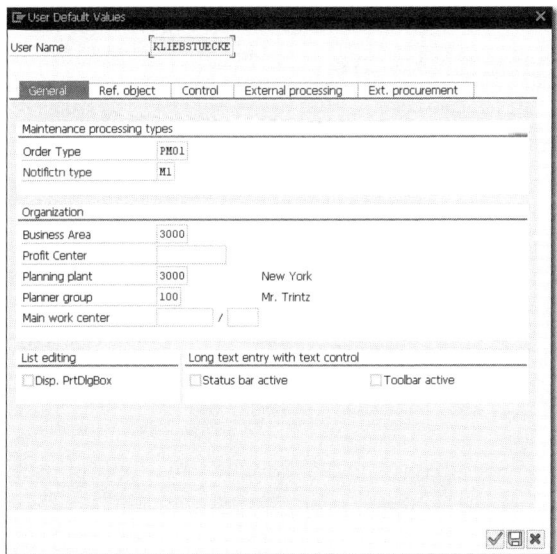

Figure 9.3 Maintenance-Specific Default Values

9 | Usability

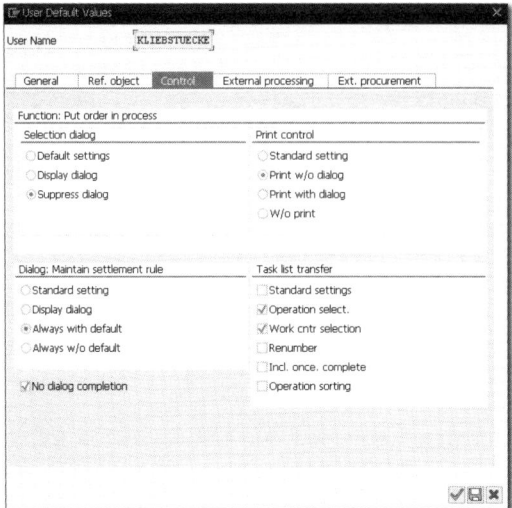

Figure 9.4 Custom Control Options

The SAP system hereby contributes to both individualization and controllability.

> [+] **Use Maintenance-Specific Parameters**
>
> Pre-assigning fields using maintenance-specific parameters reduces the processing time and allows you to control processing steps.

9.5.3 Roles and Favorites

Role menu — Transaction PFCG enables you to create role-based menus. These menus have a much more simple structure than the SAP standard menu, which in Plant Maintenance can consist of up to seven levels. Starting a transaction from a role menu is, therefore, much quicker than starting it from an SAP standard menu. If a role menu has been assigned to you, it automatically displays in the initial SAP screen (see Figure 9.5).

Favorites menu — A further simplification is provided by favorites, whereby the user adds only the required transactions (see Figure 9.6). Favorites menus can consist of one or several levels. Launching a transaction from a favorites menu is generally much quicker than doing so from the SAP standard menu.

9.5 SAP System Options to Improve Usability

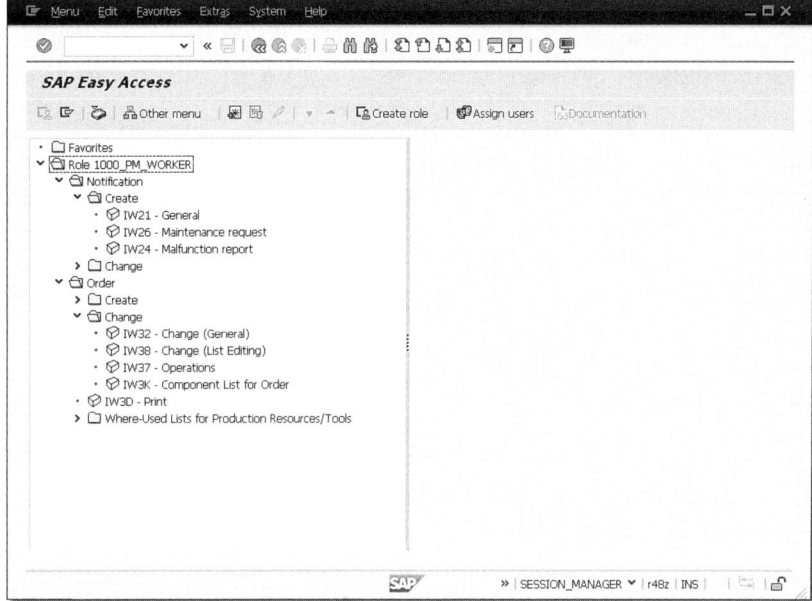

Figure 9.5 Role Menu

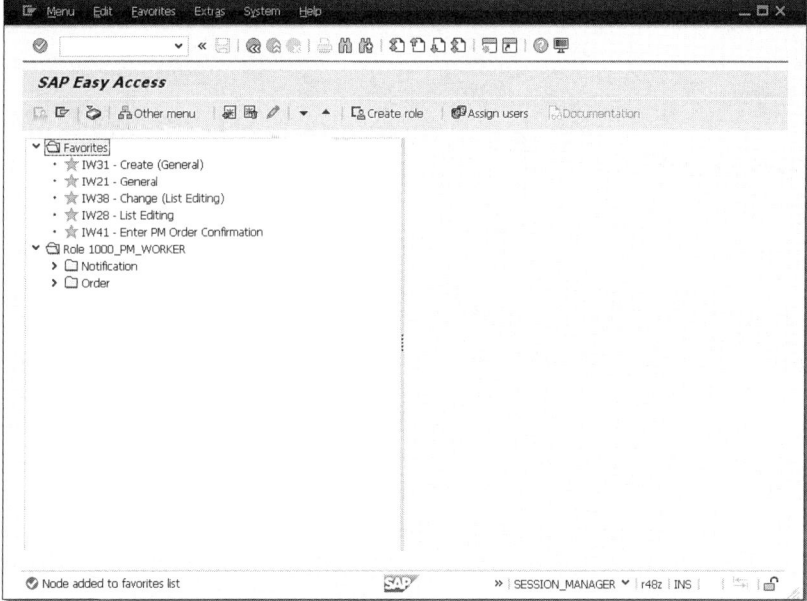

Figure 9.6 Favorites Menu

Note the following restriction: each user creates his or her own favorites menus, which means no other user can access them. However, you can copy favorites menus to other users via FAVORITES • DOWNLOAD TO PC or UPLOAD FROM PC.

[+] **Use Roles and Favorites Menus**

Role-based menus and favorites reduce the launch time of transactions. Favorites menus can be copied to other users using the download and upload functions.

9.5.4 List Variants

You can save a lot of time by providing your users with the relevant selection and display variants. Section 7.2.1 has already introduced you to the options provided by SAP List Viewer.

[!] **Guidelines for List Variants**

When creating list variants, you should follow the guidelines below.

- Find out what information your users need. Use this to define selection variants and the appropriate display variants.
- The selection variants should not contain more than one page of selection criteria.
- Users should be able to save the most commonly used selection variant as U_USERNAME and select the most commonly used display variant as a default setting.

9.5.5 Personalizing Input Help

Long F4 help — An [F4] help usually displays all entries. This list of all entries can be very long (for example, material groups, object type, and damage), although the user typically needs only a few entries from the list.

Value list — However, you can define a personal value list. From the relevant field (for example, material group), access the [F4] help, highlight the required entries, and add them to your personal value list using the 🗒 button.

The next time you call the F4 help for this field again, your personal value list, instead of the entire list, is displayed automatically (see Figure 9.7). You can use the ⊗ button any time to return to the complete value list.

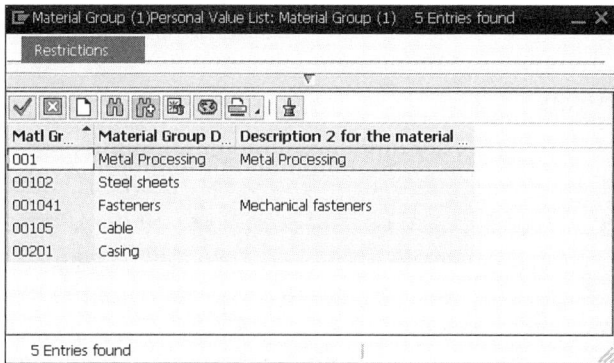

Figure 9.7 Personal Value List

| Use the Personal Value Lists | [+] |

In an F4 help, a personal value list saves time finding the correct entry.

9.5.6 Buttons and Key Combinations

Ever since the mouse has been introduced as a control element for computers, opinions have been divided about whether operation is quicker with or without a mouse. All users have to answer this question for themselves. But if you prefer using the keyboard to enter data, you should consider using key combinations and buttons.

| Create Key Combinations | [+] |

You should provide important and generally valid key combinations for users who prefer using the keyboard.

Examples — not only in the area of plant maintenance — include the following:

- Use the `F11` key to save a document. This function corresponds to the disk icon in the system toolbar.
- Another popular trick is the key combination `F4` + `Enter` in date and time fields. This copies the current date or time into these fields.
- The `F4` key generally calls a value list.

9.5.7 Table Controls

Table controls represent a generally unknown and, thus, unused option personalize the SAP system according to an end-user's specific requirements. Whereas SAP screens used to be hard coded, i.e., all fields were located in a firm position, today many screens have been switched to the table control technology, which enables the user to personalize the layout and sequence of fields.

Examples of table controls in plant maintenance and related areas include the following:

- Operations list (see Figure 9.8), components list, service specification, and object list in the order
- All partner overviews
- Item, causes, measures, and activities overviews in the notification
- Time confirmation, measurement reading entry, goods issues, and activities in the overall completion confirmation
- Item overview in the maintenance plan
- Operation overview, component overview, maintenance packages, and service specifications in the maintenance task list
- Collective confirmation
- Item overview for goods issue
- Item overview in purchase requisitions
- Item overview in purchase orders

Op...	Work ctr	Plant	Co...	Operation short text	LT	Work	Un	N...	Dur.	Un
0010	MECHMNT	3000	PM01	disconnect electrical supply			30MIN			30MIN
0020	MECHMNT	3000	PM01	external inspection: rust , leaks			30MIN			30MIN
0030	MECHMNT	3000	PM01	internal inspection: erosion, rust			30MIN			30MIN
0040	MECHMNT	3000	PM01	inspect wiring, insolation			30MIN			30MIN
0050	MECHMNT	3000	PM01	change brushes			30MIN			30MIN
0060	MECHMNT	3000	PM01	safety test , motor operational			15MIN	1		15MIN
0070	MECHMNT	3000	PM01				HR			HR
0080	MECHMNT	3000	PM01				HR			HR
0090	MECHMNT	3000	PM01				HR			HR
0100	MECHMNT	3000	PM01				HR			HR

Figure 9.8 Table Control—Operations List

All these and many other table controls allow you to make the following settings:

- You can drag and drop the columns in order to arrange their sequence to your specific requirements.
- You can change the width of each column so that it corresponds to the length of your data entries.
- You can hide unneeded fields by sliding the margins of a column together so that it completely disappears.

The most important of all these options is that you can save these settings as a user-specific variant. For this purpose, there is the 🔳 button in the top right-hand corner of each table control. This button allows you to open a detail screen in which you can create your settings as a variant and thereby overrule the default settings (see Figure 9.9).

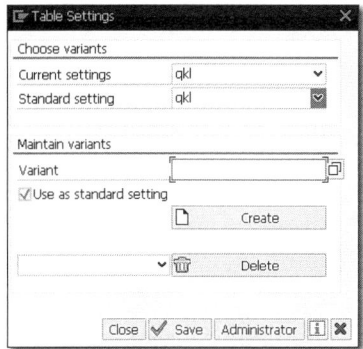

Figure 9.9 Table Settings in Table Controls

> **[+] Use the Table Controls Extensively**
>
> Individualized table controls that have been saved as variants enable you to substantially reduce the time needed for entering and finding data in the screen templates and, thus, increase the system usability to a great extent.

New in EHP 6 — SAP ERP 6.0 with EHP 6 provides a special feature for you and your users: previously, the operation overview and component overview table controls contained only a selection of fields predefined by SAP. The purchasing data, in particular, was sorely missed. This has changed in EHP 6 so that now you can maintain all relevant purchasing data in these two table controls, such as vendors, material groups, goods recipients, unloading points, or purchasing groups (see Figure 9.10).

To be able to maintain the purchasing data in the operation overview and components overview table controls, you must activate the LOG_EAM_CI_5 Business Function.

At this point, the options of Category 1 in which each user can make his or her own specific settings come to an end. Let us now take a look at the options of Category 2, which, in most companies, are the responsibility of the IT department but do not require any programming work. The following sections describe the functionality of these options, as well as of those of Category 3 (IT including programming), which means that only the *what* will be described. You can find detailed information about *how* you should use these options in the book *Configuring SAP Plant Maintenance*.

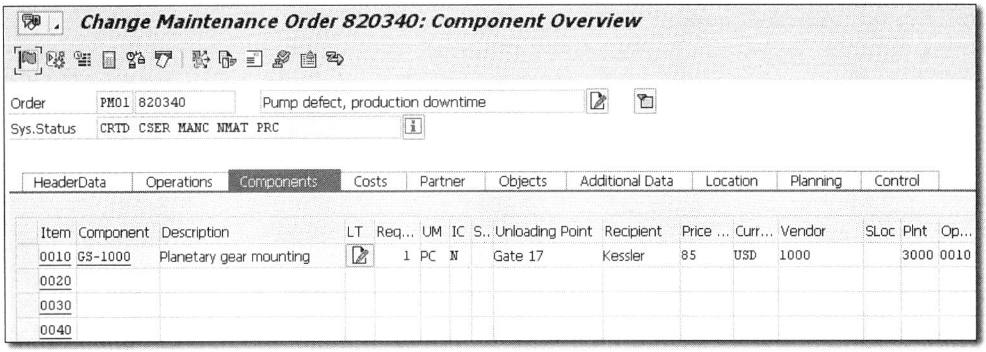

Figure 9.10 Purchasing Data in the Component Overview

The first option you may want to look at is that you can create any number of variants for an original transaction, the so-called transaction variants.

9.5.8 Transaction Variants

If a transaction—a typical case would be Transaction IW31 (Create Order)—is used to process different business transactions and is used by different user groups, it often makes sense to adjust the transaction flow to the respective business transaction or the respective user group. For example, the process of creating an order would vary depending on which of the following user groups creates an order:

- Customer or provider
- Electrician or mechanic
- Planner or technician

This is where transaction variants come in handy.

Transaction Variants Allow you to Customize Any Transaction [+]
You can create any number of transaction variants for an original transaction. In a transaction variant, you can do the following: - Hide entire screens - Hide individual tabs - Disable menu functions - Disable buttons - Set the field selection control for individual fields (display, required, hide) - Populate the field content - Modify the column sequence, change the column width, and hide columns for table controls - Assign a name to the transaction

Figure 9.11 shows an example of Transaction IW31, for which a transaction variant has been created.

9 Usability

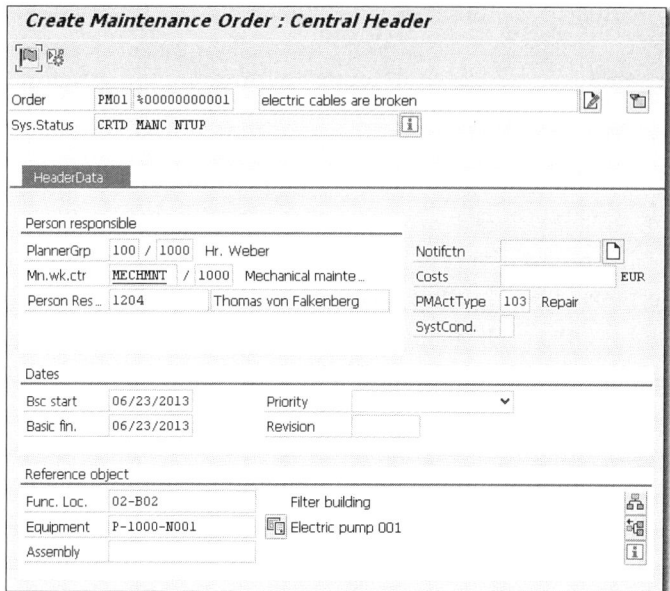

Figure 9.11 Transaction Variant for Transaction IW31

The following measures have been taken to simplify the screen:

- The initial screen for Transaction IW31 has been skipped.
- The content of certain fields has been populated (for example, the ORDER TYPE and PRIORITY).
- Apart from one tab, all the other tabs have been hidden (for example, OPERATIONS and MATERIAL).
- Menu functions and buttons have been disabled (for example, SETTLEMENT RULE, SCHEDULE, and PAGING).
- Subscreens have been hidden (for example, the operation detail in the order header).
- Some fields have been hidden (for example, PERSON RESPONSIBLE).
- A unique transaction name (here: Transaction ZW31) has been assigned, from which the transaction variant can be called.

The result is a transaction that has been significantly reduced compared to the original and contains only the screens, fields, and functions the user needs.

9.5.9 Customizing

Customizing also provides many possibilities to improve usability. In the following list, you will find the most important Customizing functions including a description of their functionality wherever the function names are not self-explanatory. The sequence of the Customizing functions in this list corresponds to the sequence of Customizing functions in the SAP Reference IMG.

- **Set View Profiles for Technical Objects**
  Screen layout for equipment and functional locations
- **Define Field Selection for Functional Locations**
  Define required fields and hide fields
- **Define Field Selection for Equipment Master Record**
  Define required fields and hide fields
- **Define Transaction-Based Default Values for Object Types**
  Populate equipment type or type of functional location
- **Maintain Settlement Profile**
  Default values for account assignment
- **Overview of Notification Type · Screen Areas in Notification Header**
  Reference object of the notification
- **Set Screen Templates for the Notification Type**
- **Set Field Selection for Notifications**
  Define required fields and hide fields
- **Assign Transaction Start Values**
  Populate notification type and skip initial screen
- **Assign Notification Types to Order Types**
  Populate order type for notification type
- **Configure Order Types**
  Reference object of the order
- **Create Default Value Profiles for External Procurement**
  Default values for material and service procurements
- **Define Notification and Order Integration**
  Enter notification and order data in one screen; automatically transfer long text from notification to order

- **Basic Order View · Define View Profiles**
  Define screen layout for orders
- **Define Default Values for Component Item Categories**
  Default value for item category for each material type
- **Message Control**
  Control whether a warning, error, or no message is to be issued
- **Define Field Selection for Order Header Data (PM)**
  Define required fields and hide fields
- **Define Field Selection for Order Operations (PM and CS)**
  Define required fields and hide fields
- **Define Field Selection for Components (PM and CS)**
  Define required fields and hide fields
- **Set Screen Templates for Completion Confirmation**
  Screen layout for overall completion confirmation
- **Set Field Selection for Completion Confirmation**
  Define required fields and hide fields

[+] **Goal-Oriented Customizing Improves Usability**

Customizing provides many possibilities to enhance the usability of SAP EAM. Especially note the options for adjusting the screen layout in notifications, orders, and overall completion information.

In addition, you should make specific use of field selection control, particularly for hiding information.

9.5.10 Action Box

When you process messages, you can use the action box in order to carry out subsequent actions that may facilitate the message processing. Once finished, these subsequent actions are documented as actions or measures.

You can launch the functions directly from within the notification, which is where you will return automatically once the function is completed. Figure 9.12 shows some examples of actions in the action box:

- Create an internal note
- Log a telephone call
- Trigger a telephone call via SAPhone
- Send an SAP mail or email
- Post a goods issue
- Create a repair order
- Search for a problem or solution in the solution database
- Create a quality notification
- Generate an 8D report
- Create a maintenance plan
- Assign a bill of material

As you can see, these are all functions for which you would normally have to leave the notification processing and that, thus, facilitate the processing of a business process.

The DEFINE ACTION BOX Customizing function enables you to store additional functions apart from the ones shown in Figure 9.12.

Prerequisites

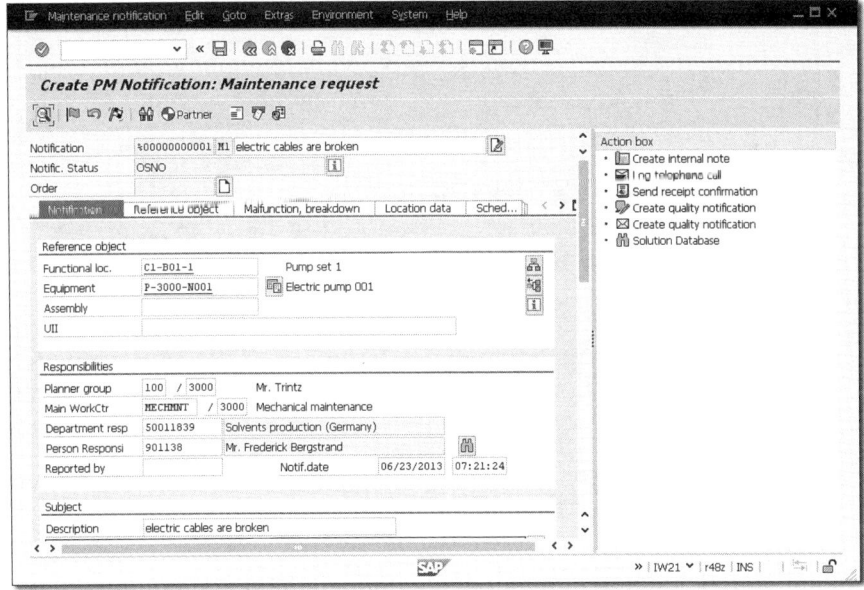

Figure 9.12 Action Box in the Notification

9.5.11 GuiXT

GuiXT is an SAP GUI component enabling you to customize your SAP transactions to suit your daily tasks. The following options are available (see Figure 9.13[2]):

- Populate fields with values
- Hide fields and field groups
- Move fields
- Add and change text
- Add field help
- Add new screen elements (for example, checkboxes, buttons, graphics, and documentation)
- Adjust tables
- Change field labels throughout the system

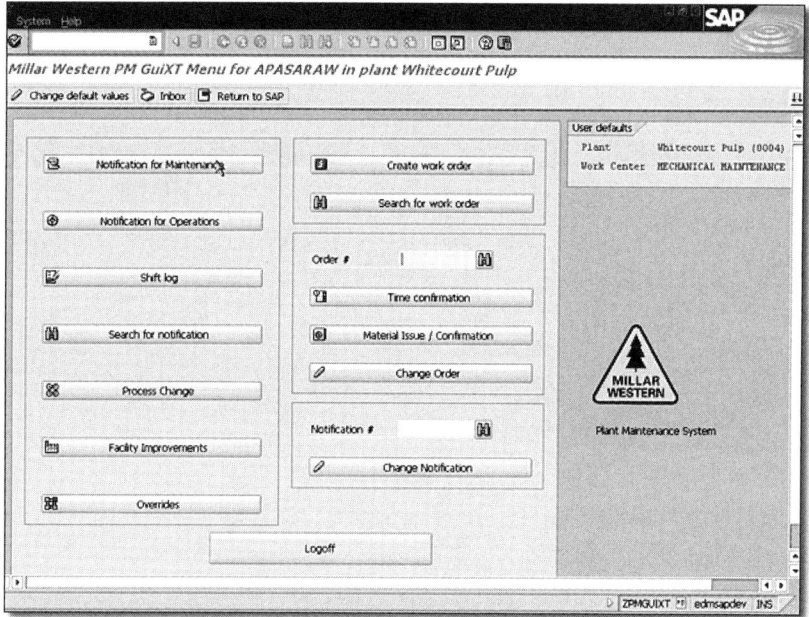

Figure 9.13 User Interface Customized via GuiXT

---

2 http://www.guixt.com/Screencams/library/NotificationMiller/NotificationMiller.html

> **GuiXT Enables You to Customize Screen Layouts** [+]
>
> GuiXT could also help you to customize processing of business transactions to suit your needs and to simplify and accelerate processing.

The following sections describe the functionality of these options, as well as those of Category 3 (IT including programming), which means that only the *what* will be described, whereas you can find detailed information about *how* you should use these options in the book *Configuring SAP Plant Maintenance*.

9.5.12 Upstream Transactions

During processing of business transactions, several transactions usually have to be called one after another. Within each transaction, the fields to be entered are distributed over several screens. The basic idea of upstream transactions is to create a custom transaction containing only one or a few screens. This transaction calls the original SAP transactions in the background and passes the data. Or this custom transaction is used to simplify the process flow of the original SAP transactions.

The calibration of test equipment is a highly complex process requiring several SAP transactions to be called in sequence (see Section 5.10). For an automotive supplier who needs to manage more than 20,000 pieces of measuring equipment per plant, the standard process flows would not be manageable. Therefore, the upstream Transaction ZMV01 (see Figure 9.14) was created to do the following:

Example

- Issue pieces of test equipment from a warehouse and install them in a functional location
- Dismantle the pieces of test equipment from the functional location and return them to the warehouse
- Generate an inspection order from the maintenance plan
- Record the measuring results
- Make a usage decision
- Confirm the inspection order

9 | Usability

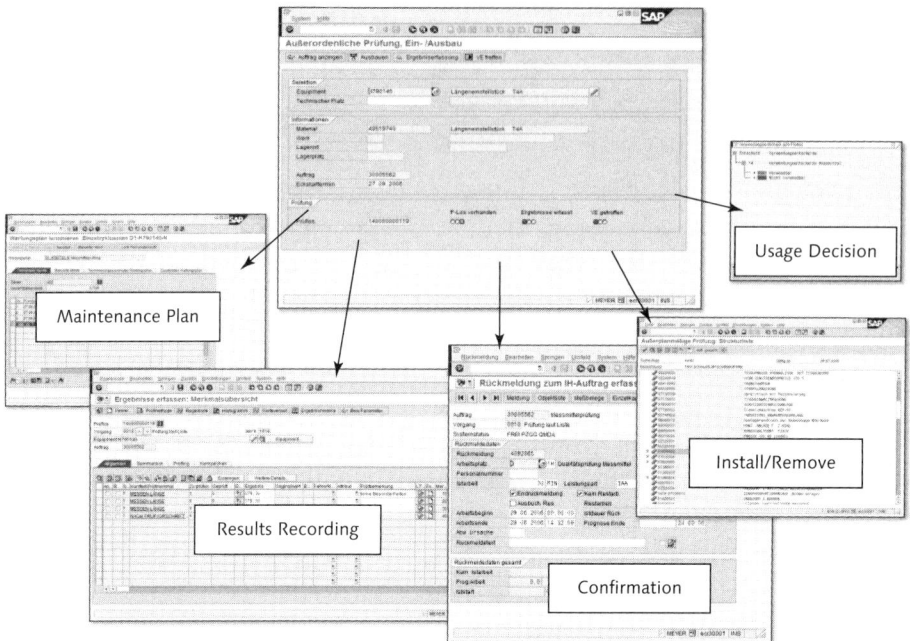

Figure 9.14 Upstream Transaction

[+] **The Effort for Programming an Upstream Transaction is Often Worthwhile**

An upstream transaction should substantially accelerate the processing of a business transaction, or else it misses the point.

BAPI SAP provides a range of business application programming interfaces (BAPIs) to simplify the process of developing upstream transactions.

BAPIs can be used for the following purposes:

- Connect SAP systems to the Internet
- Allow SAP components to communicate with one another
- Connect third-party software and legacy systems to SAP systems
- Allow PC programs to be used as a "frontend" for SAP systems
- Allow workflow applications to communicate across system boundaries
- Allow WebFlow applications to communicate using the Internet

In the plant maintenance area, SAP offers BAPIs for the following objects:

- Notifications
- Orders
- Confirmations
- Equipment
- Functional locations
- Materials
- Bills of material
- Maintenance task lists

You can call the BAPI Explorer in Transaction BAPI (see Figure 9.15). Navigating through the hierarchy is a simple way of obtaining an overview of all available BAPIs.

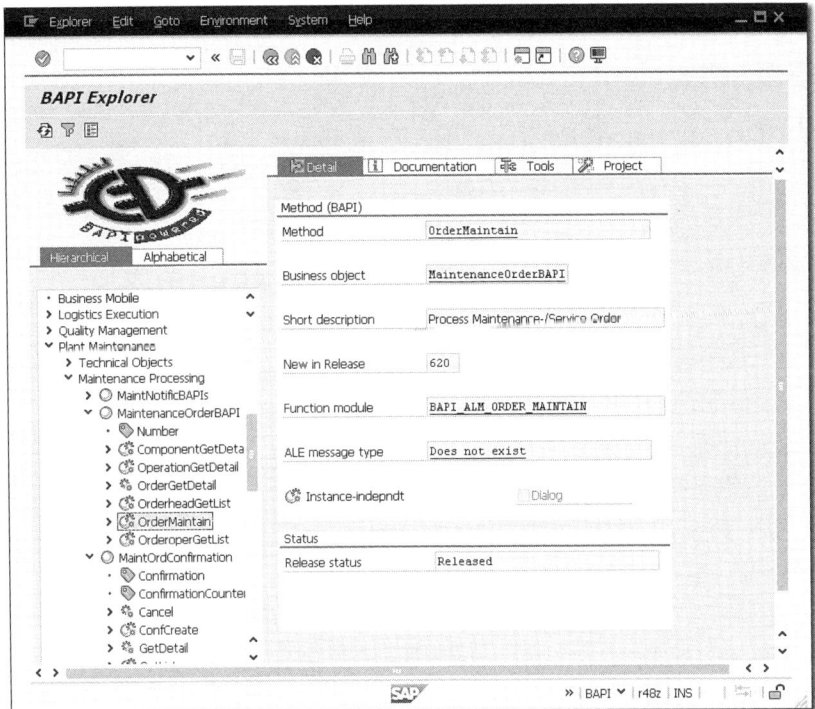

Figure 9.15 BAPI Explorer

9.5.13 Web User Interface

You can also use a similar procedure for a web environment outside the SAP system.

App for iPad and iPhone

Figure 9.16[3] shows the example of an after-event recording that was developed as an app for iPad and iPhone:

Figure 9.16 Web User Interface for After-Event Recording

- On the iPad, you can enter all the data that was generated during the processing of a damage (personnel number, work center, time required, equipment, functional location, spare parts, and so on).
- BAPIs are used to check the validity of the entered data (for example, whether the equipment number is valid).
- BAPIs are also used to pass the data on to the SAP system where it is posted.

Then, the following process occurs in the SAP system: notification is created → order is created → order is released → goods issue is posted

---

[3] I would like to thank the three researchers at IDIS (Florian Wolf, Tobias Schlereth, and Daniel Schwarz) for developing this app.

→ time confirmation is posted → order and notification are completed.
- The app was developed for HTML5 and can, therefore, be used not only on an iPad or iPhone, but also on desktop computers or Android smartphones.

Web Applications Are Widely Accepted among Users	[+]
Almost every user knows web applications or apps for iPhone, iPad, or smartphones from their private environment. This is why users can also quickly familiarize themselves with these applications in a professional environment and why the user acceptance is very high.	

9.5.14 Customer Exits

You can use customer exits to add custom functionality to SAP standard applications without modifying the original SAP programs. In standard applications, SAP creates customer exits for certain programs, screens, and menus. Initially, these exits do not have any function; they serve as a predefined entry and exit point at which you can add your own additional functionality to the SAP system.

You can call customer exits via Transaction SMOD. More than 100 customer exits are provided for plant maintenance. You can view them by entering the following:

- Technical objects: ITOB*, IEQM*, ILOM*, IHCL*, CCM*
- Measuring points/counters: IMRC*
- Warranties: BG*
- Maintenance task lists: IAIH*
- Maintenance plans: IPRM*, CI*
- Notifications: QQMA*
- Orders: IWO*, CNEX*, COZF*, IREV*
- Capacity requirements planning: COI*, CYPP*
- Confirmations: CMFU*, CONFPM*
- CATS: CATS*

- Information system: MCI*
- Data transfers: IBIP*
- Graphics modules: IMSM*

Examples

As an example, five applications that helped to simplify entries and considerably enhance user acceptance will be described.

Transfer characteristics

Customer Exit IHCL0001 allows you to transfer the characteristic valuation from the material master to the characteristic valuation of a piece of equipment. If you often add new equipment with reference to a material number, you can simplify maintenance of the classification data by storing information such as performance, type specification, or other technical data once in the material master as a classification and then prepopulating these characteristics for your new piece of equipment. Ideally, you then no longer have to modify the classification.

Right plant, right storage location

Customer Exit CNEX0027, which, strictly speaking, is part of the SAP project system but can also be used for plant maintenance, supports you in entering the right plant and the right storage location during material planning. This may be useful when a spare part is stored only in one plant to which all other plants have access. By programming a smart search function for your company in this customer exit, you no longer have to worry about the right plant in the material planning for the order.

Right task list

A significant improvement is also provided by Customer Exits IWO10021 and IWO20001. The combination of these two customer exits, for example, ensures that the right task list is generated from the damage or cause code of a malfunction report. When the order is opened from the malfunction report, the correct tasks are already listed in the order. This eliminates the need for finding the right task list and including it in the order so that order processing is accelerated, particularly for standardized processes.

Right data in notification and order

Although they do not make data entry any quicker, customer exits that can run customized data checks when saving orders (IWO10009) or notifications (QQMA0014) help to eliminate data corrections. For example, you can check straight away in the notification whether certain combinations of incident and cause codes make sense. These checks help inexperienced users to allay their fears about operating the system.

Customer Exits COZF0001 and COZF0002 allow you to automatically populate certain fields for purchase requisitions (PReq), which are generated from within the order, according to your own specifications. For example, you can populate the REQUESTER field with the name of the logged-on user or automatically enter your department acronym in the REQUIREMENT NUMBER field. This may not sound like much progress, but if a user has to enter the same department acronym 35 times for 35 non-stock items, it is easy to see why optimization becomes a priority.

Right data in purchase requisitions

These examples clearly show how varied the uses of customer exits are and that there are no limits but your imagination.

> **Customer Exits Simplify the Standard System and Enhance Its Security** [!]
>
> Customer exits allow you to customize the processing of business transactions in plant maintenance to your needs and simplify and accelerate them. But you need to consider carefully whether custom programming really has the desired effect and increases user acceptance.

9.5.15 Other Programming Techniques

For the sake of completeness, the following sections briefly describe other programming techniques that enable you to enhance the standard SAP system without having to modify it. You can find further details and information about using these tools in the book *Configuring SAP Plant Maintenance*.

BAdI stands for Business Add-in. These enable you to create predefined enhancement options in SAP components. In contrast to customer exits, BAdIs are based on ABAP Objects.

BAdIs

Unlike customer exits, Business Add-ins are not based on a two-level system landscape (SAP, customer), but on a multilevel one (SAP, country versions, industry solutions, partners, customer, and so on). You can create definitions and implementations of Business Add-ins at each level of the system landscape. Consequently, BAdIs can be implemented multiple times, whereas you can implement customer exits only once.

You can create BAdIs via Transaction SE19 (BAdI Builder).

BAdIs are available in two versions:

- Classical BAdIs (from 4.6C)
- New BAdIs (from SAP NetWeaver 2004s, also referred to as *enhancement points*)

Enhancement point

The following list contains some examples of new BAdIs (enhancement points) from the point of view of plant maintenance:

- EAM_EHP4_CI_SFWS_SC_LIST_ENH for enhancing lists in plant maintenance (e.g., to view maintenance plans, maintenance items, and maintenance packages in multilevel lists)
- EAM_EHP4_CI_SFWS_SC_INSP_ROUND for enhancing inspection rounds (e.g., to activate production resources or tools as measuring points)
- EAM_WS_ORDER_RELEASE_IMPL for security-relevant enhancements in order releases
- COCF_ES_SN_LIST for defining custom selection options in the shift notes list

Workflow

SAP Business Workflow allows you to define business processes that have not been previously mapped in the system. These processes can involve simple release or approval procedures, as well as more complex business processes, such as creating a material master record and the related coordination of involved departments. SAP Business Workflow becomes increasingly efficient with an increasing number of workflow repetitions and if the business process requires a large number of processors in a precisely defined sequence.

From a plant maintenance perspective, two workflows are especially relevant:

- **Process a Maintenance Notification**
  The *Process a Maintenance Notification* scenario is supposed to support users in processing, monitoring, and completing newly created

notifications. For example, you can notify specific persons or groups of persons when a new notification has been created or a notification has been technically completed.

▶ **Process a Maintenance Order**
The *Process a Maintenance Order* scenario is supposed to support users in processing, monitoring, and completing newly created notifications. For example, you can notify the creator of the order when the order has been released or technically completed.

You can call and configure workflows in the SAP menu via TOOLS • BUSINESS WORKFLOW. Figure 9.17 shows Transaction SWDD (Workflow Builder).

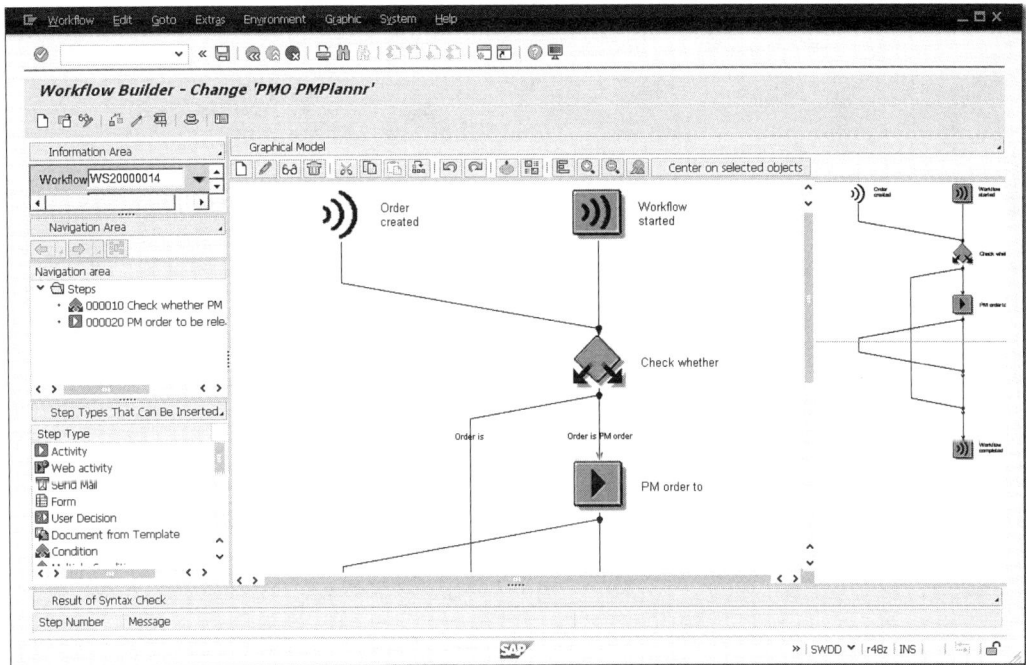

Figure 9.17 Workflow Builder

Let's now have a look at tuning measures to find out whether they contribute to improving usability and if so, to what degree: the usability test.

9.6 Usability Study for SAP ERP 6.0

To provide quantitative evidence of the effects of tuning measures, I conducted a laboratory test at the Würzburg-Schweinfurt University of Applied Sciences under real-world conditions and involving more than 40 test subjects. It was intended to answer the following question: how does processing time in a tuned system differ from processing time in an un-tuned system?

The following section introduces the test and deals particularly with the following questions:

- What preparatory measures were taken?
- How was the test conducted?
- What were the results of the usability test?
- What conclusions can we draw from the results?

9.6.1 Preparation and Execution

This section introduces the steps involved in preparing the study — business process selection and tuning measures.

Selecting Business Processes

We first had to select business processes that were a representative reflection of the maintenance process in a company. We ensured that business processes were selected from both plant maintenance and the area of master data. Business processes involving plant maintenance are often used in daily operations, so they should be given more attention when you consider possible optimization measures. We included three such processes.

Business processes involving master data are not as widely used in day-to-day operations, so we included only one such process. Based on these criteria, we selected the following business processes:

- Business process01 (Create a piece of equipment)
- Business process02 (Breakdown maintenance)

- Business process03 (External processing)
- Business process04 (Planned repair)

Tuning Measures

After selecting the business processes, we applied the appropriate tuning measures to each business process. To do so, two users who served as sample users for the tuned and un-tuned business processes were created in the system.

For user01, the SAP system default settings, such as SAP standard menu or parameters, were not stored. Moreover, the default SAP settings were used in an un-tuned state by this user for the processing of business processes.

For user02, on the other hand, a number of tuning measures were implemented that correspond to Category 1 in Section 9.5:

Tuning measures for the user

- Favorites were created for each business process.
- General parameters were defined, including cost center, company code, plant, maintenance plant, planning plant, controlling area, storage location, and so on.
- Maintenance-specific parameters were maintained, including parameters for external processing and procurement, as well as order type, notification type, organization, and reference object.
- Pop-up windows were suppressed at specific locations.
- The history was enabled.

In addition, tuning measures were applied to this user's business processes, which correspond to Category 2 in Section 9.5:

Tuning measures for business processes

- The screen layout was simplified in Customizing (tabs, field selection upon notification, order, and equipment, among others).
- The INTEGRATION OF ORDERS AND NOTIFICATIONS option was enabled in Customizing.
- A transaction variant was created for order entry.
- External processing profiles were configured in Customizing.

- A personalized selection variant was defined for selecting notifications.
- Default values were enabled for confirmations (services, backflush).

No measures from Category 3 — programming — were applied.

[!] **The Same Results without Programming**

The following principle was applied: no programming is supposed to take place. The tuning measures are limited to Customizing and similar functions and user settings. In addition, the following principle was applied: the results of a tuned business process and the results of an un-tuned business process have to be identical.

Selecting the Test Subjects

For the results to be considered representative, we had to find a sufficient number of test subjects with the appropriate qualifications.

- We assumed that five test subjects per business process would suffice.
- To be considered valid from a statistical point of view, the test subjects had to be able to work independently of each other for each business process and user type, so we recruited a total of 40 test subjects among information management students.
- For the results to be reliable, the test subjects had to have the same previous knowledge. This condition is best met if none of the test subjects has previous SAP knowledge.

[!] **Suitable Test Subjects**

To ensure that the results were representative qualitatively and quantitatively, 40 test subjects who should have no previous knowledge were required to participate in the usability test.

Description of the Business Processes

Because the test subjects were not meant to have any previous SAP knowledge, they needed a proper description of the business processes to be performed.

> **Processes Based on Documents Only**
>
> The test subjects were meant to perform the business processes on their own, relying exclusively on the description of the processes.

[!]

The description of a business process was similar to the following (an excerpt of business process02: breakdown maintenance for user01):

Example

- In the SAP menu, double-click the following menu path: LOGISTICS • PLANT MAINTENANCE • MAINTENANCE PROCESSING • NOTIFICATION • CREATE GENERAL.
- In the screen that opens, click the NOTIFICATION TYPE entry field. Then, click on the ▢ button, [F4] help, to select a valid value. In the displayed list, double-click M1 MAINTENANCE REQUEST. Now, press the [↵] key to confirm your selection.
- This brings you to the screen for creating a maintenance request notification.
- In the field highlighted in yellow, enter the text "defective pump" next to the notification number.
- On the NOTIFICATION tab, in the REFERENCE OBJECT field group, enter the value "P-1000-N003" in the EQUIPMENT field. Then, press [Enter] to confirm. The system now automatically populates the field for the functional location.
- In the RESPONSIBILITIES field group, enter the value "I01" in the PLANNING GROUP field and the value "A-01" in the MAIN WORK CENTER field. Press the [Enter] key.

Recording Tool

It seemed too inaccurate and error prone to measure the processing time using a stopwatch. We therefore had to find a tool that allowed us to record the activities of our test subjects and obtain clear readings for the time it took them to complete a business process.

After selecting different tools and testing them internally, we decided to use the keylogger tool PC Agent by Blue-Series.

This software program records a user's activities in the background with a time stamp. The recording files are saved in a proprietary format in a previously defined folder as user-dependent items. They can be converted to many other formats, including a spreadsheet-readable format.

> **[!] Only a Tool Delivers Safe and Objective Results**
>
> Using a keylogger tool ensures that the following:
>
> ▶ Data remains permanently available after you complete the test runs.
> ▶ The evaluation can be substantiated with raw data at any time.
> ▶ The results are safe and accurate.

Procedure

The tests were carried out in the SAP Laboratory at the Würzburg-Schweinfurt University of Applied Sciences during two consecutive days. On the first day, the business processes *Planned repairs* and *Breakdown Maintenance* were performed, and on the second day, the business processes *External processing* and *Create Equipment*.

The previously created users were assigned to the individual business processes so that which user performed which business process was clearly defined and could be tracked easily. This made it easier to evaluate and document the test.

Right before the test, the project team logged the users on to the terminal server and to the SAP system so that the participants could start with their assigned business processes. During logon, the project team also checked that the keylogger software was enabled in the background so that the times and activities of the users were recorded properly for later evaluation.

The subjects received a brief introduction to the SAP system regarding navigation in the system; elements such as the title bar, menu bar, user-defined favorites, the SAP menu, the system tool bar and the status bar, and direct transaction calls.

Armed with this knowledge and the descriptions of the business processes, each subject performed his business process 10 times, and PC Agent worked quietly in the background.

9.6.2 Results

From the recorded raw data, the average processing time of the five subjects who had completed a business process was calculated. The results are described below, with user01 (un-tuned) directly compared to user02 (tuned).

Business process01 (Create equipment) (see Figure 9.18): in this business process (and also in the others), you can clearly observe a steep decline in the time curve, which stabilizes after five to six test runs due to the learning effect.

Creating an equipment

So, we want to calculate the average values of test runs 6 to 10. The average time for test runs 6 to 10 is 1 minute, 35 seconds for user01 and 0:45 secondsfor user02. This results in the following relation:

$M(U)/M(T) = 2.11$

where $M(U)$ = average value of test runs 6 to 10 in an un-tuned state, and $M(T)$ = average value of test runs 6 to 10 in a tuned state.

Figure 9.18 Business Process01 — Create Equipment

> **Result for the Creation of an Equipment**
>
> Business process01 (create equipment) takes user01 about twice as long as user02.

Business process02 (breakdown maintenance; see Figure 9.19): the average time for test runs 6 to 10 is 6 minutes and 28 seconds for user01 and 1 minute and 40 seconds for user02. This results in the following relation:

$$M(U)/M(T) = 3.88$$

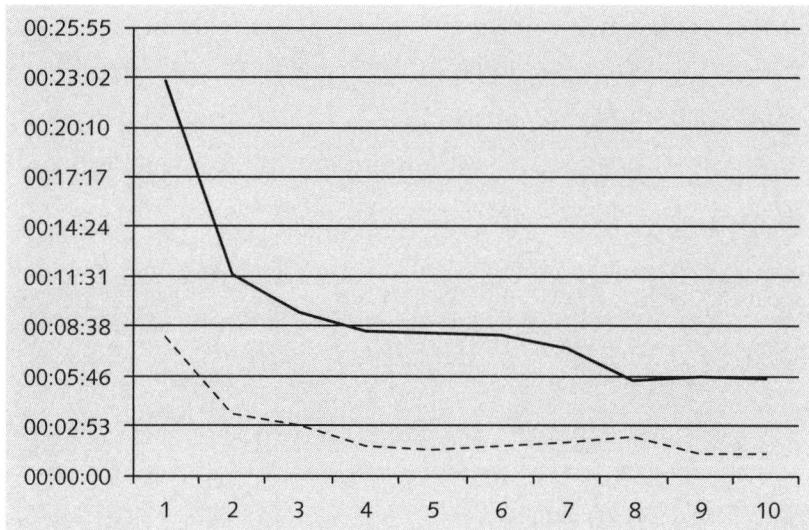

Figure 9.19 Business Process02—Breakdown Maintenance

where $M(U)$ = average value of test runs 6 to 10 in an un-tuned state, and $M(T)$ = average value of test runs 6 to 10 in a tuned state.

> **Result for Breakdown Maintenance**
>
> Business process02 (breakdown maintenance) takes user01 almost four times as long as user02.

Business process03 (External processing; see Figure 9.20): the average time for test runs 6 to 10 is 1 minute and 42 seconds for user01 and 0:26 seconds for user02. This results in the following relation:

External processing

$M(U)/M(T) = 3.92$

where $M(U)$ = average value of test runs 6 to 10 in an un-tuned state, and $M(T)$ = average value of test runs 6 to 10 in a tuned state.

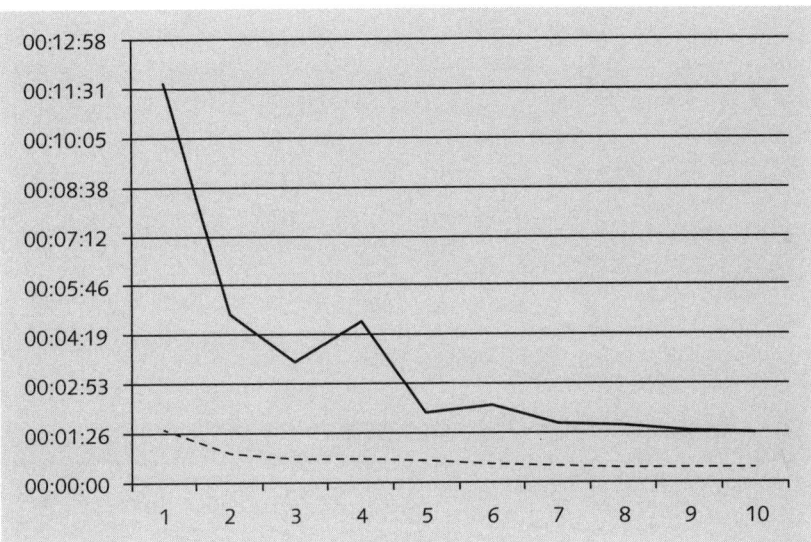

Figure 9.20 Business Process03—External processing

Result for External processing [+]

Business process03 (external commissioning) takes user01 almost four times as long as user02.

Business process04 (planned repair; see Figure 9.21): the average time for test runs 6 to 10 is 5 minutes and 53 seconds for user01 and 2 minutes and 22 seconds for user02. This results in the following relation:

Planned repair

$M(U)/M(T) = 2.49$

where $M(U)$ = average value of test runs 6 to 10 in an un-tuned state, and $M(T)$ = average value of test runs 6 to 10 in a tuned state.

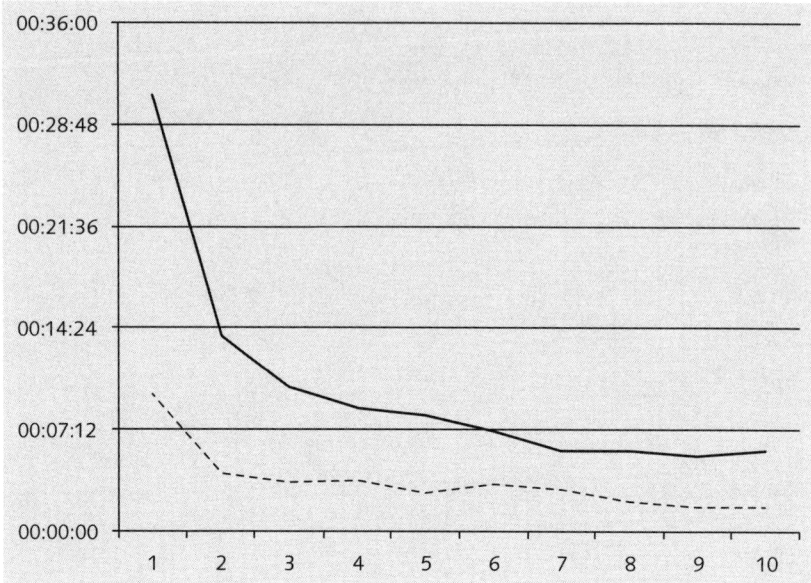

Figure 9.21 Business Process04 — Planned repair

[!] **Result for Planned repair**

Business process04 (planned repair) takes user01 almost 2.5 times as long as user02.

Figure 9.22 shows a summary of the results.

In addition to the processing time, another key figure was recorded and evaluated: control entries (mouse clicks, buttons, Keyboard, and Enter keys). Figure 9.23 shows a summary of the results. Here, too, the average values for test runs 6 to 10 are displayed.

Concerning the control entries, the difference between a tuned and an un-tuned system is almost as great.

[!] **Result for Control Entries**

The un-tuned system requires 1.5 to 2.5 as many control entries as the tuned system.

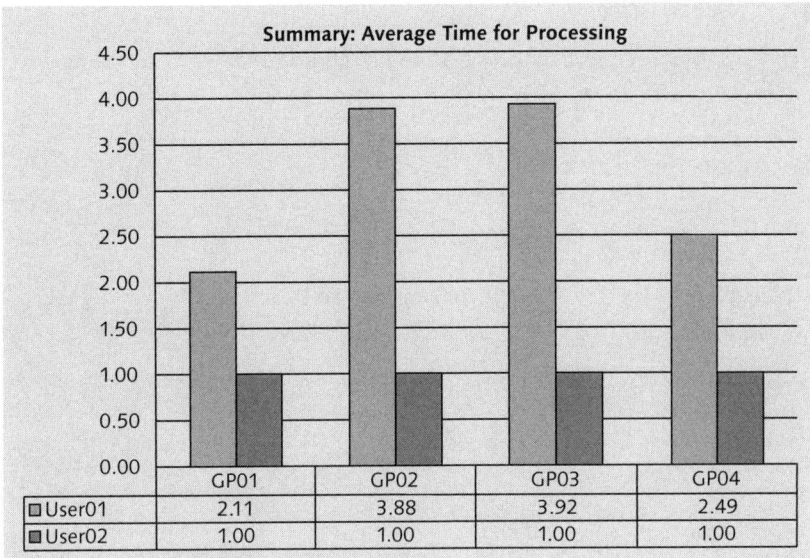

Figure 9.22 Average Processing Time

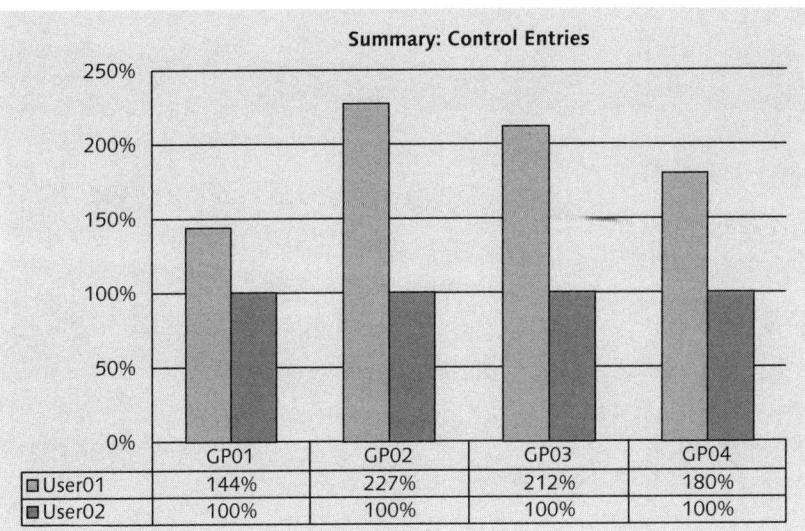

Figure 9.23 Number of Control Entries

9.6.3 Conclusions

After completing the usability test and evaluating the results, the following statements can be proven and result in the following conclusions.

[!] **Statement 1**

When processing SAP business processes, there is a fast learning effect.

This is proven by all learning curves. The sixth test run yields a processing time that can hardly be improved upon in subsequent runs.

[!] **Conclusion 1.1**

A minimum of training can achieve a lot.

[!] **Conclusion 1.2**

Your users should not get discouraged by initial failed attempts and wait before they complain about the SAP system.

[!] **Statement 2**

Tuning measures reduce the number of control entries for SAP business processes.

This is proven by all the statistics. No matter whether it was the first or tenth test run, and no matter which business process was performed: user01 always had to click the mouse and press buttons, ⇆, and ↵ keys 1.5 to 2.5 times more often than user02.

[!] **Conclusion 2**

Check whether you have implemented all tuning measures that do not require any programming. This can be very helpful.

[!] **Statement 3**

Tuning measures help reduce the processing time of SAP business processes.

This is proven by all the statistics. No matter whether it was the first or tenth test run, and no matter which business process was performed, user02 was always two or four times faster than user01.

Conclusion 3	[!]
Check whether you have implemented all tuning measures that do not require any programming. This can be very helpful.	

Statement 4	[!]
The level of improvement depends not only on the state of your system before tuning measures are applied, but also on the tuning measures you implement.	

In our laboratory test, the original state was the SAP standard version, and we used tuning measures that did not require any programming. We have thereby fully utilized an improvement potential of 222% to 396%. If you have already implemented certain tuning measures in your company, your improvement potential might be lower. However, by using additional measures and/or programming, you might also achieve a higher improvement potential than in the laboratory test.

Conclusion 4	[!]
Never settle with what you have achieved. Improvement potential can be found everywhere.	

Appendices

A	**List of Sources**	631
B	**Overviews**	637
C	**The Author**	651
D	**Acknowledgments**	653

A   List of Sources

Anschütz, O.; Junior, J.: *Die Fremdleistungsbeschaffung beim Großkraftwerk Mannheim*, DSAG-Arbeitskreis, Frankfurt 2003.

Baumgartl, A.; Mebus, F.; Seemann, V.: *Das SOA-Praxisbuch für SAP*, Bonn: SAP PRESS 2010.

Beckert, A.; Beckert, S.; Escherich, B.: *Mobile Lösungen mit SAP*, Bonn: SAP PRESS 2012.

Bock, W.: *SAP EHSM und SAP EAM Integrations-/Prozessszenarien*, DSAG-Arbeitskreis am 29.11.2012 in Mannheim.

Bradler, J.; Mödder, F.: *SAP Supplier Relationship Management*, 2. Auflage, Bonn: SAP PRESS 2013.

Brück, U.: *Praxishandbuch SAP-Controlling*, 4. Auflage, Bonn: SAP PRESS 2011.

Brumby, L.: *Optimierte Instandhaltungsbeauftragung durch den Einsatz mobiler IT*, in: 11. SAP-Kongress Instandhaltung, Berlin 2006.

Buck, M.: *Einsatz mobiler Szenarien mit SAP am Flughafen Frankfurt*, in: Effiziente Instandhaltung mit SAP, Frankfurt 2006.

Buck, M.: *RFID at Fraport AG*, in: Effiziente Instandhaltung mit SAP, Frankfurt 2005.

Deppe, B.: *Verknüpfung von PM-Aufträgen mit der Katalogbeschaffung*, in: 9. Kongress Instandhaltung und Servicemanagement mit SAP, Berlin 2004.

DIN Deutsches Institut für Normung (Hrsg.): DIN31051:2012-09: *Grundlagen der Instandhaltung*, 2012.

Eisenacher, S.; Kammerer, K.; Riepe, A.; Schuur, J.: *SAP Environment, Health, and Safety Management*, Bonn: SAP PRESS 2012.

Forum Vision Instandhaltung (FVI): Pressemitteilung vom 24.08.2007.

Franke, W.; Dangelmaier, W.: *RFID – Leitfaden für die Logistik*, Wiesbaden 2006.

Franz, M.: *Projektmanagement mit SAP Projektsystem*, 3. Auflage, Bonn: SAP PRESS 2012.

Gertz, W.: *E-Commerce*, in: Maintenance 2010, Berlin 2000.

Gillert, F.; Hansen, W.: *RFID – für die Optimierung von Geschäftsprozessen*, München 2006.

Götz, T.: *SAP-Logistikprozesse mit RFID und Barcodes*, 2. Auflage, Bonn: SAP PRESS 2010.

Hanhart, D.; Jinschek, R.; Kipper, U.; Österle, H.: *Mobile und Ubiquitous Computing in der Instandhaltung der Fraport AG*, in: Mobile Anwendungen, Heidelberg: dpunkt Verlag 2004.

Heck, Rinaldo: *Geschäftsprozessorientiertes Dokumentenmanagement mit SAP*, Bonn: SAP PRESS 2009.

Heilig, L.; John, P.; Kessler, T.; Knötzele, T.; Thaler-Mieslinger, K.: *SAP NetWeaver BW und SAP BusinessObjects*, 2. Auflage, Bonn: SAP PRESS 2013.

Heilig, L.; Karch, S.; Böttcher, O.; Hofmann, C.; Pfennig, R.: *SAP NetWeaver Master Data Management*, Bonn: SAP PRESS 2006.

Henneboel, G.: *Mobile Lösungen für das technische Anlagenmanagement*, in: 7. mySAP.com-Instandhaltungs- und Servicemanagement-Kongress, Potsdam 2002.

IKB-Report *Automobilindustrie – Neue Chancen, zunehmender Investitions- und Finanzierungsbedarf*, Düsseldorf 2003.

Institut für Wirtschaftsforschung (IFO): Pressemitteilung vom 21.11.2005.

ISO International Organization for Standardization: ISO 9241-110: *Ergonomics of human-system-interaction*, Genf 2007.

Jakowski, J., Binder, C.: *SAP NetWeaver Business Client – Einsetzen und Nutzen*, DSAG-Webinar am 26.10.2011.

Kaudewitz, R.; Theis, S.: *Mobile Instandhaltung und Service Provider Portal*, in: 11. SAP-Kongress Instandhaltung, Potsdam 2006.

Kempchen, M.: *Praxisbericht Abwicklung von Instandhaltungsmaßnahmen*, in: SAP R/3 PM in der Instandhaltung, München 2007.

Kessler, T.; Hügens, T.; Delgehausen, F.; Abdel Hadi, M.: *Reporting mit SAP NetWeaver BW und SAP BusinessObjects*, Bonn: SAP PRESS 2012.

Klauer, A.: *Mobile Instandhaltung bei Roche Diagnostics GmbH*, DSAG-Arbeitskreis am 29.11.2012 in Mannheim.

Krämer, J.: *Vorbeugende Instandhaltung mit SAP R/3 PM*, in: Workshop Instandhaltung mit SAP, Berlin 2006.

Krüger, A.: *SAP HANA und die Instandhaltung*, DSAG-Arbeitskreis am 29.11.2012 in Mannheim.

Lehnert, V.; Stelzner, K.; John, P.; Otto, A.: *SAP-Berechtigungswesen*, 2. Auflage, Bonn: SAP PRESS 2013.

Liebstückel, K.: *Anwendungssysteme in Produktentstehung und Logistik*, Modul: Beschaffung und Lagerhaltung, Stuttgart: AKAD-Verlag 2005.

Liebstückel, K.: *Anwendungssysteme in Produktentstehung und Logistik*, Modul: Produktion und Fertigung, Stuttgart: AKAD-Verlag 2005.

Liebstückel, K.: *Technisches Controlling liefert konkrete Entscheidungsunterlagen*, in: Die Industrie – Fachzeitschrift für Wirtschaft und Technik (48) 2002.

Litzinger, J.; Naumann, K.: *Höhere Flexibilität und Produktivität in der Instandhaltung mit Mobile Asset Management 2.0*, in: 9. Kongress Instandhaltungs- und Servicemanagement mit SAP, Berlin 2004.

Matyas, K.: *Taschenbuch Instandhaltungslogistik*, 4. Auflage, München/Wien: Hanser-Verlag 2010.

Müller, F.: *Mobile Instandhaltungsabwicklung bei Solvay*, in: 11. SAP-Kongress Instandhaltung, Potsdam 2006.

Nettlenbusch, M.: *Mobile Lösungen*, in: Effiziente Instandhaltung mit SAP R/3, Wiesbaden 2004.

Neumann, A: *SAP liefert Appliance für In-Memory Computing aus*, heise.de, 1.12.2010.

Nicolescu, V.; Klappert, K.; Krcmar, H.: *SAP NetWeaver Portal*, 2. Auflage, Bonn: SAP PRESS 2012.

Oswald, G.: *Innovationen von heute für die Welt von morgen*, Keynote auf dem DSAG-Jahreskongress am 26.09.2012.

Psion (Hrsg.): Radio Frequency Identification (RFID) Solutions, London 2012.

Raap, H.: *SAP Product Lifecycle Management*, Bonn: SAP PRESS 2013 (in Vorbereitung).

Rabeder, H.: *Mobile Asset Management bei voestalpine*, in: 10. Instandhaltungs- und Servicemanagement-Kongress mit SAP, Berlin 2005.

Rölleke: *IH-Optimierung mit Mobile Service und Add-ons*, in: 11. SAP-Kongress Instandhaltung, Berlin 2006.

SAP AG (Hrsg.): *Enterprise Services Repository – An Overview*, Walldorf 2007.

SAP AG (Hrsg.): SAP Business Suite powered by SAP HANA ermöglicht Unternehmensführung in Echtzeit, Pressemitteilung vom 10.01.2013.

SAP AG (Hrsg.): *SAP Enhancement Package 6 für SAP ERP 6.0, Version für SAP HANA*, Walldorf 2013.

SAP AG (Hrsg.): *SAP ERP 6.0 mit Enhancement Package 6*, Walldorf 2012.

SAP AG (Hrsg.): *SAP NetWeaver Business Warehouse 7.3 mit Enhancement Package 1*, Walldorf 2013.

SAP AG (Hrsg.): *SAP NetWeaver Master Data Management (MDM) 7.1 mit Support Package 09*, Walldorf 2012.

SAP AG (Hrsg.): *SAP Supplier Relationship Management 7.0 mit Ehancement Package 2*, Walldorf 2012.

Scheller, U.: *Mobile Lösung für die Instandhaltung*, in: 2. ETP-Fachkonferenz: Optimierung der Instandhaltung mit SAP PM für Energieversorger, Düsseldorf 2005.

Schneider, H.-J.: *Visuelles Lifecycle Management*, DSAG-Arbeitskreis, Berlin 2002.

Stengele, H.: *mySAP Product Lifecycle Management*, DSAG-Arbeitskreis, Frankfurt 2004.

Toman, S.; Köppe, A.; Lukowsky, J.: *Immobilienmanagement mit SAP*, Bonn: SAP PRESS 2010.

Vieweg, N.: *Mobile Szenarien in der Instandhaltung*, in: DSAG-Arbeitskreis, Berlin 2003.

Weber, A.: *Risikomanagement in Standardsoftware-Einführungsprojekten – Konzept und empirische Studie*, Würzburg 2003.

Weber, S.: *Praxishandbuch Kundenservice mit SAP*, Bonn: SAP PRESS 2012.

Wessendorf, M.: *Die Einbindung von Technikern in den SAP-Prozess*, in: 10. Kongress Instandhaltungs- und Servicemanagement mit SAP, Berlin 2005.

Wessendorf, M.: *Die mobile Plattform muss her*, in: SAP.info vom 6.11.2012.

Westermayr, S.: *Mobile Instandhaltung mit SAP Work Manager by Syclo*, Walldorf 2012.

Woods, D.; Mattern, T.: *Enterprise SOA – Design IT for Business Innovation*, Sebastopol: O'Reilly 2006.

B   Overviews

Appendix B contains useful additional information. Here, you will find overviews of structuring resources, the functions of notifications and orders, options for integrating SAP Plant Maintenance, and PMIS analyses.

B.1   Functional Comparison of Structuring Resources

	Functional Location	Equipment	Assembly
Measuring points and counters	+	+	–
Classes and characteristics	+	+	+
Partners	+	+	–
Address management	+	+	–
Permits	+	+	–
Warranties	+	+	–
Multilingual short texts	+	+	+
Multilingual long texts	+	+	+
Object information	+	+	–
External number assignment	+	+	+
Internal number assignment	–	+	+
Alternative labeling	+	–	–
Document links	+	+	+
Vendor data	+	+	–
Account assignment	+	+	–
Responsibilities	+	+	–
Usage history	–	+	–

	Functional Location	Equipment	Assembly
Usability period	–	+	+
Change documents	+	+	+

B.2 Functions of Notifications and Orders

Object	Function	A	B	C
Notification	User status			
	Reference objects			
	Priorities			
	Partners			
	Telephone integration			
	Paging			
	Addresses			
	Object parts			
	Damages			
	Causes of damage			
	Measures			
	Activities			
	Notification items			
	Classification			
	Printing			
	Fax			
	Download			
	Malfunctions			
	Permits			
	Response time monitoring			

Object	Function	A	B	C
	Revisions			
	Solution database			
Order	Reference objects			
	User status			
	Priorities			
	Partners			
	Telephone integration			
	Paging			
	Addresses			
	Printing			
	Fax			
	Download			
	Permits			
	Operations			
	Scheduling			
	Relationships			
	Capacity requirements planning			
	Capacity availability check			
	Reservation of stock material			
	Stock material availability check			
	Ordering of non-stock material			
	Catalog integration (Internet and intranet catalogs, vendor catalogs)			
	Estimated costs			
	Planned/actual costing			
	Order budgets			
	Object list			

Object	Function	A	B	C
	Production resources/tools			
	Production resources/tools availability check			
	Suborders			
	Utilization of production capacities			
Confirmation	Time confirmations			
	Technical completion confirmations			
	Goods receipts			
	Goods issue			
	Overhead costing			
	Order settlement			
Immediate Repairs	Historical orders			
	After-event recording in SAP NetWeaver Portal			
	Confirmation of unplanned job in SAP NetWeaver Business Client			
Shift Notes and Shift Reports	Shift notes for work centers			
	Shift notes for technical objects			
	Shift reports			
External services	External processing via service specifications			
	External processing as purchase order			
	External processing via work centers			
	Revisions			
Preventive maintenance	General maintenance task lists			
	Equipment task list			
	Functional location task list			
	Maintenance strategies			

Object	Function	A	B	C
	Time-based maintenance plans			
	performance-based maintenance plans			
	Single-cycle plans			
	Strategy plans			
	Simple multiple counter plans			
	Enhanced multiple counter plans			
	Order maintenance call object			
	Notification maintenance call object			
	Inspection lot maintenance call object			
	Service entry sheet maintenance call object			
	Simulation of capacity utilization			
	Simulation of planned costs			
	Automatic deadline monitoring			
Condition-based maintenance	PM-PCS interface			
Refurbishment	Refurbishment of serial numbers			
	Refurbishment of material			
	Production of spare parts			
	Settlement based on standard price			
	Settlement based on moving average price			
	Subcontracting			
Production	Spare part production using a refurbishment order			
	Spare part production using a production order			

Object	Function	A	B	C
Calibration of test equipment	Test equipment			
	Inspection plans			
	Inspection maintenance plans			
	Results recording			
	Confirmation			
	Usage decision			
Pool Asset Management	PAM requirements			
	PAM planning table			
Project-based maintenance	WBS elements			
	Networks			
	Manual assignment			
	Automatic assignment			
	Maintenance event builder			

B.3 Integration Aspects

The table is structured in the following manner:

- Column 1: Which department is affected?
- Column 2: Which type of information exchange should be used?
- Column 3: Will the information flow from Plant Maintenance to the department (←), will it flow from the department to Plant Maintenance (→), or will it flow in both directions (↔)?
- Columns 4 to 6: Does the integration take place within SAP ERP (E), are other SAP systems affected by it (S), or will a non-SAP system be needed (N)?
- Column 7: Which is the relevant application or system?

1	2	3	4	5	6	7
Department	Information	Flow	E	S	N	System
Inventory Management, Warehouse	Spare parts management	↔	X			MM
	Standardization of spare parts master data (e.g., avoiding duplicates, distribution of master data)	↔		X		SAP NetWeaver MDM
	Inventory management for equipment	↔	X			MM
	Creating reservations for stock materials	→	X			MM
	Availability check for stock material	←	X			MM
	Planned or unplanned goods issue	←	X			MM
	MRP for spare parts, including the triggering of procurement orders	←	X			MM
	Serial numbers in Warehouse Management	→	X			WM
	Serial numbers in handling units	→	X			MM
	Refurbishment of spare parts	↔	X			MM
	Management of materials as production resources/tools	↔	X			MM
Purchasing	Triggering of purchase requisitions for materials	→	X	X		MM, SAP SRM
	Goods receipt of external materials	←	X	X		MM, SAP SRM
	Triggering of purchase requisitions for services	→	X	X		MM
	Periodic creation of service entry sheets	→	X			MM

Department	Information	Flow	E	S	N	System
	Service entry and release	←	X	X	X	MM, SAP SRM
	Integration of spare parts catalogs	←		X		OCI interface
	Goods receipt–based invoice verification	←	X			MM
Production	Assignment of production resources to plant maintenance objects	←	X			PP
	Notification of Production in case of continued maintenance activities	→	X			PP
	Data transfer from production systems to trigger malfunction reports or update measurement and counter readings	←			X	Process control systems, diagnostics, network monitoring systems, and others PM-PCS interface
	In-house production of spare parts	←	X			PP
	Service activities, such as modifications, in the context of production orders	→	X			PP
	Usage of plant data collection to confirm plant maintenance orders	←	X			BDE systems
Quality Management	Management of test equipment	↔	X			QM
	Periodic creation of inspection orders or inspection lots	→	X			QM
	Results recording and usage decision for test equipment	←	X			QM

1	2	3	4	5	6	7
Department	**Information**	**Flow**	**E**	**S**	**N**	**System**
EH&S	Safety measures as PRTs	←	X			SAP EHS Management
	Safety plan	←	X			SAP EHS Management
Controlling	Assignment of Plant Maintenance as a service provider to the cost center structure	←	X			CO
	Assignment of plant maintenance objects as service recipients to the cost center structure	←	X			CO
	Internal orders as account assignment objects	←	X			CO
	Definition of required cost elements	←	X			CO
	Definition of activity types	←	X			CO
	Planning of prices	←	X			CO
	Definition of costing procedures	←	X			CO
	Settlement of plant maintenance orders	→	X			CO
	Allocation of overhead costs	→	X			CO
Financial Accounting	Assignment of plant maintenance objects to asset master data	←	X			FI-AA
	Creation or modification of asset master records during the creation or modification of equipment master records	→	X			FI-AA
	Assignment of orders to investment programs	→	X			IM

1 Department	2 Information	3 Flow	4 E	5 S	6 N	7 System
	Creation of assets under construction	→	X			FI-AA
	Creation or modification of equipment master records during the creation or modification of asset master records	←	X			FI-AA
	Capitalization of plant maintenance services in fixed assets	→	X			FI-AA
	Definition of required G/L accounts	←	X			FI
	Invoice receipt (without goods receipt)	←	X			FI
Personnel	Assignment of personnel numbers to plant maintenance work centers	←	X			HCM
	Assignment of personnel numbers or positions to technical objects	←	X			HCM
	Planning of personnel numbers in notifications, orders, and order operations	←	X			HCM
	Confirmation including personnel number	←	X			HCM
	Planning of qualifications in order and task list operations	←	X			HCM
	Update of employee time accounts	→	X			HCM

1	2	3	4	5	6	7
Department	Information	Flow	E	S	N	System
Real Estate Management	Assignment of functional locations to real estate objects	→	X			RE-FX
	Data transfer from building control systems to trigger malfunction reports or update measurement and counter readings, and so on	←			X	Building control systems, PM-PCS interface
	Settlement of plant maintenance orders (for instance, for further clearing in service charge settlement)	→	X			RE-FX
Construction, Network Building, or similar	Creation of functional locations, equipment, and bills of materials from upstream systems	←			X	CAD, GIS, network monitoring systems, or similar
	Triggering of notifications or orders from within upstream systems	←			X	CAD, GIS, NIS systems, or similar; PM-PCS interface
	Assignment of work breakdown structures and/or networks	↔	X			PS
	Scheduling of plant maintenance orders for projects	←	X			PS
Service and sales	Quotations, sales orders, and invoices for plant maintenance services for third parties	↔	X			CS or SD
	Maintenance of customer data in functional locations and equipment	←	X			CS

B.4 Standard Reports of PM-IS

Standard Analysis	Info-structure	Characteristics	Key figures
Object class Vendor	S062	Object class, Material, Vendor, Year of construction, Assembly	Closed notifications, Completed orders, Number of actions, Processing days, Service costs
Location	S061	Maintenance plant, Plant section, Location, PM planning plant, PM planner group, Functional location, Equipment, Assembly	Service price, Degree of urgency, Internal wage costs, Internal material costs, Internal materials quota, Internal staff quota, Recorded breakdown duration, Orders entered, Recorded breakdowns, Notifications entered, External wage costs, External material costs, External materials quota, External staff quota, Planned orders, Total actual revenues, Total actual costs, Total planned costs, Planning degree, Number of damages, Number of damage causes and actions, Immediate orders, Other costs, Unplanned orders
Maintenance planner group	S061	Planning plant, Planner group, Maintenance plant, Plant section, Location, Functional location, Equipment, Assembly	

Standard Analysis	Info-structure	Characteristics	Key figures
Damage analysis	S063	Notification type, Functional location, Equipment	Number of actions, Number of damages, Number of damage causes
Object statistics	S065	Object class, Material, Vendor, Year of construction	Acquisition value, Number of pieces of equipment, Number of functional locations with single installation, Number of functional locations without equipment installation, Number of functional locations with collective installation, Number of functional locations
Breakdown statistics	S070	Object class, Functional location, Equipment	Actual breakdowns, Meantime between Repair, Meantime to Repair, Time between Repair, Time to Repair

Standard Analysis	Info-structure	Characteristics	Key figures
Cost analysis	S115	Order type, Plant Maintenance service type, Functional location, Equipment	Service costs, Internal wage costs, Internal material costs, External wage costs, External material costs, Planned orders, Total actual revenues, Total actual costs, Total planned costs, Total estimated costs, Other costs
Fuel consumption analysis	S114	Maintenance plant, Equipment category, Vendor, Year of construction, Equipment	Mileage, Operating hours, Fuel quantity, Fuel volume

C The Author

Dr. Karl Liebstückel is a Professor of Information Management and Business Software at the Würzburg-Schweinfurt University of Applied Sciences, Germany. From 2003 to 2012, he was a member of the board of directors of the German SAP User Group (DSAG) and was its chairman from 2007 to 2012. From 2001 to 2008, he led its Plant Maintenance and Service Management working group. Dr. Liebstückel owns his own consulting company and is the author of several books on the subject of logistics. Previously, he worked at SAP AG for 13 years in the areas of development, consulting, and training in plant maintenance and service management. During this period, he gained extensive practical experience as a Platinum Consultant in more than 70 plant maintenance projects, and toward the end of his time at SAP, Dr. Liebstückel was global product manager for the Plant Maintenance and Service Management applications. You are welcome to contact the author by email at *karl@liebstueckel.com*.

D   Acknowledgments

I would like to thank all the people who made a contribution to the success of this book:

- My editor at SAP PRESS, **Eva Tripp**, for having so much patience with me and for her advice and help at all times.
- My former SAP colleagues, **Stephan Bantlin, Christian Baust, Wolfgang Bock, Gerd Hartmann, Walter Kienle, Markus Seidl, Hermann Weinmann, Michael Wessendorf,** and **Stefan Westermayr** for providing me with information and images, including previously unpublished material.
- My English translation editor, **Katy Spencer**, for making the book available in English.
- My colleague in the German SAP User Group, **Ingo Teschke**, not only for editing the content of the book with much investment of time and great meticulousness, but also for his many creative suggestions on how the content could be improved.
- The three researchers at the Institute for Design and Information Systems (IDIS), **Daniel Schwarz, Tobias Schlereth,** and **Florian Wolf,** for developing the after-event recording app for iPhone and iPad.
- My former boss, **Rolf-Peter Westhues,** for two things: first, for willingly accepting my request that he write the preface to this book, and second, for giving me every facility during my time at SAP to get the best from my role. Without the freedom he gave me, the experiences on which this book is based would not have been possible.
- Lastly, my family: my wife **Brigitta** and sons **Justin** and **Jonas,** for doing without my presence on many occasions while I was preparing the manuscript for this book, and for their moral support from beginning to end.

Index

(F4) help, 596
3-D Model, 132, 558

A

ABC analysis, 452, 464
Acceptance of services performed, 260, 379
Account assignment, 637
Action, 227
Action Box, 604
Action log, 231, 293
Activities, 638
Activity type, 405, 407
Actual costing, 409
Address, 59, 76, 137, 164, 173, 177
Address management, 137
ADPMPS Workbench, 369
After Event Recording, 236, 507, 509, 610
Agentry server, 551
Aggregation level, 444
Annual estimate, 318
App for iPhone and iPad, 610
ASCII handheld device, 540
Asset accounting, 402, 645
Asset Lifecycle Management, 34
Asset master record, 402
Asset number, 402
Asset under construction, 402, 487
Asset value, 405
Asset Viewer, 529, 531
Assignment of documents, 173, 196
ATP, 214
Attachment list, 206
Availability check, 181, 212, 378
  dynamic, 213
  global, 214
  material, 213
  production resources/tools, 213
  static, 213

Availability control, 482, 486, 490, 497
  active, 490
  passive, 490
Available capacity, 50, 210, 387
Available-to-Promise → ATP

B

BAdI, 613
BAPI, 440, 569, 608
BAPI Explorer, 609
Bar Chart, 189
BCS, 343
BEx, 471
BEx Map, 479
Bill of material, 58, 64, 65, 110, 436, 518
  functional location BOM, 58, 111
  material BOM, 58, 111
  use, 112
  vs. equipment, 66
  vs. functional location, 65
BOM
  category, 111
  equipment BOM, 58, 111
  item, 65
  multiple BOMs, 113
  spare parts BOM, 111
  structure, 113
  variant BOM, 113
Bottom-up budgeting, 493
Budget category, 495
  planned, 495
  preventive, 495
  unplanned, 495
Budget use, 495
Budgeting, 481, 488, 499
Budgeting group, 494
Building control system, 343, 431, 432, 647
Building control system → BCS
Business Add-in → BAdI

Business Application Programming Interface → BAPI
Business content for EAM, 472
Business content for MCB, 496
Business Explorer → BEx
Business Function, 37, 126, 156, 194, 195, 197, 207, 231, 244, 267, 268, 280, 294, 303, 333, 341, 363, 374, 400, 498, 505, 509, 510, 531, 534
Business partner → Partner
Business process modeling, 156
Business Workplace, 515
BW, 493, 504, 507
BW-BPS, 492

C

CAD, 36, 431, 436, 570, 647
Calibration, 344
Call horizon, 301, 311, 319, 321
Capacity availability check, 212
Capacity Leveling, 210, 211
Capacity Overview, 210
Capacity Requirements Planning, 50, 208, 209
Catalog, 167
Catalog group, 169
Catalog Profile, 167, 169, 171
CATS, 422, 424
CBM, 33, 341, 560
Cellular telephone, 540
Central building control system, 33
cFolders, 516
Characteristic, 100, 115, 461, 471, 473, 637
Check resources, 373
Class, 171, 518, 637
  standard class, 118
Class name, 117
Class system
  template, 118
  use, 117
Class type, 116

Classification, 114, 118, 170, 437, 518, 638
  characteristic, 115
  equipment, 119
  notification, 171
  search functions, 119
Classification system, 115
CO, 35, 181, 405, 410, 645
Code group, 169
Collaboration Folders → cFolders
Collective Time Confirmation, 224
Combined order/operation list, 447
Company code, 44
Completion
  business, 229
  cancel, 229, 230
  order, 235
  technical, 228
Completion confirmation
  technical, 227
Completion Counter Reading, 325
Completion requirement, 300
Component maintenance, 27
Component overview, 195
Composite role, 503
Computer-aided design → CAD
Condition-based Maintenance → CBM
Configuration Panel, 551
Confirmation, 216, 223, 230, 354, 393, 395, 422, 611, 640
  collective time confirmation, 224
  individual time confirmation, 224
  inspection rounds, 336, 340
  overall completion confirmation, 225, 236
Confirmation of reservation, 360
Conformity with user expectations, 580
Construction type, 78, 111, 288
Consumption billing, 434
Content of orders, 181
Control entry, 584, 624
Control key, 49, 183, 186, 210, 247, 249, 348
Controllability, 580
Controlling, 207, 405, 441, 570, 645
  area, 44, 46, 473

Controlling (Cont.)
　commercial, 443
　Information System, 414
　measure-based, 443
　MRP-based, 442
　object-based, 444
　operational, 441
　period-based, 444
　strategic, 442
　tactical, 442
　technical, 443
Cost Analysis, 463
Cost Center, 405, 406, 414
　budget, 483
　Report, 415, 485
Cost element, 201, 405, 406, 414
Costing, 52, 181, 198, 254, 272, 294, 408
Counter
　annual estimate, 129
　counter overflow reading, 129, 317
　counter reading, 130, 528, 574
　entry of counter readings, 320, 322
Counters, 126, 129, 317, 341, 510, 611, 637
Creating linear object, 98
Cross-Application Time Sheet → CATS
CS, 35, 647
CS order, 425
Customer exit, 344, 611
Customizing, 603
Cycle modification factor, 312
Cycle set, 326, 330

D

Data
　linear, 98
Data acquisition system
　mobile, 33
Data archiving, 70
Data exchange, 439
Data transfer
　hierarchical, 123
　horizontal, 123
Data Transfer Workbench, 69

Data Warehousing Workbench, 471
Database Table, 454
DataStore Object, 471
Date, scheduled, 187
DDIC table, 466
Deadline Monitoring, 285, 303, 574
Decision
　operational, 446
　strategic, 446
　tactical, 446
Default value, 250, 593
Defining work package, 372
Diagnostic assembly, 432
Diagnostic system, 160, 431
DIN 31051, 28, 31
DIN EN ISO 9241-110, 578
Display variant, 452
Displaying costs, 201
Document, 173, 196, 509, 517, 528, 637
Document flow, 230
Document master record, 132
DSO → DataStore Object
Duration of internal processing, 50
Dynamic data calculation, 450, 451
Dynamic segmentation, 115

E

EAM, 35
EAM lists, 447
EAM order, 388, 425
Early warning system, 467
Easy Web Transaction, 160, 514
ECC, 35
eClass, 118, 518
E-learning, 524
Electronic Data Exchange, 518
Electronic parts catalogs, 519
Electronic signature, 549, 555
EN standard 13306, 28
Enhancement Package 2, 38
Enhancement Package 3, 38
Enhancement Package 4, 38
Enhancement Package 5, 39
Enhancement Package 6, 39, 195, 398, 600

657

Enterprise Asset Management → EAM
Enterprise bundle, 569
Enterprise Core Component → ECC
Enterprise Extension, 37
Enterprise service, 527, 566, 567
Entry of services performed, 260, 438, 439
Environment, Health, and Safety, 397
Equipment, 56, 62, 65, 83, 91, 164, 169, 196, 346, 379, 402, 436, 468, 473, 637, 648
  delete, 70
  external, number, 68
  group, 91
  hierarchy, 89
  install/dismantle, 84
  lock, 355
  mass change, 125
  placing in storage/removing from storage, 86, 88
  restructure, 86
  serial data, 87
  stock overview, 89
  usage list, 86
  vs. bill of material, 66
  vs. functional location, 63, 91
Equipment Master Record, 402
Ergonomics, 578
Error tolerance, 580
E-Selling, 523
Estimated costs, 198, 202
ETL, 469
EWT, 519
Extension EA-PLM, 37
External assignment
  external work center, 253
External processing, 245
  control key, 247
  default value, 250
  individual purchase order, 248
  order type, 249
  process flow, 248
  reasons, 245
External project systems, 370
External service
  goods receipt, 379

External service (Cont.)
  individual purchase order, 378
  invoice receipt, 379
  service specification, 257, 378
External work center, 253
  prerequisites, 254
  shop papers, 255
Extraction, transformation, and loading → ETL
Extractor, 472

F

Failure analysis, 463
Failure mode and effects analysis → FMEA
Favorite, 594
Favorites menu, 594
FI, 35, 400
FI-AA, 402, 645
Field selection, 69, 156, 381
Finish-finish relationship, 188
Finish-start relationship, 188
First Line Maintenance, 27
FMEA, 34
Follow-up action, 354
Follow-up buffer, 313
Fuel consumption analysis, 463
Functional location, 56, 62, 63, 64, 71, 91, 164, 169, 436, 473, 637, 648
  alternative labeling, 80, 82
  delete, 70
  layout, 75
  List editing create, 79
  mass change, 125
  number, 67
  number assignment, 66
  real estate object, 416
  rename, 81
  scrap yard, 74
  single entry, 74
  superior, 74
  vs. bill of material, 65
  vs. equipment, 63, 91

G

General ledger accounts, 400
General maintenance task list, 288, 393
GEO data, 478
Geographical information systems → GIS
GIS, 160, 431, 435, 436, 549, 647
Goods issue, 222, 270, 386
Goods receipt, 251, 270, 278, 379, 386, 393, 395, 431
Graphical handheld device, 540
Guided Procedure, 507, 509
GuiXT, 606

H

Handling unit, 384
HCM, 35, 418, 646
Human Capital Management, 418, 646
Human Resources, 35

I

IAC, 261, 440
IM, 485
IM program, 485
Immediate Repairs, 158, 232, 236, 528
Improvement, 31
Individual purchase order, 247, 378
Individual time confirmation, 224
InfoCube, 471, 472
InfoObject, 472
Information Structure, 461
In-house production of spare parts, 389, 391
Initial Counter Reading, 318
In-memory, 571
Input help, 596
Inspection, 29
 lot, 286, 351, 397, 641
 operation, 348
 plan, 347
 point, 347
Inspection rounds, 333
 advanced, 336
 using maintenance task list, 334, 336

Inspection rounds (Cont.)
 using object list, 334
Integration, 375, 642
 non-SAP systems, 431
 SAP systems, 426
 within SAP ERP, 376
Interface, 436, 438
Internal activity allocation, 406
Internal service request, 515
Internally processed activity, 51
Internet Application Component → IAC
Internet catalog, 512
Internet Transaction Server → ITS
Inventory, 56, 83
Inventory management, 89
Inventory management of equipment, 379
Investment management → IM
Invoice receipt, 251, 255, 262, 379, 400, 431
Invoice without purchase order, 401
iPad, 540, 558
iPhone, 540
ITS, 514

K

Key combination, 597
Key figure, 461, 471, 473

L

Labeling
 alternative, 637
Lead float and follow-up buffer, 313, 328
Lead time scheduling, 50, 185
Linear asset, 57, 94
Linear Asset Management, 57, 94
Linear characteristic, 100
Linear data, 98
Linear reference patterns, 102
Linear technical system structure, 100
Link to document, 131
LIS, 481
 arithmetic operation, 465
 flexible report, 465

659

Index

LIS (Cont.)
 information structure, 461
 limits, 465
List of
 actions, 447
 attachments, 136
 components, 447
 confirmations, 447
 equipment, 447
 functional locations, 447
 goods movements, 447
 maintenance items, 447
 maintenance plans, 447
 maintenance task lists, 447
 material serial numbers, 447
 materials, 447
 measurement documents, 447
 measuring points, 447
 notification items, 447
 notifications, 447
 object links and object network, 447
 order operations, 447
 orders, 447
 permits, 447
 reference functional locations, 447
 reference measuring points, 447
 shift notes, 448
 shift reports, 448
 tasks, 447
 vehicles, 447
List variant, 596
Location, 43
Location analysis, 462
Long text
 multilingual, 637

M

Machine data acquisition → MDA
Maintenance, 30
 business factors, 25
 condition-based, 33, 283, 434, 560
 cross-plant, 45
 definition, 29
 economic factors, 25
 mobile, 33

Maintenance, 30 (Cont.)
 performance-based, 32, 283, 560
 plant-specific, 45
 preventive, 32, 280, 316, 326
 project-based, 363
 reactive, 32
 reliability-based, 33
 technological factors, 26
 time-based, 32, 283
Maintenance call object, 305
Maintenance Cost Budgeting → MCB
Maintenance Event Builder, 364, 370, 642
 process flow, 371
 resource view, 373
 revision, 372
Maintenance item, 284
Maintenance order
 displaying costs, 401
Maintenance package, 310, 312
 hierarchy, 312
Maintenance plan, 285, 297, 339, 350, 397, 574, 611
 cost display for maintenance plan, 306
 maintenance plan category, 286, 338
 maintenance plan scheduling, 573
 multiple counter plan, 285, 326, 330
 single cycle plan, 285, 316
 strategy plan, 285, 309, 323
Maintenance planner group, 141, 184, 296, 473, 648
Maintenance planning
 performance-based, 434
Maintenance planning and control system, 69
Maintenance plant, 42
Maintenance strategy, 32, 283, 309, 323, 342, 574, 640
Maintenance task list, 193, 284, 287, 296, 309, 310, 324, 330, 347, 533, 611
Maintenance task list type, 287
Malfunction report, 477
MAM, 538, 543, 555, 570
MAM layout, 546
Manufacturer analysis, 462
Manufacturer guidelines, 28

660

Index

Manufacturing execution system → MES
Mass change, 125, 207, 295
Mass maintenance of linear data, 102
Master data, 68, 427
   functions, 71
   layout, 69
   recording, 71
Master data consolidation, 427
Master data harmonization, 427
Master data maintenance, 428
Master data management, 426
Master inspection characteristic, 347
Master record, 83
   delete, 70
   stored information, 68
Master warranty, 140
Material
   material issue, 221
   material reservation, 190
   material type, 105
   material where-used list, 193
   non-stock material, 192
   stock material, 189
   user departments, views, and data, 107
Material Availability Check, 213
Material BOM, 392, 393
Material issue, 379, 393, 395
   unplanned, 221
Material master, 103, 108, 266, 380
Material number, 105
Material planning, 192
Material provision, 277
Material requirements planning, 268, 381
Material type, 105
Material Type for Spare Parts, 380
Material where-used list, 114
Material withdrawal, 230
Materials, 57, 103, 154, 196, 204, 289, 380, 436, 473
Materials Management, 35, 377, 643
MCB, 492
MDA, 343, 432
Mean time between failures → MTBF
Meantime between Repair, 531
Meantime to Repair, 531
Measurement document transfer, 130

Measurement reading, 128, 528
Measuring point, 126, 127, 338, 341, 510, 611, 637
MEB Workbench, 372
MES, 432, 570
MM, 35, 377, 643
Mobile Engine Server, 544
Mobile GIS, 549
Mobile maintenance, 33, 535, 537, 540
   devices, 540
   offline scenario, 538
   online scenario, 538
Mobile push alert, 548, 555
Model service specifications, 258, 259
MRP, 268
MRP type, 382
MTBF, 444
Multiple Counter Plan, 641
Multiple counter plan, 285
   basic, 326
   enhanced, 330

N

Network, 364
Network graphic, 189
Network information system → NIS
Network monitoring system, 431, 432
Network scheduling, 185
Networks, 642
NIS, 436
Notebook, 540
Notification, 151, 152, 160, 230, 234, 286, 370, 420, 473, 509, 514, 569, 611, 638
   action, 168
   activities, 152
   catalog, 167
   catalog profile, 167
   classification, 171
   item, 152, 167
   notification type, 161, 169, 357
   paper, 174
   print, 174
   refurbishment, 264
   screen layout, 161

Notification (Cont.)
  system status, 175
  task, 152, 164, 168
  technical completion confirmation, 227
  user status, 175
Number assignment
  external, 66, 68, 637
  internal, 66, 68, 637

O

Object
  assign class, 118
  classify, 116
  linear, 98
Object class analysis, 462
Object Information, 165, 177, 181, 637
Object link, 57, 93, 132
Object list, 153, 197
Object network, 93, 94
Object service, 135, 206
Object statistics, 462
Occupational health and safety, 398
OCI interface, 644
Offset, 314
OLAP, 460
OLTP, 460
Online Analytical Processing → OLAP
Online Transaction Processing → OLTP
Operating Condition Indicator, 388
Operating hours counter, 129
Operation, 204, 289
Operation overview, 195
Operation selection, 292
Operation type, 328
Operations information system, 431, 435
Operations monitoring system, 431, 432
Order, 151, 234, 286, 322, 351, 370, 421, 473, 509, 569, 611, 639
  address, 177
  after-event recording, 236
  assign network, 366
  assign WBS element, 365
  availability check, 212
  availability list, 216

Order (Cont.)
  bar chart, 189
  business completion, 229
  capacity requirements planning, 208
  CATS, 225
  completion, 223, 235
  confirmation, 223, 423
  content of orders, 181
  costing, 198
  costs, 154
  create, 177, 372
  document, 196, 218
  estimated costs, 198
  inspection rounds, 335, 340
  mass change, 207
  material availability check, 213
  material list, 154
  material planning, 189
  network graphic, 189
  object information, 177
  object list, 153, 197
  operation, 153
  order budget, 481
  order hierarchy, 204
  order operation, 182
  order settlement, 181
  order type, 180, 219, 249, 264, 296, 351
  overall completion confirmation, 225, 236
  partners, 177
  permit, 203
  production resources/tools, 154, 195
  reference object, 176
  refurbishment, 268
  release, 216
  responsibility, 183
  settlement, 393, 410
  settlement rule, 154
  suborder, 205
  system status, 177
  technical completion, 228
  unplanned material issue, 221
  user status, 177
Order budgeting, 481

Order hierarchy, 204, 206
Order layout, 234
Order operation, 182
Order release, 216
Order Service Specification, 260
Organizational structure, 41
Overall Completion Confirmation, 225, 236
Overhead rate, 409, 410

P

Packaging material, 384
Paging, 541, 638
Partner, 142, 164, 172, 177, 473, 637, 638
  external, 142
  internal, 142
  transfer, 172
Partner determination procedure, 142, 420
Partner role, 47, 142, 172, 420
Partner type, 142
Parts catalog, electronic, 511
PCS, 343, 434
PDA, 540
PDC, 343, 432, 644
PDE, 432
PDM, 35
Performance-based maintenance, 560
Period accruals, 412
Permit, 143, 203, 225
Permits, 637, 638
Persistent Staging Area → PSA
Person, 184, 419, 420, 421, 422
  as work center, 47
  group, 47
  responsible, 421
  responsible for executing, 421
Personal value list, 597
Personnel capacity
  virtual, 522
Personnel data entry → PDE
Personnel number, 419, 420, 421, 422
  confirmation list, 422
  legislation, 422

Plan-driven procurement, 429
Planned repairs, 158
Planner group, 43
Planning, 176
Planning board, 359, 388
Planning group analysis, 462
Planning plant, 42
Plant, 42, 473
  maintenance plant, 42
  planning plant, 42
  the spare parts storage, 45
Plant data collection → PDC
Plant maintenance
  Business Functions, 38
  costs, 282
  SAP releases, 34
Plant maintenance controlling → Controlling
Plant maintenance information system → PM-IS
Plant section, 43, 648
PM assembly, 57, 103, 164, 637, 648
PM/PS reference element, 367
PM-IS, 459, 460, 462, 465, 467, 648
PM-PCS interface, 344, 434, 519, 571, 641, 644, 647
Pool asset management, 356
  confirmation, 360
  issue, 361
  planning board, 359
  process flow, 357
  reservation, 360
  settlement, 362
Pool category, 362
Position number, 77
PP, 35, 386, 644
PP order, 390
PP Planning Board, 388
Preventive maintenance, 27, 158, 233, 280, 640
Price, 407
  fixed, 200
  variable, 200
Print, 174, 638
  output media, 175, 219

663

Index

Printing
  shop paper, 217
Priority, 181, 638
Process control system, 33, 160, 343, 431, 432
Process Control System → PCS
Process control system → PCS
Processing time, 584, 625
Product structure browser, 120
Production order, 389, 390, 391, 392, 396
Production planning and control → PP
Production resources/tools, 154, 195, 204, 289
Programming, 613
Project definition, 364
Project System → PS
Project-based maintenance, 363
PS, 35, 364, 488, 647
PSA, 471
Purchase order, 230, 248, 250, 260, 273, 277, 380, 429
Purchase order requisition, 192, 229, 230, 248, 250, 260, 273, 275, 377, 380, 429
Purchasing, 35, 377, 643
Purchasing document, 380

Q

QM, 35, 396, 644
Quality Management, 396, 644
Quality management, 35
Query, 472

R

Radio Frequency Identification → RFID
Rate of capacity utilization, 51
RBM, 33
RE, 35, 415
Real Estate Management, 415, 647
Real estate management, 35
Real estate object, 416
Reference
  functional location, 56, 71, 80

Reference object, 164, 176
Refurbishment, 262, 273, 379, 641
  costs, 272
  flow, 262
  material, 270
  notification, 264
  order, 268, 393, 396
  order type, 264
  settlement, 273
RE-FX, 415, 647
Relationship, 188
Release
  automatic, 217
Reliability-based maintenance → RBM
Reliability-centered maintenance, 569
Remote Function Call → RFC
Remote service, 524
Reorder point planning, 381
Repetition factor, 332
Requirements of internal processing, 51
Reservation, 190, 216, 221, 229, 360, 377
Restart costs, 28
Results Recording, 352, 397
RFC, 433
RFID, 562, 564
RM-INST, 34
Role, 472, 502, 527, 594
  composite role, 503
  single role, 503
Role menu, 594
Routing, 392

S

Safety measure list, 398
Safety plan, 398
Sales, 35, 423, 647
Sales order, 424, 425
SAP Business Suite, 36
SAP Business Suite on HANA, 572
SAP CRM, 36
SAP Customer Relationship Management → SAP CRM
SAP EarlyWatch, 467
SAP Easy DMS, 133

SAP Easy Document Management →
   SAP Easy DMS
SAP Environment, Health, and Safety
   Management, 397, 645
SAP HANA, 571
   for EAM, 573
   integrated scenario, 572, 573
   side-by-side scenario, 572, 573
SAP industry solutions, 36
SAP Inventory Manager app, 555
SAP List Viewer, 446
   further processing, 453
   list display, 451
   monitor, 451
   selection option, 450
   selection variant, 449
SAP Mobile Asset Management → MAM
SAP Mobile Infrastructure, 543
SAP NetWeaver, 39, 566
SAP NetWeaver Business Client, 501,
   507, 524, 528, 529, 558
   for HTML, 524
   for Windows, 524
SAP NetWeaver BW, 469, 481
SAP NetWeaver MDM, 426, 427,
   428, 643
SAP NetWeaver Portal, 501, 502, 507,
   509, 514, 524, 529
SAP PLM, 36
SAP Quick Viewer, 454
   keyword search, 455
   limit, 457
   table determination, 454
   table join, 456
SAP Rounds Manager, 551, 560
SAP SCM, 37
SAP SRM, 36, 426, 428, 643
SAP Supplier Relationship Management
   → SAP SRM
SAP Supply Chain Management →
   SAP SCM
SAP Visual Enterprise, 531, 534, 558
SAP Visual Enterprise Viewer, 532
SAP Work Manager, 538, 550, 555
   3-D model, 559
   GIS Integration, 556

SAP Work Manager (Cont.)
   iPad, 552
   iPhone, 553, 557
   local layout, 552
   timesheet, 557
SCADA, 33, 433
Scheduled maintenance, 30
Scheduling, 50, 181, 185, 204, 319, 331
   basic date, 187, 194
   indicator, 298, 311, 323
   lead time, 185
   list, 302
   log, 305
   measurement document, 321
   network, 185
   overview, 307
   parameters, 298, 311, 319, 328
   period, 301, 312
   scheduling type, 187
Scrap yard, 74
Screen control, 77
Screen layout, 181
Screen template, 156
SD, 35, 424, 647
Segmentation
   dynamic, 100
Selection variant, 449
Self-descriptiveness, 579
Serial number, 42, 57, 83, 262, 265, 279,
   385, 641
   history, 386
   profile, 87, 278
Service, 35, 423, 647
Service entry sheet, 286
Service Map, 504
Service specifications, 247, 378, 438, 640
Service-oriented architecture → SOA
Settlement, 361
   fixed price, 413
   full settlement, 412
   periodic, 412
   result, 414
Settlement by amount, 412
Settlement cost element, 410
Settlement profile, 411
Settlement Rule, 154

Index

Settlement rule, 405, 411, 412, 425
Settlement type, 412
Shared procurement, 524
Shift factor, 299, 311
Shift note, 238
Shift report, 238, 242
Shop paper
 printing, 175, 217
Short text
 multilingual, 637
Side panel, 531
Single cycle plan, 285, 335
 performance-based, 316
 time-based, 296
Single role, 503
Single-cycle plan, 641
SMART administration tool, 551
Smartphone, 540
SMS, 548
SOA, 566
Source of data, 124
Spare part, 262, 265, 389, 533
Spare Part Class Code, 267
Spare part production
 production order, 391
 refurbishment order, 393
Spare parts management, 380
Spare parts storage
 virtual, 521
Standard class, 118
Standard report, 462, 648
Start in cycle, 315, 324
Start-start relationship, 188
Statistics, 477
Status, 201, 213, 216, 228, 229, 352, 355, 372, 386, 517
 automatic assignment, 148
 several, 148
 status profile, 147, 161, 181
 system status, 145, 175, 177
 user status, 145, 146, 175, 177, 638
Stock overview, 89, 278
Strategy plan, 285, 309, 323, 324, 641
Structure indicator, 66
Structure level, 60, 61
Structuring elements, 58
Structuring of technical systems, 55
 criteria, 61
 depth, 58
 resources, 71
Subcontracting, 273, 380
Subcontracting monitor, 276
Suborder, 205
Supervisory Control and Data Acquisition Systems → SCADA
Supplier relationship, 428
Switch Framework, 38, 511
Syclo, 550
System availability, 27, 164, 227
System Monitor, 552
Systems for entry of services performed, 431

T

Table control, 598
Task, 227, 638
Task List Transfer, 292
Technical structure view, 509
Technical system structure
 detailed, 59
 linear, 100
 rough, 59
Test equipment, 345, 396, 607, 642
Time leveling, 423
Time recording, 225
Time series, 478
Timesheet, 557
TM, 35
Tolerance, 300, 311
Top-down budgeting, 493
Training, 586
Transaction AC03, 258
Transaction ADPMPS, 366, 368, 370
Transaction ADSUBCON, 276, 277
Transaction analysis, 148
Transaction AS01, 403
Transaction AS03, 402
Transaction BAPI, 609
Transaction BGM1, 140
Transaction BGM3, 140
Transaction CA01, 392

Index

Transaction CA77, 295
Transaction CA87, 295
Transaction CAT2, 225, 422
Transaction CAT9, 225
Transaction CC04, 120
Transaction CJ01, 488
Transaction CJ06, 364
Transaction CJ11, 364, 488
Transaction CJ30, 489
Transaction CL02, 116
Transaction CL20, 119
Transaction CL20N, 118
Transaction CL30N, 119
Transaction CL6B, 119
Transaction CM01, 210
Transaction CM21, 78, 388
Transaction CN21, 365
Transaction CO01, 389, 392
Transaction CO11, 396
Transaction CO15, 393
Transaction CO1F, 393
Transaction CS01, 111, 392, 393
Transaction CS15, 113
Transaction CT04, 115, 317
Transaction CV01N, 132
Transaction CV04N, 132
Transaction F-43, 401
Transaction FB60, 101
Transaction IA01, 287, 347
Transaction IA05, 288, 347
Transaction IA06, 393
Transaction IA08, 447
Transaction IA09, 447
Transaction IA11, 287
Transaction IA16, 294
Transaction IA21, 293
Transaction IB01, 111
Transaction IB11, 111
Transaction IBIP, 69
Transaction IBIPA, 305
Transaction IE01, 98
Transaction IE02, 85, 86, 118, 317
Transaction IE05, 102, 119, 125, 447
Transaction IE20, 120
Transaction IE36, 447
Transaction IE37, 447

Transaction IE4N, 88
Transaction IH01, 73, 80, 100, 121, 509
Transaction IH03, 121, 509
Transaction IH04, 113
Transaction IH06, 120
Transaction IH07, 447
Transaction IH08, 119, 447
Transaction IH09, 447
Transaction IK07, 447
Transaction IK07R, 447
Transaction IK08, 447
Transaction IK08R, 447
Transaction IK11, 318
Transaction IK17, 447
Transaction IK18, 447
Transaction IK81, 102
Transaction IK82, 102
Transaction IK83, 102
Transaction IL01, 74, 98
Transaction IL02, 85, 317
Transaction IL03, 416
Transaction IL04, 79
Transaction IL05, 80, 102, 120, 125, 447
Transaction IL06, 447
Transaction IL07, 86, 101
Transaction IL15, 447
Transaction IM01, 485
Transaction IM11, 485
Transaction IM32, 486
Transaction IN04, 93
Transaction IN07, 93
Transaction IN15, 447
Transaction IN16, 447
Transaction IN18, 447
Transaction IN18/19, 94
Transaction IN19, 447
Transaction IP10, 297, 315, 324, 329, 332
Transaction IP11, 309, 323
Transaction IP11Z, 326
Transaction IP15, 447
Transaction IP16, 447
Transaction IP17, 447
Transaction IP18, 447
Transaction IP19, 307
Transaction IP24, 447

667

Index

Transaction IP30, 302, 303, 574
Transaction IP30H, 574
Transaction IP31, 306
Transaction IP41, 296, 318
Transaction IP42, 310, 324
Transaction IP43, 327, 331
Transaction IPM2, 447
Transaction IPM3, 447
Transaction IQ08, 120, 447
Transaction IR01, 48, 419
Transaction IR02, 419
Transaction ISHN1, 239
Transaction ISHN4, 240, 448
Transaction ISHR1, 242
Transaction ISHR4, 244, 448
Transaction IW21, 160, 357
Transaction IW22, 228
Transaction IW24, 160
Transaction IW26, 160
Transaction IW28, 179, 447, 514, 515
Transaction IW29, 447
Transaction IW31, 179, 238, 275, 291, 337, 486, 511, 526, 601
Transaction IW32, 215, 217, 227, 228, 229, 230, 291, 365, 366, 511
Transaction IW36, 204
Transaction IW37, 447
Transaction IW37N, 447
Transaction IW38, 207, 215, 217, 220, 229, 447, 448
Transaction IW39, 447
Transaction IW3D, 220
Transaction IW3K, 447, 511
Transaction IW3L, 447
Transaction IW3M, 447
Transaction IW41, 224, 255, 396, 422
Transaction IW42, 225, 228, 238, 255, 335, 340, 341, 395, 422
Transaction IW44, 224, 255, 422
Transaction IW47, 447
Transaction IW48, 224, 255, 422
Transaction IW49, 447
Transaction IW49N, 447
Transaction IW61, 238
Transaction IW64, 447
Transaction IW65, 447

Transaction IW66, 447
Transaction IW67, 447
Transaction IW81, 269, 394
Transaction IW8W, 395
Transaction KGI2, 410, 411
Transaction KGI4, 410
Transaction KL01, 407
Transaction KO22, 481
Transaction KO88, 389, 393, 395, 404, 414
Transaction KO8G, 414
Transaction KP06, 483
Transaction KP26, 200, 254, 363, 407, 483
Transaction KP46, 483
Transaction KPZ2, 483
Transaction LSMW, 69
Transaction MC=E, 468
Transaction MCI1, 462
Transaction MCI2, 462
Transaction MCI3, 462
Transaction MCI4, 462
Transaction MCI5, 462
Transaction MCI6, 462
Transaction MCI7, 463
Transaction MCI8, 463
Transaction MCIZ, 463
Transaction MD04, 267
Transaction ME21N, 380
Transaction ME51N, 380
Transaction MEW10, 440
Transaction MIGO, 88, 221, 251, 270, 393, 395, 396
Transaction MIRO, 253
Transaction ML10, 258
Transaction ML12, 258
Transaction ML33, 258
Transaction ML39, 258
Transaction ML45, 258
Transaction ML81N, 260
Transaction MM02, 118
Transaction MMBE, 89
Transaction N15/16, 94
Transaction OLI5N, 201
Transaction PAM01, 363
Transaction PAM02, 363

Transaction PAM03, 358
Transaction PFCG, 594
Transaction PW61, 423
Transaction QA11, 354
Transaction QDV1, 349
Transaction QE17, 352
Transaction QE51N, 352
Transaction QS21, 347
Transaction QS23, 347
Transaction QS41, 168
Transaction REISCOLIBD, 418
Transaction S_ALR_87012824, 487
Transaction S_ALR_87013557, 490
Transaction S_ALR_87013611, 414, 484
Transaction SBWP, 515
Transaction SE93, 459
Transaction SFP, 244
Transaction SFW5, 37, 511
Transaction SHN1, 239
Transaction SHN4, 240, 448
Transaction SHN5, 240
Transaction SHR1, 242
Transaction SHR4, 244, 448
Transaction SQ01, 459
Transaction SQVI, 454
Transaction SU01, 542
Transaction SU3, 592
Transaction SWDD, 615
Transaction SXDA, 118
Transaction variant, 601
Transaction WPS1, 370
Transfer, 557
Tuning measure, 617

U

Upstream transactions, 607
Usability, 577, 583, 587, 590
  period, 637
  study, 616
Usage, 49
  decision, 354, 397
  history, 86
User acceptance, 584, 587
User parameters, 592, 593

V

Valuation category, 265
Valuation type, 265, 394
Value category, 202
Value list, personal, 597
Vehicle scheduling, 358
Vendor
  connection, 439, 520
  data, 637
  data exchange, 439
  Invoice, 401
  portal, 439, 520
Virtual personnel capacity, 522
Virtual spare parts storage, 521
Voice picking system, 540

W

Warehouse Management, 35
Warranty, 139, 569, 637
  customer warranty, 139
  for the technical object, 141
  manufacturer warranty, 139
  master warranty, 140
  performance-based, 140
  vendor warranty, 139
Warranty counters, 140
WBS element, 364, 486, 488, 642
Web Dynpro, 505
Web service, 568, 569
Web template, 472
Web user interface, 610
WM, 35, 643
Work center, 43, 47, 78, 141, 184, 247,
  254, 296, 386, 388, 419, 640
  basic data, 48
  creating, 48
  default value, 49
  executing, 47
  main, 47, 78, 387
  number, 48
  selection, 294
Workflow, 614
Workflow builder, 615
Workshop, 47

669

- Discover the power of SAP MM

- Explore how Materials Management works and integrates with other key SAP software

- Master core functionalities and configuration techniques to streamline your organization's processes

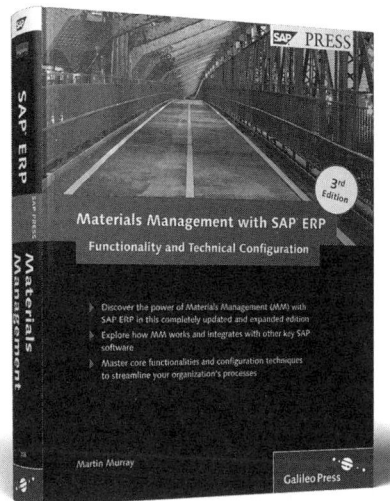

Martin Murray

Materials Management with SAP ERP: Functionality and Technical Configuration

If you are using or need to get up to speed on Materials Management in SAP ERP, this is your must-have resource. This book provides a comprehensive and expanded overview of the various functionalities and configurations needed for MM in SAP ERP. In its third edition, this book is the ultimate reference for anyone looking for MM information, dealing with everything from goods receipt and invoice verification to balance sheet valuation and the material ledger.

666 pp., 3. edition 2011, 69,95 Euro / US$ 69.95
ISBN 978-1-59229-358-2
www.sap-press.com

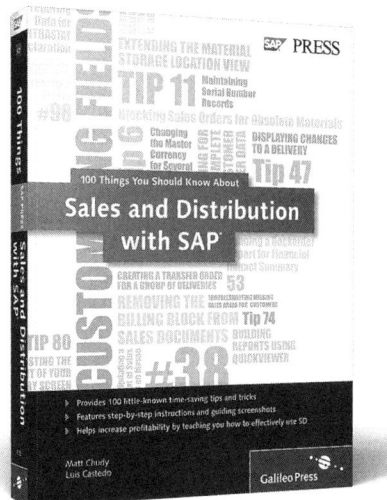

- Provides 100 little-known time-saving tips and tricks

- Features step-by-step instructions and guiding screenshots

- Helps increase profitability by teaching you how to effectively use SD

Matt Chudy, Luis Castedo

Sales and Distribution with SAP
100 Things You Should Know About...

If you've worked with Sales and Distribution in SAP ERP, you know it can sometimes be overwhelming, but it doesn't have to be. This book unlocks the secrets of SD. It provides users and super-users with 100 tips and workarounds to increase productivity, save time, and improve overall ease-of-use of SAP SD. The tips have been carefully selected to provide a collection of the best, most useful, and rarest information.

363 pp., 2012, 49,95 Euro / US$ 49.95
ISBN 978-1-59229-405-3
www.sap-press.com

Interested in reading more?

Please visit our website for all new
book and e-book releases from SAP PRESS.

www.sap-press.com